Schriften zur
rechtswissenschaftlichen Innovationsforschung

Band 12

Maximilian von Grafenstein

The Principle of Purpose Limitation in Data Protection Laws

The Risk-based Approach, Principles, and Private Standards as Elements for Regulating Innovation

Nomos

The Deutsche Nationalbibliothek lists this publication in the Deutsche Nationalbibliografie; detailed bibliographic data are available on the Internet at http://dnb.d-nb.de

a.t.: Hamburg, Univ., Diss., 2017

ISBN 978-3-8487-4897-6 (Print)
978-3-8452-9084-3 (ePDF)

British Library Cataloguing-in-Publication Data
A catalogue record for this book is available from the British Library.

ISBN 978-3-8487-4897-6 (Print)
978-3-8452-9084-3 (ePDF)

Library of Congress Cataloging-in-Publication Data
Grafenstein, Maximilian von
The Principle of Purpose Limitation in Data Protection Laws
The Risk-based Approach, Principles, and Private Standards as Elements for Regulating Innovation
Maximilian von Grafenstein
675 p.
Includes bibliographic references and index.

ISBN 978-3-8487-4897-6 (Print)
978-3-8452-9084-3 (ePDF)

1st Edition 2018

To my father

The principle of purpose limitation in data protection law is usually considered as a barrier to data-driven innovation. According to this principle, data controllers must specify the purpose of the collection at the latest when collecting personal data and must not process the data in any way that does not comply with the original purpose. Whether the principle of purpose limitation conflicts with data-driven innovation, however, depends on two sub-questions: On the one hand, one has to know how precisely a data controller must specify the purpose and under which conditions the subsequent processing is fully compatible or incompatible with that purpose. On the other hand, one has to understand the effects of a legal principle such as the principle of purpose limitation on innovation processes. Surprisingly, despite the long-standing and ongoing debate, there is little research that thoroughly examines the regulatory concept of the principle of purpose limitation, and even less its actual impact on innovation. To close this gap, was the aim of this dissertation, which reflects the debate until January 2017.

This dissertation evolved in the context of the interdisciplinary research project "*Innovation and Entrepreneurship*" at the Alexander von Humboldt Institute for Internet and Society. The main research question of this thesis was the result of hands-on observations in our Startup Clinics that we created and carried out for more than four years in order to empirically research the disabling and facilitating factors of internet-enabled innovation. In the Startup *Law* Clinic, where I helped more than 100 startups to cope with the legal challenges they faced during their innovation processes, I realised quite early that most of the startup founders were able to do a great variety of things in a very efficient and creative way, except one: Reliably expect what will happen next month, next week, or even the next day. Under these circumstances of knowledge uncertainty, I wondered how these founders should be able to reliably assess what their future data processing purposes would look like. This hands-on observation served as an inspiring research question and pushed me throughout the four years of its production. The result of this research process was in some way even puzzling to me: As a legal principle, the principle of purpose limitation is not only a highly efficient instrument to protect individuals against the risks caused by data-driven innovation but it can even enhance innovation processes of data controllers, when combined with co-regulation instruments.

For the inspiring *tour de force* of these four years, I would like to thank, first and foremost, Prof. Dr. Wolfgang Schulz who not only aroused my interest in regulation as a research discipline but also always immediately and constructively helped me with his oversight, precision in the details and humour. I would also like to especially thank Prof. Dr. Dr. Thomas Schildhauer who has given me the economic perspective on innovation and who in turn has always been pro-actively open to my regulatory viewpoints and ideas. Furthermore, I would like to thank Prof. Dr. Marion Albers, without whose contributions to informational self-determination and data protection my own work would not have been possible, and who compiled the second vote very quickly. Furthermore, I am very thankful and honoured to be included in Prof. Dr. Wolfgang Hoffmann-Riem's, Prof. Dr. Dr. h.c. Karl-Heinz Ladeur's and Prof. Dr. Hans-Heinrich Trute's publication series Legal Research on Innovation ("Rechtswissenschaftliche Innovationsforschung") on that my dissertation is based on. I would also like to thank the German Ministry of the Interior for the financial support of the publication of my thesis.

Finally, I want to thank my colleagues: Elissa Jelowicki, who helped me to revise my thesis throughout the creation process, Jörg Pohle, the "walking library" (I think I do not have to explain that) and all my other colleagues for the endless and inspiring discussions.

Last but not least, I am grateful to my wonderful fiancée Eva Schneider, who in countless evenings of discussions helped me to structure my ideas, and above all motivated me to keep on going.

Content Overview

Table of Content

A. Introduction

Dating back to the early discussions regarding the concept of data protection, the so-called "principle of purpose limitation" is one of the fundamental principles of data protection law.[1] The principle essentially requires that personal data may only be processed for the original purpose of collection of the data,[2] or in the words of the OECD Privacy Guidelines, at least, so long as it is not incompatible with the original purpose.[3] In light of our ever increasing digitization of society, the principle of purpose limitation is more and more debated amongst legal scholars.[4] The most recent motivations behind these discussions arose because the European Council's draft of the General Data Protection Regulation was leaked in the beginning of 2015 by the non-profit association European Digital Rights (EDRi).[5] Article 6 sect. 4 of the European Council's draft widely abandoned the principle of purpose limitation by stating that personal data can be used, even if it is incompatible with its original purpose, so long as it can be based on a legal provision in accordance with Article 6 sec 1 lit a-e. An exception to this rule is Article 6 sect. 1 lit. f of the draft, which provides that the collection of data is legal if it is "necessary for the purposes of the *legitimate interests* pursued by the controller (underlining by the author)". Only if the collection of personal data is based on this provision,

1 See Article 29 Data Protection Working Group, Opinion 03/0213 on purpose limitation, pp. 4 and 6 ff.; Handbook on European data protection law, p. 68; De Hert and Gutwirth, Data Protection in the Case Law of Strasbourg and Luxemburg: Constitutionalisation in Action, p. 4; Bygrave, Data Privacy Law, p. 153; v. Zezschwitz, Concept of Normative Purpose Limitation, cip. 1; Pohle, Purpose limitation revisited, p. 141; contrary, Härting, Purpose limitation and change of purpose in data protection law, who affirms the requirement of purpose limitation only applicable to the legislator but not to the data controller.

2 Cf. v. Zezschwitz, Concept of Normative Purpose Limitation, cip. 14.

3 See no. 9 of part two of the OECD Privacy Framework, p. 14.

4 See, instead of many, Cate/Cullon/Viktor Mayer-Schönberger, Data Protection Principles for the 21st Century, p. 11.

5 See the documents linked by Naranjo, Leaked documents: European data protection reform is badly broken, retrieved on the 2nd of February 2016 from https://edri.org/broken_badly/.

then the principle of purpose limitation should apply.[6] European Digital Rights particularly criticized this extensive abandonment of the principle of purpose limitation because it would undermine "control and predictability" as "the core of data protection".[7] In essence, this doctoral thesis addresses the question of whether this consideration is true or not, or from a more academic point of view, what the function of the principle of purpose limitation actually is.

I. Problem: Conflict between innovation and risk protection

From an academic perspective, there are two main aspects of the principle of purpose limitation that are particularly interesting: Firstly, the principle of purpose limitation appears to conflict with the societal needs for innovation and is the perfect example of a more general conflict for the regulators: How can the legislator enable or enhance innovation and, simultaneously, protect against its risks? The second aspect refers to the uncertainty of how to apply the principle of purpose limitation in general. Only if the principle of purpose limitation was clear and we knew what is actually meant, would it be possible to answer the preceding question.

1. Innovation as an economic driver for public welfare

A multitude of international studies and policy recommendations brings the importance of innovation for the public welfare more and more into public debate. For instance, the OECD Science, Technology and Industry Outlook 2014 considers: "Innovation is a major driver of productivity and economic growth and is seen as a key way to create new business values."[8] Another OECD report focusing on data-driven innovation considers its positive effects as "significantly accelerating research and the development of new products, processes, organisational methods and markets".[9]

---

6 See Grafenstein, The Principle of Purpose Limitation between Openness toward Innovation and the Rule of Law, DuD 2015 (12), p.789.
7 See EDRi / access / Privacy International / Fundacja Panoptykon: Data Protection Broken Badly.
8 See OECD Science, Technology and Industry Outlook 2014, p. 21.
9 See OECD: Data-Driven Innovation for Growth and Well-Being.

The World Economic Forum draws, in its 2014 report on how to enhance Europe's competitiveness, the attention to entrepreneurship as the key source of innovation.[10] From an entrepreneurial perspective, however, the law is usually not perceived as a driver of but rather barrier for innovation. The Eurobarometer on "Entrepreneurship in the EU and beyond" surveyed that a "large majority of respondents (..) agreed that business start-ups were difficult due to complex administrative procedures: 71%, in total agreed and 29% strongly agreed."[11] Similarly, the Global Entrepreneurship Monitor 2014 surveyed, amongst others, "the lowest evaluation corresponded to government policies toward regulation".[12]

2. Protection against the risks of innovation

This perception corresponds to the general view amongst innovation researchers who consider that the law actually acts as a barrier rather than as a pro-active instrument which would influence and develop, besides other factors, the process of innovation. The reason for this perception might be that the term "innovation" usually refers to something unexpected and new, while the law seeks to guarantee a certain and expected outcome.[13] The principle of purpose limitation restraining the later use of personal data to the original purpose of collection indeed appears to be diametrically opposed to such unexpected outcomes of innovation. However, the public discussion also recognizes the risks caused by innovation. The above-mentioned OECD report not only considers the positive effects of data-driven innovation but also its risks, in particular, for privacy and security.[14] Having applied a "bottom-up cultural analysis of historical, philosophical, political, sociological, and legal sources", Solove elaborated in his book *Understanding Privacy* on a taxonomy of 16 privacy risks and/or harms, from the collection of information to its processing and distribution as well as invasion.[15] In this regard, two terminological issues shall briefly

10 See World Economic Forum: Insight Report: Enhancing Europe's Competitiveness – Fostering Innovation-Driven Entrepreneurship in Europe.
11 See Eurobarometer: Entrepreneurship in the EU and beyond, p. 75.
12 See Singer et al., Global Entrepreneurship Monitor – 2014 Global Report, p. 14.
13 See Eifert, Innovation-enhancing Regulation, p. 11 and 12; cf. also Lipshaw, Why the Law of Entrepreneurship Barely Matters.
14 See OECD: Data-Driven Innovation for Growth and Well-Being.
15 Solove, Understanding Privacy, pp. 101 ff. as well as 171 ff.

be clarified: so far, this thesis does not (yet) differentiate between the terms *data* and *information*;[16] second, except of this differentiation, this doctoral thesis does not make a difference between the terms "processing", "treatment", "use" and "usage" of data and/or information. In any case, the study "Commercial Digital Surveillance in Daily Life" summarizes the most common or, at least, commonly known cases of *data mining techniques* (for example, predictive analytics about one's pregnancy, status of relationship or emotional state of mind based on purchase behavior, Facebook likes or keyboard usage patterns) and its commercial exploitation in the insurance, finance or HR industry.[17] Boyd and Crawford stress in particular the high subjectivity and potential inaccuracy of those data mining techniques.[18] The regulator must thus not only seek to enable and enhance innovation but also to protect against the risks caused by innovation.[19] In conclusion, the question therefore is which role the principle of purpose limitation plays within this regulatory conflict between enhancing innovation and protecting individuals against its risks.

3. Uncertainty about the meaning and extent of the principle of purpose limitation

This leads to the second reason that makes an academic examination of the principle of purpose limitation interesting: the uncertainty about its precise meaning and extent. In order to apply the principle of purpose limitation, it is necessary to determine the original purpose of collection. The main question hence is how precisely the original purpose must or, vice versa, how broadly it can be specified: the wider that the original purpose is specified, for example, the purpose of money making, the broader the scope of action will be for the controller and/or others to be able to use that data for the same purpose.[20] However, the question how precisiely a

16 See the differentiation below under point C. I. 3. c) cc) (1) "The reason for why the scope is too vague: Difference between data and information".
17 See Christl, Commercial Digital Surveillance in Daily Life.
18 Boyd and Crawford, Critical Questions for Big Data, pp. 666 ff.
19 See Hoffmann-Riem, Innovation Responsibility, p. 16.
20 See Forgó et al., Purpose Specification and Informational Separation of Powers, p. 34; Mehde, Handbook of European Fundamental Rights, cip. 24; in contrast, see Bygrave, Data Privacy Law, p. 155, who considers this first component of the principle of purpose limitation "relatively free of ambiguity".

processing purpose must be specified is an open question. Comparably, regarding the second component of the principle of purpose limitation, i.e. the question of under which conditions another (later) purpose is compatible with the original purpose, there are only few reliable criteria, if at all, that help really answer this question. The Article 29 Data Protection Working Party refers in its "Opinion 03/2013 on purpose limitation" to a bundle of criteria (see, now, also Art. 6 sect. 4 GDPR) such as the relationship between the original purpose and the further processing, the context of collection, the nature of the data and the impact caused by the later use on the individual, as well as the safeguards applied in order to prevent any undue impact.[21] However, these criteria also pose two problems: First, each criteria lacks an objective scale which would help to determine, for instance, the "relationship" between the purposes; and second, the fact that all criteria together can be used as an entire basis to reach a decision, produces different results amongst decision makers who weigh the criteria against each other. Interestingly, there is little academic literature on the precise meaning and extent of the principle purpose limitation that allows one, in light of the fundamental rights concerned, to determine reliable criteria.[22] This is particularly the case since most of the publications refer to the processing of personal data by the State, and not in the private sector, which is what this thesis focuses on.

4. Practical examples referring to two typical scenarios

Both aspects, i.e. the appearing conflict of the principle of purpose limitation together with the openness of innovation processes, and the ever increasing uncertainty about how to apply this principle within our current technological environment, result from the ambiguity of the current legal concept of protection. The following examples shall give the reader of this thesis an impression of the effects of this ambiguity in today's business world.

---

21 See Opinion 03/2013 on purpose limitation, pp. 23 to 27.

22 See only Hofmann, Purpose Limitation as Anchor Point for a Procedural Approach in Data Protection; Forgó et al., Purpose Specification and Informational Separation of Powers; Eifert, Purpose Compatibility instead of Purpose Limitation; Albers, Treatment of Personal Information and Data, cip. 123.

a) Coming from a practical observation: Startups and non-linear innovation processes

Practically, for the past three years, I have often discussed this issue with founders of Internet-enabled startups in the *Startup Law Clinic* of the *Alexander von Humboldt Institute for Internet and Society* (HIIG), and the specific legal challenges they face in trying to develop and implement their business model in today's society.[23] The *Startup Law Clinic* is part of the interdisciplinary research project *Innovation and Entrepreneurship.*[24] Based on empirical data gathered in these Startup Clinics, the research project aims to understand, on a more efficient level, Internet-enabled entrepreneurship. In doing so, the project focuses on Internet-enabled startups that are, pursuant to some business observers "turning the conventional wisdom about entrepreneurship on its head."[25] For instance, Blank observes that startups differ to traditional larger companies, amongst other aspects, in how they react or adapt to uncertainties: While traditional companies create long-term business plans based on the "assumption (..) that it's possible to figure out most of the unknowns of a business in advance" and then execute such plans, step-by-step, according to the so-called waterfall principle, "lean" startups *search* for a business model going "quickly from failure to failure, all the while adapting, iterating on, and improving their initial ideas as they continually learn from customers."[26] Such a methodological difference does not mean that traditional larger companies are not able to apply the same methods as startups do. In contrast, authors like Blank, as well as Ries, argue that traditional companies more and more apply this methodology.[27] However, startups are known to apply this methodology most rigorously in light of the particular uncertainty they face. Ries, at least, defines a startup, amongst others, as being "designed to confront situations of extreme uncertainty."[28] Unlike a "clone of an existing business", an innovative startup is always looking for "novel scientific

23 See the preliminary findings in the Working Paper by Dopfer et al., Supporting and Hindering Factors for Internet-Enabled Startups, pp. 23.

24 See the description of the research project retrieved on the 4th of February 2016 from: http://www.hiig.de/en/project/innovation-and-entrepreneurship/

25 See Blank, Why the Lean Start-Up Changes Everything; cf. also Blank, Four Steps to the Epiphany, as well as Ries, The Lean Startup.

26 See Blank, ibid.

27 See Blank, ibid.; Ries, ibid, pp. 36 and 37.

28 See Ries, ibid., p. 38.

discoveries, repurposing an existing technology for a new use, devising a new business model that unlocks value that was hidden, or simply bringing a product or service to a new location or a previously underserved set of customers" and, thus, confronted with constant change.[29] Indeed, this phenomenon also became apparent in the *Startup Law Clinic*.[30] Therefore, with respect to startups developing their business models based on the processing of personal data, it was interesting to figure out how far they were, in effect, able to apply the principle of purpose limitation. Not surprisingly, there essentially were two types of cases particularly relevant when seeking to find an answer to this question: The first case refers to situations where startups want to process data of its own users but cannot yet specify the purpose of the later processing; the second case concerns situations where startups want to process personal data that was originally collected by a third party. In this second case, the problem for the startups was not only their own inability to specify the new purposes, but also the high uncertainty about the precise meaning and extent of the legal requirement to restrict their processing to the purposes initially specified by the third party when the data was first collected.

b) First scenario: Purpose specification by the controller concerning the use of data of its users

In the first case, the main problem exists in the controller's limitations to specify the purpose of collection. The main reason for this limitation is the openness of its entrepreneurial process. The following example shall illustrate this process and the resulting problem with respect to the requirement of purpose specification.

aa) The unpredictable outcome of entrepreneurial processes

One startup, which exemplifies this conceptual issue, was started in early 2014 with the idea to develop a wallpaper app for smartphones with android operating systems. Android operating systems allow the user (and their apps) to interact on the home screen of the smartphone with the un-

29 See Ries, ibid., p. 38.
30 Cf. Dopfer et al., Supporting and hindering factors for internet-enabled startups.

derlying interface. In essence, the mobile app enabled its user to choose different background pictures (via a double tap on the home screen), to zoom into certain parts of the picture, to fade out to full screen, to like and to share it. The pictures were tagged with certain categories such as "red" for the main colour or "car" for the theme so that they could be matched with profiles of the users.

The startup wanted to create these profiles in order to deliver image advertising pursuant to the users' usage behavior. The startup's business model consisted in the revenues received from its advertising partners paying for the personalized advertising space. So far, this purpose, the collection of personal data for advertising as explained before, and the way of how this data was processed, could easily be specified before the start of the closed beta test using 20 users. Indeed, as a result of the closed beta test, the startup decided in the middle of 2014, to broaden its concept: Instead of a pure wallpaper app, the app should become a new media format enabling its users to explore different kinds of media. The wallpaper picture should serve as the visual entry point for the user to follow, still via the double tap on the home screen, a link to the actual media format such as the new album of a music band, the newspaper article or, still, the image advertising. Even if this concept was still based on the profiles of the app users, the business model has now changed. Now, not only advertisers should pay for advertising space, but also additional business partners, such as newspapers and music editing houses, should pay the startup a percentage of the price received for selling their online offers to the app users. Hence, the question was whether or not the original purpose still covered the new purpose and the processing operations. Taking into account possibly later changes, the startup had, in the first *Startup Law Clinic* session, before the closed beta test, used an umbrella: Before the startup specifically described the concrete purpose, data and means of the processing, it had clarified that the whole processing pursues the purpose of "personalized marketing". However, the Article 29 Data Protection Working Group stated in its "Opinion 03/2013 on the principle of purpose limitation" that the term of "marketing purposes" would be too broad.[31]

In the course of the following months, the startup started an open beta test for its app, which quickly got up to 30.000 users, and therefore looked

31 See Article 29 Data Protection Working Group, Opinion 03/0213 on purpose limitation, p. 16.

for further private investors. However, the search for a working business model remained very difficult. In April 2015, the startup joined, having now around 100.000 users, a round table discussion with finance experts organized by the *HIIG Business Model Innovation Clinic*. On this occasion, one founder of the startup gave a short presentation, in particular, about the success regarding the user growth and the on-going struggle to find a functioning business model. After a brief discussion, one finance expert provided a solution for the problem: Why spend so many efforts on finding the business model if the user growth was still exploding? The experts' advice was simply to focus, so far, on the user growth. The expert continued to advise and stated that as soon as the number of users was large enough, the startup would only then find out which revenue model would work later on. Equipped with such advice, indeed, the startup was not able to definitely specify the purpose of its later use of the collected data. Even the broad purpose of "personalized marketing" was just a guess. In beginning 2016, the startup had 180.000 users and was still looking for the business model.

bb) Excursus: In which circumstances do data controllers actually need "old" data?

This example of an iterative development process for a mobile app illustrates how difficult it may become, if not impossible, to specify the purpose of all-later processing operations when the data is collected. However, data-driven innovation does not require, in general, that the entrepreneur must be able to use all personal data that has ever been collected. In contrast, for many innovations, it may be sufficient to use data that was only recently collected: If the qualitative data gathered by the startup is just good enough or the user base just large enough, the startup might be able to find its business model or even deliver personalized marketing on an "almost-real time" basis. In conclusion, even if an iterative process principally hinders entrepreneurs to specify the purpose of a later processing, this must not necessarily be so in each particular case.

c) Second scenario: The limitation of the later use of data collected by third parties

As mentioned previously, the second constellation refers to controllers processing personal data that another entity collected originally. In these cases, the problem is not only the iterative entrepreneurial process itself which hinders the controller to specify the purpose of the later processing. Rather, the purpose originally specified by another entity might hinder the controller in its entrepreneurial process. Indeed, it is characteristic for a law to hinder someone's action in order to protect another one.[32] However, the essential point here is to illustrate the uncertainty accompanying entrepreneurial activity when controllers seek to apply the principle of purpose limitation. Two further examples shall illustrate this conceptual uncertainty.

aa) No foreseeable negative impact on individuals

The first example is about a startup that retrieved personal data from social network communities such as Facebook and Twitter via a public API, in order to create so-called *social heat maps*. The social heat map was designed to predict not only the places, but also how many people would be and at what time and for what reason at a certain establishment. One economic business idea of the startup was to sell this information to taxi drivers enabling them to plan their driving routes in a more efficient manner. In order to achieve this objective, the startup transferred data from the social networks' servers to their own servers. The transferred datasets contained data that related to geo-locations of events organized by users via the networks, as well as of users themselves sending a signal from where they were (so-called check-ins). The moment that the data was transferred to the startup's own servers, a self-learning algorithm sorted out the specific data which was useful in order create the social heat map. So far, the participants of the *Startup Law Clinic* sessions, could not see a negative impact on the users' concerned. Indeed, it was the opposite. The participants could only actually see a positive effect in that the users, possibly, will more likely find a taxi, for example, when they come out of a concert

32 Cf. Hoffmann-Riem, Openness toward Innovation and Responsibility for Innovation by means of Law, p. 258.

or a restaurant. The participants particularly came to this conclusion because the startup anonymized the data the moment it had retrieved it from the social networks (via the public API). However, with respect to the current data protection framework, the problem was that the data was not made anonymous before its retrieval. This lead to directive 95/46/EC (Data Protection Directive) being applicable, in principle.[33] As a consequence, two legal issues arose.

The first issue concerned the legitimate basis of the data processing intended by the startup. Social networks usually base their processing of data on their users consent. However, the consent given produced two problems. On the one hand, the consent may not cover the later use of the data intended by the startup, because the social network could not foresee the later usage. On the other hand, the purpose may be specified as being so broad that it ran the risk of not being sufficiently precise (e.g. the purpose of 'transfer to third parties'). Therefore, the startup had either to base its data processing on an additional consent given by the users concerned, or on another legitimate basis provided for by law, (as stipulated in Art. 7 of the Data Protection Directive, as well as in Article 6 of the General Data Protection Regulation). Since the startup would have had, in light of the amount of data concerned, practical difficulties to get the consent of all users' concerned, the startup focused on another legitimate basis provided for by law. Indeed, whether this 'secondary option', i.e. referring to a legal provision when the individual's consent does not cover the intended processing, would have been legal was also questionable because it might be seen as a circumvention of the original consent.[34] In any event, even if this had been possible, it was unclear whether or not the startup could base the data processing on, in particular, the general clause of Article 7 lit. f of the Data Protection Directive (correspondingly, Article 6 sect. 1 lit. f of the

33 The directive itself was, indeed, not directly applicable since it must be transposed into national law in order to directly bind the data controller; for the sake of simplicity, however, this thesis does refer, so far, to the directive and not national law; with respect to the transposition into national German law, see, in more detail, point C. II. 1. c) "Transposition of the requirement of purpose specification into German law".

34 Cf. Gola/Schomerus, Federal Data Protection Law, § 4 cip. 16; in contrast, see Article 17 sect. 1 lit. b GDPR, which excludes the individual's right to require from the controler, based on an objection to his or her consent, to delete the personal data if the controller can base the processing on another legitimate ground foreseen by law.

General Data Protection Regulation). This Article allows the data processing if it "is necessary for the purposes of the legitimate interests pursued by the controller (…), except where such interests are overridden by the interests for fundamental rights and freedoms of the data subject". Whether or not this provision covered the intended data processing was doubtful because the balancing exercise based on the bundle of criteria again produces legal uncertainty.

In the *Law Clinic* Session the participants examined the users consent and it became apparent that the original purpose was not identical with the later use intended by the startup or was not sufficiently precise. Therefore, the second question became additionally relevant: whether or not the later processing intended by the startup was in accordance with the compatibility assessment proposed by the Article 29 Data Protection Working Party with respect to Article 6 sect. 1 lit. b of the Data Protection Directive (correspondingly, Article 5 sect. 1 lit. b of the General Data Protection Regulation).[35] On the one hand, there was no negative impact on the individuals concerned; it seemed to be the same context (communicating with friends and going to social events = private/leisure life?); and the data was, once retrieved by the startup, immediately anonymized. On the other hand, the relationship between the original purpose of collection (connecting friends) with the later processing by the startup (creating social heat maps) was disconnected; the data was sensitive (geo-location data)[36]; and the users of the social networks did not probably expect this kind of usage. Hence, even if there was no intended negative impact on the users of the social networks concerned and the data was immediately anonymized, there was enough legitimate criteria resulting in the finding that the later use was incompatible with the original purpose of collection.

bb) Negative impact foreseeable on the individuals

In the second example, the participants of the *Startup Law Clinic* session could clearly target a possible impact on the individuals concerned by the

---

35 See the Art. 29 Data Protection Working Party, Opinion 03/2013 on the principle of purpose limitation, pp. 20 ff.

36 Cf. the Article 29 Data Protection Working Party, Opinion 06/2014 on the notion of legitimate interests of the data controller under Article 7 of the Directive 95/46/EC, p. 38.

data processing. A startup retrieved generally accessible personal data from professional networks. The startup created, in a first version, profiles based on the data that users of the professional networks have made publically available. The profiles contained predictions about three characteristics of the users of the professional networks that could potentially interest future employers: First, the probability that the user changes his or her current employment; second, the probability that the user would also change the city for a new employment; and third, the degree of expertise in a certain professional domain or area. The startup sought to sell the access to these profiles to the human resources departments of companies in the private market as the access to the profiles, would enable the human resources departments to make better decisions when finding and/or considering the right candidate for a certain job. Since the employer was intended to connect the profile with the candidate, the data could not be considered anonymous. Additionally, in light of the fact that the focus was to sell the product to employers, only, the potential employees (i.e. the users of the professional networks) would not be able to gain access to the database as a whole or to their specific profiles. Similar to the preceding example, two main questions arose.

First, whether or not the later use of the personal data could be based on the users' consent or another legitimate basis provided for by law. Here again, the consent sought by the professional networks from its users did not either cover the later use or was too broad in its purpose. Hence, the startup had to base its data processing either on Article 7 lit. b or f of the Data Protection Directive (correspondingly, Article 6 sect. 1 lit. b or f of the General Data Protection Regulation). The first provision allows the processing if it "is necessary (…) in order to take steps *at the request of the data subject* prior to entering into a contract (underlining by the author)". In the example, the creation of the profiles and the access to it could hence only be necessary for the potential employer if the employee takes the initiative of actually applying for a job. For other cases where the employer searches for new potential employees based on their own initiative, only the general clause under Article 7 lit. f of the Data Protection Directive (and Article 6 sect. 1 lit. f of the General Data Protection Directive, correspondingly) came into question. Insofar, the participants of the *Startup Law Clinic* considered the search (and help) for potential employees indeed was a legitimate interest. However, it was arguable whether or not the potential employee had an overriding interest, for example, for his or her freedom to choose an occupation protected under Article 15 ECFR.

This interest might have overridden the potential employer's (and the startup's) interest because of one particular reason. There was no reason for why the potential candidate could not be able to correct inaccurate data and add further advantageous information or do anything else which could improve his or her chances for being invited to the interview.

With respect to the compatibility of the purposes at hand, it was unclear whether or not the profiling of potential employees in order to find the right job applicants could be seen as a sub-category of the original purpose of the professional network to connect professionals and, thus, identical. In order to avoid any doubts, the participants of the *Law Clinic* session sought to apply the compatibility test proposed by the Article 29 Data Protection Working Party. The question of whether or not the later processing was compatible with the original purpose of the professional networks depended, indeed, on a bundle of criteria which was very similar, if not identical, to the balancing test required under Article 7 lit. f of the Data Protection Directive (and Article 6 sect. 1 lit. f of the General Data Protection Regulation).[37] There were several reasons in favour of the application: 1) the relationship between the later processing and the original purpose was close because the latter processing could have been considered as a subcategory of the first; 2) the data appeared not to be sensitive since it was published by the users and the categories of the profiles did not reveal any information about race, geo-location or similar information; 3) the later processing seemed to belong to the same context (professional life?); and 4) the user might consequently have expected the later use. On the other hand, the impact on the individual concerned could have been significant if he or she was filtered out, only for the reason that his or her profile did not match with the potential employer's expectations. This was even more the case if there was no official proof of whether or not the profile really mirrored the likeliness that the employee would not have the expected attributes.

37 Cf. the criteria proposed by the Article 29 Data Protection Working Group, Opinion 03/0213 on purpose limitation, p. 20 ff., and Opinion 06/2014 on the notion of legitimate interests of the data controller under Article 7 of Directive 95/46/EC, pp. 33 ff.

5. Interim conclusion: Uncertainty about the concept of protection and its legal effects

In conclusion, albeit both of the two last examples significantly differed to each other with respect to the impact, it was hard, if not impossible, to answer the question if the later data processing was legal or not. Similarly, the first example already illustrated that the requirement to specify the purpose creates uncertainty in itself. This sheds light on what startups might mean when they express hope for improvement in political regulations and bureaucracy, rather than for social or advisory support.[38] However, it shall again be stressed that these examples should only *illustrate* the general questions of how to specify the purpose and determine which later use is compatible with the original purpose and which is not. An answer to these general questions does not depend on the practical examples but on the legal concept of protection. However, finding an answer to these questions is highly important for companies and organizations. These entities try to apply the law because of their reputation, amongst other factors.[39] If a data protection authority examines their use of data and comes to the conclusion that they are using that data illegally, there is a high risk of losing their reputation in the market. Consequently, the higher the risk of a loss of reputation, the more important it is for the processing entity to rely on clear criteria that would assist in correctly applying the law.

Correspondingly, the same uncertainty is true with respect to the individuals concerned by the processing of data. Hallinan and Friedewald examined in one of their works more than ten public opinion surveys supplemented by further sources such as ethnographic studies and focus groups regarding the European public perception on the data environment. One of their aims was to find out why individuals' behavior "at first sight appears erratic and even contradictory to declared privacy preferences."[40] Irrespec-

38 See Kollmann et al., European Startup Monitor 2015, pp. 62 and 63, indeed showing financial support as the even higher ranked hope.

39 Cf. Jarchow and Estermann, Big Data: Chances, Risks and Need for Action of the Swiss Confederation, pp. 14 and 15.

40 See Hallinan and Friedewald, Public Perception of the Data Environment and Information Transactions – A selected-survey analysis of the European public's views on the data environment and data transactions, pp. 62 and 76/77.

tive of differences in national perceptions,[41] the European public considers the protection of personal data as very important and that the disclosure of personal data raises significant concerns. However, individuals appear to accept the disclosure of personal data considering it as being "simply a part of modern life".[42] In order to explain the individual logic behind these contradictory observations, Hallinan and Friedewald referred to economic considerations proposed by Acquisti and Grossklags about potential limiting factors for rational decision-making.[43] In light of these considerations, the contradictions between general privacy awareness and specific disclosure of personal data result, in particular, from the following three aspects: First, individuals often only have a limited understanding of the risks implied in data transactions.[44] For example, while they are specifically aware of ID fraud as a serious threat, only few individuals consider or understand "the more abstract, invisible and complex aspects" such as "the value of the data, the nature of the technologies involved or the shape or nature of data flows – that is to say, (…) the critical parts of the data environment".[45] The second reason, besides limited information or conceptual understanding, is psychological distortion. Individuals tend, for instance, to prefer certain short-range rewards, such as an online service "for free", to uncertain long-range risks caused by a potential misuse of data. Finally, ideological or personal attitudes constitute another factor for why an individual might either not disclose personal data at all, albeit the benefits are higher than potential losses, or vice versa.[46]

Hallinan and Friedewald stress that these factors challenged the common understanding of economic behavior that the current data protection

---

41 See, for example, Vodafone Institute for Society and Communications: Big Data – A European Survey on the Opportunities and Risks of Data Analytics, p. 17, showing that "Germans are especially critical concerning privacy issues", while "South Europeans in the survey are generally more relaxed as far as the collection and use of their data is concerned".

42 See Hallinan and Friedewald, ibid., p. 65 and 68.

43 See Hallinan and Friedewald, ibid., pp. 70 et al. with reference to Acquisti, Alessandro and Grossklags, Jens, "Privacy Attitudes and Privacy Behavior: Losses, Gains, and Hyperbolic Discounting", in: Camp, J. L. and Lewis, S. (eds.), The Economics of Information Security, 2004 Kluwer, as well as ibid., "Privacy and rationality in individual decision making", IEEE Security and Privacy 2005, pp. 26 to 33.

44 See Hallinan and Friedewald, ibid., pp. 72 to 74.

45 See Hallinan and Friedewald, ibid., p. 75.

46 See Hallinan and Friedewald, ibid., p. 74.

system is actually built on. The misconception by the legislator about the individual's behavior might be the reason for why the European public has the feeling that the current laws do not fulfill their objective.[47] In light of this, critics recognize that current data protection law suffers, from both the individual's perspective and the controller's perspective, a "credibility crisis".[48]

Several legal scholars stress that this credibility crisis results from the uncertainty about the conception behind data protection law.[49] In particular, v. Lewinski unfolds, in detail, the different dimensions of protection covered by the broad term *"data protection"*. While data protection laws are typically meant to regulate the relationship between individuals, on the one hand, and companies and the State, on the other hand, the object of protection, as well as the concept of protection is less clear.[50] In v. Lewinski's opinion, the term "data protection" refers to several objects of protection (i.e. the question of "what is protected") such as the individual's dignity, his or her private sphere, or the societal balance of informational power.[51] Similarly, there are several possible concepts of protection (i.e. referring to the question of "how to protect the objects") as: first, practical protection mechanisms such as self-protection; second, normative mechanisms such as social, technical and legal norms but also mechanisms of self-regulation such as standards, codes of conduct, and certificates; third, institutions that enable, for example, individual's self-protection, limit informational power, or enforce legal requirements; and fourth, the range of protection such as protection against concrete infringements, or specific risks and dangers, or even precautionary protection against unspecific risks and abstract dangers.[52]

---

47 See Hallinan and Friedewald, ibid., pp. 65 and 71.

48 See Kuner et al., The Data Protection Credibility Crisis, IDPL 2015 Vol. 5 no. 3, pp. 161.

49 Cf. Stentzel, The Fundamental Right to ...? The Search of the Object of Protection of Data Protection in the European Union, PinG 05.15, pp. 185; cf. Solove, Understanding Privacy; cf. v. Lewinski, The Matrix of Data Protection.

50 See v. Lewinski, ibid., pp. 1 to 16.

51 See v. Lewinski, ibid., pp. 7 as well as 17 to 63; see also De Hert and Gutwirth, Data Protection in the Case Law of Strasbourg and Luxemburg: Constitutionalisation in Action, p. 5.

52 See v. Lewinski, ibid., pp. 64 to 85.

Irrespective of whether or not this "matrix of data protection" is correct and comprehensive,[53] it does help clarify the question that the meaning and extent of the principle of purpose limitation cannot be answered without being clear on the object and concept of protection of data protection law. Only if the object and concept of protection are sufficiently precise, it is possible to answer the question of how to balance the need for innovation against its risks with respect to the processing of personal data.

II. Research questions and approach

Therefore, the research questions of this doctoral thesis are:

1. *What is the meaning and function of the principle of purpose limitation on the private sector, in light of the object and concept of protection of data protection law?*
2. *In order to find a balance between the societal need for data-driven innovation and protection against its risks, what regulation instruments should transpose the principle of purpose limitation in the private sector?*

In order to answer these questions, this doctoral thesis builds upon the research approach regarding innovation developed by the *Center of Law and Innovation* (CERI) in Hamburg, Germany.

1. Legal research about innovation

The CERI research project "Law and Innovation" reacted to the situation that at the beginning of 1990, legal scholarship had not yet started, at least not in Germany, doing research about innovation, in contrast to other research disciplines such as technical, economic, and social sciences.[54] Consequently, the object of this research approach does not primarily look to innovate the law, but rather how the regulator can regulate technological,

53 See v. Lewinski, ibid., pp. 87 to 90 commenting on the deficits of such a matrix and highlighting, however, its main use for structuring the public debate, enhancing legal comparison on an international level, and discovering deficits of legal protection.

54 See Hoffmann-Riem, Openness toward Innovation and Responsibility for Innovation by means of Law, p. 256.

economic and social innovation in today's society.[55] This approach acknowledges that the primary objective of the law is to protect against harm and risks and, thus, restricts the scope of action of entities that actual cause these harms and risks. Such a restriction, is in particular, at stake if the law expands its scope of protection from known risks to even unknown risks. One instrument for expanding the scope of protection, can be the so-called precautionary principle (as discussed in chapter B. II. Data protection as a risk regulation). However, regulating innovation, not only leads to the question of how to protect against the actual risks caused by innovation, but also how to enable the development of innovation within society.[56] Contrary to the common prejudice that the law is an inherent barrier for innovation, the law levels, protects and enforces innovation.[57] Taking both of these effects of law into account, i.e. those restricting the scope of action of risk-causing innovators, as well as those leveling, protecting, and enforcing innovation, Hoffmann-Riem summarizes this approach by posing the essential question: How should legal instruments be shaped in order to enable and even promote innovation without denying necessary protection? From this point of view, only those regulations that do not take particularities of innovation processes into account, and, thus, are badly drafted, are an unjustified barrier for innovation.[58]

2. The regulator's perspective

Referring to theories of evolutionary economics, the research approach that focuses on innovation builds upon modern movements in administrative law that seek to cope with the problem that the regulator has limited knowledge of future events.[59] With respect to German law, Voßkuhle pinpoints the essential differences between this new and the traditional approach by giving a brief summary of its historical development. The tradi-

---

55 See Hoffmann-Riem, ibid., p. 257.

56 See Hoffmann-Riem, ibid., pp. 256 ff.

57 See, instead of many, Mayer-Schönberger, The Law as Stimulus: The Role of Law in Fostering Innovative Entrepreneurship, pp. 159 to 169; Gasser, Cloud Innovation and the Law: Issues, Approaches, and Interplay, pp. 19 and 20.

58 Hoffmann-Riem, ibid., 260 and 261; cf. also Brownsword and Yeung, Regulating Technologies: Tools, Targets, and Thematics, p. 21.

59 See Hoffmann-Riem, ibid., pp. 259 to 262; Appel, Tasks and Procedures of the Innovation Impact Assessment, p. 149.

tional approach mainly concentrates on the judicial act and examines its conformity with law. This examination is based on a systematic review of positive law and the elaboration of underlying principles. This examination results, in essence, with either a yes or no answer. Its primary aim is binding the executive to the rule of law.[60] Several studies from the 1970's had proved, however, high execution deficiencies of this classic form of imperative public law, particularly in the environmental sector. Upcoming new forms of informal cooperation, between the public and private sector appeared, at the time, to function better than these classic forms of regulation. Researchers started, therefore, to thoroughly investigate the interrelationship between legislative rule making, administrative, as well as judicial decision-making, and its implementation within society. As a main starting point for alternative strategies and forms of regulation, they discovered that the regulator, in particular, did not have the full knowledge of a situation caused by more and more complex environments (particularly in the environmental, telecommunications, and other technique-driven sectors), its increasing non-linear dynamics, and, thus, (objectively) unforeseeable and (sometimes) irreversible effects.[61]

Methodologically, the new regulatory approach ties into the concept of control theory developed in political sciences.[62] Elaborating on this approach, German legal scholars in administrative law usually build on a concept of control focusing on the actions of those individuals or entities that are affected by it. This concept differentiates between the individuals and entities, aim, and instruments of control, as well as the controlling entity. Indeed, the term "controlling entity" should not conceal the fact that there often is no single entity but rather an interactive process that consists of several entities, working together and against each other, and producing regulatory outputs.[63] Similarly, with respect to the individuals and entities affected by the regulation, legal scholars recognize that society finds its solutions for problems in complex structures and a central regulator, in particular the legislator, may have difficulties to appropriately address the individuals in order to achieve its regulatory aims. Keeping this in mind,

---

60 See Voßkuhle, New Regulatory Approach of Administrative Law, cip. 2 to 8.

61 See the summary of the evolvement at Voßkuhle, ibid., cip. 10 and 11; cf. also Hoffmann-Riem, ibid., pp. 261 to 265; Eifert, New Regulatory Approach of Administrative Law, cip. 1 and 2.

62 See Voßkuhle, ibid., cip. 18.

63 See Voßkuhle, ibid., cip. 20.

the modern regulatory approach nevertheless focuses on the state's point of view and on legislative measures as its main regulation instrument. With these measures, the state seeks to create a certain impact on the individual or entity by focusing on their legal liability should they not adhere to the system. This is the main conceptual difference to the so-called governance perspective, which applies a different point of view that is not restricted in pursuing specific aims by legal means.[64] Focusing on Internet governance, Hofmann, Katzenbach and Gollatz, advocate that the governance perspective instead focuses on reflexive coordination and, thus, "refers to addressing, questioning, and renegotiating Internet-related coordination practices."[65] However, despite or rather because of the analytical difference between both perspectives, the new regulatory approach may refer well to theoretical concepts and empirical findings of the governance approach in order to find out whether "self-regulation" processes already fulfill the regulator's aims or whether there is a need for state regulatory support.

On an international level, legal scholars equally elaborate on the functions, modes, and strategies coming into question for regulation in complex and non-linear environments, however, not always using the same terminology.[66] The common starting point consists in, as mentioned previously, the knowledge deficiencies of regulators acting in these environments. Raab and De Hert describe this common starting point promoting that any understanding of the functioning of regulation (and its "tools") requires one to consider the regulatory activity as a process "in which, in

64 See Eifert, ibid., cip. 5 and 6; Voßkuhle, ibid., cip. 21; cf. also Braithwaite et al., Can regulation and governance make a difference?, p. 3; Hofmann, Katzenbach and Gollatz, Between coordination and regulation: Finding the governance in Internet governance, pp. 6 and 7.

65 See Hofmann, Katzenbach and Gollatz, ibid., p. 13.

66 Cf. Baldwin and Cave, Understanding Regulation – Theory, Strategy and Practice; Raab and De Hert, Tools for Technology Regulation: Seeking Analytical Approaches Beyond Lessig and Hood; Murray, Conceptualising the Post-Regulatory (Cyber)state, with further references, amongst others, to Black, Decentring Regulation: Understanding the Role of Regulation and Self Regulation in a 'Post-Regulatory' World' as well as Scott, Regulation in the Age of Governance: The Rise of the Post Regulatory State', further developed, ibid, The Regulation of Cyberspace – Control in the Online Environment; Franzius, Modes and Impact Factors for the Control through Law; Eifert, Regulation Strategies.

theory, several actors may participate in the making, using, and governing of each tool".[67]

The terminology regarding the regulatory functions, modes, and strategies, is often not comprehensively clear. The German scholar Eifert explains the terminological ambiguity with respect to the diversity of theoretical concepts applied, respectively. He favors to determine, at least, the regulatory strategies pursuant to the state role within the regulation distinguishing, though, between imperative law ("command and control", often also described as "rules), state regulated self-regulation ("co-regulation", often referring to "principles" or "standards"), and societal self-regulation. Focusing on two main types of regulation, i.e. imperative law (command-and-control) and instruments of regulated self-regulation (co-regulation),[68] Eifert sums up the positive and negative aspects of these two types of regulation.

On the one hand a command-and-control regulation provides for high legal certainty (given by the clarity of legal *"if-then"*-rules and the direct effects of its execution). On the other hand, this kind of regulation might be inefficient because it does not take into consideration individuals' economic behaviour. The inflexibility of this kind of regulation constrains more intensively an individual's actions. This restriction leads to three effects: First, it lowers the acceptance of the regulation amongst individuals; second, this increases the probability that the individuals will try to circumvent the regulation; and finally, it increases the efforts of the state to hinder the individuals' circumvention of the law itself. Therefore, this kind of regulation is considered to work best when the following two conditions are met: first, the regulator aims to prohibit third parties' rights or interests being harmed; and, second, the regulator has sufficient knowledge about the effectiveness and efficiency of the corresponding protection instruments. In contrast, if the regulator does not possess sufficient knowledge, such as in a dynamic and non-linear environment, and creativ-

---

67 See Raab and De Hert, ibid., p. 282.

68 See Eifert, ibid., cip. 13 to 15; focusing on privacy-related principles, Maxwell, Principles-based regulation of personal data: the case of 'fair processing', pp. 212 to 214, referring to J Black, 'Forms and Paradoxes of Principles Based Regulation', LSE Law, Society and EconomyWorking Paper 13/2008, SSRN abstract n8 1267722, L Kaplow, 'Rules Versus Standards: An Economic Analysis' (1992) 42 Duke L. J. 557; R Posner, Economic Analysis of Law (8th edn., Aspen/Wolters Kluwer, New York, 2011), p. 747.

ity is needed in order to solve a variety of problems, this kind of command and control regulation does not provide for the appropriate instruments.[69]

Instead, in order to enhance problem-solving creativity, Eifert stresses co-regulation as the more appropriate regulation strategy. Thereby, taking the decentralized knowledge of private entities into account does not only increase the problem-solving capacities in the society. Rather, the fact that the regulator adapts its regulation instruments to the inherent logics of the entities acting on the private market also increases their acceptance of the regulation instruments. Furthermore, this kind of regulation decreases the administrative costs because the private structures used for it are often also financed privately. Finally, instruments of co-regulation can provide a solution for the territorial problem of "command and control" regulation because its execution does not depend, at least not directly, on the State but private entities not being bound to national territories.[70] However, a possible disadvantage is that this kind of regulation does not meet the regulator's expectations but, instead, makes the regulation more complex, opaque and less effective or efficient than the classic form. Another risk is that the regulated private entities abuse their knowledge advantage toward the State. This could be the case, for example, if the State gives privileges to these private entities because it thinks that their solutions really serve society, but in reality serves their particulars interests, only.[71]

In any case, Eifert stresses, like Franzius, that the complexity of this form of regulation requires the regulator to learn. This means to frequently evaluate its effectiveness and efficiency of its regulation instruments.[72] Such an evaluation should refer to other disciplines, such as to social and economic sciences, and build upon their validated knowledge. The moment when the legislator extends its view to the effects of its regulation, reference to these other disciplines and their methodologies included will increase the rationality of law.[73]

---

69 See Eifert, ibid., cip. 25 and 26.

70 See Eifert, ibid., cip. 59.

71 See Eifert, ibid., cip. 60.

72 Cf. Eifert, ibid., cip. 60; Franzius, ibid., cip. 81 to 103.

73 See Hoffmann-Riem, Innovation Responsibility, p. 39.

3. Possible pitfalls taking the effects of regulation instruments into account

In conclusion, Voßkuhle summarizes the promises and possible pitfalls of this legal research approach seeking to gain deeper knowledge about the complex effects of law as a regulation instrument. He considers the promises as: first, this approach broadens the scope in which the law is just one regulation mechanism amongst others, such as beside further mechanisms of economic markets, networks or within organizations; second the approach enables researchers to ascertain and take the effects and efficiency of legal instruments into account, and their interplay with further mechanisms; and third, in doing so, the approach enables legal researchers to interconnect with other research disciplines. This last aspect enables researchers to build on theoretical frameworks and empirical methodologies already elaborated on in other disciplines. However, the possible pitfalls of this approach are: On the one hand, legal scholars considering the effects of regulation instruments may over-simplify the complex interplay of cause and effect. The reason is that all theoretical models mirror just one part of the reality and the choice of regulation instruments based on them thus runs the risk of not being able to meet the legislator's goal. On the other hand, the regulatory function of the law is not the only function. The law also serves as an expression of the values provided for by the constitution. This means that legal provisions do not lose their validity just because in some circumstances it has little effect, only, for example, because of inefficient execution of the law.[74]

These considerations are important for the examination of the principle of purpose limitation pursued in this thesis. The principle of purpose limitation suffers, indeed, from a lack of execution in the private market. And this may result from the uncertainty about its precise meaning and extent.[75] However, this lack of execution does not mean, per se, that the principle of purpose limitation should be abandoned as a whole. This hesitation is particularly justified because the uncertainty about its meaning and

---

74 See Voßkuhle, ibid., cip. 22 to 28.

75 See, in general, the above-mentioned studies as well as, in particular, the observations made in the HIIG Law Clinic where startups simply went on developing their products if they could not definitely clarify how to apply the principle of purpose limitation and expected that data protection authorities would not become aware of their practice, anyway.

extent is not a special problem of the principle of purpose limitation but of all legal principles in general. The less imperative law and its conditional if-then-scheme serves as regulation instrument, the more important instruments, such as legal principles, become. Principles do not provide for a binary scheme that will answer the question of whether an act is legal or not but allows individuals to explore different, and in the best possible outcome an optimal solution.[76] Indeed, with the abandonment of imperative law and its conditional decision rule, the individuals' legal uncertainty increases because individuals do not know whether the solution found meets the regulators expectations. Consequently, individuals and the regulator have to start an interactive process reconstructing together, the certainty of legal rules.[77] The answer of whether or not or in which way the regulator meets its expectations regarding the principle of purpose limitation depends, in the first instance, on the above-mentioned research questions of this thesis.

III. Course of examination

In order to answer the research questions, the next chapter clarifies the conceptual definitions which provides a basis for regulation of innovation. The first sub-chapter illustrates how economic theories define and conceptualize "innovation" and "entrepreneurship" and which role the law plays in these conceptualizations of "innovative entrepreneurship". In doing so, one particular focus is on the illustration of economic models describing the non-linearity of innovative entrepreneurship processes. Subsequently, the examination goes on to review literature from both economic and legal perspectives and examines the effects of legal certainty on "innovative entrepreneurship". The first sub-chapter concludes with the appearing regulatory conflict: On the one hand, as discussed, regulation instruments, such as the principle of purpose limitation, is open toward innovation but decreases legal certainty; on the other hand, legal uncertainty hinders innovation. Therefore, it will be key to explore mechanisms that combine both aspects, i.e. being open toward innovation but also ensuring legal certainty and, thus, even promoting innovation. The second sub-chapter draws at-

76 See Franzius, ibid., cip. 7; cf. Raab and De Hert, ibid., p. 278.
77 Cf. Franzius, ibid., cip. 17.

tention to the other side of the "innovation" coin, i.e. data protection law as a regulation of risks caused by innovation. This sub-chapter clarifies the terms "risks" and "dangers", as well as the often correspondingly used protection mechanisms "prevention" and "precaution". This distinction is highly relevant for exploring the function of the principle of purpose limitation at a later stage. The discussion on various protection instruments for different types of threats leads to the last sub-chapter that clarifies the conceptual definitions for the regulation of data-driven innovation: The question of what is threatened, in terms of data protection and, thus, which object of protection the principle of purpose limitation serves. Based on Nissenbaum's work *Privacy in Context*, this last sub-chapter provides an overview about the prevailing theories, concepts, and approaches on the value of privacy. So far, this work does hence not yet clarify the distinction between privacy and data protection and, correspondingly, privacy and data protection laws; this distinction is an essential element of the conceptual work of this thesis and will be proposed later on. This sub-chapter finally gives a first response to Nissenbaum's critique on the purpose-oriented concept of protection by clarifying the relationship between the terms "purpose" and "context". This will lead to a first insight into the function of the principle of purpose limitation.

The third chapter contains the main part of this thesis: An analysis of the legal framework determining the meaning and function of the principle of purpose limitation. Elaborating on the object and concept of protection of data protection law, this chapter seeks to clarify three main question: first, the precise meaning and extent of the requirement to specify the purpose; second, the precise meaning and extent of the requirement to limit the later use of data to the purposes originally specified; and third, which specific instruments are appropriate for establishing these two requirements in the private sector in order to find a sound balance between enabling innovation and protection against its risks in society. In doing so, the first sub-chapter clarifies the interrelationship between the different regimes of fundamental rights focusing on the European Convention on Human Rights (ECHR), the European Charta of Fundamental Rights (ECFR), and German Basic Rights (GG). Furthermore, it treats the question of the effects of these fundamental rights in the private sector, in particular, of the right to privacy under Article 8 ECHR, the rights to privacy and data protection under Article 7 and 8 ECFR, as well as the German right to informational self-determination under Article 1 sect. 1 in combination with 2 sect. 1 GG. The question is whether these fundamental rights directly bind private entities that process personal data, like the State, or whether they have only an indirect effect in the private sector. The thought behind this question is that the second alternative gives the legislator more room for transposing the constitutional requirements into secondary and/or ordinary law. The sub-chapter goes on to analyze the object and concept of protection developed by the European Court of Human Rights (ECtHR), the European Court of Justice (ECJ), and the German Constitutional Court (BVerfG), with respect to each of the above-mentioned fundamental rights. This parallel analysis will effectively allow one to compare the differences between the corresponding objects, as well as concepts of protection. The first sub-chapter concludes with an analytical result on the challenges facing, in general, from these objects and concepts of protection being very broad and vague. A theoretical solution provides a first hint on how this may also affect the determination of the function of the principle of purpose limitation.

The next sub-chapter draws the attention to the main problem resulting from such concepts of protection that are intrinsically broad and/or vague: The uncertainty about how to legally specify the purpose of the data processing. On a European level, the analysis will illustrate that there are almost no criteria which help specify the purpose, provided for by the judicial courts in light of the corresponding fundamental rights. However, it will be illustrated that the specification of the purpose is an essential element in secondary law because several further definitions and requirements, such as the scope of application, refer to the purpose specified. Despite this essential role, the Article 29 Data Protection Working Party, having an advisory status for questions about the interpretation of the Data Protection Directive, does not provide reliable criteria for the specification of the purpose, either (nor does the General Data Protection Regulation address this issue). Therefore, the sub-chapter continues to examine how the secondary law itself specifies certain purposes of processing such as for "marketing electronic communications services", pursuant to Art. 6 sect. 3 of the Directive 2002/58/EC of the European Parliament and of the Council of 12 July 2002 concerning the processing of personal data and the protection of privacy in the electronic communications sector (ePrivacy Directive). Subsequently, the examination turns into the question of how the German legislator transposes these requirements into German ordinary law. This allows the comparison, since there are almost no criteria provided for by European fundamental rights, of the concept of protection established within ordinary law, at least, with German basic rights. The analysis of European secondary and German ordinary law, as well as its comparison with the (so far developed) constitutional requirements, alludes to the fact that there are several flaws in the concept of protection. The results not only confirm the general challenges stemming, as concluded previously, from the object and concept of protection as being very broad and vague, now with particular respect to the requirement of purpose specification. Rather, it is apparent from the results that these flaws consist, in essence, in the fact that the constitutional requirements for the processing of data by the State are, in essence, equally applied to private entities. Since private entities have different means for specifying purposes at their disposal than the State, this leads to the situation that the effects of the requirements are even stricter for private entities than for the State. This sub-chapter hence concludes, with a particular focus on the European Charta of Fundamental Rights, with a refinement of the object and concept of protection serving a better scale to private entities for the specification of the purpose of their data processing.

The following sub-chapter treats the second component of the principle of purpose limitation, i.e. the question on the precise meaning and extent of the requirement to limit the later processing to the purpose(s) initially specified. The examination exemplifies two different models: The European model of purpose compatibility and the German model requiring strict purpose identity allowing, however, a change of purpose if this change is proportionate. With regard to the European model, this doctoral thesis examines the criteria developed by the European Court of Human Rights, as well as the European Court of Justice in light of the corresponding fundamental rights. While the European Court of Human Rights mainly refers to the "reasonable expectations" of the individual concerned by the processing of data related to him or her, the European Court of Justice does not. Interestingly, the Article 29 Data Protection Working Party nevertheless refers, proposing their criteria helping answer the extent of the requirement of purpose compatibility, to the individual's "reasonable expectations",[78] albeit the Data Protection Directive does not either (interestingly, Article 6 sect. 4 lit a-e of the General Data Protection Regulation also lists all criteria but the "reasonable expectations" criterion). It is apparent from the analysis that the criteria proposed do not actually help in

78 See the Art. 29 Data Protection Working Party, Opinion 03/2013 on the principle of purpose limitation, pp. 24 and 25.

answering the question on the extent of the requirement of purpose compatibility. This doctoral thesis therefore continues, in order to receive inspiration on which functions the limitation of purposes can have, to examine the German model. Interestingly, albeit German ordinary law transposes the European directive, it deviates, at least formally, from the compatibility requirement. The examination therefore draws the attention to the concept of protection provided for by the German basic right to informational self-determination in order to find the reason for the deviation. Since the reason for the deviation appears to come, indeed, from the application of the German basic right (and not of the European fundamental rights), this thesis presents three alternative approaches proposed within German legal literature in order to get a clearer understanding about the possible functions of the principle of purpose limitation. Indeed, all three approaches refer to the processing of data by the State. Taking the results of the preceding analysis into account, the thesis concludes this sub-chapter with a new approach defining the meaning and extent of the principle of purpose limitation for the private sector.

On the basis of the own approaches developed in the two last-preceding sub-chapters, the last sub-chapter treats the question of which specific regulation instruments serve best in order to establish this new understanding of the meaning and extent of the principle of purpose limitation in the private sector. Here, the thesis exemplifies, iteratively, the impact of this understanding on the following elements: first, the scope(s) of application of all protection instruments; second, the specific application of the protection instruments in the private sector (in particular, the necessity as well as interplay of the individual's consent and other legitimate basis laid down by law); and third, on particular aspects of the consent, its withdrawal, and a right to object to the data processing, as well as on further protection instruments such as rights of information, participation, and deletion of personal data, by taking the individual's decision-making process as a whole into account.[79]

Finally, on the basis of the refined concept of protection regarding the principle of purpose limitation and related protection instruments, the last chapter of this thesis comes back to answer questions about the effects of these instruments. These questions refer to both sides of the "innovation"

---

79 Cf. the concept and terminology of "choice architectures" at Thaler and Sunstein, Nudge – Improving Decisions About Health, Wealth, and Happiness.

coin, i.e. the effects on processes of "innovative entrepreneurship" as well as on the efficiency of risk protection instruments. The preceding chapters will have made certain remaining questions apparent that cannot sufficiently be answered by legal analysis alone. This last chapter therefore proposes an empirical methodology that helps answer the remaining questions. On the basis of these results, the regulator might answer the overarching question of which instruments fits best its regulatory aims.

B. Conceptual definitions as a link for regulation

This chapter clarifies the conceptual definitions that provide a link for the regulation of innovation. While the first sub-chapter refers to economic theories defining the terms "innovation" and "entrepreneurship", the second sub-chapter draws the attention to the other side, i.e. data protection law as a regulation of risks caused by innovation. This sub-chapter illustrates the discussion on various protection instruments for different types of threats, such as prevention and precaution or dangers and risks. This leads to the last sub-chapter treating the question of what is actually threatened. The clarification of the interplay between "context" and "purpose" provides a first understanding of the meaning and extent of the principle of purpose limitation.

I. Innovation and entrepreneurship

If the regulator refers, at least implicitly, to entrepreneurial innovation, it permits one to tie definitions that have been developed by other research disciplines.[80] Indeed, in other disciplines, there is not a common definition of "innovation" or "entrepreneurship". Scholars consider that innovation and entrepreneurship are phenomena that can and should be analyzed from various, interdisciplinary perspectives. This might be the reason for the lack of common definitions.[81] However, as one of the first economists, Schumpeter recognized, coming from an evolutionary understanding of private markets, innovation as an essential force for societal change. In his work *Capitalism, Socialism & Democracy*, he disagreed with the common view on price competition as the main driver of economy and determined, instead, "the new consumers' goods, the new methods of production or transportation, the new markets, the new forms of industrial organization

80 See Hoffmann-Riem, Openness toward Innovation and Responsibility for Innovation by means of Law, p. 257.

81 See regarding the first term at Fagerberg, Innovation: A Guide to the Literature, p. 1, and regarding the second term at Fueglistaller et al., Entrepreneurship – Basics, p. 6.

that capitalist enterprise creates" as the fundamental impulse "that sets and keeps the capitalist engine in motion".[82] From this perspective, the "function of entrepreneurs is to reform or revolutionize the pattern by exploiting an invention or, more generally, an untried technological possibility for producing a new commodity or producing an old one in a new way (...) and so on."[83]

Hence, Schumpeter differentiated between inventions, i.e. the first realization of a solution for a problem, and the innovation bringing an invention to the market.[84] This differentiation is, until today, widely recognized. Today's economists are focusing, in essence, on four types of innovations: First, product and service innovations; second, process innovations; third, business model innovations; and fourth, social innovations which often refer to new forms of communication or cooperation being mostly considered, actually, either as the basis for the before-mentioned types of innovations or as their result.[85] Further categories classify innovations pursuant to their impact on current production processes or market structures. This perspective differentiates between: on the one hand, "incremental" or "marginal" innovations describing continuous improvements of one or more innovation types listed previously; and on the other hand, "radical" innovations or "technological revolutions" referring to the introduction of a new technology or cluster of technologies which did not exist before in society.[86] Keeping this in mind, it is common ground today that data provides, more and more, the basis for many, if not once most, of these types or categories of innovation.[87]

---

82 See Schumpeter, Capitalism, Socialism & Democracy, pp. 82 and 83.

83 See Schumpeter, ibid., p. 132.

84 See Fagerberg, ibid., p. 5; Fueglistaller et al., Entrepreneurship – Innovation and Entrepreneurship, p. 98.

85 See Fueglistaller, ibid., pp. 99 and 100; cf. also Neveling et al., Economic and Sociological Approaches of Innovation Research, pp. 369 and 370, as well as Fagerberg, ibid., pp. 8 and 9.

86 See Fagerberg, ibid., p. 9 referring to Schumpeter.

87 See, instead of many, at Mayer-Schönberger and Cukier, Big Data: A Revolution That Will Transform How We Live, Work, and Think, in particular at pp. 6 to 35 and 322 to 336.

1. Process of innovative entrepreneurship

Entrepreneurship research poses, in particular, the question of how entrepreneurs create such innovation.[88] After researchers had initially focused on the personality of the entrepreneur per se, Drucker stressed, in his influential article *The Discipline of Innovation*, that it is less the personality per se that constitutes entrepreneurship than the entrepreneurial activity.[89] Over time, several economics had elaborated on models describing the entrepreneurial process as the overarching unit of analysis encompassing entrepreneurial phenomena such as activity, novelty, and change.[90] In order to extract a common model being both generic, i.e. describing the common patterns of all different kinds of entrepreneurial processes, as well as distinct, i.e. differentiating entrepreneurial from non-entrepreneurial processes, Moroz and Hindle analyzed more than 32 of existent models. They came to the result, however, that the models analyzed were too fragmented in order to achieve the initial aim of building a common model being both generic and distinct.[91] Despite this fragmentation, or rather because of it, three aspects shall be explained in more detail because they may serve as reference points for answering the question of how legal regulation instruments function with respect to the logics of entrepreneurs creating innovation.

a) Key Elements for the entrepreneurial process

The first aspect being of interest for this doctoral thesis refers to key elements which are decisive for entrepreneurship. Gartner elaborated on several of these key elements, who conducted, in the 1980's, a study with academics, practitioners and politicians related to the entrepreneurial field in order to gain a more comprehensive understanding about what kind of ac-

---

88 See Drucker, The Discipline of Innovation, p. 3.

89 See Drucker, The Discipline of Innovation, p. 3.

90 See Moroz and Hindle, Entreneurship as a Process: Toward Harmonizing Multiple Perspectives.

91 See Moroz and Hindle, Entreneurship as a Process: Toward Harmonizing Multiple Perspectives, p. 781.

tivity or situation is considered as entrepreneurial.[92] Pursuant to this model, entrepreneurs locate business opportunities, accumulate resources, and build organizations in order to produce and market products or services, while constantly responding to their environment.[93] Moroz and Hindle stress that this model does not actually describe a behavior being distinct to others, such as pure managerial activities. However, they also point to the implicit distinctness of this model describing the entrepreneur as being "involved in a multidimensional process of organizational emergence that is focused upon the creation of a new venture that is independent, profit oriented, and driven by individual expertise. The newness attached to this process is linked to products, processes, markets, or technologies where the firm is considered a new entrant or supplier to a market."[94]

Fueglistaller proposes a very similar process model determined by the following five key elements: The entrepreneur, a business opportunity, sufficient resources, a form of organization, and a supportive environment.[95]

---

92 See Gartner, What are we talking about when we talk about entrepreneurship?, as well as, A Conceptual Framework for Describing the Phenomenon of New Venture Creation.

93 See Gartner, A Conceptual Framework for Describing the Phenomenon of New Venture Creation, p. 702.

94 See Moroz and Hindle, ibid., p. 800.

95 See Fueglistaller et al., Entrepreneurship – Basics, p. 7.

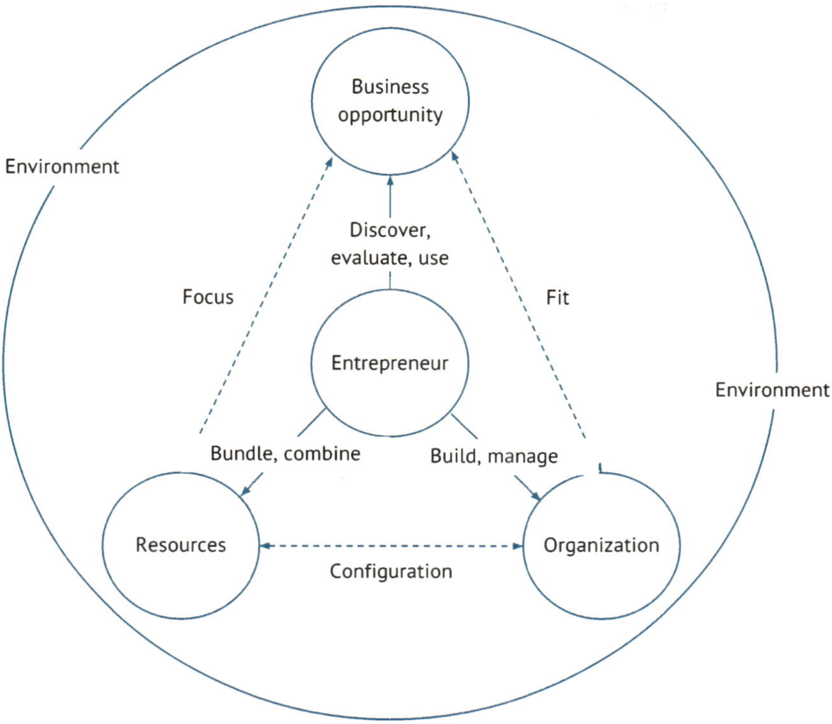

Graphic: Key Elements for Entrepreneurial Process[96]

Consequently, the entrepreneur constitutes the core of an enterprise discovering or creating business opportunities, evaluating and using them. In such an emergent process, the individual capacities, capabilities, and attitudes play a decisive role. The entrepreneur's cognitive capacities influence the identification or creation of business opportunities; the evaluation of the opportunity depends, on the one hand, on the characteristics of the opportunity and, on the other hand, on the individual attitude such as toward risks; and the use of the opportunities depends on the abilities of how to practically organize the process as a whole.[97]

96 Following Fueglistaller et al., ibid., p. 8.
97 See Fueglistaller et al., ibid., pp. 7 to 14.

b) Business Opportunities: Discovery and creation

The second aspect focuses on how entrepreneurs identify or create business opportunities. Economics usually consider the existence of a "business opportunity" if "there is an opportunity to introduce a new product, new service, or new method and to sell it for a higher price than its production costs".[98] They also agree on the assumption that such an opportunity arises "whenever competitive imperfections in an industry or market exist".[99] However, economics argue about from where these market imperfections come: Does an entrepreneur discover or create these market imperfections and, as a consequence, the business opportunity?

There are two main theories seeking to answer this question, the Discovery- and Creation Theory. Tying into teleological theories of human action, both theories aim to explain the relationship between entrepreneurial action and the ability to produce innovation.[100] Alvarez and Barney summarize the essential differences between both theories as:[101]

	Discovery Theory	**Creation Theory**
Nature of Business Opportunities/Market Imperfections	Caused by exogenous shocks to pre-existing industries or markets	Caused by endogenous actions of individuals to produce new products or services
Nature of Entrepreneurs	Entrepreneurs are different than non-entrepreneurs in some critical and enduring ways	Entrepreneurs may be the same or different than non-entrepreneurs; any differences, ex ante, may be magnified by entrepreneurial actions
Nature of Decision Making	Those who are aware of and seek to exploit opportunities operate under conditions of risk	Those creating opportunities act under conditions of uncertainty

Table: Differentiating aspects of Discovery and Creation Theories[102]

98 See Fueglistaller et al., ibid., p. 10: "Im Allgemeinen spricht man von einer unternehmerischen Gelegenheit, wenn sich die Möglichkeit bietet, ein neues Produkt, eine neue Dienstleistung oder eine neue Methode einzuführen und zu einem höheren Preis als die Produktionskosten zu verkaufen."

99 See Alvarez and Barney, Discovery and Creation: Alternative Theories of Entrepreneurial Action, p. 6.

100 See Alvarez and Barney, ibid., p. 2 to 4.

101 See Alvarez and Barney, ibid., pp. 2 and 6.

102 Following Alvarez and Barney, ibid., p. 6.

The last category, i.e. the nature of decision making, clarifies the interplay of both theories. Alvarez and Barney differentiate, pursuant to the possibility and probability of outcomes, between the terms "certainty", "risk", "ambiguity", and "uncertainty": While the term "certainty" refers to situations were a certain outcome is sure, entrepreneurs act under conditions of "risk" if they know (or are able to know) which outcome is possible and under which degree of probability; in contrast, an outcome is "ambiguous" if an entrepreneur has sufficient information (or are at least is able to retrieve it) in order to foresee that an outcome is possible but does not have enough information that he or she would able to determine its probable or likely outcome. Finally, an entrepreneur acts under "uncertainty" if he or she does not even know that outcome is possible). This differentiation allows one to clarify the knowledge-related pre-conditions of each theory: While the Discovery Theory assumes that entrepreneurs are able, principally, "to predict both the range of possible outcomes associated with producing new products or services, as well as the probability that these different outcomes will occur"[103], the Creation Theory "assumes that the end of an emergent process cannot be known from the beginning."[104] In such an uncertain situation, entrepreneurs are, hence not able to calculate, based on a risk-calculation methodology the opportunity costs related to their actions. As a consequence, the Creation Theory instead proposes focusing on the losses an entrepreneur can accept if his or her actions do not lead to a successful outcome.[105]

Alvarez and Barney draw from these assumptions the following implications: "Discovery Theory suggests that entrepreneurs maximize their probability of success by (1) carefully collecting and analyzing information about opportunities to calculate their return and possible opportunity costs, (2) developing a rigorous business plan that describes the opportunities they are going to pursue, and (3) obtaining capital to execute these plans from outside sources. Creation Theory suggests that entrepreneurs maximize their probability of success by (1) engaging in iterative, incremental, and inductive decision making, (2) developing very flexible and constantly adjusting business plans, and (3) obtaining capital from friends and family—people who are willing to bet on them and not on the oppor-

---

103 See Alvarez and Barney, ibid., p. 13.
104 See Alvarez and Barney, ibid., p. 20.
105 See Alvarez and Barney, ibid., pp. 20 and 21.

tunities they may or may not exploit."[106] Alvarez and Barney stress that the Creation Theory may also solve problems that appear to arise in other economic research fields, such as in strategic management theories. For example, these theories could not explain, so far, the reason for the empirical finding that entrepreneurs generate competitive advantages by using "valuable, rare, and costly to imitate resources".[107] The Creation Theory can explain such phenomena, arguing that the path dependency of a process emerged under uncertainty "is likely to generate resources that, from the point of view of potential competitors, are intractable (...) and causally ambiguous (...)."[108]

The differences between both theories do not mean that they must be considered, practically, as exclusive to each other. Instead, the conditions under which entrepreneurs act rather clarify which theory is more appropriate for predicting successful entrepreneurial behavior in specific situations. In situations where the entrepreneur has sufficient knowledge or, at least, is able to retrieve it in order to determine the risks, his or her actions lead more likely to successful innovation if they are consistent with the Discovery Theory; in contrast, if the entrepreneur acts under uncertainty, thus, is not even able to foresee that a specific outcome is possible, he or she will more likely be successful when acting consistent with Creation Theory.[109] Indeed, Alvarez and Barney also stress for cases in between: First, ambiguous situations where an entrepreneur has enough information to foresee that an outcome is possible, but not its probability; in these cases their predictions are less clear.[110] Second, there are also situations where the advantage of one process methodology toward the other one may change over time if entrepreneurs are moving from "risky" to "uncertain" situations, and vice versa.[111] In any case, both theories provide illustrative examples of how economics conceptualize the action-related logics of entrepreneurs and which role legal regulation may play with respect to the knowledge base for their activities.

---

106 See Alvarez and Barney, ibid., p. 32.
107 See Alvarez and Barney, ibid., p. 36.
108 See Alvarez and Barney, ibid., pp. 36 and 37.
109 See Alvarez and Barney, ibid., pp. 33 and 34.
110 See Alvarez and Barney, ibid., p. 35.
111 See Alvarez and Barney, ibid., p. 34.

c) Strategic management: Causation and effectuation

This leads to the third aspect being of interest for this thesis. Economics discuss two approaches describing in more detail the different logics of how entrepreneurs may decide and act in specific situations named "causation" and "effectuation". Sarasvathy describes these two approaches as: "Causation processes take a particular effect as given and focus on selecting between means to create that effect. Effectuation processes take a set of means as given and focus on selecting between possible effects that can be created with that set of means."[112] Sarasvathy exemplifies the implications of this approach as:

	Causation Processes	**Effectuation Processes**
Givens	Effect is given	Only some means or tools are given
Decision-making selection criteria	Help choose between means to achieve the given effect Selection criteria based on expected return Effect dependent: Choice of means is driven by characteristics of the effect the decision maker wants to create and his or her knowledge of possible means	Help choose between possible effects that can be created with given means Selection criteria based on affordable loss or acceptable risk Actor dependent: Given specific means, choice of effect is driven by characteristics of the actor and his or her ability to discover and use contingencies
Competencies employed	Excellent at exploiting knowledge	Excellent at exploiting contingencies
Context of relevance	More ubiquitous in nature **More useful in static, linear, and independent environments**	More ubiquitous in human action **Explicit *assumption* of dynamic, nonlinear and ecological environments**
Nature of unknowns	Focus on the predictable aspects of an uncertain future	Focus on the controllable aspects of an unpredictable future
Underlying logic	To the extent we can predict future, we can control it	To the extent we can control future, we do not need to predict it
Outcomes	Market share in existent markets through competitive strategies	New markets created through alliances and other cooperative strategies

Table: Differentiating Aspects of Causation and Effectuation Processes (words in bold and/or italic highlighted by the author)[113]

112 See Sarasvathy, Causation and Effectuation, p. 245.
113 Following Sarasvathy, ibid., p. 251.

Fueglistaller et al. refer to both approaches in order to illustrate the process of strategic management. They define the term "strategy" as the "systematic planning of all business activities and processes in order to pursue long-term competitive advantages."[114] The classic strategic management process is usually categorized along four phases: Analysis, development of strategic goals, strategic execution, and control.[115] In contrast to such a linear-causal approach, the effectuation approach focuses on the means available in a specific situation and the iterative-nonlinear development of the strategic aims. The effectuation approach thus, fits well situations defined by many unknown factors in which, for example, startups mainly operate.[116]

d) Entrepreneurial contexts: The Law as one influencing factor in innovation processes amongst others

Focusing on specific situations and the means actually available for an entrepreneur, the context plays a more important role. Welters highlights the importance that specific historical, institutional, societal and social contexts can have in determining the resources, as well opportunities and boundaries for entrepreneurial activities. From this perspective, the legal regulatory framework is, as an example of formal institutions, one impact factor for "entrepreneurship as taking place in (further) intertwined social, societal, and geographical contexts, which can change over time and all of them which can be perceived as an asset or a liability by entrepreneurs" (word in brackets added by the author).[117] Welters also stresses the recursivity of links between these contexts during the entrepreneurial process.[118] Innovation produced by entrepreneurs hence, is not the result of a one-dimensional and linear process, but of a multi-factor-based non-linear process.[119] Fagerberg highlights this interdependency as an essential rea-

---

114 See Müller et al., Entrepreneurship – Strategy and business model, p. 138: "Strategie: Die planvolle Ausrichtung sämtlicher Unternehmensaktivitäten und -prozesse zur Erzielung langfristig wirkender Wettbewerbsvorteile."

115 See Müller et al., ibid., p. 143.

116 See Müller et al., ibid., p. 147 to 150.

117 See Welter, Contextualizing Entrepreneurship, pp. 172 and 176.

118 See Welter, ibid., pp. 177.

119 See Neveling et al., ibid., pp. 371 and 372 with references to J. S. Metcalfe, Impulse and Diffusion in the Study of Technical Change, Futures 13 (1981), p. 347,

son for why many inventions take time turning, if at all, into an innovation as: "There may not be sufficient need (yet!) or it may be impossible to produce and/or market because some vital inputs or complementary factors are not (yet!) available."[120] Mayer-Schönberger concludes from this that many current laws suffer from a conceptual flaw because they would imply, in his opinion, a linear model of innovation processes. Taking the multi-dimensional and non-linear model seriously, the legislator should give up its reactive approach and understand itself, instead, as proactive actor directly creating – equally beside the other mechanisms (be they technical, social, cultural etc.) – business opportunities, and not only facilitating them.[121]

2. Regulation of innovative entrepreneurship

The preceding illustration of Entrepreneurship theories provides several links in order to answer the question of how innovation may be regulated through the law. First, considering entrepreneurs as the main driver of innovation (in which organizational form ever this occurs)[122] they appear to be appropriate addressees of laws aiming to regulate such innovation. Second, the action-oriented approach of entrepreneurship theories, in particular, the Discovery and Creation Theory corresponds to the regulatory approach applied in this thesis, which focuses, equally, on action.[123] Third, entrepreneurship models describing the entrepreneurial process correspond with the observation made in practice, as well as in regulation theory, that innovation often, if not mainly, occurs in highly dynamic non-linear processes, and not in causal-linear ways.[124] There are indeed causal-linear innovation processes, such as in research science; however, academics stress that most innovations do not occur in research settings but instead is driven by the experience of users and, thus, in more non-linear

---

as well as K. J. Schmidt-Tiedemann, A New Model of the Innovation Process 25 (1982), pp. 18 ff.

120 See Fagerberg, ibid., pp. 5 and 6.

121 See Mayer-Schönberger, The Law as Stimulus: The Role of Law in Fostering Innovative Entrepreneurship, pp. 180 to 183.

122 See Fueglistaller et al., Entrepreneurship – Basics, pp. 12 and 13.

123 See above under point A. II. Research questions and approach.

124 Cf. above under point A. I. 4. Practical examples referring to two typical scenarios, and A. II. Research questions and approach.

environments.[125] Finally, the context-oriented view of entrepreneurship research corresponds with the self-understanding of the regulatory approach considering the law as just one mechanism beside further ones, such as informal norms or geographical conditions.[126] Even if there is neither a common understanding of innovation or entrepreneurship research, in general, nor a holistic theory of entrepreneurial processes and its contextualization, in particular, the preceding aspects make it suitable as a conceptual model of reality for doing research on the effects of legal regulation instruments on processes of innovation.[127] The following paragraphs shall shed further light on the various effects of regulation on "innovative entrepreneurship" discussed in entrepreneurship as well as legal literature.

a) Do laws simply shift societal costs either protecting against or being open to innovation?

The legislator may shape laws conflicting with the non-linearity of innovation processes in order to protect individuals concerned. The principle of purpose limitation could be considered as an example for such a law, at least so long as it requires from the controller to exactly specify the intended use of personal data and then strictly limit the later use to this initial specification. Such an understanding of the principle of purpose limitation principally conflicts with the openness of innovation processes because it does not allow controllers to use the data for purposes other than for those that the controller could foresee when the data is collected. Mayer-Schönberger describes such a law as simply shifting costs between different groups in society. He gives an example of labor law in order to illustrate his opinion: The legislator can structure labor law in such a way, allowing entrepreneurs to easily hire and fire employees. On the one hand, this would enable entrepreneurs to save costs, i.e. constantly adapt expenses for human resources to the actual need at low transaction costs. On the other hand, either the employee concerned has to bear the costs for finding new employment (or other ways of financing his or her living expenses) or

125 See Fagerberg, ibid., Box 1.3 "What innovation is not: the linear model", p. 11.

126 Cf. above under point A. II. Research questions and approach.

127 See again Fagerberg, ibid., p. 1; Fueglistaller et al., ibid., p. 6; Moroz and Hindle, ibid., p. 781; Welter, ibid., p. 177.

the state for supporting the unemployed.[128] In light of this, the principle of purpose limitation as described before may be considered as simply shifting costs from the individual concerned to the controller referring to an assumption as: If the later use of personal data is limited to the originally specified purpose, the individual (or the social welfare state) may suffer less harm and though have less costs; the controller bears these costs, in turn, being limited in its innovation process.

b) Principles between openness toward innovation and legal uncertainty

In contrast, the legislator might also choose another way and decrease costs overall. Instead of shaping a law that only shifts costs from one group in society to another, the legislator might "also influence the probability of incurring a cost even when holding expected values (and thus costs for taxpayers) constant, thus prompting more people to engage in entrepreneurial activity".[129] In the first instance, principles may be considered as such a regulation instrument. As illustrated in the introduction, the legislator does not often have sufficient knowledge for determining precisely the circumstances of an entrepreneurial process and its impact on society. Therefore, the legislator can choose to establish principles, which leaves private companies more room in finding the best solutions themselves in order to meet the regulatory aim. Indeed, this form of regulation decreases legal certainty because the companies are not able to state whether or not they actually meet the regulator's exact expectations.[130] So far, at least, from this perspective, the principle of purpose limitation does not simply shift costs from the individuals to the controllers. Instead, it gives controllers room to find the best solution to apply the principle of purpose limitation and, thus, different ways of avoiding costs, not only for themselves, but also for the individuals concerned. This approach assumes that it is possible, in principle, for the controller to use, for example, personal data in a very broad way, or even for another purpose than initially specified, so that the way the data is being used does not harm the individual, and thus, does not lead in an increase in costs for the individual or so-

128 See Mayer-Schönberger, ibid., with further examples on pp. 175 ff.

129 See Mayer-Schönberger, ibid., p. 180, see also pp. 176/177.

130 Cf. again Raab and De Hert, ibid., p. 278; Eifert, ibid., cip. 25 and 26; Franzius, ibid., cip. 7, 17, 81 to 103;.

ciety. If this assumption turned out to be correct, i.e. no costs for the individual or society, the subsequent question is: what impact the decrease of legal certainty has on entrepreneurial activity.

aa) Legal (un)certainty as a factor that mediates the regulatory burden

In order to answer this question, two empirical studies shall be highlighted. First, the study conducted by Hartog et al. examined the impact of the regulatory burden and rule of law on entrepreneurial activity. Their results confirmed previous works "suggesting that social security entitlements, taxes, and employment protection legislation are negatively associated with (different forms of) entrepreneurial activity."[131] This result corresponds to Mayer-Schönberger's understanding of the type of regulation that shifts costs from one group in society to another. However, their study additionally came to the (seemingly) counter-intuitive result that countries with stronger rule of law had lower entrepreneurial activities. The authors considered this result as counter-intuitive because they assumed that a strong rule of law would not only hinder entrepreneurial activity, but would also help entrepreneurs, for example when they want to enforce their own contracts that they have concluded with third parties.[132] Hartog et al. considered that a possible reason for this result was that because, in developed countries, primarily large enterprises profit from the benefits of a strong rule of law.[133] The second study, which was conducted by Levie and Autio, proposes a more detailed explanation for this phenomenon: "Entrepreneurial and new ventures face disproportionately high compliance costs, because their small initial size makes it costly for them to maintain compliance functions internally. For industry incumbents, whose large size permits a greater degree of internal specialisation and the maintenance of a larger administrative function in absolute terms, compliance costs are less significant."[134] If one were to pre-suppose that there is a causal relationship, these considerations lead to the result that higher legal

131 See Hartog et al., Institutions and Entrepreneurship: The Role of the Rule of Law, p. 3.
132 See Hartog et al., ibid., p. 8.
133 See Hartog et al., ibid., p. 3.
134 See Levie and Autio, Regulatory Burden, Rule of Law, and Entry of Strategic Entrepreneurs: An International Panel Study, p. 1411.

certainty hinders innovative entrepreneurs, rather than enabling them to pursue their activity. At least this is the case, so long as the entrepreneur's organizational structure remains so small, that the bearing of compliance costs still is disproportionate.

In this study, Levie and Autio however, came to a more nuanced result. They took a deeper look at the particular interplay between the regulatory burden and the rule of law and its effects on strategic entrepreneurial decisions. Referring, amongst other unities of analysis, to an individual's decision to enter into business and, conceptually, to Signaling Theory, they assumed that individuals, who aim to profit most from their decisions, make their decisions in light of how they perceive the influence of institutional factors within society in relation to their activities. Similar to Mayer-Schönberger's understanding of a regulation shifting costs between different societal groups, the way how entrepreneurs perceive these factors regulates "the distribution of profits between stakeholders and, thus, the accumulation and approbiability of returns to entrepreneurial efforts."[135] Levie and Autio concluded a further conceptual dimension from this: their findings confirmed, firstly, the already known assumption that a "lighter regulatory burden (is) associated with a higher rate and relative prevalence of strategic entrepreneurial entry (word in brackets added by the author)."[136] However, the new finding was that rule of law "moderates this effect such that regulation has a significant effect on strategic entry only when rule of law is strong."[137] Instead of a weaker rule of law, as considered by Hartog et al., Levie and Autio thus suggest that a stronger rule of law enables entrepreneurship, under the condition that the regulatory burden is low.

In order to explain this suggestion, Levie and Autio generally considered four different types of interrelationships: First, if the rule of law is weak and the regulatory burden is heavy, corrupt officials get the opportunity to siphon off entrepreneurial rents; even if corruption is low, strategic entrepreneurs are more likely to interact with officials than non-strategic entrepreneurs and, thus, run a higher risk of being regulated heavily. Second, if the rule of law is weak and the regulatory burden is light, corrupt officials have fewer opportunities to siphon off entrepreneurial rents; however, entrepreneurs are less able to defend their own interests against other private parties by means of law. Third, if the rule of law is strong and the

135 See Levie and Autio, ibid., p. 1395.
136 See Levie and Autio, ibid., p. 1392.
137 See Levie and Autio, ibid., p. 1392.

regulatory burden is heavy, officials have fewer opportunities to siphon off entrepreneurial rents and entrepreneurs are able to defend their interests against other parties by legal means; however, they must pay the costs resulting from a heavy (effective) regulation. Consequently, Levie and Autio promote the fourth case as the best solution; if the rule of law is strong and the regulatory burden is low, entrepreneurs do not end up paying for corruption costs resulting from heavy regulation, but they also have sufficient legal means to defend their interests.[138] Even if their study referred to the distribution of profits between entrepreneurs and employees and, thus, to the choice of being a potential employer or an employee,[139] they draw a more general conclusion as: "Bureaucracy and red tape hamper entrepreneurial growth and divert scarce resources of potentially high-growth entrepreneurial firms away from their core business. Regulations, then, can adversely affect the prevalence and anatomy of entrepreneurial activity, particularly in countries in which the rule of law is respected."[140] Thus, in their opinion, if the regulatory burden is low, high legal certainty not only enables innovative large companies, but also small and middle-sized companies.

bb) Conditioning further legal certainty as a promoting factor for entrepreneurial activity

These results lead back to Mayer-Schönberger's approach. He considers a strong rule of law as an incentive for entrepreneurial activity. He argues that in light of the many uncertainties entrepreneurs are confronted with, they generally prefer to precisely know what the law expects from them. In Mayer-Schönberger's opinion, this knowledge would enable them to calculate their legal risks and associated costs. From this point of view, "the role of the legal system in facilitating entrepreneurial activity is to reduce the uncertainties that entrepreneurs perceive."[141] Mayer-Schönberger refers, similarly to Levie and Autio, to the Expected Utility Theory. How-

---

138 See Levie and Autio, ibid., pp. 1400 and 1401.

139 See Levie and Autio, ibid., pp. 1395 and 1396.

140 See Levie and Autio, ibid., p. 1411.

141 See Mayer-Schönberger, ibid., pp. 177 and 178; cf. also Kloepfer, Law enables Technology – About an understimated function of environmental and technology law, p. 417 and 418.

ever, he emphasises that the focus should be on how the law may play a decisive role in entrepreneurial risk calculation: In light of the individually different capabilities of evaluating risks, Mayer-Schönberger clarifies, at first, that more legal certainty does not necessarily lead to better entrepreneurial decisions but, at least, to more entrepreneurial activities. Second, in light of empirical findings demonstrating that individuals become more risk-averse the higher the potential payoff is, he suggests to increase legal predictability if entrepreneurs face high benefits or costs. Third, since individuals are more risk-averse when they evaluate potential benefits and more risk-taking regarding possible losses, he proposes "that lawmakers should focus on making legal rules more certain for financial benefits offered to entrepreneurs, like subsidies, rather than costs, like taxes".[142] He concludes that this perspective would enable the regulator to enhance entrepreneurial activity without decreasing protection, i.e. increasing costs, for third parties.[143]

c) Interim conclusion with respect to the principle of purpose limitation

So far, there appears to be a conflict. In the first instance, the principle of purpose limitation is principally open toward innovation because it leaves data controllers enough room to find the most cost effective way of applying the principle. However, in the second instance, the principle of purpose limitation decreases legal certainty and therefore fails in enhancing entrepreneurial activity. However, the previous considerations allows us to come to the conclusion that there are different hypotheses regarding the interplay between the principle of purpose limitation and data-driven innovation:

First, legal certainty acts as an incentive for entrepreneurs to apply the law, so long as the regulatory burden does not turn red tape. Whether this is the case or not with respect to the principle of purpose limitation depends on its interpretation and application in the specific case. Second, the higher the potential payoff for entrepreneurs is, the better legal certainty can act as an incentive to apply the principle of purpose limitation. This means that mechanisms clarifying how to apply the principle of purpose

142 See Mayer-Schönberger, ibid., pp. 179 and 180.
143 See Mayer-Schönberger, ibid., p. 180.

limitation only work better the more the data controllers potentially stand to lose or gain. The first might be the case if the penalties for non-compliance with the principle of purpose limitation are so high that the controller would consider its execution as a real loss. The second might be the case if the controller is going to break through in gaining users, customers or financial investors for their product, service or enterprise and these parties require, in exchange for giving data controllers their trust (i.e. personal data, money or investment), an assurance that the controller is applying the law (the principle of purpose limitation). This second case refers to the so-called competitive advantage of data protection law:[144] Users may only disclose their data to the data controller or customers may only pay for the product if certain data protection principles are met. Financial investors might verify whether the data controller has complied with data protection law, similarly to compliance with copyright law, as a condition for their investment. Indeed, there is little scientific evidence to what extent users, customers, or investors really expect such a compliance with data protection law. However, there is at least a study which demonstrates that users prefer products from online merchants with better privacy policies even if they have to pay a higher price for the product.[145] In any case, so long as a user or customer base does not yet constitute a real asset for the data controller or it does not need an external investment, these requirements do not serve an incentive per se. However, the moment where these factors constitute an asset for the controller, the second hypothesis becomes relevant: Since potential gains serve better than potential losses as incentive, the legislator should focus more, if it had to choose, on increasing legal certainty enabling entrepreneurs to exploit a competitive advantage than on penalties.

---

144 See, instead of many others, the "Statement by Vice President Neelie Kroes, on the consequences of living in an age of total information"" from the 4th of July 2013, retrieved on the 10th of March 2016 from http://europa.eu/rapid/press-release_MEMO-13-654_en.htm.

145 See Nissenbaum, Privacy in Context, p. 106 referring to Tsai, J., Egelman, S., Cranor, L., and Acquisti, A. 2007. The Effect of Online Privacy Information on Purchasing Behavior: An Experimental Study. Paper presented at the 6th Workshop on the Economics of Information Security (WEIS), Carnegie Mellon University, Pittsburgh, PA, p. 35.

II. Data protection as a risk regulation

After having illustrated how economic models about innovative entrepreneurship provide links for doing research on the regulation of innovation, this sub-chapter draws the attention to the other side of the regulation of data-driven innovation, i.e. the protection against the risks. In the preceding considerations, the terms "risks", "dangers", "threats" and "harms" were already mentioned frequently, even if, however, rather casually. The following considerations clarify the meaning of these terms and how they serve, conceptually, as links for regulation.

1. Risk terminology oscillating between "prevention" and "precaution"

Legal scholars stress the function of data protection law as a regulation of risks.[146] And many data protection sources indeed aim to regulate risks caused by the processing of personal data. The revised OECD Guidelines Governing the Protection of Privacy and Transborder Flows of Personal Data define, for example, its scope of application by referring to personal data as "which, because of the manner in which they are processed, or because of their nature or the context in which they are used, pose a risk to privacy and individual liberties."[147] With respect to the EU directive 95/46/EC on the protection of individuals with regard to the processing of personal data and on the movement of data (Data Protection Directive), the Article 29 Data Protection Working Party stresses that the risk-based approach is "not a new concept, since it is already well known under the current Directive 95/46/EC."[148] Indeed, in several provisions, the Data Protection Directive explicitly refers, for instance, to "the risks represented by the processing" (regarding data security under Article 17), to "specific risks to the rights and freedoms of data subjects" (regarding prior checking under Article 20), and to the proportionality test (general clause

---

146 See Kuner et al., Risk management in data protection; Costa, Privacy and the precautionary principle; Gellert, Data protection: a risk regulation? Between the risk regulation of everything and the precautionary alternative.

147 See OECD Guidelines Governing The Protection Of Privacy And Transborder Flows Of Personal Data in Article 2.

148 See the Article 29 Data Protection Working Party, Statement on the role of a risk-based approach in data protection legal frameworks, p. 2.

for the controller's legitimate interests under Article 7 lit. f) that is typical for risk regulation regimes.[149] In the forthcoming General Data Protection Regulation (GDPR), risks play an even more important role, in particular, with respect to the so-called risk-based approach. Veil categorizes the multitude of terms referring to the risk-based approach and its legal consequences. For example, while one category referring to high risks can lead to the application of specific requirements, another category referring to low risks may result in the exclusion of requirements; yet another category determines, for instance, the extent and manner of how data controllers must implement measures protecting against risks.[150] In this last regard, Article 24 of the General Data Protection Regulation provides for a central provision stating as:

> "*Taking into account the nature, scope, context and purposes of the processing as well as the risks of varying likelihood and severity for the rights and freedoms of individuals, the controller shall implement appropriate technical and organisational measures to ensure and be able to demonstrate that the processing of personal data is performed in compliance with this Regulation. These measures shall be reviewed and updated where necessary.*"[151]

The Article 29 Data Protection Working Party stresses that such a risk-based approach "goes beyond a narrow 'harm-based-approach' that concentrates only on damages and should take into consideration every potential as well as actual adverse effect, assessed on a very wide scale ranging from an impact on the personal concerned by the processing in question to a general societal impact (e.g. loss of social trust)."[152]

From a historical perspective, indeed, it is not a new idea to focus on risks, thus, on a moment before a danger occurs. The idea behind such a temporal extension of protection is that a protection for an individual, who might be the subject of the use of information, could be too late if he or she was only able to claim against the specific use of that information after it had been collected. Legal scholars had recognized, very early in the discussions about data protection, as well as privacy that a protection against

149 With respect to the last aspect, see Kunert et al., ibid., p. 98, as well as Costa, ibid., p. 19.

150 See Veil, GDPR: Risk-based approach instead of rigid principle of prohibition, pp. 351 and 352.

151 Cf. already the Article 29 Data Protection Working Group, Opinion 3/2010 on the principle of accountability.

152 See the the Article 29 Data Protection Working Group, Statement on the role of a risk-based approach in data protection legal frameworks, p. 4.

the collection of the data (providing the basis for the information), can instead be more effective. For instance, in 1969, Miller highlighted that "the most effective privacy protection scheme is one that minimizes the amount of potentially dangerous material that is collected and preserved; a regulatory scheme that focuses on the end use of the data by governmental or private systems might be a case of too little, too late."[153] The reason for this fear is that once information is spread, in metaphorical words, the cat is led out of the bag, and it is difficult to get it back. Once the State or a private entity knows something about somebody else, it can base its decisions (with all possibly negative consequences for the individual concerned) on this knowledge.[154] Thus, from a regulatory perspective, it seems to be more difficult to enforce the State or a private entity not to base its decisions on this knowledge than to regulate the collection of the personal data as the source of this informational risk.

Such a risk-related regulatory approach plays also an important role in Germany. Costa refers to the so-called precautionary principle that was first formalized by Germany during the 1970's in environmental law;[155] and Gellert quotes the "pioneering" data protection legislation established by the German Land Hessen that "implicitly frames data protection as a risk regulation regime since one of its purposes is to: 'safeguard the constitutional structure of the state (…) against all risks entailed by automatic data processing'."[156] The German legal scholar Roßnagel draws the attention to the regulator's protection instruments resulting from such a risk approach. He highlights the principle of data minimization as an example for the precautionary principle because it extends, similar to the minimization principle in environmental law, the protection provided for by preventative means by adding precautionary means. In his opinion, the requirement of data minimization particularly goes beyond the *necessity requirement* (i.e. that the data processing must be necessary for achieving the purpose of the

---

153 See Miller, Personal Privacy in the Computer Age: The Challenge of a New Technology in an Information-Oriented Society, p. 1221.

154 See Grimm, Data protection before its refinement, p. 586.

155 See Costa, ibid., p. 4, referring to Olivier Godard, "Introduction générale", in: "Le principe de précaution dans la conduite des affaires humaines" (Paris: Editions de la Maison des sciences de l'homme Institut National de Recherche Agronomique, 1994), p. 25.

156 See Gellert, ibid., p. 5, referring to Lee A Bygrave, Data Protection Law—Approaching Its Rationale, Logic, and Its Limits (Kluwer, The Hague; London; New York 2002), 39, at 5.

processing intended) because the latter depends on a specific purpose while the first questions the purpose per se. Thus, the principle of data minimization does not require asking whether or not the processing is necessary for a given purpose but whether the purpose as such can be formulated more narrowly in order to minimize the data collection as a whole. In light of this, Roßnagel differentiates between both principles pursuant to their range of protection: while the necessity requirement serves the prevention of dangers, the requirement of data minimization is a means of precaution.[157] This consideration leads to the question of how to differentiate, actually, between prevention and precaution.

2. Sociological approaches defining "dangers" and "risks"

The German legal scholar Jaeckel considers the difference between prevention and precaution as corresponding to the question of how to differentiate between dangers and risks.[158] Indeed, while there is common sense in the meaning of an actual harm or damage, e.g. "a loss to a person or their property"[159], the precise meaning of terms like danger and risk referring to a potential harm (i.e. overall threat) is less clear. Jaeckel gives an overview about sociological and legal conceptions of how to differentiate between dangers and risks.[160] From a sociological perspective, she highlights the concepts proposed by Evers and Novotny, on the one hand, and Luhmann, on the other hand.

Evers' and Novotny's starting point is to define "risk" as a term seeking to make dangers calculable. Thus, the specific knowledge about the probability and severity of a threat turns dangers into risks.[161] Subsequently, Evers and Novotny draw the attention to the normative dimension of risks.

---

157 See Roßnagel, The Requirement of Data Minimization, pp. 43 to 45.

158 See Jaeckel, Differentiating between Danger and Risk, p. 117; Prevention of Danger through Law and Legal Conceptualization of Risk, p. 70.

159 See, for example, Costa, ibid., p. 14.

160 See Jaeckel, Prevention of Danger through Law and Legal Conceptualization of Risk, pp. 49 ff.

161 See Jaeckel, ibid., pp. 51 and 52, by referring to Evers and Novotny, Umgang mit Unsicherheit, Suhrkamp 1987, Berlin; cf. also Gellert, ibid., pp. 7 and 13, referring to Patrick Peretti-Watel, La société du risque (Repères. La Découverte, Paris 2010); Olivier Borraz, Les politiques du risque (Presses de Sciences Po, Paris 2008), Jenny Steele, Risks and Legal Theory, vol 68 (Hart Publishing, Oxford,

They stress that the difference between dangers and risks depends on its general perception in today's society. For example, citizens express their concerns and fears about a certain issue like environmental pollution or state surveillance based on an abuse of personal data because there is a societal consensus that environmental health or privacy or autonomy in a democratic civil society is a value. Thus, the moment citizens perceive a non-calculable threat for environmental health, their privacy or autonomy, this perception can turn a risk back to a danger for these values. Jaeckel stresses Evers' and Novotny's conclusion that mathematic and system-analytical methods of calculating risks alone can hence not explain the treatment of uncertainties in a society; instead, this treatment also depends on its normative expectations.[162]

Luhmann, in contrast, differentiates between dangers and risks pursuant to the question of who is considered as responsible for the (potential) harm. If the harm is considered as resulting from an external factor, Luhmann refers to the term "danger"; instead, there is a risk if the harm is considered as resulting from a human decision. Jaeckel considers this perspective as interesting from a legal viewpoint because it illustrates that not only decisions which lead to active action but also decisions not to act, may in itself be considered as causing risks. For example, the prohibition of a certain medicine against a certain disease can avoid risks resulting from unwanted side effects but, simultaneously, create or increase the risk caused by the disease itself. This nature of decisions as a two-sided sword

UK; Portland, Oregon 2004) 21, Jacqueline Peel, Science and Risk Regulation in International Law (Cambridge University Press, Cambridge, UK 2010) 79–80.

162 See Jaeckel, ibid., pp. 51 and 52, by referring to Evers and Novotny, Umgang mit Unsicherheit, Suhrkamp 1987, Berlin; cf. also van Dijk, Gellert and Rommetveit, A risk to a right? Beyond data protection risk assessments, p. 13, referring, amongst others, to Felt U,Wynne B, Callon M, Gonçalves ME, Jasanoff S, Jepsen M, et al. Taking European knowledge society seriously (report of the expert group on science and governance to the science, economy and society directorate, directorate-general for research). Luxembourg: European Commission; 2007, as well as Irwin A,Wynne B, editors. Misunderstanding science? – the public reconstruction of science and technology. Cambridge: Cambridge University Press; 1996; see, regarding the German perspective, at Forum Privatheit, White Paper – Data Protection Impact Assessment, pp. 29 and 30.

leads to the result that potential negative effects must always be weighed against potential positive effects in order to determine the overall risk.[163]

In any case, Jaeckel comes to the conclusion that both concepts do actually not correspond to approaches developed so far in (German) legal literature: Luhmann's concept does not help, in her opinion, determine the real risk or danger and, therefore, does not answer the question of which protection instruments are needed in order to establish against real risks or dangers. And the concept by Evers and Novotny contradicts the legal discussion considering the relationship between danger and risk in the reverse direction. In Germany, at least, the legal discussion considered that a danger was the calculable threat, whereas a risk was considered as an uncertain threat that could not comprehensively be grasped.[164]

3. German legal perspectives: Different protection instruments for different types of threat

In Germany, initially focusing on police law, the debate centered, for more than a century, on the notion of *prevention of danger*. In contrast, the legal debate started to develop the notion of *precaution against risks* in the 1980's, holding the reference to this relatively new term as a necessary answer to the scientific and technological progress.[165] This progress produced a new type of threat that did not appear to fit to the classic understanding of a *danger*. The debate discovered, in particular, the following characteristics: First, these threats only become apparent after a long period had lapsed and/or when it is looked at from a global perspective; second, only the combination of several issues, which are, per se, not risky if they remain a singular phenomenon, together cause a threat; or third, a threat is indeed extremely unlikely but runs the risk of causing an ex-

163 See Jaeckel, ibid., pp. 53 to 56, referring, amongst others, to Luhmann, Soziologie des Risikos, pp. 30 ff, as well as, ibid., Die Moral des Risikos and das Risiko der Moral, in: Bechmann, Risiko und Gesellschaft, pp. 327 and 331.

164 See Jaeckel, ibid., pp. 52 as well as 55 and 56.

165 See Jaeckel, ibid., p. 57, referring, amongst others, to decisions of the Prussian Higher Administrative Court (Preußisches Oberverwaltungsgericht) as well as to Murswiek, Die staatliche Verantwortung für die Risiken der Technik, p. 80, and Kloepfer, Umweltrecht, 1. Auflage 1989, p. 45 cip. 46.

tremely severe and irreparable harm.[166] In light of the perception of such risks in society as a new form of threat, the legislator started to use the term in law, and the legal discussion started to react to this term by clarifying its precise meaning and extent.

a) Protection pursuant to the degree of probability

At first, the legal discussion elaborated on a three-layered model differentiating between dangers, risks, and remaining risks combined with different legal consequences: While a regulator had to strictly prevent a danger, it could only minimize a risk; and there also is a *remaining risk* that had to be accepted without protection against it. On the basis of this differentiation, this model defined the term *danger* as a situation that may turn, with sufficient probability, into a harm for a specific object of protection if nobody were to stop this causal chain. Certainty about the harm, thus, is not necessary; however, the concept of harm as being an only possible threat was considered as insufficient for regulation. Between these two poles, i.e. certainty and possibility, the regulation depended on the probability of the harm. Indeed, there is no fixed probability required, instead, the following balancing exercise had to be carried out: The more severe the potential harm is, the less probable it had to be in order to create a state duty of protection, and vice versa. Indeed, the moment the existence of a danger could be determined, the State had to prevent it, irrespective of how much effort had to be spent on prevention; in the worst case scenario, the State or any other party had to refrain from the action or decision that caused the danger.[167]

In contrast to such a prevention of dangers, precaution against risks takes place before preventative measures can protect against threats. Pursuant to the three-layered model, a situation is risky if harm is possible but the methods elaborated with respect to a danger cannot determine its probability. This might be the case because of one of the following three reasons, which were mentioned previously: First, the negative effects of an action or decision may take place too far in the future; second, its causality is hard to determine because there are too many factors leading to the po-

---

166 See Jaeckel, ibid., p. 58 with reference to Murswiek, Die staatliche Verantwortung für die Risiken der Technik, p. 80.

167 See Jaeckel, ibid., pp. 57 to 60 with further references.

tential harm; or third, its probability is just too low. In light of the lower threat of a risky situation than of a dangerous one, the regulator does not have to prevent the threat as a whole but only to minimize it. Furthermore, this duty depends on the technical possibilities, as well as the proportionality between efforts and utility. Another difference between prevention of a danger and precaution against risks is that the individual concerned has a subjective right to protection only against dangers but not against risks. Finally, this three-layered model acknowledged a third category of threat, i.e. *remaining risks* that must be socially accepted without having protection measures against it. This results from the fact that no technology can guarantee full protection against all threats imaginable. A duty of protection against such threats would therefore be disproportionate and lead to a prohibition of technology development.[168]

Jaeckel confirms that this three-layered approach brought to light the issue that there are different kinds of threats that require different protection instruments. However, the problem of this model was that it only superficially provided a clear differentiation between dangers, risks, and remaining risks. In fact, it was hardly possible to precisely determine which situation bears a danger, or a risk, or only a remaining risk. This uncertainty was problematic because the three-layered model tied precise legal requirements to these three categories: If one type of threat (i.e. danger) requires preventative protection measures, another type of threat (i.e. risk) requires minimizing measures, only, and a third type of threat (i.e. remaining risk) requires no protection at all, then its differentiation should be clear.[169] In order to minimize this problem, legal scholars had therefore proposed, a two-layered model that mainly differentiated between dangers and risks, on the one hand, and remaining risks, on the other. This two-layered model considered a risk as the umbrella term and a danger as a specific type of risk. From this perspective, the term *risk* meant all possible threats, whereas a danger is a threat with a certain probability.[170] Jaeckel affirms that this concept enables one to tie different proportionate protection instruments to different types of threats, without drawing an artificial and over-formalistic line of distinction. However, in her opinion, it would nevertheless be helpful to clearly differentiate between dangers and

168 See Jaeckel, ibid., pp. 60 and 61 with further references.
169 See Jaeckel, ibid., pp. 62 to 63.
170 See Jaeckel, ibid., p. 66 referring to Murswiek, Die staatliche Verantwortung für die Risiken der Technik, pp. 80 ff. and 335 ff.

risks in order to choose the adequate and proportionate protection instruments.[171]

b) Protection pursuant to the available knowledge in linear-causal and non-linear environments

Tying into the conceptual approaches developed by Di Fabio and Ladeur, Jaeckel finally comes to the conclusion that the actual difference between dangers and risks consists in the methodologies for (administrative) "decisions under uncertainty":[172] A danger refers to a type of threat that is, based on individual and societal experience, which is already known so that the State is able to react to it with an experienced set of methodologies. In contrast, the term "risk" refers to knowledge that is not certain. This perceived uncertainty results from the conceptual shift from a linear and causal approach to a non-linear and dynamic approach in understanding the world.[173] In a non-linear dynamic world, "the loose connection between cause and effect requires new concepts for actions or decisions based on uncertain knowledge: 'The connection between action and knowledge, which was made in the past through the term of danger, has to be made today, under the conditions of increased complexity and uncertainty, through the term of risk.'"[174] From this knowledge perspective, the main difference between a danger and a risk hence is that an objective observer having all the knowledge of the world is principally able to determine under which conditions a danger turns into harm; in contrast, regarding risks, there is no objective knowledge horizon about the outcome of a risk, instead, there principally is only a subjective point of view. In Jaeckel's opinion, the regulator reacts to this paradigm shift (i.e. with respect to the knowledge uncertainties) by introducing, more and more, subjective elements into the law: First, by accumulating knowledge through the integration of expert groups and private entities and by stretching, second, these procedures from a time perspective, as well as by binding them to

171 See Jaeckel, ibid., pp. 69 and 70.
172 See Jaeckel, ibid., p. 77.
173 See Jaeckel, ibid., pp. 78 to 80.
174 See Jaeckel, ibid., p. 81, quoting Ladeur, The Environmental Law of the Knowledge Society: From the protection against dangers to the management of risks, p. 78.

procedural rules; and third, by acknowledging that the introduction of legal objectives, like broad legal terms and principles, corresponds with a certain limitation of the judicial review. If knowledge is exclusively subjective, then the Courts have to acknowledge this subjectivity and cannot substitute it by their own "objective" point of view. Indeed, Jaeckel stresses that this limitation of judicial review only applies insofar as there really is an uncertainty that limits the construction of an objective knowledge horizon.[175]

c) Interim conclusion: Fundamental rights determining the appropriateness of protection

With respect to the protection instruments, preventative measures thus seek to directly protect against dangers, i.e. linear-causal threats of sufficient probability for specific objects of protection. In contrast, precautionary measures react to the knowledge deficiencies resulting from dynamic and non-linear environments. They serve to maintain possibilities for action if there is, for example, no objective proof for a causal connection between a certain action and a later harm for a specific object of protection. Therefore, they often refer, at first, to informational measures rather than control. Jaeckel advocates that this conceptual difference enables the regulator to choose, with respect to the particularities of a certain area of life, the proportionate protection instruments for the different types of threats.[176] Indeed, the choice for the proportionate protection instruments consists, of two different questions: The first question refers to the duty of protection of the State. This question posed is: which type of threat requires which protection instrument, in other words, whether preventative or precautionary measures are necessary in order to (finally) avoid a potential harm. The answer depends, similarly for the actual harm, on the fundamental rights of the individuals concerned or other constitutional guarantees (e.g. environmental protection under Article 37 of the European Charta of Fundamental Rights).[177] The second question posed is:

175 See Jaeckel, Differentiating between Danger and Risk, p. 120.

176 Jaeckel, ibid., p. 123.

177 See Jaeckel, Duties of Protection in German and European Law, pp. 85 to 88 as well as 165 and 166; cf. also van Dijk, Gellert and Rommetveit, A risk to a right? Beyond data protection risk assessments, pp. 17 and 18.

whether the protection instrument established in order to fulfill a State duty of protection is proportionate or not. The answer to this question does not only refer to the fundamental rights of the individual concerned, but also on the fundamental rights of the entities (e.g. entrepreneurs), which must apply this protection instrument. Thus, this answer therefore depends on the balancing exercise between the opposing fundamental rights. This balancing exercise may result in the fact that the prevention of a certain action (e.g. its prohibition) that leads to a risk (not a danger) would be disproportionate. In contrast, a precautionary measure, which only seeks to gather information in order to potentially discover a danger is proportionate. The reason is that the requirement to gather information infringes the fundamental rights of the entrepreneur less, than the prohibition of its actions.[178]

4. Searching for a scale in order to determine the potential impact of data protection risks

The essential point here is that this doctoral thesis does not purport to decide which definition of risks and dangers is appropriate. However, its aim is to illustrate that there are different kinds of threats that require different protection instruments. Therefore, this thesis mainly refers to the term, "threat" or uses both terms "risks" and "dangers", synonymously, unless stated otherwise. In conclusion, amongst these threats, there are particular situations where there is insufficient knowledge in order to specify an object of protection threatened by a certain action or to determine a causal link between this action and a potential harm. Costa describes the precaution against these kind of threats, giving yet another definition, as based on "hypotheses that have not been scientifically confirmed", in contrast to the prevention of "identifiable risks".[179] In other words, "while the prevention is the remedy against the exposure with regard to a known harm, precaution is meant to avoid the mere possibility of suffering harm or

178 See Jaeckel, Duties of Protection in German and European Law, pp. 85 to 88 as well as 165 and 166; Dietlein, The Doctrine of Duties of Protection of Basic Rights, pp. 105 to 109; cf. Kuner et al., ibid., p. 98; see below in more detail regarding the duties of protection point C. I. b) The effects of fundamental rights on the private sector.

179 See Costa, ibid., p. 15.

loss."[180] From this point of view, both approaches of protection, i.e. prevention of known risks and precaution against unknown risks, do not exclude each other but, instead complement each other. Thus, when the risk is "known" or "identified", this is the essential moment when there is a switch from precautionary to preventative measures. It is at this moment, when the protection instruments do not primarily aim to identify a risk anymore but instead to prevent it.[181] Such a differentiating approach is particularly important if protection measures shall not forbid all future innovations, but instead, the protection instruments applied shall be proportionate, respecting the conflicting constitutional positions, such as fundamental rights.[182]

However, the most urgent challenge of such a "risk-based" approach applied to data protection law is the question of how to determine the potential harm, i.e. the object of protection that actually is threatened by a certain action or decision. Many scholars stress that beyond common sense, i.e. that not only material but also immaterial harm must be considered, there is little agreement on how to determine the corresponding threats.[183] This is a desperate situation for a regulation aiming to protect against threats caused by the processing of personal data. The reason is that effective protection is possible only if it is clear which of these threats are legally relevant. The answer to this general question may lead, in particular, to further answers to more specific questions, such as: what kind of information is actually needed in order to discover threats; which threats must be accepted without having protection instruments against it; how to avoid "rabulistic games" with numbers determining the probability and severity of threats; and thus, how to avoid, firstly, that the risk-based approach undermines rights and duties provided for by fundamental rights and, second, risk management processes provided for by ordinary data protection law "may be perverted into a self-legitimation exercise that serves no other purpose than that of managing operational and reputational

180 See Costa, ibid., p. 5.

181 Cf. Costa, ibid., pp. 2, 5, and 14 to 18.

182 See the criticism of the precautionary principle provided for by data protection, in particular, at Thierer, Privacy Law's Precautionary Principle Problem.

183 See, for example, Kuner et al., ibid., p. 97; Center for Information Policy Leadership, The Role of Risk Management in Data Protection – Paper 2 of the Project on Privacy Risk Framework and Risk-based Approach to Privacy, p. 13.

risks, and which, ultimately, is itself a risk to the management of (primary) risks."[184]

III. Theories about the value of privacy and data protection

In order to answer this question, it is necessary to determine the overall objective that data protection actually serves. It is necessary to stress that this chapter does not yet precisely differentiate between theories, concepts, or approaches of privacy, on the one hand, and data protection, on the other. Both terms are therefore (still) synonymously used.[185]

1. The individual's autonomy and the private/public dichotomy

Without requiring a complete and detailed description of each single theory on this matter, Nissenbaum provides, in her book *Privacy in Context*, an overview about "predominant themes and principles, as well as a few of the well-known theories that embody them."[186] In doing so, Nissenbaum organizes these theories into two categories: First, theories that consider privacy as related or even necessary for further moral or political values; and, second, theories that attribute the legitimacy question of privacy to the individual's capacity to control a certain "private zone".[187]

With respect to the first category, i.e. theories connecting privacy with further moral or political values, the individual's autonomy plays an important role. There can be several threats endangering the autonomy of individuals who are concerned by the processing of personal data. Quoting Stanley Benn, Nissenbaum defines autonomy as "self-determination embodied in the individual 'whose actions are governed by principles that are his own' and who 'subjects his principles to critical review, rather than

184 See Gellert, ibid., pp. 14 to 17, referring, with respect to the quote, to Michael Power, The Risk Management of Everything – Rethinking the Politics of Uncertainty (Demos, London 2004), p. 19.

185 See, for example, in relation to EU law, the discussion about the terminological (and conceptual) shift from "privacy" to "data protection" at González-Fuster, The Emergence of Data Protection as a Fundamental Right of the EU.

186 See Nissenbaum, Privacy in Context, p. 13.

187 See Nissenbaum, ibid., p. 73.

taking them over unexamined from his social environment'".[188] Nissenbaum acknowledges that such an understanding of autonomy might indeed be endangered in light of the thought experiment proposed by Jeffrey Reiman called the "informational panopticum":[189] Similar to Jeremy Bentham's panoptic prison, the life of an individual trapped in an informational panopticum can be observed from one single point of view. Given the current development of collection, aggregation, and analysis of personal data, Nissenbaum considers such a thought experiment not as unreasonable.[190] Instead, she delves deeper into the four types of risks that Reiman considers for an individual's autonomy caused by the informational panopticum: "risks of extrinsic and intrinsic losses of freedom, symbolic risks, and risks of 'psycho-political metamorphosis'".[191]

An extrinsic loss of freedom arises when an individual suffers from negative decisions by third parties due to information third parties are able to gather about the individual. For example, an employer receives information (that could be true or untrue) about the work performance of a potential employee and decides not to give the potential employee the job based on this information. An intrinsic loss of freedom results from anteceding self-censorship because the individual fears such potential external losses and therefore omits behaviors that could lead, once somebody else is informed about it, to a negative decision made by others. The symbolic risk refers to a lack of institutional bodies and concepts affirming the right of the individual to act autonomously without having to fear losses of their freedom. The fourth risk of psycho-political metamorphosis finally "follows Reiman's speculation that if people are subjected to constant surveil-

188 See Nissenbaum, ibid., p. 81 quoting Stanley Benn (1971), Privacy, Freedom and Respect for Persons, in: Privacy, ed. J. R. Pennock and J. W. Chapman, New York: Atherton Press, pp. 1 to 27 (p. 24), reprinted in Philosophical Dimensions of Privacy: An Anthology, ed. F. Schoeman. Cambridge: Cambridge University Press, 1984, pp. 223– 244.

189 See Nissenbaum, ibid., quoting Jeffrey Reiman (1995), Driving to the Panopticum: A Philosophical Exploration of the Risks to Privacy Posed by the Highway Technology of the Future, Santa Clara Computer and High Technology Law Journal 11(1): pp. 27 to 44 (p. 33).

190 See Nissenbaum, ibid., p. 75 referring to Jeffrey Bentham (1995), The Panopticon Writings. M. Bozovic, ed. London: Verso.

191 See Nissenbaum, ibid., pp. 75 and 76 referring to Jeffrey Reiman (1995), Driving to the Panopticum: A Philosophical Exploration of the Risks to Privacy Posed by the Highway Technology of the Future, Santa Clara Computer and High Technology Law Journal 11(1): pp. 27 to 44 (p. 42).

lance, they will be stunted not only in how they act, but in how they think. They will aspire to a middle-of-the-road conventionality — to seek in their thoughts a 'happy medium.'"[192] From this perspective, a right to privacy and/or data protection protecting against these threats indeed serves an individual's autonomy.[193] However, Nissenbaum concedes that autonomy does not require that individuals are totally free from any social influence. It is a thin line to draw between coercion, manipulation, and deception, on the one hand, and respecting the individual's autonomy, on the other. In particular, there is no proof that the processing of personal data leads, in general and automatically, to harm for the autonomy, but only that it may.[194]

The preceding considerations about the individual's autonomy lead to the second value of privacy, for human relationships. Several theorists stress the value of privacy which enables individuals to decide who they want to trust or not, i.e. it is the individuals who decide who they want to share personal information with. Autonomy therefore is an important precondition for developing relationships.[195] Finally, and equally related to the concept of autonomy, Nissenbaum refers to another scholar who stresses the importance of privacy for society as a whole: Priscilla Regan considers and promotes the notion that privacy enables individuals to decide on which aspects of their personal life they want to place in the background, distinguishing them from others, and which aspects they choose to share with others in order to signal their commonalities. This ability is an essential pre-requisite for being a citizen in a democracy, which becomes particularly obvious with respect to the freedom of association. However, there are further constitutional positions related to or even dependent on privacy such as the fundamental right to anonymous speech or the institution of the secret ballot. These examples make apparent that privacy per se must not be at the complete disposal of individuals, who use their privacy or may abandon it, but has to be considered as a collective good. Regan

---

192 See Nissenbaum, ibid.

193 Cf. Nissenbaum, ibid., p. 81.

194 See Nissenbaum, ibid., p. 83 and 84.

195 See Nissenbaum, ibid., pp. 84 and 85 referring to Charles Fried (1986), Privacy: A Moral Analysis, Yale Law Journal 77(1): pp. 475– 493 (pp. 477 ff.) as well as Ferdinand Schoeman (1984), Privacy and Intimate Information, in: Philosophical Dimensions of Privacy: An Anthology, ed. Ferdinand Schoeman, Cambridge University Press, pp. 403 to 418 (p. 408) and James Rachels (1975), Why Privacy Is Important, Philosophy & Public Affairs 4(4): pp. 383 to 423 (p. 326).

advocates that this nature of privacy "as a non-excludable, indivisible collective good like clean air and national defense" gives a good reason for concluding that the legislator should regulate privacy by public law and not completely leave it to mechanisms of the private market.[196]

The second category of theories equally considers privacy as important for an individual's ability to avoid scrutiny, approbation and hence, in more general words, threats for his or her autonomy. However, these theories consider privacy and how it is conceptualized by the preceding theories as too broad and therefore focus on its function to define a specific "private zone". From this point of view, all concepts of privacy can only refer to a private realm but not to the public sphere. Nissenbaum calls this approach the "private/public dichotomy".[197] Pursuant to her analysis, there are three basic strands defining this private/public dichotomy. The first strand defines the dichotomy by distinguishing between private and public "actors". The second strand defines it by distinguishing between private and public spaces. And the third strand refers to the distinction between private and public information.[198] Pursuant to these theories, a right to privacy shall exist only for these private zones, otherwise the value of privacy and, thus, protection for it is unclear.[199]

2. Criticism: From factual to conceptual changes

Nissenbaum criticizes all of these approaches. With respect to the second category, theories referring to the private/public dichotomy, in her opinion, these theories are not problematic as such, but are not useful in today's world for elaborating on a normative concept of protection. She argues: "Although, in the past, it might have served as a useful approximation for delineating the scope of a right to privacy, its limitations have come to light as digital information technologies radically alter the terms under which others – individuals and private organizations as well as government – have access to us and to information about us in what are traditionally understood as private and public domains. In the period before such

196 See Nissenbaum, ibid., p. 87 referring to Priscilla Regan (1995), Legislating Privacy, Chapel Hill: University of North Carolina Press, pp. 226 and 227.

197 See Nissenbaum, ibid., pp. 89 and 90.

198 See Nissenbaum, ibid., pp. 91 ff.

199 See Nissenbaum, ibid., pp. 98.

technologies were common, people could count on going unnoticed and unknown in public arenas; they could count on disinterest in the myriad scattered details about them."[200] Today, in contrast, personal data can be, once it is collected in a certain context, permanently stored and can always be analyzed and used in another context. In light of this "always-possible context change", the linear private/public dichotomy, hence, does not serve as a useful criterion reliably distinguishing, for example, between private and public spaces or private and public information anymore.[201] However, the theories described before, which focus on the value of privacy in relation to further moral or political values, in particular to autonomy, do not provide reliable criteria in order to distinguish various forms of data processing from others either. Nissenbaum summarizes, in particular, the following weaknesses of these theories as: "One recurring skeptical challenge, for instance, cites the lack of concern many people seem to demonstrate in day- to-day behaviors, contradicting claims that privacy is a deeply important moral and political value that deserves stringent protection. Another is the clearly evident cultural and historical variation in commitments to privacy, hard to explain if privacy is supposed to be a fundamental human right. A third points to the difficulty of resolving conflicts between privacy and other moral and political values, such as property, accountability, and security."[202]

The shortcomings of all these theories become, in Nissenbaum's opinion, most apparent in light of their inappropriate answers to the threats to privacy caused by modern Internet and Information technologies. The existing theories lead to the result that the public discourse discusses some of the new technologies with great anxiety even if they do actually not pose a significant risk to privacy. In contrast, existing concepts do not provide for sufficient protection measures against other technologies, which heavily put traditional understandings of privacy in question, only because their principles are "'blind' to essential elements and differences" of these technologies.[203] As a consequence of all these challenges, Nissenbaum finally develops her approach not by creating her own new principles of privacy, but rather by reacting to altered factual conditions and, thus, elaborating

200 See Nissenbaum, ibid., pp. 116 and 117.
201 Cf. Nissenbaum, ibid., pp. 113 ff.
202 See Nissenbaum, ibid., p. 14.
203 See Nissenbaum, ibid., pp. 103 and 104.

on the existing principles:[204] the framework of "contextual integrity".[205] One essential element of this approach is to specify conditions for the flow of personal information with respect to a certain context. From this point of view, a right to privacy is not a right to secrecy or to control of certain information, but to appropriate flow of information.[206]

Interestingly, Nissenbaum also heavily criticizes the purpose-based approach. However, before analyzing this criticism and, as a consequence, coming to the question of the relationship between a "context" in which the data processing (aka information flow) takes place and the "purpose" of this processing, the next paragraph delves deeper into the approach of contextual integrity. The reason is that this approach may help, once the question of the context-purpose-relationship is clarified, find an answer to the research question about the meaning and extent of the principle of purpose limitation.

3. Nissenbaum's framework of "contextual integrity"

Elaborating on her framework of contextual integrity, Nissenbaum underlines, as mentioned previously, that she does not want to substitute current intuitive principles of privacy. In contrast, she seeks to provide a concept, which functions better than current theories, in order to evaluate whether or not a certain flow of information infringes such intuitive principles of privacy. Pursuant to her framework, a certain use of information infringes "contextual integrity" only if it conflicts with "informational norms" that exist in specific contexts. These informational norms are specified by the

---

204 See Nissenbaum, ibid., p. 118 quoting Lawrence Lessig (1999), Code and Other Laws of Cyberspace, New York: Basic Books, p. 116 as: "This form of argument is common in our constitutional history, and central to the best in our constitutional tradition. It is an argument that responds to changed circumstances by proposing a reading that neutralizes those changes and preserves an original meaning... It is reading the amendment differently to accommodate the changes in protection that have resulted from changes in technology. It is translation to preserve meaning'"; cf. the same approach in German law, Grimm, Data protection before its refinement, p. 585, who differentitates between the over-arching aim specified by the object of protection of fundamental rights and the concept of protection that must be adapted, from time to time, to the changes of the environment.

205 See Nissenbaum, ibid., p. 14.

206 See Nissenbaum, ibid., pp. 127 and 239.

following factors: First, the corresponding context; second, the actors involved; third, attributes such as the type of information; and fourth, principles for the transmission of the information.[207]

Nissenbaum proposes the following explanations for these factors: the term "context" refers to "structured social settings with characteristics that have evolved over time (sometimes long periods of time) and are subject to a host of causes and contingencies of purpose, place, culture, historical accident, and more."[208] By way of example, she names contexts such as health care, education, employment, religion, family, and the commercial marketplace.[209] The second factor, i.e. the type of information, can refer to the dichotomy between private and publically available information, but it is however, not restricted to these types. Instead, further types can equally be relevant. In this regard, Nissenbaum provides examples that friends might share intimate information amongst each other but not, for example, their salaries; in contrast, the same people might share the information about their salaries with their bankers or tax lawyers, but not the intimate information shared with their friends; similarly, the information exchange about religious affiliation might be appropriate amongst friends, but not between an employer and his or her employee; and finally, a physician might ask for medical information but not about the religious or financial matters of an individual.[210]

Correspondingly, the definition of the social role by the individual also depends on the context. For example, in a health-care context it is decisive in order to define the social norms, whether the doctor, receptionist, nurse, or bookkeeper receives certain types of information.[211] This example also points to the fourth factor, i.e. the transmission principle. Nissenbaum stresses that her framework of contextual integrity is not restricted to a binary transmission principle, such as having access or not having access to information. Instead, she stresses the point that there are several possible conditions governing how in a certain context, certain types of information might be shared amongst certain actors. For instance, there may be a principle of reciprocity for sharing information, such as amongst friends; or rights of receiving certain information; or duties of providing for certain

207 See Nissenbaum, ibid., p. 181.
208 See Nissenbaum, ibid., p. 130.
209 See Nissenbaum, ibid., p. 130.
210 See Nissenbaum, ibid., pp. 143 and 144.
211 See Nissenbaum, ibid., pp. 141 and 142.

information; or a right for individuals to determine by themselves the conditions of a certain information flow; there may be a principle requiring that information is shared voluntarily or consensually or based on the knowledge of the individual concerned ("notice") or on his or her permission ("consent"), or a combination of all or some of these conditions.[212] In any event, Nissenbaum stresses that "contexts are not formally defined constructs, but (…) are intended as abstract representations of social structures experienced in daily life. (…). In other words, the activity of fleshing out the details of particular types of contexts, such as education or health care, is more an exercise of discovery than of definition."[213]

Irrespective of whether this statement is correct or not, and supposing that the particularities of a specific context is fleshed out in detail, and its informational norms are determined, the next step in the framework of contextual integrity is to evaluate whether or not a certain flow of information challenges the corresponding norms and therefore violates its contextual integrity. Nissenbaum recognizes the fact that if all information flows that challenge an already existing norm were considered as violating its contextual integrity, the evolvement of new norms, i.e. change per se, would be problematic. In order to avoid a "lock-in effect" in entrenched norms that hinders new developments, Nissenbaum hence adds to her framework a normative component: the value of a specific context. In light of this component, new informational norms challenging existing ones "can be justified on moral grounds insofar as they support the attainment of general as well as context-based values".[214] Thus, coming from her approach that existing informational norms are presumed to be appropriate norms, she considers that new norms can also be justified, so long as they are more effective in supporting, promoting or achieving context-related values than existing informational norms.[215] These contextual values, in other words, purposes, objectives or ends hence play an essential role for evaluating whether or not a new informational norm within a given context violates the contextual integrity. Nissenbaum stresses, referring to Schatzki's "teleology", the function of these contextual values as necessary for any understanding of why individuals behave in certain contexts in a certain way, in more abstract words, why certain context-related infor-

212 See Nissenbaum, ibid., pp. 145 to 147.
213 See Nissenbaum, ibid., p. 134.
214 See Nissenbaum, p. 181 and pp. 158 ff.
215 See Nissenbaum, p. 181 and pp. 158 ff.

mational norms exist. She comes to the conclusion that even if "settling on a definitive and complete list of contextual values is neither simple nor non-contentious, the central point is that contextual roles, activities, practices, and norms make sense largely in relation to contextual teleology, including goals, purposes, and ends."[216]

4. Clarifying the relationship between "context" and "purpose"

Promoting this approach of contextual integrity, Nissenbaum also criticizes, as mentioned previously, the purpose-based approach. In her opinion, the principle of purpose limitation that consists of the two requirements, first, to specify the purpose of the processing of personal data and, second, to limit the later use of the data to the purpose initially specified, has "only indexical meaning".[217] She stresses that so long as there is no substantive criteria in order to specify a purpose, privacy and/or data protection laws "constitute a mere shell, formally defining relationships among the principles (that refer to the purpose of the data processing) and laying out procedural steps to guide information flows."[218] Since such a concept of protection leaving the specification of the purpose to the controller's will serve a "glaring loophole",[219] Nissenbaum comes to the conclusion that another concept focusing on a principle for "respect for context" is "something materially different, something better."[220]

In essence, Nissenbaum's criticism of the principle of purpose limitation refers to the same challenges as mentioned in the introduction of this thesis. However, considering a context-based approach as materially different and (sic!) better than a purpose-based approach requires, at first, determining the "tertium comparationis" (i.e. the commonality allowing a

216 See Nissenbaum, p. 134 referring to Schatzki, T (2001), Practice Minded Orders, in: The Practice Turn in Contemporary Theory, ed. T. R. Schatzki, K. K. Cetina, and E. von Savigny, London: Routledge, pp. 42 to 55.

217 See Nissenbaum, Respect for Context as a Benchmark, p. 291.

218 See Nissenbaum, ibid., p. 292.

219 See Nissenbaum, ibid., p. 291, referring to Fred Cate (2006), "The failure of Fair Practice Information Principles," Consumer Protection in the Age of the Information Economy, July 8. Accessed July 1, 2013 from http://papers.ssrn.com/sol3/papers.cfm?abstract_id=1156972.

220 See Nissenbaum, ibid., p. 292.

comparison) of both approaches.[221] In addition, such a conclusion presupposes that there is no framework for helping to determine, similar to the approach of contextual integrity, substantive criteria for the specification of the purpose. Such an implicit presumption is particularly important for Nissenbaum's conclusion, since she admits that the success of her approach also depends on how the "context" is interpreted.[222] However, her observation that the principle of purpose limitation constitutes, without such a framework providing for substantive criteria, a mere shell remains valid. In 1989, the German legal scholar Badura equally criticized the legislation process of the German Federal Data Protection Law and at the time stated that it remained unclear "what the term 'purpose' actually means (…)".[223] However, the term "context", with respect to its function to a right to privacy, today is clearer in particular in light of Nissenbaum's approach. Thus, it should be possible to elaborate on a concept that equally clarifies the term "purpose". Indeed, before turning to this task it is necessary to clarify the interrelationship between both terms "context" and "purpose" because legal scholars, as well as data protection authorities, often use these terms 'simultaneously, at least, without explicitly clarifying the precise differences in their meaning.[224]

In its "Decision on Population Census", the German Constitutional Court provided the first and, compared to its following decisions, most comprehensive approach in defining both terms and explaining their interrelated functions. In order to determine the extent of the basic right to informational self-determination, it held that "it is not only necessary to examine the type of the data provided but also to examine the possibilities of

221 Cf. Bygrave, p. 157, associating the criteria of „context“ with „purpose compatibility“ and also the individual's „reasonable expectations“ (with respect to this latter relationship, see in particular below under C. II. 1. a) ECtHR and ECJ: Almost no criteria.

222 See Nissenbaum, ibid., p. 292.

223 See Albers, Treatment of Personal Information and Data, cip. 124 quoting Peter Badura, Anhörungsbeitrag in der öffentlichen Anhörung des Innenausschusses des Deutschen Bundestages vom 19. Juni 1989, in: Deutscher Bundestag (Hrsg.), Fortentwicklung der Datenverarbeitung und des Datenschutzes, Zur Sache 17/1990, S. 15 (16): "Es sei unklar, was denn Zweck überhaupt ist, wie eng oder wie weit der Zweck zu sehen ist, ob Zweck etwa gleich Aufgabe ist oder organisatorisch definiert werden kann usw."

224 See, instead of many, the Article 29 Data Protection Working Grouop, Opinion 03/2013 on purpose limitation, pp. 23 and 24.

its usage. *These depend, on the one hand, on the purpose of the collection and, on the other hand, on* the possibilities of the specific technique of processing the data and on the possibilities of its combination. Consequently, a datum that is, per se, irrelevant can become relevant; insofar, under the conditions of automated data processing, there is no 'irrelevant' data. Whether information is sensitive cannot only depend on the intimacy of the events. In order to determine the relevance of the datum for the personality right, it is rather necessary to know *the context of its usage.* Only when it is clear for which purpose the information is required and which possibilities of linking and usage exist, it is possible to answer the question of whether the infringement of the right to informational self-determination is constitutionally legal or not (underlining by the author)."[225] In essence, the Court clarified that the relevance of data with respect to the personality right of the data subject does not only depend, similar to Nissenbaum's approach, on the type of data or the intimacy of the event, but also on further factors.

One decisive factor for determining the legal relevance of data is, from the Court's perspective, the context of its usage. Interestingly, the Court determines the context by referring to the purpose of the collection of the data, as well as referring to the actual technical possibilities of how the data can be combined and used.[226] Therefore, in order to answer the question of what the term purpose really means, it seems plausible to refer to contexts in the meaning that Nissenbaum describes. The specification of the

---

225 See BVerfG, 15th of December 1983, 1 BvR 209, 269, 362, 420, 440, 484/83, cip. 176 and 177: "(...) Dabei kann nicht allein auf die Art der Angaben abgestellt werden. Entscheidend sind ihre Nutzbarkeit und Verwendungsmöglichkeit. Diese hängen einerseits von dem Zweck, dem die Erhebung dient, und andererseits von den der Informationstechnologie eigenen Verarbeitungsmöglichkeiten und Verknüpfungsmöglichkeiten ab. Dadurch kann ein für sich gesehen belangloses Datum einen neuen Stellenwert bekommen; insoweit gibt es unter den Bedingungen der automatischen Datenverarbeitung kein ‚belangloses' Datum mehr. Wieweit Informationen sensibel sind, kann hiernach nicht allein davon abhängen, ob sie intime Vorgänge betreffen. Vielmehr bedarf es zur Feststellung der persönlichkeitsrechtlichen Bedeutung eines Datums der Kenntnis seines Verwendungszusammenhangs: Erst wenn Klarheit darüber besteht, zu welchem Zweck Angaben verlangt werden und welche Verknüpfungsmöglichkeiten und Verwendungsmöglichkeiten bestehen, lässt sich die Frage einer zulässigen Beschränkung des Rechts auf informationelle Selbstbestimmung beantworten. (...)"

226 See also Britz, Informational Self-Determination between Legal Doctrine and Constitutional Case Law, p. 575.

purpose serves, from this perspective, to pre-determine the (future) context of the intended use of data and, thus, the context-related informational norms. Indeed, Hofmann already stated in his work *Purpose Limitation as Anchor Point for a Procedural Approach in Data Protection* from 1991 that the specification of the purpose serves to create "well-designed, transparent and controllable structures" and its limitation to "maintain the original context of collection".[227] Pohle stresses the similarity, if not equality, of these functions with Nissenbaum's approach of "contextual integrity".[228] In any event, the determination of a future context in advance through the specification of the purpose makes it possible to determine, for example, the transmission principles before the use of data takes actually place. Having the considerations on the regulation of risks in mind, referring to the purpose of the data processing enables the data controller to apply the transmission principles (or to prepare their application) in advance in order to avoid the (potential) later harm, that means, a later violation of contextual integrity. So far, the requirement to specify the purpose would not be a mere shell as Nissenbaum promotes. Instead, it is just another legal link for regulation. This approach focuses, by expanding legal protection before the violation of contextual integrity can take place, on the prevention of or precaution against risks for the individual's autonomy.

However, despite the German Constitutional Court's elaborated approach, the difference between both terms "context" and "purpose" is not sufficiently clear when reviewing the different acts of data treatment, i.e. stages of the information flow: Firstly, there is no clear distinction between contexts of different acts of data treatment over time. The Court only refers to the context of later usage. In contrast, the collection of data is also embedded in a certain context. This differentiation is important in order to exactly determine, as Nissenbaum proposes, the context in which the data usage precisely occurs and whether this use challenges the corresponding informational norms or not. Furthermore, the difference is im-

---

227 See Hofmann, Purpose Limitation as Anchor Point for a Procedural Approach in Data Protection, p. 25/26 regarding the first quote, and p. 126 regarding the second quote; cf. Bygrave, Data Privacy Law, p. 153, who highlights the importance of the principle of purpose limitation "ensuring adequate information quality and that the data-processing outcomes conform with the expectations of data controllers".

228 See Pohle, Purpose limitation revisited, footnote 24, referring to Helen Nissenbaum, Privacy as contextual integrity, Washington Law Review 79, pp. 101 to 139.

portant in order to obtain a clear distinction between the purpose specified the moment the data is collected and each later use of data. The reason is that one must be clear about the fact that each time the data is used, this use might pursue another purpose which would then determine another future context of the data treatment etc. etc. The second unclear aspect is that there is no specific explanation for the interplay between, *the purpose of the collection and (...) the possibilities of the specific technique of processing the data and on the possibilities of its combination*. The Court thus differs between the usage intended by the data controller and the usages that are factually possible. In doing so, the Court appears to imply that all factual possibilities of data processing could be pre-determined. Such an implication becomes reasonable in light of the data processing techniques that had existed at the time. In the 1980's, data processing was based on very few large central-computing systems. These central systems determined the different phases and possibilities of the processing of data and its possible combination. The legal terms of *collection, storage, processing, change, usage, and deletion of personal data* actually followed the technical environment at the time. Instead, today, the treatment of personal data often takes place in highly decentralized and non-linear environments. The different stages of the treatment of data, such as the collection, changing, combination, and transfer of data – how it is often described in literature and within the German law – do not necessarily succeed in this linear direction. Instead, in today's non-linear environment, these different types of data processing occur simultaneously or parallel and are intertwined, again and again, with the information constantly retrieved. Consequently, the information depends, more than before, on the corresponding context of usage.[229] This leads to the result that the computing system as such cannot determine all factual possibilities of data processing. A concept protecting (in other words, preserving) principles of privacy and/or data protection and, thus, a definition of the terms "context" and "purpose" must mirror this consequence.

In conclusion, in light of the fact that de-centralized and non-linear environments do not allow for the pre-determination of all factual possibilities of data processing, one has to, firstly, focus on examining the present

229 See Albers, ibid., cip. 121 and 122; highlighting the current change of the computational systems and environments compared to the times of the first "*Decision on Population Census*" in 1983, Hoffmann-Riem, Protection of the Confidentiality and Integrity of Information Technological Systems, pp., 1009 and 1010.

context in which the data is currently processed. Secondly, an appropriate legal link for determining the future context, is the present purpose. Therefore, in this thesis, the term "purpose" means the intended reason behind the data controller's treatment of the data referring to a future context; from this point of view, the realization of the purpose is a causal process with, at least an analytical final end that is determined by this purpose. The purpose serves to bundle the different acts of the data processing to a meaningful unity. From the perspective of the entity setting the purpose, the purpose thus decides on whether the means, which are used in order to reach the purpose, are appropriate or not.[230] In contrast, the term "context" does not primarily refer, be it a present or future one, to a certain result of a human-caused process but, as quoted previously, to "structured social settings with characteristics that have evolved over time (sometimes long periods of time) and are subject to a host of causes and contingencies of purpose, place, culture, historical accident, and more."[231]

So far, this definition of the term "purpose" does not exclude or substitute the "context" as defined within the framework of contextual integrity but rather incorporates it. Indeed, Nissenbaum also refers, in turn, to the term "purpose" when she elaborates on the definition of context. However, it is obvious that her context definition referring to the 'causes and contingencies of purpose' rather means the value, objective or end of a specific context than the subjective purpose formulated by an individual within that context. In any event, this thesis explicitly ties into the definition by the German Constitutional Court considering a purpose set by an individual not only referring to a future context of the data use, but also as another factor characterizing the present context. The reason is that a determination of the legal responsibility of the entity processing personal data, must also take its purpose into account. Without the knowledge about the purpose of the processing, it would be hard to determine the reason of the entrepreneurs behavior and, thus, at least, the entrepreneurs social role.[232] Hence, the context of a data treatment includes the purpose of the data processing – and this purpose characterizes, together with further circum-

230 See Albers, ibid., cip. 123; Pohle, Purpose limitation revisited, pp. 142 and 143; see, from a sociological perspective, Luhmann, The Concept of Purpose and the Rationality of Systems, in particular, pp. 1 ff., 9 ff. and 114 ff.

231 See Nissenbaum, ibid., p. 130.

232 Cf. Nissenbaum herself with respect to the necessity of knowing the purpose of a context in order to understand it, ibid., p. 134.

stances, the corresponding context. A purpose thus links the existent context of the current act of data treatment to a future, intended one.[233]

By means of an example: The startups mentioned in the introduction each publish their own websites, in order to improve the process and experience of users of their websites, and use the service of a provider of analytical tools, who in turn analyze the behavior of the users visiting the website. This analysis is based on the collection and processing of user data, such as the time and date of his or her visits, the visit behavior (for example, from which page does the user come from, on which page does he or she start, how much time does the user stay and when does he or she leave) as well as, possibly, the user's IP address, the location and type of his or her device and the browser ("attributes"). The moment a user's data is collected, the context is determined by: the publisher of the website using the service of the service provider, the service provider itself (both with respect to their corresponding purposes) and the social role of the data subject the moment when he or she uses the website ("actors"); the general expectations of whether the data might be collected or under which conditions and for which purposes it might be used ("norms"). Thus, the purposes of the website publisher and the service provider determine, amongst others, the context of the data collection. The future contexts can be, given that the website publisher and the service provider constantly develop their products further, mainly prescribed by these purposes. The way the website is developed and the analytical software used per se, only allows in a limited way to pre-determine, pursuant to the technical environment, the future context of the concrete data processing.

5. Values as a normative scale in order to determine the "contexts" and "purposes"

However, this example evidences that there is, over time, not only an unlimited number of contexts in which the data processing may occur but also, an unlimited number of purposes which pre-determine these contexts. Accordingly, the service provider collects the data, deletes certain other data and combines it with further data, firstly, for the purpose of analyzing it. The analysis as such takes place for the purpose of transferring

233 Cf. Albers, ibid., cip. 121 and 122.

the analytical results to the website publisher and, possibly, in order to improve the functioning of its analytical software. While all purposes take place in order to maintain the corresponding businesses, the service provider may know or not know the true purposes of the website publisher using the analytical results. The publisher of the website might use them, as described above, for the purpose of improving the user experience of its website but also in order to present it to (potential) cooperation partners and financiers. Even the storage of the data for an unknown purpose is, as such, a purpose. Hence, there are many acts of a data treatment occurring iteratively or simultaneously for many different purposes and, consequently, in corresponding contexts. For example, the purpose of a preceding act can lead to a following one, i.e. a subsequent purpose, or be completely different. Depending on the respective purposes, data may not only be intended to be transferred from one context into another one, but also the context in which the processing occurs may remain the same or turn into another one. The reason for this change is that the determination of the context depends on the perspective of the observer (whoever exercises this judgment task), just like the specification of the purpose depends on the actors' point of view. The question therefore is how to distinguish the different purposes and contexts, as well as the different acts of data treatment from a legal point of view: Which acts of the data treatment, which corresponding purposes, which contexts are legally relevant?

Nissenbaum herself provides a solution to this question: The values serve as the main criteria for determining a context as a common unity of analysis. Values explain the reason of behavior in a context and, thus, which elements observed are relevant within this context and which are not. Values hence not only help answer the question of which new informational norms that challenge entrenched ones are justified, but already, in a preceding step, the question of how to determine the specific context, i.e. which elements observed belong to a specific context and which not. As a consequence, values may fulfill the same function in order to determine the relevance of the purpose of data processing. From this perspective, the main task of this thesis is then to elaborate on such values as a normative concept that can assist in determining context-relative informational norms and, in this framework, the function of the principle of purpose limitation.[234] This may imply answers to the question of how precisely purposes of data processing must or how broadly they may be specified.

234 Cf. De Hert and Gutwirth, Data Protection in the Case Law of Strasbourg and Luxemburg: Constitutionalisation in Action, p. 4, summarizing how data protection regulation "formulates the conditions under which processing is legitimate."

C. The function of the principle of purpose limitation in light of Article 8 ECFR and further fundamental rights

As a main part of this thesis, this chapter illustrates the legal framework surrounding the collection and processing of personal data with respect to the principle of purpose limitation. Seeking to prove the hypothesis made in the preceding chapter that values define the contexts in which data is being processed and, consequently, define the purposes for why the data is processed, this chapter elaborates on a normative concept for the definition of purposes and contexts. This concept intends to clarify, which informational norms govern certain contexts and, consequently, what legal function the principle of purpose limitation has in our digital society.

In order to elaborate on such a normative concept, the first sub-chapter examines the constitutional framework that is applicable, in general, to the processing of personal data in the private sector within the European Union. On this basis, the second chapter draws the attention to the first component of the principle of purpose limitation, i.e. the requirement to specify the purpose, in light of the specific fundamental rights concerned. The third chapter focuses on the second component, i.e. the requirement to limit the later processing to the purpose initially specified. Finally, the fourth chapter treats the question of which regulation instruments come into question for establishing, by means of ordinary law, the principle of purpose limitation in the private sector.

I. Constitutional framework

Any ordinary law and, consequently, regulation instrument, as well as its interpretation, must correspond to our current notation of fundamental rights. Thus, the constitutional framework, such as the European Charter of Fundamental Rights not only serves as a scale of control for the interpretation of ordinary law by the judiciary and the executive, such as the (independent) data protection authorities, but it also determines the scope of decision making for the legislator.[235] Even if all fundamental rights regimes treated in this thesis cover, in principle, privacy and/or data protection, there are essential differences with respect to the respective objects and concepts of protection. These differences are highly relevant in determining the function of the principle of purpose limitation with respect to the European Charter of Fundamental Rights. This sub-chapter attempts and starts, hence, to clarify the scope of application of the different fundamental rights regimes and its legal effects in the private sector. The analysis continues to examine the object and concept of protection of the German right to informational self-determination. In light of the extensive case law provided for, in the last 30 years, on this right, this examination serves as a starting point for analyzing the different objects and concepts of protection of the fundamental regimes provided for on a European level. From this perspective, it may hence serve as a source of inspiration.[236] In this regard, it must be stressed that the subsequent analysis is not a complete evaluation of all existing case law regarding data protection and/or privacy in the European Union. Instead, the analysis concentrates on those Court decisions that appear to be most suitable in providing guidance in order to answer the main research question of this thesis.

1. Interplay and effects of fundamental rights regimes

Consequently, the following three constitutional frameworks are relevant, surrounding privacy and/or data protection in the European Union, as well as in Germany (as one of its Member States): The European Convention for Human Rights, the European Charter of Fundamental Rights of the European Union and, as an example for the national level, German Basic Rights.[237] In contrast, in this thesis, international treaties such as the

235 Cf. Britz, Informational Self-Determination between Legal Doctrine and Constitutional Case Law, pp. 562 and 563; Burgkardt, Data Protection between the German Basic Law und Union Law, p. 29.

236 Cf. Rouvroy and Poullet, The Right to Informational Self-Determination and the Value of Self-Development: Reassessing the Importance of Privacy for Democracy, p. 49; Bäcker, Constitutional Protection of Information regarding Private Parties, pp. 115 and 116.

237 See Burgkardt, ibid., p. 53 and 81.

OECD Guidelines play a role, only, so long as the Courts, which interpret the fundamental rights, explicitly refer to it.[238]

a) The interplay between European Convention for Human Rights, European Charter of Fundamental Rights and German Basic Rights

In this triangle, the European Convention for Human Rights affects both the legal frameworks of the European Union, as well as its Member States, which also are members of the European Council and, as such, addressees of the European Convention. The European Convention has the status of constitutional or, at least, ordinary law in most members of the European Council.[239] In contrast, the European Union has not yet acceded to the European Council. Therefore, the European Convention does not directly bind the European Union.[240] However, Article 6 sect. 3 of the Treaty on European Union and Article 52 sect. 3 ECFR require the European Court of Justice to interpret the European Charter of Fundamental Rights in light of the European Convention.[241] Historically, this requirement results from the fact that the European Convention for Human Rights served as a source for the establishment of the Charter of Fundamental Rights.[242]

The European Charter of Fundamental Rights primarily binds the institutions, bodies, offices and agencies of the European Union. It also binds Member States, but only when the respective Member State is implementing Union law, Article 51 sect. 1 sent. 1 ECFR.[243] This principle of "primacy of application" seeks to avoid the divergent application of Union law amongst the EU Member States. If each Member State could interpret Union law under the light of their national constitutions, Union law would run the risk of being applied differently within each Member State.[244] Given that there is no legal definition in relation to the question of how each Member State is implementing Union law, the European Court of Justice

238 See, however, on the general impact of the OECD guidelines, Kirby, The history, achievement and future of the 1980 OECD guidelines on privacy.

239 Cf. Schweizer, European Convention and Data Protection, pp. 462 and 463.

240 See Burgkardt, ibid., p. 246.

241 See Streinz/Michl in: Streinz, EUV/AEUV, EUV Art. 6 cip. 25, 21 ff.

242 See Niedobitek, Development and General Principles, cip. 95.

243 See Streinz/Michl, ibid., GR-Charta Art. 51 cip. 3.

244 See Streinz/Michl, ibid., EUV Art. 4 cip. 35 (and the following).

has developed a solution through several types of cases whereby Union law was considered and deemed to apply.

Firstly, European fundamental rights undoubtedly govern European regulations that are directly applicable in all Member States.[245] An important example in this context is the General Data Protection Regulation that will come into force on 25 May 2018, pursuant to Article 99. Less certain is the scale of control in relation to the application of European directives within Member States, such as the Data Protection and ePrivacy Directives. Directives are not directly applicable within the Member States. Instead, they must be transposed into national law through the national legislator. This leads critics to come to various opinions, as summarized by Burgkardt: While some critics come to the conclusion that the transition into national law falls under the scope of national constitutional law. In contrast, the prevailing opinion argues that many directives are so precise in their wording, which means that the directive can almost be translated on a literal basis into national law. If the national legislator has no room to interpret a directive, national fundamental law does, in consequence, not apply. These critics therefore differentiate between the parts of the directive that must be identically transposed and the other parts that have to be interpreted. While European fundamental rights govern the first, national basic rights principally provide a scale of control for the latter.[246] Indeed, the European Court of Justice stresses that this room of interpretation does not apply to notions being autonomously interpreted in light of European law.[247] Thus, if the ePrivacy Directive authorizes, for example, the processing of personal data for "marketing electronic communications services or for the provision of value added services", these terms appear to leave no room for interpretation by the Member States.[248]

245 See Burgkardt, ibid., p. 33.

246 See Burgkardt, ibid, pp. 34, with further references, and who stresses that the European Court of Justice holds European fundamental rights as binding for national legislators even in the case that there is a certain scope of transition because the transition must never contradict the directive that consists, on its part, of the purposes of European fundamental rights.

247 See Britz, The Fundamental Right to Data Protection in Article 8 ECFR, p. 8 and 9.

248 See Article 6 sect. 3 sent. 1 of the Directive 2002/58/EC of the European Parliament and of the Council of 12 July 2002 concerning the processing of personal data and the protection of privacy in the electronic communications sector (Directive on privacy and electronic communications).

This leads to the situation whereby the scope of the directive defines whether the European Charter of Fundamental Rights or national constitutional law, such as the German Basic Law, applies. The application of the European Charter of Fundamental Rights upon Member States depends, therefore on two prevailing factors. The first factor pertains to the scope of the directive. The second relates to the room of interpretation that the European legislator left to the national legislator for transposing the secondary law.[249]

In conclusion, both the European Union, as well as its Member States, have to respect the European Convention. The European Charter of Fundamental Rights binds, in any case, the European Union. Whether the European Charter of Fundamental Rights also bind the Member States, depends on the fact of whether or not they are implementing Union law. This will undoubtedly be the case, if Member States execute European regulations such as the General Data Protection Regulation. In contrast, if Member States transpose European directives into national law, it will depend on the scope and room of interpretation of the directive.

b) The effects of fundamental rights on the private sector

The different fundamental rights regimes undoubtedly address the public bodies, i.e. the legislator, the executive, and the judiciary. Indeed, the subject-matter of this thesis is not to examine the effects of the principle of purpose limitation on the collection and processing of personal data by the State but private companies operating through the private sector. The way in which fundamental rights affect private parties depends on the concept of protection provided for by the respective constitutional regimes.[250]

---

249 Cf. Grimm, Data protection before its refinement, pp. 589 to 592, who stresses the extreme wide scope of application of the right to data protection under Article 8 ECFR because this right covers, across to normal fundamental rights, all areas of social life under the only condition that the processing of personal data is at stake; Burkhardt, ibid., pp. 53 and p. 59.

250 Cf. Britz, ibid., pp. 562 and 563.

aa) Third-party effect, protection and defensive function

The basic differentiation is whether or not fundamental rights have an *indirect or direct effect to third-parties*. In the latter case, fundamental rights not only bind the State but also private entities. This leads to the situation where not only the State, but also private parties have to justify any harm caused against an individual's fundamental right. In the former case, in contrast, it is only the public bodies bound by fundamental rights. In this case, only the State is bound to justify all infringements, whereas private parties are principally free, for example, to process personal data even if this harms another's fundamental right to privacy and/or data protection.[251] Another terminological issue shall be stressed in this regard: this thesis calls a State intrusion into the scope of protection of a fundamental right an "infringement"; in contrast, if a private party intrudes into the scope of protection this intrusion is called a "harm" for the fundamental right.[252] In any case, if a private party harms another party's fundamental right(s), the public bodies must balance, through the establishment and execution of regulation instruments, the colliding fundamental rights of these private entities interacting on the private sector.[253]

This duty of balance can also be described by two different functions of fundamental rights. Firstly, there is a defensive function that enables the private party to defend him or herself against actions of the State. Secondly, there is a protection function that obliges the State to protect an individual's fundamental right against threats caused by sources other than that of the State if the individual is not able to protect him or herself against this threat.[254] This can be the case with respect to natural disasters for example, because a person alone is not able to protect his or her house against a flood. However, in situations where a threat does not result from natural sources but from third parties' behavior, both the protection and

251 See Papier, Third-Party Effect of German Basic Rights, cip. 23/24; cf. Bethge, Collision of Fundamental Rights, cip. 9 to 11, who apparently refers in his criticism to the direct third-party effect; with particular respect to the processing of personal data, see Gusy, Informational Self-Determination and Data Protection: Continuing or New Beginning?, p.60.

252 Cf. Eckhoff, The Infringement of Fundamental Rights, pp. 288 to 290; ; Grimm, Data protection before its refinement, p. 587.

253 See Papier, ibid., cip. 23/24; cf. Bethge, ibid., cip. 9 to 11.

254 See with regard to German Basic Rights, Dietlein, The Doctrine of Duties of Protection of Basic Rights, pp. 103 and 104.

defensive functions potentially come into conflict to each other: in these situations, the same State action intending, on the one side, to protect the basic rights of individuals against harmful behavior of third parties may infringe, on the other side, the defensive function of the third parties' basic rights. The State hence has to weigh these colliding fundamental rights in order to make both rights as effective as possible in practice.[255]

Amongst the Member States of the European Union, an indirect effect of fundamental rights on the private sector is widely recognized only with regard to the laws of torts. However, critics believe that there is a general tendency amongst countries to transfer the concept to further areas of law. Germany, Switzerland, the United Kingdom, Italy, France, Spain (and the USA as well) appear, more or less, to principally acknowledge an indirect effect of their fundamental rights.[256] In contrast, the concept of the protection function of fundamental rights is less acknowledged, in general. Leading Scholars of Constitutional Law consider that only Germany, Austria, France, and Ireland recognize the protection function as a basic principle within their constitutional regimes.[257] Given the diversity of the doctrinal concepts amongst these countries, it is worth illustrating to what extent the fundamental rights regimes considered in this thesis, generally provide for an indirect effect or even the protection function, and, in particular, to what extent, their respective fundamental rights to privacy and/or data protection do so.

(1) European Convention on Human Rights

While the European Convention on Human Rights does not directly bind third parties, the European Court of Human Rights recognizes the protection function by establishing what are called "positive obligations" on the members of the Council of Europe. The term "positive obligations" means

255 Cf. Callies, regarding to German Basic Rights, Duties of Protection, cip. 3 and 5 as well as 18 and 22; Jaeckel, Duties of Protection in German and European Law, pp. 63 to 79, who also stresses the frequent difficulties when trying to clearly differentiate between both functions.
256 See Papier, ibid., cip. 47 and 48.
257 See Calliess, ibid., cip. 15.

that the members have to establish protective measures against the harm of fundamental rights by third parties in the private sector.[258]

(a) Positive obligations with respect to Article 8 ECHR

Indeed, the extent of such a protection function differs to the corresponding fundamental rights in question. The protection function of Article 2 ECHR only protects against intentional harm or intentional killing. In contrast, the protection function of the right to respect for private and family life under Article 8 ECHR protects not only against intentional but also non-intentional harms.[259] In the case of "*López Ostra vs. Spain*", the Court considered that "naturally, severe environmental pollution may affect individuals' well-being and prevent them from enjoying their homes in such a way as to affect their private and family life adversely, without, however, seriously endangering their health."[260] Indeed, the Court appears not to conceptually differentiate between the protection and the defensive function in light of the following reasoning: "whether the question is analysed in terms of a positive duty on the State – to take reasonable and appropriate measures to secure the applicant's rights under paragraph 1 of Article 8 (...) -, as the applicant wishes in her case, or in terms of an 'interference by a public authority' to be justified in accordance with paragraph 2 (...), the applicable principles are broadly similar. In both contexts regard must be had to the fair balance that has to be struck between the competing interests of the individual and of the community as a whole, and in any case the State enjoys a certain margin of appreciation."[261] Critics stress that even if the positive function of Article 8 ECHR is therefore recognized, its concept of protection with respect to its effects in the private sector is not comprehensively clear.[262]

---

258 See Schweizer in: Handbook of Basic Rights – Europe I, § 138 cip. 64 (and the following); however, see also Linskey, The Foundations of EU Data Protection Law, pp. 115-118 (referring to further sources) who also applies the concept of "mittelbare Drittwirkung" to the ECHR.

259 See Calliess, ibid., cip. 16.

260 See ECtHR "López Ostra vs. Spain" (Application nr 16798/90), cip. 51.

261 See ECtHR, ibid., cip. 51.

262 See Calliess, ibid., cip. 16; ECtHR "Guerra et alt. Vs. Italy" (Application nr. 14967/89), cip. 58 and 60; Jaeckel, ibid., pp. 179 to 181.

(b) Right to respect for private life under Article 8 ECHR

Legal scholars stress the importance of the positive duties of protection in Article 8 ECHR in light of the wording 'right to *respect* for private life' (underlining by the author).[263] Thus, regarding the different guarantees mentioned before, they consider two substantial elements which undoubtedly fall under Article 8 ECHR: The right for private life serves, firstly, a defensive function (also called negative duty of protection) and, secondly, a protection function (also called positive duty of protection).[264] With regard to the private sector, for example, in the case of "*Craxi vs. Italy*", the press published information that originally stemmed from private documented court files. The European Court of Human Rights held, in general, that the public bodies concerned were obliged, pursuant to Article 8 ECHR, to provide measures that are necessary for the protection of private life.[265] With a particular view to the processing of personal data, the protection function of the right to respect for private life may also provide, for instance, for the right to access to personal data, the deletion of personal data, the correction of inaccurate data, and even the need for a supervisory authority can result from this right.[266]

With respect to the balancing of colliding fundamental rights, in the case of "*K. U. vs. Finland*", the European Court of Human Rights had in particular to balance the right of private life in Article 8 ECHR between two private parties.

> In this case, information about a 12 year old boy, such as his age, physical data, telephone number, address and his pretended desire for an intimate relationship with another coeval or older boy, were published, without the boy's knowledge, on a dating website. The boy subsequently became a victim of an apparent pedophile. Despite the gravity of the harm caused, the service

---

263 See Schweizer, DuD 2009, Decisions of the European Court of Human Rights on the Fundamental Rights to Personality and Data Protection (Die Rechtsprechung des Europäischen Gerichtshofs für Menschenrechte zum Persönlichkeits- und Datenschutz), p. 464.

264 See Burgkardt, ibid., pp. 247.

265 See ECtHR, Case of Craxi vs. Italy from 17 July 2003 (application no. 25337/94), cip. 73.

266 See De Hert and Gutwirth, Data Protection in the Case Law of Strasbourg and Luxemburg: Constitutionalisation in Action, p. 7 and 19.

> provider for the website did not provide the dynamic IP address of the person who published the information.[267]

The European Court of Human Rights finally weighed the right of confidentiality in favor of the, so far, unknown person who published the data against the right of physical integrity of the violated boy.[268] Legal scholars stress that the Court, at least, indirectly balanced the defensive and the protection function of the right of private life of Article 8 ECHR, on the one side, in favor of the person who published the information and, on the other side, in favor of the violated boy.[269] Thus, even if the concept of protection regarding the negative and positive duties of a Sate is not comprehensively clear, structurally, the Court applies the general principle weighing the colliding fundamental rights.

(2) European Charter of Fundamental Rights

Amongst legal scholars, it is heavily debated, whether the European Constitution directly applies to the private sector or not. While some critics deny a third-party effect, in general, in relation to the lack of application of Union Law on private parties, others confirm it, at least, with regard to market freedoms.[270]

(a) Market freedoms and fundamental rights

Interestingly, the European Court of Justice affirmed in several decisions a direct third-party effect of two market freedoms: the freedom to provide services and the freedom of movement for workers, under Article 49 and 45 of the Treaty on the Functioning of the European Union. In the cases of "*Walrave and Koch vs. Association Union Cycliste Internationale*" and "*Gaeton Donà vs. Mario Mantero*", the Court affirmed the third-party effect for collective agreements on the sector of services and employment.

---

267 See ECtHR, Case of K.U. vs. Finland from 2 December 2008, (application no. 2872/02), cip. 6 to 14.

268 See ECtHR, Case of K.U. vs. Finland from 2 December 2008, (application no. 2872/02), cip. 48.

269 See Burgkardt, ibid., pp. 280 to 282.

270 See Niedobitek, ibid., cip. 103 with further references.

In addition, in the case of "*Angonese vs. Cassa de Risparmio*", the Court finally confirmed the third-party effect even for agreements that were concluded on an individual basis.[271]

In contrast, with regard to the principle of free movement of goods, the European Court of Justice denied the direct third-party effect in the private sector. In the case of "*Dansk Supermarked vs. Imerco*", the Court stated that the breach of an individual agreement prohibiting the commercial exploitation of a good in a certain Member State must not be considered as an infringement of unfair competition law. The decision clearly addressed the referring court, which had to interpret the national unfair competition clause, with the result that the principle of free movement of goods had only an indirect effect on the private sector. In the case of "*Bayer vs. Süllhöfer*", the European Court of Justice explicitly denied a direct third-party effect of the principle of free movement of goods. In the case of "*Commission vs. France*", the Court finally stated that there was an obligation of the Member State to guarantee the free movement of goods on the single market and that it had to, given that private parties hinder such free movement, weigh this freedom with the colliding fundamental rights.[272] In conclusion, the European Court of Justice affirmed the third-party effect, however, only in relation to the freedom to provide services and for the movement of workers. In relation to the principle of free movement of goods, the Court denied the direct-third party effect and instead appeared to favor the protection function. This means that it is not the private parties, but the Member States who are bound and must balance the fundamental freedoms with the fundamental rights of the private parties concerned.

The decisions described above concerned, primarily, the fundamental freedoms and not the fundamental rights. Critics conclude that the European Court of Justice will apply, at least, the protection function for the fundamental rights also.[273] Calliess stresses, in particular, the wording and importance of Article 1 ECFR which states that "Human Dignity is inviolable (and/..) must be respected and *protected*" (underlining by the author). From his point of view, this duty of protection implies, in light of the fact

271 See Papier, ibid., cip. 50 to 54 with references to ECJ C36/74, ECJ 13/76, ECJ C-415/93, and ECJ C-281/98.

272 See Papier, ibid., cip. 55 to 59 with references to ECJ 58/80, ECJ 65/86, and ECJ C-295/95.

273 See Jaeckel, ibid., pp. 279 to 281.

that human dignity is inherent in all fundamental rights,[274] that the protection function applies, in general, to fundamental rights of the European Charter.[275] The European Court of Justice did not clearly comment on the effects of the fundamental rights to private life under Article 7 ECFR and to data protection provided for by 8 ECFR between private parties, for example, in the cases "*Lindqvist*" and "*PROMUSICAE*". Since these and further decisions all referred, so far, to the European directives applicable to both the public and private sector, it is not exactly clear which kind of effects the European Court of Justice considers for the fundamental rights to private life and data protection.[276] In any case, in order to illustrate, in more detail, how the European Court of Justice weighs the opposing fundamental rights of the private parties involved, the subsequent few decisions of the European Court of Justice shall be discussed.

(b) The right to data protection under Article 8 ECFR and/or the right to private life under Article 7 ECFR

In these decisions, it becomes clear that the European Court of Justice does not (yet) clearly differentiate between the right to private life and to data protection, under Article 7 and 8 ECFR. In the cases "*Telekom vs. Germany*", "*SABAM vs. Scarlet*" and "*SABAM vs. Netlog*", for example, the Court referred to the right to data protection under Article 8 ECFR, only.

In the first-mentioned case "*Telekom vs. Germany*", a German telecommunications network provider, Deutsche Telekom AG, published, based on the individuals' consent, the names and telephone numbers of its own customers as

274 Cf. Papier, ibid., cip. 23.

275 See Calliess, ibid., cip. 17.

276 See Britz, Europeanisation of Data Protection Provided for by Fundamental Rights?, p. 8; v. Danwitz, The Fundamental Rights to Private Life and to data Protection, p. 585; ECJ C-101/01 (Lindqvist); ECJ C-275/06 (PROMUSICAE); See Kokott and Sobotta, The distinction between privacy and data protection in the jurisprudence of the CJEU and the ECtHR, p. 225, stressing an only indirect effect on the private sector; in contrast, De Hert and Gutwirth, Data Protection in the Case Law of Strasbourg and Luxemburg: Constitutionalisation in Action, pp. 9 and 10, seem to assume a direct effect on the private sector stating that the "Charter extends the protection of personal data to private relations and to the private sector."

> well as those of third parties in the public directory. The claimant's, Go Yellow GmbH and Telix AG, operated an Internet inquiry service and a telephone directory enquiry service, offering the said data in return for payment. The companies demanded, on the grounds of Article 25 section 2 Universal Service Directive 2002/22/EC, from Deutsche Telekom that it must provide not only the data of the customers of Deutsche Telekom AG but also of the third parties. Pursuant to Article 25 section 2 Universal Service Directive 2002/22/EC, "Member States shall ensure that all undertakings which assign telephone numbers to subscribers meet all reasonable requests to make available, for the purposes of the provision of publicly available directory enquiry services and directories, the relevant information in an agreed format on terms which are fair, objective, cost oriented and non-discriminatory." The referring German court asked the European Court of Justice to consider whether Article 12 Directive on privacy and electronic communications 2002/58/EG hindered, in light of the fact that the Defendant lacked the explicit consent or objection from the said third parties or their customers, the transfer of the data concerned.[277] Article 12 sect. 2 Directive on privacy and electronic communications 2002/58/EC only obliges the Member States, amongst others, to "ensure that subscribers are given the opportunity to determine whether their personal data are included in a public directory."

In order to answer this question, the Court stated, referring only to Article 8 ECFR, as: "Article 8(2) of the Charter authorizes the processing of personal data if certain conditions are satisfied. It provides that personal data 'must be processed fairly for specified purposes and on the basis of the consent of the person concerned or some other legitimate basis laid down by law'. (…) Moreover, the Directive on privacy and electronic communications makes it clear that that directive makes the publication, in printed or electronic directories, of personal data concerning subscribers conditional on the consent of those subscribers."[278] The decision appears, in the first instance, to presume a direct effect of Article 8 section 2 ECFR between the parties involved. Since it is not public bodies but private companies that collected and transferred the data in question, the Court seems to presume that Article 8 ECFR addresses these private parties. However, from a second perspective, such a third-party effect becomes arguable by focusing on which entity actually caused the transfer of data. Article 25 section 2 Universal Service Directive establishes an obligation for private undertakings to make the personal data available to third parties. Due to the fact that the law obliged these private companies to transfer the data,

---

277 See ECJ C-543/09 cip. 19, 20, and 27.

278 See ECJ C-543/09 cip. 52 and 54.

they had no choice in the matter of whether or not to transfer the same. It is hence the legislature establishing the obligation and not the private company that infringes the right of Article 8 ECFR. The right to data protection therefore had, so far, no direct effect on the private parties.

In the next case "*SABAM vs. Scarlet*", Scarlet was an Internet Service provider offering its customers access to the Internet. SABAM was an association of authors, composers and publishers representing the interests of its members in the field of copyright. SABAM had noticed that Internet users used the service of Scarlet by downloading copyright protected works by members of SABAM without any authorization or payment of royalties. SABAM filed an injunction against Scarlet to block any illegal file sharing. The referring Belgian court asked the European Court of Justice to consider whether such a filtering system harmed the fundamental right for the protection of personal data in Article 8 ECFR, since such a filtering system implied the processing of certain IP addresses.[279] Similarly, in the case of "*SABAM vs. Netlog*", Netlog was a social online community where users were able to set up a personal profile and communicate to each other sharing all sorts of information. SABAM was of the opinion that users on Netlog shared copyright protected works of its members and filed an injunction against Netlog in order for it to cease illegally making available the said musical and audiovisual content of SABAM's repertoire by installing a filter system. The Belgian court also referred this case to the European Court of Justice asking whether, amongst other matters, the Data Protection Directive and the Directive on privacy and electronic communication "permit Member States to authorize a national court (…) to order a hosting service provider to introduce, for all its customers, *in abstracto* and as a preventive measure (…) a system for filtering most of the information which is stored on its servers in order to identify" works of the said repertoire.[280]

The European Court of Justice balanced the right to data protection of the individuals using the Internet service and the social network, respectively, as well as the rights of the providers with the opposing fundamental rights of the claimant, i.e. the association of authors, composers, and publishers. The Court stated, at first, that "such an injunction would result in a serious infringement of the freedom of the ISP concerned to conduct its business since it would require that ISP to install a complicated, costly, permanent computer system at its own expense (…). In those circumstances, it must be held that the injunction to install the contested filtering system is to be regarded as not respecting the requirement that a fair balance be struck between, on the one hand, the protection of the intellectual-property right en-

279 See ECJ C-70/10 cip. 15 to 26.
280 See ECJ C-360/10 cip. 15 to 25.

joyed by copyright holders, and, on the other hand, that of the freedom to conduct business enjoyed by operators as ISPs. Moreover, the effects of that injunction would be limited to the ISP concerned, as the contested filtering system may also infringe that fundamental rights of that ISP's customers, namely their right to protection of their personal data and their freedom to receive or impart information, which are rights safeguarded by Articles 8 and 11 of the Charter respectively." In the case of "*SABAM vs. Netlog*", the Court considered in more detail how such a filtering system would harm the fundamental right to data protection of users in the social network in question: "Indeed, the injunction requiring installation of the contested filtering system would involve the identification, systematic analysis and processing of information connected with the profiles created on the social network by its users. The information connected with those profiles is protected personal data because, in principle, it allows those users to be identified". The Court concluded, referring to the preceding case of "*SABAM vs. Scarlet*", that the injunction would not be in line with the requirement of a fair balance between, on the one side, the copyright of the SABAM members and, on the other, the right to protection of personal data of the users of the social network.

While the European Court of Justice referred in the preceding cases to the right to data protection under Article 8 ECFR, only, it additionally referred, in the cases of "*ASNEF vs. FECEMD*" and "*González vs. Google Spain*", to the right to private life provided for by Article 7 ECFR. The first case of "*ASNEF vs. FECEMD*" is interesting because the Court did not weigh the opposing rights itself. Instead, the Court decided on the question of whether or not the Spanish legislator was correct in the way it has balanced the opposing rights, in light of Articles 7 and 8 ECFR, in accordance with Article 7 lit. f) of the Data Protection Directive.

> Article 7 lit. f) of the directive states that the Member States shall provide, transposing the directive into national law, that personal data may be processed only if the "processing is necessary for the purposes of the legitimate interests pursued by the controller or by the third party or parties to whom the data are disclosed, except where such interests are overridden by the interests for fundamental rights and freedoms of the data subject which require protection under Article 1 (1)" of the directive. The Spanish legislator transposed this provision into Spanish law excluding, in general, the processing of personal data that not has been made publicly available before.[281]

281 See ECJ C-468/10 and C-469/10, cip. 22.

The European Court of Justice stated, at first, that the "Member States must, when transposing Directive 95/46, take care to rely on an interpretation of that directive which allows a fair balance to be struck between the various fundamental rights and freedoms protected by the EU legal order". The Court agreed with the national legislator that the fact that the data was already publically available before might influence the intensity of the harm of the fundamental rights of the individual concerned. The intensity of harm for the individual is much higher if the data was not publically available before its processing. This higher intensity of harm must be taken into account balancing the individual's rights with the opposing rights of the third parties. However, the Court stated that the Spanish legislator interfered with Article 7 lit. f) of the Data Protection Directive by "excluding, in a categorical and generalized manner, the possibility of processing certain categories of personal data, without allowing the opposing rights and interests at issue to be balanced against each other in a particular case." The Court added that this might be only different, in accordance with Article 8 of the Data Protection Directive, with respect to special categories of data revealing racial or ethnic origin, political opinions, religious or philosophical beliefs, trade-union membership, and the processing of data concerning health or sex life.

While the European Court of Justice decided this case in favor of the data controllers,[282] it followed, in the case of "*González vs. Google Spain*", a more restrictive approach in favor of the individual concerned by the data processing.

> In this case, the claimant was involved, in 1998, in a real estate-auction as a measure for recovering social security debts. A Spanish newspaper had published articles about the auction that Internet users could find, until 2012, under the claimant's name, via Google's search engine. The claimant requested not only from the newspaper to delete his name in the articles or, at least, to use technical tools so that Google's search engine could not find the articles but also from Google itself to delete the links to the articles. The case ended up before the European Court of Justice, which finally denied the first but affirmed the second request: Google had to delete the links.[283]

The European Court of Justice weighed the fundamental rights to privacy and data protection of Mr. González against the fundamental rights of the search engine operator linking to the articles, and the Internet users who

282 See the similar case of ECJ C-582/14, cip. 50 to 64.

283 See ECJ C-131/12 cip. 14 to 20.

could find these articles searching for his name. In doing so, the Court clearly differentiated not only between the interests of the publishers of the articles and the operator of the Internet search engine but also between the effects of the publication of the articles, as such, and the fact that they can be found by means of the search engine.[284] In the Court's opinion, the increased possibilities of finding and interconnecting the articles within the Internet can even have a worse affect on the claimant than the first publication of the articles within the newspaper itself. The Court concluded from this that Articles 7 and 8 ECFR "override, as a rule, not only the economic interest of the operator of the search engine but also the interest of the general public in having access to that information (...)."[285] From the Court's point of view that might be only different "if it appeared, for particular reasons, such as the role played by the data subject in public life, that the interference with his fundamental rights is justified by the preponderant interest of the general public in having, on account of its inclusion in the list of results, access to the information in question."[286]

(3) German Basic Rights

On the German level, finally, constitutional law primarily binds, pursuant to Article 1 sect. 3 GG, the State and not private parties. However some critics believe that German Basic rights not only address the State but also private individuals. They argue that, nowadays, it is not only the State but also private entities that are able to infringe fundamental rights.[287] Simitis, who also chaired the Expert Group set up by the European Commission in order to prepare the European Charter of Fundamental Rights, particularly considers that the personality right, more precisely, the right to informational self-determination guaranteed in Article 2 sect. 1 and Article 1 sect. 1 GG serves as "classic link for the third-party effect of constitutional rights".[288] Nevertheless, the prevailing opinion denies such a direct effect of fundamental rights on the private sector, even if third parties have com-

284 See ECJ C-131/12 cip. 87.
285 See ECJ C-131/12 cip. 97.
286 See ECJ C-131/12 cip. 97.
287 See Papier, ibid., cip. 4 to 6.
288 See Expert Group on Fundamental Rights, p. 27; Simitis, NJW 1984, p. 401; denying Wente, NJW 1984, 1446.

prehensive power of control. A direct third-party effect is only recognized in exceptions explicitly provided for by the German Basic Rights.[289]

Irrespective of the question of the direct third-party effect of German Basic Rights, it is common ground that these rights have an indirect effect on third parties. The legal doctrine elaborated several objective and subjective functions of the Basic Law. In light of these functions, the Basic Rights do not only serve, as illustrated previously, the defensive function that is at stake if someone seeks to defend him or herself against state regulation, but also serves a protection function. This function results from the "objective order of values" provided for by German Basic Law. The justification of the protection function refers especially to Article 1 sect. 1 sent. 1 GG, which requires, similarly to Article 1 ECFR, that all state authorities must respect and protect human dignity.[290]

(a) Protection function of the right to informational self-determination

In the decision of "*Release of Confidentiality*" (Schweigepflichtentbindung), the German Constitutional Court affirmed this concept of protection with particular respect to the data processing by private parties.

> In this case, the claimant complained about a certain contractual obligation in her disability insurance contract that contained an authorization for the release of her confidential information of the insurance policy. The claimant reached an agreement with the insurance company for a life policy with a supplementary insurance for occupational disablement.[291] The contract for this supplementary insurance consisted of the claimant's duty to authorize the insurance company to "retrieve appropriate information from all doctors, hospitals, nursing homes, where I (the claimant) was or will be treated, as well as from my (the claimant's) health insurance company and other personal insurance companies, social insurance companies, public agencies, current and former employers."[292] When an insurance event occurred, the claimant refused to authorize the general release of confidential information and instead offered to authorize the respective entities to disclose her personal information on a case-by-case basis. The defendant refused to do this and, consequently, refused to pay out the policy. The claimant brought an action against the insurance company declaring that the specific clauses of the agreement in

289 See Jarass in: Jarass/Pieroth, GG, Art. 1 cip. 50; Jaeckel, ibid., pp. 100/101.
290 See Papier, ibid., cip. 7 to 10.
291 See BVerfG, 1 BvR 2027/02 (Release of Confidentiality), cip. 1 to 11.
292 See BVerfG, ibid., cip. 13.

> question were illegal and demanded that the insurance company pay out according to the policy. After the civil courts denied the claim in all instances, the claimant brought a constitutional complaint about the decisions of the civil courts on the grounds that the decisions would infringe the claimant's basic right to informational self-determination.[293]

The Constitutional Court affirmed the claim stating that the decisions of the civil courts infringed the claimant's general personality right in its specific form as the right to informational self-determination. The Court incorporates the state duty of protection regarding the right to informational self-determination with the following reasoning:

> "The judgments in question of the Regional Court and Higher Regional Court must be conform with the duty of the public authorities resulting from Art. 2 sect. 1 in combination with Art. 1 sect. 1 GG to guarantee the individual's informational self-determination in relation to third parties (…). The general personality right consists of the right of the individual to determine by him or herself the disclosure and usage of his or her personal data (…). This right also affects (…) the private law. If the judge, who decides on a case according to private law, misunderstands the object of protection of the general personality right, he or she infringes, by means of his or her decision, the protection function of the citizen's basic right (…). Indeed, especially on the private sector, the general personality right does not constitute an absolute control about certain information. The individual has to be rather considered as a personality that develops within the social community and depends on communication (…). This might result in the situation in which the individual has to respect the interests of communications by others. Principally, it belongs to the individual to form his or her communicational relationships and to decide whether he or she discloses or keeps certain information secret. Also the freedom to release information is protected by basic rights. For the individual, it is generally possible and reasonable to take preventative measures in order to maintain his or her interests of confidentiality. The general personality right safeguards that the legal order provides and maintains the legal conditions under which the individual is able to participate in communicational processes in a self-determined way and to develop his or her personality. In order to fulfill this duty, the individual must be reasonably enabled to protect him or herself in informational matters. If this is not the case, there is a responsibility of the State to establish the conditions for a self-determined participation in communication. In this case, the State cannot deny persons concerned protection under reference to the only seemingly voluntariness of the disclosure of certain information. The duty of protection that results from the general per-

293 See BVerfG, ibid., cip. 12 to 23.

sonality right rather requires from the responsible public agencies to provide the legal pre-conditions for an efficient informational self-protection."[294]

Thus, the duty of protection resulting from the right to informational self-determination obliges the State to establish and safeguard mechanisms that enable the individual concerned to protect him or herself against the threats resulting from the data processing by third parties.

---

294 See BVerfG, ibid., cip. 27 to 33: "Die angegriffenen Urteile des Landgerichts und des Oberlandesgerichts sind an der aus Art. 2 Abs. 1 in Verbindung mit Art. 1 Abs. 1 GG folgenden Pflicht der staatlichen Gewalt zu messen, dem Einzelnen seine informationelle Selbstbestimmung im Verhältnis zu Dritten zu ermöglichen. Das allgemeine Persönlichkeitsrecht umfasst die Befugnis des Einzelnen, über die Preisgabe und Verwendung seiner persönlichen Daten selbst zu bestimmen (...). Dieses Recht entfaltet als Norm des objektiven Rechts seinen Rechtsgehalt auch im Privatrecht. Verfehlt der Richter, der eine privatrechtliche Streitigkeit entscheidet, den Schutzgehalt des allgemeinen Persönlichkeitsrechts, so verletzt er durch sein Urteil das Grundrecht des Bürgers in seiner Funktion als Schutznorm (...). Gerade im Verkehr zwischen Privaten lässt sich dem allgemeinen Persönlichkeitsrecht allerdings kein dingliches Herrschaftsrecht über bestimmte Informationen entnehmen. Der Einzelne ist vielmehr eine sich innerhalb der sozialen Gemeinschaft entfaltende, auf Kommunikation angewiesene Persönlichkeit (...). Dies kann Rücksichtnahmen auf die Kommunikationsinteressen anderer bedingen. Grundsätzlich allerdings obliegt es dem Einzelnen selbst, seine Kommunikationsbeziehungen zu gestalten und in diesem Rahmen darüber zu entscheiden, ob er bestimmte Informationen preisgibt oder zurückhält. Auch die Freiheit, persönliche Informationen zu offenbaren, ist grundrechtlich geschützt. Dem Einzelnen ist es regelmäßig möglich und zumutbar, geeignete Vorsorgemaßnahmen zu treffen, um seine Geheimhaltungsinteressen zu wahren. Das allgemeine Persönlichkeitsrecht gewährleistet, dass in der Rechtsordnung gegebenenfalls die Bedingungen geschaffen und erhalten werden, unter denen der Einzelne selbstbestimmt an Kommunikationsprozessen teilnehmen und so seine Persönlichkeit entfalten kann. Dazu muss dem Einzelnen ein informationeller Selbstschutz auch tatsächlich möglich und zumutbar sein. Ist das nicht der Fall, besteht eine staatliche Verantwortung, die Voraussetzungen selbstbestimmter Kommunikationsteilhabe zu gewährleisten. In einem solchen Fall kann dem Betroffenen staatlicher Schutz nicht unter Berufung auf eine nur scheinbare Freiwilligkeit der Preisgabe bestimmter Informationen versagt werden. Die aus dem allgemeinen Persönlichkeitsrecht folgende Schutzpflicht gebietet den zuständigen staatlichen Stellen vielmehr, die rechtlichen Voraussetzungen eines wirkungsvollen informationellen Selbstschutzes bereitzustellen."

(b) Priority of contractual agreements and the imbalance of powers

Subsequently, the German Court specified under which conditions the decision of an individual, in relation to a contractual agreement, has to be considered as voluntary or 'only seemingly voluntary', which finally lead to the infringement of the basic right by the deciding courts:

> "The contract is the essential instrument in order to develop free and self-responsible actions in relation to third parties. The contract, which mirrors the harmonious will of the contracting parties generally, allows the assumption of a fair balance of their interests and must be principally respected by the State. However, if it is apparent that one party of the contract is so powerful that he or she can, in fact, unilaterally determine the contract, the law must safeguard both constitutional positions in order to avoid that the self-determination of one party perverts into being completely controlled by the other party. Such unilateral power of determination can result, amongst others, from the fact that the service offered by one party for the maintenance of the personal circumstances of the other is so essential that the latter cannot reasonably refuse to conclude the contract and, subsequently, to disclose the information demanded by the first. If those contract clauses – which concern the right to informational self-determination – are, in fact, not negotiable, the corresponding duty of protection requires the judge to weigh the interests of confidentiality of the one party with the other's interests of disclosure."[295]

---

295 See BVerfG, ibid., cip. 34 to 36:"Der Vertrag ist das maßgebliche Instrument zur Verwirklichung freien und eigenverantwortlichen Handelns in Beziehung zu anderen. Der in ihm zum Ausdruck gebrachte übereinstimmende Wille der Vertragsparteien lässt in der Regel auf einen sachgerechten Interessenausgleich schließen, den der Staat grundsätzlich zu respektieren hat (...). Ist jedoch ersichtlich, dass in einem Vertragsverhältnis ein Partner ein solches Gewicht hat, dass er den Vertragsinhalt faktisch einseitig bestimmen kann, ist es Aufgabe des Rechts, auf die Wahrung der Grundrechtspositionen beider Vertragspartner hinzuwirken, um zu verhindern, dass sich für einen Vertragsteil die Selbstbestimmung in eine Fremdbestimmung verkehrt (...). Eine solche einseitige Bestimmungsmacht eines Vertragspartners kann sich auch daraus ergeben, dass die von dem überlegenen Vertragspartner angebotene Leistung für den anderen Partner zur Sicherung seiner persönlichen Lebensverhältnisse von so erheblicher Bedeutung ist, dass die denkbare Alternative, zur Vermeidung einer zu weitgehenden Preisgabe persönlicher Informationen von einem Vertragsschluss ganz abzusehen, für ihn unzumutbar ist. Sind in einem solchen Fall die Vertragsbedingungen in dem Punkt, der für die Gewährleistung informationellen Selbstschutzes von Bedeutung ist, zugleich praktisch nicht verhandelbar, so verlangt die aus dem allgemeinen Persönlichkeitsrecht folgende Schutzpflicht eine gerichtliche Überprüfung, ob das Geheimhaltungsinteresse des unterlegenen Teils dem Offenbarungsinteresse des überlegenen Teils angemessen zugeordnet wurde. Dazu sind

The Court finally came to the conclusion that the power of negotiation of the contracting parties was so unbalanced that the claimant could not safeguard her informational self-protection on her own. The Court stated that in light of the current low level of state insurance for occupational disability, professionals have to, in order to safeguard their living standard, take out private insurance policies. Furthermore, the Court held the clause in question as not negotiable. Even if the claimant could choose between different policies which were offered by different insurance companies, the differences in the policies on the market, referred only to the conditions and the extent of the services of the policy as such but not to the collection and processing of the personal data. Thus, the Court did not see that competition which existed in the market with regard to the clauses that were relevant with respect to data protection law.[296]

(c) Balancing the colliding constitutional positions

Consequently, the German Constitutional Court stated on how the constitutional positions of the contracting parties may be weighed against each other. On the one hand, the Court considered, with the following reasoning, that the contractual obligation of release of confidentiality did essentially harm the claimant's right to informational self-determination:

> "The persons and institutions that are, in part, rather generally listed in the authorization of release from confidentiality can have sensible information about the claimant which dramatically affects her development of personality. (…) (Given the release of confidentiality), the claimant looses the possibility to control her interests of confidentiality by her own because of the general wording of the authorization, which does not determine specific inquiry offices nor specific inquiries, so that she cannot foresee which information about her will be demanded by whom. (…) The authorization demanded by the defendant is comparable with a general authorization to retrieve sensitive information with respect to the insurance event which extent is merely foreseeable by the claimant. (…) Because of the broad term 'appropriate', the policy-holder is not able to estimate which information can be retrieved on the basis of the authorization. The district court considered 'all facts which might be, even indirectly, legally relevant for the approval and execution of the policy services' as appropriate. As a consequence, actually each reference to the

---

die gegenläufigen Belange einander im Rahmen einer umfassenden Abwägung gegenüberzustellen (...)."

296 See BVerfG, ibid., cip. 37 to 40.

> event of insurance suffices in order to allow the inquiry. (…) Mechanisms of control to prove whether the collection of the data occurs in accordance to the (… /clause) are lacking. (…) The contract does not provide any duties of special information in favor of the policy-holder about specific collections of the data. The insurant has only after the disclosure of the information, given that he or she becomes aware of it, the possibility to control its legitimacy and to bring judicial action against it. However, at this moment, his or her interest can be already irreparably harmed (… /by the insurance company)."[297]

On the other hand, the German Constitutional Court considered that the defendant has an equally essential interest to obtain the information:

> "It is of high relevance for the insurance company to verify whether the event of insurance really occurred. (…) In addition, the insurance company is, in light of the variety of the events, not able to pre-list, already in the contract

297 See BVerfG, ibid., cip. 43, 45 to 48: "Wenn die Beklagte von der Beschwerdeführerin die Abgabe der begehrten Schweigepflichtentbindung verlangen kann, wird deren Interesse an wirkungsvollem informationellem Selbstschutz in erheblichem Ausmaß beeinträchtigt. Die in der formularmäßigen Erklärung der Schweigepflichtentbindung genannten, zum Teil sehr allgemein umschriebenen Personen und Stellen können über sensible Informationen über die Beschwerdeführerin verfügen, die deren Persönlichkeitsentfaltung tief greifend berühren. (...) Dabei begibt sie sich auch der Möglichkeit, die Wahrung ihrer Geheimhaltungsinteressen selbst zu kontrollieren, da wegen der weiten Fassung der Erklärung, in der weder bestimmte Auskunftsstellen noch bestimmte Auskunftsersuchen bezeichnet sind, für sie praktisch nicht absehbar ist, welche Auskünfte über sie von wem eingeholt werden können. (...) Die von der Beklagten verlangte Ermächtigung kommt damit einer Generalermächtigung nahe, sensible Informationen mit Bezug zu dem Versicherungsfall zu erheben, deren Tragweite die Beschwerdeführerin kaum zuverlässig abschätzen kann. (...) Es fehlt an einem wirksamen Kontrollmechanismus für die Überprüfung der Sachdienlichkeit einer Informationserhebung. (...) Aufgrund der Weite des Begriffs der Sachdienlichkeit kann der Versicherungsnehmer nicht im Voraus bestimmen, welche Informationen aufgrund der Ermächtigung erhoben werden können. Das Landgericht hat ausgeführt, sachdienlich seien "alle Tatsachen, die für die Feststellung und Abwicklung der Leistungen aus dem Versicherungsvertrag rechtserheblich sein können, und sei es auch nur mittelbar als Hilfstatsachen". Damit reicht praktisch jeder Bezug zu dem behaupteten Versicherungsfall aus, um eine Auskunftserhebung zu begründen. (...) Eine gesonderte Aufklärung des Versicherungsnehmers über die einzelnen Erhebungen ist in den Vertragsbedingungen nicht vorgesehen. Allenfalls nach einer Auskunftserteilung hat der Versicherte, soweit er von ihr erfährt, die Möglichkeit, deren Berechtigung zu prüfen und gegebenenfalls gerichtlichen Rechtsschutz in Anspruch zu nehmen. Zu diesem Zeitpunkt kann sein Interesse jedoch bereits irreparabel geschädigt sein, wenn das Versicherungsunternehmen unbefugt sensible Informationen erhoben hat."

> clause, all the information that might become relevant for the subsequent verification. Evaluating the importance of the defendant's interests, also the organizational and financial efforts that result from different possibilities of verification may come into consideration."[298]

In conclusion, the German Constitutional Court examines, first, whether or not the State actually infringes a State duty of protection and, in doing so, whether or not the individual concerned is really able to protect him or herself. Only if this is not the case, the State then has the duty to weigh itself (in this case, the Constitutional Court) the opposing fundamental rights, instead of the private parties.

bb) Balance between defensive and protection function

As demonstrated so far, the European Court of Human Rights does not precisely differentiate between the defensive and the protection function of human rights. In turn, the European Court of Justice does not even clarify, at least not explicitly, the type of effect of the fundamental rights to private life and/or data protection on the private sector. In contrast, the German Constitutional Court explicitly applies an indirect effect of basic rights, elaborating, precisely on the protection and defensive function in order to balance the basic rights opposing the German right to informational self-determination. Therefore, even if not all fundamental rights regimes recognize the defensive and protection function as applicable principles, it is worth examining their interplay, in general, which can serve as a structural aid in order to find a sound balance between the colliding fundamental rights.[299]

---

298 See BVerfG, ibid., cip. 50 to 52: "Dem Interesse der Beschwerdeführerin an informationeller Selbstbestimmung steht ein Offenbarungsinteresse der Beklagten von gleichfalls erheblichem Gewicht gegenüber. Es ist für das Versicherungsunternehmen von hoher Bedeutung, den Eintritt des Versicherungsfalls überprüfen zu können. (...) Zudem ist es aufgrund der Vielzahl denkbarer Fallgestaltungen dem Versicherer nicht möglich, bereits in der Vertragsklausel alle Informationen im Voraus zu beschreiben, auf die es für die Überprüfung ankommen kann. Im Rahmen der Gewichtung des Interesses der Beklagten kann auch der organisatorische und finanzielle Aufwand berücksichtigt werden, den verschiedene Prüfungsmöglichkeiten erfordern."

299 Cf. Jaeckel, ibid., p. 103, who stresses the many commonalities of all three fundamental rights regimes, i.e. the ECHR, the ECFR, and the German Basic Rights

(1) The 3-Step-Test: Assessing the defensive and protection function

There is a rough consensus on how to assess both the protection function and the defensive function of fundamental rights.[300] Both assessments usually follow three steps: Firstly, it is necessary to determine the scope of protection of the fundamental right in question. The second step requires examining whether or not a certain action invades into the scope. So far, the first and second steps are very similar in its approach. The third step seeks to assess whether or not the invasion into the scope of protection leads to a disproportionate violation of the fundamental right or not. It is the third step of this test where the assessment is different between the defensive and protective function as demonstrated below.

As mentioned previously, like the defensive function, the protection function applies to all three state powers, i.e. the legislator, the executive, and the judiciary. Regarding the *protection* function, the third step of the assessment refers to the question of whether or not the harm caused by a private party to another private party must be considered as a non-fulfillment of the duty of protection by the State. However, with respect to an legislator's action, or rather omission, the protection function is particular. In Germany, it can be assessed pursuant to the principle called "prohibition of insufficient means". The German Constitutional Court requires, in essence, only "an – under respect of colliding objects of protection – adequate level of protection; it is essential, that such protection is effective. The measures provided for by the legislator must be sufficient for an adequate and effective protection and must be, in addition, based on an accurate investigation of facts and on reasonable estimations."[301] Hence, the duty of protection principally follows the objects of protection guaranteed

regarding the state duty of protection; Eckhoff, ibid, regarding the terminology, pp. 288 to 290.

300 See Jaeckel, ibid., examining in detail the criteria for the distinction between the protection and defensive function in the light of German Basic Rights, pp. 63 to 79, the ECHR, pp. 141 to 154, and the ECFR, pp. 247 to 159.

301 See Calliess, ibid., cip. 6 with reference to BVerfGE 88, 203, cip. 159: "Notwendig ist ein – unter Berücksichtigung entgegenstehender Rechtsgüter – angemessener Schutz; entscheidend ist, daß er als solcher wirksam ist. Die Vorkehrungen, die der Gesetzgeber trifft, müssen für einen angemessenen und wirksamen Schutz ausreichend sein und zudem auf sorgfältigen Tatsachenermittlungen und vertretbaren Einschätzungen beruhen".

by the fundamental rights.[302] Consequently, these guarantees also determine the so-called range of protection. The following three questions essentially determine the range of protection in order to provide for an adequate level of protection: Is a subsequent protection against a harm that already had occurred sufficient?; or is a preventative protection against specific risks necessary?; or is a precautionary protection against unspecific risks even required?[303]

Calliess stresses a further factor determining the duty of protection: the state "monopoly on the use of force".[304] This monopoly forbids individuals to execute their rights themselves. Therefore, the less private individuals are legally allowed to protect themselves against harms by third parties, the more the State is in charge of controlling the protection of their fundamental rights. In contrast, the more the legislator provides mechanisms enabling private parties to protect themselves, e.g. by self-regulation mechanisms such as codes of conducts, certificates or the individual's consent, the less strict is the state duty of protection.[305] Similarly, if private entities become so powerful that they can unilaterally determine the conditions on the market, the state duty of protection requires rebalancing this market power.[306] Overall, the State must safeguard that the legal system effectively and efficiently enables the individual to protect him or herself; the system of protection provided for must be suited to repel the harm (depending on its risk and intensity that it poses), according to the fundamental right in question.[307]

However, even if the duty of protection is strict, the legislator always has a certain margin of discretion for how to fulfill its duty of protection. This is the particularity of the protection function with respect to the legislator, compared to the executive or the judiciary. This margin results from the separation of powers: A Constitutional Court belonging to the Judiciary must not substitute the legislator which is democratically empowered

---

302 See Dietlein, The Doctrine of Duties of Protection of Basic Rights, pp. 86 and 87.

303 See above under point B. II. 3. c) Interim conclusion: Fundamental rights determining the appropriateness of protection; Jaeckel, ibid., regarding the German Basic Rights, pp. 85 to 88, the ECHR, pp. 165 and 166, and the ECFR, pp. 260 to 265; cf. Kuner et al., Risk management in data protection, p. 98.

304 See Calliess, ibid., cip. 2.

305 See Calliess, ibid., cip. 20 to 22.

306 Cf. v. Danwitz, The Fundamental Rights to Private Life and to Data Protection, pp. 584 and 585.

307 See Calliess, ibid., cip. 20 to 22, 25, and 26.

by its citizens. The Constitutional Court would substitute the legislator if it made an order as to how the legislator has to fulfill its protection function.[308] Only the importance of the substantial guarantee in question, the severity of the infringement, and the importance of opposing constitutional guarantees can restrict the margin of appreciation.[309]

In contrast, the assessment of whether or not a state action conflicts with the *defensive* function of a fundamental right generally foresees a narrow margin of discretion, thus, it is stricter. Here, the assessment always refers to a specific state action. If this specific action infringes the scope of protection of a fundamental right, the question is whether or not the infringement is legitimate or not. In answering this last question, a proportionality test plays a decisive role.[310] This proportionality test refers to the following four questions:

1. Does the action intruding into the scope of the fundamental right follow a legitimate aim? (Pre-question)
2. If so, is the action adequate in order to achieve this aim?
3. If so, is the action necessary for this aim, in other words, is there no other action being equally efficient in achieving the legitimate aim *and* intruding less into the scope of the fundamental right?
4. If so, is the action proportionate with respect to the colliding fundamental rights?

In conclusion, the regulator has to balance the colliding fundamental rights by respecting, with regard to the protection function, the "prohibition of insufficient means" and, with respect to the defensive function, the proportionality test.[311] In this regard, it is the legislator who is primarily in charge of balancing the colliding fundamental rights through means of implementing ordinary law, be it civil, administrative, or penal law. And even if it is the classic role of civil law to solve conflicting interests

---

308 See, with respect to German law, Callies, ibid., cip. 6; Rupp, The State Duty of Protection for the Right to Informational Self-Determination in the Press Sector, pp. 46 to 53.

309 Cf. v. Danwitz, The Fundamental Rights to Private Life and to Data Protection, p. 582.

310 See, regarding the European Convention on Human Rights, Matscher, Methods of Interpretation of the Convention, p. 67; regarding the European Charter of Fundamental Rights, González-Fuster, The Emergence of Data Protection as a Fundamental Right of the EU, pp. 200 to 205, who also stresses the uncertainties on the interplay of Article 8 sect. 2 and 3 ECFR and Article 52 ECFR.

311 See Grimm, Data protection before its refinement, p. 587 and 588.

amongst private individuals, it does not have to be considered as the only regime of regulation instruments. Administrative law, comparably, serves to prevent such conflicts, especially with regard to relationships where multiple individuals are involved.[312] This might be in particular the case if the object of regulation concerns a collective good so that it must not completely depend on the disposal by private parties. As mentioned previously, Regan promotes to consider privacy as such a collective good because it constitutes the pre-conditions for being a citizen in a democracy.[313] In any event, the legislator provides this legal framework on both an abstract and a general level and has, therefore, a wide scope with respect to the consideration of the relevant facts, its evaluation, and finally the establishment of the regulation instruments.[314]

(2) A first review: decomposing the object and concept of protection

Weighing both functions in a correct way thus is a rather complex task. It does not only depend on the object of protection guaranteed by the fundamental right concerned, but also on the specific protection instruments. The challenge of drawing the line between efficient protection of fundamental rights and an infringement of opposing fundamental rights because of over-regulation, becomes particularly apparent with respect to privacy and data protection, in other words, threats caused by the "processing of personal data".

(a) Which instruments actually protect which object of protection?

With respect to the German right to informational self-determination, the way the State balances the duty of protection with opposing fundamental rights, can be differentiated, in essence, pursuant to the following categories: First, a ban to disclose personal data (e.g. by legal prohibitions or technical means); and second, support for informational self-protection

---

312 See Bethge, § 72 – Collision of Basic Rights, cip. 16, 17, 22, and 24; Dietlein, The Doctrine of Duties of Protection of Basic Rights, pp. 109 and 110.

313 See Nissenbaum, ibid., p. 87, referring to Priscilla Regan (1995), Legislating Privacy, Chapel Hill: University of North Carolina Press, pp. 226 and 227.

314 Cf. Jarass, ibid., Vorb. vor. Art. 1 cip. 56; Callies, ibid, cip. 6.

(e.g. by information or technical self-protection).[315] The State is usually able to fulfill its duty of protection by the second mean, i.e. supporting measures. Only if these supporting measures are not effective, or in order to protect the fundamental rights of third parties who were concerned by the disclosure, then the State is allowed to prohibit the self-disclosure of personal data. In any case, abstract constitutional aims (such as environmental protection), do not create a duty of protection. Such constitutional positions can only help justify provisions, which infringe the defensive function of fundamental rights, in the balancing exercise of the colliding fundamental rights.[316]

(b) Example: "Commercialized" consent threatening the object of protection including…

Regarding the abstract constitutional positions, Buchner unfolds the diverse aspects that are discussed in German literature, focusing on the consent, regarding the object of protection of the right to informational self-determination. In particular, the following aspects of the object of protection are discussed: a protection of individuality, of solidarity, and of democracy in society. Promoters of these positions argue that the focus on the individual's consent as the main self-regulation instrument of informational self-determination inevitably leads, in the private market, to its commercialization and as a consequence, endangers not only the dignity of the individual but also society as a whole. The individuals would degrade themselves to a mere economic asset, which simultaneously disintegrates the basis for a democratic civil society.[317] Buchner does not negate these criticisms per se, but stresses that this discussion actually refers to the relationship between reality and law. He asserts that the economic exploitation of personal data is a fact. Meanwhile, there is a long-standing market in which its participants trade data as economic goods. Conse-

315 Cf. Sandfuchs, Privacy against one's will?, pp. 299 to 302.

316 See Dietlein, The Doctrine of Duties of Protection of Basic Rights, pp. 104 and 105.

317 See Buchner, ibid., pp. 183, with further references to the German discussion; Rouvroy and Poullet, The Right to Informational Self-Determination and the Value of Self-Development: Reassessing the Importance of Privacy for Democracy, p. 50.

quently, he poses the question for the legislator: "Should its regulatory function focus on guaranteeing, by means of certain procedural rules, a minimum of balance between the market participants? Or should the legislator also be in charge of setting up ethical rules and enforcing them, eventually, even against the actual covetousness of the market?"[318] Buchner responds to these questions by referring to the decision of "*Marlene Dietrich*" by the German Federal Court of Justice, i.e. the highest civil court in Germany: The legal order must restrain the commercialization of the personality right "where superior legal or ethic principles require this".[319] Buchner then unfolds these principles, with respect to the commercialization of the right to informational self-determination.

(c) … individuality?

At first, Buchner refers to the criticism that individuals would degrade themselves, resulting from the commercialization, to mere economic assets. From this perspective, human life would be, more and more, interpreted pursuant to economic categories and human beings, which are reduced to mere rates and, thus, are quantitatively measurable and comparable. Critics therefore assume that the economic exploitation of personal data automatically increases the pressure of homogenization and eliminates qualitative differences. In contrast, Buchner challenges this mechanism by stressing the factual development of personalized marketing. Its aim is not to equalize the individual but to capture his or her particularities in order to increase the customer's loyalty. From this point of view, indeed, the commercialization of personal data leads less to a homogenization of individuals than to an individualization of production and marketing processes.[320] However, besides the marketing, Buchner admits there is a pressure of adaptation: Private parties decide with whom and under which conditions they want to contract on the basis of the available information. For instance, the more information private companies (such as insurance companies, creditors, landlords or employers) have or gain about individuals (such as debtors, tenants and employees), the higher the pres-

318 See Buchner, ibid., pp. 185 and 186.
319 See Buchner, ibid., p. 187 with reference to BGHZ 143, 214 (225) – Marlene Dietrich.
320 See Buchner, ibid., pp. 184, 189, and 190.

sure becomes for those individuals to comply with those expectations. However, Buchner considers that this pressure is not arguable in itself or new, at least, so long as it safeguards proper legal or contractual behavior and the processing of data is correct and fair. In contrast, the new issue raised by the processing of personal data is the increasing differentiation with respect to how certain characteristics of the potential contractual partner are pre-determined and, consequently, of contractual relations.[321]

(d) … solidarity?

The last aspect leads to another criticism regarding the commercialization of personal data: The disintegration of the community of solidarity. The more individuals can profit, in the form of economic advantages, from the disclosure of their personal data, the less they will be willing to accept common (contractual) conditions protecting others who cause higher risks or costs. Buchner concludes from this that the more information can principally be retrieved, be it by better algorithms or a higher willingness of individuals to share their data, the more difficult it will be, by means of law, to impose an artificial ignorance in favour of the equality between or amongst the individual.[322] In essence, there are two, partly intertwined, categories of law covering this phenomenon: The rights of equality and non-discrimination and the Social State Principle guaranteed by the German Basic Law. Buchner stresses that even if the increased differentiations do not infringe the rights to equality and non-discrimination of the individuals concerned, it increases the challenges for those individuals who do not fit into the advantageous expectations of the economy. Consequently, Buchner recognizes an increasing social gap between individuals within an economic meaning, 'good' and 'bad' data, respectively. However, he sees in this phenomenon that it is primarily a problem related to the Social State principle. Therefore, he asks whether the State can or should impose, by means of data protection law, its social responsibility on private companies. Buchner favors a solution for this social problem by public social law and not by data protection law regulating interactions between private parties.[323]

---

321 See Buchner, ibid., pp. 190 and 191.
322 See Buchner, ibid., p. 194.
323 See Buchner, ibid., pp. 197 and 198.

(e) … democracy?

Finally, Buchner deals with the criticism whether, and if so, to which extent the commercialization of personal data on the private sector endangers the pre-conditions of a democratic civil society. Accordingly, he determines, as a main source of this criticism, the "*Decision on Population Census*" by the German Constitutional Court that stated that:

> "In light of the right to informational self-determination, no social or legal order would be possible if citizens would not be able to know what information others have about them. The person who is unsure if their deviant behavior will be noted and permanently stored, used or transferred will attempt not to attract attention with such behavior. The person who is aware of being registered by the State when he or she takes part at an assembly or is part of an association will possibly give up on exercising his or her corresponding fundamental rights (…). This would not only restrict the chances of individual freedom of development but also the common welfare because self-determination is an essential condition for a free and democratic civil society that builds upon the ability of action and participation of its citizens."[324]

---

324 See BVerfG, 15th of December 1983, 1 BvR 209, 269, 362, 420, 440, 484/83 (Decision on Population Census), retrieved on the 7th of February 2016 from https://openjur.de/u/268440.html, cip. 172: "Wer nicht mit hinreichender Sicherheit überschauen kann, welche ihn betreffende Informationen in bestimmten Bereichen seiner sozialen Umwelt bekannt sind, und wer das Wissen möglicher Kommunikationspartner nicht einigermaßen abzuschätzen vermag, kann in seiner Freiheit wesentlich gehemmt werden, aus eigener Selbstbestimmung zu planen oder zu entscheiden. Mit dem Recht auf informationelle Selbstbestimmung wären eine Gesellschaftsordnung und eine diese ermöglichende Rechtsordnung nicht vereinbar, in der Bürger nicht mehr wissen können, wer was wann und bei welcher Gelegenheit über sie weiß. Wer unsicher ist, ob abweichende Verhaltensweisen jederzeit notiert und als Information dauerhaft gespeichert, verwendet oder weitergegeben werden, wird versuchen, nicht durch solche Verhaltensweisen aufzufallen. Wer damit rechnet, daß etwa die Teilnahme an einer Versammlung oder einer Bürgerinitiative behördlich registriert wird und daß ihm dadurch Risiken entstehen können, wird möglicherweise auf eine Ausübung seiner entsprechenden Grundrechte (Art. 8, 9 GG) verzichten. Dies würde nicht nur die individuellen Entfaltungschancen des Einzelnen beeinträchtigen, sondern auch das Gemeinwohl, weil Selbstbestimmung eine elementare Funktionsbedingung eines auf Handlungsfähigkeit und Mitwirkungsfähigkeit seiner Bürger begründeten freiheitlichen demokratischen Gemeinwesens ist."

These considerations are similar to the approach promoted by Priscilla Regan.[325] However, Buchner stresses that the Constitutional Court developed this reasoning with respect to the State. He agrees that treatment of data by a State endangers a free political discourse but doubts that the treatment of personal data in the private sector is relevant for the individual's ability to freely participate in public discourses. Buchner argues that private legal transactions primarily serve the exchange of goods and services but not the execution of civil rights. Even if the concepts of private and public autonomy would be inextricably linked to each other, he doubts that the commercialization of personal data would hinder the individual's autonomy. In his opinion, while the disclosure of personal data indeed increases the knowledge of third parties, this does not automatically hinder the autonomy of the individual concerned. Autonomy does not require individuals to know anything about other individuals, nor does one's own knowledge always leads to another's manipulation. Therefore, Buchner advocates that it is important to only concentrate on the real problematic cases and not on every single aspect of the processing of data by private parties because each social interaction in a digitized society would be problematic.[326]

cc) Equal or equivalent level of protection compared to state data processing?

Before coming to a first conclusion on the previous considerations, there is still another question to be considered. Given that there is an only indirect effect of fundamental rights, and the object of protection is so broad covering abstract constitutional positions (such as individuality, solidarity, and democracy), the question to consider is: whether or not the data protection instruments established in the private sector should be identical to the public sector or, at least, equivalent. There are two contrasting opinions in relation to this issue amongst legal scholars. Pursuant to the first opinion, the level of protection and regulation instruments are the same for both the public and private sector. An 'equal level' of protection is considered because the imbalance of power caused by the processing of personal

325 See above point B. III. 1. The individual's autonomy and the private/public dichotomy.
326 See Buchner, ibid., pp. 193 and 194.

data is the same on the public and the private sector. De Hert and Gutwirth give a vivid explanation why data protection law is often considered as equally applicable in the public and in the private sector, as: "The power of those, be it in the public or in the private sector, who process personal data concerning others (whether with the help of information technology or not) is generally already greater to begin with. The stream of personal data primarily flows from the weak actors to the strong. Citizens not only need to provide information to the authorities, but they also need to do so as a tenant, job seeker, customer, loan applicant and patient. That is precisely why legal tools of transparency and accountability under the form of data protection regulations were devised for application both in the public and in the private sector."[327] In contrast, legal scholars promoting an 'equivalent level' of protection do not require the same protection instruments but consider different protection instruments to be implemented in the private or public sector. This might result, pursuant to the particular circumstances of the case, to a higher, equal or lower level of protection. Others finally doubt that these questions make sense at all. Buchner argues, for example, that such a comparison of different levels of protection implies an objective scale. In the private sector, such an objective scale does not exist, in his opinion, because the fundamental right of the individual concerned is not an 'absolute' right but must instead be weighed against the opposing fundamental rights. The result is that fundamental rights always lack an objective scale that would actually be the pre-condition in order to answer the question of whether there should be a higher, lower or equivalent level of protection.[328]

c) Interim conclusion: Interdisciplinary research on the precise object and concept of protection

The previous discussion illustrates the difficulties in deciding the appropriate regulation instruments, whilst balancing on the one hand, in the private sector, the opposing fundamental rights and further constitutional

327 See De Hert and Gutwirth, Privacy, data protection and law enforcement. Opacity of the individual and transparency of power, p. 78.

328 See above C. I. 1. b) cc) Equal or equivalent level of protection compared to state data processing?, referring to Buchner, Informational self-determination in the private sector, pp. 44 and 45 with further references, as well as pp. 57 and 58.

positions. All three fundamental rights regimes, i.e. the European Charter on Human Rights, the European Charter of Fundamental Rights, and the German Basic Rights, tend to apply an only indirect effect of fundamental rights between private parties. Even if not all particularities are comprehensively clarified, the 3-step-tests assessing a protection and defensive function of fundamental rights can provide structural help for this balancing exercise. In this regard, the question of how the legislator should provide for protection against threats resulting from the processing of personal data by private entities depends on the objects and concepts of protection of the fundamental rights.

However, already defining the object of protection of privacy and/or data protection is a difficult task. Buchner decomposes the object of protection of the German right to informational self-determination considering individuality, solidarity and democracy as abstract constitutional positions, in his words, superior legal or ethic principles. Indeed, these constitutional positions do not create per se a state duty of protection. However, the legislator may refer to these positions justifying its protection instruments established, primarily, in order to protect an individual's fundamental right. And in doing so, the legislator has a wide margin of discretion for establishing the adequate protection instruments. Therefore, the legislator can indeed decide to impose certain mechanisms on the private sector, supplementing the social basis for a democratic and supportive Civil Society. Even if Buchner's observations are principally correct, the legislator can therefore well decide, for example, to implement certain Social State principles by means of data protection law and not by Social Law. At least, this thought applies so long as these objective constitutional aims are not the only reason for the regulation, but are additional to the protection of an individual's fundamental right. Equally, this idea applies, in principle, to the discussion on whether the data protection instruments applied on the public and private sector should be, in light of the same (or similar) imbalances of informational power, the same or equivalent. If the legislator comes to the conclusion that there are informational imbalances on both the public and the private sector, it can well address these imbalances with the same or different protection instruments.

However, there is another aspect to this regulation which is problematic: All of the negative effects discussed in legal discourse regarding the processing of personal data in the private sector, are mainly grounded on assumptions. For example, do contractual differentiations between private parties, such as in the insurance industry, really increase the pressure of social adaptation, and if so, to what extent? If private parties are able to more and more pre-control their contractual partners, instead of retrospectively sanctioning them for disappointing trustful expectations, does this destroy social trust as a pre-condition for autonomous behaviour? How much do imbalances of information threaten the balance of public discourses? Are there informational power inequalities? And how do we actually capture these inequalities in our theoretical concepts?

The concepts underlying these questions are similar, if not the same, to the concepts proposed previously: Nissenbaum summarized these concepts referring to autonomy, human relationships, and the society as a whole, as the actual values of privacy. If such concepts serve as a basis for the legislator, then actually, it is absolutely necessary to clarify and validate both its theoretical as well as empirical presumptions in order to improve the rationality of law.[329] Only if it is clear what the fundamental rights protect, it is possible to validate, first, the actual threats for these objects of protection; and second, the efficiency of the protection instruments applied in order to achieve these aims, such as the principle of purpose limitation.[330]

2. The object and concept of protection of the German right to informational self-determination

Clarifying the object and concept of protection hence, is key, in order to help data controllers apply the principle of purpose limitation. As illustrated in the introduction, data controllers often have difficulties in precisely specifying the purpose of the processing intended. The German Constitutional Court has developed the object and concept of protection of the German right to informational self-determination over three decades. Examining these decisions shall thus serve as a comparison with (or even a source of inspiration for the development of) the rights to private life and data protection under Articles 7 and 8 ECFR.

329 See Hoffmann-Riem, Innovation Responsibility, p. 39.

330 See above point B. II. 4. Searching for a scale in order to determine the potential impact of data protection risks.

a) Genesis and interplay with co-related basic rights

The German State of Hessen established, in 1970, the first data protection law in the world.[331] However, interestingly, German Basic Law does not explicitly state that an individual's data is protected. Legal scholars consider that the various plans to introduce the right to data protection in German Basic Law became superfluous in light of the comprehensive definition provided for by the German Constitutional Court in the "*Decision on Population Census*" (Volkszählungsurteil) from 1983. In this case, the German Constitutional Court recognized the so-called right to informational self-determination as an autonomous guarantee provided for by the general personality right.[332] The right to informational self-determina-tion primarily served to protect the individual against the informational interest of the State. Under German Basic Law, there are several rights that mirror this purpose of protection with regard to specific aspects of life, such as the right to privacy of correspondence, posts and telecommunication under Article 10 GG, as well as the right to the inviolability of the home under Article 13 GG.[333] Another fundamental right related to the right to informational self-determination refers to the protection of the confidentiality and integrity of information technological systems (Grundrecht auf Vertraulichkeit und Integrität informationstechnischer Systeme). This fundamental right extends the general scope of protection for the individual's personality to the moment *before* the personal data is collected. This right protects the individual's trust that the information technological system used by him or her functions properly. Recognizing this kind of protection, the German Constitutional Court decided not to discuss this issue under the right to informational self-determination, because this would have meant extending its already broad scope of protection even further. Instead, the Court decided to establish a new guarantee, which indeed is also provided for by the general personality right.[334] Despite the different guarantees provided for by the German basic rights surrounding the protection of personal data, the German Constitutional Court often connects them in order to evaluate an infringement by the State. For example, the Court

331 See Rudolf, Right to Informational Self-Determination, cip. 8.
332 See Rudolf, ibid., cip. 8 and cf. Burgkardt, ibid., p. 85.
333 Cf. Burgkardt, ibid., p. 85.
334 See Hoffmann-Riem, Protection of the Confidentiality and Integrity of Information Technological Systems, p. 1015.

considers the basic right to privacy of telecommunications under Article 10 GG and the basic right to privacy of the home under 13 GG as "specifications of the basic right to informational self-determination", and applies their principles to the more general right to informational self-determi-nation, at least, "as long as they are not the result of the particularities of the special guarantees."[335]

Before the recognition of the basic right to informational self-determination, the German Constitutional Court referred in similar cases to the protection of being private, comparable to Art. 8 ECHR and Art. 7 ECFR. This right resulted in a "right to be left alone."[336] Pursuant to the so-called theory of spheres, the more that the data was considered as being connected to the individual concerned, the stricter the protection of personal data was. Despite the clarity of this concept, the theory of spheres failed to provide clear criteria in order to differentiate between the different spheres. Some scholars view this as the essential problem that finally lead to the development of the right to informational self-determination, and was recognized by the German Constitutional Court in the famous "*Decision on Population Census*".[337] In light of the development of both the following constitutional decisions, as well as the technical possibilities of data collection and processing today, the introduction of this decision is worth being quoted in this thesis. In this case, citizens within Germany filed several constitutional complaints against a law for a state census including population, housing, profession and work areas. The German Court described the social backgrounds that lead to the constitutional complaints in the introduction of its judgment as:

> "*The data collection intended by this law caused anxiety even in those parts of the population who respect as loyal citizens the right and duty of the State*

335 See BVerfG, 4th of April 2006, 1 BvR 518/02 (Dragnet Investigation), cip. 90: "Da diese Grundrechte spezielle Ausprägungen des Grundrechts auf informationelle Selbstbestimmung darstellen (...), sind diese Maßstäbe auch auf das allgemeinere Grundrecht anwendbar, soweit sie nicht durch die für die speziellen Gewährleistungen geltenden Besonderheiten geprägt sind." as well as BVerfG, 14th of July 1999, 1 BvR 2226/94 (Surveillance of Telecommunications), cip. 137, and BVerfG, 3rd of March 2004, 1 BvR 2378/98 (Big Eavesdropping Operation), cip. 169.

336 See Burgkardt, ibid., p. 87.

337 See Albers, Informational Self-Determination, pp. 211 and 212; Burgkardt, ibid., p. 88; cf. the criticism of the "private/public dichotomy" by Nissenbaum above under point B. III. 2. "Criticism: From factual to conceptual changes".

to collect the information necessary for reasonable public action. This might result from the fact that the extent and purpose of the census was, to a great extent, unknown and that the necessity to reliably inform the citizens concerned was not taken early enough into account despite the fact that public awareness (...) increased in view of the development of automated data processing. Nowadays, the possibilities of modern data processing are, to a large extent, transparent only to experts and can provoke the fear of uncontrolled profiling, even if the legislator demands the collection of such information which is necessary and reasonable."[338]

Thus, in this decision, the Court stated, with respect to the public sector, that the "free development of the personality requires, under the modern conditions of data processing, the protection of the individual against unlimited collection, storage, usage and transfer of his or her personal data."[339] In this statement, the Court does not want to protect the individual against all kinds of treatment of 'his or her' data but instead, only wants to protect the individual against the unlimited treatment of data.[340] The subsequent analysis will therefore illustrate how the German Court frames the principle of purpose limitation in light of the object and concept of protection of the right to informational self-determination in order to protect against an unlimited use of personal data.

---

338 See BVerfG, 15th of December 1983, 1 BvR 209, 269, 362, 420, 440, 484/83 (Decision on Population Census), cip. 8: "Die durch dieses Gesetz angeordnete Datenerhebung hat Beunruhigung auch in solchen Teilen der Bevölkerung ausgelöst, die als loyale Staatsbürger das Recht und die Pflicht des Staates respektieren, die für rationales und planvolles staatliches Handeln erforderlichen Informationen zu beschaffen. Dies mag teilweise daraus zu erklären sein, daß weithin Unkenntnis über Umfang und Verwendungszwecke der Befragung bestand und daß die Notwendigkeit zur verläßlichen Aufklärung der Auskunftspflichtigen nicht rechtzeitig erkannt worden ist, obwohl sich das allgemeine Bewußtsein durch die Entwicklung der automatisierten Datenverarbeitung (...) erheblich verändert hatte. Die Möglichkeiten der modernen Datenverarbeitung sind weithin nur noch für Fachleute durchschaubar und können beim Staatsbürger die Furcht vor einer unkontrollierbaren Persönlichkeitserfassung selbst dann auslösen, wenn der Gesetzgeber lediglich solche Angaben verlangt, die erforderlich und zumutbar sind. (...)"

339 See BVerfG, ibid., cip. 173: "Freie Entfaltung der Persönlichkeit setzt unter den modernen Bedingungen der Datenverarbeitung den Schutz des Einzelnen gegen unbegrenzte Erhebung, Speicherung, Verwendung und Weitergabe seiner persönlichen Daten voraus."

340 Cf. Hoffmann-Riem, ibid., p. 1015.

b) Autonomous substantial guarantee

In this same "Decision on Population Census", the Court firstly determined on the conceptual provenance and normative aim of the right to informational self-determination. In this regard, it must be stressed that this thesis uses, so far, the terms "object of protection" and "substantial guarantee" provided for by fundamental rights, synonymously. Both the meaning and differences of the terms shall be examined, later on, with respect to the differentiation of the fundamental rights to privacy and data protection under Article 7 and 8 ECFR.[341] In any case, the German Constitutional Court considers the normative substance of the right to informational self-determination as:

> "*The human dignity of a person who acts as a member of a free society in a free and self-determined manner constitutes the center of the constitutional order. Besides specific guarantees of freedom, the general personality right of Art. 2 sect. 1 in combination with Art. 1 sect. 1 GG serves as a protection (of human dignity) and can become relevant especially in the light of modern developments and new dangers for the human personality. (...) Stemming from the idea of self-determination, it (the general personality right) contains (...) the right of the individual to basically decide by him or herself when and to what extent personal facts about his or her live are revealed. (...) Individual self-determination requires (...) that the individual can freely decide on his or her actions, including the freedom to genuinely act corresponding to their decisions.*"[342]

---

341 See under point C. I. 3. c) cc) "Referring to substantial guarantees as method of interpreting fundamental rights in order to avoid a scope of protection that is too broad and/or too vague".

342 See BVerfG, 15th of December 1983, 1 BvR 209, 269, 362, 420, 440, 484/83 (Decision on Population Census), cip. 170 to 172: "Im Mittelpunkt der grundgesetzlichen Ordnung stehen Wert und Würde der Person, die in freier Selbstbestimmung als Glied einer freien Gesellschaft wirkt. Ihrem Schutz dient - neben speziellen Freiheitsverbürgungen - das in Art 2 Abs. 1 in Verbindung mit Art 1 Abs. 1 GG gewährleistete allgemeine Persönlichkeitsrecht, das gerade auch im Blick auf moderne Entwicklungen und die mit ihnen verbundenen neuen Gefährdungen der menschlichen Persönlichkeit Bedeutung gewinnen kann (...). (Die bisherigen Konkretisierungen durch die Rechtsprechung umschreiben den Inhalt des Persönlichkeitsrechts nicht abschließend.) Es umfaßt (...) auch die aus dem Gedanken der Selbstbestimmung folgende Befugnis des Einzelnen, grundsätzlich selbst zu entscheiden, wann und innerhalb welcher Grenzen persönliche Lebenssachverhalte offenbart werden (...). Diese Befugnis bedarf unter den heutigen und künftigen Bedingungen der automatischen Datenverarbeitung in besonderem Maße des Schutzes. Sie ist vor allem deshalb gefährdet,

The phrase 'that the individual can freely decide on his or her actions, including the freedom to genuinely act corresponding to their decisions' appears to mean that the right to informational self-determination primarily serves to protect the individual's freedom of action. In this sense, the specific rights of freedom could add to a differentiated scale that helps determine the extent of the right and, thus, the specification of the purpose as required for the data processing.[343] In other words, the specific rights to freedom may define the informational norms governing a certain context. However, in the following decisions, the Court clarified that the extent of the right to informational self-determination does not depend on a specific risk for other basic rights. This becomes particularly apparent in the case of "*License Plate Recognition*" (Kennzeichenerfassung).[344]

In this case dated 11 March 2008, the constitutional action was brought against provisions of police law, which authorized the automated recognition of license plates of cars. Using this method, video cameras record the passing cars on the street. Certain software extracts the code with numbers and figures of the license plates and is then automatically checked against police investi-

---

weil (bei Entscheidungsprozessen nicht mehr wie früher auf manuell zusammengetragene Karteien und Akten zurückgegriffen werden muß, vielmehr) heute mit Hilfe der automatischen Datenverarbeitung Einzelangaben über persönliche oder sachliche Verhältnisse (einer bestimmten oder bestimmbaren Person (personenbezogene Daten (vgl. § 2 Abs. 1 BDSG)) technisch gesehen unbegrenzt speicherbar und jederzeit ohne Rücksicht auf Entfernungen in Sekundenschnelle abrufbar sind. Sie können darüber hinaus - vor allem beim Aufbau integrierter Informationssysteme - mit anderen Datensammlungen zu einem teilweise oder weitgehend vollständigen Persönlichkeitsbild zusammengefügt werden, ohne daß der Betroffene dessen Richtigkeit und Verwendung zureichend kontrollieren kann. Damit haben sich in einer bisher unbekannten Weise die Möglichkeiten einer Einsichtnahme und Einflußnahme erweitert, welche auf das Verhalten des Einzelnen schon durch den psychischen Druck öffentlicher Anteilnahme einzuwirken vermögen. Individuelle Selbstbestimmung setzt aber (- auch unter den Bedingungen moderner Informationsverarbeitungstechnologien -) voraus, daß dem Einzelnen Entscheidungsfreiheit über vorzunehmende oder zu unterlassende Handlungen einschließlich der Möglichkeit gegeben ist, sich auch entsprechend dieser Entscheidung tatsächlich zu verhalten. (...)"

343 Cf. Grimm, Data protection before its refinement, p. 585 and 586, who stresses, first, the delimited scope of protection in the light of the fact that all personal data are relevant and, second, considers the specific rights to freedom and possible legal links determining the scope of protection.

344 In this regard, it must be stressed that the German Constitutional Court does not differentiate, terminologically, between risks and dangers as elaborated on in the preceding chapter B. II. Data protection as a risk regulation.

gation data. In the case of a match, the software delivers a report, stores the data together with further information such as the time and place of the car recorded and provides, in doing so, the basis for potentially follow up investigations. If there is no match, the records, as well as the code of the license plates, are immediately deleted. The wording of the provisions authorizing the automatic license plate recognition stated: "The police authorities are authorized to automatically collect on public streets and spaces data from license plates of cars for the purpose of checking the data against the data files for open investigations. Data that is not part of the data files for open investigations must immediately be deleted."[345]

The German Constitutional Court affirmed that the legal provisions, which the claimant addressed in its constitutional claim, infringed the general personality right, more precisely, the right to informational self-determination. Pursuant to the Court's decision, this right "meets the threats of dangers of infringements of the personality which for the individual results, especially under the conditions of modern data processing, from informational measures. This right supplements and broadens the protection of freedom of action and of being private; it (the protection) already begins as soon as there is danger to the personality. Such a danger may already exist before there is a specific threat for an object of protection."[346] Thus, the right to informational self-determination is conceptually independent from the other basic rights and only indirectly serves to protect the specific rights of freedom. Consequently, these further rights do not add, so far, to a differentiated scale in order to determine its scope, the purpose of the data processing or the context in which the processing occurs. However, it is clear that the object and concept of protection of the right to informational self-determination is very similar to the other rights to privacy. This

345 See BVerfG, 11th of March 2008, 1 BvR 2074/05 and 1 BvR 1254/07 (License Plate Recognition), cip. 1, 2 and 9: "Die Polizeibehörden können auf öffentlichen Straßen und Plätzen Daten von Kraftfahrzeugkennzeichen zum Zwecke des Abgleichs mit dem fahndungsbestand automatisiert erheben. Daten, die im Fahndungsbestand nicht enthalten sind, sind unverzüglich zu löschen."

346 See BVerfG, ibid., cip. 63: "Das Recht auf informationelle Selbstbestimmung trägt Gefährdungen und Verletzungen der Persönlichkeit Rechnung, die sich für den Einzelnen, insbesondere unter den Bedingungen moderner Datenverarbeitung, aus informationsbezogenen Maßnahmen ergeben (...). Dieses Recht flankiert und erweitert den grundrechtlichen Schutz von Verhaltensfreiheit und Privatheit; es lässt ihn schon auf der Stufe der Persönlichkeitsgefährdung beginnen. Eine derartige Gefährdungslage kann bereits im Vorfeld konkreter Bedrohungen von Rechtsgütern entstehen."

becomes particularly apparent in the decision of "*Retrieval of Bank Account Master Data*" (Kontostammdatenabfrage) from 2007.

In this case, a German financial institution and two individuals who received social security benefits filed a constitutional complaint against the "law for the advancement of the financial market" and the law "for the encouragement of tax compliance". The law for the advancement of the financial market obliged each financial institution to store certain master data relating to its bank accounts. The Federal Financial Supervisory Authority (BaFin) was authorized to automatically retrieve these data as long as it was necessary for purposes of its supervision. The data only referred to the existence of the bank account and the person(s) who was authorized to view it. The law did not authorize the use of further information such as account activities. The use of information by BaFin occurred without notifying the financial institution that stored the data, because they did not want to alert the financial institutions unnecessarily. BaFin was allowed to transfer the data to public state agencies, such as competent courts for international legal assistance in criminal matters. The law for the encouragement of tax compliance then broadened the circuit to which the data could be transmitted, such as to tax or social security authorities. In order to authorize the transfer of data all that was required was that authorization had to refer to a notion or term contained in the Income Tax Act.[347]

In this case, the Constitutional Court clarified the differences, or better, interplay between the various basic rights as: "The general personality right guarantees elements of the personality which are not protected by special guarantees of freedom but are, nevertheless, not less constitutive for the personality. (...) The acknowledgement of a concrete claim by the claimant in relation to the different aspects of the personality right hence depends on the different threats for the personality that result from the circumstances of the individual case. (…) The right to informational self-determination complements prevailing special guarantees of being private such as the right to privacy of correspondences, posts and telecommunications of Art. 10 GG and the right to spatial privacy guaranteed by Art. 13 GG. It exists beside other basic rights typifying the general personality right which can also guarantee constitutional protection of being private against revelation and usage of information, such as the protection of the private sphere or the right to the spoken word."[348]

---

347 See BVerfG, 13th June 2007, 1 BvR 1550/03 (Retrieval of Bank Account Master Data), cip. 10 to 29.

348 See BVerfG, ibid., cip. 62 and 63: "Das allgemeine Persönlichkeitsrecht gewährleistet Elemente der Persönlichkeit, die nicht Gegenstand der besonderen

c) Right to control disclosure and usage of personal data as protection instrument?

Similarly to other rights to privacy enabling the individual to decide on whether or not someone else intrudes into his or her private sphere, the right to informational self-determination provides an individual's 'right to basically determine by him or herself the disclosure and the usage of his or her personal data'.[349] The German Constitutional Court justifies this right of control, particularly, with the 'increased danger which is based on the technical possibilities under modern conditions of data processing' resulting in the situation that the 'data are not only, on a second-by-second basis, retrievable at any time and place but can also be, especially in the case

---

Freiheitsgarantien des Grundgesetzes sind, diesen aber in ihrer konstituierenden Bedeutung für die Persönlichkeit nicht nachstehen (...). (Einer solchen lückenschließenden Gewährleistung bedarf es insbesondere, um neuartigen Gefährdungen zu begegnen, zu denen es im Zuge des wissenschaftlich-technischen Fortschritts und gewandelter Lebensverhältnisse kommen kann (...).) Die Zuordnung eines konkreten Rechtsschutzbegehrens zu den verschiedenen Aspekten des Persönlichkeitsrechts richtet sich daher vor allem nach der Art der Persönlichkeitsgefährdung, die den konkreten Umständen des Anlassfalls zu entnehmen ist (...). (Das allgemeine Persönlichkeitsrecht trägt in seiner Ausprägung als Recht auf informationelle Selbstbestimmung Gefährdungen und Verletzungen der Persönlichkeit Rechnung, die sich für den Einzelnen aus informationsbezogenen Maßnahmen, insbesondere unter den Bedingungen moderner Datenverarbeitung, ergeben (...). Es gibt dem Einzelnen die Befugnis, grundsätzlich selbst über die Preisgabe und Verwendung seiner personenbezogenen Daten zu bestimmen (...).) Das Recht auf informationelle Selbstbestimmung ergänzt besonders geregelte Garantien der Privatheit, die ihm vorgehen, insbesondere das Post- und Fernmeldegeheimnis nach Art. 10 GG (...) und den durch Art. 13 GG gewährleisteten Schutz der räumlichen Privatsphäre des Wohnungsinhabers (...). Es steht neben anderen Ausprägungen des allgemeinen Persönlichkeitsrechts, die als Gewährleistungen von Privatheit gleichfalls grundrechtlichen Schutz gegenüber Kenntnisnahme und Verarbeitung von Informationen vermitteln können, wie dem Schutz der Privatsphäre (...) oder dem Recht am gesprochenen Wort (...)."

349 See BVerfG, 15th of December 1983, 1 BvR 209, 269, 362, 420, 440, 484/83 (Decision on Population Census), cip. 173; cf. equally BVerfG, 14th of July 1999, 1 BvR 2226/94 (Surveillance of Telecommunications), cip. 136 and BVerfG, 3rd of March 2004, 1 BvR 2378/98 (Big Eavesdropping Operation), cip. 132 and BVerfG, 4th of April 2006, 1 BvR 518/02 (Dragnet Investigation), cip. 64 and BVerfG, 13th June 2007, 1 BvR 1550/03 (Retrieval of Bank Account Master Data), cip. 63; BVerfG, 1 BvR 2027/02 (Release of Confidentiality), cip. 31.

of integrated information systems, combined with other data collections leading to multiple possibilities of usage and linking'.[350]

Some legal scholars praise, even on an international level, this object and concept of protection (which was actually advocated already by Westin in 1967)[351] in light of its "intermediate value" serving the final values of "dignity", "autonomy" and, therefore, the "free and democratic society" as a whole.[352] And indeed, the construction of this right and the considerations behind it appear to be very similar to some of the conceptual thoughts surrounding the value of privacy as summarized by Nissenbaum and illustrated previously in chapter "Theories about the value of privacy and data protection".[353]

However, the German Court seems to have foreseen that such a concept might lead to far-reaching effects in social interactions. It already stressed in its first "*Decision on Population Census*" not to guarantee the individual an absolute control over his or her social representation (i.e. how he or she is perceived by others), which is based on data related to him or her. Rather, the concept only guarantee certain 'chances of individual freedom of development'.[354] It explicitly stated "the individual does not have a right in the meaning of an absolute and boundless control about 'his or her' data; (conceptually), he or she rather has to be considered as a personality developing within the social community who depends on communication. Information constitutes, even if it is related to a person, a picture of social reality that cannot be exclusively contributed only to the person concerned."[355] In the decision of "*Release of Confidentiality*" (Schweigepflichtent-bindung), the Constitutional Court stressed this thought with particular respect to the data processing by private parties.

---

350 See only BVerfG, 4th of April 2006, 1 BvR 518/02 (Dragnet Investigation), cip. 65.

351 See Westin, Privacy and Freedom, p. 7: "Privacy is the claim of individuals, groups, or institutions to determine for themselves when, how, and to what extent information about them is communicated to others."

352 See Rouvroy and Poullet, The Right to Informational Self-Determination and the Value of Self-Development: Reassessing the Importance of Privacy for Democracy, p. 57 and 58.

353 See above under point B. III. 1 The individual's autonomy and the private/public dichotomy.

354 See BVerfG, 15th of December 1983, 1 BvR 209, 269, 362, 420, 440, 484/83 (Decision on Population Census), cip. 174.

355 See BVerfG, ibid., cip. 174.

The Court stated "especially on the private sector, the general personality right does not constitute an absolute control about certain information. The individual has to be rather considered as a personality that develops within the social community and depends on communication (…)."[356]

Despite these statements about the individual's dependency on communications in the social community, the scope of application of the right to informational self-determination remains rather broad. As noted above, specific rights of freedom do not determine the same. Even more so, the scope is wider than certain prevailing rights to privacy. In the case of "*Big Eavesdropping Operation*" (Großer Lauschangriff) in 2004, the Court decided that an eavesdropping operation occurring from outside protected rooms, infringes the right to privacy of the home under Article 13 GG, only if the communication could not be – naturally – recognized by acoustic means.

> In this case, the objects of the constitutional complaint related to several provisions of the German Code of Criminal Procedure. The complaint focused on the central provision of § 103 c sect. 1 nr. 3 StPO, which authorized the State to record non-public communications of a suspected person in his or her home if certain facts justified the suspicion that the person committed a crime listed by the law with respect to organized crime. The State measure referred only to the suspected person. Nevertheless, the law also authorized the observation of homes of third parties if the suspected person was staying in the third party's home. The observation was exclusively used for state investigative purposes. The data could only be transferred, in principle, for criminal proceedings. In addition, the law restricted the duty to notify the person being surveyed. If an operator received a special authorization by the competent court, the state could hold back from notifying the particular for a period of six months or more after the end of the observation.[357]

The German Constitutional Court clarified in this decision that "even the perception of such a communication that can be heard from outside without acoustic means can infringe the guarantee of being private. However, such communication is not protected by Article 13 GG if the person concerned makes the perception of the communication from outside by him or

356 See BVerfG, 1 BvR 2027/02 (Release of Confidentiality), cip. 32: "Gerade im Verkehr zwischen Privaten lässt sich dem allgemeinen Persönlichkeitsrecht allerdings kein dingliches Herrschaftsrecht über bestimmte Informationen entnehmen. Der Einzelne ist vielmehr eine sich innerhalb der sozialen Gemeinschaft entfaltende, auf Kommunikation angewiesene Persönlichkeit (...)."

357 See BVerfG, 3rd of March 2004, 1 BvR 2378/98 (Big Eavesdropping Operation), cip. 14, 20 and 21.

herself possible and thus, does not actually use the spatial sphere of privacy in order to protect him or herself."[358] In contrast, in "*License Plate Recognition*", the Court stated that the right to informational self-determination is not restricted to personal data originating from the private sphere. It equally protects personal data that is publicly available: "(…) even if the individual takes him or herself to the public, the right to informational self-determination protects his or her interest that the related personal information is not automatically collected for the purpose of storage enabling to further use."[359] In the case of "*Video Surveillance*" (Videoüberwachung), the Court finally clarified that the right to informational self-determination protects an individual against being recorded in public even if the person concerned knows that he or she will be recorded the moment he or she enters a monitored space.[360]

> In this case, a city installed an artwork at one of its main squares. It was a relief on the soil mirroring the rest of the medieval synagogue hidden under the ground. The artwork should serve as a meeting place for the public. After several incidences, the city decided to implement video cameras in order to police the place. A citizen filed a complaint against the video surveillance before the administrative court.[361] When the case finally came to the Constitutional Court, the Constitutional Court affirmed that the right to informational self-determination also protects against such a collection of personal data in the public.[362]

The Court clarified in this case also the question of whether the individuals recorded by the video camera gave their consent to the recording because they knew that they were being filmed. From the Court's point of

358 See BVerfG, ibid., cip. 138: "Zwar kann auch die Wahrnehmung der aus der Wohnung nach außen dringenden und ohne technische Hilfsmittel hörbaren Kommunikation deren Privatheit beeinträchtigen. Solche Lebensäußerungen nehmen aber nicht am grundrechtlichen Schutz des Art. 13 GG teil, weil der Betroffene die räumliche Privatsphäre nicht zu seinem Schutz nutzt, wenn er die Wahrnehmbarkeit der Kommunikation von außen selbst ermöglicht."

359 See BVerfG, ibid., cip. 67: "Auch wenn der Einzelne sich in die Öffentlichkeit begibt, schützt das Recht der informationellen Selbstbestimmung dessen Interesse, dass die damit verbundenen personenbezogenen Informationen nicht im Zuge automatisierter Informationserhebung zur Speicherung mit der Möglichkeit der Weiterverwertung erfasst werden (...)."

360 See BVerfG, 23rd of February 2007, 1 BvR 2368/06 (Video Surveillance), cip. 39 and 40.

361 See BVerfG, ibid., cip. 2 to 14.

362 See BVerfG, ibid., cip. 39 and 40.

view, a person who does not explicitly disagree with the recording, does not automatically consent to it.[363] Thus, even if the individual has a choice of not entering the monitored space and voluntarily enters that space, the right to informational self-determination still protects him or her. So far, the Court's statement that the individual has no "right in the meaning of an absolute and boundless control about 'his or her' data"[364] has little effect on the scope of protection.

Comparably, the Court's statements that the right to informational self-determi-nation seeks to guarantee "that the individual can freely decide on his or her actions, including the freedom to genuinely act corresponding to their decisions"[365] and, therefore, "supplements and broadens the protection of freedom of action and of being private"[366] does not determine the scope of application. In the opposite, in "*Big Eavesdropping Operation*" as well as in the case of "*Surveillance of Telecommunications*" (Telekommunikationsüberwachung I), the Court actually applies the opposite methodology: in these cases, not the right to informational self-determination supplements the rights to freedom but, vice versa, the rights to freedom supplement the right to informational self-determination.

In this second-mentioned case of "*Surveillance of Telecommunications*", the Constitutional Court decided on the synchronicity between the right to informational self-determination and the right to privacy of correspondences, posts and telecommunications of Art. 10 GG. The claimants filed an ultra vires action against the surveillance, data collection and processing of telecommuni-

363 See BVerfG, ibid., cip. 39 and 40.

364 See again BVerfG, 15th of December 1983, 1 BvR 209, 269, 362, 420, 440, 484/83 (Decision on Population Census), cip. 174: "(…) Der Einzelne hat nicht ein Recht im Sinne einer absoluten, uneinschränkbaren Herrschaft über "seine" Daten (…)."

365 See BVerfG, ibid., cip. 172: "(…) daß dem Einzelnen Entscheidungsfreiheit über vorzunehmende oder zu unterlassende Handlungen einschließlich der Möglichkeit gegeben ist, sich auch entsprechend dieser Entscheidung tatsächlich zu verhalten."

366 See BVerfG, 11th of March 2008, 1 BvR 2074/05 and 1 BvR 1254/07 (License Plate Recognition), cip. 63: "Das Recht auf informationelle Selbstbestimmung trägt Gefährdungen und Verletzungen der Persönlichkeit Rechnung, die sich für den Einzelnen, insbesondere unter den Bedingungen moderner Datenverarbeitung, aus informationsbezogenen Maßnahmen ergeben (...). Dieses Recht flankiert und erweitert den grundrechtlichen Schutz von Verhaltensfreiheit und Privatheit; es lässt ihn schon auf der Stufe der Persönlichkeitsgefährdung beginnen. Eine derartige Gefährdungslage kann bereits im Vorfeld konkreter Bedrohungen von Rechtsgütern entstehen."

> cations by the German Federal Bureau of Investigation. The so-called law for the suppression of crime expanded, amongst other issues, the legal possibility to collect and process personal data that was provided for by means of telecommunications. On the one hand, this law added several purposes for the collection and processing of data, such as the prevention, intelligence, and criminal prosecution of: international terrorist attacks, international distribution of weapons of war, exports of drugs into the Federal Republic, and of counterfeiting of currencies committed abroad. On the other hand, this law only applied to non-cable based telecommunications and, amongst other issues, under the pre-condition that only concrete facts arising from the data about the planning or commitment of one of the crimes mentioned. The law did not authorize the observation of single connections of telecommunications, but it enabled the selection via certain key words in order to fulfill the purposes described. Nevertheless, the observation of single connections of telecommunications of foreigners abroad was possible. Finally, the observation did not have to be communicated to the person concerned if the data was deleted within three months.[367] Several of the claimants, who were journalists living in Germany and abroad, who carried out research and published news articles in the field of international terrorism, argued that their conversations with contacts in Germany and abroad could potentially contain key words which fit those key words provided by the German Federal Bureau of Investigation. They argued that the general collection, the selection corresponding to the key words and acts following those collections would consequently infringe their right to privacy of correspondence, posts and communications in Art. 10 GG.[368]

In this case, the German Constitutional Court explicitly stressed the significance of other fundamental rights, such as the freedom of the press stating that "the protection of Art. 10 GG can be supplemented by further fundamental guarantees which depends on the specific content and context of the communication or on the negative effects resulting from the usage of the information which is used in new contexts."[369] And in the case of "*Big Eavesdropping Operation*", the Court provided the example of a conversation between a married couple at home which could not only fall, from its point of view, under the right to privacy of the home pursuant to Article 13 section 1 GG but also under Article 6 section 1 GG which provides for special protection of a marriage. Comparably, the protection of conversations with people who have to respect professional secrets can equally be supplemented by further basic rights such as, for example, clerical people,

367 See BVerfG, 14th of July 1999, 1 BvR 2226/94 (Surveillance of Telecommunications), cip. 11 to 14, 16 to 18.

368 See BVerfG, ibid., cip. 28, 28, 49 to 51.

369 See BVerfG, ibid., cip. 154.

by the freedom of faith and conscience under Article 4 GG. The Court also set down certain criteria in order to determine when the general personality right is supplemented by further special guarantees, which is "the special necessity for protection of the communicating people".[370] Indeed, both decisions referred to the prevailing rights to privacy of Article 10 and 13 GG. Since the principles of these two basic rights and of the right to informational self-determination (of Article 2 section 1 in combination with Article 1 section 1 GG) can be transposed between each other,[371] it is very likely that the specific rights of freedom also supplement the right to informational self-determination. Thus, in light of these considerations, not the right to informational self-determination supplements the rights to freedom but, in the opposite, the rights to freedom supplement the right to informational self-determination.

d) Infringement by 'insight into personality' and 'particularity of state interest'

In summary, the broad scope of the right to informational self-determination protects against all threats against the individual's personality by automated data processing, irrespective of whether or not there is a specific risk in relation to specific rights of freedom or privacy. Consequently, the German Constitutional Court principally considers each act of collection and processing – such as the storage, filtering, and transferal – of personal data as an infringement of its scope. In the case of "*Surveillance of Telecommunications*", the Court clarified that the collection of personal data can also infringe Article 10 GG, if it cannot immediately be related to

370 See BVerfG, 3rd of March 2004, 1 BvR 2378/98 (Big Eavesdropping Operation), cip. 135: "Auch in Bezug auf die Kommunikation mit Berufsgeheimnisträgern können neben dem grundrechtlichen Schutz der räumlichen Privatsphäre Grundrechte in Betracht kommen, die - wie etwa Art. 4 GG im Hinblick auf das Gespräch mit einem Geistlichen - der besonderen Schutzbedürftigkeit der Kommunizierenden Rechnung tragen."

371 See BVerfG, 14th of July 1999, 1 BvR 2226/94 (Surveillance of Telecommunications), cip. 137, BVerfG, 3rd of March 2004, 1 BvR 2378/98 (Big Eavesdropping Operation), cip. 169, and BVerfG, 4th of April 2006, 1 BvR 518/02 (Dragnet Investigation), cip. 90.

a person at that time but easily at a later stage.[372] However, the Court also acknowledged that certain acts of data treatment do not infringe the scope of protection. With respect to telecommunication data, it decided that "the collection does not infringe Art. 10 GG, so long as the telecommunication between German connection points is only unintentionally collected because of technical reasons and is, directly after the conditioning of the signal, technically eliminated without a trace."[373]

This exception was particular to the case at hand. The question therefore is whether, and if so, there exists a more general principle in order to answer the question whether an act of data treatment infringes the scope of protection of the right informational self-determination. With respect to a similar situation, the Court argued, slightly different, in the case of "*License Plate Recognition*", that the collection and processing of personal data does not infringe the right to informational self-determination "if checking against key investigation words immediately occurs after the collection, that leads to a negative result (…) and if it is legally and technically safeguarded that the data remain anonymous and is immediately deleted without leaving the possibility to relate it to a person. In contrast, the storage of the license plate that was recorded, which provides the basis for potentially further measures, infringes the basic right."[374] The Court justified this differentiation stating that "this is the intended goal of the measure if the license plate matches the key words (…). From this point in time, the license plate recorded is available for the processing by state agencies and the specific danger for the freedom of action and of being private occurs,

372 See BVerfG, 14th of July 1999, 1 BvR 2226/94 (Surveillance of Telecommunications), cip. 160.

373 See BVerfG, ibid., cip. 160.

374 See BVerfG, 11th of March 2008, 1 BVR 2047/05 and 1 BvR 1254/07 (License Plate Recognition), cip. 69: "(Zu einem Eingriff in den Schutzbereich des Rechts auf informationelle Selbstbestimmung kommt es daher in den Fällen der elektronischen Kennzeichenerfassung dann nicht,) wenn der Abgleich mit dem Fahndungsbestand unverzüglich vorgenommen wird und negative ausfällt (sogenannter Nichttrefferfall) sowie zusätzlich rechtlich und technisch gesichert ist, dass die Daten anonym bleiben und sofort spurenlos und ohne die Möglichkeit, einen Personenbezug herzustellen, gelöscht werden. Demgegenüber kommt es zu einem Eingriff in das Grundrecht, wenn ein erfasstes Kennzeichen im Speicher festgehalten wird und gegebenenfalls Grundlage weiterer Maßnahmen werden kann."

which justifies the protection of the basic right to informational self-determination."[375]

In other cases, such as of "*Dragnet Investigation*" (Rasterfahndung), in order to determine an infringement, the Court had also referred to the state's intended purpose and the fact that the data treatment would provide a basis for further measures.

> In this case from 2006, the claimant contested judicial decisions in relation to police orders of the so-called "Rasterfahndung" (dragnet investigation). The dragnet investigation is a special tracing method based on data processing for wanted people whereby the data of a large number of people are checked against existing data in a database. There are two types of laws that permit the use of this tracing method in Germany. Firstly, § 98 StPO permits the Dragnet investigation for criminal proceedings. Secondly, Police Law permits it in order to prevent the commitment of crimes. Originally, most of these provisions required an existing danger to the security of the State or for life, health or freedom of a natural person and referred to certain types of data that could be collected and processed. Most of the States (Länder) in Germany changed these requirements as they abandoned the need to use the criteria of "existent" or of "existent danger" entirely. After the terrorist attacks carried out on 11th of September 2001, the States within Germany organized together, with the Federal Bureau of Investigation a German-wide dragnet investigation. The "Internal Security team", defined national-wide criteria in order to discover potential Islamistic terrorists. The State demanded from universities, registration of addresses offices and the central register of foreigners, data relating to the following: whether the person was male, those aged between 18 to 40, whether or not he was a student or former student, whether or not he was from the Islamic religion, his country of birth or nationality of states with mainly Islamic population. These data were collected on a State level and were then transferred to the Federal Bureau of Investigation where it was stored in a network file named "Schläfer" (sleeper).[376] The State of Nordrhein-Westfalen authorized, via its own law, the collection and processing not only of certain types of data but also 'other data which are necessary for the concrete case'. It collected approximately 5.2 million data sets fitting to several pre-criteria defined by its public agencies. These data were then automatically checked against the criteria defined by the working group "Internal

---

375 See BVerfG, ibid, cip. 69: "Darauf vor allem ist die Maßnahme gerichtet, wenn das Kraftfahrzeugkennzeichen im Fahndungsbestand aufgefunden wird (sogenannter Trefferfall). Ab diesem Zeitpunkt steht das erfasste Kennzeichen zur Auswertung durch Staatliche Stellen zur Verfügung und es beginnt die spezifische Persönlichkeitsgefährdung für Verhaltensfreiheit und Privatheit, die den Schutz des Grundrechts auf informationelle Selbstbestimmung auslöst."

376 See BVerfG, 4th of April 2006, 1 BvR 518/02 (Dragnet Investigation), cip. 7 to 12.

> Security" with the result of around 11.000 data sets (the persons concerned were, afterwards, informed about the collection and treatment of their data); the rest was deleted. More than 1,000 of these data sets transferred to the Federal Bureau of Investigation did not fit the requirements of the judicial order, either because the people concerned were female or Christians. Consequently, these data sets were deleted, and the rest were transferred to the competent police station, which manually checked the personal identity of the individuals concerned. The remaining 816 cases were sent back to the Federal Bureau of Investigation who started further investigations into 72 cases.[377] In conclusion, German-wide data of 200,000 to 300,000 people were temporarily stored. None of the further investigations revealed "sleepers" or led to prosecutions of any individuals.[378] The claimant in the particular case fit several of the criteria defined by the working group "Internal Security" as he was born in 1978, of Moroccan nationality and Islamic faith. While the judicial orders that he contested by the constitutional complaint came into force, he studied at the University Duisburg in Germany.[379]

In this case the German Constitutional Court firstly considered whether "the information about each of the single data (concerned) provides, in combination with other data, a separate insight into the personality" and then held it as essential "to determine whether the state interest, with respect to the overarching context and with respect to the purpose of surveillance and usage, for the data concerned is so particular that it qualitatively affects a person's fundamental right."[380] The Court came to the conclusion that "the combination of the data in question – name, address, day and date of birth – combined with other data such as (…) nationality, religion or field of studies can and shall provide information about personal conducts and, by these means, suspicious facts and especially – how it is stated within (…/the law offended by the claimant) – about 'danger-increasing characteristics of this person'."[381] Similar, in the before-mentioned case of "*Retrieval of Bank Account Master Data*", the Court examined

377 See BVerfG, ibid., cip. 22 to 27.

378 See BVerfG, ibid., cip. 12 and 13.

379 See BVerfG, ibid., cip. 29.

380 See BVerfG, ibid., cip. 67 and 69: "Maßgeblich ist, ob sich bei einer Gesamtbetrachtung mit Blick auf den durch den Überwachungs- und Verwendungszweck bestimmten Zusammenhang das behördliche Interesse an den betroffenen Daten bereits derart verdichtet, dass ein Betroffensein in einer einen Grundrechtseingriff auslösenden Qualität zu bejahen ist."

381 See BVerfG, ibid., cip. 67: "Die Kombination der (ausdrücklich in § 31 Abs. 2 PolG NW 1990) benannten Daten - Name, Anschrift, Tag und Ort der Geburt - mit anderen, etwa, (wie im vorliegenden Fall,) der Staatsangehörigkeit, der Reli-

whether the collection and processing of the claimant's personal data provided an insight into his personality and why the state's interest in it became so specific that it 'qualitatively affected his fundamental right': "Corresponding to the current customs, most of the payments (…) are processed via banking accounts. If information about the content of the accounts of one person is collected for a common purpose, this collection provides an insight into the economic situation and the social contacts of the person concerned, given that these (…/social contacts) consist of a financial dimension. Some of the account data could also allow for further conclusions about the conduct of the person concerned. The state investigations (…) based on the provisions of those offended can prepare measures, which can essentially concern the individual's interests and would have not been possible without the knowledge retrieved."[382]

The considerations described made it apparent that the criteria developed by the German Court in order to determine whether a state act of data treatment infringes the individual's right to informational self-determination are not clear. At least, there appear to be four requirements: First, the data treatment must provide an insight into the personality of the individual concerned. This is the case if the data reveal, for example, the person's personal conducts, economic situation or social contacts. Second, the Court considers not only the enforced revelation of data by the State, but also the factual treatment of data such as by secret or public observa-

gionszugehörigkeit oder der Studienfachrichtung, kann und soll Aufschluss über Verhaltensweisen und damit Verdachtsmomente und insbesondere (- wie es in § 31 Abs. 1 PolG NRW 2003 nunmehr ausdrücklich heißt -) über "gefahrenverstärkende Eigenschaften dieser Personen" ermöglichen."

382 See BVerfG, 13th June 2007, 1 BvR 1550/03 (Retrieval of Bank Account Master Data), cip. 68 and 69: "Nach den gegenwärtigen Gepflogenheiten werden die meisten Zahlungsvorgänge, die über Bargeschäfte des täglichen Lebens hinausgehen, über Konten abgewickelt. Werden Informationen über die Inhalte der Konten einer bestimmten Person gezielt zusammengetragen, ermöglicht dies einen Einblick in die Vermögensverhältnisse und die sozialen Kontakte des Betroffenen, soweit diese - etwa durch Mitgliedsbeiträge oder Unterhaltsleistungen - eine finanzielle Dimension aufweisen. Manche Konteninhaltsdaten, etwa die Höhe von Zahlungen im Rahmen verbrauchsabhängiger Dauerschuldverhältnisse, können auch weitere Rückschlüsse auf das Verhalten des Betroffenen ermöglichen. Die auf der Grundlage der hier angegriffenen Normen erfolgenden behördlichen Ermittlungen über Kontostammdaten können anschließende Maßnahmen vorbereiten, die ohne die erlangten Kenntnisse nicht möglich wären und die die Belange der Betroffenen erheblich berühren können."

tions.[383] Third, the Court requires that there must be an intention or a purpose behind the collection of data when it refers to the 'intended goal' or 'state interest, with respect to the overarching context and with respect to the purpose'. The collection of data by coincidence without further interests of usage, does not infringe the right to informational self-determination.[384] Finally, the Court does not consider each act of data treatment intended by the state as an infringement. An infringement will occur only if it either constitutes a 'specific danger for the freedom of action and of being private'; or if it 'qualitatively affects a person's fundamental right' or if it can 'essentially concern the individual's interests'.

Indeed, it remains unclear in what way these last criteria relate to each other and what they actually mean. For example, does the term 'specific danger for the freedom of action and of being private' only require the data to be stored for the purpose of providing the basis for potential further measures, or must these measures be specific? Does the term 'particularity of the state interest qualitatively affecting a fundamental right' mean that there must be a specific threat for another fundamental right, be it a specific right to privacy, freedom or equality or is any type of unspecific threat sufficient? Finally, does the term 'individual's interests' cover more aspects than a fundamental right?

One thought seems at least to be clear. The Court considers the accumulation of data related to the same person, as well as the retrieval of information through combining data, as different types of one infringement. In contrast, the Court considers subsequent measures, which are based on an infringement as previously described, as a separate infringement. For example, if license plates recorded are combined with further data, such as the type of car etc., this means that there has been an extension of the infringement of the right to informational self-determination. If these different types of data are combined and processed retrieving further information regarding, for instance, the driver, the court considers this a deepening of the infringement. In contrast, if this gathered information leads to the result that the police stops the car in order to, for example, check the driver's license, this is seen as a separate infringement.[385]

---

383 See Bechler, Informational Harm by Intransparent Treatment of Personal Data, pp. 58 f.

384 Cf. Bechler, ibid., pp. 60 ff.

385 See BVerfG, 11th of March 2008, 1 BVR 2047/05 and 1 BvR 1254/07 (License Plate Recognition), cip. 74.

e) Purpose specification as the essential link for legal evaluation

Last but not least, these considerations lead to another important aspect of the object and concept of protection of the right to informational self-determination: The relevant moment for the legal evaluation, in particular, of whether the principle of purpose limitation is met or not.

aa) In the public sector: Interplay between the three principles clarity of law, proportionality, and purpose limitation

The relevant moment regarding the legal evaluation becomes particularly apparent with respect to infringements by the State. The German Constitutional Court combines the principle of clarity of law, the principle of proportionality and the principle of purpose limitation essentially resulting in the requirement that all future acts of usage of personal data must be predetermined when it is collected.

(1) Principles of clarity of law and purpose limitation referring to the moment when data is collected

This requirement already becomes apparent in the Court's first "*Decision on Population Census*". With respect to individualized data, i.e. data which is not anonymized, the Court stated:

> "An obligation for the provision of personal data requires that the legislator precisely and specifically determines in certain areas the purpose of usage and should ensure that the information is suitable and necessary for achieving this purpose. The collection ahead of non-anonymized data for an undetermined or not yet determinable purpose is disproportionate with this (requirement). All (public) agencies collecting personal data in order to perform their tasks are restrained to the minimum which is necessary for achieving their given goals. The usage of the data is restricted to the purpose provided for by the provision. In the light of the dangers of automated data processing, it is necessary to establish protection, by means of transfer and usage bans, against the misuse of data for other purposes other than originally determined. Obliga-

tions to clarify and to inform those about the data processing and to delete the data are essential measures for procedural protection."[386]

Indeed, the Court does not forbid the State to collect data in advance for non-pre-determined purposes if the State only processes anonymized data for statistical purposes. However, the Court limits this broader range of action through other procedural restrictions and specifies the general objective aim of these requirements as: "Clearly defined requirements for the processing of data are necessary in order to guarantee that the individual does not become, under the conditions of automated collection and processing of his or her personal data, a mere object of information."[387]

Consistent with these requirements, the Court handed down its reasoning in the case of "*License Plate Recognition*". In this case, the Court stressed again that the moment personal, non-anonymized data is collected, is the cardinal point for the question of whether or not later acts of data processing is constitutionally legitimate or not: "The concrete requirements for the pre-determined clarification of the authorizing provision depend on the type and intensity of the infringement. Hence, the authorizing provision must especially pre-determine whether it allows serious infringements. If it does not exclude such (serious) infringements in a sufficiently clear manner, the provision has to also meet the legal requirements

386 See BVerfG, 15th of December 1983, 1 BvR 209, 269, 362, 420, 440, 484/83 (Decision on Population Census), cip. 179 and 180: "Ein Zwang zur Angabe personenbezogener Daten setzt voraus, daß der Gesetzgeber den Verwendungszweck bereichsspezifisch und präzise bestimmt und daß die Angaben für diesen Zweck geeignet und erforderlich sind. Damit wäre die Sammlung nicht anonymisierter Daten auf Vorrat zu unbestimmten oder noch nicht bestimmbaren Zwecken nicht zu vereinbaren. Auch werden sich alle Stellen, die zur Erfüllung ihrer Aufgaben personenbezogene Daten sammeln, auf das zum Erreichen des angegebenen Zieles erforderliche Minimum beschränken müssen. Die Verwendung der Daten ist auf den gesetzlich bestimmten Zweck begrenzt. Schon angesichts der Gefahren der automatischen Datenverarbeitung ist ein - amtshilfefester - Schutz gegen Zweckentfremdung durch Weitergabeverbote und Verwertungsverbote erforderlich. Als weitere verfahrensrechtliche Schutzvorkehrungen sind Aufklärungspflichten, Auskunftspflichten und Löschungspflichten wesentlich."

387 See BVerfG, ibid., cip. 167: "Es müssen klar definierte Verarbeitungsvoraussetzungen geschaffen werden, die sicherstellen, daß der Einzelne unter den Bedingungen einer automatischen Erhebung und Verarbeitung der seine Person betreffenden Angaben nicht zum bloßen Informationsobjekt wird."

which apply to these (serious) infringements."[388] In the case of "*Data Retention*", the Court provided its reasoning on the function of such requirement.

In this case, the German Court had to decide on the validity of the German provisions transposing the European Data Retention Directive into German law – before the High Court of Ireland referred the homonymous case to the European Court of Justice.[389] According to Article 1 of that directive, Member States were hold to oblige network and service providers to retain data for "the purpose of the investigation, detection, and prosecution of serious crime, as defined by each Member State in its national law." The directive should apply to traffic and location data but not to the content of electronic communications, Article 1 section 2 of the Data Retention Directive. Pursuant to its Article 4, Member States should "adopt measures to ensure that data retained in accordance with this Directive are provided only to competent national authorities in specific cases and in accordance with national law. The procedure to be followed and the conditions to be fulfilled in order to gain access to retained data (…) shall be defined by each Member State". While Article 6 of the directive required the duration of the data being retained between six months up to two years, its Article 7 regulated certain data protection and security measures. In contrast to the Irish Court, the German Constitutional Court did not stay its proceedings in order to let prove the validity of the directive according to the European Charter of Fundamental Rights by the European Court of Justice but decided the case, autonomously, on the grounds of the German Basic Law. The German Court argued it could autonomously decide the case because the Data Retention Directive left enough room for the national legislator in order to implement it in accordance with German basic rights.[390] In its opinion, the German Basic Law did not prohibit per se the transposition of the Data Retention Directive into German law so that the 'pri-

---

388 See BVerfG, 11th of March 2008, 1 BVR 2047/05 and 1 BvR 1254/07 (License Plate Recognition), cip. 95: "Die konkreten Anforderungen an die Bestimmtheit und Klarheit der Ermächtigung richten sich nach der Art und Schwere des Eingriffs (...). Die Eingriffsgrundlage muss darum erkennen lassen, ob auch schwerwiegende Eingriffe zugelassen werden sollen. Wird die Möglichkeit derartiger Eingriffe nicht hinreichend deutlich ausgeschlossen, so muss die Ermächtigung die besonderen Bestimmtheitsanforderungen wahren, die bei solchen Eingriffen zu stellen sind (...)."

389 See beneath, under point C. I. 3. c) aa) (2) (b) Protection against collection, storage, and subsequent risk of abuse, the homonymous case of "*Digital Rights vs. Ireland*", decided by the ECJ in 2014, ECJ C-293/12 and C-594/12.

390 See BVerfG, 2nd March 2010, 1 BvR 256/08, 1 BvR 263/08, and 1 BvR 586/08 (Data Retention), cip. 186, discussed above under point C. I. 2. d) aa) (1) Principles of clarity of law and purpose limitation referring to the moment when data is collected.

macy of application' of European fundamental rights did not become relevant.[391]

At first, the German Constitutional Court clarified the retention of the data by providers as a direct state interference because the providers pursued public purposes only, and there was no room left to make their own decisions. Furthermore, albeit other laws should provide pre-conditions for a concrete request of data by the state authorities, it already considered the provisions regarding the transfer as an infringement because these provisions already listed the general purposes for the later use of data. Consequently, these provisions released the providers from their duty of confidentiality.[392] However, regarding the later usage of the data that was collected, i.e. its treatment by Intelligent Services that provide their results to state authorities, the Court clarified that "the constitutional limits of these authorities using the data must not be undermined by a wider authorization for the preceding usage (by the Intelligence Services)."[393] Thus, the flux of data and the retrieval of information are principally bound to the constitutional evaluation the moment it is first collected and stored.

(2) The proportionality test also takes the use of data at a later stage into account

In relation to the test of proportionality of the legal provisions that authorize the collection of personal data, the Constitutional Court takes several criteria into account: First, who and how many individuals are concerned; second, under which circumstances the data is collected, e.g. whether the individuals gave a reason or not or whether the data collection occurs secretly or open; and third, the intensity of the infringement.[394] With regard to the last aspect, i.e. the intensity of the infringement, the Court considers the essential criteria as: first, how relevant the information is for the per-

391 See BVerfG, ibid., cip. 187.

392 See BVerfG, ibid., cip. 192 to 194.

393 See BVerfG, 2nd March 2010, 1 BvR 256/08, 1 BvR 263/08, and 1 BvR 586/08 (Data Retention), cip. 233: "(Dies ist erst möglich durch Folgemaßnahmen der für die Gefahrenabwehr zuständigen Behörden,) deren verfassungsrechtliche Begrenzungen bei der Datenverwendung nicht durch weitergehende Verwendungsbefugnisse im Vorfeld unterlaufen werden dürfen."

394 See BVerfG, 14th of July 1999, 1 BvR 2226/94 (Surveillance of Telecommunications), cip. 192.

sonality of the individuals, in particular, if it is combined with further data; and second, whether or not the individuals could expect that the data about them would be treated in a certain way.[395] In this last respect, the intensity of an infringement is particularly high if it interferes with the expectation of privacy in the home or regarding the use of telecommunications.[396] In contrast, an infringement in relation to an individual's conduct within the public is less intensive.[397] The possibilities of later usage of the data also play an essential role.[398] Consequently, the Court takes the disadvantages caused by the later usage for the individual into account. In doing so, the Court considers not only real disadvantages but also potential disadvantages that the individuals have reasonably to fear in order to determine the intensity of the infringement. The Court justifies the first aspect, i.e. real disadvantages, by considering that the state treatment of data related to unsuspicious individuals leads to their risk of being an object of state investigations, which adds to their general risk of being unreasonably suspected.[399] It also indirectly increases the risk of being stigmatized in daily or professional life, in particular, if the treatment of data refers to criteria, such as religion or ethnic origin, listed in Article 3 of the German Basic Law, which guarantees the freedom of equality.[400] The Court also takes into account whether or not the individual is able to defend him or herself against the current or following state measures.[401] With respect to the second aspect, i.e. potential disadvantages, the Constitutional Court stresses that the individual's fear of being surveyed can lead, in advance, to a bias in communication and to adaptations of personal conduct. These chilling effects concern not only the individual but also communication in society

395 See BVerfG, 4th of April 2006, 1 BvR 518/02 (Dragnet Investigation), cip. 92 and 93.

396 See BVerfG, ibid., cip. 93.

397 See BVerfG, 11th of March 2008, 1 BVR 2047/05 and 1 BvR 1254/07 (License Plate Recognition), cip. 83.

398 See BVerfG, 13th June 2007, 1 BvR 1550/03 (Retrieval of Bank Account Master Data), cip. 109; cf. also BVerfG, 11th of March 2008, 1 BVR 2047/05 and 1 BvR 1254/07 (License Plate Recognition), cip. 82.

399 See BVerfG, 3rd of March 2004, 1 BvR 2378/98 (Big Eavesdropping Operation), cip. 227; BVerfG, 4th of April 2006, 1 BvR 518/02 (Dragnet Investigation), cip. 103.

400 See BVerfG, 4th of April 2006, 1 BvR 518/02 (Dragnet Investigation), cip. 106.

401 See BVerfG, 13th June 2007, 1 BvR 1550/03 (Retrieval of Bank Account Master Data), cip. 111.

as a whole.[402] Comparably, it takes into account the 'diffuse threat' for the individual. This threat results from the fact that the individuals know that the State has some information about them but do not know the precise information it has and what it will do with it.[403]

However, if the State meets certain requirements, the treatment of data can nevertheless be proportionate. In the decision of "*Data Retention*", the Court precisely elaborated on the procedural measures coming into account in order to meet the principle of proportionality. The Court stressed that this can be, in particular, the case, if the authorizing law provides sufficiently clear rules, beside the extent and purpose of the data processing, on the security, transparency, and sanctions of the treatment of the data itself.[404] With respect to the first point, data security requirements, the Court was of the opinion that the retention required an especially high standard of data security, because the collected data attracted, in light of its multifunctional informative value, the attention of many different stakeholders. Given that these stakeholders are private entities, they have little incentive to maintain a high level of data security. In order to maintain a particularly high standard of data security, for example, the following issues come into question: the systemic separation of the data, its encryption, a secure access control, and an irreversible documentation.[405] Regarding the transparency of the data retention, the Court stressed, at first, that "the legislator must tackle the diffuse threat, which results from the data storage, by effective transparency rules. These serve to diminish the unspecific threat resulting from the lack of knowledge about the real relevance of the data, to counter unsettling speculations, and to enable the individuals concerned to question these measures in a public discourse. Furthermore, these requirements result from the principle of effective judicial relieve, pursuant to Art. 10 sect. 1 GG in combination with Art. 19 sect. 4 GG. Without corresponding knowledge, the individuals concerned can neither claim against an illicit usage of data by the authorities nor for

---

402 See BVerfG, 14th of July 1999, 1 BvR 2226/94 (Surveillance of Telecommunications), cip. 207; BVerfG, 3rd of March 2004, 1 BvR 2378/98 (Big Eavesdropping Operation), cip. 230.

403 See BVerfG, 2nd March 2010, 1 BvR 256/08, 1 BvR 263/08, and 1 BvR 586/08 (Data Retention), cip. 241.

404 See BVerfG, ibid., cip. 220.

405 See BVerfG, ibid., cip. 222 and 224.

their rights to deletion, rectification or compensation."[406] Finally, the Court stressed the importance of effective sanctions in order to meet the principle of proportionality as "if even severe infringements of the privacy of telecommunications were not sanctioned, with the result that the protection of the personality right specified in Art. 10 sect. 1 GG became stunted in light of its immaterial nature, this would contradict the state duty to enable the individual developing his or her personality and to protect him against dangers for his or her personality caused by third parties. This might be in particular the case if illicitly retrieved data could be freely used or an illicit usage of data remained without compensation, serving the satisfaction of the individual concerned, because there is no material damage."[407]

In the most recent case of "*Federal Criminal Police Office Act" (*Bundeskriminalamtgesetz), the Constitutional Court consolidated its previous decisions, and highlighted another aspect being relevant for meeting the principle of proportionality.

In this case, several individuals, such as politicians, lawyers, psychologists and journalists lodged a constitutional complaint against the law for the prevention of dangers of international terrorism through the Federal Criminal Po-

406 See BVerfG, ibid., cip. 241: "Der Gesetzgeber muss die diffuse Bedrohlichkeit, die die Datenspeicherung hierdurch erhalten kann, durch wirksame Transparenzregeln auffangen. (...) Sie haben zum einen die Aufgabe, eine sich aus dem Nichtwissen um die tatsächliche Relevanz der Daten ergebende Bedrohlichkeit zu mindern, verunsichernde Spekulationen entgegenzuwirken und den Betroffenen die Möglichkeit zu schaffen, solche Maßnahmen in die öffentliche Diskussion zu stellen. Zum anderen sind solche Anforderungen auch aus dem Gebot des effektiven Rechtsschutzes gemäß Art. 10. Abs. 1 GG in Verbindung mit Art. 19 Abs. 4 GG herzuleiten. Ohne Kenntnis können die Betroffenen weder eine Unrechtmäßigkeit der behördlichen Datenverwendung noch etwaige Rechte auf Löschung, Berichtigung oder Genugtuung geltend machen."

407 See BVerfG, ibid., cip. 252: "Würden auch schwere Verletzungen des Telekommunikationsgeheimnisses im Ergebnis sanktionslos bleiben mit der Folge, dass der Schutz des Persönlichkeitsrechts, auch soweit er in Art. 10 Abs. 1 GG eine spezielle Ausprägung gefunden hat, angesichts der immateriellen Natur dieses Rechts verkümmern würde (...), widerspräche dies der Verpflichtung der staatlichen Gewalt, dem Einzelnen die Entfaltung seiner Persönlichkeit zu ermöglichen (...) und ihn vor Persönlichkeitsgefährdungen durch Dritte zu schützen (...). Dies kann insbesondere der Fall sein, wenn unberechtigt gewonnene Daten weitgehend ungehindert verwendet werden dürften oder eine unberechtigte Verwendung der Daten mangels materiellen Schadens regelmäßig ohne einen der Genugtuung der Betroffenen dienenden Ausgleich bliebe."

lice Office (Gesetz zur Abwehr von Gefahren des internationalen Terrorismus durch das Bundeskriminalamt). This law authorizes, amongst others, secret measures carried out by the German Federal Criminal Police Office, such as long-term observations, acoustic and optical surveillance of the home, online investigations, and surveillance of telecommunications as well as the later use of the data for other purposes than for that it was originally collected.[408] The claimants argued that this law would infringe their basic right to inviolability of the home, Art 13 GG, right to privacy of correspondence, posts and telecommunication of Article 10 GG, and their rights to the confidentiality and integrity of information technological systems informational as well as to informational self-determination, both provided for by Article 2 sect. 1 in combination with Article 1 sect. 1 GG. They justified their claim because they could get, in light of their human rights-related activities, in contact with individuals whom the law considers, pursuant to its broad provisions, as international terrorists and therefore could be also concerned by the surveillance measures.[409]

In this case, the Court stressed, beside the requirements mentioned previously, the importance of supervisory authorities to control the treatment of data, and reporting duties before the parliament and the public. The particularity of these additional requirements results, in the Court's opinion, from the fact that the measures foreseen in the law are usually taken in secret and, though, the individuals concerned cannot defend themselves.[410]

bb) In the private sector: The contract as an essential link for legal evaluation

The concept of protection of the right to informational self-determination in relation to the private sector is similar to the approach described with respect to the public sector. In the private sector, from the Court's point of view, "the contract is the essential instrument in order to develop free and self-responsible actions in relation to third parties."[411] Taking the contract into the center of the execution of the right to informational self-determination, the Court declares, in comparison to the public sector, that the es-

---

408 See BVerfG, 20th of April 2016, 1 BvR 966/09 and 1 BvR 1140/09 (Federal Bureau of Investigation Law), cip. 1 to 5.

409 See BVerfG, ibid., cip. 79 to 84.

410 See BVerfG, ibid., cip. 140 to 143.

411 See BVerfG, 23rd of October 2006, 1 BvR 2027/02 (Release of Confidentiality), cip. 34: "Der Vertrag ist das maßgebliche Instrument zur Verwirklichung freien und eigenverantwortlichen Handelns in Beziehung zu anderen."

sential determining point is the moment that a contract has been concluded. This means, since the conclusion of the contract usually precedes the collection of data, the essentially moment for legal evaluation is thus, before the data is collected.

However, it recognized that the conclusion of the contract is not the only possible moment for evaluating the treatment of data at a later stage. With respect to the release of confidential information, the Court weighed the effects of the release of confidential information about the individual concerned against the equally important interest of the insurance company to receive the information.[412] Balancing the opposing constitutional positions, the Court also considered that the point after the contract had been concluded was also relevant in respect of evaluating the legal relevance of the later treatment of data. In the Court's opinion, such moments would have been possible by using alternative or supplementary mechanisms as: First, by means of specific releases of confidentiality for the particular request, referring to the specific institutions involved; second, by an information mechanism which enables the policy holder to object to the retrieval of data intended; third, by a mechanism where the institution involved does not provide the information about the policy holder directly to the insurance company but, before, to the policy holder who can then decide to add information and forward it to the insurance company or not, with the possible result that it looses the insurance claim.[413]

f) Interim conclusion: Conceptual link between 'privacy' and 'data processing'

In conclusion, the concept of protection of the German right to informational self-determination establishes an autonomous substantial guarantee providing the individual a right to 'basically determine by him or herself the disclosure and later usage of 'his or her' data'. This concept leads to several problematic aspects of protection:

First, the concept leads to a rather broad scope of protection of the basic right. The broad scope results in the situation that each treatment of personal data must be justified. If the State treats personal data, this basically

412 See BVerfG, ibid., cip. 43, 45 to 48 as well as 50 and 51.
413 See BVerfG, ibid., cip. 59 and 60.

constitutes an infringement of the basic right and consequently must be justified by a parliamentary law.[414] Given that such a right shall not be an absolute right but rather be considered with regard to its function in society as a whole, the German Constitutional Court seeks to restrain the broadness of its scope in two ways. First, by determining what acts actually infringe the scope of protection. Second, when using a balancing exercise, by taking the intensity of the infringement into account. In the public sector, the essential moment for this examination is at the point of collection.[415] In the private sector, a private party's treatment of data related to an individual does not infringe his or her basic right, but can harm this basic right. Because of the protection function of the basic right, the State has to provide for protection instruments that enable the individual to effectively protect him or herself. A main protection instrument is the private contract. The broad scope principally leads, also in the private sector, to the situation that an individual can 'basically determine by him or herself the disclosure and later usage of 'his or her' data'. However, in the private sector, the moment of legal evaluation of the data processing does not have only to be when the data is first collected, but also at later stages, depending on the specific contractual arrangement in question.

This leads to the second problematic aspect of the concept of protection: that the specification of the purpose, which serves as an essential link for determining the legal relevance of the treatment of data, mainly refers to the moment of collection. Critics give two reasons for this approach: The first reason is, here again, that the concept of protection provides for an individual's right to control over the collection and usage of 'his or her' data; such a control right naturally begins with the data collection. The second reason is that the concept of protection actually implies a centralized and linear environment where the data processing takes place. Critics consider this as problematic because the requirement of purpose specification should rather be considered, in light of the de-centralized and non-linear environment today, as a regulation instrument serving to structure the

414 See Härting, Purpose limitation and change of purpose in data protection law, p. 3284.

415 See Hoffmann-Riem, Protection of the Confidentiality and Integrity of Information Technological Systems, p. 1014.

non-linear processes regarding the data treatment.[416] Thus, the requirement of purpose specification should not focus on the moment that personal data is collected, as this results in the situation that all possible future purposes must be pre-determined the moment it is collected. Rather, it should refer to the specific data processing and usage of information, irrespective of the moment it occurs.

3. Different approach of Article 7 and 8 ECFR with respect to Article 8 ECHR

The challenges described with respect to the concept of protection of the German right to informational self-determination raise the question of how they might be avoided. The German Constitutional Court has developed the concept of protection of the right to informational self-determination over decades, starting in a time of non-linear environments. This makes it difficult for private data controllers to apply, in particular today, the requirements surrounding the principle of purpose limitation in innovative non-linear environments. The previous insights thus constitute a great opportunity for elaborating on the object and concept of protection of the new fundamental right to data protection under 8 ECFR. The object and concept of protection of this right, in particular, with respect to the fundamental right to private life in Article 7 ECFR is still not sufficiently clear.[417] It is therefore a not only demanding but even more so promising task to elaborate on Article 8 ECFR as a fundamental right that fits the needs in non-linear environments.

---

416 See Albers, Treatment of Personal Information and Data, cip. 121 to 123; highlighting the current change of the computational systems and environments compared to the times of the first "*Decision on Population Census*" in 1983, Hoffmann-Riem, Protection of the Confidentiality and Integrity of Information Technological Systems, pp. 1009 and 1010.

417 See, instead of many, Schneider, Status of and Perspectives for the European Data Traffic and Data Protection Law, pp. 515 and 516.

a) Genesis and interplay of both rights

Before the European Charter of Fundamental Rights came into force, the European Court of Justice referred to the right to private life under Article 8 ECHR when it had to decide on cases in which data protection and/or privacy played a role. Under normal circumstances, the European Court of Justice also referred to the constitutional traditions amongst the Member States in order to develop, on the level of the European Union, the respective definition of fundamental rights. However, in relation to the definition of "data protection" there were, and still are, no common principles in the constitutional traditions. For example, while there is an explicit fundamental right for data protection in the Netherlands, Finland, Austria, Belgium and Greece treat it as part of the right of private life. Denmark, Estonia and Italy frame data protection under the right of communication, and in Germany, it results from the general personality right.[418] In light of these different concepts, the European Court of Justice could not refer to a common tradition amongst Member States but had to focus on the European Convention. Today, after the European Charter of Fundamental Rights came into force, the wording of Article 8 ECHR reappears, almost literally, in the right to private life under Article 7 ECFR.[419] However, beside that Article, the European legislator established the right to data protection under Article 8 ECFR in order to harmonize the different approaches of data protection amongst the Member States by strengthening the protection of individuals against the new risks caused by the processing of personal data. Some critics stress that it is, actually, this new right that enables judicial courts to interpret internal market instruments, such as the Data Protection Directive in a way that effectively protects the individual's fundamental rights.[420]

---

418 See Bernsdorff, European Charter of Fundamental Rights, cip. 3; see also De Hert and Gutwirth, Data Protection in the Case Law of Strasbourg and Luxemburg: Constitutionalisation in Action, p. 14; and Lynskey, The Foundations of EU Data Protection Law, p. 89.

419 See Burgkardt, ibid., p. 343.

420 Cf. De Hert and Gutwirth, Data Protection in the Case Law of Strasbourg and Luxemburg: Constitutionalisation in Action, pp. 8 and 9; De Hert and Gutwirth, Privacy, data protection and law enforcement. Opacity of the individual and transparency of power, p. 81; Tzanou, Data protection as a fundamental right next to privacy? 'Reconstructing' a not so new right, p. 94.

In light of the above, it is necessary to examine whether, and if so, to what extent the objects and concepts of protection of Articles 8 and 7 ECFR, as well as of Article 8 ECHR differ to each other. Article 52 section 3 ECFR states, in this regard: "in so far as this Charter contains rights which correspond to rights guaranteed by the Convention for the Protection of Human Rights and Fundamental Freedoms, the meaning and scope of those rights shall be the same as those laid down by the said Convention. This provision shall not prevent Union law providing more extensive protection." The explanations of the European Charter of Fundamental Rights provide further assistance in order to answer the question of whether or not Articles 7 and/or 8 ECFR correspond to Article 8 ECHR. Pursuant to the Explanations of the European Charter of Fundamental Rights, only "the rights guaranteed in Article 7 (ECFR) correspond to those guaranteed by Article 8 of the ECHR." In relation to Article 8 ECFR, the Explanations of the European Charter of Fundamental Rights state that "this Article has been *based on* (…) Article 8 of the ECHR" (underlining by the author).[421] With respect to further systematic reasons, legal scholars conclude from this wording that Article 8 ECFR does not exactly correspond to Article 8 ECHR, but is interpreted by the European Court of Justice within the general framework provided for by the European Convention on Human Rights.[422] Legal scholars stress that the establishment of the new right to data protection solves several problems that existed with respect to the protection of personal data under the right to private life in Article 8 ECHR. For example, the right to access to personal data and to have it rectified, pursuant to section 2, tackles problems that remain unanswered by the European Court of Human Rights.[423]

However, the precise interplay between the right to data protection under Article 8 ECFR and the right to private life provided for by Article 7 ECFR is heavily debated amongst legal scholars.[424] Eichenhofer and González-Fuster summarize the spectrum of opinions pursuant to three

421 See Explanations of the European Charter of Fundamental Rights, 2007/C 303/02.

422 See Burgkardt, ibid., p. 348 with further references.

423 See De Hert and Gutwirth, Privacy, data protection and law enforcement. Opacity of the individual and transparency of power, p. 81.

424 See also the unclear interplay between privacy and data protection in the OECD Guidelines, Tzanou, Data protection as a fundamental right next to privacy? 'Reconstructing' a not so new right, p. 91.

categories: First, approaches considering both rights either as exclusive or, second, complementary to each other, or third, understanding one right as prevailing the other one.[425] The so-called exclusivity approach considers the right to private life as solely covering aspects of private life, whereas the right to data protection only protects against risks caused by the processing of personal data.[426] In contrast, the second approach advocates that the right to data protection covers a special part of the broader right to private life and, thus, prevails the right to private life so long as the processing of personal data is the matter of the case.[427] This opinion is supported by the fact that more recently established secondary law refers to the right to data protection, only, and not to the right to private life anymore.[428] Indeed, this approach foresees an exception from the exclusive attribution of the processing of personal data to the fundamental right to data protection, if the data processing constitutes a particular risk to the personality of the individual concerned. For instance, this can be the case if the processing leads to extensive profiles of the individuals concerned. In such a case, as an exception, the fundamental right to private life prevails.[429]

The third approach finally considers both rights as intersecting with each other in certain cases. Pursuant to this opinion, both rights may cover, jointly, certain situations while having, each of them, an autonomous scope of application. On the one hand, the right to private life is wider than the right to data protection because it protects an individual's private life, irrespective of the processing of personal data. On the other hand, the right to data protection is wider than the right to private life because it also

425 See Eichenhofer, Privacy in the Internet as Protection of Trust, p. 61; González-Fuster, The Emergence of Data Protection as a Fundamental Right of the EU, p. 200; cf. also Lynskey, The Foundations of EU Data Protection Law, pp. 89-130, regarding the case law provided by the ECtHR with respect to the right to private life under Art. 8 ECHR

426 See Eichenhofer, ibid., p. 61, referring to González-Fuster, ibid., p. 200, referring, in turn, to Carlos Ruiz-Miguel, El derecho a la protección de los datos personales en la Carta de Derechos Fundamentales de Unión Europea: Análisis crítico, p. 8.

427 See Bernsdorff, European Charter of Fundamental Rights, Art. 8 cip. 13; Mehde, Handbook of European Fundamental Rights, § 21 cip. 13; Eichenhofer, ibid., p. 61, with further references.

428 See Eichenhofer, ibid., p. 61, referring to González-Fuster, ibid., pp. 243 ff.

429 See Eichenhofer, ibid., p. 61, referring, amongst others, to Opinion of Advocate General Cruz Villalón, 12th of December 2013, Case C-293/12 (Digital Rights vs Ireland), cip. 65.

protects against risks caused by data processing that do not refer to the individual's private life. A certain action can therefore either only conflict with the right to private life under Article 7 ECFR or with the right to data protection of Article 8 ECFR, or, simultaneously, with both fundamental rights.[430]

b) Concept of Article 8 ECHR: Purpose specification as a mechanism for determining the scope of application (i.e. the individual's 'reasonable expectation')

Before analyzing in detail how the European Court of Justice constructs the interplay of both rights to private life and to data protection under Articles 7 and 8 ECFR, so far, it is essential to examine the decisions of the European Court of Human Rights with respect to the right to private life under Article 8 ECHR. Regarding the European Convention for Human Rights, data protection falls under the right for private life and family in Article 8 ECHR. As mentioned before, only Article 7 ECFR corresponds to Article 8 ECHR, whereas, Article 8 ECFR is only based on it. Furthermore, the right to data protection of Article 8 ECFR explicitly mentions the requirement of purpose specification, while the right to private life under Article 7 ECFR does not. Therefore, it is helpful to first understand the function of purpose specification applied by the European Court of Human Rights with respect to Article 8 ECHR. As a second step, this analysis can further help answer the question about the interplay of Articles 7 and 8 ECFR.

aa) Substantial guarantee of "private life": Trust in confidentiality and unbiased behavior

In 1950, when the European Convention on Human Rights was signed, data protection as such, was not publically discussed. Therefore, beside

430 See, for example, De Hert and Gutwirth, Data Protection in the Case Law of Strasbourg and Luxemburg: Constitutionalisation in Action, p. 6; Kokott and Sobotta, The distinction between privacy and data protection in the jurisprudence of the CJEU and the ECtHR; Albers, Treatment of Personal Information and Data, cip. 43; Eichenhofer, ibid., p. 61, with further references.

the terms "private and family life", "correspondences", and the "home", data protection is not explicitly set out or conceptualized in the text of the convention. Nevertheless, the scope of application of Article 8 ECHR is considered to be broad enough to cover the recent technical and social development of data processing and accordingly, is interpreted by the European Court of Human Rights. In doing so, the Court does not always clarify whether it considers the processing of personal data as falling under "correspondences" or "private life".[431] In any case, with respect to the term "private life", the Court has developed its definition through case law, instead of providing for a common definition that is generally applicable to all types of cases.[432] This approach has meant that there is now a fairly ambiguous and wide scope of application of Article 8 ECHR that appears to repel several particular risks for its substantial guarantee(s).[433]

In the case of "*Gillan and Quinton vs. The United Kingdom*", the European Court of Human Rights summarized, for example, several guarantees, which it has elaborated on the term "private life", and clarified that "(…) the concept of 'private life' is a broad term not susceptible to exhaustive definition. It covers the physical and psychological integrity of a person. The notion of personal autonomy is an important principle underlying the interpretation of its guarantees (…). The Article also protects a right to identity and personal development, and the right to establish relationships with other human beings and the outside world. It may include activities of a professional or business nature. There is, therefore, a zone of interaction of an individual with others, even in a public context, which may fall within the scope of 'private life'."[434]

---

431 See De Hert and Gutwirth, Data Protection in the Case Law of Strasbourg and Luxemburg: Constitutionalisation in Action, p. 18; Burgkardt, ibid., pp. 247 with further references.

432 See Matscher, Methods of Interpretation of the Convention, pp. 63/64, with respect to the method of interpretation of the European Court of Human Rights, in general.

433 See, instead of many, Schweizer, European Convention and Data Protection, p. 464; Eichenhofer, Privacy in the Internet as Protection of Trust, p. 58, with further references; regarding the fact that not all data processing falls under the scope of protection, see De Hert and Gutwirth, Privacy, data protection and law enforcement. Opacity of the individual and transparency of power, pp. 80 and 81.

434 See ECtHR, Case of Gillan and Quinton v. The United Kingdom from 12 January 2010 (application no. 4158/05), cip. 61.

Indeed, it is a difficult task to generalize certain rulings of the European Court of Human Rights because those are based on a case-by-case approach. Legal scholars, however, stress that the principle of autonomy plays a significant role in all rulings of the European Court of Human Rights on the right to private life.[435] From this perspective, the general objective of the right to private life is to protect the individual's interest that certain actions and opinions by him or her remain confidential.[436] This aspect becomes particularly apparent in a case where the European Court of Human Rights decided about the treatment of medical data. In this case of "*Z. vs. Finland*", the Court stated that "the protection of personal data, not least medical data, is of fundamental importance to a person's enjoyment of his or her right to respect for private and family life as guaranteed by Article 8 of the Convention (...). Respecting the confidentiality of health data is a vital principle in the legal systems of all the Contracting Parties to the Convention. It is crucial not only to respect the sense of privacy but also to preserve his or her confidence in the medical profession and in the health services in general. Without such protection, those in need of medical assistance may be deterred from revealing such information of a personal and intimate nature as may be necessary in order to receive appropriate treatment and, even, from seeking such assistance, thereby endangering their own health and, in the case of transmissible diseases, that of the community."[437] In light of these considerations, Article 8 ECHR provides individuals with confidence that their privacy is respected in order for them to act within society on an unbiased basis which is necessary to protect themselves and the society as a whole.

bb) Criteria established for certain cases: Context of collection, nature of data, way of usage, and results obtained

In light of such a guarantee, which is relatively broad, but also takes into account the case-by-case approach, the question is the following: What

435 See De Hert and Gutwirth, Data Protection in the Case Law of Strasbourg and Luxemburg: Constitutionalisation in Action, p. 15, with further references to corresponding considerations by the ECtHR.

436 See Schweizer, ibid., p. 466.

437 See ECtHR, Case of Z. vs. Finland from 25 February 1997 (application no. 22009/93), cip 95.

kind of data is precisely protected against which kind of usage? The European Court of Justice, indeed, does not recognize all types of personal data as being protected.[438] Hence, in order to answer this question, it is necessary to examine in detail the types of cases the European Court of Human Rights has considered as falling under the scope of application of Article 8 ECHR.

One type of case concerns telecommunication data, which is protected insofar as participants of telecommunication processes usually expect their data to be confidential.[439] Therefore, both the content of the communication, as well as its meta data is protected, for example, phone numbers, as well as the time and the duration of the call.[440] Beside telecommunication data, other forms of "correspondences" fall under Article 8 ECHR as, for instance, letters, documents, and files.[441] Another type of case refers to the term "physical and psychological integrity" of the individual. The Court elaborated in several cases on what this term means.

In the case of "*S. and Marper vs. The United Kingdom*", the European Court of Human Rights lists, in particular, the following aspects covered by this term: "Elements such as, for example, gender identification, name and sexual orientation and sexual life fall within the personal sphere protected by Article 8 (…). Beyond a person's name, his or her private and family life may include other means of personal identification and of linking to a family (…). Information about the person's health is an important element of private life (…). The Court furthermore considers that an individual's ethnic identity must be regarded as another such element (see, in particular, Article 6 of the Data Protection Convention quoted in paragraph 41 above, which lists personal data revealing racial origin as a special category of data along with other sensitive information about an indi-

438 See De Hert and Gutwirth, Data Protection in the Case Law of Strasbourg and Luxemburg: Constitutionalisation in Action, pp. 24 to 26.

439 Cf. ECtHR, Case of Copland vs. The United Kingdom from 3 April 2007 (application no. 62617/00), cip. 41 and 42; ECtHR, Case of Halford vs. The United Kingdom from 25 June 1997 (application no. 20606/92), cip. 42 to 46.

440 See ECtHR, Case of Copland vs. The United Kingdom from 3 April 2007 (application no. 62617/00), cip. 43.

441 See examples at Schweizer, ibid., p. 465.

vidual).”[442] Legal critics stress that the European Court of Justice acknowledged the category of sensitive data in its decision.[443]

In any case, the European Court of Human Rights clarified that “in determining whether the personal information retained by the authorities involves any of the private-life aspects mentioned above, the Court will have due regard to the specific context in which the information at issue has been recorded and retained, the nature of the records, the way in which these records are used and processed and the results that may be obtained (…).”[444] Thus, the above-listed categories of personal information is not protected *per se*. Instead, its protection must be examined, again, on a case-by-case basis, pursuant to the context of collection, the nature of the data, and the results retrieved from it.

cc) Particular reference to the individual’s “reasonable expectations”

When undertaking this exercise, the European Court of Human Rights often grounds its decision in further cases, by also referring to the “reasonable expectations” of the individual concerned. In this regard, the purpose of the data processing can play a decisive role.[445]

---

442 See ECtHR, Case of S. and Marper vs. the United Kingdom from 4 December 2008 (application nos. 30562/04 and 30566/04), cip. 66.

443 See Schweizer, ibid., p. 466; with respect to genetic data, see ECtHR, Case of S. and Marper vs. the United Kingdom from 4 December 2008 (application nos. 30562/04 and 30566/04), cip. 70 to 77.

444 See ECtHR, Case of S. and Marper v. The United Kingdom from 4 December 2008 (application nos. 30562/04 and 30566/04), cip. 67.

445 The following categorization is not the only possible one, of course. For example, Lindsay categorizes possible infringements of the right to private life under Art. 8 ECHR along the five elements: „storage of data relating to the private life of an individual“, „systematic collection and storage of (non-private) data“, „use of collected data infringing the individual’s ‚reasonable expectations‘“, „concerned data constitute sensitive personal information“, and „whether consent was given“ - see at Linskey, The Foundations of EU Data Protection Law, pp. 108-110. The most apparent difference to Linskey’s scheme is that the following criteria are altogether categorized under the umbrella criterion of the „individual’s reasonable expectations“.

(1) 'Intrusion into privacy'

The Court refers, for instance, to the individual's "reasonable expectations" in order to determine whether or not an intrusion into his or her private sphere infringes the right to private life. The Court hence does not affirm that each intrusion into the individual's privacy is an infringement of the individual's right to private life. However, in the case of "*Copland vs. The United Kingdom*", the Court affirmed that such an infringement took place.

> In this case, the claimant worked at a state college in England. When her supervisor suspected that she had an "improper relationship" with another male employee at the college, the supervisor started to monitor her telephone, email and Internet usage.[446]

In this case, the European Court of Human Rights affirmed that the claimant's right to private life under Article 8 ECHR had been infringed considering that "the applicant in the present case had been given no warning that her calls would be liable to monitoring, therefore she had a reasonable expectation as to the privacy of calls made from her work telephone. The same should apply in relation to the applicant's email and Internet usage."[447]

In the case of "*Halford vs. The United Kingdom*", the Court also examined further factors, beside the mere use of telecommunications by the individual, which reinforced her "reasonable expectations" to privacy.

> In this case, the claimant was an Assistant Chief Officer at the Merseyside police office in England. When her supervisor refused to promote the claimant, despite existing vacancies, the claimant started proceedings before the judicial court on the grounds of gender discrimination. The claimant furthermore alleged that her employer intercepted the telephones that she had used in her office in order to use that information against her in the discrimination proceedings. The claimant had two telephones, one for business and one for private use. There were no restrictions or guidance given by her employer for the use of these phones.[448]

---

446 See ECtHR, Case of Copland vs. The United Kingdom from 3 April 2007 (application no. 62617/00), cip. 6 to 17.

447 See ECtHR, ibid., cip.z 41.

448 See ECtHR, Case of Halford vs. The United Kingdom from 25 June 1997 (application no. 20606/92), cip. 8 to 20.

The Court confirmed that an infringement had taken place: "There is no evidence of any warning having been given to Ms. Halford, as a user of the internal telecommunications system operated at the Merseyside police headquarters, that calls made on that system would be liable to interception. She would, the Court considers, have had a reasonable expectation of privacy for such calls, which expectation was moreover reinforced by a number of further factors. As Assistant Chief Constable she had sole use of her office where there were two telephones, one of which was specifically designated for her private use. Furthermore, she had been given the assurance, in response to a memorandum, that she could use her office telephones for the purposes of her sex-discrimination case."[449] Both cases illustrate that the Court does not strictly differentiate between the two legal terms "private life" and "correspondences". However, the Court examines an infringement of Article 8 ECHR took place, by referring, commonly, to the individual's "reasonable expectations".

(2) Public situations: 'Systematic or permanent storage' vs. 'passer-by situations'

In cases related to public situations, the European Court of Human Rights elaborates on the criteria regarding the individual's "reasonable expectations" extensively. This was in particular the case in the decision of "*P.G. and J.H. vs. The United Kingdom*".

> In this case, the police wanted to compare the voice samples of the applicants with voices recorded during a conversation held on the occasion of an earlier event. In light of that the applicants had denied, during their arrest, to voluntarily provide such voice samples, the police installed covert listening devices in order to record their voices while police officers asked them formal questions. Hence, the applicants did not know that their voices were recorded during that conversation.[450]

In order to determine the scope of protection of Article 8 ECHR, the Court took into account that "there are a number of elements relevant to a consideration of whether a person's private life is concerned in measures effected outside a person's home or private premises. Since there are occa-

449 ECtHR, ibid., cip. 45.

450 See ECtHR, Case of P.G. and J.H. vs. The United Kingdom from 25 September 2001 (application no. 44787/98), cip. 15 and 16.

sions when people knowingly or intentionally involve themselves in activities that are or may be recorded or reported in a public manner, a person's reasonable expectation as to privacy may be a significant, although not necessarily conclusive, factor. A person who walks down the street will, inevitably, be visible to any member of the public who is also present. Monitoring by technological means of the same public scene (for example, a security guard viewing through closed-circuit television) is of similar character. Private-life considerations may arise, however, once any systematic or permanent record comes into existence of such material from the public domain. It is for this reason that files gathered by security services on a particular individual fall within the scope of Article 8, even where the information has not been gathered by an intrusive or covert method (…)"[451]

The Court referred in this decision to the precedent cases of "*Amann vs. Switzerland*" and "*Rotaru vs. Romania*": While in the first case, "the storing of information about the applicant on a card in a file was found to be an interference with private life, even though it contained no sensitive information and had probably never been consulted"[452], the Court had stressed in the second case that the systematic or permanent storage of public information especially falls under Article 8 if "such information concerns a person's distant past (…,) some of the information has been declared false and is likely to injure the applicant's reputation."[453] Consequently, in the case of "*Herbecq vs. Belgium*", the European Court of Justice decided that a video system controlling a public space does not fall under Article 8 ECHR if the visual data is not recorded because "it is difficult to see how the visual data obtained could be made available to the general public or used for purposes other than to keep a watch on places."[454] From the Court's point of view, "the data available to a person looking at monitors is identical to that which he or she could have ob-

---

451 See ECtHR, Case of P.G. and J.H. vs. The United Kingdom from 25 September 2001 (application no. 44787/98), cip. 57.

452 See ECtHR, Case of P.G. and J.H. vs. The United Kingdom from 25 September 2001 (application no. 44787/98), cip. 57.

453 See ECtHR, Case of Rotaru vs. Romania from 4 May 2000 (application no. 28341/95), cip. 43 and 44.

454 See ECtHR, Case of Herbecq and the Association League des Droits de l'Homme vs. Belgium from 14 January 1998 (application nos. 32200/96 and 32201/96), p. 97.

tained by being on the spot in person (…). Therefore all that can be observed is essentially, public behavior."[455]

(3) 'Data relating to private or public matters', 'limited use' and/or 'made available to the general public'

While in the case of "*Herbecq vs. Belgium*" the right to private life under Article 8 ECHR did not apply because there was no "systematic or permanent storage" of personal data at all, the Court denied the application of Article 8 ECHR in the cases of "*Lupker vs. the Netherlands*" and "*Friedl vs. Austria*" for further reasons.

> The Court stated that these decisions "concerned the unforeseen use by authorities of photographs which had been previously voluntarily submitted to them (…/for example, during an application process for a passport or drivers license) and the use of photographs taken by the authorities during a public demonstration (…)."[456] In these cases, the photographs taken during an application process were later used for criminal proceedings; and the photographs taken by the authorities during a public demonstration were used for policing the demonstration, only.

The Court decided this case by referring to the following criteria as: "In those cases, the Commission attached importance to whether the photographs amounted to an intrusion into the applicant's privacy (as, for instance, by entering and taking photographs in a person's home), whether the photograph related to private or public matters and whether the material thus obtained was envisaged for a limited use or was likely to be made available to the general public. In (../the second case) the Commission noted that there was no such intrusion into the 'inner circle' of the applicant's private life, that the photographs taken of a public demonstration related to a public event and that they had been used solely as an aid to policing the demonstration on the relevant day. In this context, the Commission attached weight to the fact that the photographs taken remained anonymous in that no names were noted down, the personal data recorded and pho-

---

455 See ECtHR, Case of Herbecq and the Association League des Droits de l'Homme vs. Belgium from 14 January 1998 (application nos. 32200/96 and 32201/96), p. 97.

456 See ECtHR, Case of Peck vs. the United Kingdom from 28 January 2003 (application no. 44647/98), cip. 61.

tographs taken were not entered into a data-processing system and no action had been taken to identify the persons photographed on that occasion by means of data processing (ibid.). Similarly, in (../the first case), the Commission specifically noted that the police used the photographs to identify offenders in criminal proceedings only and that there was no suggestion that the photographs had been made available to the general public or would be used for any other purpose."[457] Consequently, the Court considered the use of the data was not infringing the right to private life under Article 8 ECHR.

In the next case of "*Peck vs. The United Kingdom*", the European Court of Human Rights at first tied into the criteria considered in the case of "*Herbecq vs. Belgium*" – whether the treatment of data is comparable to a passer-by or security situation – and then explicitly differentiated between the moment the data is collected and its later usage.

> In this case, the camera of a CCTV-system had filmed the applicant walking around at a junction with a kitchen knife in his hand, directly after he tried to commit suicide.[458] The defendant published the record in its *CCTV News* publication while the identity of the applicant was not appropriately masked.[459] The Court stressed in its decision that the "applicant did not complain that the collection of data through the CCTV-camera monitoring of his movements (…) amounted to an interference to his private life. (…) Rather, he argued that it was the disclosure of that record of his movements to the public in a manner in which he could never have foreseen which gave rise to such an interference."[460]

The Court affirmed a serious infringement of Article 8 ECHR had occurred taking into account that "the footage was disclosed to the media for further broadcasting and publication purposes. Those media included the audiovisual media: Angelia Television broadcast locally to approximately 350,000 people and the BBC broadcast nationally, and it is 'commonly acknowledged that the audiovisual media have often a much more immediate and powerful effect than the print media' (…). (…/The applicant) was

457 See ECtHR, Case of Peck vs. the United Kingdom from 28 January 2003 (application no. 44647/98), cip. 61.
458 See ECtHR, Case of Peck vs. the United Kingdom from 28 January 2003 (application no. 44647/98), cip. 10.
459 See ECtHR, Case of Peck vs. the United Kingdom from 28 January 2003 (application no. 44647/98), cip. 62.
460 See ECtHR, Case of Peck vs. the United Kingdom from 28 January 2003 (application no. 44647/98), cip. 60.

recognized by certain members of his family and by his friends, neighbours and colleagues."[461] The Court therefore decided that "the relevant moment was viewed to an extent which far exceeded any exposure to a passer-by or to security observation (…) and to a degree surpassing that which the applicant could possibly have foreseen when he walked (…/in the moment he was filmed)."[462] In light of the seriousness of the infringement, that being: the applicant's identity was not appropriately masked, and that the footage was not published for purposes of crime detection or prevention, the Court came to the conclusion that the infringement was not justified.[463]

(4) 'Unexpected use' pursuant to the purpose perceptible by the individual concerned

In the cases described, the European Court of Human Rights more or less implicitly referred to the purpose of the collection and usage of the personal data in order to examine whether the individual could reasonably expect the collection and, more importantly, the later usage or not. In all of the cases, the Court examined whether the data 'amounted to an intrusion into the applicant's privacy, related to private or public matters and whether the information obtained was envisaged for a limited use or was likely to be made available to the general public'.[464] However, even a limited use, not being a publication of data, can interfere with an individual's 'reasonable expectation'. In the above-mentioned case of "*P.G. and*

461 See ECtHR, Case of Peck vs. the United Kingdom from 28 January 2003 (application no. 44647/98), cip. 62 and 63.

462 See ECtHR, Case of Peck vs. the United Kingdom from 28 January 2003 (application no. 44647/98), cip. 62.

463 See ECtHR, Case of Peck vs. the United Kingdom from 28 January 2003 (application no. 44647/98), cip. 79, 85, and 87.

464 Cf. ECtHR, Case of Herbecq and the Association League des Droits de l'Homme vs. Belgium from 14 January 1998 (application nos. 32200/96 and 32201/96), p. 97; ECtHR, Case of P.G. and J.H. vs. The United Kingdom from 25 September 2001 (application no. 44787/98), cip. 58; ECtHR, Case of Peck vs. the United Kingdom from 28 January 2003 (application no. 44647/98), cip. 61 referring to the Case of Friedl vs. Austria from 31 January 1995 (Series A no. 305-B) and Case of Lupker vs. the Netherlands from 7 December 1992 (application no. 18395/91); see also, for example, ECtHR, Case of von Hannover vs. Germany from 24 June 2004 (application no. 59320/00), cip. 52.

J.H. vs. The United Kingdom", the Court came to the conclusion that the covert recording of voices during a conversation in the police station fell within the scope of Article 8 ECHR. In conclusion, the Court did not follow the opinion of the defending government that the applicants could not expect their privacy in that context.[465] From the Court's point of view, "a permanent record has nonetheless been made of the person's voice and it is subject to a process of analysis directly relevant to identifying that person in the context of other personal data. Though it is true that when being charged the applicants answered formal questions in a place where police officers were listening to them, the recording and analysis of their voices on this occasion must still be regarded as concerning the processing of personal data about the applicants."[466]

While the Court referred in this case only to the fact that the covert voice sample became "subject to a process of analysis directly relevant to identifying (…/the applicant) in the context of other personal data"[467], the purpose of the data treatment played in the other decisions a more explicit role. In the case "*Herbecq vs. Belgium*", the Court held it as essential that the visual data from the video camera control could not be, in light of the fact that it did not record the data, "used for purposes other than to keep a watch on places."[468] In the cases of "*Friedl vs. Austria*" and of "*Lupker vs. the Netherlands*", the Court considered that the photographs had been used, in the first case, "solely as an aid to policing the demonstration on the relevant day" and, in the other case, "to identify offenders in criminal proceedings only (…/without giving) suggestion that the photographs (…) would be used for any other purpose."[469] In the case of "*Peck vs. the United Kingdom*", the Court finally came to the conclusion that the usage of the visual data had clearly surpassed what the applicant could have fore-

465 Cf. ECtHR, Case of P.G. and J.H. vs. The United Kingdom from 25 September 2001 (application no. 44787/98), cip. 54.

466 See ECtHR, Case of P.G. and J.H. vs. The United Kingdom from 25 September 2001 (application no. 44787/98), cip. 59.

467 See ECtHR, Case of P.G. and J.H. vs. The United Kingdom from 25 September 2001 (application no. 44787/98), cip. 59.

468 See ECtHR, Case of Herbecq and the Association League des Droits de l'Homme vs. Belgium from 14 January 1998 (application nos. 32200/96 and 32201/96), p. 97.

469 See ECtHR, Case of Peck vs. the United Kingdom from 28 January 2003 (application no. 44647/98), cip. 61.

seen because it was not only recorded for security reasons, but also "disclosed to the media for further broadcasting and publication purposes."[470]

Finally, the purpose plays an even more explicit and decisive role in the decisions of "*Perry vs. the United Kingdom*" and of "*M.S. vs. Sweden*".

> In the case of "*Perry vs. the United Kingdom*", the applicant had, in connection of a robbery for which he was accused, refused an identity parade. The police therefore decided to indirectly make the identity parade possible by means of a tape record: An engineer adjusted a custody suite camera in the police station in order to ensure that it took clear pictures of the applicant in the moment when he, being arrested, entered the police station. After the record, the police prepared a compilation video in which other persons mimicked the actions of the applicant how it was recorded. When this compilation was shown to witnesses of the robbery, some of them positively identified the applicant.[471]

Similar to the case of "*P.G. and J.H. vs. The United Kingdom*"", the defending Government argued that the police station "could not be regarded as a private place, and that as the cameras which were running for security purposes were visible to the applicant he must have realized that he was being filmed, with no reasonable expectation of privacy in the circumstances."[472] In contrast, the European Court of Human Rights had a more differentiated approach on privacy within the meaning of Article 8 ECHR. It affirmed, at first, that "the normal use of security cameras, whether in public or on premises, such as shopping centres, or police stations, where they serve a legitimate and foreseeable purpose, do not raise issues under Article 8 § 1 of the Convention. However, the police regulated the security camera so that it could take clear footage of the applicant in the custody suite and inserted it in a montage of film of other persons to show to witnesses for the purposes of seeing whether they identified the applicant as the perpetrator of the robberies under investigation. The video was also shown during the applicant's trial in a public court room. (…) The Court recalls that the applicant had been brought to the police station to attend an identity parade and that he had refused to participate. Whether or not he was aware of the security cameras running in the custody suite, there is no

470 See ECtHR, Case of Peck vs. the United Kingdom from 28 January 2003 (application no. 44647/98), cip. 62.

471 See ECtHR, Case of Perry vs. the United Kingdom from 17 July 2003 (application no. 63737/00), cip. 14 and 15.

472 See ECtHR, Case of Perry vs. the United Kingdom from 17 July 2003 (application no. 63737/00), cip. 39.

indication that the applicant had any expectation that footage was being taken of him within the police station for use in a video identification procedure and, potentially, as evidence prejudicial to his defence at trial. This ploy adopted by the police went beyond the normal or expected use of this type of camera, as indeed is demonstrated by the fact that the police were required to obtain permission and an engineer had to adjust the camera. (…) The Court considers therefore that the recording and use of the video footage of the applicant in this case discloses an interference with his right to respect for private life."[473] This interference was not justified because the police did not inform the applicant about the actual purpose of the filming before it, which is required by the national law concerned.[474]

> Finally, in the case of "*M.S. vs. Sweden*", a medical clinic has sent, without prior notice of the applicant, the applicant's medical records to a Social Insurance Office. The Office had requested the data because of a claim of the applicant for compensation after she had an accident at work.[475]

In this case, the European Court of Human Rights examined whether the transfer constituted an infringement of Article 8 ECHR taking into account "that the medical records in question contained highly personal and sensitive data about the applicant (…). Although the records remained confidential, they had been disclosed to another public authority and therefore to a wider circle of public servants (…). Moreover, whilst the information had been collected and stored at the clinic in connection with medical treatment, its subsequent communication had served a different purpose, namely to enable the Office to examine her compensation claim. It did not follow from the fact that she had sought treatment at the clinic that she would consent to the data being disclosed to the Office (…). Having regard to these considerations, the Court finds that the disclosure of the data by the clinic of the Office entailed an interference with the applicant's right to respect for private life guaranteed by paragraph 1 of Article 8."[476] However, the Court considered that the inference was justified within Ar-

---

473 See ECtHR, Case of Perry vs. the United Kingdom from 17 July 2003 (application no. 63737/00), cip. 40, 41, and 43.

474 See ECtHR, Case of Perry vs. the United Kingdom from 17 July 2003 (application no. 63737/00), cip. 47 and 49.

475 See ECtHR, Case of M.S. vs. Sweden from 27 August 1997 (74/1996/693/885), cip. 8 to 14.

476 See ECtHR, Case of M.S. vs. Sweden from 27 August 1997 (74/1996/693/885), cip. 35.

ticle 8 ECHR because the Office had a legitimate interest in the data as it could not have checked otherwise whether the applicant's claim for the compensation was well-founded or not. Furthermore, the receiving office was under a duty to verify that the pre-conditions for the transfer were met. In addition, they were also under a duty to keep this information confidential, so that limitations for further use existed, as well as safeguards against abuse.[477]

dd) Consent: Are individuals given a choice to avoid the processing altogether?

In the same case, the European Court of Human Rights also examined, in more detail, the pre-conditions and extent of a potential waiver of the individual's right to private life. The Court discussed, in particular, whether the applicant consented to the transfer of her medical data in what would have excluded, in the Court's opinion, the application of Article 8 ECHR. In doing so, it took into account that the "communication of such data by the clinic to the Office would be permissible under the Insurance Act only if the latter authority had made a request and only to the extent that the information was deemed to be material to the application of the Insurance Act (…). This assessment was left exclusively to the competent authorities, the applicant having no right to be consulted or informed beforehand (…). It thus appears that the disclosure depended not only on the fact that the applicant had submitted her compensation claim to the Office but also on a number of factors beyond her control. It cannot therefore be inferred from her request that she had waived in an unequivocal manner her right under Article 8 § 1 of the Convention to respect for private life with regard to the medical records at the clinic. Accordingly, the Court considers that this provision applies to the matters under consideration."[478]

The Court similarly focused on the question of whether or not the individual is able to control the collection of his or her data in the case of "*Gillan and Quinton vs. the United Kingdom*".

---

477 See ECtHR, Case of M.S. vs. Sweden from 27 August 1997 (74/1996/693/885), cip. 42 to 44.

478 See ECtHR, Case of M.S. vs. Sweden from 27 August 1997 (74/1996/693/885), cip. 32.

> In this case, the police has stopped, on the grounds of the Terrorism Act 2000, passers-by and searched their bags in connection with a demonstration.[479] The government argued that the individual's concerned had given their consent to the search because they would have "brought themselves into contact with the public sphere through their voluntary engagement with a public demonstration."[480]

The Court of Human Rights did not accept this argument nor, in particular, "the analogy drawn with the search to which passengers uncomplainingly submit at airports or at the entrance of a public building. It does not need to decide whether the search of the person and of his bags in such circumstances amounts to an interference with an individual's Article 8 rights, albeit one which is clearly justified on security grounds, since for the reasons given by the applicants the situations cannot be compared. An air traveller may be seen as consenting to such a search by choosing to travel. He knows that he and his bags are liable to be searched before boarding the aeroplane and has a freedom of choice, since he can leave personal items behind and walk away without being subjected to a search. The search powers under section 44 are qualitatively different. The individual can be stopped anywhere and at any time, without notice and without any choice as to whether or not to submit to a search."[481] The Court concluded from this that the searches interfered with Article 8 ECHR and were, not justified on the grounds of the authorizing law (section 44 of the Terrorism Act 2000). The reason was that the searches were "neither sufficiently circumscribed nor subject to adequate legal safeguards against abuse".[482] As it had already affirmed that an infringement of Article 8 ECHR had taken place, the Court held that it was not necessary to examine further rights under ECHR, such as the freedom of expression or assembly.[483]

---

479 See ECtHR, Case of Gillan and Quinton vs. the United Kingdom from 12 January 2010 (application no. 4158/05), cip. 7 to 9.

480 See ECtHR, Case of Gillan and Quinton vs. the United Kingdom from 12 January 2010 (application no. 4158/05), cip. 60.

481 See ECtHR, Case of Gillan and Quinton vs. the United Kingdom from 12 January 2010 (application no. 4158/05), cip. 65.

482 See ECtHR, Case of Gillan and Quinton vs. the United Kingdom from 12 January 2010 (application no. 4158/05), cip. 87.

483 See ECtHR, Case of Gillan and Quinton vs. the United Kingdom from 12 January 2010 (application no. 4158/05), cip. 88 to 90.

ee) Conclusion: Assessment of 'reasonable expectations' on a case-by-case basis

In conclusion, the European Court of Human Rights does not, in general, define but rather examines, on a case-by-case basis, which acts of data treatment are legally relevant: Be it medical or communication data, or a human action in public. The Court tends to answer the question of whether or not the treatment of data is legally relevant by determining the specific context. In doing so, it takes into account "whether the (… / personal data) amounted to an intrusion into the applicant's privacy, whether (… / it) related to private or public matters and whether the material thus obtained was envisaged for a limited use or was likely to be made available to the general public."[484] In this examination exercise, the Court does not explicitly refer to the principle of purpose limitation, but rather to the individual's "reasonable expectations". In this regard, indeed, the purpose of the data processing plays an important instrumental role.[485] The explicit purpose of the collection for the individual concerned provides a link for examining whether or not he or she could expect an intrusion into his or her private sphere or, respectively, could expect how their data was used later on. However, the European Court of Human Rights does not refer to any further human rights in order to determine the impact resulting from the treatment of the data for the individual. In the case of "*Gillan and Quinton vs. The United Kingdom*", the Court rather, concluded that it did not have to examine any further rights of the European Charter on Human Rights, such as the freedom to expression or to assembly, since it had already affirmed a violation under Article 8 ECHR.[486]

484 See ECtHR, Case of Peck vs. the United Kingdom from 28 January 2003 (application no. 44647/98), cip. 61.

485 However, see Bygrave, Data Privacy Law, p. 154, who sees the principle of purpose limitation "far from salient in ECtHR case law".

486 See ECtHR, Case of Gillan and Quinton vs. the United Kingdom from 12 January 2010 (application no. 4158/05), cip. 88 to 90.

c) Concept of Articles 7 and 8 ECFR: Ambiguous interplay of scopes going beyond Article 8 ECHR

After having examined the reasons developed by the European Court of Human Rights with respect to Article 8 ECHR, it is now possible to analyze how the European Court of Justice transposes these functions of purpose specification into the concept of protection of Articles 7 and 8 ECFR, respectively.

aa) Comparing the decisions of the European Court of Justice with the principles developed by the European Court of Human Rights

A comparison of the decisions held, on the one hand, by the European Court of Human Rights and, on the other hand, the European Court of Justice, reveals more differences than commonalities. One reason for this is that the European Court of Justice clearly developed the concept of protection further by referring, either, to the right to private life under Article 7 ECFR, or to the right to data protection under Article 8 ECFR, or to both fundamental rights.

(1) General definition of the term 'personal data' under Article 7 and 8 ECFR instead of case-by-case approach

The first difference concerns the way how the European Court of Justice constructs the scope of protection of the fundamental rights, respectively. After the European Charter of Fundamental Rights came into force, the European Court of Justice commonly defined the scope(s) of protection of both rights to private life under Article 7 ECFR and data protection under Article 8 ECFR by referring to the term 'personal data'. In doing so, the European Court of Justice principally applies the reasoning of the European Court of Human Rights. This becomes particularly apparent in the case of "*Schecke vs. Land Hessen*".

> In this case, the applicants of the main proceedings were a group of agricultural companies that were financially supported by the department of European agricultural funds. According to the corresponding European regulation, the executive public agency published data about the applicants, such as their names, their place of establishment and residence, as well as the annual amounts of the money received from the department. The claimants brought

an action against the publication of their information, which was finally referred by the national court to the European Court of Justice.[487]

The European Court of Justice explicitly referred to the decisions of "*Amann vs. Switzerland*" and "*Rotaru vs. Romania*" of the European Court of Human Rights stating not only that the right to data protection under Article 8 ECFR "is closely connected with the right to private life expressed in Article 7 ECFR"[488] but also "that the term 'private life' must not be interpreted restrictively".[489] The Court appears to construct one common fundamental right, stressing: "The right to respect for private life with regard to the processing of personal data, recognized by Article 7 and Article 8 of the Charter, concerns any information relating to an identified or identifiable individual (…) and the limitations which may lawfully be imposed on the right to the protection of personal data correspond to those tolerated in relation to Article 8 of the Convention."[490] While some critics consider that the Court "assimilates Article 7 and 8 of the Charter to create an unprecedented right",[491] others stress that the unclear reasoning does not automatically mean that the Court assumes both Articles 7 and 8 ECFR as one fundamental right in relation to the meaning of Article 8 ECHR.[492]

The European Court of Justice affirmed this combination of Article 7 and 8 ECFR in the case of "*FECEMD and ASNEF*".[493] However, the Court basically applies the same definition for affirming the scope of protection in decisions where it refers to the right to data protection under Article 8 ECFR, only. This is the case, for example, in the decisions of "*SABAM vs. Scarlet*" and "*SABAM vs. Netlog*".[494] In both cases, the European Court of Justice simply affirmed that the IP addresses concerned did

487 See ECJ C-92/09 and C-93/09 (Schecke vs. Land Hessen), cip. 25 to 28.

488 See ECJ C- 92/09 and C-93/09 cip. 47 and 52.

489 See ECJ C-92/09 and C-93/09 cip. 59.

490 See ECJ C-92/09 and C-93/09 cip. 52.

491 See González-Fuster, The Emergence of Data Protection as a Fundamental Right of the EU, pp. 234 to 236.

492 See Burgkardt, ibid., pp. 349 to 356 with further references.

493 See ECJ C-468/10 and C-469/10, cip. 40 to 42, and the facts of the case above under point C. I. 1. b) aa) (2) (b) The right to data protection under Article 8 ECFR and/or the right to private life under Article 7 ECFR.

494 See the facts of the case above under point C. I. 1. b) aa) (2) (b) The right to data protection under Article 8 ECFR and/or the right to private life under Article 7 ECFR.

indeed fall under Article 8 ECFR "because (they) allow those users to be precisely identified."[495] Legal critics are of the opinion that this reasoning indicates a rather broad interpretation of the term 'personal data' without any further requirements, such as a link to the private sphere or data sensitivity.[496]

So far, the essential aspect is that the European Court of Justice uses the term 'personal data' for defining both scopes of protection of Article 7 and Article 8 ECFR, like the European Court of Human Rights with respect to Article 8 ECFR, but uses a different method for constructing the scopes. The European Court of Human Rights constructs the scope of protection of the right to private life on a case-by-case basis and does not provide for a definition of private life that is capable of a general application.[497] Consequently, the legal doctrine elaborating on such a general definition plays a much smaller role at the European Court of Human Rights level than it does in the continental European traditional level. Based on the more empirical approach of common law, there is, consequently, no "general formula" determining the "implicit limitations" of fundamental rights. Instead, these limitations must be defined for each (type of) case(s), for example, by means of affirming or denying the scope of protection.[498] In contrast, scholars stress that the European Court of Justice does not sufficiently take into account the particularities of the case at hand.[499] Therefore, even if there is not yet a commonly accepted normative methodology of interpreting union law,[500] the European Court of Justice shows a strong tendency – at least, with respect to the rights to private life and data protection under Articles 7 and 8 ECFR – to apply another method of interpretation than the European Court of Human Rights. The European Court of Justice defines the scopes of protection of both fundamental rights un-

495 See ECJ C-70/10 cip. 51 and ECJ C-360/10 cip 49.

496 See Burgkardt, ibid., pp. 349 to 356 with further references.

497 See above under point C. I. 3. c) aa) (1) General definition of the term 'personal data' under Article 7 and 8 ECFR instead of case-by-case approach.

498 See Matscher, Methods of Interpretation of the Convention, pp. 63 to 67, who also stresses that a comparative analysis with the judicature by the European Court of Justice would be interesting.

499 See Fleischer, European Methodology, p. 717, referring to Vogenauer, Die Auslegung von Gesetzen in England und auf dem Kontinent I und II (2001), pp. 255 ff.

500 See Fleischer, ibid., pp. 707 to 710, referring, indeed, to prescriptive methodologies such as at Ulla B. Neergaard, Ruth Nielsen, Lynn M. Rosenberry, European legal Method: Paradoxes and Revitalisation (2011).

der Article 7 and 8 ECFR referring, in general, to the term of "personal data". This term serves as the Court's main starting point when considering, by means of its deductive method, all processing of personal data as falling under the scope(s) of protection. This leads to the result that the European Court of Human Rights remains, in light of its case-by-case approach, relatively free in examining the particularities of the case at hand and, though, affirming or denying the scope of application of the right to private life under Article 8 ECHR. In contrast, the European Court of Justice, which refers to its general definition of the term of "personal data", is bound, once personal data is the main focal point of the case, to affirm the scope of protection of the rights to private life and/or data protection under Article 7 and 8 ECFR.

(2) Differences between private life and data protection under Articles 7 and 8 ECFR

The second difference concerns the elements that were originally covered, all together, by the right to private life under Article 8 ECHR and are now located, in one part, under the homologue right of Article 7 ECHR and, in another part, under the new right to data protection of Article 8 ECFR. So far, this re-location is not a substantive further development regarding the concept of protection provided for by Article 8 ECHR. It rather, is a formal change due to the explicit wording of Article 8 sect. 2 and 3 ECFR. However, since the European Court of Justice does not apply a case-by-case approach, as the Court of Human Rights does, but sets up a common definition for both fundamental rights, it is necessary to examine how the European Court of Justice differentiates between both fundamental rights.

(a) Protection against first publication and profiles based on public data

At first, the European Court of Justice affirms, similar to the European Court of Human Rights, an infringement of the right to private life under Article 7 ECFR if personal data is firstly published. In doing so, the Court basically considers, such as in its decision of "*Schecke vs. Germany*", the right to data protection as "closely connected with the right to private life".[501] However, in the case of "*González vs. Google Spain*", the data was in fact already published. In this case, sort of an instrumental character of the (new) right to data protection for the (old) right to private life becomes apparent. Here in particular, the purpose of the data processing is also an essential element behind the Court's reasoning.[502]

The European Court of Justice examined, at first, the effects of data processing by Google's search engine on Mr. González' right to private life. It then considered and answered the question of whether or not Mr. González could request Google to delist the articles containing information about him from its search results. In particular, the Court took into account the purpose of the initial publication and the time that had elapsed after the first publication of the article (16 years). Referring to the Data Protection Directive, the Court stressed that "it follows from those requirements, laid down in Article 6(1) lit. c) to (e) (…), that even initially lawful processing of accurate data may, in the course of time, become incompatible with the directive where those data are no longer necessary in the light of the purposes for which they initially were collected or processed. That is in particular where they appear to be inadequate, irrelevant or no longer relevant, or excessive in relation to those purposes and in the light of the time that has elapsed."[503] The Court went on to state that such a right to be delisted does not require "that the inclusion of the information in question in the list of results causes prejudice to the data subject. As the data subject may, in the light of his fundamental rights under Articles 7 and 8 of the Charter, request that the information in question no longer made available to the general public by its inclusion in such a list of results, it should be held (…) that those rights override, as a rule, not only the economic interest of the operator of the search engine but also the interest of the general public in finding that information".[504] The specification of the purpose basically required by Article 8 sect. 2 ECFR thus played an instrumental role in order to safeguard Mr. González' right to private life.

---

501 See ECJ C- 92/09 and C-93/09 cip. 47 and 52, and the facts of this case above under point C. I. 3. c) aa) (1) General definition of the term 'personal data' under Article 7 and 8 ECFR instead of case-by-case approach.

502 See the facts of this case above under point C. I. 1. b) aa) (2) (b) The right to data protection under Article 8 ECFR and/or the right to private life under Article 7 ECFR.

503 See ECJ C-131/12, cip. 93.

504 See ECJ C-131/12, cip. 96 and 97.

Indeed, the Court did not discuss whether this requirement directly applies to the private sector nor did it examine what the initial purpose was and why the later usage of that data by the search engine operator actually conflicted with this initial purpose. However, so far, the reasoning appears to be consistent with the principles provided for by the European Court of Human Rights. The Court of Human Rights would probably have considered whether the constant availability of these articles through Google's search engine interfered with the "reasonable expectations" of Mr. González' or not.[505] This might have been the case because the "processing enables any internet user to obtain through the list of results a structured overview of the information relating to that individual that can be found on the internet — information which potentially concerns a vast number of aspects of his private life and which, without the search engine, could not have been interconnected or could have been only with great difficulty — and thereby to establish a more or less detailed profile of him. Furthermore, the effect of the interference with those rights of the data subject is heightened on account of the important role played by the internet and search engines in modern society, which render the information contained in such a list of results ubiquitous (...)."[506] When the newspapers initially published the information 16 years ago, Mr. González therefore had probably not expected the profile that was later created through the Internet search engine when Internet users typed in the claimant's name. In addition, from the point of view of the European Court of Human Rights, it might have played a role that the first publication "took place upon order of the Ministry of Labor and Social Affairs and was intended to give maximum publicity to the auction (in that Mr. González was involved at the time) in order to secure as many bidders as possible". The first publication, hence, depended not only on the fact that Mr. González could not pay his security debts 'but also on a number of factors beyond his control.'[507]

505 Cf. ECtHR, Case of Peck vs. the United Kingdom from 28 January 2003 (application no. 44647/98), cip. 62.

506 See ECJ C-131/12 cip. 80.

507 Cf. ECtHR, Case of M.S. vs. Sweden from 27 August 1997 (74/1996/693/885), cip. 32.

(b) Protection against collection, storage, and subsequent risk of abuse

The right to data protection under Article 8 ECFR, in particular, the requirement to specify the purpose, can therefore play an important role in the Court's reasoning in order to determine an infringement of the right to private life under Article 7 ECFR. In the subsequent case "*Digital Rights vs. Ireland*", the Court again refers to the purpose of the data processing in order to examine an infringement of the right to private life. However, in this case, the Court more precisely differentiates between both fundamental rights.

> In this case, Digital Rights Ireland Ltd. lodged a complaint before an Irish court challenging national legislative and administrative measures regarding the retention of data related to electronic communications. These measures were based on the Data Retention Directive.[508] In light of the broad scope of the directive, the Irish court referred the decision, unlike the German Constitutional Court, to the European Court of Justice asking on its legality with respect to the right to privacy in Article 7 ECFR, the right to data protection in Article 8 ECFR, and the freedom of expression in Article 11 ECFR.[509]

With respect to the scopes of application of the fundamental rights, the European Court of Justice stressed, at first, that the "data, taken as a whole, may allow very precise conclusions to be drawn concerning the private lives of the persons whose data has been retained, such as the habits of everyday life, permanent or temporary places of residence, daily or other movements, the activities carried out, the social relationships of those persons and the social environments frequented by them."[510] The Court concluded from this that, albeit no content of the communication should have been retained, "it is not inconceivable that the retention of the data in question might have an effect on the use, by subscribers or registered users, of the means of communication covered by that directive and, consequently, on their exercise of the freedom of expression guaranteed by

---

508 See ECJ C-293/12 and C-594/12 cip. 17; Directive 2006/24/EC of the European Parliament and of the Council of 15 March 2006 on the retention of data generated or processed in connection with the provision of publicly available electronic communications services or of public communications networks and amending Directive 2002/58/EC (Data Retention Directive).

509 Cf. above under point Principles of clarity of law and purpose limitation referring to the moment when data is collected, referring to BVerfG, 2nd March 2010, 1 BvR 256/08, 1 BvR 263/08, and 1 BvR 586/08 (Data Retention), cip. 186.

510 See ECJ C-293/12 and C-594/12 cip. 27.

Article 11 of the Charter."[511] The Court continued to state that "the retention of data for the purpose of possible access to them by the competent authorities (…) directly and specifically affects private life and, consequently, the rights guaranteed by Article 7 of the Charter."[512] With respect to Article 8 ECHR, the Court finally added that "such a retention of data also falls under Article 8 of the Charter because it constitutes the processing of personal data within the meaning of that article and, therefore, necessarily has to satisfy the data protection requirements arising from that article (…)."[513]

Regarding an infringement of these rights, the Court stressed, at first, "the fact that data retained and subsequently used without the subscriber or registered user being informed is likely to generate in the minds of the persons concerned the feeling that their private lives are the subject of constant surveillance."[514] However, the Court clarified that "it does not matter whether the information on the private lives concerned is sensitive or whether the people concerned have been inconvenienced in any way".[515] As a consequence, both the obligation to retain the data, as well as to grant access to it interferes "with the rights guaranteed by Article 7 of the Charter."[516] With respect to the right to data protection, the Court simply considered that "likewise, (…/the Data Retention Directive) constitutes an interference with the fundamental right to the protection of personal data guaranteed by Article 8 of the Charter because it provides for the processing of personal data."[517]

Examining whether these infringements are justified, the ECJ principally upheld the distinction between the right to private life in Article 7 ECFR and of the right to data protection in Article 8 ECFR. At first, it determined whether the Data Retention Directive affects the essence of the corresponding fundamental right: "So far as concerns the essence of the fundamental right to privacy and the other rights laid down in Article 7 of the Charter, it must be held that, even though the retention of data required (…) constitutes a particularly serious interference with those rights, it is

511 See ECJ C-293/12 and C-594/12 cip. 28.
512 See ECJ C-293/12 and C-594/12 cip. 29.
513 See ECJ C-293/12 and C-594/12 cip. 29.
514 See ECJ C-293/12 and C-594/12 cip. 37.
515 See ECJ C-293/12 and C-594/12 cip. 33.
516 See ECJ C-293/12 and C-594/12 cip. 34 and 35.
517 See ECJ C-293/12 and C-594/12 cip. 36.

not such as to adversely affect the essence of those rights given that, as follows from Article 1(2) of the directive, the directive does not permit the acquisition of knowledge of the content of the electronic communication as such. Nor is that retention of data such as to adversely affect the essence of the fundamental right to the protection of personal data enshrined in Article 8 of the Charter, because Article 7 of (…/the Data Retention Directive) provides, in relation to data protection and data security, that, without prejudice to the provisions adopted pursuant to (…/the Data Protection Directive) and (…/the ePrivacy Directive), certain principles of data protection and data security must be respected by (…/service and network providers). According to those principles, Member States are adopted against accidental or unlawful destruction, accidental loss or alteration of data."[518] Thus, while Article 7 ECFR contains the essence that nobody else gets access to the content of communication, the essence of Article 8 ECFR requires a minimum set of data protection principles and data security.

However, coming to the question of whether the interferences of Article 7 and 8 ECFR are proportionate, the European Court of Justice again interconnects both rights. The Court considered, at first, that the Member States' margin of discretion implementing the Data Retention Directive into national law is limited and can therefore be strictly reviewed by the Court because "of the important role played by the protection of personal data in the light of the fundamental right to respect for private life and the extent and seriousness of the interference with that right caused by (…/the directive)".[519] It then goes on to state that "the fight against serious crime, in particular against organized crime and terrorism (…), however fundamental it may be, does not, in itself, justify a retention measure such as that established by (…/the directive)".[520] The Court stressed that "so far as concerns the right to respect for private life, the protection of that fundamental right requires, according to the Court's settled case-law, in any event, that derogations and limitations in relation to the protection of per-

518 See ECJ C-293/12 and C-594/12 cip. 39 and 40; Directive 2002/58/EC of the European Parliament and of the Council of 12 July 2002 concerning the processing of personal data and the protection of privacy in the electronic communications sector (ePrivacy Directive).

519 See ECJ C-293/12 and C-594/12 cip. 45 to 48.

520 See ECJ C-293/12 and C-594/12 cip. 51.

sonal data must apply only in so far as is strictly necessary (…).”[521] While it referred, in this respect, only to the right to privacy in Article 7 ECFR, it continued, taking the right to data protection into account, as: “In that regard, it should be noted that the protection of personal data resulting from the explicit obligation laid down in Article 8(1) of the Charter is especially important for the right to respect for private life enshrined in Article 7 of the Charter.”[522]

In conclusion, the European Court of Justice tends to refer to the fundamental right to private life if there is a direct effect on the individual's privacy, such as conclusions to be drawn, based on the collection of the personal data, about “the private lives of the persons whose data has been retained, such as the habits of everyday life.”[523] In contrast, the court rather refers to the right to data protection under Article 8 ECFR if there are no “sufficient safeguards (…) to ensure effective protection (…) against the risk of abuse and against any unlawful access and use of that data.”[524] The Court thus appears to focus on the right to private life as protecting against the direct impact of the collection of data on the individual, while focusing on the right to data protection as an instrument protecting against potential threats caused by the storage and potential later usage of the data. In its essence, the European Court of Justice affirmed this differentiation in the subsequent decision of “*Schrems vs. Facebook*”.

> In this case, Mr. Schrems, an Austrian resident as well as national, has been a user of the social network Facebook. Facebook concludes with its users, at the beginning of their registry for the platform, a contract regulating, amongst others, the processing of their personal data. This data is transmitted from the subsidiary Facebook Ireland to the Facebook Inc. in the USA, and stored there. Mr. Schrems lodged a complaint to the Data Protection Commissioner in Ireland demanding to stop Facebook Ireland transferring the personal data related to Mr. Schrems to the USA. He argued, based on Mr. Snowden's revelations about the processing of personal data by the National Security Agency (NSA), that the level of protection in the USA is not adequate to the level within the European Union and the data transfer therefore conflicts with the

---

521 See ECJ C-293/12 and C-594/12 cip. 52; affirmed in the subsequent case of “*Digital Rights vs. Ireland*”, ECJ C-293/12 and C-594/12, cip. 92.

522 See ECJ C-293/12 and C-594/12 cip. 53.

523 See ECJ C-293/12 and C-594/12 cip. 27; see also Kokott and Sobotta, The distinction between privacy and data protection in the jurisprudence of the CJEU and the ECtHR, p. 224, giving further examples of similar wordings.

524 See ECJ C-293/12 and C-594/12 cip. 66, cf. also ECJ C- 92/09 and C-93/09 cip. 52 as well as ECJ C-468/10 and C-469/10, cip. 41.

Data Protection Directive. The Data Protection Commissioner refused the complaint. From the Commissioner's view point, it was hindered to validate the facts of Mr. Schrems' complaint because, amongst others, the European Commission had found in its Decision 2000/520 (so-called Safe Harbour decision) that the level of data protection in the USA was adequate. Mr. Schrems lodged a claim against this decision of the Commissioner before the High Court of Ireland that finally referred the case to the European Court of Justice.[525]

In this decision, the Court took into account, one the one hand, "the important role played by the protection of personal data in the light of the fundamental right to respect for private life"[526] and concluded from this that an "interference with the fundamental rights guaranteed by Articles 7 and 8 of the Charter must (…) lay down clear and precise rules governing the scope and application of a measure and imposing minimum safeguards, so that the persons whose personal data is concerned have sufficient guarantees enabling their data to be effectively protected against the risk of abuse and against any unlawful access and use of that data."[527] On the other hand, the Court affirmed a separate infringement of the essence of the fundamental right to private life under Article 7 ECFR because the legislation in question allowed "the public authorities to have access on a generalised basis to the content of electronic communications".[528]

(3) Reference to further fundamental rights under Article 7 and/or 8 ECFR

In the same cases, the European Court of Justice additionally referred to further fundamental rights, beside the right to private life and the right to data protection under Article 7 and 8 ECFR. This reference to further fundamental rights constitutes a third difference of the decisions by the European Court of Human Rights with respect to the right to private life protected by Article 8 ECHR.

---

525 See ECJ C-362/14 (Schrems vs. Facebook), cip. 26 to 36.
526 See ECJ C-362/14 (Schrems vs. Facebook), cip. 78.
527 See ECJ C-362/14 (Schrems vs. Facebook), cip. 91.
528 See ECJ C-362/14 (Schrems vs. Facebook), cip. 94.

(a) Which right is used to discuss other fundamental rights?

In the case of "*Schrems vs. Facebook*", the European Court of Justice pointed, in relation to the right to data protection under Article 8 ECFR, to further fundamental rights, beside the right to private life under Article 7 ECFR. In doing so, the European Court of Justice referred, at first, to Article 1, as well as Recitals 2 and 10 of the Data Protection Directive, which state to protect not only the fundamental rights to private life and data protection under Article 7 and 8, but also all other fundamental rights.[529] However, the European Court of Justice makes it clear that this function of data protection instruments referring to all fundamental rights does not only result from secondary law, but also from the fundamental right to data protection under Article 8 ECFR. From its point of view, if the Safe Harbour decision hindered a national data protection commissioner to examine an individuals' claim, these individuals "would be denied the right, guaranteed by Article 8(1) and (3) of the Charter, to lodge with the national supervisory authorities a claim for the purpose of protecting their fundamental rights."[530] The European Court of Justice also examines, in more detail, which further fundamental right comes into question being supplemented by the rights guaranteed by Article 8 sect. 1 and 3 ECFR. In this case, for instance, the Court referred to Article 47 ECFR as: "legislation not providing for any possibility for an individual to pursue legal remedies in order to have access to personal data relating to him, or to obtain the rectification or erasure of such data, does not respect the essence of the fundamental right to effective judicial protection".[531]

The European Court of Justice also took, in its preceding decision of "*Digital Rights vs. Ireland*", further fundamental rights into account. Indeed, the European Court of Justice discussed the fundamental right of freedom to expression provided for by Article 11 ECFR in relation to the right to private life under Article 7 ECFR. In particular, the Court considered the unspecified threat of being constantly surveyed, as well as that individuals are likely to limit their communication. Even if the Court did not use these considerations in order to determine the scope of Article 7 ECFR, it referred to it in order to determine the intensity of the infringe-

529 See ECJ C-362/14 (Schrems vs. Facebook), cip. 39.

530 See ECJ C-362/14 (Schrems vs. Facebook), cip. 58 as well as 56.

531 See ECJ C-362/14 (Schrems vs. Facebook), cip. 95.

ment.[532] However, the reason for the different attribution of further fundamental rights, on the one hand, to the right to private life and, on the other hand, to the right to data protection, appears to lie in the different type of threat: As analyzed before, the European Court of Justice tends to refer to the right to private life if the collection of personal data leads to a direct effect on the individual's privacy.[533] Or how the Advocate General Cruz-Villalón puts it in its Opinion to the case of "*Digital Rights vs. Ireland*": In this case, "it is not the processing of the data retained, (..) in terms of the manner in which they are used (…), which requires the utmost vigilance, but the actual collection and retention of the data at issue, as well as the data's impact on the right to privacy".[534] The reason for this is that these "are data which, qualitatively, relate essentially to private life, to the confidentiality of private life (…). The issue which arises in such cases is not yet that of the guarantees relating to data processing but, at an earlier stage, that of the data as such, that is to say, the fact that it has been possible to record the circumstances of a person's private life in the form of data, data which can consequently be subject to information processing."[535] Thus, the deterring effect of this kind of data collection on the exercise of the freedom of expression "would be merely a collateral consequence of interference with the right to privacy".[536] In contrast, the European Court of Justice tends to refer to the right to data protection if the threat results from the storage and later use of the data retained rather than from the collection per se.[537]

(b) The answer depends on the type of threat posed

Indeed, the preceding decisions do not definitely clarify under which circumstance the reference to further fundamental rights should be related to

532 See ECJ C-293/12 and C-594/12 cip. 37 referring to Opinion of Advocate General Cruz Villalón delivered on 12 December 2013 on Case C-293/12, cip. 52.

533 See above under point C. I. 3. c) aa) (2) (b) Protection against collection, storage, and subsequent risk of abuse.

534 See Opinion of Advocate General Cruz Villalón delivered on 12 December 2013 on Case C-293/12, cip. 59.

535 See ibid., cip. 65.

536 See ibid., cip. 52.

537 See above under point C. I. 3. c) aa) (2) (b) Protection against collection, storage, and subsequent risk of abuse.

Article 7 and to Article 8 ECFR. However, the idea of referring privacy and/or data protection to further areas of social life protected by other fundamental rights already became apparent in an earlier case, which was decided before the European Charter of Fundamental Rights came into force. Thus, at the time of this decision, i.e. the case of "*Rechnungshof vs. ORF*", the European Court of Justice still decided on the grounds of the European Convention on Human Rights. It was thus still unclear whether the European Court of Justice would refer to other fundamental rights under the angle of the right to private life protected by Article 7 ECFR or the right to data protection under Article 8 ECHR.

> In this case, an Austrian law obliged institutions subject to the control of the Austrian Court of Audit to inform the Court of the salaries and pensions of employees that superseded a certain amount. Several institutions denied the information or provided the information but without personal data such as the names of the employees concerned. The Court of Audit insisted in receiving all information required and, as a consequence, brought an action before the Austrian Constitutional Court which finally stayed the proceedings asking the European Court of Justice whether the duty of information provided for by the Austrian law interfered with Community law, in particular, with Article 8 ECHR.[538]

Before treating the hypothetical question about the fundamental rights angle possibly chosen by the European Court of Justice if the European Charter of Fundamental Rights had already been in force, it is necessary to examine, in more detail, the Court's reasoning in the case. Referring, here again, to the decisions "*Amann vs. Switzerland*" and "*Rotaru vs. Romania*" decided by the European Court of Human Rights, the European Court of Justice stated: "First of all, the collection of data by name relating to an individual's professional income, with a view to communicating it to third parties, falls within the scope of Article 8 of the Convention." Subsequently, the Court differentiated, pursuant to the context in which the data was processed, stressing that "while the mere recording by an employer of data by name relating to the remuneration paid to his employees cannot as such constitute an interference with private life, the communication of that data to third parties, in the present case a public authority, infringes the right of the persons concerned to respect for private life, whatever the subsequent use of the information thus communicated, and constitutes an interference

538 See ECJ C-465/00, C-138/01 and C-139/01 (Rechnungshof vs. ORF), cip. 3, 18 to 21, and 48.

within the meaning of Article 8 of the Convention."[539] Examining the intensity of the infringement, the Court took into consideration that the individuals concerned by the disclosure of the information required "may suffer harm as a result of the negative effects of the publicity attached to their income from employment, in particular on their prospects of being given employment by other undertakings, whether in Austria or elsewhere, which are not subject to control by the Rechnungshof."[540] The Court concluded from this that the referring Austrian Constitutional Court had to examine whether not only the disclosure of the salaries and pensions exceeding the certain thresholds defined by the Austrian law, but also the names of the employees concerned, is really necessary and appropriate in order to meet the aim of the law in question.[541]

In conclusion, the European Court of Justice did not consider each act of data treatment as legally relevant. The collection and processing of personal data by the employer for purposes of payroll accounting did not amount to a harm under Article 8 ECHR. In contrast, the transfer of that data for the purpose of its publication did.[542] The decision is interesting, compared with the decisions developed by the European Court of Human Rights: While its conclusion was in line with the concept of protection developed by the European Court of Human Rights, its reasoning was different. Both Courts principally consider that the publication of personal data infringes the right to private life of the individuals concerned.[543] However, if the European Court of Human Rights had affirmed a violation of the right to private life, it did not examine whether or not there is an additional violation of another human right.[544] In contrast to this approach, the European Court of Justice also took, at least implicitly, other fundamental rights into account. The court considered that the publication of the individual' salaries in relation to their names could have negative effects on

539 See ECJ C-465/00, C-138/01 and C-139/01 cip. 73 and 74.

540 See ECJ C-465/00, C-138/01 and C-139/01, cip. 89.

541 See ECJ C-465/00, C-138/01 and C-139/01, cip. 90.

542 See ECJ C-465/00, C-138/01 and C-139/01 cip. 73 and 74.

543 See, on behalf of the European Court of Justice, also ECJ C-92/09 and C-93/09 cip. 58; on behalf of the European Court of Human Rights, ECtHR, Case of Peck vs. the United Kingdom from 28 January 2003 (application no. 44647/98), cip. 61.

544 Cf. ECtHR, Case of Gillan and Quinton vs. the United Kingdom from 12 January 2010 (application no. 4158/05), cip. 88 to 90.

their chances of being given employment by other undertakings.[545] Indeed, in the case of "*Rotaru vs. Romania*", the European Court of Human Rights also considered that the 'systematic and permanent storage' of personal data falls under Article 8 ECHR especially if the "information concerns a person's distant past (…) has been declared false and is likely to injure *the applicants reputation* (underlining by the author)."[546] However, the individual's reputation rather belongs to the individual's 'psychological or social integrity' protected by Article 8 ECHR than to another fundamental right. In contrast, the individual's chances of 'being employed by an other undertaking' rather fall under a fundamental right related to work. Indeed, when the European Court of Justice decided on the case of "*Rechnungshof vs. ORF*", the European Charter of Fundamental Rights was not yet in force. However, the Charter already existed as a draft.[547] In light of this, it appears reasonable that the European Court of Justice thought, at least, about the freedom to choose an occupation and the right to engage in work provided for by Article 15 ECFR.

Presupposing that the European Charter of Fundamental Rights had already been in force, these considerations may allow the following hypothetical analysis: The fact that the Court considered the later usage of the information, and not the data collection, as legally relevant, principally speaks in favor of Article 8 ECFR that provides the instrument for protection for the right to work. Instead, in favor of the right to private life, it can be stressed that the publication of information already leads to the risk for the individual's right to engage in work. In this instance, the Court usually considers the publication as an infringement of the right to private life under Article 7 ECFR in combination with Article 8 ECFR. Therefore, it is also possible that the European Court of Justice had discussed the freedom to find an occupation protected by Article 15 ECFR in relation to both rights to data protection and to private life.[548] In any case, the essential point here is that the concept of referring to the right to engage in work in

545 See ECJ C-465/00, C-138/01 and C-139/01, cip. 89.

546 See ECtHR, Case of Rotaru vs. Romania from 4 May 2000 (application no. 28341/95), cip. 43 and 44.

547 The decision was ruled on 20th May 2003, while the proclamation of the Charter of Fundamental Rights was in 2000, retrieved from http://ec.europa.eu/justice/fundamental-rights/charter/index_en.htm.

548 Cf. Tzanou, Data protection as a fundamental right next to privacy? 'Reconstructing' a not so new right, pp. 94 and 95.

order to examine the effects of the data processing on the individual concerned can easily be transferred to further fundamental rights of freedom or equality.[549]

(4) Protection in (semi)-public spheres irrespective of 'reasonable expectations'?

Another difference between the decisions of the European Court of Justice and the European Court of Human Rights concerns the mechanism of the individual's "reasonable expectations" when determining the scope of protection of the fundamental rights. This mechanism was already mentioned, briefly, with respect to the case of "*Mr. González vs. Google Spain*".[550] By conducting a thought experiment, the following question was raised: whether the European Court of Human Rights would have come to the same or a different result as the European Court of Justice if it had referred to Mr. González' "reasonable expectations". This decision was based on both the right to private life and the right to data protection under Articles 7 and 8 ECFR. The same thought experiment conducted in "*González vs. Google Spain*" will now be also be transcribed in the three following cases of "*Telekom vs. Germany*", "*SABAM vs. Scarlet*", and "*SABAM vs. Netlog*" where personal data was also already published, at least, in (semi)-public spheres. In these cases, the European Court of Justice referred only to Article 8 ECFR.[551]

In the case of "*Telekom vs. Germany*", the European Court of Justice does not explain why it refers only to the right to data protection under Article 8 ECFR. One reason might be that the personal data in question was already made publically available so that the second publication of the personal data simply in another directory did not reveal any more aspects

549 Cf. Britz, Europeanisation of Data Protection Provided for by Fundamental Rights?, p. 11; De Hert and Gutwirth, Data Protection in the Case Law of Strasbourg and Luxemburg: Constitutionalisation in Action, p. 44.

550 See above under point C. I. c) aa) (2) (a) Protection against first publication and profiles.

551 See the facts of these cases above under point C.I. 1. b) aa) (2) (b) The right to data protection under Article 8 ECFR and/or the right to private life under Article 7 ECFR.

of the individual's private life.[552] Another reason might be that the decision depended on the individual's consent, which is explicitly foreseen under Article 8 ECFR, and not under Article 7 ECFR. Indeed, in the subsequent cases of "*SABAM vs. Scarlet*" and "*SABAM vs. Netlog*", the Court equally referred only to Article 8 ECFR even if, here, the consent of the individuals did not play a role. Therefore, regarding the case of "*Telekom vs. Germany*", the reason might be that the Court implicitly considered that the personal data identifying the individuals concerned was already public, at least, within the sharing communities, so that the filtering of the data did not reveal information of their private life.

If we were to suppose that this consideration is correct, the decisions in "*SABAM vs. Scarlet*" and "*SABAM vs. Netlog*" appear to deviate from the principles developed by the European Court of Human Rights. The European Court of Human Rights usually refers, if the data is collected in public spheres, to the individual's "reasonable expectations". If the data controller reveals its real purpose of the processing, the individual concerned is principally able to avoid the processing for this purpose by not entering the sphere where the data is collected: The purpose recognizable for the individual concerned frames his or her "reasonable expectations".[553] In contrast, the European Court of Justice does not refer, so far, to the individual's "reasonable expectations". This observation is interesting in light of the same thought experiment as conducted with respect to the decision of "*Mr. González vs. Google Spain*": In the cases "*SABAM vs. Scarlet*" and "*SABAM vs. Netlog*", the filtering systems would probably not infringe the users' right to private life under Article 8 ECHR if the Internet access provider and the social network had informed them of the processing and further usage of the data through these systems. This information would thus have framed their expectations. Indeed, such an approach would probably have far reaching effects for the users and even for the Internet Society as a whole. If just the information about the existence and purpose of the filtering system excluded an infringement of the fundamental right,

552 Cf. Opinion of Advocate General Cruz Villalón delivered on 12 December 2013 on Case C-293/12, cip. 65.

553 Cf. above under point C. I. 3. b) cc) Particular reference to the individual's "reasonable expectations"; cf. Kokott and Sobotta, The distinction between privacy and data protection in the jurisprudence of the CJEU and the ECtHR, p. 227, who argue, in a similar way, with respect to the decision of "González vs. Google Spain".

most Internet access providers and social networks would likely start to filter the information in order to avoid damage claims by copyright holders for the copyright infringements conducted by the users.[554] Therefore, potentially the European Court of Justice had the same reasoning as the German Constitutional Court in mind, considering a negative impact on the users 'becoming an object of copyright enforcement which adds to their general risk of being unreasonably suspected'.[555]

Suppose that all Internet access and social network providers install such systems, it might, furthermore, be arguable whether or not the users really had a choice of avoiding the treatment of 'their' data by these systems. Indeed, in light of the reasoning given by European Court of Human Rights in "*Gillan and Quinton vs. The United Kingdom*", a rather liberal approach has been applied. In this case, the Court considered, as stressed before, that the individuals concerned by the airplane access control could avoid this by choosing not to travel by plane.[556] Given this, Internet users equally have a choice of not using Internet access services or social networks, respectively, or, at least, of not sharing content through these services. Like air travellers who could choose to travel by train or by boat, Internet users could use, instead, classic means of communications such as postal services. The European Court of Justice might have foreseen the far-reaching consequences. If the pure information about the filtering systems excluded an infringement of the Internet users' "reasonable expectations" and, consequently, their fundamental right to data protection, there would be no protection against these surveillance measures, and the risk of being unreasonably suspected.

It might be for this reason why the European Court of Justice does not refer, so far, to the "reasonable expectations"-mechanism determining the scope of protection of the right to data protection of Article 8 ECFR. In the case of "*Mr. González vs. Google Spain*" the same thought experiment was applied. However, the European Court of Justice had the chance to

554 Cf. Rouvroy and Poullet, The Right to Informational Self-Determination and the Value of Self-Development: Reassessing the Importance of Privacy for Democracy, p. 48.

555 Cf. BVerfG, 3rd of March 2004, 1 BvR 2378/98 (Big Eavesdropping Operation), cip. 227; BVerfG, 4th of April 2006, 1 BvR 518/02 (Dragnet Investigation), cip. 103.

556 See ECtHR, Case of Gillan and Quinton vs. the United Kingdom from 12 January 2010 (application no. 4158/05), cip. 65.

circumvent the question on Mr. González' "reasonable expectations" – or other individuals who must expect, at least today, that almost everything is re-published on the Internet. The Court was able to avoid this question by referring to the direct impact on the individual concerned; it clearly differentiated between the effects of the publication of the articles, as such, and the fact that they can be found by means of an Internet search engine. Since the latter effects can be even worse for the claimant than the publication of the articles per se, the Court makes it clear that Article 7 ECFR particularly protects against such profiling, even if the information was known before.[557] In contrast, in the cases of "*Telekom vs. Germany*", "*SABAM vs. Scarlet*", and "*SABAM vs. Netlog*", the Court did not refer to such an impact of data processing on the individuals concerned – and probably could not because the filtering per se does not constitute a profile and has no comparable impact – but to the right to data protection, only. Since all these cases related, at least, to situations in semi-public-spheres, the question is why the European Court of Justice did not refer to the users' "reasonable expectations". The reasons might be that the application of this mechanism would have far too reaching effects on the scope of protection of the fundamental right to data protection overall. Even if it had been possible to deny such expectations in the present cases, the pure reference to this mechanism principally opens a floodgate for legitimizing the processing of personal data in the future: The pure information about the filtering systems can 'frame' the individuals' "reasonable expectations".[558] The Court therefore appears to have used the opportunity to elaborate on the right to data protection as a fundamental right distinctive to the right to private life of Article 8 ECHR and, consequently, to Article 7 ECFR.

(5) Going beyond the requirement of consent provided for under Article 8 ECHR

With respect to the individual's consent, the decision of "*Telekom vs. Germany*" reveals another and, so far, final difference to the concept applied

557 See ECJ C-131/12 cip. 87.

558 Cf. Rouvroy and Poullet, The Right to Informational Self-Determination and the Value of Self-Development: Reassessing the Importance of Privacy for Democracy, p. 48.

by the European Court of Human Rights. As set out previously, the referring national court asked the European Court of Justice to consider whether the ePrivacy Directive hindered the defendant from transferring personal data for the purpose of, again, publishing it in another directory. The reason for this doubt was that the Defendant lacked the individuals' explicit consent for the transfer and second publication.[559] In order to answer this question, the European Court of Justice referred only to Article 8 ECFR and affirmed, implicitly, here again, that the nature of the customers' names and telephone numbers were considered as personal data.[560]

Referring exclusively to Article 8 ECFR, the Court examined, in more detail, the purpose that essentially determined the extent and function of the individual's consent. The Court stated that "where a subscriber has consented to the passing of his personal data to a given undertaking with a view to their publication in a public directory of that undertaking, the passing of the same data to another undertaking intending to publish a public directory without renewed consent having been obtained from that subscriber is not capable of substantively impairing the right to protection of personal data, as recognized in Article 8 of the Charter."[561] The Court also clarified what requirements were needed for the information to be provided for by the private company. It must inform, "before the first inclusion of the data in the public directory, of the purpose of that directory and of the fact that those data will may be communicated to another telephone service provider and that it is guaranteed that those data will not, once passed on, be used for purposes other than those for which they were collected with a view to their first publication."[562]

Even if this decision principally applies the logic of the European Court of Human Rights, it seems to refine the requirement of purpose specification in one aspect: Principally, the European Court of Human Rights considers an un-consented publication of personal data as an infringement of Article 8 ECHR because it usually interferes with the "reasonable expectation" of the individual concerned. However, the moment when the data

559 See ECJ C-543/09 cip. 19,20, and 27, and see above the further facts of this case under point C. I. 1. b) aa) (2) (b) The right to data protection under Article 8 ECFR and/or the right to private life under Article 7 ECFR.

560 See ECJ C-543/09 cip. 49 to 54.

561 See ECJ C-543/09 cip. 66.

562 See ECJ C-543/09 cip. 66 and 67.

controller communicates the purpose to the individual, this information frames his or her expectation of how the data will be used and, as a consequence, does not infringe his or her right to private life. In this regard, it should be stressed that the pure information about the purpose already excludes an interference with the individual's expectation. The individual must not give his or her consent in a certain form. It is sufficient that he or she has an initial choice of avoiding how the data will be treated and the possibility to refuse the same.[563] However, the European Court of Justice goes one step beyond this. In the Court's judgment, it is not only necessary to inform the individual concerned about the concrete purpose but also 'of the fact (…) that it is guaranteed that those data will not, once passed on, be used for purposes other than those for which they were collected'. Thus, while the European Court of Human Rights only requires that the data should not be factually used at a later stage, for other purposes, the European Court of Justice requires that this fact must be explicitly stated in the initial information provided to the individual. Whether this statement means that the treatment of data infringes the right to data protection under Article 8 ECFR, if the information only does inform the individual about the positive purposes, but not of the fact that it is guaranteed that the data is not used for further purposes, must, so far, remain open.

563 Cf., on the one hand, under point C. I. 3 b) dd) "Consent: are individuals given a choice to avoid the processing altogether?", as well as ECtHR, Case of Gillan and Quinton vs. the United Kingdom from 12 January 2010 (application no. 4158/05), cip. 87; ECtHR, Case of Rotaru vs. Romania from 4 May 2000 (application no. 28341/95), cip. 46; Case of Leander vs. Sweden from 26 March 1987 (application no. 9248/81), cip. 48; Case of Kopp vs. Switzerland from 25 March 1998 (application no. 13/1997/797/1000), cip. 53; Case of Amann vs. Switzerland from 16 February 2000 (application no. 27798/95), cip. 69; and, on the other hand, Article 2 lit. h of the Data Protection Directive stating that "'the data subject's consent shall mean any freely given specific and informed indication of his whishes by which the data subject signifies his agreement to personal data relating to him being processed" and, finally, § 13 sect. 2 of the German Telemedia Law that states that the consent must be given, at least, in electronic form.

bb) Interim conclusion: Article 8 ECFR as a regulation instrument?

In conclusion, it became apparent that the European Court of Justice does not strictly apply the principles developed by the European Court of Human Rights with respect to Article 8 ECHR, but instead has started to elaborate on the particularities of the concept of protection provided for by Article 7 and Article 8 ECFR.

(1) Location of protection instruments under Article 8 ECFR

One important difference is that the European Court of Justice discusses 'effective protection of the data retained against the risk of abuse and against any unlawful access and use of that data', not with respect to Article 7 ECFR protecting, correspondingly to Article 8 ECHR, the right to private life but in the new right to data protection provided for by Article 8 ECFR.[564] The decisions developed by the European Court of Human Rights equally foresees such safeguards against abuse by further usage of the data.[565] However, this re-location is not a substantive further development regarding the concept of protection provided for by Article 8 ECHR, but rather a formal change. With respect to the publication of personal data, it essentially applies the principles developed by the European Court of Human Rights.[566] For example, just like the publication of an individual's name and salary interferes with Article 8 ECHR so does, after the European Charter of Fundamental Rights has come to force, the publication of an individual's name and the amount of funding received from the State interfere with Article 7 in combination with Article 8 ECFR.[567] However, when it comes to the question of the extent of the consent limiting a protection against the publication, the European Court of Justice only refers to Article 8 ECFR. According to these decisions, Article 8 ECFR appears

564 See ECJ C-293/12 and C-594/12 cip. 66.

565 See, for example, ECtHR, Case of Z. vs. Finland from 25 February 1997 (application no. 22009/93), cip 95; ECtHR, Case of M.S. vs. Sweden from 27 August 1997 (74/1996/693/885), cip. 41.

566 See above under point C. I. 3. b) cc) (3) 'Data relating to private or public matters', 'limited use' and or 'made available to the general public'.

567 See, regarding the first case, ECJ C-465/00, C-138/01 and C-139/01 (Rechnungshof vs. ORF), and with respect to the second case, ECJ C-92/09 and C-93/09 (Schecke vs. Land Hessen).

to provide for regulation instruments that are necessary in order to protect, at least, the right to private life under Article 7 ECFR.[568]

(2) Protection going beyond Article 8 ECHR

However, this mediating function of the right to data protection of Article 8 ECFR does not mean that its level of protection would be lower than that of the right to private life under Article 8 ECHR. In contrast, with respect to the individual's "reasonable expectations", the European Court of Justice appears, so far, to not apply the principles developed by the European Court of Human Rights under Article 8 ECHR. In the cases of "*SABAM vs. Scarlet*" and "*SABAM vs. Netlog*", the European Court of Justice confirmed that there was an infringement of the right to data protection under Article 8 ECFR, albeit providers of the Internet access or social network, respectively, would be able, in the future, to inform their users about the filtering systems and, though, frame the users' "reasonable expectations". The Court might have foreseen the negative effects in the future for the Internet Society that the introduction of the "reasonable expectations"-mechanism into the concept of protection of Article 8 ECFR would have caused. This mechanism is principally able to open the floodgates for surveillance measures essentially making Internet users, in terms of the German Constitutional Court, 'an object of surveillance that adds to their general risk of being unreasonably suspected'.[569] The European Court of Justice might therefore have avoided referring to the individuals' "reasonable expectations". Similarly, in the case of "*Mr. González vs. Google Spain*", the Court did not explicitly or, at least, not precisely elaborate on the function of the requirement of purpose specification provided for by Article 8 ECFR. It might have implicitly considered that Mr. González could not reasonably expect that Internet search engines will once make use of the information initially published about him in newspa-

568 See above under point C. I. 3. c) aa) (2) (b) Protection against collection, storage, and subsequent risk of abuse, referring, for example, to ECJ C-293/12 and C-594/12 cip. 53.

569 Cf. BVerfG, 3rd of March 2004, 1 BvR 2378/98 (Big Eavesdropping Operation), cip. 227; BVerfG, 4th of April 2006, 1 BvR 518/02 (Dragnet Investigation), cip. 103, and see above under point C. I. 2. d) aa) (2) The proportionality test also takes the use of data at a later stage into account.

pers. However, it is arguable that the Court would deny protection only because individuals today can expect the profiling of information by Internet search engines. In contrast, in this case, the Court appears to apply a different approach referring to the individual's 'social and/or psychological integrity' protected by Article 7 ECFR and using the principle of purpose limitation provided for by Article 8 ECFR in order to evaluate the infringement of the right to private life and the justification from a time perspective.

These differences between the concept of protection under Article 8 ECHR and under Article 7 and 8 ECFR do not interfere with Article 52 sect. 3 ECFR. Article 52 section 3 ECFR states, as stressed before, that this "provision shall not prevent Union law providing more extensive protection." Following the explanations of the European Charter of Fundamental Rights, the European Court of Justice therefore appears to apply the principles of the European Court of Human Rights when interpreting the corresponding right to private life but elaborates further on the concept of protection under Article 8 ECFR which is only "based on (...) Article 8 of the ECHR".[570]

This development leads to a more extensive protection and becomes particularly apparent if the regulation instruments provided for by Article 8 ECFR serves not only to protect the right to private life of Article 7 ECFR, but also the other fundamental rights to freedom and non-discrimination. This leads to the last important difference between the concept of protection under Article 8 ECHR and that provided for by Article 7 and 8 ECFR. In contrast to the European Court of Human Rights, the European Court of Justice also takes other fundamental rights into account. In the case of "*Rechnungshof vs. ORF*", it considers the negative effects for the individuals concerned by the publication of their salaries with respect to the risk of 'being employed by an other undertaking'. Since the European Charter of Fundamental Rights only existed, at the time of this decision, as a draft, the European Court of Justice appears to have, at least, thought about the freedom to choose an occupation and the right to engage in work under Article 15 ECFR. In contrast, during the case of "*Digital Rights vs. Ireland*" the Charter of Fundamental Rights was already in force. In this case, the court explicitly referred to the right to freedom and expression

570 See Explanations of the European Charter of Fundamental Rights, 2007/C 303/02; Burgkardt, ibid., p. 348, with further references.

under Article 11 ECFR. The Court considered the collection and storage of the telecommunication data is likely to lead to a bias in communication. Indeed, the Court took these effects into account in order to determine the intensity of the infringement of the right to private life under Article 7 and not to orient the protection instruments provided for by Article 8 ECFR toward the substantial guarantees endangered by the later usage of the data. However, the reason likely is that the treatment of personal data in question essentially consisted in the collection and not the later usage of the data. In contrast, in the case of "*Schrems vs. Facebook*", the European Court of Justice considered that the rights under Article 8 sect. 1 and 3 ECFR also serve to "lodge (…) a claim for the purpose of protecting their fundamental rights" and, in particular, "the fundamental right to effective judicial protection, as enshrined in Article 47 of the Charter."[571] Whether the European Court of Justice discusses further fundamental rights in relation to the right to private life under Article 7 ECFR or the right to data protection under Article 8 ECFR appears, thus, to depend on the type of threat caused by the data processing.[572]

(3) Remaining uncertainty about the interplay between Article 7 and 8 ECFR

In light of these decisions, there is indeed a tendency by the European Court of Justice to differentiate between Article 7 and Article 8 in the following way: while Article 8 ECFR, rather, provides regulation instruments for the treatment of personal data, the right to private life provides protection for a more substantial guarantee. This becomes, for example, apparent in the case of "*Digital Rights vs. Ireland*" where it states that the Data Retention Directive offended "does not provide for sufficient safeguards (…) to ensure effective protection (…) against the risk of abuse and against any unlawful access and use of that data"[573] and that Article 8 ECFR is, in this regard, "especially important for"[574] the right to private life in Article

571 See ECJ C-362/14 (Schrems vs. Facebook), cip. 56, 58, and 95.

572 See above under point C. I. 3. c) aa) (3) (b) The answer depends on the type of threat posed.

573 See ECJ C-293/12 and C-594/12 cip. 66, Cf. also ECJ C- 92/09 and C-93/09 cip. 52 as well as ECJ C-468/10 and C-469/10, cip. 41.

574 See ECJ C-293/12 and C-594/12 cip. 53.

7 ECFR. However, the Court does not clarify what is actually threatened. It only refers to the causes of threat, i.e. 'unlawful access and use of (…) data'. The Court only states that Article 8 ECFR is "especially important for"[575] the right to private life in Article 7 ECFR. Its precise functioning with respect to this right remains unclear.

The problem of such an unclear concept of protection becomes obvious in the case of "*González vs. Google Spain*". The European Court of Justice affirmed Mr. González' right to require Google Spain to delist him from the search results because the right to private life and to data protection "override, as a rule, not only the economic interest of the operator of the search engine but also the interest of the general public in finding that information."[576] The Court considered that this might exceptionally not be the case "if it appeared, for particular reasons, such as the role played by the data subject in public life, that the interference with his fundamental rights is justified by the preponderant interest of the general public in having (…) access to the information in question."[577] The result of this reasoning is that the European Court of Justice provides, by tying into its definition of personal data in both Articles 7 and 8 ECFR, the individual concerned a rather comprehensive right to control the social interaction that others have with him or her.[578] If the relationship of rule and exception developed by the European Court of Justice in the case of "*González vs. Google Spain*" generally applies – 'as a rule' – to any other situation where personal data is treated, the extent of such a right risks conflicting with the often-repeated statement of the European Court of Justice that this right "is not an absolute right but must be considered in relation to its function in society."[579]

One technical reason for this conflict is that the European Court of Justice does not define, unlike the European Court of Human Rights, the scope of protection on a case-by-case basis. Instead, it sets out a general definition, referring to the term "personal data", for both Articles 7 and 8 ECHR. This difference has far-reaching consequences on the scopes:

575 See ECJ C-293/12 and C-594/12 cip. 53.

576 See ECJ C-131/12, cip. 97.

577 See ECJ C-131/12, cip. 97.

578 See v. Grafenstein and Schulz, The right to be forgotten in data protection law: a search for the concept of protection, pp. 262 to 264; cf. Grimm, Data protection before its refinement, p. 588.

579 See, for example, ECJ C-92/02 and C-93/09, cip. 48.

While the European Court of Human Rights is principally free, based on its case-by-case approach, to deny or affirm protection referring to certain type of cases, the deductive method of the European Court of Justice leads to the situation that any processing of personal data generally falls under the scope of protection.[580]

cc) Referring to substantial guarantees as method of interpreting fundamental rights in order to avoid a scope of protection that is too broad and/or too vague

A potential solution for this conflict might be not to focus on the term 'personal data' as the only criteria for determining the scope of protection of both fundamental rights, but on their substantial guarantees. In order to explain this idea, it is necessary to illustrate in more detail how the scope of protection of a fundamental right can be constructed.

Usually, the definition of the scope of protection has two functions. First, the definition determines the threshold of constitutional protection. Judicial courts defining the scope of protection therefore dispose of a mechanism in order to decide whether fundamental rights protect individuals against certain acts of others, be it by the State or private parties, or not. The individual concerned can claim protection against it only if a certain act falls under the scope of a fundamental right. Secondly, the scope of protection determines which fundamental right is applicable in a particular case. This second issue is paramount with respect to Articles 7 and 8 ECFR. The European Court of Justice defines by commonly referring to the term 'personal data', both rights under the same scope of protection. This raises the question of how to distinguish these fundamental rights from each other. The approach referring to a substantial guarantee provided for by fundamental rights provides an alternative method of distinguishing fundamental rights. It is more normative than the method of defining the scope pursuant to certain ontological categories. While the latter usually refers to pre-known phenomena as so-called objects of protection, such as 'family', 'privacy' or 'personal data', the method falls short if the object of protection is too broad or too vague. The object of

580 See above under point C. I. 3. c) aa) (1) General definition of the term 'personal data' under Article 7 and 8 ECFR instead of case-by-case approach.

protection of personal data is, as such, a pure ontological category, both too broad and too vague.[581]

(1) The reason for why the scope is too vague: Difference between data and information

The term is too vague, at least, with respect to the legal effects of the treatment of data for the individual concerned. Legal scholars stress, in this regard, the difference between data and information.[582] In particular, the German scholars Albers and Britz conclude from this differentiation that it is not data as such, but the information retrieved from data which provides the basis for social interaction.[583] Thus, it is not the data but the information that leads, possibly, to an infringement of fundamental rights. While data are signs stored on physical carriers, be it analogously in the form of text, audio or video documents or as digital data retained in memory chips, they must, at first, be interpreted corresponding to the social context in order to make sense. The interpretation constitutes the information serving a basis for the social interaction, which possibly infringes the fundamental rights of the individual concerned by the treatment of 'his or her' data.[584]

Focusing on the German right to informational self-determination, Britz concludes from this: that a concept of protection directly referring to an individual's right to determine data guarantees what is not necessary; in contrast a concept of protection providing for an individual's right to determine information, is not possible. While basic rights can only guarantee

---

581 See v. Grafenstein and Schulz, ibid., pp. 254 to 257, with further references; cf. also Dietlein, The Doctrine of Duties of Protection of Basic Rights, pp. 78 to 81, stressing, amongst others, "property", "marriage and family", "free press" as well as "free research" as so-called institutional guarantees that cannot be pre-determined pursuant to ontological categories but must be normatively specified by the legislator.

582 See Pombriant, Data, Information and Knowledge – Transformation of data is key, pp. 97 and 98, who adds, furthermore, the third dimension of subjective "knowledge"; Albers, Treatment of personal information and data, cip. 8 to 15; Britz, Informational Self-Determination between Legal Doctrine and Constitutional Case Law, pp. 567 and 568.

583 See Albers, ibid.; Britz, ibid; Grimm, Data protection before its refinement, p. 586.

584 See Albers, ibid., cip. 8 to 15 and 68; Britz, ibid., pp. 567 and 568; Grimm, ibid., p. 586.

the determination of data by individuals because data as such does not depend on subjective interpretation, data has no direct relevance for constitutional protection. Consequently, an individual's right to dispose of data must mainly be considered as an instrument of protection for specific guarantees provided for (also) by other fundamental rights.[585]

Albers does not consider the German right to informational self-determination as purely instrumental. However, she particularly criticizes that the concept of protection, developed so far by the German Constitutional Court, focuses on data instead of information. This leads to a flood of protection instruments that have no substantive object of protection and therefore miss the actual threats caused by the use of context-related information.[586] Britz similarly argues that the German Constitutional Court had principally acknowledged the social pre-condition of information quoting the "*Decision on Population Census*" as:[587] "The individual does not have a right in the meaning of an absolute and boundless control about 'his or her' data; (conceptually), he or she rather has to be considered as a personality developing within the social community who depends on communication. Information constitutes, even if it is related to a person, a picture of social reality that cannot be exclusively contributed only to the person concerned. The Basic Law decided (…) that the field of tension between the individual and the community has to be solved in the way that the former is related and bound to the latter."[588] However, Britz considers that the German Court does not actually transpose this reasoning into its concept of protection. Instead, it falls short by affirming the fact that an individual's right to comprehensively determining the disclosure and, even more important, the usage of 'his or her' personal data.[589] The result of this inconsequent concept of protection is that the individual does not have certain chances of influencing the social interaction but can determine it in a rather comprehensive way.[590]

585 See Britz, ibid., pp. 567 and 568.
586 See Albers, ibid, cip. 68.
587 See Britz, Informational Self-Determination between Legal Doctrine and Constitutional Case Law, p. 566.
588 See BVerfG, 15th of December 1983, 1 BvR 209, 269, 362, 420, 440, 484/83 (Decision on Population Census), cip. 174.
589 See Britz, ibid., p. 567.
590 Cf. Rouvroy and Poullet, The Right to Informational Self-Determination and the Value of Self-Development: Reassessing the Importance of Privacy for Democracy, pp. 51 and 52.

These considerations comparably apply to the, so far, ambiguous concept of protection developed by the European Court of Justice. As stressed above, the European Court of Justice also acknowledges that the right to data protection under Article 8 ECFR 'is not an absolute right but must be considered in relation to its function in society'.[591] Despite this asseveration, it also essentially affirms, particularly in the case of "*González vs. Google Spain*", an individual's right to comprehensively control the social interaction based on the processing of personal data. The European Court of Justice is doing so by affirming that an individual who is concerned by the processing of 'his or her personal data' has a right, which supersedes, as a rule, the opposing fundamental rights of others using that data. Thus, so long as the term 'personal data' serves the only and common link in order to define the scopes of both the right to private life under Article 7 ECFR and the right to data protection under Article 8 ECFR, it is, at least, too vague to determine the scope of protection of both rights in light of its functioning in society.

(2) The reason for why the scope is too broad: Increasing digitization in society

The vagueness of the term 'personal data' additionally results, in combination with the ambiguous concept of protection, in an object of protection that is too broad. The reason for this is that both rights to private life and to data protection under Article 7 and 8 ECFR risk to substitute, in light of increasing digitization in society, the other fundamental rights more and more. The more digitization overlaps into different areas of social life, the broader the scope of application of both rights becomes.[592] In light of the broad definition of the term 'personal data' by the European Court of Justice, both rights 'concern any information relating to an identified or identifiable individual'.[593] Given this broad definition, and in light of the in-

---

591 See above under point C. I. 3. c) bb) (3) Remaining uncertainty about interplay between Article 7 and 8 ECFR, referring, for example, to ECJ C-92/02 and C-93/09, cip. 48.

592 See already v. Grafenstein and Schulz, The right to be forgotten in data protection law: a search for the concept of protection, p. 262.

593 See, for example, ECJ C-92/09 and C-93/09 cip. 52, ECJ C-70/10 cip. 51, and ECJ C-360/10 cip 49.

creasing digitization, Articles 7 and 8 ECFR apply more and more to any given social interaction. The reason for this is that the diversity of social interaction consists, more and more, on the processing of personal data. Before digitization, in contrast, different areas of social life were covered by the diversity of all fundamental rights. For example, in the "analogue world", concluding contracts in the private sector actually falls under the private autonomy guaranteed by fundamental rights. The fundamental right to the physical integrity of a person usually covers health related situations. The freedom to choose an occupation and the right to engage in work principally protects against actions, be it by the State or private parties, hampering the individual in conducting his or her work. Cases of discrimination are normally answered in light of the fundamental rights of non-discrimination.[594] Instead, in a digital world, the more digitization penetrates all these different areas of social life, the more comprehensively the rights to private life and to data protection apply, superseding the other fundamental rights.

(3) Advantages and challenges: 'Personal data' as legal link for a subjective right

However, the term 'personal data' as an essential link for legal regulation also has advantages. Information provides the basis for social interaction, not data, which possibly leads to an infringement of fundamental rights. Even if information provides a more direct link for legal instruments regulating informational social interaction, it cannot be the direct reference point of an individual's subjective right. Since information builds on data that must be interpreted pursuant to social contexts in order to make sense, the individual to whom the information is related cannot directly refer to it, at least, cannot determine it.[595] In contrast, linking the regulation instruments not to information, but to specific data enables an individual to directly enforce his or her subjective right: While the individual cannot determine interpretations of third parties by him or herself, he or she can in-

594 See, for example, Folz, Article 16 ECFR – Freedom to Conduct a Business, cip. 3, and Article 3 ECFR – Freedom to Integrity, cip. 1 to 3, and Article 15 ECFR – Freedom to Work, cip. 4, and Article 21 – Freedom to non-discrimination, cip. 1 to 5.

595 Cf. Albers, ibid., cip. 68.

deed determine the disclosure and use of data on which the information is built on.[596] In this thesis, this is the legal link that will be taken up in light of the explicit wording of Article 8 sect. 1 ECFR, which states: "Everyone has the right to the protection of personal data concerning him or her." Indeed, since it is not data, but information that possibly leads to harm or an infringement of fundamental rights, a "right to the protection of personal data" must be understood as just a certain legal link for regulating the use of information.[597] At this moment, indeed, the question again is how to avoid that the scope of application of such a protection instrument becomes too broad and vague.

With respect to the German right to informational self-determination, the legal scholar Albers therefore promotes a combination of an objective and a subjective regulatory approach: On a first level, the German general personality right shall mainly provide the necessary regulation instruments. These are: First, the objective requirement that data and information is only processed and used in an appropriate and transparent manner; second, an individual's guarantee that he or she is able being informed of the informational actions related to him or her; and third, an individual's guarantee that he or she can participate in the informational process, be it through a claim of cease and desist of certain usages of information, of deletion and rectification of certain information or positively influence the information. On a second level, all other German basic rights shall provide the scale determining the contexts for informational protection and, as a consequence, which kind of informational action and, consequently, which kind of informational protection is legally relevant.[598]

Britz builds upon Albers' approach proposing a compromise between the two-level concept by Albers and the more subjective approach applied by the German Constitutional Court. As mentioned previously, in order to avoid a scope of protection becoming too broad and vague, Britz advocates that the German right to informational self-determination should be considered, at least partly, as an accessory right, which provides for protection for the other "more specific" constitutional norms.[599] Indeed, the

596 Cf. Albers, Treatment of Personal Information and Data, cip. 11; as well as Hoffmann-Riem, Protection of the Confidentiality and Integrity of Information Technological Systems, p. 1010.
597 Cf. Britz, ibid., pp. 573 and 574.
598 See Albers, ibid., cip. 69 to 83.
599 See Britz, ibid., pp. 573 and 574.

German Constitutional Court actually seeks, already, to determine the right to informational self-determination by referring to other basic rights.[600] However, in Britz' opinion, the German Court does so only when balancing, as a last step of the proportionality assessment, the right with opposing constitutional positions. In contrast, Britz stresses the other basic rights should already determine its scope, thus, as a first step of the assessment.[601]

So far, this thesis does not decide for one or the other approach. Rather, this thesis seeks to illustrate different ways of how a broad and vague scope of protection, which results from a commingling of the phenomena and terms "data" and "information", could be avoided. In this regard, however, there is one aspect regarding Britz' concept that shall be clarified: Even if her considerations are principally correct, she however overlooks that the German Court does not only refer to other basic rights in its balancing exercise, but already before, as a second step of the proportionality assessment, when examining whether or not harm or an infringement exists.[602] Indeed, as was stressed before, the Court appears to be reluctant to narrow the scope, at this level. The ambiguity possibly results from the far-reaching effects that the indirect restriction of the scope – by narrowly defining harm or an infringement – has on the concept of protection. The moment where certain acts of usage of personal data do not fall under the scope of application, the Constitutional Court is not able to react to the same with its corresponding regulations.[603]

---

600 See above under point C. I. 2. d) Infringement by 'insight into personality' and 'particularity of state interest', and C. I. 2. e) aa) (2) The proportionality test also takes takes the use of data at a later stage into account.

601 See Britz, ibid., pp. 566 to 568 as well as 573 and 574.

602 See above under point C. I. 2. d) Infringement by 'insight into personality' and 'particularity of state interest'.

603 Cf. above under point C. I. 1. b) bb) (1) The 3-Step-Test: Assessing the defensive and protection function; v. Grafenstein and Schulz, The right to be forgotten in data protection law: a search for the concept of protection, pp. 254 to 257 with further references.

(4) Possible consequence: A legal scale provided for by all fundamental rights which determine the regulation instruments under Art. 8 ECFR

In conclusion, a concept of protection that refers to data, not to information, in order to provide for an individual's subjective right bears two risks: Either, it is too vague and broad and, therefore, inefficient; or, a narrow determination of which act constitutes a harm or an infringement restricts the scope and therefore fails, perhaps too early, in providing for protection at all. One solution for this conflict could be to open, first, the scope of application of the fundamental right to data protection at a very early stage. So far, the reference to the term 'personal data' indeed opens a broad and vague scope of protection. However, the other fundamental rights of privacy, freedom and non-discrimination could then determine. As a second step, which specific data protection instruments are necessary in order to efficiently protect against the threats for the provided substantial guarantees.[604]

Such a concept serves three advantages compared, at least, to the current concepts of protection: First, it focuses not only on the scope(s) per se which is, so far, mainly determined by the term 'personal data', but on the substantial guarantees allowing one more precisely to differentiate between fundamental rights. In this respect, it should be noted that the distinction between the guarantees help not only to see whether an individual's behavior is principally covered by the scope, but also whether it (e.g. a certain processing of personal data), conflicts with this guarantee and whether or, more precisely, under which conditions it might legitimately limit this fundamental right.[605] In light of this normative approach, the right to data protection under Article 8 ECFR could be considered as a regulation instrument serving to protect the substantial guarantees provided for by all the other fundamental rights. In this respect, Article 8 ECFR would not only serve to protect the guarantees to respect for private and family life, home and communications in Article 7 ECFR, but also substantial guarantees provided for by further fundamental rights. This protection function serving all fundamental rights could help avoid the scope of application being too vague and broad.

---

604 See v. Grafenstein and Schulz, ibid., pp. 260.

605 See v. Grafenstein and Schulz, ibid., pp. 254 and 255.

Second, such a concept of protection would avoid the situation where it provides either too much (i.e. ineffective and inefficient) or too little protection. As shown before, it would open the scope of protection at a very early stage but determine its specific protection instruments pursuant to the other fundamental rights. And third, if all fundamental rights provide a scale in order to determine the legal relevance of data processing, Article 8 ECFR is not exclusively linked to privacy.[606] Instead, the fundamental right to data protection can equally serve specific rights to freedom and non-discrimination. The fundamental right to data protection hence does not provide a right to informational self-determination with the result that the individual had a 'right to basically determine by him or herself about the disclosure and the usage of his or her personal data'[607]. It does not merely focus on the individual's consent as the main regulation instrument but provides for further regulation instrument for the treatment of personal data constituting a "heading of a set of rights and obligations and limitations to these which are put together as an elaborated system of checks and balances."[608]

In conclusion, such a concept of protection corresponds to the different contexts of social life that are endangered by a data treatment and correspondingly protected by the substantial guarantees provided for by all fundamental rights. Regarding Nissenbaum's context-based approach, all the fundamental rights could thus provide a normative scale in order to determine the context-relative informational norms.[609] And as a possible consequence, the diversity of all fundamental rights may also help determine the function of the principle of purpose limitation.

---

606 Cf. above under point C. I. 2. f) Interim conclusion: Conceptual link between 'privacy' and 'data processing'.

607 See BVerfG, 15th of December 1983, 1 BvR 209, 269, 362, 420, 440, 484/83 (Decision on Population Census), cip. 173; cf. equally BVerfG, 14th of July 1999, 1 BvR 2226/94 (Surveillance of Telecommunications), cip. 136 and BVerfG, 3rd of March 2004, 1 BvR 2378/98 (Big Eavesdropping Operation), cip. 132 and BVerfG, 4th of April 2006, 1 BvR 518/02 (Dragnet Investigation), cip. 64 and BVerfG, 13th June 2007, 1 BvR 1550/03 (Retrieval of Bank Account Master Data), cip. 63.

608 See Kranenborg, Article 8 – Protection of Personal Data, cip. 8.176.

609 See above under point B. III. 5. Values as a normative scale in order to determine the "contexts" and "purposes".

II. The requirement of purpose specification and its legal scale

The vague and broad nature of scope of protection of the fundamental right to private life under Article 7 ECFR and/or the fundamental right to data protection under Article 8 ECFR, which was, so far, considered from a theoretical point of view, becomes obvious, in practice, in relation to the requirement of purpose specification. As mentioned in the introduction of this thesis, private entities often have difficulties answering the question of how precisely they have to specify the purpose of their data processing. Neither the decisions of the European Court of Human Rights nor of the European Court of Justice provide reliable criteria, in order to answer this question, albeit the purpose plays a central role in secondary and ordinary data protection laws. Therefore, this sub-chapter will analyze how European secondary laws themselves specify purposes of data processing. It will also illustrate how the German legislator transposes the requirements of the European directives into national law. In light of the conceptual differences between European and German laws, the German provisions will then be compared to the concept of protection of the German right to informational self-determina-tion. The idea behind this is that the German legislator rather tied, perhaps, into the German concept of protection than that of Article 8 ECFR, since the latter was not yet as developed as the German right. In any case, the comparison will reveal several flaws in the current concepts of protection when applied to the requirement of purpose specification in the private sector. On the basis of these results, this sub-chapter concludes with refining the object and concept of protection of the fundamental right to data protection of Article 8 ECFR, with respect to the function of the requirement of purpose specification.

1. Main problem: Precision of purpose specification

The following sections will, firstly, illustrate the criteria provided for by the European Court of Human Rights and the European Court of Justice. So far, in fact, there are only few criteria that help determine the purpose. In light of this, it is necessary to examine which requirements are established by European secondary law and how, in particular, the Article 29 Data Protection Working Group interprets the same. The next chapter will examine how the German legislator transposed the requirements provided for by the European directives into German ordinary law. It will become apparent that the German discussion on how to interpret the German requirements refers less to European constitutional law than to the German right to informational self-determination. Therefore, the criteria developed by the German Constitutional Court in relation to purpose specification assists in providing a deeper understanding of the requirements discussed in German legal literature. However, in light of its comprehensive decisions, it might also provide a further source in order to develop criteria for the precision of purpose specification with respect to Articles 7 and 8 ECFR.

a) ECtHR and ECJ: Almost no criteria

The European Court of Human Rights does not explicitly deal with the issue of how precise the purpose needs to be in relation to the processing of data. The reason for this is that it does not explicitly require the controller to specify the purpose, but instead, examines the purpose imposed by the controller in order to evaluate an infringement under Article 8 ECHR.[610] In doing so, the range of purposes classified by the Court in order to undertake the evaluation is limited. The collection of data intruding into the individuals' privacy, as well as the purpose of publishing personal data, usually infringes Article 8 ECHR. With regard to the State, the Court also has confirmed that there will be an infringement of Article 8 ECHR if the data is 'systematically and permanently' stored. This is the case even if "it contained no sensitive information and had probably never been consulted".[611] However, the limited re-use of data, which was collected and stored for another limited purpose, usually does not infringe the scope of protection of Article 8 ECHR. The only exception to this rule is if the later use of data differs considerably from the supposed purpose interfering with the individual's 'reasonable expectation'. From a data controller's perspective, it might be clear enough how to avoid an infringement of Article 8 ECHR by not intruding in someone's privacy and not publishing 'his or her' personal data. In contrast, a data controller might have difficulties defining which purpose is limited and which one goes beyond an individual's 'reasonable expectation'. This might less be the case if the

610 See above the analysis under point C. I. 3. b) cc) Particular reference to the individual's "reasonable expectations".

611 See ECtHR, Case of P.G. and J.H. vs. The United Kingdom from 25 September 2001 (application no. 44787/98), cip. 57.

controller has, the moment that the data is collected, the intended use of that data already in mind. Instead, if the controller wants to re-use the data at a later stage, going beyond the initial purpose, the controller might have more difficulties in defining the criteria for its legitimate usage. Applying its case-by-case approach, the European Court of Human Rights does not provide more general criteria in order to determine which purposes and, correspondingly, which acts of usage interfere with the individual's right to private life.[612]

The European Court of Justice provides even fewer criteria. Similar to the European Court of Human Rights, the European Court of Justice considers the publication of personal data as infringing the right to private life provided for by Article 7 ECFR with respect to the right to data protection in Article 8 ECFR.[613] However, with particular view to the private sector, even if the Court examines, in the case of "*Telekom vs. Germany*", the purpose in more detail, it does actually not provide any criteria for determining the precision of the purpose in general. The Court stated that the data controller must inform, in essence, the individual about the publication of the data before its first inclusion in the public directory.[614] This case hence refers again only to a publication of the data. Comparably, in the case of "*Mr. González vs. Google Spain*", the Court did not precisely examine what the initial purpose of the newspaper publishing the articles and the later purpose of the Internet search engine were and why this resulted in an infringement of Mr. González' right to private life in Article 7 ECFR combined with Article 8 ECFR.[615]

With respect to the processing of personal data by the State, the European Court of Justice does also not elaborate on precise criteria in order to specify the purpose. In the case of "*Digital Rights vs. Ireland*", the Court examined whether or not the legislator of the Data Retention Directive met the requirement that: limitations of the right to data protection, with respect to the protection of the individuals' private life, must be limited to what is strictly necessary in order to reach the legislator's objective. In this

---

612 See above under point C. I. 3. b) ee) Conclusion: Assessment of ‚reasonable expectations' on a case-by-case basis.

613 See ECJ C-465/00, C-138/01 and C-139/01 (Rechnungshof vs. ORF), and ECJ C-92/09 and C-93/09 (Schecke vs. Land Hessen).

614 See ECJ C-543/09 cip. 66 and 67.

615 See above under point C. I. 3. c) aa) (2) (a) Protection against first publication and profiles.

regard, the Court simply criticized the following failures: first, the directive did not differentiate between the specific crimes in question; second, the directive did not limit the authorities obtaining access to the data, in light of their specific tasks; third, it did not require that a control mechanism be put in place prior to accessing the data, for example by the Court or another independent public authority. Finally, the directive did not provide any criteria in order to limit the period of time the data could be held that would be strictly necessary for the aim pursued in the case.[616] The Court referred to these considerations in the later case of "*Schrems vs. Ireland*" stating "that legislation is not limited to what is strictly necessary where it authorises, on a generalised basis, storage of all the personal data (…) without any differentiation, limitation or exception being made in the light of the objective pursued and without an objective criterion being laid down by which to determine the limits of the access of the public authorities to the data, and of its subsequent use, for purposes which are specific, strictly restricted and capable of justifying the interference which both access to that data and its use entail".[617] These considerations do not, in any detail, treat the issue of the degree of precision in which the State has to specify the purpose of the processing of data.

b) Requirements provided for by European secondary law

Irrespective of the few criteria provided for by the European Courts, European secondary law (i.e. the Data Protection Directive, the ePrivacy Directive, the Civil Rights Directive, and the upcoming General Data Protection Regulation) foresees a comprehensive system regulating data processing in the private sector, which circles around the purposes of the processing. This system serves several goals: The Data Protection Directive generally pursues, on the one hand, the free traffic of personal data in the European Single Market and, on the other hand, the protection of individuals in relation to the treatment of 'their personal data'.[618] The ePrivacy Directive establishes further requirements with respect to personal data processed by means of information and communication technologies (ICT), in particu-

616 See ECJ C-293/12 and C-594/12 cip. 56 to 64.

617 See ECJ C-362/14 (Schrems vs. Facebook), cip. 92 and 93.

618 Regarding the Data Protection Directive, Ehmann/Helfrich, EU Data Protection Directive, Introduction, cip. 4.

lar, Internet and electronic messaging services. The Civil Rights Directive finally amended several provisions of the ePrivacy Directive. It reacted to technological development, particularly, with respect to "new applications based on devices for data collection and identification, which could be contactless devices using radio frequencies" such as Radio Frequency Identification Devices (RFIDs).[619] Finally, the General Data Protection Regulation, which shall apply, pursuant to Article 99, from the 25th of May 2018, will substitute the Data Protection Directive and be directly applicable in all EU Member States.

Pursuant to the principles of these laws, the processing of personal data must apply certain principles and requirements for lawfulness within society. In particular, the data controller must apply the following two requirements together: first, that the processing must be either based on the individuals consent or on an authorizing law. The general prohibition to process personal data therefore applies not only to the public but also to the private sector.[620] Second, Article 6 sect. 1 lit. b of the Data Protection Directive and Article 5 sect. 1 lit. b of the General Data Protection Regulation requires that personal data must be "collected for specified, explicit and legitimate purposes". In the subsequent chapters, we will review; first, the role of this requirement within the current legal framework in relation to data protection; second, the criteria discussed in order to specify the purpose, and finally the purposes specified within the laws itself.

aa) Central role of purpose specification within the legal system

In relation to European Data Protection Law, the specification of the purpose plays a decisive role. Amongst several other factors, it determines the scope of application of the applicable laws, and which entity is legally responsible for applying the laws (i.e. who is the 'controller', and who is the 'processor').

619 See recital 56 of the Civil Rights Directive.

620 See, regarding Article 7 of the Data Protection Directive, Ehmann/Helfrich, ibid, Art. 7, cip. 1; Dammann/Simitis, EU Data Protection Directive, Art. 7, Explanations sect. 1, and regarding Article 6 GDPR, Härting, Data Protection Regulation: The new data protection law in operational practice, cip. 318.

(1) Scope of protection: 'Personal data'

The definition of the term 'personal data' plays an essential role because it determines the scope of application. Article 2 lit. a of the Data Protection Directive, and Article 4 sect. 1 of the General Data Protection Regulation, essentially define the term 'personal data' as "any information relating to an identified or identifiably natural person ('data subject'); an identifiable person is one who can be identified, directly or indirectly, in particular by reference to **an identifier such as a name,** an identification number**, location data, an online identifier** or to one or more factors specific to the physical, physiological, **genetic,** mental, economic, cultural or social identity (bold words added in the General Data Protection Regulation)".

(a) 'All the means reasonably likely to be used'

Recital 26 of the Data Protection Directive further clarifies that in order "to determine whether a person is identifiable, account should be taken of all the means likely reasonably to be used either by the controller or by any other person to identify the said person". In its recital 26, the General Data Protection Regulation ties into these considerations (sent. 3), and adds (sent. 4): "To ascertain whether means are reasonably likely to be used to identify the natural person, account should be taken of all objective factors, such as the costs of and the amount of time required for identification, taking into consideration the available technology at the time of the processing and technological developments."

(b) Example: IP addresses as 'personal data'?

One prominent example of this assessment concerns the question of whether IP addresses constitute personal data or not; the same question arises with respect to 'unique device identifiers' (UID or UDID), used for portable devices, and 'media access control' (MAC) addresses used for network technologies, such as Ethernet and Wifi.[621] In relation to IP addresses, the prevailing opinion considers static IP addresses as 'personal

621 See, for example, Schreibauer, Federal Data Protection Law and further Provisions, § 11 TMG, cip. 4.

data', as long as they relate to natural individuals. The reason for this is that the individuals behind the static addresses can always be identified by means of Who-Is search requests, for example on www.ripe.net. This opinion leads to the situation that IP addresses accessible on the new Internet protocol IPv 6 are automatically 'personal data' because, with IPv 6, each device receives one single address. In light of the sheer amount of addresses available through the implementation of IPv 6, in contrast to IPv 4, which provides for approximately 4.3 billion addresses, IPv 6 provides around 340 sextillion addresses[622] – critics argue that the relation of an IP address to a natural person becomes so complex that IP addresses of IPv 6 should be considered as anonymized data.[623] However, with respect to IPv 4, which is still mainly used, IP addresses are not statically but dynamically, that means only for a certain period of time, related to individuals or, in more precise words, to the devices used by individuals. Indeed, some legal scholars advocate a rather strict approach: As long as it is theoretically possible to identify the individual, IP addresses must be considered as 'personal data'. In contrast, other legal scholars argue that IP addresses can only be considered as 'personal data' if the data controller is able to identify itself the individual using the address.[624]

The European Court of Justice stated in the above-illustrated cases of "*SABAM vs. Scarlet*" and "*SABAM vs. Netlog*" that the IP addresses concerned did fall under Article 8 ECFR "because (they) allow those users to be precisely identified."[625] Some legal scholars conclude from this that the European Court of Justice generally considers all IP addresses as 'personal data'. In contrast, other legal scholars argue that the Court only affirmed the nature of IP addresses as 'personal data' because the providers of the Internet access and the social network had the registration data and could only therefore identify the individuals.[626] In light of this, the European Court of Justice had indeed not yet answered this question, explicitly – until the case of "*Breyer vs. Germany*".

622 See Federal Communications Commission: Internet Protocol Version 6: IPv 6 for Consumers.

623 See Schreibauer, ibid., cip. 5 with further references.

624 See Schreibauer, ibid., cip. 7 and 8, who summarizes the spectrum of opinions, with further references.

625 See ECJ C-70/10 cip. 51 and ECJ C-360/10 cip 49.

626 See Schreibauer, ibid., cip. 9 with further references.

(c) The case of "Breyer vs. Germany"

In the case of "*Breyer vs. Germany*", the entity processing the IP addresses could not identify the users itself. This decision therefore sheds further light on how the Court elaborates on the definition of the scope of application of the Data Protection Directive in light of the right to data protection under Article 8 ECFR.

> In this case, the referring German Civil Supreme Court asked the European Court of Justice whether IP addresses have to be considered as personal data within the meaning of the Data Protection Directive. Pursuant to the facts of the case, a public agency processed IP addresses of the users of its website. In particular, the agency recorded which IP addresses accessed the website at which time and date in order to guarantee not only the specific but also more general functionality of the website, for instance, in order to prosecute potential cyber attacks against the website in the case of denial-of-service attacks. As stressed before, the public agency providing the website could not identify the user behind the IP address by itself. For identifying the user, the agency had to combine the IP address with further data stored at and by the Internet service provider. The question of the referring German court therefore was whether the definition of "personal data" in the Data Protection Directive requires that the public agency itself is able to identify the user or whether it is sufficient that the agency can identify the user through the Internet service provider as a middle-man.[627]

Referring to recital 26 of the Data Protection Directive, the European Court of Justice affirms that additional information held by an internet service provider can be sufficient in order to identify the individual.[628] The Court affirmed, in particular, that the combination of that data is a 'reasonable means' because it is not "prohibited by law or practically impossible on account of the fact that it requires a disproportionate effort in terms of time, cost and man-power, so that the risk of identification appears in reality to be insignificant."[629] In this decision the Court explicitly refers to the General Advocate who has stated, in its opinion: "Just as recital 26 refers not to any means which may be used by the controller (in this case, the provider of services on the Internet), but only to those that it is likely 'reasonably' to use, the legislature must also be understood as referring to 'third parties' who, also in a reasonable manner, may be approached by a

627 See Opinion of Advocate General Campos Sánchez-Bordona, C-582/14, 12th of May 2016, cip. 1 to 10 as well as 79 and 80.

628 See ECJ C-582/14, cip. 40 to 44.

629 See ECJ C-582/14, cip. 46.

controller seeking to obtain additional data for the purpose of identification. This will not occur when contact with those third parties is, in fact, very costly in human and economic terms, or practically impossible or prohibited by law. Otherwise, as noted earlier, it would be virtually impossible to discriminate between the various means, since it would always be possible to imagine the hypothetical contingency of a third party who, no matter how inaccessible to the provider of services on the Internet, could — now or in the future — have additional relevant data to assist in the identification of a user."[630] Referring to these considerations, the European Court of Justice came, in the present case, to the conclusion "that, in particular, in the event of cyber attacks legal channels exist so that the online media services provider is able to contact the competent authority, so that the latter can take the steps necessary to obtain that information from the internet service provider and to bring criminal proceedings. Thus, it appears that the online media services provider has the means which may likely reasonably be used in order to identify the data subject, with the assistance of other persons, namely the competent authority and the internet service provider, on the basis of the IP addresses stored."[631]

In conclusion, this decision applies the same reasoning as considered by the European Commission which has stressed that the processing of the IP address is, in particular, reasonable because it was stored exactly for that purpose to identify the user, in the case of cyber attacks.[632] Thus, it would be contradictory not to consider the IP addresses as personal data, albeit they are collected for the purpose to identify the user. The purpose hence plays, here again, an essential role in order to ascertain whether the scope of protection applies or not. However, as the General Advocate correctly stressed, this case concerns a situation where an internet service provider is the middle-man. Thus, it does not refer to other situations where further individuals or entities might be able to identify the user.[633] How far these considerations can be transferred to further cases, in particular, in light of

---

630 See Opinion of Advocate General Campos Sánchez-Bordona, C-582/14, 12th of May 2016, cip. 68.

631 See ECJ C-582/14, cip. 47 and 48.

632 See Opinion of Advocate General Campos Sánchez-Bordona, C-582/14, 12th of May 2016, cip. 38.

633 See Opinion of Advocate General Campos Sánchez-Bordona, C-582/14, 12th of May 2016, cip. 63.

the upcoming General Data Protection Regulation must remain, so far, an open question.

(2) Liability for 'data processing': 'Controller' and 'processor'

In order to determine who is responsible for the data processing, the purpose also plays an essential role. In this regard, it must first be clarified what the term "data processing" means. Pursuant to Article 2 lit. b of the Data Protection Directive, the "'processing of personal data' (..) shall mean any operation or set of operations which is performed upon personal data **or sets of personal data**, whether or not by automatic means, such as collection, recording, organization, **structuring,** storage, adaptation, or alteration, retrieval, consultation, use, disclosure by transmission, dissemination or otherwise making available or combination, blocking (or **restriction**), erasure or destruction (bold words in brackets added or changed in Article 4 sect. 2 GDPR)". Some legal scholars believe that this definition covers as many acts of data processing as possible: For example, even the act of deletion of data or the mere reading of data by an individual falls under the scope of protection.[634]

In order to determine who is responsible for the processing, Article 2 lit. d of the Data Protection Directive, and Article 4 sect. 7 sent. 1 of the General Data Protection Regulation, define the 'controller' as "the natural or legal person, public authority, agency or any other body which alone or jointly with others determines the purposes and means of the processing of personal data". This definition implies a dynamic and non-linear understanding regarding the concept of data processing, which results in the situation that different controllers might be involved in one process.[635] In contrast to the "controller", a "processor" essentially is, pursuant to Article 2 lit. e of the Data Protection Directive and Article 4 sect. 8 of the General Data Protection Regulation, a "natural or legal person, public authority, agency or any other, body which processes personal data on behalf

---

634 See Ehmann/Helfrich, ibid., Art. 2, cip. 27 et seqq; Dammann/Simitis, EU Data Protection Directive, Art. 2 cip. 5 et seqq.

635 Cf. Ehmann/Ehrlich, ibid., cip. 39 et seqq.,; Dammann/Simitis, ibid., cip. 11 et seqq.; see also "Opinion 1/2010 on the concepts of 'controller' and 'processor' " by the Article 29 Data Protection Working Party, p. 12; also affirmed in Article 26 GDPR ('joint controllers').

of the controller." This definition implies several aspects: First, amongst other requirements, the controller must contractually bind the processor to its purpose of the data processing. The moment the processor determines itself the purposes and means, the processor becomes a controller and thus is more liable in relation to data protection compliance. This is decisive because even if the General Data Protection Regulation stipulates that the processor must adhere to several duties, in contrast to the Data Protection Directive, the liability is still much more extensive for the controller than for the processor.[636] For example, while the requirement to implement appropriate measures of security-by-design applies to both the controller and the processor, pursuant to Article 32 GDPR, the requirement to implement measures of data protection-by-design provided for by Article 24 GDPR applies to the controller, only.

In conclusion, the specification of the purpose plays an important role in order to determine the contractual powers of the processor and which legal requirements the controller and/or processor has to fulfill in order to protect the individual concerned by the data processing.

(3) Further legal provisions referring to the purpose

There are further requirements provided for by law, which also depend on the purpose. For example, the principles of data-minimisation and storage-limitation provided for by Article 6 lit. c and e of the Data Protection Directive and Article 5 sect. 1 lit. c and e, requires that personal data must be "adequate, relevant and not excessive in relation to the purposes for which they are ~~collected and further~~ processed" and "kept in a form which permits identification of data subjects for no longer than is necessary for the purposes ~~for which they were collected or for which they were collected or~~ for which they are ~~further~~ processed" (words crossed-out only mentioned in the directive).

The first principle means that the individual concerned must be able, before the data is collected about him or her, to determine whether the collection is relevant with respect to the purposes specified by the controller. From a formalistic point of view, legal scholars admit that the collection of data for the purpose of simply 'storing' it would actually be sufficiently

636 See Härting, ibid., cip. 577 to 584.

relevant. However, since these scholars also pre-suppose that the Data Protection Directive requires a strict purpose limitation, any later usage going beyond the storage would not be allowed.[637] Other scholars provide further considerations regarding the terms "adequate" and "excessive". For example, the data collected related to an individual's health or political views is, principally, not adequate in order to evaluate him or her as a potential employee; and therefore, more general, the processing of personal data in more detail than is necessary for the purpose is deemed excessive. The second principle adds a time dimension to the first: the moment when the purpose is fulfilled, the further storage of personal data is only allowed if it cannot be related to the individual in the first instance. While some legal scholars stress that this requires that the data gets completely anonymized[638], others consider that the Member States has to answer this question transposing the directive into national law.[639] In any case, Article 17 of the General Data Protection Regulation essentially builds upon this requirement and establishes an individual's right to have personal data deleted, amongst other factors, if the data is no longer necessary in relation to the purposes for which the data was collected or otherwise processed in the first place; this so-called right to be forgotten does not apply, for example, if the processing is necessary for exercising the freedom of expression. The European Court of Justice explicitly referred, in the case of "*Mr. González vs. Google Spain*", to these principles without precisely examining, indeed, what the initial and the current purposes were.[640]

The principle of accuracy under Article 6 lit. d of the Data Protection Directive and Article 5 sect. 1 lit. d of the Data Protection Regulation states that personal data must be "accurate and, where necessary, kept up to date; every reasonable step must be taken to ensure that personal data that are inaccurate ~~or incomplete~~, having regard to the purposes ~~for which they were collected or~~ for which they are ~~further~~ processed, are erased or rectified **without delay**" (words crossed-out only mentioned in the directive, bold words added in the regulation). Based on this principle, the individual concerned has the right to rectify incorrect data or to complete incomplete data, pursuant to Article 16 of the regulation.

---

637 Cf. Ehmann/Helfrich, ibid., cip. 24.

638 See Dammann/Simitis, ibid., cip. 17.

639 See Ehmann/Helfrich, ibid., cip. 31.

640 See above under point C. I. 3. c) aa) (2) (a) Protection against first publication and profiles.

Beside these principles, there are further requirements for the "legitimate" processing of personal data and further rights and duties, which refer to the purpose specification requirement. Article 7 lit. a of the Data Protection Directive and Article 6 sect. 1 lit. a of the General Data Protection Regulation state that processing of personal data is lawful only if the individual concerned has provided their consent to the actual processing of his or her personal data for one or more specific purposes. Article 7 lit. f of the Data Protection Directive and Article 6 sect. 1 lit. f of the General Data Protection Regulation authorize the processing of personal data if it "is necessary for the purposes of the legitimate interests pursued by the controller or by a third party, except where such interests are overridden by the interests or fundamental rights and freedoms of the data subject which require protection of personal data". Articles 10 lit. b and 11 sect. 1 b of the Data Protection Directive, as well as Article 13 sect. 1 lit. c and sect. 3, and Article 14 sect. 1 lit. c, and sect. 4 of the General Data Protection Regulation, require the controller to provide information about the purpose of processing their data. Article 12 lit. a of the directive and Article 15 sect. 1 lit. a of the regulation provide that an individual also has the right to that information.

Furthermore, the General Data Protection Regulation provides, in its Articles 24 and 32, for the following: „Taking into account the nature, scope, context and purposes of processing as well as the risks of varying likelihood and severity for the rights and freedoms of natural persons, the controller shall implement appropriate technical and organisational measures to ensure and to be able to demonstrate that processing is performed in accordance with this Regulation. Those measures shall be reviewed and updated where necessary." The data protection impact assessment required under Article 35 of the regulation also refers to the purpose, providing for the duty of prior consultation of the data protection authority if the assessment reveals a high risk under Article 36. Pursuant to Article 29 sect. 2 of the regulation, a data protection officer must "have due regard to the risk associated with processing operations, taking into account the nature, scope, context and purposes of processing". The controller's duty to designate a representative, provided for by Article 27 sect. 2 lit. a of the regulation, also depends on the risks for the individual in light of the purpose of the processing. Finally, the administrative fines foreseen under Article 83 equally refer to the nature, gravity and duration of the infringement taking into account the nature, scope or purpose of the processing.

All these requirements refer to the purpose specified by the controller. However, if the data protection laws itself determine the purpose, it is, in principle, not so difficult for the entities processing personal data to fulfill the purpose specification requirement.[641] In contrast, if the purpose is not determined by law, the question is how the entities have to specify the purpose (on which, as shown before, all the before-mentioned requirements depend).

bb) Criteria discussed for purpose specification

Unfortunately, data protection laws do not provide explicit criteria in order to determine how precisely the purposes should be specified.[642] With respect to the Data Protection Directive, legal critics stress that the term 'collected for specified and explicit purposes' requires that the purpose of the data processing is made explicit to the data subject before its collection. These critics explain this requirement by referring to the legislation process. The European Parliament stated with respect to the first draft of the Data Protection Directive that there must be as much transparency as possible about which data is stored, about whom, and for which purpose; if individuals shall have the right to contest the storage, it must firstly be clear what shall be contested in the first place.[643] While some legal scholars advocate further that the purposes must usually be specified in written form[644], others stress that this requirement was actually abandoned

641 See, for example: Article 2 sect. 2 lit. b GDPR (material scope of the regulation regarding purposes of the prevention, investigation, detection or prosecution of criminal offences or the execution of criminal penalties, including the safeguarding against and the prevention of threats to public security); Article 4 sect. 9 GDPR (recipient of personal data); Article 85 (journalistic, academic, artistic or literacy purposes); Article 88 GDPR (recruitment purposes and purposes of exercise of rights and benefits related to employment); Article 89 GDPR (archiving, scientific or historical research, or statstical purposes).

642 Cf. regarding the Data Protection Regulation, Härting, ibid., cip. 95.

643 See "Allgemeine Beobachtungen des Berichterstatters" in der Begründung zur Stellungnahme im Bericht des Ausschusses für Recht und Bürgerrechte (Hoon-Report) vom 15. Januar 1992, S. 16: "Es muss die größtmögliche Transparenz darüber bestehen, welche Daten über welche Personen und für welche Zwecke gespeichert werden. Wenn Menschen das Recht erhalten sollen, Einspruch zu erheben, so muss zuerst feststehen, wogegen Einspruch erhoben werden soll."

644 See Ehmann/Helfrich, ibid., cip. 13.

in the course of the legislation process.[645] However, if the purpose is not clear, some critics consider that the controller is not allowed to process the data.[646] Regarding the precision of the purpose specified by the controller, scholars provide an example that the purpose must not be so broad that it implicitly includes unlawful sub-purposes.[647] And the legal scholars Ehmann and Helfritz quote the European Commission as: "A general or vague definition or description of the object of the processing (such as for "commercial purposes") does not meet the principle of purpose specification required by Article 6 lit. b" of the directive.[648] Correspondingly, recital 28 of the Data Protection Directive states that "(…) purposes must be explicit and legitimate and must be determined at the time of collection of the data". The General Data Protection Regulation only slightly liberalizes this approach by changing, pursuant to its recital 39 sent. 6, the "must"-requirement into a "should"-recommendation. None of these considerations effectively help answer the question of how specific the purpose must be specified.

(1) Preliminary note: Clarifying conceptual (mis)understandings

The Article 29 Data Protection Working Group seeks to provide further guidance in order to determine the requirement to specify the purpose. In its "Opinion 03/2013 on purpose limitation", the Working Group principally differentiates between the requirement of purpose specification and limitation even if it intermingles, conceptually, and in the wording, both requirements from time to time.

For example, while the Group structures the role of the concept of the principle of purpose limitation in a 'first building block: purpose specification' and a ‚second building block: compatible use', it states with respect to Article 8 ECFR that the "Charter clearly establishes the principle

---

645 See Dammann/Simitis, ibid., cip. 6.

646 See Ehmann/Helfrich, ibid., cip. 13.

647 See Dammann/Simitis, ibid., cip. 7.

648 See Ehmann and Helfrich, EU Data Protection Directive, Article 6 cip. 12, referring to "Geänderter Vorschlag der Kommission, ABl. EG Nr. C 311 v. 27.11.1992, S. 15: "Eine allgemeine oder vage Definition oder Beschreibung des Gegenstandes einer Verarbeitung (beispielsweise "für kommerzielle Zwecke") entspricht dem Grundsatz der Definition der Zweckbestimmung nach Artikel 6 Buchstabe b nicht."

of purpose limitation, specifying that personal data must be processed 'fairly for specified purposes'."[649] In fact, Article 8 ECFR does not refer to the requirement of purpose limitation, but only of purpose specification (at least with respect to its explicit wording). Comparably, the Working Group does not refer, in a precise way, to the decisions developed by the European Court of Human Rights with respect to the right to private life under Article 8 ECHR. From its point of view, the approach provided for by Article 8 ECHR "is based on a general prohibition of interference with the right of privacy and allows exceptions only under strictly defined conditions. In cases where there is 'interference with privacy' a legal basis is required, as well as the specification of a legitimate purpose as a precondition to assess the necessity of the interference."[650] It adds that "in the course of time, the European Court of Human Rights also developed the test of 'reasonable expectations of privacy' to help decide whether there had been an interference with the right to privacy."[651]

The Working Group hence appears to consider two arguable aspects: First, that the concept of protection developed by the European Court of Human Rights 'is based on a general prohibition of' data processing; and second, that there is a *requirement* of purpose specification, which functions in order to evaluate, first, the necessity of an infringement of Article 8 ECHR and, second, its justification. In contrast, as shown previously, the European Court of Human Rights mainly examines the purpose pursued by the data controller in order to determine whether there is an infringement at all.[652] More importantly: even if the case-by-case approach of the European Court of Human Rights has led to a rather wide scope of protection, it cannot be concluded from its decisions that the right to private life under Article 8 ECHR is based on a general prohibition of data process-

649 See the Article 29 Data Protection Working Group, Opinion 03/2013 on purpose limitation, with respect to the first aspect, pp. 11 to 12, and, with respect to the second aspect, p. 10.

650 See the Article 29 Data Protection Working Group, Opinion 03/2013 on purpose limitation, p. 7, as well as Opinion 06/2014 on the notion of legitimate interests of the data controller under Article 7 of Directive 96/46/EC, p. 6.

651 See the Article 29 Data Protection Working Group, Opinion 03/2013 on purpose limitation, p. 6.

652 See above under point C. I. 3. b) cc) Particular reference to the individual's "reasonable expectations".

ing.[653] This is in particular the case with respect to the private sector where the Court instead refers to the 'positive obligations' of the States to establish safeguards protecting the interests of confidentiality of individuals against a misuse of 'their' data by third private parties.[654]

However, despite these ambiguous considerations, the opinion of the Working Party on the requirement of purpose specification is highly important in order to understand the concept provided for by the European data protection laws. The Working Party felt compelled to elaborate on its opinion in light of the divergent interpretations existing amongst the EU Member States. It stated: "In some countries, specific rules may apply to the public sector. In others, purposes may sometimes be defined in very broad terms. The approaches in the different Member States also vary as to how the purposes are made explicit, for example, whether specification of purpose is required in the notification to the data protection authority or in the notice to the data subject."[655] Thus, in order to give guidance for a consistent interpretation, the Working Group stresses, at first, the connection between the requirement of purpose specification and related concepts: Transparency, predictability, and user control. In its opinion "there is a strong connection between transparency and purpose specification. When the specified purpose is visible and shared with stakeholders such as data protection authorities and data subjects, safeguards can be fully effective. Transparency ensures predictability and enables user control. (…) If data subjects fully understand the purposes of the processing, they can exercise their rights in the most effective way. For instance, they can object to the processing or request the correction or deletion of their data."[656]

(2) Legal opinion on the function of the specification of a purpose

Subsequently, the Group elaborates on the meaning and function of the terms 'specified, explicit and legitimate' purposes. From its point of view,

653 See above under point C. I. 3. b) ee) Conclusion: Assessment of 'reasonable expectations' on a case-by-case basis.

654 See above under point C. I. 1. b) aa) (1) European Convention on Human Rights.

655 See the Article 29 Data Protection Working Group, Opinion 03/0213 on purpose limitation, p. 10.

656 See the Article 29 Data Protection Working Group, ibid., pp. 13 and 14.

the requirement to specify the purpose serves to "determine whether data processing complies with the law, and to establish what data protection safeguards should be applied (.../and therefore is) a necessary precondition to identify the specific purpose(s) for which the collection of personal data is required."[657] It adds: "Purpose specification requires an internal assessment carried out by the data controller and is a necessary condition for accountability. It is a key first step that a controller should follow to ensure compliance with applicable data protection law. The controller must identify what the purposes are, and must also document, and be able to demonstrate, that it has carried out this internal assessment."[658] The Working Group also advocates "that the purposes must be specified prior to, and in any event, not later than, the time when the collection of personal data occurs" and "must be detailed enough to determine what kind of processing is and is not included within the specified purpose, and to allow that compliance with the law can be assessed and data protection safeguards applied".[659]

The Group concludes from this function that purposes "such as, for instance 'improving users' experience', 'marketing purposes', 'IT-security purposes' or 'future research' will – without more detail – usually not meet the criteria of being 'specific'."[660] However, it recognizes that "the degree of detail in which a purpose should be specified depends on the particular context in which the data are collected and the personal data involved."[661] With respect to the fact that data is usually processed for several purposes, it states as: "Personal data can be collected for more than one purpose. In some cases, these purposes, while distinct, are nevertheless related to some degree. In other cases the purposes may be unrelated. A question that arises here is to what extent the controller should specify each of these distinct purposes separately, and how much additional detail should be provided."[662] Coming to these questions, the Working Group points to the core challenge of the requirement of purpose specification. However, so far, it only provides a method for applying this requirement as: "For 'related' processing operations, the concept of an overall purpose,

657 See the Article 29 Data Protection Working Group, ibid., p. 13.
658 See the Article 29 Data Protection Working Group, ibid., p. 15.
659 See the Article 29 Data Protection Working Group, ibid., p. 15.
660 See the Article 29 Data Protection Working Group, ibid., p 16.
661 See the Article 29 Data Protection Working Group, ibid., p 16.
662 See the Article 29 Data Protection Working Group, ibid., p 16.

under whose umbrella a number of data processing operations take place, can be useful. That said, controllers should avoid identifying only one broad purpose in order to justify various further processing activities which are in fact only remotely related to the actual initial purpose."[663]

In conclusion, the Article 29 Data Protection Working Group only provides a rather superficial objective scale in order to determine the degree of precision of a purpose as: "Ultimately, in order to ensure compliance with Article 6(1)(b), each separate purpose should be specified in enough detail to be able to asses whether collection of personal data for this purpose complies with the law, and to establish what data protection safeguards to apply."[664]

(3) Legal opinion on the function of 'making a specified purpose explicit'

The Working Group also elaborates on the meaning and function of the requirement that the specified purpose must be made explicit to the individual. In its opinion "the purposes of collection must not only be specified in the minds of the persons responsible for data collection. They must also be made explicit. In other words, they must be clearly revealed, explained or expressed in some intelligible form. It follows from the previous analysis that this should not happen later than the time when the collection of personal data occurs. (…) The requirement that the purposes be specified 'explicitly' contributes to transparency and predictability. (…) It helps all those processing data on behalf of the controller, as well as data subjects, data protection authorities and other stakeholders, to have a common understanding of how the data can be used. This, in turn, reduces the risk that the data subject's expectation will differ from the expectations of the controller. In many situations, the requirement also allows data subjects to make informed choices – for example, to deal with a company that uses personal data for a limited set of purposes rather than with a company that uses personal data for a wider variety of purposes."[665]

In this regard, the Working Group also stresses how differently Member States transposed this requirement into national laws. While some Member States, often linguistically originating from the Latin family of lan-

663 See the Article 29 Data Protection Working Group, ibid., p 16.
664 See the Article 29 Data Protection Working Group, ibid., p 16.
665 See the Article 29 Data Protection Working Group, ibid., p. 17.

guages, refer to the requirement in the meaning of 'unfold, unravel, and explain', other countries such as Germany or Hungary understand this to mean 'unambiguous'. This second understanding does not necessarily require that the purpose must be expressed in a certain form.[666] However, the Working Group exemplifies how the specified purpose may be made explicit as: "Describing the purposes in a notice provided to the data subjects, in a notification provided to the supervisory authority, or internally in the information provided to a data protection officer."[667] It also stresses the function of the requirement with respect to accountability. For example, on the one hand, purposes made explicit in written form or another appropriate documentation, help data controllers to verify that they had fulfilled the requirement of purpose specification. On the other hand, it equally helps data subjects to exercise their rights. However, the Working Group clarifies that such documentation might not be necessary in every case. In some cases, it is sufficiently clear for which purpose the controller uses the data.[668]

(4) Legal opinion on the reconstruction of a purpose and its legitimacy

The Working Group considers that data processing that does not meet the specified requirements is not automatically unlawful. Instead, "it will be necessary to reconstruct the purposes of processing, keeping in mind the facts of the case. While the publicly specified purpose is the main indicator of what the data processing will actually aim at, it is not an absolute reference: where the purposes are specified inconsistently or the specified purposes do not correspond to reality (for instance in case of a misleading data protection notice), all factual elements, as well as the common understanding and reasonable expectations of the data subjects based on such facts, shall be taken into account to determine the actual purposes."[669]

---

666 See the Article 29 Data Protection Working Group, ibid., footnote 42.

667 See the Article 29 Data Protection Working Group, ibid., p. 18.

668 See the Article 29 Data Protection Working Group, ibid., p. 18; cf. the reasoning of the German Constituional Court, 16th of June 2009, 2 BvR 902/06 (Email Confiscation), cip. 102, illustrated beneath under point C. III. 1. b) bb) (3) Identification marks as control-enhancing mechanisms.

669 See the Article 29 Data Protection Working Group, ibid., p. 18.

Finally, the Working Group states on the legitimacy requirement as: “In order for the purposes to be legitimate, the processing must – at all different stages and at all time – be based on at least one of the legal grounds provided for by Article 7 (of the Data Protection Directive). However, the requirement that the purposes must be legitimate is broader than the scope of Article 7. In addition, Article 6(1)(b) also requires that the purposes must be in accordance with all provisions of applicable data protection law, as well as other applicable laws such as employment law, contract law, consumer law, and so on. (…) This includes all forms of written and common law, primary and secondary legislation, municipal degrees, judicial precedents, constitutional principles, fundamental rights, other legal principles, as well as jurisprudence, as such ‘law’ would be interpreted and taken into account by competent courts. Within the confines of law, other elements such as customs, codes of conduct, codes of ethics, contractual arrangements, and the general context and facts of the case, may also be considered when determining whether a particular purpose is legitimate. This will include the nature of the underlying relationship between the controller and the data subjects, whether it be commercial or otherwise.”[670]

cc) Purposes of processing specified when consent is given

In addition to the requirements described, data processing must either be based on the consent of the individual concerned or an authorizing law. With respect to the consent, Article 2 lit. f of the ePrivacy Directive refers to the same requirements as provided for by the Data Protection Directive. Article 2 lit. h of the Data Protection Directive states: “‘The data subject’s consent’ shall mean any freely given specific and informed indication of his whishes by which the data subject signifies his agreement to personal data relating to him being processed.” Regarding the term ‘specific’, the Working Group considers that a “blanket consent without determination of the exact purposes does not meet the threshold.”[671] Legal scholars refine this criteria by stressing that the individual must be informed not only about the specific data processing, but also about its consequences. In their

---

670 See the Article 29 Data Protection Working Group, ibid., pp. 19 and 20.
671 See the Article 29 Data Protection Working Group, ibid., p. 34.

opinion, the term 'specific' does not exclude future acts of usage but rather means concrete circumstances, including the purpose of the processing. In addition, the question of how detailed the controller must specify the consequence, depends on how intensively the later usage affects the individuals fundamental rights.[672] However, the term 'specific' does not reveal, so far, further criteria determining the purposes provided for within the consent.

dd) Purposes of data processing authorized by legal provisions

As mentioned previously, the limited criteria set out in order to determine the precision of the purpose is less problematic for the controller (and further entities) if the law itself defines the purpose. The ePrivacy Directive, the Data Protection Directive and the General Data Protection Regulation provide for several provisions authorizing the processing of personal data for specific purposes.

(1) ePrivacy Directive

The ePrivacy Directive provides, in its current version amended by the Civil Rights Directive, several authorizations for the processing of personal data that prevail over the general provisions in the Data Protection Directive. These provisions mainly concern four types of data:

1. 'Communications and the related traffic data' and, with a particular view to cookies, 'information stored in the terminal equipment of a subscriber or user', Article 5;
2. 'traffic data relating to subscribers and users processed and stored by the provider of a public communications network or publicly available electronic communication service', Article 6;
3. 'location data other than traffic data', Article 9; and
4. 'information provided for by electronic calling and communication systems without human intervention (automatic calling machines), facsimile machines (fax) or electronic mail, Article 13 ('unsolicited communications').

---

672 See Dammann/Simitis, ibid., cip. 22.

Article 2 lit. d defines the term 'communication' as "any information exchanged or conveyed between a finite number of parties by means of a publicly available electronic communications service"; pursuant to Article 2 lit. b, the term of 'traffic data' means "any data processed for the purpose of the conveyance of a communication on an electronic communications network or for the billing thereof"; Article 2 lit. c states on the definition of the term of 'location data' as "any data processed in an electronic communications network, indicating the geographic position of the terminal equipment of a user of a publicly available electronic communications service"; and Article 2 lit. h defines the term of 'electronic mail' as "any text, voice, sound or image message sent over a public communications network which can be stored in the network or in the recipient's terminal equipment until it is collected by the reception."

Regarding the first type of data, Article 5 of the ePrivacy Directive requires EU Member States to ensure that communication and related traffic data remain confidential. This kind of data may be processed only, in the private sector, under the following conditions:

1. Always if it is based on the user's consent (sect. 1 sent. 2);
2. Its storage only if it is necessary for the conveyance of a communication without prejudice to the principle of confidentiality (sect. 1 sent. 3);
3. The recording of communications and related traffic data carried out in the course of lawful business practice for the purpose of evidence of a commercial transaction or of any other business communication if it is legally authorized (sect. 2); and
4. Finally, the storing of information, or the gaining of access to information already stored, in the terminal equipment of a subscriber or user, here again, either on the basis of his or her consent, or for the sole purpose of carrying out the transmission of a communication over an electronic communications network, or if it is strictly necessary for the provider of an Information Society service explicitly requested by the subscriber or user to provide the service' (sect. 3).

Regarding the second type, traffic data, Article 6 of the ePrivacy Directive authorizes, in essence, it's processing only if it is:

1. Made anonymous the moment where it is no longer needed for the purpose of the transmission of a communication (sect. 1);
2. For the purposes of subscriber billing and interconnection payments (sect. 2); and

3. For the purposes of marketing electronic communications services or for the provision of value added services, as long as it is necessary for the marketing or service or if the subscriber or the user has given his or her prior consent (sect. 3); in the last respect, article 2 lit. g of the directive defines the term of 'value added service' as "any service which requires the processing of traffic data or location data beyond what is necessary for the transmission of a communication or the billing thereof."

Concerning the third type of data, i.e. location data other than traffic data, the requirements are the strictest: Article 9 of the ePrivacy Directive authorizes its processing only if it is made anonymous or with the consent of the subscribers or users to the extent and for the duration necessary for the provision of a value added service. Finally, regarding the fourth type of data, unsolicited communications, Article 13 of the ePrivacy Directive authorizes the use of automated calling machines, fax or email for the purposes of direct marketing only if the subscribers or users has given their prior consent.

(2) Data Protection Directive and General Data Protection Regulation

As far as the prevailing provisions of the ePrivacy Directive do not apply, the Data Protection Directive provides several purposes under which the processing of personal data is justified. In essence, the upcoming General Data Protection regulation corresponds to these provisions. Irrespective of the processing of special categories of data, Article 7 of the Data Protection Directive, as well as Article 6 sect. 1 of the General Data Protection Regulation generally authorize the processing of personal data as:[673]

1. If it is necessary for the performance of a contract (lit. b);
2. If it is necessary for the compliance of a legal obligation of the data controller (lit. c);
3. If it is necessary in order to protect the vital interests of the individual concerned (lit. d);
4. If it is necessary for a task carried out in the public interest (lit. e);
5. Or, if it is necessary for the purposes of the legitimate interests pursued by the controller or by the third party to whom the data are disclosed,

673 See Dammann/Simitis, ibid., cip. 4 referring to the Explanation sect. 4.

except where such interests are overridden by the individual's interests for fundamental rights and freedoms which require protection under Article 1 sect. 1 of the directive or Article 1 sect. 2 of the regulation.

Pursuant to Article 1 sect. 1 of the directive, Member States transposing the directive into national law are required to not only protect the individual's right to privacy with respect to the processing of personal data, but also the other fundamental rights and freedoms. And Article 1 sect. 2 of the regulation states: "This Regulation protects fundamental rights and freedoms of natural persons and in particular their right to the protection of personal data."

(a) Preliminary note: Clarifying conceptual (mis)understandings

The Article 29 Data Protection Working Group also provides in this regard, in its "Opinion 06/2014 on the notion of legitimate interests of the data controller under Article 7 of Directive 96/46/EC", guidance on how to interpret these purposes specified within the laws itself. Comparably to its "Opinion 03/2013 on purpose limitation", the Working Group briefly refers, at first, to the European Convention on Human Rights and the European Charter of Fundamental Rights in order to explain the conceptual background of its recommendations. With respect to the European Convention on Human Rights, the Working Group is, here again, of the opinion that the approach developed by the European Court of Human Rights "is based on a general prohibition of interference with the right of privacy and allows exceptions only under strictly defined conditions."[674] It adds: "In cases where there is 'interference with privacy' a legal basis is required, as well as the specification of a legitimate purpose as a precondition to assess the necessity of the interference."[675] In the Working Group's opinion, "this approach explains that the ECHR does not provide for a list of possible legal grounds but concentrates on the necessity of a legal basis, and on the conditions this legal basis should meet."[676] Similarly, the Group refers to the European Charter of Fundamental Rights stating: "The

674 See the Article 29 Data Protection Working Group, Opinion 06/2014 on the notion of legitimate interests of the data controller under Article 7 of Directive 96/46/EC, p. 6.

675 See the Article 29 Data Protection Working Group, ibid., p. 6.

676 See the Article 29 Data Protection Working Group, ibid., p. 6.

Charter enshrines the protection of personal data as a fundamental right under Article 8, which is distinct from the respect for private and family life under Article 7. Article 8 lays down the requirement for a legitimate basis for the processing. In particular, it provides that personal data must be processed 'on the basis of the consent of the person concerned or some other legitimate basis laid down by law'. These provisions reinforce both the importance of the principle of lawfulness and the need for an adequate legal basis for the processing of personal data."[677] The Working Group hence appears to conclude from both the European Charter on Human Rights, as well as the European Charter of Fundamental Rights, a general prohibition about the processing of personal data even for the private sector. In any event, it does not treat the question of whether these rights have a direct or an indirect effect on private parties processing personal data.[678]

However, the respectable aim of the Working Group is to "clarify the relationship of the 'legitimate interests' ground with the other grounds of lawfulness – e.g. in relation to consent, contracts, tasks of public interest" in order to "contribute to legal certainty". This is highly creditable since the Data Protection Directive, as well as the General Data Protection Regulation establishes a general prohibition of the processing of personal data, not only for the public, but also for the private sector, and the data controller therefore heavily depends on these legitimate grounds.[679] Though, the Working Group firstly states (in relation to the interplay between the consent and the other legal grounds) provided for by the directive "the first ground, Article 7(a), focuses on the self-determination of the data subject as a ground for legitimacy. All other grounds, in contrast, allow processing – subject to safeguards and measures – in situations where, irrespective of consent, it is appropriate and necessary to process the data within a certain context in pursuit of a specific legitimate interest."[680]

677 See the Article 29 Data Protection Working Group, ibid., p. 8.

678 Cf. above under points C. I. 1. b) The effects of fundamental rights on the private sector, and C. I. 3. b) Concept of Article 8 ECHR: Purpose specification as a mechanism for determining the scope of application (i.e. the individual's 'reasonable expectation', and C. I. 3. c) Concept of Articles 7 and 8 ECFR: Ambiguous interplay of scopes going beyond Article 8 ECHR.

679 See the Article 29 Data Protection Working Group, ibid., p. 10.

680 See the Article 29 Data Protection Working Group, ibid., p. 13.

(b) Legal opinion on 'performance of a contract'

Article 7 lit. b of the directive provides, and allows, the processing of certain data which is necessary for the performance of a contract. In relation to a contract that had already existed before the data was processed, the Working Party provides examples about which situations may meet this requirement (i.e. for the 'performance' of a contract) and which do not: The profiling of an individual regarding his or her purchase behavior usually does not meet the requirement because the contract most often refers to the delivery of products or services and not to profiling (in the Working Group's opinion, this is not even the case if the profiling is explicitly mentioned "in the small print of the contract");[681] while "a company-wide internal employee database containing the name, business address, telephone number and email address of all employees, to enable employees to reach their colleagues may in certain situations be considered as necessary"[682], "electronic monitoring of employee internet, email or telephone use, or video-surveillance of employees" is more likely not to be necessary for the performance of the employment contract; while formal reminders referring to outstanding contractual obligations usually meet the requirement, the transfer of personal data to external debt collection or lawyers' companies do not.[683] However, other legal grounds such as for the 'legitimate interests' might authorize these kinds of data processing.[684] Regarding data processing prior to the entering of a contract, these considerations comparably apply: "If an individual requests a retailer to send her an offer for a product, processing for these purposes, such as keeping address details and information on what has been requested, for a limited period of time, will be appropriate". In contrast, "detailed background checks, for example, processing the data of medical check-ups before an insurance company provides health insurance", "credit reference checks prior to the grant of a loan" or "direct marketing at the initiative of the retailer/controller" is not necessary for the contract that shall be conclud-

681 See the Article 29 Data Protection Working Group, ibid., p. 17.
682 See the Article 29 Data Protection Working Group, ibid., p. 17.
683 See the Article 29 Data Protection Working Group, ibid., pp. 17 and 18.
684 See the Article 29 Data Protection Working Group, ibid., pp. 17 and 18.

ed.[685] Of course, again, the 'legitimate interests' in Article 7 lit. f of the directive might authorize the data processing.[686]

(c) Legal opinion on 'legal obligation', 'vital interests', and 'public task'

With respect to the other purposes of data processing authorized by Article 7 lit. c to e of the directive, the Working Group provides further guidelines regarding its interpretation of the same. Article 7 lit. c of the directive provides for the processing of personal data in order to fulfill a legal obligation. The Working Group regards this as "the data controller must not have a choice whether or not to fulfill the obligation. Voluntary unilateral engagements and public-private partnerships" do not meet this provision. Consequently, "Article 7(c) (only) applies on the basis of legal provisions referring explicitly to the nature and object of the processing. The controller should not have an undue degree of discretion on how to comply with the legal obligation. The legislation may in some cases set only a general objective, while more specific obligations are imposed at a different level, for instance, either in secondary legislation or by a binding decision of a public authority in a concrete case."[687]

Article 7 lit. d of the directive authorizes the processing of personal data if it is necessary in order to protect the vital interests of the data subject. In this regard, the Working Party essentially considers this to be as: first, referring to recital 31 of the directive, the term 'vital interest' limits the scope only to questions of life and death situations; second, the situation must refer to a specific threat to the individuals life (an abstract threat is not sufficient); and third, the controller is allowed to refer to this legal provision only if it cannot seek consent from the data subject.[688] Article 7 lit. e of the directive furthermore authorizes data processing by private parties in relation to a 'public task'. The Working Party clarifies that this provision particularly becomes relevant if "there is no requirement for the controller to act under a legal obligation", for example, if the controller becomes aware of a fraud and wants to inform public authorities, even if it is not legally obliged to do so. Here again, the Working Group stresses

685 See the Article 29 Data Protection Working Group, ibid., p. 18.
686 See the Article 29 Data Protection Working Group, ibid., p. 18.
687 See the Article 29 Data Protection Working Group, ibid., pp. 19 and 20.
688 See the Article 29 Data Protection Working Group, ibid., p. 20.

that the "official authority or public task will have been typically attributed in statutory laws or other legal regulations. If the processing implies an invasion of privacy or if this is otherwise required under national law to ensure the protection of the individuals concerned, the legal basis should be specific and precise enough in framing the kind of data processing that may be allowed."[689]

(d) Legal opinion on 'legitimate interests'

Finally, Article 7 lit. f of the directive authorizes the data processing which 'is necessary for the purposes of the legitimate interests pursued by the controller or by the third party or parties to whom the data are disclosed'. In this regard, EU Member States are only allowed to specify these interests but not to broaden or limit the provision.[690] Concerning this last authorization, the European Court of Justice came to the conclusion in the case of "*ASNEF vs. FECEMD*" that the Spanish legislator had not found an adequate balance between the opposing fundamental rights.[691] Transposing Article 7 lit. f of the Data Protection Directive into Spanish ordinary law, the Spanish legislator had excluded the processing of personal data, which had not been made publically available before, from this provision.[692] This general exclusion of this type of data, not yet made publically available, conflicted, in the European Court of Justice' opinion, with the general clause of Article 7 lit. f.

Similarly, in the case of "*Breyer vs. Germany*", the German legislator cannot restrict, when transposing this provision into national law, the storage of personal data to such cases where it is necessary for guaranteeing the specific operability of a certain service. In contrast, Article 7 lit. f of the directive may also authorize the storage of that data if it is necessary for the general operability of the service.[693] In contrast, in the case of "*Mr. González vs. Google Spain*", the Court decided, turning the relationship between rule and exception provided for by Article 7 lit. f on its head, that the fundamental rights to private life and to data protection "override, as a

689 See the Article 29 Data Protection Working Group, ibid., pp. 21 and 22.
690 See Dammann/Simitis, ibid., cip. 2.
691 See ECJ C-468/10 and C-469/10, cip. 43 to 48.
692 See ECJ C-468/10 and C-469/10, cip. 22.
693 See ECJ C-582/14, cip. 50 to 64.

rule, not only the economic interest of the operator of the search engine but also the interest of the general public in having access to that information".[694]

The Article 29 Data Protection Working Party provides further guidance on how to interpret Article 7 lit. f of the directive. At first, regarding the requirement that the data processing must be 'necessary' for the purpose of the legitimate interest, the Working Party states that "this condition complements the requirement of necessity under Article 6 (of the directive), and requires a connection between the processing and the interests pursued. (…) As in other cases, this means that it should be considered whether other less invasive means are available to serve the same end."[695] With respect to the question on how precisely the 'interest' must be articulated, the Working Party advocates that there must be "a real and present interest, something that corresponds with current activities or benefits that are expected in the very near future. In other words, interests that are too vague or speculative will not be sufficient."[696] The Working Party also promotes that the term 'legitimate' interest can "include a broad range of interests, whether trivial or very compelling, straightforward or more controversial. It will then be a second step, when it comes to balancing these interests against the interests and fundamental rights of the data subjects, that a more restricted approach and more substantive analysis should be taken."[697] Consequently, it exemplifies several 'legitimate interests' as: the exercise of the right to freedom of expression or information, including in the media and the arts; conventional direct marketing and other forms of marketing or advertisement; unsolicited non-commercial messages, including for political campaigns or charitable fundraising; enforcement of legal claims including debt collection via out-of-court procedures; prevention of fraud, misuse of services, or money laundry; employee monitoring for safety or management purposes; whistle-blowing schemes; physical security, IT and network security; processing for historical, scientific or statistical purposes; processing for research purposes (including marketing research).

Whatever the specific interest might be, the Working Group stresses that "an interest can be considered as legitimate as long as the controller

694 See ECJ C-131/12, cip. 92 to 99.
695 See the Article 29 Data Protection Working Group, ibid., p. 29.
696 See the Article 29 Data Protection Working Group, ibid., p. 24.
697 See the Article 29 Data Protection Working Group, ibid., p. 24.

can pursue this interest in a way that is in accordance with data protection and other laws. In other words, a legitimate interest must be 'acceptable under the law'."[698] This is in particular the case if the interests are guaranteed by fundamental rights such as: the freedom of expression and information; the freedom of the arts and sciences; the right to access to documents; the right to liberty and security; the freedom of thought, conscience, and religion; the freedom to conduct a business; the right to property; the right to effective remedy and to a fair trial; and the presumption of innocence and right of defense.[699]

In conclusion, the Working Party provides several examples for legitimate interests: a company's interest to know the 'needs and desires' of their customers is principally allowed. In contrast, 'unduly monitoring' their online and offline activities is not allowed. Similarly, the combination of vast amounts of data from different sources, that were initially collected in other contexts and for different purposes is not allowed. The creation – with the involvement of data brokers as intermediaries – of complex profiles' might also not be allowed.[700] With respect to the interests of third parties, the Working Party also takes the interests of the public into account. In this regard, it takes into consideration transparency and accountability of private entities. For example, the salaries of top managers within large corporations might be disclosed; the re-publication of data, such as by the press or in general in a more innovative and user-friendly way is another example. Finally, and in addition, historical or other kinds of research might be a legitimate interest under Article 7 lit. f of the Data Protection Directive.[701] Interestingly, the European Court of Justice came, in the cases of "*Rechnungshof vs. ORF*" and "*González vs. Google Spain*" to a contrasting result to the above. The publication of the salaries of the individuals concerned in combination with their name was not proportionate; and the re-publication of personal data via an Internet search engine did not override the interests of the individual concerned. With respect to the second aspect, the Court indeed considered that this re-publication was very user friendly. However, this did not lead to being deemed a legitimate

698 See the Article 29 Data Protection Working Group, ibid., p. 25.
699 See the Article 29 Data Protection Working Group, ibid., p. 34.
700 Cf. the Article 29 Data Protection Working Group, ibid., p. 26.
701 Cf. the Article 29 Data Protection Working Group, ibid., pp. 27 and 28.

interest. Rather, it was the opposite, as it was deemed a particular severe harm for the individual concerned.[702]

c) Transposition of the requirement of purpose specification into German law

The German legislator transposed these requirements into German ordinary law, as set out in the following sections. In contrast to the two directives on the European Level, which currently apply, in Germany, there essentially are three laws regulating the processing of personal data in the private sector: The Federal Data Protection Law, the Telemedia Law, and the Telecommunication Law. The dispersion of data protection instruments over several laws makes it very difficult to decide which law actually applies. Consequently, the potential interplay of these laws, and with respect to a particular case (whatever that may be), is highly debated in German legal literature.[703]

In principle, the Federal Data Protection Law provides the basic regulation instruments for any kind of processing of personal data.[704] However, pursuant to Article 3 sect. 3 sent. 1 of the Federal Data Protection Law, other, more specific laws must prevail if applicable. This regulation leads to a prevalence of the more specific Telemedia Law and the Telecommunication Law over the Federal Data Protection Law. Telemedia Law and the Telecommunication Law differ from each other in terms of the different services regulated by these laws: While the Telemedia Law applies – correspondingly to Information Society services – to so-called telemedia services, the Telecommunication Law applies to telecommunication services. Article 1 sect. 1 sent. 1 of the Telemedia Law defines the term 'telemedia' as "any electronic information and communication service as long as it is not a telecommunication service (…) or a telecommunication-based service in the meaning of the Telecommunication Law

---

702 See above under points C. I. 3. c) aa) (3) (b) The answer depends on the type of threat posed, and C. I. 3. c) aa) (2) (a) Protection against first publication and profiles based on public data.

703 See, for example, Boos et al., Data protection and cloud computing pursuant to the Telecommunication Law, Telemedia Law, and Federal Data Protection Law.

704 See v. Lewinski, Federal Data Protection Law and further Provisions, § 1 BDSG, cip. 31.

(…)".[705] Thus, the Telemedia Law partly defines its scope negatively to the Telecommunication Law. Article 3 no. 24 of the Telecommunication Law states, in turn, on the term of 'telecommunication services' as "services (…) which totally or mainly consist in the transfer of signals via telecommunication networks".[706] Applying these definitions, legal scholars provides the following examples for telecommunication services: Cloud services, as long as they provide the infrastructure but not the hosting as such; email services, as long as they consist in the transport, but not the storage and administration; Voice over IP, Internet VPN, and messaging services, as long as they control the transfer even if it is based on a third party's infrastructure.[707] In contrast, telemedia is considered as, for example: Chat rooms, blogs, Internet search engines, online shops, advertising emails, wikis, and online games.[708]

The principles of the telecommunication law and telemedia law could potentially lead to the situation where a provider combines both telemedia and telecommunication services and therefore has to apply all laws simultaneously when offering its services.[709] However, all three laws apply the systematic approach of the directives: The processing of personal data, irrespective of the specific type of data, is only allowed on the basis of a legal provision or if the individual provides the necessary consent to the processing.

---

705 See Article 1 sect. 1 sent. 1 TMG states: "Dieses Gesetz gilt für alle elektronischen Informations- und Kommunikationsdienste, soweit sie nicht Telekommunikationsdienste nach § 3 Nr. 24 des Telekommunikationsgesetzes, die ganz in der Übertragung von Signalen über Telekommunikationsnetze bestehen, telekommunikationsgestützte Dienste nach § 3 Nr. 25 des Telekommunikationsgesetzes oder Rundfunk nach § 2 des Rundfunkstaatsvertrages sind (Telemedien)."

706 See Article 3 no. 24 TKG states as: "Im Sinne dieses Gesetzes ist oder sind ‚Telekommunikationsdienste' in der Regel gegen Entgelt erbrachte Dienste, die ganz oder überwiegend in der Übertragung von Signalen über Telekommunikationsnetzwerke bestehen, einschließlich Übertragungsdienste in Rundfunknetzen."

707 See v. Lewinski, ibid., Vor. zu § 88 TKG, cip. 37 to 60 as well as 23.

708 See Schreibauer, Federal Data Protection Law and further Provisions, Vor. zu § 11 TMG, cip. 8 with further references.

709 See v. Lewinski, ibid, cip. 61.

aa) Purposes of processing authorized by the Telecommunication Law

The most restrictive law, the Telecommunication Law, differentiates between three different types of data: Personal data in relation with a contract, traffic data, and location data. In comparison to the ePrivacy Directive, the Telecommunication law authorizes the processing of personal data for specifically listed purposes within these three categories. At first, article 88 sect. 1 and 2 of the Telecommunication Law generally protects the content of telecommunication, as well as its 'closer circumstances' against any kind of processing. Pursuant to sect. 3, providers of telecommunication services are only allowed to process such data:

1. In order to provide the telecommunication service;
2. For safeguarding protection of the technical system; and
3. Or for other purposes authorized by legal provisions that explicitly limit the scope of application; such provisions are, amongst others, Articles 96 regarding traffic data and, concerning location data, Article 98 of the Telecommunication Law.

In contrast, data collected in relation to a contract does not necessarily fall under Article 88 of the Telecommunication Law, because in principle, it does not directly relate to a specific communication process.[710] Article 3 no. 3 of the Telecommunication Law defines the term 'data in relation to a contract' as "data of a participant (of the telecommunication network) which is collected for the conclusion, alignment, changing, or termination of a contract." Legal scholars exemplify such data as: telephone numbers, email addresses, personal names, addresses or birthdays, device numbers, static IP addresses, passwords, or bank account and credit card data. Even if this kind of data does not fall under Article 88 of the Telecommunication Law, its Article 95 sect. 1 requires that:

1. This data may be, in essence, used only for the purposes of the contract agreed between the service provider and the participant;
2. Section 2 of this article states that, for purposes of marketing or market research, the usage of that data related to participants of other networks is allowed only based on their consent;

710 See Heun, Federal Data Protection Law and further Provisions, § 88 TKG, cip. 7 to 13, and § 95 cip. 1.

3. In contrast, the provider may use the data related to participants of its own network for purposes of marketing or market research as long as the participants do not object.[711]

After the termination of the contract, the service provider must delete the data after a certain period of time as set out under Article 95 sect. 3 of the Telecommunication Law.

Articles 96 and 98 of the Telecommunication regulate the processing of traffic and location data. Legal scholars justify the strictness of the provisions because of the vast amount of information that this kind of data may reveal and the private companies and the Police, which therefore have a particularly high interest in the data.[712] This is why the provisions authorizing the processing of such data are especially restrictive. Just as Article 6 of the ePrivacy Directive, Article 96 sect. 1 of the Telecommunication Law essentially allows collecting and processing traffic data only as:

1. For the purpose of transferring the telecommunication signals and for billing purposes;[713]
2. The processing of traffic data for purposes of marketing, improving the service or for the provision of value added services is allowed only if the participant belonging to the network consented to it; since their consent also authorizes the processing of data related to the individuals who are called or contacted, sentence 2 states that their personal data must immediately be anonymized.[714]

Equal to the provisions provided for by Article 9 of the ePrivacy Directive, the requirements regarding location data are even stricter. Pursuant to Article 98 sect. 1 of the Telecommunication Law, the collection and processing of location data is allowed only in anonymized form or with the participants' consent. In addition, providers of value-added services collecting location data regarding its participants or users have to inform them about each collection, for example, via text messages. Only if the telecommunication service provider uses the location data exclusively for showing the participant his or her location, the text message is not required.[715] These provisions lead to the result that providers of value-added

711 See Heun, ibid., § 95 TKG, cip. 8 et seqq.
712 See Heun, ibid., § 96 cip. 1 and § 98 cip. 1.
713 See Heun, ibid., § 96 sect. 1 cip. 12.
714 See Heun, ibid., cip. 18 to 23.
715 See Heun, ibid., cip. 22 referring to Article 98 sect. 1 sent. 3 of the Telecommunication Law.

services most often require the user's consent because their product or business model needs the user to be identified (e.g. for location based marketing), and so, the data collected cannot be anonymized.[716] In addition, if the provider of the value-added service is not the provider of the telecommunication network, but a third party, the consent must be, amongst other requirements, given in writing.[717] This results in the situation whereby many value-added services can hardly be offered because the requirement of submitting a written confirmation to use the data enforces users to get in contact with the value-added service provider by post. The only solution for this problem seems to be that the telecommunication service provider includes the purpose of processing for such a value-added service offered by third parties in the contracts with its own participants.

bb) Purposes of processing authorized by the Telemedia Law

European directives do not regulate data processing in relation with 'telemedia services'; however, the German legislator decided to nevertheless apply certain regulatory principles for these services.[718] The provisions of the German Telemedia Law refer to data processing in relation with a contract (article 14) and to 'usage data' (article 15). In contrast, 'content data' do not fall under these provisions but under the Federal Data Protection Law. Legal scholars define the term of 'content data' as data referring to a transaction where the Telemedia service is not the object of the contract but is only used during the process of agreement. Hence, data referring to a contract that could also have been concluded in the offline world, for example, the online contract of an offline purchase (such as an Amazon or Ebay purchase), are considered to be 'content data'.[719] If 'content data' is not at stake, but data in relation to a contract or 'usage data' is, providers of Information Society services are allowed to only process this kind of data, pursuant to Article 12, as:

---

716 See Heun, ibid., cip. 12 to 14.

717 See Heun, ibid., cip. 18 referring to the electronic consent regulated in Article 94 of the Telecommunication Law.

718 See Schreibauer, Federal Data Protection Law and further Provisions, § 11 TMG, cip. 2.

719 See Schreibauer, ibid., cip. 11 with further references.

1. On the basis of the user's consent;
2. Or a provision explicitly limiting the scope of application; in German law, so far, there are only Articles 14 and 15 of the Telemedia Law limiting this scope.[720]

Article 14 sect. 1 of the Telemedia Law only allows the data processing if it occurs in relation with a contract. Legal scholars consider, comparably to Telecommunication Law, the following data as falling under the provision: names, addresses, email addresses, user names, or passwords.[721] The collection and processing of that data is only allowed if it is necessary for the conclusion, alignment, or changing of a contract between the user and the service provider. Indeed, the meaning of the term 'necessary' is discussed in German legal literature: While some legal scholars require that the data must be necessary for the provision of the service itself, others consider that a legitimate interest in the data with respect to the conclusion, alignment, or changing of the contract is sufficient.[722]

Article 15 sect. 1 of the Telemedia Law only allows the processing of 'usage data' if it is necessary for the provision of the telemedia service or for its billing.[723] The provision exemplifies usage data as: Identifiers referring to the user; information about the beginning, the end, and the extent of the concrete usage, for example, the time, data volume or downloads; and information about the concrete usage of the services, such as the specific websites visited by the user. The record of which fields the user tapped on the websites and the information provided for by cookies can also be usage data. The definition makes it principally possible that this kind of data simultaneously relates to the contract and the usage. In these cases both Articles 14 and 15 of the Telemedia Law apply.[724]

The term 'necessary' means, here again that the provider has a legitimate interest in the data for providing the service. Legal scholars argue that the collection and processing of this kind of data is necessary, at least, if there is no reasonable technical alternative. In order to ascertain if there is a technical alternative, it must be taken into account whether it is possi-

720 See Schreibauer, ibid., cip. 9.

721 See Schreibauer, ibid., cip. 6 and 7 with further references.

722 See Schreibauer, ibid., cip. 15 with further references.

723 See also the discussion on the extent of security purposes covered by this provision above under point C. II. 1. b) dd) (2) (d) Opinion on 'legitimate interests', referring to ECJ C-582/14, cip. 50 to 64.

724 See Schreibauer, ibid., cip. 6 to 10 with further references.

ble to irreversibly anoymize personal data or, at least, to pseudonymize it.[725] Pseudonymization is a technical term which means, the data is separated from the identifier, such as the name or the email address of the person concerned.[726] Consequently, as far as IP addresses are considered as personal data, their processing is allowed only if it is necessary for the provision of the service. For example, web tracking including IP addresses is usually not necessary because the provision of the service would also be possible without the tracking. In contrast, session cookies are allowed as long as they serve the user process from one sub-website to another or the purchase process in an online shop. In this last respect, of course, it is only allowed when the user has really chosen certain products to buy. Comparably, log data including IP addresses or user profiles are not allowed, pursuant to Article 15 sect. 1 of the Telemedia Law. However, in these cases either the user's consent or Article 15 sect. 3 of the Telemedia Law might authorize the processing.[727]

Article 15 sect. 3 of the Telemedia Law allows the processing of 'usage data' for the purposes of advertising, market research and technical improvements of the user experience under the following conditions:

1. First, the data is pseudonymized;
2. Second, the user does not object to the processing of his or her data; and
3. Third, the transfer of such data to third parties is only allowed in anonymized form.

If these conditions are met, the data controller does not need the user's consent. In contrast, if these purposes also cover other types of data, such as 'content data' or data in relation to a contract, the processing must also be based on the user's consent. Hence, analytical tools for websites do not require consent if the data are anonymized or, at least, pseudonymized.[728] Pursuant to Article 15 sect. 3 sent. 3 of the Telemedia Law, the re-pseudonymization (i.e. combining the data with the identifier) is forbidden. This is only allowed if the user requires information about the data stored under his or her pseudonym, pursuant to Article 15 sect. 7 of the Telemedia Law in combination with article 34 of the Federal Data Protection Law.

725 See Schreibauer, ibid., cip. 13.
726 Cf. Article 4 no. 5 of the General Data Protection Regulation.
727 See Schreibauer, ibid., cip. 14 to 16.
728 See Schreibauer, ibid., cip. 19 to 22 with further references.

cc) Purposes of processing authorized by the Federal Data Protection Law

If both the Telecommunication Law and Telemedia Law do not apply, the processing of personal data possibly falls under the scope of the Federal Data Protection Law. The Federal Data Protection law principally differentiates, in contrast to the European Data Protection laws, between the public and private sector.[729] However, the principle that data processing is only allowed on the basis of an authorizing law or the individual's consent applies not only to the public but also to the private sector.[730] For the private sector, Article 27 et seqq. of the Federal Data Protection Law provide several of these authorizing provisions. Here, the purpose of the data processing again plays a decisive role because it provides a link for the degree of regulation. The legislator principally differentiates between data processing for the data controller's 'own' purposes and that for third parties. Legal scholars justify this disparity with the different levels of risk posed for the individual. As soon as the data processing does not occur for the controller's own purpose but for the purpose of third parties, the risk significantly increases. If the data is used for different purposes by third parties, the individual concerned has less overview and can control the later usage of the data less. In light of this, the German regulation applies a stricter approach if the data controller pursues the interest of a third party instead of its own.[731]

(1) Three basic legitimate grounds

Irrespective of legal provisions in other data protection laws and the individual's consent, the Federal Data Protection Law establishes, in essence, three different legitimate grounds for the processing of personal data as:[732]

1. The processing occurs in relation with a legal or quasi-legal obligation (article 28 sect. 1 sent. 1 no. 1);

729 See Simitis, Federal Data Protection Law, § 27, cip. 1.

730 See Kramer, Federal Data Protection Law and further provisions, § 28 BDSG, cip. 1.

731 See Simitis, ibid., cip. 4 and 5.

732 See Kramer, ibid., cip. 7.

2. The legitimate interests of the data controller are not overridden by the interests of the individual concerned (article 28 sect. 1 sent. 1 no. 2);
3. The data processed is generally accessible (article 28 sect. 1 sent. 1 no. 3);

Beside the type of data (e.g. special categories of data such as health data regulated under article 28 sect. 6 to 9), the legitimate grounds are more or less limited pursuant to further (more specific) purposes. The Federal Data Protection Law differentiates, in essence, between: the processing of personal data for the controller's purpose of address trading and marketing (article 28 sect. 3 to 3b); the transfer of data to credit agencies (article 28a); the processing of data for scoring (article 28b); the collection, storage and transfer of data to third parties, in particular, for purposes of marketing, credit agencies, or address trading (article 29); the treatment of data for purposes of market research for third parties (article 30a); the treatment of data for purposes of an employment (article 32); the treatment of data for scientific research (article 40); and the treatment of data for purposes of journalism and literature (article 41).

In principle, the data controller is not obliged to explicitly say on which of these legitimate grounds it bases its treatment of data. However, pursuant to article 28 sect. 1 sent. 2, the controller must stipulate, as soon as the data is collected, the purpose of the data processing.[733] Before addressing the restrictions or privileges under legislation, in relation to the abovementioned purposes, the next paragraphs will provide a summary about the pre-conditions provided for by the basic legitimate grounds listed above.

(2) 'Performance of a contract', Article 28 sect. 1 sent. 1 no. 1 BDSG

Comparably to the European directives, Article 28 sect. 1 sent. 1 no. 1 of the Federal Data Protection Law states that the data processing is allowed if it is 'needed to create, carry out or terminate a legal obligation or quasi-legal obligation with the data subject'. The reference to 'legal and quasi-legal obligation' includes not only contracts, but also transactions which do not require a contract, for instance, price competitions or spontaneous

733 See Kramer, ibid., cip. 8.

associations.[734] With respect to the term 'needed', there is an ongoing discussion in German legal literature about what this term actually means. At least, it seems to be common ground that there must be a direct relationship between the processing intended and the concrete purpose of usage.[735]

However, the following examples might illustrate the difficulties in defining this requirement: While the contracting parties usually disclose their names and contact addresses, the shipping address is undoubtedly necessary for the delivery; in contrast, the complete address is 'only' useful, for example, when it comes to enforcement proceedings.[736] Another example is the credit assessment before the conclusion of a contract: Since the provider of a product or service could always retain the purchase until full payment, the assessment would not be necessary.[737] Therefore, legal scholars stress that the requirement actually leads to a balancing act of the colliding interests of the data subject and the data controller. In so doing, they consider that the interests of the data controller might often prevail the interests of the data subject because the data subject can, in principle, decide whether or not to enter into the contract.[738]

(3) 'Justified interests of the controller', Art. 28 sect. 1 sent. 1 no. 2 BDSG

With respect to the second legitimate ground listed above, Article 28 sect. 1 sent. 1 no. 2 of the Federal Data Protection Law authorizes the processing of personal data "in so far as this is necessary to safeguard justified interests of the controller (…) and there is no reason to assume that the data subject has an overriding legitimate interest in his data being excluded from processing or use". This provision provides an equivalent legitimate basis similar to the other legal grounds. However, legal scholars stress that the legal ground provided for by Article 28 sect. 1 sent. 1 no. 2 should usually be examined after the other legal grounds. The reason is that a contract, for example, concluded between the data subject and the

734 See Kramer, ibid., cip. 39 with further references.
735 See Kramer, ibid., cip. 30 with further references.
736 See Kramer, ibid., cip. 32 with further references.
737 See Kramer, ibid., cip. 50 with further references.
738 See Kramer, ibid., cip. 31 with further references, particularly, to contra opinions.

controller might reveal interests or even contain explicit clauses of confidentiality which prevail the general weighing of interests foreseen in article 28 sect. 1 sent. 1 no. 2.[739] If this is not the case, the data controller can pursue any interest so long as their interests do not conflict with the law.[740] Article 28 sect. 1 sent. 1 no. 3 of the Federal Data Protection Law structures the weighing in two steps: At first, the data processing must be, here again, 'necessary' to safeguard the justified interests. If this is the case, the data controller must examine whether there is a 'reason to assume' that the individual has an overriding interest in that the data controller does not use the individual's personal data. This means, on the one hand, that the individual's interest must override the controller's interest, not the reverse; on the other hand, the moment the data controller assumes that an overriding interest for the individual exists, it cannot base its processing on this provision.[741]

(4) 'Generally accessible data', Art. 28 sect. 1 sent. 1 no. 3 BDSG

In contrast to this rather differentiated approach, article 28 sect. 1 sent. 1 no. 3 of the Federal Data Protection Law provides, with respect to generally accessible data, a priority rule when weighing the interests. Article 10 sect. 5 sent. 2 of the Federal Data Protection Law defines the term of 'generally accessible data' as: "Data which anyone can use, be it with or without prior registration, permission or the payment of a fee." This is, for instance, the case with respect to data stemming from public registers, such as the population register. Secondly, private databases are generally accessible as long as the access does not depend on an arbitrary decision of the provider. Therefore, for example, the processing of data stemming from public profiles in social networks usually falls under this provision.[742]

However, there are two restrictions provided for by Article 28 sect. 1 sent. 1 no. 3 of the Federal Data Protection Law: First, the processing must exclusively refer to the type of data that is collected i.e. the publically available data. That means that the controller is not allowed, on the basis of this provision, to combine publically made available data with data

739 See Kramer, ibid., cip. 57 with further references.
740 See Kramer, ibid., cip. 57 with further references.
741 Cf. Kramer, ibid., cip. 59 and 74 whose methodology is even more complex.
742 See Kramer, ibid., cip. 16 to 20 with further references.

that is not publically available.[743] Some legal scholars are of the opinion that this provision does not even cover the combination of data stemming from different generally accessible sources.[744] Second, this kind of data may only be processed on the basis of article 28 sect. 1 sent. 1 no. 3 of the Federal Data Protection Law "unless the data subject's legitimate interest in his data being excluded from processing or use clearly outweighs the justified interest of the controller of the filing system." Thus, the priority rule does not apply if an 'objective and impartial observer' would identify an issue of confidentiality.[745] This might be the case, for instance, if information about an individual is stored in online or in offline archives and should, from an objective perspective, be 'forgotten'; or if information about an individual in public rating portals harms his or her social reputation. This is in particular the case if the individual has objected to any further publication.[746]

(5) Privileges and restrictions pursuant to the purpose

These three basic legitimate grounds are more or less restricted with respect to the (further) specific purposes described above. The following sections will highlight few of these specific purposes in order give an impression of the idea (and complexity) of the regulatory approach.

Article 28 sect. 3 to 4 of the Federal Data Protection Law essentially regulates the processing of data for the purpose of marketing and address trading, on the one hand, in the controller's interest, and on the other hand, in the interest of a third party. In principle, this kind of processing is only allowed on the basis of the consent of the individual concerned (sect. 3 sent. 1). However, the data controller is allowed to process the data without consent if the following conditions are met (sent. 2): First, if the data refers only, amongst others, to the individual's name, title, academic degree, profession, address, year of birth, as well as the name of his or her branch, business, and profession. And second, this data is used only for

743 See Kramer, ibid., cip. 14; Simitis, Federal Data Protection Law, § 28 cip. 164.

744 See Gola/Schomerus, Federal Data Protection Law, § 28 BDSG cip. 31; Wolff/Brink, Federal Data Protection Law, § 28 BDSG cip. 84; contra opinion by Kramer, ibid., cip. 14.

745 See Kramer, ibid., cip. 23 with further references.

746 See Kramer, ibid., cip. 24 to 27 with further references.

purposes, first, of marketing of the controller's offers, and second, of marketing in relation to the profession of the individual and under his or her professional address, or third, marketing for donations. In light of both the restriction (sent. 1) and the privilege (sent. 2), it is decisive to define the term 'marketing or address trading for own purposes'. If Article 28 sect. 3 to 4 do not apply, the processing may only be based under Article 28 sect. 1 and 2 (the 'basic legitimate grounds') or Article 30a ('market research for third parties') or Article 29 ('address trading for third parties'). This complicated systematic approach has lead to a heavy debate within German literature. In conclusion, the following 'rules of thumb' apply: in terms of marketing, if the controller uses the customer primarily in order to sell new products, Article 28 sect. 3 to 4 apply – in contrast, if the customer contact primarily occurs for the service regarding products already sold, the processing falls under Article 28 sect. 1 and 2; in terms of market research, if the market research is conducted for third parties, Article 30a applies – in contrast, the treatment of data for an internal market research falls under Article 28 sect. 1 or 2; and in terms of address trading, this falls only under Article 28 sect. 3 to 4 if it occurs for the purpose of direct marketing – if not, Article 29 applies.[747]

The transfer of personal data to credit agencies regarding a legal claim is, pursuant to Article 28a of the Federal Data Protection Law, essentially allowed if the obligation is not fulfilled in time and the claim is, either (first), officially verified by a judicial court, or (second) during the course of an insolvency procedure, or (third) by the individual concerned. For "scoring purposes" (similar to profiling), in relation to the conclusion, execution or termination of a contract, Article 28b of the Federal Data Protection Law essentially establishes the following procedural requirements: First, the data is, pursuant to an established mathematical-statistical method, relevant in order to calculate the probability of a particular behavior; second, the profiling is not only based on address data (such as a home address); and third, if the home address of an individual concerned is used, he or she is informed about the usage before the calculation. Article 29 of the Federal Data Protection Law authorizes the commercial collection and processing of personal data for the purpose of transferring it to third parties under similar conditions as provided for by Article 28 sect. 1 ('own business purposes') as: first, there is no reason to assume that the individ-

747 See Kramer, ibid., cip. 92 to 101 with further references.

ual concerned has an interest of confidentiality; second, the data concerned stem from publically available sources and the interests of the individual concerned do not prevail; or third, the conditions provided for by Article 28a sect. 1 or 2 ('transfer to credit agencies') are met. The treatment of data for purposes of market research for third parties is, pursuant to Article 30a of the Federal Data Protection Law, allowed under similar conditions as provided for by Article 29 ('address trading for third parties'). Finally, Article 32 of the Federal Data Protection Law regulates the processing of data of employees. Section 1 sentence 1 states: "Personal data of an employee may be collected, processed or used for employment-related purposes where necessary for hiring decisions or, after hiring, for carrying out or terminating the employment contract." Legal scholars essentially discuss, in this regard, the following issues: first, the interplay of this Article with Article 28 sect. 1 and 2 ('own business purposes'); second what the term 'employment-related purposes' actually means; and third, whether there actually is a difference in the methods of how the colliding interests are weighed against each other. [748]

dd) Purposes of processing specified when consent is given

Beside all these legitimate grounds provided for by law, the data controller can also base its data processing on the consent of the individual concerned. Legal scholars stress that the data controller should only seek the individual's consent, so long as there is no legal provision authorizing the processing of the data. The reason is that the principle of good faith might prohibit the controller to fall back on the legal provisions if the consent is illegal or the individual objects to it.[749] If the individual objects to the processing, the data controller only has to stop the processing of the individual's data. If the consent, as a whole is illegal, the processing itself (from the start) would also be illegal.

748 See Kramer, ibid., cip. 60 to 61 with further references.
749 See Kramer, ibid., cip. 60 to 61 with further references; Gola/Schomerus, ibid., § 4 cip. 16.

(1) Not a waiver but execution of right to informational self-determination

Irrespective of the fact that the requirements for consent provided for by German ordinary law are based on the European directives, German legal scholars refer to the German informational self-determination right when they stress that the consent is not a waiver but a form of execution of German Basic Law.[750] They refer, in particular, to the decision of "*Release of Confidentiality*" which stated, as quoted previously: "The general personality right safeguards that the legal order provides and maintains the legal conditions under which the individual is able to participate in communicational processes in a self-determined way and to develop his/her personality. (…) The contract is the essential instrument in order to develop free and self-responsible actions in relation to third parties. The contract, which mirrors the harmonious will of the contracting parties generally allows the assumption of a fair balance of their interests and must be principally respected by the State."[751] Pursuant to the concept of protection of the German right to informational self-determination, the consent provided, thus is not a waiver, but a form of execution of this right.

In contrast, the European Court of Human Rights, appears to consider the individual's consent as a waiver of a right to private life under Article 8 ECHR. In the decision of "*M.S. vs. Sweden*", the Court explicitly dealt with this issue, as quoted previously: "It cannot therefore be inferred from her request that she had waived in an unequivocal manner her right under Article 8 § 1 of the Convention to respect for private life with regard to the medical records at the clinic."[752] Since the right to private life in Article 7 ECFR corresponds to Article 8 ECHR, the European Court of Justice might equally consider the consent as a waiver of fundamental rights, at least with respect to Article 7 ECFR. In this case, the German legislator would have to apply this concept of protection as long as there is no mar-

---

750 See Kramer, ibid., § 28 BDSG cip. 1 and 2 referring to the quoted decision "Release of Confidentiality" by the German Constitutional Court as well as to Simitis, Federal Data Protection Law, § 4a cip. 2.

751 See BVerfG, 1 BvR 2027/02, cip. 33 and 34.

752 See ECtHR, Case of M.S. vs. Sweden from 27 August 1997 (74/1996/693/885), cip. 32.

gin of discretion transposing the European directives into German law.[753] However, the European Court of Justice has not yet decided, at least not explicitly, on this issue.[754]

(2) Requirements for consent and consequences of its failure

With respect to the formal requirements, the Federal Data Protection Law, on the one hand, as well as the Telecommunication Law and the Telemedia Law, on the other hand, provide different requirements for the consent that needs to be given. While Article 4a of the Federal Data Protection Law principally requires the consent in writing, Article 94 of the Telecommunication Law and Article 13 sect. 2 of the Telemedia Law allow the user to also consent in electronic form. These two last-mentioned provisions, hence, avoid the scenario whereby the participants or users of the regulated services, have to change from the online world into the offline world.[755] In essence, the consent in electronic form is only legitimate if the service provider meets the following requirements: that the user consents to the processing of 'his or her' data explicitly and unambiguously; the consent is documented by the controller; the user is able to always access his or her consent; and the user gets the opportunity to always object the processing. In whatever form the consent is provided for, finally, the question always is: What happens with the consent from a legal perspective if the individual consenting to his or her data processing made a mistake when they initially provided their consent. Most often, legal scholars, as well as judicial courts, consider the consent given as invalid. This may be the case, for instance, if the data controller fooled the individual or did not inform him or her about relevant circumstances of the treatment of data.[756] The question thus is closely connected to the information that the data controller has to provide to the individual concerned. In this regard, Ar-

753 See above under point C. I. 1. a) The interplay between European Convention for Human Rights, European Charter of Fundamental Rights and German Basic Rights.

754 See in more detail beneath under point C. IV. 3. b) aa) Consent: "Later processing covered by specified purpose?".

755 See Schreibauer, ibid., § 12 cip. 10.

756 See Kramer, ibid., § 4a BDSG cip. 12, 13 and 22 with further references to Gola/ Schomerus, ibid., § 4a cip. 22; Plath, ibid., § 4a cip. 29; OLG Köln, decision from the 17th of June 2011 (6 U 8/11).

ticle 4a sect. 1 sent. 2 of the Federal Data Protection Law refers, in particular, to the purpose of the treatment of data as: "Data subjects shall be informed of the purpose of collection, processing or use". However, similarly to the European directives, there are no further criteria provided for by law in order to determine the purpose.

(3) Discussion on the degree of precision of a specified purpose

As a consequence, these criteria are also highly discussed in German legal literature, particularly, referring to the degree of precision. In summary, the reasoning provided for in the discussion, often appears to be circular and/or overly strict. However, some legal scholars at least refer to the constitutional concept of protection in order to justify their reasoning. As a common ground, comparably to the European discussion, these scholars stress that the individual must be able to understand the factual extent of his or her consent. However, when reviewing the details in order to determine the 'extent' of the consent, this criteria starts to get blurred. For example, Taeger summarizes that, "the consent must be so precise that the type of personal data and the purpose of collection or usage as well as, in the case of a transfer, possible recipients are sufficiently specified."[757] Däubler ads a dynamic element, referring to the intensity of the possible infringements, as: "The consent must not be, pursuant to the common understanding, a blanket; it must specify which data is processed or used for which purpose. The more the protection of the personality is concerned the more precise the possibilities of processing must be specified."[758] Däubler continues to provide examples: "This is the case (i.e. it is sufficiently precise) if a medical patient consents to the transfer of the remuneration claim for 'billing purposes' and to the transfer of the related in-

757 See Taeger/Gabel, BDSG Kommentar, § 4a, cip. 30: "Vielmehr muss die Erklärung so bestimmt sein, dass die Art der personenbezogenen Daten und der zweck der Erhebung und Verwendung sowie im Falle der Übermittlung etwaige Empfänger hinreichend genau benannt werden."

758 See Däubler/Klebe/Welde/Weichert, BDSG, § 4a cip. 18 with further references to court decisions: "Die Einwilligung nach allgemeiner Auffassung keinen pauschalen Charakter tragen; sie muss erkennen lassen, welche Daten zu welchem Zweck verarbeitet werden oder genutzt werden sollen. Je stärker der Schutz der Persönlichkeit tangiert ist, umso präziser müssen die Verarbeitungsmöglichkeiten umschrieben sein."

formation. In contrast, the consent to a transfer to 'any refinancing bank' is illicit because the individual concerned cannot overview the extent of his or her consent."[759] Däubler comes to the conclusion that "the requirement of specification is justified, at the end, because the individual is only on its basis able to overview the process (…)."[760] Kramer provides comparable examples. From his point of view, the information about the "transfer (of the data) to partner companies" is not sufficient because the recipients of the data would not be identifiable when the data is first collected. Comparably, the information given about the usage of data 'for marketing purposes' would not be sufficient because it is not clear whether the usage will be that of either the controller or that of a third party.[761] In this last respect, this reasoning clearly refers to the German legislator's thoughts that the risks for the individual caused by the processing of personal data in relation to a controller's own interest and that of a third party is different. Therefore, this legal scholar argues the controller must clarify their interest as a basis for gathering personal data.[762]

Däubler and Kramer already referred, more or less, to a broader concept of protection. However, Simitis explicitly ties into the concept of protection developed by the German Constitutional Court stating as: "The consent does only serve to safeguard and concretize the individual's right of decision if it is sufficiently specified, in other words, if it informs about under which conditions the individuals consented to the processing of

---

759 See Däubler/Klebe/Welde/Weichert, BDSG, § 4a cip. 18 with further references to court decisions: "Dem ist Rechnung getragen, wenn ein Patient in die Abtretung der Honorarforderung des Arztes ‚zu Abrechnungszwecken' und in die Weitergabe der dafür notwendigen Informationen einwilligt; eines besonderen Hinweises auf die ärztliche Schweigepflicht bedarf es nicht. Unzulässig ist dagegen eine Einwilligung zur Abtretung an jede ‚refinanzierende Bank; hier kann der Betroffene die Tragweite seiner Erklärung nicht überblicken."

760 See Däubler/Klebe/Welde/Weichert, BDSG, § 4a cip. 18 with further references to court decisions: "Das Bestimmtheitserfordernis rechtfertigt sich insgesamt damit, dass nur auf diese Weise der Vorgang für den Einzelnen überschaubar und damit der Grundsatz der Datentransparenz gewahrt bleibt."

761 See Kramer, ibid., § 4a BDSG cip. 21 with references to Wolff/Brink, ibid., § 4a cip. 44 and Plath, ibid., § 4a cip. 47.

762 See above the introduction of point C. II. 3. c) cc) Purposes of processing authorized by the Federal data Protection Law, referring to Simitis, Federal Data Protection Law, § 27, cip. 4 and 5.

which data."[763] Indeed, Simitis admits that the information is limited: "Nobody may seriously expect that the individual's consent meticulously refers to each single detail of the data process. (…) The degree of precision of the consent depends on the particular case. However, in any case, the consent has to refer not only to the information given by the individual but also to the agreed aims and phases of the processing."".[764] He therefore has a rather strict approach. In his opinion, information about the following purposes is not sufficiently precise: for 'prudent business management'; 'usual support of the authorizing person'; 'credit security'; 'market research'; not even the transfer of 'data of the debtor for credit processing' would suffice, in his opinion, to the individual's right to self-determination. Instead, the data controller must specify which concrete data is processed and used. Only in special circumstances, would the reference to a certain "type" of data could be sufficient. In summary, "only information which is as precise as possible enables the individual concerned to principally hinder the processing of single information that he or she considers as particularly dangerous, for example, the unlimited transfer of 'negative credit data' to credit agencies. The same applies with respect to a general consent to the transfer of data to other companies of the same branch. An effective protection depends, here like in other situations, on an early enough restriction of the circle of recipients."[765]

---

763 See Simitis, Federal Data Protection Law, § 4a cip. 77: "Die Einwilligung kann vielmehr die ihr zugewiesenen Aufgabe, das Entscheidungsvorrecht der Betroffenen zu gewährleisten wie zu konkretisieren, nur dann erfüllen, wenn sie hinreichend bestimmt ist, also klar zu erkennen gibt, unter welchen Bedingungen sich die Betroffenen mit der Verarbeitung welcher Daten einverstanden erklärt haben."

764 See Simitis, ibid., § 4a cip. 80: "Niemand kann ernsthaft mit einer Äußerung der betroffenen rechnen, die minutiös alle Einzelheiten des Verarbeitungsprozesses aufgreift. (...) Wie spezifiziert die Erklärung zu sein hat, lässt sich letztlich nur vor dem Hintergrund der konkreten Verarbeitungssituation beurteilen. So viel steht jedoch fest: Der Erklärung müssen in jedem Fall nicht nur die jeweils in Betracht kommenden Angaben zu entnehmen sein, sondern auch die gebilligten Verarbeitungsziele und Verarbeitungsphasen."

765 See Simitis, ibid., § 4a cip. 81 and 82: "Kurzum, nur eine möglichst präzise Aussage räumt den Betroffenen grundsätzlich die Chance ein, eine aus ihrer Sicht besonders gefährliche Verarbeitung einzelner Angaben, etwa die uneingeschränkte Übermittlung von 'Negativmerkmalen' an Kreditinformationssysteme, rechtzeitig zu verhindern."

ee) Comparison with principles developed by the German Constitutional Court

In light of the divergence of examples, more or less referring to the right to informational self-determination, it is helpful to examine, in more detail, the criteria developed by the German Constitutional Court with respect to the precision of the purpose. As set out in chapter C. I. 2. d) Purpose specification as the essential link for legal evaluation, the German Constitutional Court decided, with respect to both the public and the private sector, on this question. In this regard, the difference between the requirement of purpose specification in the public and the private sector also becomes clearer.

(1) Public sector: Purpose specification as a result of the principle of clarity of law

With respect to the public sector, the German Constitutional Court assesses the requirement of purpose specification as part of the proportionality assessment. In light of this, the requirement of purpose specification supplements the requirement to limit the later use, and is particularly strengthened by the principle of clarity of law.

(a) Function of purpose specification (basic conditions)

In the case of "*Decision on Population Census*", the German Constitutional Court stated, on the main criteria for specifying the purpose, which legal scholars many times referred to, as: "An obligation for the provision of personal data requires that the legislator precisely and specifically determines in certain areas the purpose of usage and should ensure that the information is suitable and necessary for achieving this purpose. The collection ahead of non-anonymized data for an undetermined or not yet determinable purpose is disproportionate with this (requirement)."[766]

766 See BVerfG, 15th of December 1983, 1 BvR 209, 269, 362, 420, 440, 484/83 (Decision on Population Census), cip. 179: "Ein Zwang zur Angabe personenbezogener Daten setzt voraus, daß der Gesetzgeber den Verwendungszweck bereichsspezifisch und präzise bestimmt und daß die Angaben für diesen Zweck

The Court referred to these criteria in its subsequent decisions, and particularly clarified, in its decision of "*Retrieval of Bank Account Master Data*", the interrelationship between the principle of purpose limitation and the principle of clarity of law. In the Court's opinion, "the principle of clarity of law is based, with respect to the right to informational self-determination, on Art. 2 sect. 1 in combination with Art. 1 sect. 1 GG per se. It shall guarantee that public agencies find legal criteria for the execution of the law and that the judicial courts are able to control it; furthermore, the principle of clarity of law enables the citizens concerned to be prepared by potentially infringing measures. Essentially, the reason, the purpose and the limits of the infringing measure must be provided for by the provision in a precise, legally clear manner, as well as specifically in relation to certain areas. (…) If a legal provision authorizes an infringement of the right to informational self-determination, the principle of clarity of law has a specific function to provide a sufficiently precise determination of the purpose of usage for the information concerned. It hence supplements the constitutionally required purpose limitation with respect to the information retrieved. The right to informational self-determination protects the individual against information related measures that he or she cannot foresee nor control."[767] Thus, beside further requirements, such as the specification of the reason for the infringing measure and the extent of the data col-

geeignet und erforderlich sind. Damit wäre die Sammlung nicht anonymisierter Daten auf Vorrat zu unbestimmten oder noch nicht bestimmbaren Zwecken nicht zu vereinbaren. (...)"

767 See BVerfG, 13th June 2007, 1 BvR 1550/03 (Retrieval of Banking Account Matser Data), cip. 71, 73 and 74: "Das Bestimmtheitsgebot findet im Hinblick auf das Recht auf informationelle Selbstbestimmung seine Grundlage in Art. 2 Abs. 1 in Verbindung mit Art. 1 Abs. 1 GG selbst (…). Es soll sicherstellen, dass die gesetzesausführende Verwaltung für ihr Verhalten steuernde und begrenzende Handlungsmaßstäbe vorfindet und dass die Gerichte die Rechtskontrolle durchführen können; ferner erlauben die Bestimmtheit und Klarheit der Norm, dass der betroffene Bürger sich auf mögliche belastende Maßnahmen einstellen kann (…). (…) Ermächtigt eine gesetzliche Regelung zu einem Eingriff in das Recht auf informationelle Selbstbestimmung, so hat das Gebot der Bestimmtheit und Klarheit die spezifische Funktion, eine hinreichend präzise Umgrenzung des Verwendungszwecks der betroffenen Informationen sicherzustellen. Auf diese Weise wird das verfassungsrechtliche Gebot der Zweckbindung der erhobenen Information verstärkt. Das Recht auf informationelle Selbstbestimmung schützt den Einzelnen gegen informationsbezogene Maßnahmen, die für ihn weder überschaubar noch beherrschbar sind. (…)".

lected and further processed, the requirement of purpose specification results from the principle of clarity of law.[768] However, both the principle of clarity of law and the principle of purpose limitation, are directly based in the right to informational self-determination.

The German Constitutional Court also clarified that the requirement of purpose specification, as one element of the principle of clarity of law, does not, per se, forbid the usage of undetermined legal provisions. Rather, the legislator could choose, depending on the particular issue, between different regulation instruments in order to determine the requirements of the infringement. For example, the collection of personal data for statistical purposes cannot be comprehensively pre-determined in advance.[769] In the case of "*Surveillance of Telecommunications*", the Court comparably took the concrete possibilities of pre-determining the purposes into account, as: "In view of the task and operational method of intelligence services, a more precise determination of the pre-conditions for the surveillance was not possible."[770] In contrast, state measures, such as those based on social legal provisions, could typically be categorized and consequently listed according to the matter at hand.[771]

In the case of "*License Plate Recognition*", the Court finally specified further criteria for the proportionality assessment: "The concrete requirements for the pre-determined clarification of the authorizing provision depend on the type and intensity of the infringement. Hence, the authorizing provision must especially pre-determine whether it allows serious infringements. If it does not exclude such (serious) infringements in a suffi-

---

768 Confirmed in BVerfG, 20th of April 2016, 1 BvR 966/09 and 1 BvR 1140/09 (Federal Bureau of Investigation Law), cip. 285; see also Härting, Purpose limitation and change of purpose in data protection law, p. 3285.

769 See BVerfG, 15th of December 1983, 1 BvR 209, 269, 362, 420, 440, 484/83 (Decision on Population Census), cip. 187.

770 See BVerfG, ibid., cip. 181: "(Der Gesetzgeber hat insbesondere die Zwecke, zu denen Telekommunikationsbeziehungen überwacht und die so erlangten Erkenntnisse verwendet werden dürfen, hinreichend präzise und normenklar festgelegt. Die Gefahrenlagen, auf deren Früherkennung die Beobachtung oder Überwachung zielt, werden genau genug beschrieben und durch die Bezugnahme auf andere Gesetze noch weiter verdeutlicht. Der Umfang der Überwachung ist durch die Begrenzung auf den internationalen nicht leitungsgebundenen Verkehr bestimmt.) Eine nähere Bestimmung der Voraussetzungen, unter denen die Überwachung stattfinden darf, war angesichts der Aufgabe und Arbeitsweise von Nachrichtendiensten nicht möglich."

771 See BVerfG, ibid., cip. 76 and 77.

ciently clear manner, the provision has to also meet the legal requirements which apply to these (serious) infringements."[772] Already in the "Decision on the Population Census", the Court has required, similarly: if the legislator cannot narrowly specify the purpose, "corresponding restrictions within the information system must balance the collection and processing of information. Clearly defined requirements for the processing of data are necessary in order to guarantee that the individual does not become, under the conditions of automated collection and processing of his or her personal data, a mere object of information."[773]

(b) Examples for specific purposes: Certain areas of life or explicitly listed crimes

Given these criteria, the Constitutional Court came, in the cases of "*Decision on Population Census*", "*Surveillance of Telecommunications*", and "*Big Eavesdropping Operation*" to the conclusion that the purposes, which were provided for by the corresponding law, were sufficiently precise. In the case of "*Decision on Population Census*", it clarified that "a legal provision is sufficiently determined if its purpose becomes clear with respect to the text of the provision and its legislative material; thereby, it is sufficient if the purpose results from the context of the provision with respect to the area of life that shall be regulated. The description of the data (…)

772 See BVerfG, 11th of March 2008, 1 BVR 2047/05 and 1 BvR 1254/07, cip. 95: "Die konkreten Anforderungen an die Bestimmtheit und Klarheit der Ermächtigung richten sich nach der Art und Schwere des Eingriffs (…). Die Eingriffsgrundlage muss darum erkennen lassen, ob auch schwerwiegende Eingriffe zugelassen werden sollen. Wird die Möglichkeit derartiger Eingriffe nicht hinreichend deutlich ausgeschlossen, so muss die Ermächtigung die besonderen Bestimmtheitsanforderungen wahren, die bei solchen Eingriffen zu stellen sind (…)."

773 See BVerfG, BVerfG, 15th of December 1983, 1 BvR 209, 269, 362, 420, 440, 484/83 (Decision on Population Census), cip. 184 and 185: "Ist die Vielfalt der Verwendungsmöglichkeiten und Verknüpfungsmöglichkeiten damit bei der Statistik von der Natur der Sache her nicht im voraus bestimmbar), müssen der Informationserhebung und Informationsverarbeitung innerhalb des Informationssystems zum Ausgleich entsprechende Schranken gegenüberstehen. Es müssen klar definierte Verarbeitungsvoraussetzungen geschaffen werden, die sicherstellen, daß der Einzelne unter den Bedingungen einer automatischen Erhebung und Verarbeitung der seine Person betreffenden Angaben nicht zum bloßen Informationsobjekt wird.(...)"

provided for by the law for the census from 1983 meets these requirements; the citizen is able to understand which fundamental facts of the social structure he or she will be asked. The main purposes result from the type of collection – a census for population, profession, housing, and work areas, from the program of collection and from the legislative material. The legislator is not obliged to determine the concrete purpose for each single information that must be provided for by citizens. This is especially the case with respect to the particularities of the collection of data for statistical purposes, in particular, of a census of population; the listing of the separate purposes is, given its multifunctional aims, impossible."[774]

With respect to non-statistical purposes, in the case of "*Surveillance of Telecommunications*", the Court stated "especially the purposes for which the telecommunication is controlled and the information retrieved can be used (such as the prevention, intelligence, and criminal prosecution of international terrorist attacks, of international distribution of weapons of war, of exports of drugs into the Federal Republic, and of counterfeiting of currencies committed abroad) are sufficiently precise and clear. The dangers, which the observation and surveillance seeks to discover in advance, are sufficiently pre-determined. The extent of the surveillance is determined by its restriction to traffic of international non-cable based telecommunication."[775] In the case of "*Big Eavesdropping Operation*", the legislator also met the requirements of purpose limitation and clarity of law, giv-

---

774 See BVerfG, ibid., cip. 199: "Hinreichend bestimmt ist ein Gesetz, wenn sein Zweck aus dem Gesetzestext in Verbindung mit den Materialien deutlich wird (…); dabei reicht es aus, wenn sich der Gesetzeszweck aus dem Zusammenhang ergibt, in dem der Text des Gesetzes zu dem zu regelnden Lebensbereich steht (…). Diesen Anforderungen genügt die Beschreibung der zu erhebenden Merkmale im Volkszählungsgesetz 1983; der Bürger kann erkennen, über welche Grundtatbestände der Sozialstruktur er befragt werden soll. Die Hauptzwecke lassen sich aus der Art der Erhebung - einer Volkszählung, Berufszählung, Wohnungszählung und Arbeitsstättenzählung -, dem Erhebungsprogramm und den Gesetzesmaterialien hinreichend deutlich entnehmen. Nicht erforderlich ist, daß der Gesetzgeber zu jeder einzelnen gesetzlichen Verpflichtung auch den konkreten Zweck im Gesetz selbst erläutert. Dies gilt namentlich mit Rücksicht auf die Besonderheiten der Erhebung von Daten für statistische Zwecke, zumal bei einer Volkszählung; hier ist eine Auflistung der einzelnen Zwecke aufgrund ihrer multifunktionalen Zielsetzung unmöglich."

775 See BVerfG, 14th of July 1999, 1 BvR 2226/94, cip. 181: "Der Gesetzgeber hat insbesondere die Zwecke, zu denen Telekommunikationsbeziehungen überwacht und die so erlangten Erkenntnisse verwendet werden dürfen, hinreichend präzise

en that the surveillance was only used for the investigation of explicitly listed crimes.[776]

(c) Examples for unspecific purposes: Abstract dangers or unknown purposes

In contrast, in the case of "*Dragnet Investigation*", the German Constitutional Court clarified which purpose provided for by law was sufficiently precise and which was not: "The transfer of the data serves the purpose of automated synchronization regarding other data sets so long as it is necessary for the defense of specific dangers, here, for the existence or security of the Federal State or of one Land or for physical integrity, life or freedom of a person. (…) The law determines the police as the receiving public agency. (…) Given the pre-conditions mentioned, (…/the law offended) is also sufficiently determined as it authorizes not only the retrieval and processing of the explicitly listed types of data but (…) also 'other data that are necessary for the concrete case'. The requirement of pre-determined clarification of legal rules is met because the notion of 'other data which is necessary for the concrete case' can be, with respect to the purpose of the defense of danger (…), typified in a manner that the principle of proportionality is met."[777] In contrast, the Court stressed "without restriction to a specific danger, there was not sufficient criteria in order to

---

und normenklar festgelegt. Die Gefahrenlagen, auf deren Früherkennung die Beobachtung oder Überwachung zielt, werden genau genug beschrieben und durch die Bezugnahme auf andere Gesetze noch weiter verdeutlicht. Der Umfang der Überwachung ist durch die Begrenzung auf den internationalen nicht leitungsgebundenen Verkehr bestimmt. Eine nähere Bestimmung der Voraussetzungen, unter denen die Überwachung stattfinden darf, war angesichts der Aufgabe und Arbeitsweise von Nachrichtendiensten nicht möglich."

776 See BVerfG, 3rd of March 2004, 1 BvR 2378/98, cip. 307 to 319.

777 See BVerfG, 4th of April 2006, 1 BvR 518/02, cip. 145 to 147: "Gemäß § 31 Abs. 1 PolG NW 1990 dient die Datenübermittlung dem Zweck des automatisierten Abgleichs mit anderen Datenbeständen, soweit dies zur Abwehr bestimmter Gefahren, nämlich für den Bestand oder die Sicherheit des Bundes oder eines Landes oder für Leib, Leben oder Freiheit einer Person, erforderlich ist. (Als Verwendungszweck ist damit der automatisierte Abgleich der übermittelten Daten mit anderen Datenbeständen zur Abwehr der in § 31 Abs. 1 PolG NW 1990 benannten Gefahren festgelegt. Das ist hinreichend. Auch dem für Übermittlungsregelungen geltenden Gebot einer hinreichend sicher erschließbaren

interpretatively determine the data concerned, especially with respect to the notion 'other data which are necessary for the concrete case'. If there is no specific danger, it is not possible to sufficiently pre-determine which data is necessary 'for the concrete case'. If a general terroristic danger was the reference for the dragnet investigation and consequently for the determination of the data required by the police, there would be a merely unlimited authorization (for data collection and processing). (…) This would infringe the constitutional requirements for the clarity of law."[778]

In the case of "*Retrieval of Bank Account Master Data*", the Court also affirmed the claim that the "law for the encouragement of tax compliance" infringed the requirement of purpose specification. This law required that the retrieval of data had to only relate to terms under the income tax act. The Constitutional Court stressed that such a requirement "does not determine the circuit of public agencies which shall be authorized to retrieve

---

Kennzeichnung der Empfangsbehörden, einhergehend mit Regeln, welche die Übermittlung auf deren jeweiligen spezifischen Aufgabenbereich konzentrieren (…), ist nur genügt, wenn der Gefahrenbegriff zur Einschränkung der Ermächtigung verfügbar ist.) Als Empfangsbehörde für die übermittelten Daten ist die Polizei benannt. (Der Verwendungszweck ist auf den Zweck der Abwehr von Gefahren für im Einzelnen benannte, hochwertige Schutzgüter der öffentlichen Sicherheit begrenzt, also auf einen Zweck, dessen Verfolgung zum spezifischen Aufgabenbereich der Polizeibehörden zählt (…)).§ 31 PolG NW 1990 ist unter den genannten Bedingungen auch insoweit hinreichend bestimmt, als nicht nur die ausdrücklich aufgezählten Typen von Daten, sondern nach Absatz 2 auch "andere für den Einzelfall benötigte Daten" verlangt und verarbeitet werden dürfen. Die Bestimmtheitsanforderungen sind insoweit gewahrt, weil der Begriff der "anderen für den Einzelfall benötigten Daten" unter Berücksichtigung des Normzwecks der Gefahrenabwehr und damit auch hinsichtlich der Feststellung, wozu die Daten "benötigt" werden, so konkretisiert werden kann, dass der Verhältnismäßigkeitsgrundsatz gewahrt bleibt."

778 See BVerfG, ibid., cip. 148: "Ohne die Begrenzung auf das Vorliegen einer konkreten Gefahr gäbe es demgegenüber keine hinreichenden Anhaltspunkte zur teleologischen Bestimmung der erfassbaren Daten, insbesondere soweit es sich um "andere für den Einzelfall benötigte Daten" handelt. Fehlt es an einer konkreten Gefahr, ist nicht mit verfassungsrechtlich hinreichender Bestimmtheit ermittelbar, unter welchen Bedingungen Daten "für den Einzelfall" benötigt werden. Wäre Bezugspunkt der Rasterfahndung etwa eine allgemeine Terrorismusgefahr und würde diese somit zum Bezugspunkt der Konkretisierung der Art der Daten, die von der Polizei benötigt werden, wäre eine nahezu grenzenlose Ermächtigung geschaffen. Es fehlten jegliche Anhaltspunkte für die Prüfung, ob die zu erhebenden Daten "für den Einzelfall benötigt" werden. Dies würde verfassungsrechtliche Bestimmtheitsanforderungen verletzen."

the data and the tasks for that the retrieval serves in a sufficiently precise manner. (…/The wording allows) each notional accordance between the law that shall be executed and the income tax act in order to authorize the retrieval of the account data. Consequently, the scope of application would be unlimited in light of the fact that the income tax act contains numerous notions without concrete references to tax law which also exist in a multitude of other laws with totally different objectives."[779] The Court came to the conclusion that the retrieval of data has to relate to specific terms under the Act. In the Court's opinion, there would be too many other laws containing such terms and, thus, allowing for the retrieval of data.[780]

As described above, in the case of "*License Plate Recognition*", the Court weighed the criteria of both the requirement of purpose specification and the principle of proportionality against each other. As a first step, it examined to what extent the legal provision authorizing the automated license plate recognition determined the purposes for the collection of the data. The Court came to the conclusion that the police law originally offended, did not provide "concrete requirements for the state measure, it especially did not pre-determine the reason and the purpose of usage which was sufficiently specific for certain areas and legally clear."[781] Indeed, the provision authorized the collection of data for the purpose of checking it against the data files that were open for investigation. The Court argued, however, that this term "does not determine the purpose for that the collection and the checking of the data shall finally serve. Only the manner how an investigation purpose shall be, after the collection of the data,

779 See BVerfG, 13th June 2007, 1 BvR 1550/03, cip. 79 and 80: "Auf diese Weise werden der Kreis der Behörden, die zu Abrufersuchen berechtigt sein sollen, und die Aufgaben, denen solche Ersuchen dienen sollen, nicht präzise genug festgelegt. Sollte der Wortlaut von § 93 Abs. 8 AO weit zu verstehen sein, so genügte jede begriffliche Übereinstimmung zwischen dem anzuwendenden Gesetz und dem Einkommensteuergesetz, damit ein Kontoabruf in Betracht käme. In der Folge wäre der Anwendungsbereich der Norm praktisch unübersehbar, da das Einkommensteuergesetz zahlreiche Begriffe enthält, die keinen besonderen steuerrechtlichen Bezug aufweisen und sich auch in einer Vielzahl anderer Gesetze mit völlig unterschiedlichen Regelungsgegenständen finden (...)."

780 See BVerfG, ibid., cip. 81.

781 See BVerfG, 11th of March 2008, 1 BVR 2047/05 and 1 BvR 1254/07, cip. 98: "In den angegriffenen Bestimmungen fehlt es an näheren Voraussetzungen für die Maßnahme, insbesondere an einer hinreichenden bereichsspezifischen und normenklaren Bestimmung des Anlasses und des Verwendungszwecks der automatisierten Erhebung."

achieved is mentioned. This purpose (itself) indeed remains open."[782] Pursuant to the Court's decision, the notion 'open investigation', at least, did not determine the purpose because there was no legal or commonly accepted definition of the term.[783] The broad specification of the purpose did not particularly exclude the possibility to use the collected data for police surveillance or even for purposes of criminal investigation.[784] The requirement of 'public streets and spaces' did indeed restrict the locations where the data can be legally collected but did not refine the purpose of the collection.[785] Finally, it was not possible to restrain the purpose by narrowly interpreting the provision, because there was no identifiable core objective of the regulation.[786] Consequently, the undetermined purpose of collection of the data lead to the result that the information also gathered on the basis of that data is equally illegitimate.[787] Given the broad definition of the purpose, and all potential purposes considered, the Court then examined, as a second step, whether or not the provision met the requirement of proportionality. It came to the conclusion that the provision was not proportionate in light of the following reasons: first, that the lack in the reasoning for the collection of the data could lead to chilling effects on society as a whole; second, the purpose was not restricted to the defense of concrete dangers; and third, the provision did not differentiate between the reasons for the inclusion of certain individuals in the data files for the open investigation.[788] In addition, the Court stressed that the provision did not clearly exclude the collection of the data on the basis that the reason given as to why the license plates were included in the open file for all investigations fell away. Finally, the provision did not limit the collection and usage of the data for the determined purposes. The Court pointed out that this lack in limitation could lead to roaming data. This would also lead to an infringement of the principle of proportionality.[789]

---

782 See BVerfG, ibid., cip. 99: "Erwähnt wird lediglich das Mittel, mit dem ein Ermittlungszweck nach der Erhebung weiter verfolgt werden soll. Welcher Zweck das sein soll, bleibt jedoch offen."
783 See BVerfG, ibid., cip. 100.
784 See BVerfG, ibid., cip. 136 and 149.
785 See BVerfG, ibid., cip. 144.
786 See BVerfG, ibid., cip. 153.
787 See BVerfG, ibid., cip. 157.
788 See BVerfG, ibid., cip. 170 to 176.
789 See BVerfG, ibid., cip. 177 and 178.

(d) Liberalization of the strict requirement by referring to the object of protection

In conclusion, the German Constitutional Court considers a purpose provided for by law with respect to the treatment of data by the State as sufficiently precise if they result, for example, as: from the type of collection such as a 'census for population, profession, housing, and work areas', or pursues the 'prevention, intelligence, and criminal prosecution of international terrorist attacks' or other explicitly listed crimes. Instead, the 'defense of an abstract danger' or notions which refer to unknown purposes such as 'open investigation' and, as such, only to the way of how these unknown purposes shall be achieved are not sufficiently precise.

In the case of "*Federal Criminal Police Office Act*", the Constitutional Court finally refined the general conditions as described. In this case, the Court clarified, as a first step, the criteria to be considered in order to decide whether a later use of data still pursues the same purpose or whether this usage pursues another purpose and must thus be considered as a change of purpose.[790] Pursuant to this decision, the later use of data in another procedure (other than that of the collection) but for the same purpose requires, on the one hand, a proper legal basis. However, this extension does not constitute a change of purpose and, thus, does not have to meet the strict proportionality requirements for a change of purpose. Instead, such a later use of data must strictly apply the conditions set up by the law that authorized the collection. In this regard, this law has to determine, first, the public agency that is allowed to collect the data; second, the specific purpose; and third, further requirements set up for the collection of the data. By refining these specific criteria, the Constitutional Court clarified that it is not sufficient to specify the purpose by simply referring to the abstract task of a public agency. Instead, the purpose specified within the law that authorizes the collection of data sets the limit for the later processing and must be, as a consequence, more specific than the abstract task of the public agency. However, the purpose originally specified has not always to refer, for example, to explicitly listed crimes. Instead, it can

790 See BVerfG, 20th of April 2016, 1 BvR 966/09 and 1 BvR 1140/09 (Federal Bureau of Investigation Law), cip. 277; see with respect to further refinements in this decision beneath point C. III. 1. b) bb) (2) Proportionate change of purpose.

also refer to the object of protection that is protected by these criminal provisions.[791]

This last criteria is highly important because the reference to an object of protection leaves the public agency with more room for action than a reference to an explicit provision which is established in order to protect the object of protection. The reason is that the object of protection is broader than the explicit provision. This conclusion is based on the Court's wording as: "A later usage for the same purpose is therefore only possible if it is carried out be the same public agency, for the same task, and if it serves the same object of protection as decisive for the collection: If this (the data collection) is allowed for the protection of specific objects of protection *or* for the prevention of specific crimes, only, this limits the immediate or later use even in the same public agency (… /words in brackets and underlining added by the author)".[792] Indeed, this conclusion is not free of doubt because the Court refers, in a subsequent paragraph, to both criteria not alternatively ("or") but cumulatively ("and") as: "In conclusion, it is decisive (…) that the public agency authorized for the data collection uses the data for the same task, the same objects of protection *and* for the prosecution or prevention of the same crimes as specified in the law authorizing the collection of the data. (Underlining added by the author.)"[793] In the first quote, the Court thus appears to allow both options as alternatives, whereas in the second quote both options appear to form a cumulative requirement. The second option would lead, in contrast to the conclusion drawn in this thesis, to a narrower room of action for the public agency than the first one.

---

791 Cf. BVerfG, ibid., cip. 278 and 279.

792 See BVerfG, ibid., cip. 279: "Eine weitere Nutzung innerhalb der ursprünglichen Zwecksetzung kommt damit nur seitens derselben Behörde im Rahmen derselben Aufgabe und für den Schutz derselben Rechtsgüter in Betracht wie für die Datenerhebung maßgeblich: Ist diese nur zum Schutz bestimmter Rechtsgüter oder zur Verhütung bestimmter Straftaten erlaubt, so begrenzt dies deren unmittelbare sowie weitere Verwendung auch in derselben Behörde, (soweit keine gesetzliche Grundlage für eine zulässige Zweckänderung eine weitergehende Nutzung erlaubt)."

793 See BVerfG, ibid., cip. 282: "Für die Wahrung der Zweckbindung kommt es demnach darauf an, dass die erhebungsberechtigte Behörde die Daten im selben Aufgabenkreis zum Schutz derselben Rechtsgüter und zur Verfolgung oder Verhütung derselben Straftaten nutzt, wie es die jeweilige Datenerhebungsvorschrift erlaubt."

In any case, as a second step, the Court also refines the concept of protection with respect to the reason of the data processing. This refinement does not require the same reason as required for its collection. The Court stressed, at first, that the requirement to specify the reason for State action, such as the "adequately specified danger" in the area of danger prevention or the "adequate grounds of suspicion" in the area of prosecution of crimes, does not result from the principle of purpose limitation.[794] As illustrated previously, this requirement indeed results from the principle of clarity of law, which only supplements the principle of purpose limitation, but is equally based in the right to informational self-determination.[795] As a consequence, the public agency can use the data at a later stage as a baseline for further investigation, even if there is no specific danger. The existence of a "specific investigative reason" usually suffices.[796] However, even if no specific danger is required, the object of protection must be clear because, here again, the later use must pursue the same task and serve the same objects of protection as the data collection. The Court makes it very clear that this refinement is not a further tightening of the principle of purpose limitation, but a liberalization of it.[797] The Court justifies this liberalization as: "This (liberalization) acknowledges the fact that the production of knowledge cannot be based – not least if it is about understanding terroristic structures – on the pure addition of single, separated data being taken into account only formally pursuant to criteria specified by law. (…) Through the boundaries to the tasks specified in the moment of collection and the objects of protection, the later usage of the data as a pure baseline for further investigation is adequately limited".[798]

794 See BVerfG, ibid., cip. 285.

795 See above under point C. II. 1. c) ee) (1) (a) Function of purpose specification (basic conditions), referring to BVerfG, 13th June 2007, 1 BvR 1550/03 (Retrieval of Banking Account Matser Data), cip. 71, 73 and 74.

796 See BVerfG, 20th of April 2016, 1 BvR 966/09 and 1 BvR 1140/09 (Federal Bureau of Investigation Law), cip. 289: "konkreter Ermittlungsansatz".

797 See BVerfG, ibid., cip. 292: "Hierin liegt keine Verschärfung der Maßstäbe, sondern eine behutsame Einschränkung, indem das Kriterium der hypothetischen Datenneuerhebung nicht strikt angewandt (…), sondern in Blick auf die - die zu fordernde Aktualität der Gefahrenlage bestimmenden - Eingriffsschwellen gegenüber früheren Anforderungen (…) teilweise zurückgenommen wird."

798 See BVerfG, ibid., cip. 281: "Dies trägt dem Umstand Rechnung, dass sich die Generierung von Wissen – nicht zuletzt auch, wenn es um das verstehen terroristischer Strukturen geht – nicht vollständig auf die Addition von je getrennten, nach Rechtskriterien formell ein- oder ausblendbaren Einzeldaten reduzieren

In contrast, this liberalization does not apply to data which is collected by an infringement of the right to inviolability of the home or the right to the confidentiality and integrity of information technological systems. The later use of this kind of data by the State is legitimate only if there is, additional to the before-mentioned conditions, again a specific or even urgent danger. The German Constitutional Court justifies this stricter condition in relation to this type of data with regard to the particular severity of the infringement with these fundamental rights.[799] The Court considers an infringement of these basic rights as particularly severe because it typically concerns the essence of private life, which gets supplementary protection by the right to human dignity in Article 1 GG. From this perspective, an individual's private home is particularly protected against surveillance because it typically concerns highly private or sensitive communication. Similar, information technological systems contain (typically) information stored over a longer period of time. An intrusion into these systems can reveal highly private or sensitive information, as well as, if the data is processed further, personal weaknesses and attitudes, which should be kept secret. In contrast, the German Court does not consider, for example, an infringement of the right to privacy of telecommunications as equally severe because this typically concerns single acts of immediate communication only. The essence of these rights must therefore be differently protected.[800]

(2) Private sector: 'Self-control of legitimacy'

With respect to the private sector, at first glance, the German Court pursues a similar approach. The Court refers to the same idea behind the regulation for both the private and public sector, such as: 'The right to informational self-determination protects the individual against information

lässt. (...) Durch die Bindung an die für die Datenerhebung maßgeblichen Aufgaben und die Anforderungen des Rechtsgüterschutzes hat auch eine Verwendung der Daten als Spurenansatz einen hinreichend konkreten Ermittlungsbezug, (den der Gesetzgeber nicht durch weitere einschränkende Maßgaben absichern muss)."

799 See BVerfG, ibid., cip. 283.

800 See BVerfG, ibid., cip. 119 to 129 as well 238 and 239.

related measures which he or she cannot foresee nor control'[801] and 'the general personality right consists of the right of the individual to determine by him or herself the disclosure and usage of his or her personal data'[802]. However, the mechanisms safeguarding this guarantee are different. As illustrated above, in the case of "*Release of Confidentiality*", the Court stated on the claimant's duty to authorize her insurance company to "retrieve appropriate information from all doctors, hospitals, nursing homes, where (../the claimant) was or will be treated, as well as from (../the claimant's) health insurance company and other personal insurance companies, social insurance companies, public agencies, current and former employers."[803] The Constitutional Court came to the conclusion that the authorization was too broad, despite former decisions of lower courts stating that it was legal, and consequently lead to an infringement of the claimant's right to informational self-determination.

Interestingly, the purpose itself provided for by the release of confidentiality does not appear to be broader than the purposes lawfully provided for by ordinary law regarding a State's treatment of data: The authorization, and the insurance policy, made clear that any retrieval of information would only occur with respect to the event of insurance and the approval and execution of the policy services. However, given the sensitivity of the data, the general list of rather unspecific inquiry offices and the lack of determination of the specific inquiries themselves, the Constitutional Court held the authorization as being too vague. From its point of view, the claimant lost "the possibility to control her interests of confidentiality by

801 See, for the public sector, for example, BVerfG, 4th of April 2006, 1 BvR 518/02 (Retrieval of Bank Account Master Data), cip. 74; and for the private sector, BVerfG, 1 BvR 2027/02 (Release of Confidentiality), cip. 43.

802 See, for the private sector, BVerfG, 1 BvR 2027/02, cip. 31; and for the public sector, BVerfG, 15th of December 1983, 1 BvR 209, 269, 362, 420, 440, 484/83 (Decision on Population Census), cip. 173; cf. equally BVerfG, 14th of July 1999, 1 BvR 2226/94 (Surveillance of Telecommunications), cip. 136 and BVerfG, 3rd of March 2004, 1 BvR 2378/98 (Big Eavesdropping Operation), cip. 132 and BVerfG, 4th of April 2006, 1 BvR 518/02 (Dragnet Investigation), cip. 64 and BVerfG, 13th June 2007, 1 BvR 1550/03 (Retrieval of Bank Account Master Data), cip. 63.

803 See BVerfG, ibid., cip. 13: "von allen Ärzten, Krankenhäusern und Krankenanstalten, bei denen ich in Behandlung war oder sein werde sowie von meiner Krankenkasse: … und von Versicherungsgesellschaften, Sozialversicherungsträgern, Behörden, derzeitigen und früheren Arbeitgebern sachdienliche Auskünfte einzuholen."

her own".[804] This ability of self-control apparently is the essential difference for the Court when it examines whether the control mechanisms implemented by a private data controller are sufficient. This is the reason for why the Court also examines, in detail, alternative mechanisms. As stressed previously, the Court examined, at first, whether the claimant relied on the insurance and whether there was no other insurance company offering such policy without the same authorization. Both questions referred to market mechanisms enabling the individual to control the disclosure of the information. Correspondingly, the Court considered whether the defendant had offered, on an organizational level, alternative mechanisms such as subsequent releases relating to her confidentiality that would have respected the claimant's possibility of self-determination.[805]

Thus, so far, it shall be summarized that the German Constitutional Court applies, for the public and private sector, different scales in order to answer the question of whether the processing of personal data complies with the idea of informational self-determination or not.

2. Criticism: Stricter effects on the private than the public sector

The preceding chapters illustrated the important role that the specification of purposes plays in the European data protection system. The requirement of purpose specification provides a central link for further legal requirements. First, it serves to define the scope of application through determining which data are identifiable. Second, it determines the data controller who is responsible for safeguarding the regulation. Third, it determines further requirements such as adequacy, relevance, and necessity of processing of personal data. However, despite its important role, several aspects remain unclear. First, there appears to be a different scale in determining the precision of purposes specified, on the one hand, by the legislator authorizing certain acts of data processing and, on the other hand, by data controllers which base their processing either on the law or on the individual's consent. Second, there are further ambiguities surrounding the

804 See BVerfG, 1 BvR 2027/02 (Release of Confidentiality), cip. 43: "Dabei begibt sie sich auch der Möglichkeit, die Wahrung ihrer Geheimhaltungsinteressen selbst zu kontrollieren (…)."

805 See above under point C. I. 2. d) bb) In the private sector: The contract as an essential link for legal evaluation.

specification of the purpose in light of the applicable concept of protection, in particular, regarding requirements for the consent, and consequences of its non-fulfillment. Finally, none of the concepts, be they appropriately applied or not, provide reliable criteria that help data controllers in the private sector to determine how precisely they shall specify their processing purposes. The subsequent analysis will show that it appears as though the initial concept of protection developed by the constitutional courts with respect to the processing of personal data by the State is simply transferred to the private sector.[806] The surprising bottom line of such a transfer is, given the different situations of the State and private data controllers, that the effects of the requirements discussed are even stricter for controllers acting in the private sector than for the State.

a) Difference in precision of purposes specified by legislator and data controllers

The first aspect which became apparent during the previous analysis is the divergence between the purpose being specified, on the one hand, by the legislator and, on the other hand, by data controllers in the private sector. In summary, the legislator is allowed to specify purposes in a broader way than data controllers. Examining in detail the purposes listed in the law for which certain acts of data processing are authorized, there are essentially four types. The first type refers to data processing which is necessary for the technical conveyance of a communication service.[807] The second type authorizes data processing for the necessary conclusion, execution or termination of a contract.[808] The third type refers to obligations provided for

806 Cf. above under points C. II. 1. b) bb) (1) Peliminary note: Clarifying conceptual (mis)understandings, and dd) (2) (a) Peliminary note: Clarifying conceptual (mis)understandings.

807 See in the ePrivacy Directive Article 5 sect. 1 sent. 3 and sect. 3, Article 6 sect. 1; in the German Telecommunication Law Article 88 sect. 3, Article 96 sect. 1, as well as in the Telecommunication Law Article 15 sect. 1.

808 This includes billing purposes; see in the ePrivacy Directive Article 6 sect. 2; in the Data Protection Directive Article 7 lit. b; in the German Telecommunication Law Article 95 sect. 1 and Article 96 sect. 1; in the German Telemedia Law Article 14 sect. 1 and Article 15 sect. 1; and in the German Federal Data Protection Law Article 28 sect. 1 sent. 1 no. 1.

by law and public interests.[809] Finally, the fourth type refers to the interests of data controller.

aa) Data processing for undisputed 'marketing purposes' authorized by law

In this last respect, the law provides both provisions authorizing the data processing for the data controller's interests in general, as long as they are legitimate,[810] and more specific purposes. In particular, the purposes of 'marketing' and 'market research' play a prominent role as the following provisions will illustrate:

- Article 6 sect. 3 of the ePrivacy Directive allows the processing of traffic data for the purpose of marketing or for the provision of value added services if it is based on the user's consent;
- Article 95 sect. 3 sent. 1 of the German Telecommunication Law also authorizes the processing of data in relation with a contract with telecommunication service providers for its own purposes of marketing and market research if it is based on the user's consent;
- Article 96 sect. 3 of the German Telecommunication Law equally allows the processing of traffic data for purposes of marketing of telecommunication services, technically improving the usability of the telecommunication services or for the provision of value added services if it is based on the user's consent;
- Article 15 sect. 3 of the German Telemedia Law allows the creation of user profiles with 'usage data' for purposes of marketing, market research, or technical improvement of the usability of Information Society services if it is pseudonymized and the user does not object;
- The German Federal Data Protection Law finally authorizes data processing for the data controller's own purposes of marketing and address trading (Article 28 sect. 3 to 3b); the commercial data treatment for third parties' purposes of marketing and address trading (Article

---

809 See, for example, in the ePrivacy Directive Article 15 sect. 1 referring to Article 13 sect. 1 of the Data Protection Directive; in the Data Protection Directive Article 7 lit. c and e as well as the before mentioned Article 13 sect. 1; in the German Telecommunication Law, in particular, Articles 108 et seqq.

810 See in the Data Protection Directive Article 7 lit. f and in the German Federal Data Protection Law the basic legitimate ground in Article 28 sect. 1 sent. 1 no. 3.

29); and the commercial data treatment for third parties' purposes of market research (Article 30a).

In legal literature, legal scholars do not doubt that these specified purposes within the law itself are sufficiently precise.[811]

bb) Disputed 'marketing purposes' specified by data controllers

However, it is interesting to see that while particular purposes of 'marketing' specified within the law are almost not disputed amongst legal scholars, the same purposes specified by data controllers in the private sector are disputed. The Article 29 Data Protection Working Party promotes that a controller simply using the term 'marketing purpose' does not sufficiently meet the requirement of purpose specification, pursuant to Article 6 sect. 1 lit. a of the Data Protection Directive.[812] Comparably, German legal scholars argue that the purpose of 'market research' included in the user's consent does not meet the requirement of purpose specification either.[813] This is at least the case if the data controller does not differentiate between their own and third parties' marketing purposes.[814] This second reasoning enforces the data controller to apply at least the difference between the purposes drawn by German law itself. As described above, the German Federal Data Protection Law differentiates between the controller's purposes and purposes pursued on behalf of third parties in order

811 See, for example, Simitis, Federal Data Protection Law, § 30a cip. 67 to 95, who undertakes great efforts to define and distinguish the admittedly vague statutory terms of market and opinion research as purposes of data processing while not calling into question their blatant vagueness (indeed, he interprets the terms also with respect to the type of data concerned, which is, at least, given by the law).

812 See the Article 29 Data Protection Working Group, Opinion 03/0213 on purpose limitation, p 16.

813 See Simitis, ibid., § 4a cip. 81 and 82: "Kurzum, nur eine möglichst präzise Aussage räumt den Betroffenen grundsätzlich die Chance ein, eine aus ihrer Sicht besonders gefährliche Verarbeitung einzelner Angaben, etwa die uneingeschränkte Übermittlung von ‚Negativmerkmalen' an Kreditinformationssysteme, rechtzeitig zu verhindern."

814 See Kramer, ibid., § 4a BDSG cip. 21 with references to Wolff/Brink, ibid., § 4a cip. 44 and Plath, ibid., § 4a cip. 47.

to cover different risks of the data processing for the individual concerned.[815]

Another reason for why legal scholars take such a strict view of the term 'marketing purposes' used by data controllers seems to be that it often does not refer to a certain type of data. The legal provisions authorizing the data processing for marketing purposes most often refer to certain types such as 'traffic data' (Article 6 sect. 3 of the ePrivacy Directive and Article 96 sect. 3 of the German Telecommunication Law) or 'usage data' (Article 15 sect. 3 of the German Telemedia Law). However, the German Federal Data Protection Law only partly refers to a certain type of data, such as in Article 28 sect. 3 to 3b for ones own marketing purposes, and authorizes the processing for third parties' marketing and market research purposes for any kind of data (Articles 29 and 30a). Thus, the law itself does not consequently apply such a strict approach.

cc) Further examples for different scales applied in order to specify the purpose

This difference also becomes apparent with respect to other purposes. For example, Article 96 sect. 1 of the German Telecommunication Law and Article 15 sect. 3 of the Telemedia Law refer to purposes of technical improvements of the usability for the processing of 'traffic' and 'usage' data, respectively. In contrast, the Working Group promotes that the term 'improving user experience' used by data controllers is not sufficiently precise.[816] In the German Telecommunication Law, Article 88 sect. 3 authorizes the processing of 'content data' and 'related circumstances' for the purpose of protection of the technical telecommunication system. However, the Working Party considers the purpose of 'IT security' as not sufficiently specified.[817] While Article 7 sect. 1 lit. b sent. 2 of the Data Protection Directive refers, exempting from the requirement of purpose limitation, to 'scientific purposes', the Working Party denies that the term of 'future research' used by data controllers meets the requirement of pur-

---

815 See above under point C. II. 1. c) cc) (5) Privileges and restrictions pursuant to pruposes.

816 See the Article 29 Data Protection Working Group, Opinion 03/0213 on purpose limitation, p. 16.

817 See the Article 29 Data Protection Working Group, ibid., p. 16.

pose specification in the first sentence of that article.[818] Comparably, while Article 28a of the German Federal Data Protection Law allows the transfer of certain data to credit agencies, legal scholars consider the terms of 'transfer of remuneration claim to any refinancing bank' or of 'data of the debtor for credit processing' or for the purpose of 'credit security' used by data controllers to not be sufficiently precise.[819]

dd) Can the context help interpret a specified purpose?

As mentioned above, the individual's consent to the processing of his or her data for the purposes of 'prudent business management' or 'usual support of the authorizing person' is not sufficiently precise. These two last examples are particularly interesting in light of the criteria that the German Constitutional Court developed with respect to the purposes provided for by law. This is the case because the German Constitutional Court states "that the legislator precisely and specifically determines in certain areas the purpose of usage."[820] Pursuant to this requirement, "a legal provision is sufficiently determined (…) if the purpose results from the context of the provision with respect to the area of life that shall be regulated."[821] In light of this consideration, the terms 'prudent business management' and 'usual support of the authorizing person' would, in principle, allow the individual concerned, as well as the data controller to conclude from the specific context which kind of processing shall be covered and which not. The context of the interrelationship and the area of life referred to in the individuals consent appear indeed to clarify the extent of the data processing. The Article 29 Data Protection Working Party similarly considers that "the degree of detail in which a purpose should be specified depends on the particular context in which the data are collected and the personal data involved."[822] Regarding the requirement of 'making the specified purpose explicit', it stresses that the context may be sufficient informing the indi-

818 See the Article 29 Data Protection Working Group, ibid., p. 16.
819 See Simitis, ibid., § 4a cip. 81 and 82; Däubler/Klebe/Welde/Weichert, BDSG, § 4a cip. 18.
820 BVerfG, 15th of December 1983, 1 BvR 209, 269, 362, 420, 440, 484/83, cip. 161.
821 BVerfG, ibid., cip. 180.
822 See the Article 29 Data Protection Working Group, ibid., p. 16.

vidual about the purpose of the processing.[823] Indeed, a data controller could significantly increase the probability that such purposes meet the requirement of purpose specification if it provides examples of how the data will be processed and used. In this regard, the Working Party stated: "For 'related' processing operations, the concept of an overall purpose, under whose umbrella a number of data processing operations take place, can be useful."[824] However, it ads "that controllers should avoid identifying only one broad purpose in order to justify various further processing activities which are in fact only remotely related to the actual initial purpose."[825] The context itself seems, hence, to not provide sufficient criteria in order to legitimize purposes such as 'prudent business management' or 'usual support of the authorizing person'. In conclusion, a solution for the question of how precisely the data controller has to specify the purpose, could be to have an objective scale which would assist in defining the context.[826]

ee) A different scale for 'purpose specification' pursuant to the German concept of protection

In any event, the German Constitutional Court appears to consider two different objective scales in order to determine the degree of precision of the purpose specified, on the one hand by the legislator and, on other hand, by data controllers in the private sector. It considers purposes provided for by law for the treatment of data by the State as lawful if they result, for example: from the type of collection such as a 'census for population, profession, housing, and work areas', or pursues the 'prevention, intelligence, and criminal prosecution of international terrorist attacks' or other explicitly listed crimes.[827] In this regard, the Court considers whether the collection of data occurs in order to prevent abstract or concrete dangers. The law, which was questioned in the case of "*Dragnet In-*

823 See the Article 29 Data Protection Working Group, ibid., p. 18.
824 See the Article 29 Data Protection Working Group, ibid., p. 16.
825 See the Article 29 Data Protection Working Group, ibid., p. 16.
826 See introduction under point B. III. 5. Values as normative scale defining "contexts" and "purposes".
827 See above under point C. II. 1. c) ee) Examples for specific purposes: Certain areas of life or explicitly listed crimes.

vestigation", had authorized the collection of 'other data which is necessary for the concrete case'. The Court concluded that this notion can be, in light of the overall aim, typified in a way that it is proportionate. In contrast, without reference to a concrete threat, it was not possible to interpret the notion in a way which limits the data concerned. If the notion referred to an abstract threat, only, this "would infringe the constitutional requirements for the clarity of law."[828] As a consequence, the 'defense of an abstract danger' or notions which refer to unknown purposes are not sufficiently precise.

On the other hand, the Court considered an individual's consent was not sufficiently precise if the consent given authorized his or her insurance company to "retrieve appropriate information from" certain types medical institutions from the health care sector such doctors, hospitals, etc.[829] All of this data was intended to be gathered for the purpose of 'approval and execution of the policy services'. Interestingly, if the Court had strictly applied its considerations made in the decision of "*Dragnet Investigation*", it would have probably agreed that the release of confidentiality was sufficiently precise. Indeed, the Court considered the release of confidentiality as 'comparable with a general authorization to retrieve sensitive information with respect to the insurance event (…)' because the broad term 'appropriate' did not enable the policy-holder 'to pre-estimate which information can be retrieved on the basis of the authorization'. However, the release of confidentiality required a 'concrete (insurance) case' as a pre-condition for the collection of the data. And from this angle, it would have been possible 'to sufficiently pre-determine which data is appropriate 'for the concrete case'.

In conclusion, even if the release of confidentiality required, as a precondition for the retrieval of personal data, a concrete insurance case, the Court considered the consent given as not being sufficiently precise. The reason for this appears to be that the Court referred to two different objective scales in order to determine the degree of precision of the purpose specified, on the one hand by the legislator though the means of legal provisions, and on the other hand, by the data controller in the private sector gathering the individual's consent. In the case of "*Release of Confidentiality*" which referred to the individual's consent and not an authorizing law,

828 See BVerfG, 4th of April 2006, 1 BvR 518/02, cip. 145 to 148.
829 See BVerfG, 1 BvR 2027/02, cip. 13.

the decisive fact was, in the Court's opinion, the extent of control that would have been possible, on the basis of the "consent" as a protection instrument. From the Court's point of view, the release of confidentiality was too broad because the individual concerned lost "the possibility to control her interests of confidentiality by her own".[830] Thus, this aim of enabling or giving an individual control over their own confidentiality justifies a different objective scale for determining the purpose, than if the purpose is determined by an authorizing law. If the legislator authorizes the data processing on the basis of a legal provision, the individual has lost this possibility of self-control in any case. This appears to justify that purposes can be more broadly specified in an authorizing legal provision than in the individual's consent.

ff) Interim conclusion: Do regulation instruments dictate the scale for 'purpose specification'?

In light of this reasoning, it becomes apparent that the concrete regulation instrument might dictate the degree of precision of the purpose specified. In light of the concept of protection of the right to informational self-determination, this differentiation is reasonable. The German Constitutional Court considers the individual's consent, on the private sector, as "the essential instrument in order to develop free and self-responsible actions in relation to third parties."[831] The Article 29 Data Protection Working Group also sees the individual's consent as an expression of "self-determination".[832] Thus, both ideas lead to the result that the purpose must be more precisely specified within the individual's consent than in an authorizing provision.

Indeed, whether the European Court of Justice applies a similar approach is not (yet) clear. In the decision of "*Telekom vs. Germany*", it applied a more functional approach. In this case, the Court stated that "the consent given (…) to the publication of his personal data in a public direc-

830 See BVerfG, ibid., cip. 43.
831 See BVerfG, ibid., cip. 31, 32, and 34.
832 See above under point C. II. 1. b) dd) Preliminary note: Clarifying conceptual (mis)understandings, referring to the Article 29 Data Protection Woking Group, Opinion 06/2014 on the notion of legitimate interests of the data controller under Article 7 of Directive 96/46/EC, p. 13.

tory relates to the purpose of that publication and thus extends to any subsequent processing of those data by third-party undertakings active in the market (…), provided that such processing pursues that same purpose."[833] The Court concludes from this that the transfer of personal data from one party to another one pursuing the same purpose does not harm the individual's right to data protection.[834] In this instance, the Court does not refer to an individual's self-determination but simply to his or her right to data protection. And in light of this right, the purpose specified within the individual's consent simply 'bundles', from a normative perspective, several acts of data processing. Thus, so long as the data processing occurs for the same purpose that was made explicit when the first consent was given, it does not harm Article 8 ECFR. Such a function does not, *per se*, provide for stricter requirements regarding the purpose specified in the consent than in an authorizing law.[835]

b) Further ambiguities and possible reasons behind the same

However, there are further ambiguities regarding the concept of protection that become apparent in the legal discussion on the requirement of purpose specification in the private sector. While German legal scholars and the Article 29 Data Protection Working Group have a similar understanding regarding the requirements to specify the purpose and make the specified purpose explicit, their reasoning appears to intermingle the applicable concept of protection provided for by the different constitutions. Even more so, further considerations will bring to light that certain requirements may simply be transferred from the public sector to the private sector. At least, this is the case with respect to the individual's consent, in particular, the moment where these requirements are considered to be relevant, and the legal consequences if the requirements are not applied. Examining these aspects, the subsequent considerations will, from time to time, refer to decisions by the German Constitutional Court regarding the right to informa-

---

833 See ECJ C-543/09 cip. 65.
834 See ECJ C-543/09 cip. 66.
835 However, see the discussion at Lynskey, The Foundations of EU Data Protection Law, pp. 190 et seq., whether the consent incorporates the concept of individual self-control enabling an individual not only to determine *what* can be done with data relating to him or her, but also *who* is allwowed to do that.

tional self-determination. Indeed, German basic rights do barely apply when interpreting European law.[836] However, a comparison with the German concept of protection helps one to understand better certain conceptual components and decide which of these components should be incorporated in the concept of protection provided for by the European Charter of Fundamental Rights.

aa) Common understanding about the function of 'purpose specification'

Firstly, the function of specifying purposes and making these purposes explicit and how it is interpreted on both the European and the German level shall be analyzed. As mentioned above, the Article 29 Data Protection Working Group reviewed and discussed in its "Opinion 03/2011 on purpose limitation" the function of both requirements, i.e. to specify the purpose and to limit the later processing of data to the originally specified purpose. In its opinion, the requirement to specify the purpose serves, as quoted previously, to "determine whether data processing complies with the law, and to establish what data protection safeguards should be applied (…)."[837] From this perspective, the specification of the purpose "requires an internal assessment carried out by the data controller and is a necessary condition for accountability."[838] This function is similar to the German concept of protection. The German Constitutional Court considered that "only when it is clear for which purpose the information is required and which possibilities of linking and usage exist, it is possible to answer the question of whether the infringement of the right to informational self-determination is constitutionally legal or not."[839] Therefore, the specification of the purpose plays, in relation to both concepts of protection, an essential role, because it provides the legal link for subsequent legal requirements.

---

836 See above under point C. I. 1. a) The interplay between European Convention for Human Rights, European Charter of Fundamental Rights and German Basic Rights.

837 See the Article 29 Data Protection Working Group, Opinion 03/0213 on purpose limitation, pp. 13 and 15.

838 See the Article 29 Data Protection Working Group, ibid., pp. 13 and 15.

839 See BVerfG, 15th of December 1983, 1 BvR 209, 269, 362, 420, 440, 484/83, cip. 159.

bb) Ambiguous understanding regarding the functions of 'making specified purpose explicit'

Compared with the requirement to specify the purpose, the requirement of making the specified purpose explicit has another function. The Working Party considers, in this regard: "The purposes of collection must not only be specified in the minds of the persons responsible for data collection. They must also be made explicit. In other words, they must be clearly revealed, explained or expressed in some intelligible form. (…) The requirement that the purposes be specified 'explicitly' contributes to transparency and predictability. (…) It helps all those processing data on behalf of the controller, as well as data subjects, data protection authorities and other stakeholders, to have a common understanding of how the data can be used."[840]

The German right to informational self-determination provides a function equivalent to the requirement of 'making specified purposes explicit'. However, the German Constitutional Court locates this function in the principle of clarity of law, in particular, with respect to the State. The principle of clarity of law "shall guarantee that public agencies find legal criteria for the execution of the law and that the judicial courts are able to control it; furthermore, the principle of clarity of law enables the citizens concerned to be prepared by potentially infringing measures."[841] However, while the predictability plays an important role by protecting "the individual against information related measures (by the State) which he or she cannot foresee nor control"[842], the right to informational self-deter-mination safeguards, in the private sector, "that the legal order provides and maintains the legal conditions under which the individual is able to participate in communicational processes in a self-determined way and to develop his or her personality."[843] For this approach, "the contract is the essential instrument."[844]

In light of this conceptual difference, the question is, on the European level, where the idea of the requirement to 'make the specified purpose explicit' to the individual concerned originates from. If there is no other jus-

840 See the Article 29 Data Protection Working Group, ibid., p. 17.
841 See BVerfG, 13th June 2007, 1 BvR 1550/03, cip. 71, 73.
842 See BVerfG, ibid., cip. 74.
843 See BVerfG, 1 BvR 2027/02, cip. 33.
844 See BVerfG, ibid., cip. 34.

tification for this requirement, it appears to introduce in the private sector a protection instrument that primarily protects, in Germany, individuals against data processing authorized by law. Indeed, Britz makes clear that this function may also be transposed to the private sector: the information of the individual about the harm of his or her fundamental right may diminish its intensity because it principally enables the individual to adjust to it, correct wrong data, and seek legal protection against it.[845] The European Court of Human Rights refers to a similar idea with respect to Article 8 ECHR. The European Court of Human Rights examines the purpose pursued by the data controller in order to determine whether there is an infringement at all: The information by the controller of the individual concerned about the purpose of the data processing frames the individual's "reasonable expectation", enables him or her to react to it, correspondingly, and therefore decides on whether the data processing harms his or her right to private life or not.[846] However, so far, the concept of protection provided for by the European Charter of Fundamental Rights is not sufficiently clear in order to answer the question on the precise function of the requirement to 'make the purpose explicit'. In the case of "*Digital Rights vs. Ireland*", the Court indeed considered, determining the intensity of the infringement, the unspecified threat of the individual concerned that may result from being constantly surveyed.[847] However, this decision referred to the processing of personal data by the State and it is still unclear whether, and if so, to which extent this idea can and should transferred to the private sector.[848]

cc) Arguable focus on data collection for legal evaluation in the private sector

It appears to be exactly such a transfer of certain conceptual elements, which were originally developed for the processing of personal data by the

---

845 See Britz, ibid., p. 584.

846 See above under point C. I. 3. c) b) cc) Particular reference to the individual's "reasonable expectations".

847 See ECJ C-293/12 and C-594/12 cip. 37 referring to Opinion of Advocate General Cruz Villalón delivered on 12 December 2013 on Case C-293/12, cip. 52.

848 See beneath under point C. II. 3. a) bb) (3) Function of making specified purpose explicit.

State, to the private sector, which led legal scholars and the Article 29 Working Group to conclude two further opinions on this issue. First, it is common sense to mainly focus, evaluating the legal consequences of the specified purpose, on the moment the data is collected.[849] Consequently, the specified purpose must also be explicit before the personal data is collected. Recital 28 of the Data Protection Directive states, correspondingly, that the "purposes must be explicit and legitimate and must be determined at the time of collection".[850] The Working Party also stresses that "it follows from the previous analysis that this should not happen later than the time when the collection of personal data occurs."[851] Thus, this requirement not only applies to the consent given by the individual, but also to any kind of data processing in general. Such a broad understanding of the requirement might be discussed because it refers to all data collected, irrespective of how important the data is for the individual concerned. Since the definition of the term of 'personal data' refers, potentially, to any data that more or less relates to the individual, the individual can quickly be overwhelmed by information. The reason is that the controller will be obliged, in light of the increase in digitization in our society, to, on a more and more frequent basis, inform the individual about the processing of data that is somewhat related to him or her. This is, at least the case, if the controller's information duty are not adapted to the specific risk by the processing of that data. Of course, the Article 29 Working Party considers that the context may sufficiently determine for which purpose the controller uses the data and, thus, which information the controller has to provide to the individual.[852] However, again, in order to fulfill this function its must be clear how to define the context.[853]

With respect to the general requirement of purpose specification, it was recommended, only, that the specification of the purpose should be carried

849 See above under points C. II. 1. b) bb) (2) Legal opinion on the function of purpose specification, and C. II. 1. b) cc) Purposes of processing specified when consent is given.

850 See, however, recital 39 sent. 6 of the General Data Protection Regulation, which changes the "must"-requirement into a "should"-recommendation (see the possible impact of this amendment at the end of this paragraph).

851 See the Article 29 Data Protection Working Group, Opinion 03/0213 on purpose limitation, p. 17.

852 See the Article 29 Data Protection Working Group, ibid., p. 18.

853 See above under point B. III. 5. Values as a normative scale in order to determine the "contexts" and "purposes".

out before the data is collected. However, with respect to the individuals consent, the controller must specify the purpose before the data is collected. The European Court of Justice stated in the case of "*Telekom vs. Germany*" that the individuals concerned must be "informed, before the first inclusion of their data in a public directory, of the purpose of that directory".[854] Furthermore, the European legislator clarified in Article 2 sect. 6 of the Civil Rights Directive that the marketing of electronic communication services or the provision of value-added services is only allowed on the basis of the individual's 'prior consent'. With respect to German ordinary law, legal scholars comparably agree that the consent must be given before the data is processed.[855] However, the German Constitutional Court applies a more differentiated approach in this regard. Taking the contract into the center of the execution of the right to informational self-determination, it declares, comparably to the public sector, the moment of the conclusion of the contract, i.e. the legitimate basis for the following collection of the data, as the essential anchor point. However, it admits that the moment of the conclusion of the contract must not be the only possible moment for evaluating the subsequent data treatment. In the case of "*Release of Confidentiality*", it acknowledged that the insurance company was, "in light of the variety of the events, not able to pre-list, already in the contract clause, all the information that might become relevant for the subsequent verification."[856] The Court therefore also considered moments subsequent to the conclusion of the contract in order to evaluate the final consequences of the treatment of data. In the Court's opinion, such moments would have been possible by using alternative or supplementary mechanisms.[857] In this regard, it is important to note that this decision only referred to one specific purpose. In contrast, the Article 29 Working Group promotes that the individual can only give his or her consent during the course of a data process if there is a new purpose.[858]

In conclusion, on the European level, the data controller has to comprehensively inform the individual about all purposes existing the moment that the data is collected. In the end, such a focus on the moment of collec-

---

854 See ECJ C-543/09 cip. 67.

855 See, for example, Simitis, Federal Data Protection Law, § 4a, cip. 27.

856 See BVerfG, 1 BvR 2027/02, cip. 50 and 51.

857 See BVerfG, ibid., cip. 59 and 60.

858 See the Article 29 Data Protection Working Group, Opinion 15/2011 on the definition of consent, p. 34.

tion by private parties corresponds to the strict requirement applied, in Germany, to the processing of personal data by the State.[859] From this perspective, the slight liberalization foreseen in recital 39 sent. 6 of the General Data Protection Regulation might become very relevant. As stressed before, this recital does not require, but only recommends the controller to make explicit the purpose the moment the data is collected. Thus, the European legislator now appears to have foreseen situations where it makes more sense to specify and make explicit the purpose at a later stage.

dd) Arguable legal consequences surrounding the validity of the consent

The second arguable conclusion considered by legal scholars concerns the legal consequences resulting from the fact that the data controller does not meet the requirement to make the specified purpose explicit. With respect to Article 6 sect. 1 lit. a of the Data Protection Directive, some legal scholars consider that the controller must not process the data if the purpose of the data processing is unclear.[860] In contrast, the Article 29 Working Party promotes that if a data controller fails to meet this requirement, it does not mean that the processing as such is illegal. Instead, "it will be necessary to reconstruct the purposes of processing, keeping in mind the facts of the case. While the publicly specified purpose is the main indicator of what the data processing will actually aim at, it is not an absolute reference: where the purposes are specified inconsistently or the specified purposes do not correspond to reality (for instance in case of a misleading data protection notice), all factual elements, as well as the common understanding and reasonable expectations of the data subjects based on such facts, shall be taken into account to determine the actual purposes."[861] In fact, the Working Party intermingles, here again, the requirements of 'purpose specification' and 'making the specified purpose explicit'. The reason appears to be that the Working Party itself is not clear about which functions these requirements precisely have.

---

859 See above under point C. I. 2. e) aa) (1) Principles of clarity of law and purpose limitation referring to the moment when data is collected.

860 See Ehmann/Helfrich, ibid., cip. 13.

861 See the Article 29 Data Protection Working Group, Opinion 03/0213 on purpose limitation, p. 18.

In any case, the Working Group's considerations are interesting with respect to the situation where the data processing is based on the individual's consent. Usually, German legal scholars, as well as judicial courts consider that the consent is invalid if the controller does not sufficiently inform the individual about the processing of data. This is in particular the case, if the controller does not sufficiently specify the purpose of the data processing in the consent form.[862] In light of the principles of good faith, the data controller might not be allowed to fall back on legal provisions authorizing the processing.[863] Therefore, if the controller does not or, even worse, is not able to specify all purposes the moment it collects the data, it is not allowed to adapt its processing operations at a later stage in order to legitimize its processing of the data. Instead, the data processing as a whole is forbidden. With respect to the European level, the above-mentioned recommendation that 'the purpose must not be so broad that it implicitly includes unlawful sub-purposes'[864] points into a similar direction. However, the approach is arguable because it transposes the idea of the legal consequences of an infringement of the principle of clarity of law, which undoubtedly applies to actions of the State to data controllers operating in the private sector.

On the German level, as stressed before, the Constitutional Court developed the requirements of clarity of law in combination with the principle of purpose limitation with respect to the State. In the case of "*License Plate Recognition*", the Court elaborates, on the function of this interplay as: If a processing purpose specified within the law, which shall authorize the data processing, does not exclude serious infringements for fundamental rights of the individual concerned, this authorizing provision must meet the strict proportionality requirement also for the serious infringements.[865]

---

862 See above under point C. II. 1. c) Requirements for consent and consequences of its failure; Kramer, ibid., § 4a BDSG cip. 12, 13 and 22 with further references to Gola/Schomerus, ibid., § 4a cip. 22; Plath, ibid., § 4a cip. 29; OLG Köln, decision from the 17th of June 2011 (6 U 8/11).

863 See Kramer, ibid., § 28 BDSG cip. 60 to 61 with further references; Gola/Schomerus, Federal Data Protection Law, § 4 cip. 16; in contrast, see Article 17 sect. 1 lit. b GDPR, which excludes the individual's right to require, based on an objection to his or her consent, from the controller to delete the personal data if the controller can base the processing on another legitimate ground foreseen by law.

864 See Dammann/Simitis, ibid., cip. 7.

865 See BVerfG, 11th of March 2008, 1 BVR 2047/05 and 1 BvR 1254/07, cip. 95.

And, in the case of "*Data Retention*", the Court explicitly stressed the idea behind that function. With respect to the treatment of data by the Intelligent Services, who in turn provide their results to State authorities, the Court clarified that "the constitutional limits of these authorities using the data (later on) must not be undermined by a wider authorization for the preceding usage (by the Intelligence Services)."[866] Thus, the flux of data and the retrieval of information are principally bound to the requirement that the later usage of information must already be determined the moment the data is first collected. That said, it becomes apparent that the idea that an individual's consent is illegal as a whole if it does not specify possible harm in advance, the strict requirements for state data processing equally burdens private parties: Private parties, like the State, have to specify and make explicit their purposes the moment the data is collected, by excluding all possible later processing that might harm an individual's fundamental right in another way than specified.

In contrast, the above-mentioned consideration of the Article 29 Data Protection Working Party that the purpose must be re-constructed, pursuant to the real circumstances of a data processing, points to another direction.[867] Indeed, these considerations referred to the requirement of 'making specified purposes explicit' and not to the consent. However, if transferred to the consent, these considerations could mean that the consent would not be illegal as a whole. Rather, the alternative could be, that the purpose specified in the consent simply answers the question on whether or not a later processing activity can still be covered by the consent or not. In this case, the question would not be whether the consent is illegal as a whole, but whether the specific later processing of data is legal or not.

c) The lack of a legal scale for 'purpose specification' in the private sector

The preceding criticism provided several arguments that the ambiguous understanding of the different concepts of protection (provided for by different constitutions) led to a transfer of requirements initially developed

866 See BVerfG, ibid., cip. 233.

867 See the Article 29 Data Protection Working Group, Opinion 03/0213 on purpose limitation, p. 18.

for the State to data controllers operating on the private sector. In light of this transferal, it is astonishing to note that the requirement to specify the purpose, is actually stricter for data controllers operating in the private sector, than for the legislator authorizing the data processing by law.[868] This is even more the case, since a precise look at the structural conditions surrounding the requirement of purpose specification will reveal, in this sub-chapter, that private data controllers additionally have, in practice, more difficulties to specify the purpose than the State. This result is particularly relevant since there are only few reliable criteria which help determine the precision of the purposes being specified, over all.[869] This sub-chapter therefore goes on to examine criteria that may help private data controllers fulfill their task. In doing so, the following will be examined: First, the differentiation between the terms 'purpose', 'means', and 'interests'; and second, which 'purpose' or which 'interest' is, from a time perspective sufficiently specified.

aa) No legal system providing for 'objectives' of data processing in the private sector

As mentioned above, the European Courts provide few criteria that help specify a purpose of data processing.[870] In contrast, the German Constitutional Court elaborated on, during the last 30 years, a rather detailed approach. Indeed, this approach mainly refers to purposes specified by the State. This is the crucial point because the State is able to refer, in order to specify the purposes of its processing of data, to a rather extensively developed legal system. Such a legal system helps to specify the purposes because it extensively provides for the objectives as to how the data shall be processed. In the case of "*Retrieval of Bank Account Master Data*", the German Court highlights this function, in particular. In this case, the law for the encouragement of tax compliance authorized the retrieval of data by state authorities from private banks only under the condition that the

---

868 See above under point C. II. 2. a) Difference in precision of purposes specified by legislator and data controllers.

869 See above under points C. II. 1. b) bb) Criteria discussed for purpose specification, and C. II. 1. b) cc) Purposes of processing specified when consentis given, and C. II. 1. c) dd) (3) Discussion on degree of precision of specified purpose.

870 See above under point C. II. 1. a) ECtHR and ECJ: Almost no criteria.

concrete provision had to relate to the income tax act. The German Court came to the conclusion that such a "scope of application would be unlimited in light of the fact that the income tax act contains numerous notions without concrete references to tax law which also exist in a multitude of other laws *with totally different objectives*. (Underlining by the author)"[871] Thus, the crucial point to consider here is that the objectives of a certain law, to that a legal provision authorizing a data processing refers, not only help specify the purpose for the processing, but also implies the consequences for the individuals concerned.[872] Accordingly, most German legal scholars who elaborate on a more comprehensive approach in order to determine the requirement of purpose specification, discuss this with respect to the State. In doing so, they refer to specific tasks and functions of public agencies formulated by the legislator.[873] These tasks and functions determined under State Law help resolve the purpose of the data processing, to a remarkable extent. Accordingly, Eifert highlights, in particular, that the legal order provides, "in light of the legal reservation and the principle of purpose limitation a relatively precise image of the flux of information between public agencies".[874] In contrast, data controllers operating in the private sector do not have such a reference system at their disposal; they cannot refer to established laws determining their "tasks and functions" in the private sector.[875] The consequences of data processing in the private

871 See BVerfG, 13th June 2007, 1 BvR 1550/03, cip. 79 and 80.

872 See, for example, BVerfG, 11th March 2008, 1 BVR 2047/05 and 1 BvR 1254/07 (License Plate Recognition), cip. 98 to 178; BVerfG, 13th June 2007, 1 BvR 1550/03 (Retrieval of Bank Account Master Data), cip. 79 to 124; BVerfG, 14th July 1999, 1 BvR 2226/94 (Surveillance of Telecommunications), cip. 180 and 181; BVerfG, 3rd March 2004, 1 BvR 2378/98 (Big Eavesdropping Operation), cip 307 to 319; BVerfG, 4th April 2006, 1 BvR 518/02 (Dragnet Investigation), cip. 145 to 149; cf. also the Article 29 Data Protection Working Group, "Opinion 06/2014 on the notion of legitimate interests of the data controller under Article 7 of Directive 96/46/EC", pp. 19 and 20 as well as pp. 21 and 22.

873 See, for example, Hofmann, Purpose Limitation as Anchor Point for a Procedural Approach in Data Protection, p.76 ff., Forgó/Krügel/Rapp, Purpose Specification and Informational Separation of Powers, p. 35 f. m. w. N.

874 See Eifert, Purpose Congruence instead of Purpose Limitation, p. 151: "(...) angesichts des eng verstandenen Gesetzesvorbehalts und der Zweckbindung ein relativ gutes Abbild der Informationsströme zwischen den Verwaltungen".

875 At least, such a solution is barely discussed in legal literature; however, see the approach of Buchner, ibid., pp. 262 and 263, who refers to the German Civil Law in order to assess the legitimacy of the controller's interest in the data processing.

sector are thus less predictable because the flux of information *cannot* be so extensively predicted, in light of the diversity of participants, their actions and intentions, as well as their entanglements in a free market economy.[876] Thus, in practice, private data controllers have less possibilities at their disposal in order to specify the purpose of its data processing than public agencies.

bb) Differentiating between the terms 'purpose', 'means' and 'interest'

This is an astonishing result and it gives further reasons for why it is important to elaborate on reliable criteria that help data controllers acting in the private sector to specify the purpose of their data processing activities. Therefore, it seems to be promising to examine, precisely, the terms of 'purpose', 'means', and 'interest'. Differentiating between these terms may help clarify the question of what purpose actually is legally relevant.

As highlighted before, the term 'purpose' is mentioned in various Articles provided for by law. The term 'means' is mentioned, for example, together with the term 'purpose', in Article 2 lit. d of the Data Protection Directive and Article 4 sect. 7 of the General Data Protection Regulation determining who the 'data controller' is.[877] On the German level, the German Constitutional Court also refers to the term 'means' as the way of how data is processed and, in doing so, differentiates it from the term 'purpose'.[878] Finally, while Article 28 sect. 1 sent. 1 no. 2 of the German Federal Data Protection Law only refers to 'interests', Article 7 lit. f of the Data Protection Directive refers to both terms 'purpose' and 'interests' as: "Personal data may be processed only if processing is necessary for the purposes of the legitimate interests pursued by the controller or by the third party or parties to whom the data are disclosed". It is therefore important to know how these notions can be differentiated from each other.

---

876 Cf. Bäcker, Constitutional Protection of Information regarding Private Parties, p. 100.

877 See above under point C. II. 1. b) (2) Liability for 'data processing': 'Controller' and 'processor'.

878 See above under point C. II. 1. c) ee) (1) (c) Examples for unspecific purposes: Abstract dangers or unknown purposes, referring to BVerfG, 11th of March 2008, 1 BVR 2047/05 and 1 BvR 1254/07, cip. 99.

An analysis of all three terms may provide criteria in order to determine which purpose is legally relevant.

(1) 'Interests' protected by the controller's fundamental rights

The Article 29 Data Protection Working Group provides some guidelines on how to differentiate between 'purposes', 'means' and 'interests'. With respect to the difference between the terms 'purpose' and 'means' it defined the first as an "anticipated outcome that is intended or that guides planned actions" and the second as "how a result is obtained or an end is achieved".[879] It elaborates on these definitions as: "(…) determining the purposes and the means amounts to determining respectively the 'why' and the 'how' of certain processing activities."[880] With respect to the difference between the terms of 'purpose' and 'interest', the Group furthermore states: "The concept of 'interest' is closely related to, but distinct from, the concept of 'purpose' mentioned in Article 6 of the Directive. In data protection discourse, 'purpose' is the specific reason why the data are processed: the aim or intention of the data processing. An interest, on the other hand, is the broader stake that a controller may have in the processing, or the benefit that the controller derives – or that society might derive – from the processing. For instance, a company may have an *interest* in ensuring the health and safety of its staff working at its nuclear power-plant. Related to this, the company may have as a *purpose* the implementation of specific access control procedures which justifies the processing of certain specified personal data in order to help ensure the health and safety of staff."[881]

In conclusion, the Working Group defines the 'purpose' referring to the 'why' of the data processing. It defines the 'means' by referring to 'how' this purpose is obtained. And, it defines the 'interest' by referring to the 'benefit that the controller derives' from that purpose. At a first glance, these definitions appear to provide reliable criteria in order to differentiate

879 See the Article 29 Data Protection Working Group, Opinion 1/2010 on the concepts of 'controller' and 'processor', p. 13.

880 See the Article 29 Data Protection Working Group, ibid., p. 14.

881 See the Article 29 Data Protection Working Group, Opinion 06/2014 on the notion of legitimate interests of the data controller under Article 7 of Directive 96/46/EC, p. 24.

between the terms. However, applying them to a particular case, it becomes apparent that the definitions highly depend on the circumstances of the case at hand. In the example provided for in the second chapter, the publisher of an online newspaper used an analytical tool in order to review the 'usage data' of visitors of its website.[882] While the 'purpose' might be the improvement of the website experience, the analysis would be the 'means', and the 'interest' could be to increase the user traffic. However, this 'interest' could also be the 'purpose' for the 'interest' to increase the price for banner advertisement and the improvement of the website would then be the 'means'. Accordingly, this broader 'interest' could be the 'purpose' for the even broader 'interest' to finance the costs for the journalistic labor of the website holder and the 'means' would be the efforts of increasing the user traffic. Finally, this 'interest' could again be the 'purpose' for the ultimate 'interest' of surviving on the private market and so on. In conclusion, each 'purpose' could become the 'means' for the next following 'purpose', and each 'interest' the 'purpose' for the next broader 'interest'. The question therefore remains: How to differentiate between purposes, means and interests? Or, in other words, if means and interests can also be considered as purposes, which of these purposes are deemed to be legally relevant?

In fact, this question cannot be answered by technically differentiating between the terms 'purposes', 'means' and 'interests'. Instead, it can only be answered, from a normative perspective, through an objective scale. The examples provided for by the Article 29 Working Group demonstrate that the method proposed leads to a circular reasoning. With respect to the difference between the terms of 'purpose' and 'interest', the Working Group exemplifies, as listed previously, possible 'legitimate interests' as: Conventional direct marketing and other forms of marketing or advertisement; unsolicited non-commercial messages; employee monitoring for safety or management purposes; physical security, IT and network security; processing for historical, scientific or statistical purposes; processing for research purposes (including marketing research). Most of these 'interests' are not only 'purposes' authorized by law but the Working Party itself also names them 'purposes'! However, other examples given by the Working Party for 'legitimate interests' point to a solution, which provides

882 See above under point B. III. 4. Clarifying the relationship between "context" and "purpose", and 5. Values as normative scale determining "contexts" and "purposes".

an objective scale in order to define 'interests'. In order to evaluate the importance of the 'legitimate interests' of the data controller during the balancing exercise with the opposing interests, the Working Group also refers to the data controller's fundamental rights. These indeed protect 'interests' and therefore provide an objective scale for determining the 'interests' of the data controller.

(2) Is the 'purpose' determined by the individual's fundamental rights?

With respect to the definition of the term of 'purpose', the German Constitutional Court pointed, in its decision of "*License Plate Recognition*" into the same direction, even if it did so in favor of the individual. Again, the decisions provided for by the German Constitutional Court do not provide criteria for the interpretation of European laws.[883] However, the decisions can provide a source of inspiration for how the terms could be differentiated on a European level. In the case of "*License Plate Recognition*", as illustrated before, the law offended permitted the collection of data related to license plates of cars for the purpose of checking it against police data files that were open for investigation. The Court came to the conclusion that the law offended did not provide "concrete requirements for the state measure, it especially did not pre-determine the reason and the purpose of usage which was sufficiently specific for certain areas and legally clear."[884] The law offended has indeed named the 'purpose' of the data collection as 'checking against the data stored in the police files open for investigation'. However, the Court argued that this term "does not determine the purpose for that the collection and the checking of the data shall finally serve. Only the manner how an investigation purpose shall be, after the collection of the data, achieved is mentioned. This purpose (itself) indeed remains open."[885] The Constitutional Court hence considered that the 'checking of the data collected against other data stored in police files' was not the 'purpose' but the 'means'. The actual 'purpose' instead was the notion of 'open investigation'. In the Court's opinion, this notion did

883 See above under point C. I. 1. a) The interplay between European Convention for Human Rights, European Charter of Fundamental Rights and German Basic Rights.

884 See BVerfG, 11th of March 2008, 1 BVR 2047/05 and 1 BvR 1254/07, cip. 98.

885 See BVerfG, ibid., cip. 99.

not sufficiently specify the purpose because there was no legal or commonly accepted definition of the term.[886] In particular, the fact that the purpose was so broad did not exclude the possibility to use the collected data for police surveillance purposes or even for purposes of criminal prosecution.[887]

The last two considerations finally point to the solution, which is based, again, on an objective scale and determines which purpose is legally relevant or not. As described before, the German Constitutional Court examines, whether the informational measures by the State are constitutional or not. The German Court does so, by assessing, at first, whether the information measure offended constitutes an infringement or not. This is the case if it provides 'an insight into the personality' of the individual concerned and the 'state interest, with respect to the overarching context and with respect to the purpose' either constitutes a 'specific danger for the freedom of action and of being private' or if it 'qualitatively affects a person's fundamental right' or if it can 'essentially concern the individual's interests'.[888] Whatever the concrete scale might be, evaluating the intensity of the infringement, the Court also takes the other fundamental rights of the individual concerned into account.[889] For example, it considers the right to privacy of the home or telecommunications.[890] It also takes the individual's risk of being stigmatized into account, in particular, if the treatment of data refers to criteria, such as religion or ethnic origin, listed in Article 3 of the German Basic Law, which guarantees the freedom of equality.[891] In addition, it stresses that the individual's fear of being surveyed can, in advance, lead to a bias in communication, which is protected by the freedom of opinion.[892] Finally, taking the disadvantages for the individuals into account, the Court considers their risk of being an object of state investigations, which adds to their general risk of being unreasonably

886 See BVerfG, ibid., cip. 100.
887 See BVerfG, ibid., cip. 136 and 149.
888 See above under point C. I. 2. d) Infringement by 'insight into personality' and 'particularity of state interest'.
889 See in detail above under point C. I. 2. e) aa) In the public sector: Interplay between the three principles clarity of law, proportionality, and purpose limitation.
890 See BVerfG, 4th of April 2006, 1 BvR 518/02, cip. 93 (Dragnet Investigation).
891 See BVerfG, 4th of April 2006, 1 BvR 518/02 (Dragnet Investigation), cip. 106.
892 See BVerfG, 3rd of March 2004, 1 BvR 2378/98 (Big Eavesdropping Operation), cip. 230.

suspected.[893] This last consideration refers, at least implicitly, to the right to a fair trial and/or the individual's general freedom of action.

In conclusion, be it in relation to the infringement by an informational measure, or in relation to the proportionality of the infringement, the German Constitutional Court refers to the individual's basic rights. Fundamental rights can therefore not only provide an objective scale in order to determine the 'interests' on behalf of the controller, but also, vice versa, the 'purpose' of the data processing with respect to the fundamental rights of the individual concerned. Thus, while the fundamental rights of the controller of the personal data can provide a scale for determining its interests, the opposing fundamental rights of the individual concerned could provide a legal scale in order to specify the purpose of the data processing. This differentiation at least enables one, so far, to clarify both terms used in Article 7 lit. f of the Data Protection Directive and Article 6 sect. 1 lit. f of the General Data Protection Regulation. While the term 'interest' refers to the fundamental rights of the controller, the term 'purpose' may refer to the fundamental rights of the individual who is concerned by the processing of data concerning him or her.

bb) Inclusion or exclusion of future 'purposes' and 'interests'

Another question is which 'interests' and 'purposes' are recognized in terms of time. With respect to the 'interests' mentioned in Article 7 lit. f of the Data Protection Directive, the Article 29 Working Group states that there must be "a real and present interest, something that corresponds with current activities or benefits that are expected in the very near future. In other words, interests that are too vague or speculative will not be sufficient."[894] With respect to Article 2 lit. h of the Data Protection Directive, legal scholars comparably argue that the 'specific' consent does not exclude future acts of usage, but rather must refer to concrete circumstances, including the purpose of the processing.[895] At first view, both statements

---

893 See BVerfG, 3rd of March 2004, 1 BvR 2378/98 (Big Eavesdropping Operation), cip. 227; BVerfG, 4th of April 2006, 1 BvR 518/02 (Dragnet Investigation), cip. 103.

894 See "Opinion 06/2014 on the notion of legitimate interests of the data controller under Article 7 of Directive 96/46/EC", p. 24.

895 See Dammann/Simitis, ibid., cip. 22.

seem to refer to the same question: How specific must the controller's interest be, or, how specific must the consent be specified in terms of time? However, the answer depends on the fundamental rights. If the fundamental rights provide a legal scale in order to determine, on the one hand, the 'interests' on behalf of the controller and, on the other hand, the 'purpose' of the data processing with respect to the individual concerned, it becomes clear that there actually are two different starting points for answering this question.

(1) Present interests vs. future interests

As proposed previously, a data controller's 'interest' is determined by its fundamental rights. This differentiation refers to controllers acting through the private sector. With respect to the state processing of personal data, the Data Protection Directive, as well as the General Data Protection Regulation, also use the term 'interest', in more precise words, 'public interest'.[896] However, the State, as the controller does not process personal data in favor of its own fundamental rights. Instead, the State processes personal data in order to protect the fundamental rights of third private parties or other constitutional positions conflicting with the individual's fundamental rights.[897]

In Germany, the German Constitutional Court summarizes, in its recent decision of "*Federal Bureau of Investigation Law*", how the legislator has to specify these "interests": in particular, first, it must specify the object of protection being protected by the data processing; second the task of the public agency that is allowed to process the personal data; and third, the reason given for the data processing. In the Court's opinion, the reason, such as an abstract or concrete danger for the object of protection that shall be protected, does not result from the principle of purpose limitation but from the principle of clarity of law. If the collected data is re-used, for the same purpose by the same public agency, the Court slightly liberalized, in this decision, its approach. Before this new decision, the re-use of data required the same reason to be given as the initial reason (e.g. an urgent

896 See, for example, Article 7 lit. e of the Data Protection Directive and Article 6 sect. 1 lit. e of the General Data Protection Regulation.

897 See above under point C. I. 1. b) bb) (1) The 3-Step-Test: Assessing the defensive and protection function.

danger for human life). Instead, pursuant to the recent case, the re-use of personal data does not require anymore the same reason to be given for its collection, but only for a so-called investigative reason.[898] In any case, even if the Court slightly liberalized, in this regard, the concept of protection, the duty of the legislator to specify the reason still restricts, essentially, the State from data processing and, therefore, still constitutes an important element in the proportionality assessment.[899]

The Article 29 Data Protection Working Group applies a similar approach with respect to data controllers acting through the private sector requiring "a real and present interest, something that corresponds with current activities or benefits that are expected in the very near future."[900] Again, the reasoning provided for by the German Constitutional Court shall not serve, of course, as a source for the interpretation of European secondary law. However, also with respect to the European constitution, there is a difference principally between the State and private parties being regulated.[901] Thus, the Working Group has to justify why it wants to regulate private parties similar or equal to the State. Private parties are not bound to the principle of clarity of law. In contrast, they are themselves protected by fundamental rights.[902] There must hence be another reason justifying the restriction that their 'interest' must be 'a real and present interest'. As highlighted before, fundamental rights do not only protect present interests, but also broader expectations, even against unspecific risks.[903] At least, the right to freedom to conduct a business under Article 16 ECFR covers, as the more general right compared to the fundamental rights to occupation and property under Articles 15 and 17 ECFR, all

898 See above under point C. II. c) ee) (1) (d) Liberalization of the strict requirement by referring to the object of protection, referring to BVerfG, 20th of April 2016, 1 BvR 966/09 and 1 BvR 1140/09 (Federal Bureau of Investigation Law), cip. 289.

899 See, in particular, BVerfG, 11th of March 2008, 1 BVR 2047/05 and 1 BvR 1254/07 (License Plate Recognition), cip. 75; BVerfG, 13th June 2007, 1 BvR 1550/03 (Retrieval of Banking Account Matser Data), cip. 71, 73 and 74.

900 See the Article 29 Data Protection Working Group, Opinion 06/2014 on the notion of legitimate interests of the data controller under Article 7 of Directive 96/46/EC, p. 24.

901 See above under point C. I. 1. b) The effects of fundamental rights on the private sector.

902 See above under point C. I. 1. b) aa) Third party effect, protection and defensive function.

903 See above under point B. II. 3. c) Interim conclusion: Fundamental rights determining appropriateness of protection.

kinds of business activity.[904] This right apparently protects, therefore, not only present profit prospects but also strategic aims. As a consequence, the restriction of a controller's data processing operations to 'present' interests must thus be justified by the prevailing interests of the individual concerned covered by his or her fundamental rights.

(2) Purpose specification pursuant to the type of threat?

With respect to the 'purpose' of the data processing, the question to consider is which type of threat the processing of data causes for the individual's fundamental rights. The German Constitutional Court provides for the following differentiation: "the right to informational self-determination supplements and broadens the constitutional protection of freedom of action and of privacy by extending its scope already at the level of danger for the personality. Such a danger can already exist before the concrete threat of certain objects of legal protection, especially if personal information is used and combined in a manner that the individual is unable to overview or control it."[905]

In chapter B. II. Data protection as a risk regulation, the differences that exist between the terms of 'danger' and 'risk' and which protection instruments are appropriate for these different types of threat were discussed. Different theories were presented, not in order to decide which theory prevails, but instead, in order to highlight the fact that different threats require different protection instruments. An essential difference concerned the fact of whether the object of the threat is known or not. If the threat is not known, effective instruments often require the threat-causing entity to gather or provide the information necessary in order to monitor the threats and discover, if so, the threat for a specific object of protection. This protection instrument constitutes a low regulatory burden because it only slightly restricts the room of action of the "threat causing" data controller. Simultaneously, the risk discovery function of this protection function safeguards the possibility of avoiding or at least reducing the threat before it turns into real harm. Thus, the question for example is whether the purpose specified by the controller must refer to threats for specific objects of

904 Cf. Folz, Article 15 ECFR – Freedom to Conduct a Business, cip. 3.
905 See BVerfG, 13th June 2007, 1 BvR 1550/03, cip. 64 ("Kontostammdatenabfrage").

protection, only, or whether it can also refer to unspecific threats.[906] This question leads to the function of the requirement to specify the purpose with respect to the fundamental rights of the individual concerned.

d) Summary of conceptual ambiguities

The previous criticism carved out several arguable considerations made in the legal discussion with respect to the processing of personal data in the private sector: First, the current framework mainly refers to the purpose of the collection of personal data, for the private sector just as for the public sector, in order to evaluate the need for protection against the risks caused by the processing as a whole. But focusing on the moment of collection conflicts, in principle, with innovation processes in non-linear environments. The reason for this is that focusing on the moment of collection requires the controller to predict the later use of data, albeit the outcome of innovation processes is hardly predictable. Second, some legal scholars consider the individual's consent invalid as a whole, if the private data controller did not specify the purpose in a sufficiently precise or comprehensive manner at the outset. This approach actually transfers the concept of protection, applicable for the processing of data by the State, to the private sector. Indeed, in the public sector, a law authorizing the processing of personal data is principally invalid as a whole if it is disproportionate. In contrast, in the private sector, it would be possible that an individual's consent containing a very broad purpose is not invalid as a whole. Instead, such a consent could be considered as providing the basis only for such data processing that corresponds to the purposes specified in the consent. Other data processing activities that harm the individual more than specified before, does not lead to the consent becoming void *per se*, but this processing would simply not be covered by the individual's consent. Finally, comparing the requirements considered, on the one hand, for the purpose specified in the consent, and on the other hand, within the law itself, brings to light the following result: the effects are, in practice, stricter on the private sector than on the public sector. This result is in particular surprising, in light of the fact that the legislator is, unlike private con-

906 See above under point B. II. 3. c) Interim conclusion: Fundamental rights determining appropriateness of protection.

trollers, directly bound to the individual's fundamental rights. The reason for all of these results may be that the concept of protection initially developed with respect to the processing of data by the State is directly transferred to the data processing in the private sector.[907]

However, the previous criticism also sheds light on a possible solution for this contradictory result. When elaborating on a possible solution for the problem of how one could differentiate between the terms 'purpose', 'means', and 'interest', it was found that the fundamental rights of both the individual concerned and the controller could, respectively, provide for the necessary objective legal scale. Hence, the individual's fundamental rights could also provide a legal scale in order to determine which purpose of the data processing is legally relevant, and as a consequence, how precisely a private data controller has to specify the purpose of its data processing. The subsequent analysis will demonstrate how this may work, applying the framework of the regulation of risks, as illustrated in the second chapter.

3. Solution approach: Purpose specification as a risk-discovery process

Data protection law is considered to be a regulation of risks caused by the processing of personal data. One of the challenges of such a risk-based approach is to find an objective scale for measuring the impact of risks on the individuals concerned and society as a whole. Without such an objective scale, the risk-based approach runs itself the risk of turning into a self-legitimizing procedural practice for data controllers.[908] With respect to the question of the object of data protection laws, scholars argue that these laws protect the individual's autonomy. Indeed, since the concept of individual autonomy is rather broad and therefore barely provides clear criteria for a *legal* concept of protection, scholars, as well as Constitutional Courts, refer to the specific context of a data processing activity. Nissenbaum argues, in particular, that such a "context"-based approach helps to determine the "informational norms" that govern specific contexts and, as such, provides a better framework for assessing the individual's privacy

---

907 See above under point B. II. Data protection as a risk regulation.
908 See above under point B. II. Data protection as a risk regulation.

than a “purpose” of data processing.[909] However, this thesis has clarified that the “purpose” of the processing of personal data constitutes just another legal link for regulation, focusing on risk protection. This legal link, i.e. the purpose, determines the intended “future” context of the data processing and enables regulators, data controllers, and individuals concerned to determine and adapt, in advance, to the “informational norms” that govern a certain context. Using the purpose as a legal link for determining a future context hence avoids the risk of an infringement of its “contextual integrity”.

Indeed, the definition of the context depends on “values” inherent in a social context,[910] and consequently, the definition of the purpose also requires an objective scale in order to determine which context (aka purpose) is legally relevant.[911] Therefore, the search for an objective scale draws attention to the concept of protection. Interestingly, the concept of protection elaborated on by the German Constitutional Court regarding the right to informational self-determination does not provide, so far, reliable criteria in order to determine the contexts and purposes, at least, not in the private sector.[912] Similarly, the concept of protection that the European Court of Justice had started to elaborate on with respect to the fundamental rights to private life and to data protection under Article 7 and 8 ECFR, does not provide reliable criteria either. So far, the discussion mainly treats the question of the exact interplay between the fundamental right to private life under Article 7 ECFR and the fundamental right to data protection under Article 8 ECFR.[913] However, it was demonstrated that both scopes of protection essentially are defined by referring exclusively to the

909 See above under point B. III. 4. Clarifying the relationship between ”context“ and ”purpose“, referring to Nissenbaum, Respect for Context as a Benchmark, p. 291 and 292.

910 See above under point B. III. 4. Clarifying the relationship between ”context“ and ”purpose“, referring to Nissenbaum, Respect for Context as a Benchmark, p. 292, and point B. III. Theories about the value of privacy aka data protection.

911 See above under point B. III. 4. Clarifying the relationship between ”context“ and ”purpose“, referring to Nissenbaum, Respect for Context as a Benchmark, p. 292, and point B. III. Theories about the value of privacy aka data protection.

912 See above under point C. II. 1. c) ee) Comparison with principles developed by German Constitutional Court.

913 See above under point C. I. 3. a) Genesis and interplay of both rights.

term "personal data". Such a concept of protection leads, in light of the increasing digitization of society, to the displacement of the other, eventually more specific, fundamental rights. This theoretical finding is particularly relevant because these other fundamental rights could actually provide the necessary criteria in order to determine the context in which data processing occurs and, correspondingly, the purpose of data processing.[914] On the basis of these findings, this chapter proposes, in its first sub-chapter, a concept of protection for the fundamental right to data protection under Article 8 ECFR, avoiding the criticized "broadness and vagueness" of its scope. The second part illustrates the functioning of this concept of protection with respect to the substantial guarantees provided for by the other fundamental rights to privacy, freedom, and non-discrimination of the individual concerned by the processing of data concerning him or her. The last part concludes, by emphasizing that this concept of protection corresponds with the openness of data-driven innovation in the private sector.

a) Regulative aim: Data protection for the individual's autonomy

This thesis promotes that the essential value added by the fundamental right to data protection under Article 8 ECFR consists of the following elements as subsequently assessed: The first chapter examines individual autonomy as the ultimate objective of the right to data protection, which is an essential pre-condition for a free and democratic civil society. However, since individual autonomy is itself a too broad concept in order to provide a precise scale determining specific requirements for the risks caused by the processing of personal data, the specific requirements must be determined by the totality of all fundamental rights. This leads to the second and third elements, which will be examined in the next chapter. The right to data protection under Article 8 ECFR regulates, *as a central norm*, the risks caused by the processing of personal data for all fundamental rights and freedoms and, in doing so, extends the range of protection to unspecific risks, i.e. before a specific object of protection of the

914 See above under point C. I. 3) c) cc) Referring to substantial guarantees as method of interpreting fundamental rights in order to avoid a scope of protection that is too broad and/or too vague.

other fundamental rights is threatened.[915] The concept promoted thus avoids a conceptual link between privacy and data protection, because this conceptual link would inevitably lead to an exclusive focus on privacy and the moment when the data is collected. Instead, the concept promoted in this thesis equally links data protection regulation to the other fundamental rights. Consequently, the *later* processing is equally important for the evaluation of the risks. Hence, the requirement of purpose specification serves as an instrument of risk discovery. As will be demonstrated, this concept bears several advantages with respect to the interplay of the general scope of protection of the right to data protection and the application of its protection instruments balancing the opposing fundamental rights. Finally, since there are clear tendencies by the Constitutional Courts and the legislator that can assist in refining the current concept of protection, the last chapter concludes with highlighting how this refinement might be worked out in order to balance, more appropriately, the opposing interests of data controllers and individuals concerned in the private sector.

aa) Intermediate function of data protection

As shown in chapter "C. I. 3. a) Genesis and interplay of both rights", one part of the legal discussion surrounding the right to private life under Article 7 ECFR, and the right to data protection under Article 8 ECFR, concerns their precise interplay.[916] A similar, but however distinct debate, concerns the nature of the fundamental right to data protection *per se*. This debate treats the question on the ultimate value of this right or, in other words, the object and concept provided for. Regarding this issue, Tzanou gives a dense overview and summarizes several values of data protection discussed in legal literature: First of all, the protection of privacy is deemed to be one value; another value is meant to be data security, i.e. securing personal data against its potential misuse (such as by loss or access by unauthorized persons); data quality is considered as another value, which means that personal data is accurate, relevant, and up-to-date; comparably, Tzanou mentions "transparency, foreseeability in data processing, accountability of data controllers, and (…) participation of the data subject

915 Cf. BVerfG, 11th of March 2008, 1 BvR 2074/05 and 1 BvR 1254/07 (License Plate Recognition), cip. 63.

916 See above under point C. I. 3. a) Genesis and interplay of both rights.

in the processing of his/her information" as further values (which data protection laws establish by means of fair information principles such as fair processing, purpose specification and individual participation); as yet another value is considered the principle of non-discrimination; and Tzanou even lists the proportionality principle as a value expressed within the law (in form of the necessity requirement).[917] Indeed, this multi-facetted "value collection", as discussed in legal literature, does not provide a consistent theory on the object and concept of protection of the fundamental to data protection under Article 8 ECFR. In particular, it remains unclear *why* these values, and maybe even further ones, are the values of data protection law. Tzanou therefore consequently turns to the two, so far, most-comprehensively developed theories, on the one hand, by the scholars De Hert and Gutwirth and, as a reaction to it, Rouvroy and Poullet.[918]

(1) Different functions of rights (opacity and transparency)

De Hert and Gutwirth appraise the new fundamental right to data protection,[919] and consider privacy and data protection as two distinct instruments of power control: Privacy protects, in their opinion, as a "tool of opacity", the individual by determining "what is deemed so essentially individual that it must be shielded against public and private interference";[920] in contrast, as a "tool of transparency", data protection becomes relevant "after these normative choices have been made in order still to channel the normatively accepted exercise of power".[921] In De Hert and Gutwirth's opinion, data protection laws hence are, contrary to laws legit-

---

917 See Tzanou, Data protection as a fundamental right next to privacy? 'Reconstructing' a not so new right, pp. 91 and 92 referring, amongst others, to: Lee Bygrave, 'The Place of Privacy in Data Protection Law' (2001) 24 University of New South Wales Law Journal 277, 278; Helen Nissenbaum, 'Protecting Privacy in an Information Age: The Problem of Privacy in Public' (1998) 17 Law and Philosophy 559, 576; Herbert Burkert, 'Towards a New Generation of Data Protection Legislation' in Gutwirth and others (eds), Reinventing Data Protection? (Springer: Dordrecht, 2009) 339; C Kuner and others 'The challenge of "big data" for data protection' (2012) 2 International Data Privacy Law 47–49.

918 See Tzanou, ibid., p. 92.

919 See De Hert and Gutwirth, Privacy, data protection and law enforcement. Opacity of the individual and transparency of power, p. 81.

920 See De Hert and Gutwirth, ibid., p. 70.

921 See De Hert and Gutwirth, ibid., p. 70.

imizing an interference of privacy, "based upon the assumption that the processing of personal data is in principle allowed and legal."[922] Both authors consider, thus, the logic behind current data protection laws as not being prohibitive. Indeed, it might appear prohibitive because these laws principally forbid the processing of personal data unless certain conditions are met. However, for example, the general clause of Article 7 lit. f of the Data Protection Directive "can obviously 'make data processing legitimate' for every thinkable business interest."[923] De Hert and Gutwirth consider few exceptions from this rule. In particular, they see only provisions as exceptionally prohibitive regarding sensitive data, profiling, and the principle of purpose limitation. The first exception results, in their opinion, from the nature of the data that "bears the supplementary risk of discrimination"; however, they stress that the other exceptions do actually not strictly limit the use of data. For instance, the compatibility assessment of the principle of purpose limitation foresees that certain conditions need to be met (in order to pass the test) rather than a strict limitation, for example, as the strict requirement of purpose identity does.[924]

In contrast to De Hert and Gutwirth, Rouvroy and Poullet do not appraise the new right to data protection under Article 8 ECFR, but criticize its elevation into the status of a fundamental right.[925] Rouvroy and Poullet advocate the high importance of the individual's autonomy as the final objective behind privacy, stating that the right to privacy should be understood as "essentially an instrument for fostering the specific yet changing autonomic capabilities of individuals that are (…) necessary for sustaining a vivid democracy."[926] Turning the focus on the right to data protection, Rouvroy and Poullet indeed acknowledge that data protection laws are "among the tools through which the individual exercises his right to privacy" and even that "data protection is also a tool for protecting other rights than the right to privacy".[927] However, the similarities of both rights are

922 See De Hert and Gutwirth, ibid., p. 78.
923 See De Hert and Gutwirth, ibid., p. 78 and 79.
924 See De Hert and Gutwirth, ibid., pp. 79 and 80.
925 See Rouvroy and Poullet, The Right to Informational Self-Determination and the Value of Self-Development: Reassessing the Importance of Privacy for Democracy, p. 71.
926 See Rouvroy and Poullet, ibid., p. 46.
927 See Rouvroy and Poullet, The Right to Informational Self-Determination and the Value of Self-Development: Reassessing the Importance of Privacy for Democracy, p. 70.

strong. In their opinion, it "appears obvious (…) that data protection regimes are intended both, with regard to the 'seclusion' aspect of privacy, to protect our 'private sphere' (for instance by forbidding the processing of certain sensitive data or by enlarging the secrecy of the correspondence to electronic mails) on the one hand and, on the other hand, with regard to the 'decisional autonomy' aspect of privacy, to increase the transparency of information flows and to limit them in order to prevent disproportionate informational power relationships to be developed or perpetuated between public and private data controllers and citizens."[928] Both rights thus "intersect but are also different tools for enabling individual reflexive autonomy and, as a consequence, also collective deliberative democracy."[929] Rouvroy and Poullet fear these similarities because it risks "obscuring the essential relation existing between privacy and data protection and further estrange data protection from the fundamental values of human dignity and individual autonomy, foundational to the concept of privacy and in which data protection regimes have their roots (…)."[930]

(2) Disconnecting the exclusive link between data protection to privacy

Tzanou criticizes both approaches of De Hert and Gutwirth, as well as of Rouvroy and Poullet, because they do not provide a robust analysis of the fundamental right to data protection as such.[931] With respect to Rouvroy and Poullet, she stresses that their "fears (...) remain unsubstantiated" because they do not make "clear why data protection cannot have an instrumental value, while at the same time being on an equal footing with privacy."[932] She observes that both authors obviously negate any proper value of the fundamental right to data protection "because this might allegedly end up in trumping the instrumental value of privacy, and thus undermine privacy as a fundamental right."[933] Indeed, Tzanou affirms the important values of autonomy, human dignity, and self-development that Rouvroy and Poullet highlight when discussing the appropriateness of privacy and

928 See Rouvroy and Poullet, ibid., p. 70.
929 See Rouvroy and Poullet, ibid., p. 70.
930 See Rouvroy and Poullet, ibid., p. 75.
931 See Tzanou, ibid., pp. 92 and 93.
932 See Tzanou, ibid., p. 94.
933 See Tzanou, ibid., p. 94.

data protection as fundamental rights. However, before discussing the inappropriateness of data protection as a fundamental right, it is necessary, in her opinion, to clarify the precise concept of protection of the right to data protection.[934]

Irrespective of the principle legitimacy of her criticism, Tzanou indeed overlooks one decisive aspect in the reasoning of Rouvroy and Poullet. Their fear lies, undoubtedly, in the similarity of both rights. However, the reason for this similarity (and, consequently, for their fear) is how they conceptualize both rights. They locate "the two 'aspects' of privacy (the right to seclusion and the right to decisional autonomy)" under the right to privacy *and* the right to data protection. Hence, they link data protection exclusively to privacy when they state that data protection organises, like the right to privacy (and the German right to informational self-determination), "a system of disclosure of personal data respectful of the individual's right to self-determination, as both opacity and transparency therefore contribute to sustaining the individual's self-development."[935] In Rouvroy's and Poullet's understanding, there is hence, no clear conceptual difference between both rights, and this indeed obscures the relation between the right to privacy and the right to data protection and, consequently, the overall concept of protection.

Though, this conceptual difference is exactly what makes the concept developed by De Hert and Gutwirth so important. Interestingly, Tzanou also criticizes their approach because both authors essentially define the right to data protection by referring to the right to private life, instead of elaborating on its concept of data protection independent from the right to privacy.[936] She formulates this criticism as: "There is, however, a paradox in their line of thinking: their theory, while it aims to be a theory on data protection, does not focus on data protection itself. Rather, the added value of data protection is demonstrated through its distinction from privacy. By preaching separation, they strive to show the indispensability of data protection. But, their very argument proves them wrong. In the end, according to de Hert and Gutwirth, everything will be judged on the basis of privacy, as the tool of opacity will be the benchmark for establishing prohibited interference. Data protection, as a transparency tool, merely describes the permitted level of processing; the limits will then be set on the basis of

934 See Tzanou, ibid., p. 94.
935 See Rouvroy and Poullet, ibid., p. 58.
936 See Tzanou, ibid., pp. 92 and 93.

privacy. This, however, means that data protection is not indispensable: we could live well without it. Of course we are better off with it, as it has some utility as a useful transparency tool, but still we could live without it, since every possible interference will be judged against privacy. De Hert and Gutwirth fail to prove, therefore, why data protection is so fundamental, that it explains its constitutional entrenchment."[937] Tzanou concludes from her critique that there is a necessity to elaborate on a concept of protection of the right to data protection, independently from the right to private life. This would enable one to clarify the real value added by this right. In particular, conceptualizing the fundamental right to data protection as a transparency tool, only, leads, in her opinion, to the problem that it remains dependent from other rights. Such an understanding limits the value of data protection. Therefore, she promotes the notion of elaborating on 'hard core' data protection principles that make this right autonomous from other fundamental rights.[938] In doing so, she claims, amongst others, a 'core' or 'essence' of the right to data protection and that it should be balanced per se against opposing fundamental rights, and "not through the proxy of privacy."[939]

Indeed, Tzanou's criticism highlights an important point. If the right to data protection shall add protection with respect to other fundamental rights, its concept of protection must be clear in comparison to the other fundamental rights. However, in fact, the European Court of Justice had already balanced the right to data protection per se against opposing rights.[940] And, meanwhile, the Court has also affirmed a 'core' or 'essence' of the fundamental right to data protection.[941] Both affirmations undoubtedly strengthen this fundamental right and make it more independent from other rights, such as the right to privacy. However, this is not enough in order to clarify the value added by this right in the European Charter of Fundamental Rights. Tzanou therefore stops herself too early in elaborating on the precise concept of the right to data protection and ne-

937 See Tzanou, ibid., p. 93.
938 See Tzanou, ibid., pp. 96 and 97.
939 See Tzanou, ibid., p. 98.
940 See the decisions above under point C. I. 1. b) aa) (2) (b) The right to data protection under Article 8 ECFR and/or the right to private life under Article 7 ECFR.
941 See the decisions above under point C. I. 3. c) aa) (2) (b) Protection against collection, storage, and subsequent risk of abuse, referring to ECJ C-293/12 and C-594/12 cip. 39 and 40.

glects the fact that all authors criticized by her (De Hert, Gutwirth, Rouvroy, Poullet), already point into the direction that makes this right so indispensable.

(3) Data protection for all rights to privacy, freedom, and equality

What makes the fundamental right to data protection so indispensable, is that it protects the individual against risks caused by the processing of personal data for all his or her fundamental rights. Its paramount objective is to protect the individual's autonomy. However, because individual autonomy is a concept that is too broad in order to provide a differentiated scale to determine the requirements for the processing of personal data in all particular cases, it is the diversity of all fundamental rights that provide the necessary objective scale. This is where all legal scholars referred here point to, however, they do not actually deal with it in detail.

For example, Rouvroy and Poullet stress that "autonomy and self-determination (…) cannot be characterized as legal 'rights', they are not something that the state can 'provide' the individuals with (…)."[942] Instead, the State is rather able "showing respect for individual autonomy and, as far as possible, providing some of the conditions necessary for individuals to develop their capacity for individual deliberative autonomy (…) and for collective deliberative democracy (…)."[943] Thus, the value of individual autonomy must always be intermediated by more specific rights. Unfortunately, the concept of protection considered by Rouvroy and Poullet in relation to the right to privacy does not provide clarity in this regard. In contrast, both authors believe that the natural result of the "intermediate value" of the right to privacy is indeterminate in itself. In order to tackle the ambiguous notion of privacy, both authors therefore require "taking fully into account the context in which our liberties have to express them-

942 See Rouvroy and Poullet, The Right to Informational Self-Determination and the Value of Self-Development: Reassessing the Importance of Privacy for Democracy, pp. 59 and 60.

943 See Rouvroy and Poullet, The Right to Informational Self-Determination and the Value of Self-Development: Reassessing the Importance of Privacy for Democracy, pp. 59 and 60.

selves".[944] With respect to data protection, both authors even more explicitly point to the idea that data protection laws are not only "among the tools through which the individual exercises his right to privacy" but "also a tool for protecting other rights than the right to privacy".[945] Hence, the other fundamental rights of freedom and equality can, beside the right to privacy, well provide a sufficient legal scale in order to refine the ambiguous notion of a right to data protection, which protects individual autonomy that is put at risk by automated data processing.

De Hert and Gutwirth similarly follow this trait stating: "Last and foremost, data protection has grown in response to problems generated by new technology. It brings no added value to reduce all these responses to 'privacy'. Other values and concerns are also at play. Take for instance the right not to be discriminated against that is protected by Article 15 of the European Data Protection Directive. There is also a special regime for 'sensitive data' in the Directive prohibiting processing of data relating to racial or ethnic origin, political opinions, religious or philosophical beliefs and so on. The connection with rights and liberties such as the freedom of religion, freedom of conscience and the political freedoms is obvious."[946] Both authors also highlight the instrumental value of data protection for these more substantial values and even refer to abstract constitutional claims as: "Data protection principles seem less substantive and more procedural compared to other rights norms but they are in reality closely tied to substantial values and protect a broad scale of fundamental values other than privacy. Because of its reputation of only focusing on the benefits for individuals, putting data protection in the privacy frame hampers the realization of the societal benefits of data protection rights and therefore puts these rights essentially in conflict with the needs of society."[947]

In actual fact, Tzanou also follows this approach by concluding: "Nevertheless, privacy and data protection are not identical rights. (…) Privacy

---

944 See Rouvroy and Poullet, The Right to Informational Self-Determination and the Value of Self-Development: Reassessing the Importance of Privacy for Democracy, p. 61.

945 See Rouvroy and Poullet, The Right to Informational Self-Determination and the Value of Self-Development: Reassessing the Importance of Privacy for Democracy, p. 70.

946 See De Hert and Gutwirth, Privacy, data protection and law enforcement. Opacity of the individual and transparency of power, p. 82.

947 See De Hert and Gutwirth, Data Protection in the Case Law of Luxemburg and Strasburg, p. 44.

is a much broader concept that embodies a range of rights and values, such as the right to be let alone, intimacy, seclusion, personhood, and so on according to the various definitions. (…) Furthermore, unlike privacy's elusive and subjective nature that makes the right different in different contexts and jurisdictions, data protection has an essential procedural nature that it makes it more objective as a right in different contexts. Finally, data protection is more than informational privacy itself because, as will be demonstrated below, it serves other, further fundamental rights and values besides privacy."[948] Unfortunately, in the end, and contrary to her intentions, Tzanou does not demonstrate, at least not in detail, how the fundamental right to data protection protects not only privacy, but also the other fundamental rights. This lack in detail of the concept of the right to data protection is characteristic of all approaches discussed so far. All authors stress the important function of data protection for individual autonomy and, consequently, for the other fundamental rights providing for more substantial values, be it privacy, liberties or equality. However, they do not show how this might be implemented in reality.

bb) Purpose specification as a risk regulation instrument

This sub-chapter therefore illustrates how the concept of protection of Article 8 ECFR serving the other fundamental rights to privacy, freedom, and equality can be implemented, focusing on a risk regulatory point of view. As mentioned previously, this thesis promotes individual autonomy as the ultimate objective of the fundamental right to data protection. Since the concept of individual autonomy is too broad for providing for an objective scale for each particular case of data processing, it is the diversity of all fundamental rights that provides this differentiated scale. From the perspective that data protection is a regulation of risks, the (more instrumental) right to data protection serves, as a central norm, to protect the (more substantial) values provided for by the other fundamental rights against the risks caused by the processing of personal data. In doing so, the right extends its scope of protection, even so far to unspecific risks, i.e. before the data processing threatens a specific object of protection (i.e. substantial guarantee or value) of the other fundamental rights, such as of freedom

948 See Tzanou, ibid., p. 90.

or equality. However, this type of protection is an *extension to unspecific risks but* not a substitute of protection against specific risks. Thus, it *extends* the range of protection in the sense that it *adds* a precautionary level of protection against unspecific risks *to* the preventative level of protection against specific risks. In this system, the requirement of purpose specification plays a decisive role because it determines which type of risk, unspecific or specific, is caused by the data processing, and if specific, which fundamental right is actually concerned. The type of risk and, eventually, the specific substantial guarantee of the fundamental right concerned then determine which instruments are necessary for protection. Thus, the substantial guarantees provided for by the fundamental rights to privacy, freedom, and non-discrimination determine the context and related 'informational norms' and, consequently, which purpose of the data processing is legally relevant.

(1) 'A risk to a right': Quantitative vs. qualitative evaluation?

Indeed, putting data protection within a framework of regulation of risks, can be challenging. Focusing on privacy impact assessments, as well as data protection impact assessments, van Dijk, Gellert and Rommetveit examine in more detail the relation between a risk and a right. They carve out the following conundrum which results from the conceptual link of a 'risk to a right'. In doing so, the authors stress the provenance of privacy impact assessments from technology assessments and environmental impact assessments. Thus, privacy impact assessments, import the risk management practices developed for these technology assessments into data protection regimes.[949] The authors stress the methodological challenge resulting from the fact that these risk management practices were typically "concerned with physical consequences for the natural environment and human health" and, thus, "defined through scientific concepts of probability in dealing with the possibilities" of these future events.[950] In contrast, risk management practices once introduced in the field of data protection "direct risk assessment exercises to the consequences of technologies

949 See van Dijk, Gellert and Rommetveit, A risk to a right? Beyond data protection risk assessments, pp. 287 and 288.

950 See van Dijk, Gellert and Rommetveit, ibid., p. 290.

(ICTs) upon citizens' fundamental rights".[951] In light of this conceptual shift, the authors particularly raise one question that is especially relevant for this part of this thesis:[952] how should a 'risk to a right' be conceptualized within the context of data protection law?

(a) Challenges of bridging risks to rights

The authors van Dijk, Gellert and Rommetveit particularly criticize the quantitative risk-based approach that is becoming more and more dominant within general data protection regulation. They formulate their concern as: "The basic processes of risk assessment and management are not fundamentally concerned with the *nature of rights*, but rather with the *likelihood* of certain consequences occurring. Classical statements about the nature of risk assessments typically highlight quantification as intrinsic to the risk assessment process: 'it is the major task of risk assessment to identify and explore, preferably in quantitative terms, the types, intensities and likelihood of the (normally undesired) consequences related to an activity or event'."[953] The authors conclude from this a certain shift: legal questions are not answered by legal analysis anymore but, more and more, through risk assessment practices.[954]

Several legal scholars seek to address the methodological challenge. For instance, the German White Paper on "*Data Protection Impact Assessment*" (Datenschutz-Folgenabschätzung) by the research project Forum Privatheit explicitly underlines, that the legal requirements guaranteed by fundamental rights of the individuals concerned must not be undermined by a risk assessment.[955] This argument explicitly ties into the similar paper on "*The Role of Risk Management in Data Protection*" published by the French Centre for Information Policy Leadership (CNIL), which stressed: "Risk management does not alter rights or obligations. If a law conveys a

951 See van Dijk, Gellert and Rommetveit, ibid., p. 290.

952 See van Dijk, Gellert and Rommetveit, ibid., pp. 289 and 290.

953 See van Dijk, Gellert and Rommetveit, ibid., p. 293, quoting Renn O. Risk governance coping with uncertainty in a complex world. Earthscan, London: Sterling, VA; 2008, p. 5.

954 See van Dijk, Gellert and Rommetveit, ibid., p. 293, quoting Renn O. Risk governance coping with uncertainty in a complex world. Earthscan, London: Sterling, VA; 2008, p. 5.

955 See Forum Privatheit, White Paper – Data Protection Impact Assessment, p. 18.

right to data protection, or provides individuals with specific rights, such as rights of access, correction or deletion, risk management cannot alter those rights; just as the law imposes obligations on controllers or processors, risk management does not change those obligations. Rather, risk management is a valuable tool for calibrating accountability, prioritising action, raising and informing awareness about risks, identifying appropriate mitigation measures and, in the words of the Article 29 Working Party, providing a 'scalable and proportionate approach to compliance'".[956] The German White Paper therefore proposes a risk assessment process intending to establish "a bridging of the risk-based approach and the fundamental rights approach".[957]

(b) Example: German White Paper on DPIA

However, a closer look at this approach reveals how difficult it is to consistently bridge a 'risk to a right'. The risk assessment methodology proposed by the German White Paper builds upon so-called "protection goals" (Schutzziele). German data protection experts had developed these protection goals, similar to the protection goals developed in IT security, for improving the assessment of whether specific protection instruments implemented in practice suffice the requirements of data protection law or not.[958] These data protection goals add to the already known IT security goals and create certain "fields of conflicts" between each other. This shall be illustrated as follows:[959]

956 See the Center for Information Policy Leadership, The Role of Risk Management in Data Protection, p. 13, quoting the Article 29 Data Protection Working Party, Statement on the role of a risk-based approach in data protection legal frameworks, p. 2.

957 See Forum Privatheit, White Paper – Data Protection Impact Assessment, p. 18: "Der im folgenden Kapitel skizzierte Prozess zur Durchführung von DSFAen versucht den Brückenschlag zwischen dem Risikoansatz sowie dem Ansatz zur Grundrechtsgewährleistung und kombiniert die als sinnvoll erachteten Elemente mit dem Ziel, ein für alle Beteiligten nützliches Werkzeug zu schaffen."

958 See Rost, Standardized Modeling of Data Protection; Rost and Bock, Privacy by Design and the New Protection Goals: Principles, objectives, and requirements; Rost and Pfitzmann, Data Protection Goals – revisited.

959 See Forum Privatheit, ibid., pp. 24 and 25.

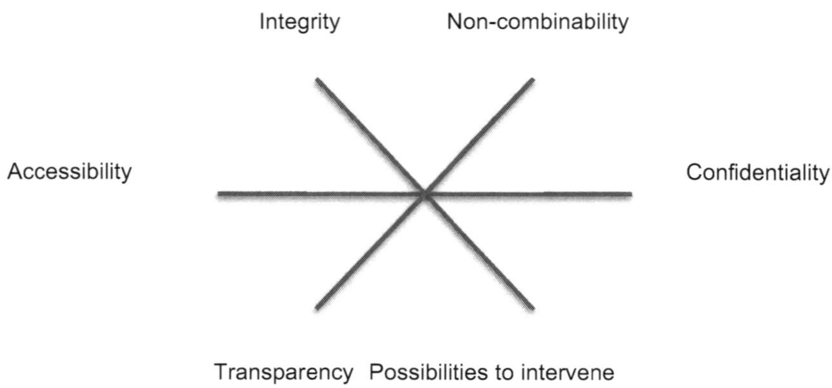

For example, the protection goal of "non-combinability" shall constitute criteria for the assessment of whether or not a data controller meets, in practice, the principle of purpose limitation on an organizational and technical level. This principally leads to a conflict with the protection goal of "transparency". The reason is that the more technical and organizational measures guarantee that personal data stored or processed by the controller cannot be combined (for instance, by means of anonymization, pseudonymization, and isolation of data sets, systems and processes), the less the controller is able to make the personal data processed transparent, as a whole, to the individual concerned.[960]

In order to assess the data protection risk, the White Paper uses the same scale as developed for IT security risks. Indeed, the scenarios set out in the paper and consequences appear from time to time to be rather random. In any case, in the opinion of the authors of the White Paper, the fundamental rights approach requires one to consider each processing of personal data, even if it is undoubtedly legal, as harming the fundamental rights to private life and data protection under Articles 7 and 8 ECFR. Therefore, the data protection risk assessment must not depend on the likelihood and the intensity of the harm, only. Instead, even the "normal" processing of personal data already requires a certain minimum level of protection. In contrast, a higher level of protection is needed if, first, personal data is processed that belongs to the especially protected categories listed in the law or, second, the individual concerned depends on the deci-

960 See Forum Privatheit, ibid., pp. 25 and 28.

sion or service of the controller. In the second scenario, there are two additional, aspects increasing the need for protection: the risk caused by the data processing either leads to significant consequences for the individual concerned or the individual has no effective means at his or her disposal in order to protect him or herself. Consequently, the need for protection is very high if the before-mentioned aspects apply at the same time, i.e. personal data belonging to a special category of data is processed and the individual concerned depends on the decision or service of the controller (plus the additional requirements). Finally, a high need for protection can also result from the cumulative effects of a certain data processing that poses only a normal level of risk for an individual. This might be the case if personal data of many individuals is processed or the data is processed for many purposes.[961]

In order to specify these protection goals, the German data protection authorities formed the so-called "Technology" working group. This working group is going to set up a manual of specific protection measures that the controller can implement in order to meet the before-mentioned goals. The manual will constantly be updated in tandem with whatever new technology is being launched in Germany. In conclusion, the risk assessment methodology enables the controller (and data protection authorities) to evaluate the risk for the data protection goals that results from deviations from this catalogue. If the data controller uses protection measures other than listed in the catalogue, the data controller bears the burden of proving that these equally meet the protection goals. A data protection authority can therefore assess, on this basis, whether or not there are deficiencies in the protection of personal data overall.[962]

(c) Criticism: Incoherence of current risk criteria

In conclusion, the German White Paper refers to criteria such as the sensitivity of data and the possible consequences for the individual concerned in order to evaluate the *level* of risk. On the other hand, the data protection goals provide a reference point for the question of *what* is at risk. This approach is rather astonishing because the criteria determining the level of

961 See Forum Privatheit, ibid., p. 27.
962 See Forum Privatheit, ibid., pp. 27 to 29.

risk are, actually, more substantial than the data protection goals, which appear here to constitute the object of protection. In contrast, one could think that the possibility to intervene (in the White Paper listed as a "goal") should enable the individual to avoid negative consequences for him or herself, be it protected in general or specifically by his or her fundamental rights. The reason for this confusion is, thus, that the White Paper mixes procedural measures, such as transparency enhancing mechanisms, with substantial aspects, such as the consequences for the individual. In summary, the data protection risk assessment proposed may therefore well serve as a "bridging" of risk assessment methodologies and the fundamental rights approach. However, the approach unfortunately lacks consistency, at least, regarding the question of why certain criteria should determine the level of risk and why other criteria serve as reference points for the object of protection.

In light of these challenges, van Dijk, Gellert and Rommetveit rightly stress how important it is to clarify and establish the risk criteria by distinguishing the following questions: Which event, if realized, should be considered as relevant (i.e. what is the harm)? Who would suffer the harm and who is responsible for it? And, how should the risk be measured?? Van Dijk, Gellert and Rommetveit propose to answer these questions by more rigorously referring to the attributes of law.[963] The second part of this thesis has already discussed this issue and that it depends, indeed, on the fundamental right "at risk" which object or substantial value is guaranteed, thus, which type of threat is relevant and, as a consequence, what kind of protection instrument is required. The discussion differentiated between preventative measures against the danger for a substantial guarantee that is already specified, i.e. specific risks, and precautionary measures for situations where it is not yet even clear which harm the situation bears. These risks were called unspecific risks. For unspecific risks, the appropriate protection instruments often refers to the gathering of information in order to discover, in a timely fashion, the specific risks. Furthermore, such instruments that gather, in the first place, information are often more proportionate with respect to opposing fundamental rights than instruments that create a higher regulatory burden, such as the precautionary prohibition of certain actions.[964]

963 See van Dijk, Gellert and Rommetveit, ibid., pp. 302 to 304.

964 See above under point B. II. 3. c) Interims conclusion: Fundamental rights determining appropriateness of protection; cf. van Dijk, Gellert and Rommetveit, ibid.,

(2) Purpose specification discovering risks posed to all fundamental rights

This thesis therefore promotes that the first component of the principle of purpose limitation, i.e. the requirement to specify the purpose of the processing, is a risk regulation instrument that primarily serves to discover the risks caused by the processing of personal data to all fundamental rights of the individual concerned. As mentioned before, the Article 29 Data Protection Working Party considers the requirement as the necessary precondition in order to "determine whether data processing complies with the law, and to establish what data protection safeguards should be applied".[965] The German Constitutional Court similarly states, regarding informational measures imposed by the State, that "only when it is clear for which purpose the information is required (…), it is possible to answer the question of whether the infringement of the right to informational self-determination is constitutionally legal or not."[966] The specification of the purpose thus serves as the essential link for evaluating the legal relevance of the data processing.

(a) Pooling different actions together in order to create meaning

German legal scholars indeed stress that the requirement of purpose specification must not be confused with the principle of clarity of law.[967] As mentioned previously, with respect to the public sector, the German Constitutional Court concludes the requirement of purpose specification from the principle of clarity of law, which strengthens the principle of purpose limitation.[968] However, Britz underlines that the requirement serves, pri-

---

p. 295, referring to the ECtHR, which also focuses, more and more, on the production of knowledge as part of the risk assessment.

965 See the Article 29 Data Protection Working Group, Opinion 03/0213 on purpose limitation, pp. 13 and 15.

966 See BVerfG, 15th of December 1983, 1 BvR 209, 269, 362, 420, 440, 484/83, cip. 159.

967 See Albers, Treatment of Personal Information and Data, cip. 123; Britz, Informational Self-Determination between Legal Doctrine and Constitutional Case Law, p. 583.

968 See above under point C. II. 1. c) ee) (1) Public sector: Purpose specification as a result of the principle of clarity of law.

marily, to diminish the intensity of an infringement by the State and therefore relates it to the principle of proportionality.[969] Albers instead highlights that the requirement serves to structure the treatment of personal data from a normative perspective determining which of the single acts are legally relevant.[970] This second function is particularly relevant for the processing of data in the private sector. As mentioned previously, the German Constitutional Court also referred to the purpose examining the processing of personal data by a private party.[971] However, the Court did not explicitly explain the specific function of the requirement to specify the purpose in the private sector. Here, the function therefore is more uncertain than on the public sector because private parties are undoubtedly not bound to the principles of clarity of law and proportionality.[972] In light of this, the main function of the requirement to specify the purpose seems, in the private sector, indeed to be the structuring function promoted by Albers. This function is also supported by a historical point of view. Pohle stresses the historical provenance of the principle of purpose limitation in the individual's consent. In this regard, the requirement to specify the purpose was considered, in particular, to define the context and conditions under that the controller should be allowed to use the data.[973] If this function is transferred, in general, to the processing of data,[974] the specification of the purpose indeed serves to pre-determine the conditions of the processing of data with respect to a specific context and, thus, the "informational norms" governing this context.[975]

However, this structuring function in the private sector does not answer the question of how precisely the controller has to specify the purpose.

---

969 See Britz, Informational Self-Determination between Legal Doctrine and Constitutional Case Law, pp. 583 and 584.

970 See Albers, Treatment of Personal Information and Data, cip 123.

971 See above under point C. II. 1. c) ee) (2) Private sector: 'Self-control of legitimacy'.

972 At least, so long as private parties are not directly bound to fundamental rights, see the discussion above under point C. I. 1. b) aa) Third-party effect, protection and defensive function.

973 See Pohle, Purpose limitation revisited, p. 141, referring to Oscar M. Ruebhausen und Orville G. Brim Jr. (1965), "Privacy and Behavioral Research", Columbia Law Review 65.7, p. 1199.

974 See this conceptual shift from the historical perspective at Pohle, ibid., pp. 141 and 142.

975 See above under point B. III. 4. Clarifying the relationship between "context" and "purpose".

The preceding chapters made it clear that the task to precisely specify the purpose is, from a practical viewpoint, even more difficult for data controllers operating in the private sector than for the legislator. In contrast to the legislator, a private data controller is not able to refer to a legal system that comprehensively and precisely determines the objectives of different laws and, subsequently, the consequences for the individual concerned. If the legislator refers, for example, to the income tax act in a sufficiently precise way in order to authorize the processing of certain data, the individual concerned is able to foresee the consequences if/and when the tax authorities retrieve their data. In contrast, a private data controller does not have such a legal system at its disposal and is, in exaggerating words, on a stand-alone basis. In addition, the flux of data in the private sector is less predictable, in light of the diversity of the participants, their actions and intentions, as well as their interconnections in a free market economy. For the data controller operating in the private sector, the need for reliable criteria therefore is even more important.[976] Thus, which criteria could help the controller specify the purpose operating in the private sector?

(b) Separating unspecific from specific risks (first reason why data protection is indispensable)

The following two slight shifts regarding the concept of protection discussed so far assists in answering the above question. On the one hand, there is the intermediate function of the right to data protection for individual autonomy, which is determined by all further fundamental rights. As quoted previously, Rouvroy and Poullet seek to determine, for example, the indeterminateness of the right to privacy by "taking fully into account the context in which our liberties have to express themselves".[977] This sentence points to what has been already presumed with respect to Nissenbaum's approach: Since the definition of a context and, thus, the purpose referring to the context depends on values, it is necessary to elab-

976 See above under point C. II. 2. c) aa) No legal system providing for 'objectives' of data processing in the private sector.

977 See Rouvroy and Poullet, The Right to Informational Self-Determination and the Value of Self-Development: Reassessing the Importance of Privacy for Democracy, p. 61.

orate on an objective concept for this definition.[978] It is the liberties of the individual, in other words, his or her fundamental rights to freedom, but also privacy and non-discrimination, that define which context, and which purpose is legally relevant when the data is processed. On the other hand, the concept of protection of the right to data protection builds upon the regulation of risks. De Hert and Gutwirth do not explicitly mention this function but elaborate on the particularity of the concept of protection of the right to data protection compared to the right to privacy. In their opinion, the right to data protection provides, as a "tool of transparency", more for procedural protection than the right to privacy, as a "tool of opacity". However, with this procedural function, the right to data protection is also closely linked to further substantial values, beside the right to privacy.[979] Indeed, De Hert and Gutwirth do not compare the concept of the right to data protection with other fundamental rights, even if they mention them. This deficiency lead Tzanou to criticize the fact that both authors define in a negative manner "the added value of data protection (…) through its distinction from privacy."[980] However, considering the transparency tools provided for by the right to data protection, not only protecting the right to privacy but also to the other fundamental rights, i.e. to freedom and non-discrimination, verifies that 'we cannot live without it' (i.e. the right to data protection). The reason is that the right to data protection protects, perceived as a risk regulation instrument, against the risks caused by the processing of personal data for all fundamental rights. Since this kind of protection already starts before a specific object of protection of one of the other fundamental rights is threatened, other fundamental rights cannot provide for similar protection.[981] There must be an autonomous fundamental right if it shall protect, as a precautionary measure, further rights before there is a specific threat for them.

The indispensability of the right to data protection, which protects the individual against risks to all his or her fundamental rights, becomes par-

---

978 See above under point B. III. 5. Values as normative scale determining "contexts" and "purposes".

979 See De Hert and Gutwirth, Privacy, data protection and law enforcement. Opacity of the individual and transparency of power, pp. 69 and 70; and, ibid., Data Protection in the Case Law of Luxemburg and Strasburg, p. 44.

980 See Tzanou, ibid., p. 93.

981 Cf. BVerfG, 11th of March 2008, 1 BvR 2074/05 and 1 BvR 1254/07 (License Plate Recognition), cip. 63.

ticularly apparent with respect to the requirement of purpose specification. From the perspective of the regulator of risks, the requirement to specify the purpose primarily serves as a function to discover the risks for the other fundamental rights. So long as the purpose specified by the controller does not concern one of the further fundamental rights of the individual concerned, data processing does not bear a specific risk but an unspecific risk. In this regard, the requirement to specify the purpose is a risk regulation instrument that primarily serves to gather information. However, the moment where the purpose of the data processing concerns one of the other fundamental rights, the substantial guarantee of this fundamental right determines the further protection instruments necessary in order to prevent the individual, i.e. the carrier of this fundamental right, against the specific risk. The answer to the question of how precisely the purpose must be specified hence is twofold: So long as the processing intended does not bear a specific risk for the other fundamental rights, there are no specific requirements related to the precision of the purpose specified by the controller. So far, the requirement to specify the purpose only constrains the controller to constantly assess whether its data processing bears a specific risk for the individual's fundamental rights. In the end, this function appears more or less to correspond to the conclusion that Kokott and Sobotta draw after having compared the fundamental right to data protection with that to private life. They stress "the requirements that personal data must be processed fairly and for a specified purpose cover many instances where an interference with privacy would have to be justified. These specific requirements of data protection help to focus the debate on areas that are particularly susceptible to interference with fundamental rights."[982] This might mean, in the moment the purpose specified discovers a specific risk to one of the fundamental rights, the substantial guarantee of this right determines, amongst others, how precisely the purpose must be specified. Albers sums up this result, with respect to the German right to informational self-determination and to the public sector, as: "The required degree of specification thus depends on the needs for protection and the context of regulation."[983]

982 See Kokott and Sobotta, The distinction between privacy and data protection in the jurisprudence of the CJEU and the ECtHR, p. 228.

983 See Albers, Treatment of Personal Information and Data, cip. 124: "Der gebotene Konkretionsgrad hängt also von den Schutzerfordernissen und vom

(c) Central function with respect to all fundamental rights (second reason why data protection is indispensable of data protection)

This function is an illustrative example for why there must be a right, which is autonomous from the other fundamental rights, at least, to freedom and equality. However, this does not yet explain why this function explained above must also be autonomous from the right to privacy. Since each kind of processing of personal data starts with the collection, indeed it seems possible that the right to privacy might equally provide for this protection function. This corresponds, in principle, to the concept of the right to private life under Article 8 ECHR, even if the European Court of Human Rights does not determine the protection instruments by referring to the other fundamental rights.[984] Furthermore, this approach appears to correspond to what Rouvroy and Poullet promote when referring to the fundamental right to privacy and, correspondingly, to the German right to informational self-determination. However, there is one important reason why it makes sense that a right to data protection should also be autonomous from the right to privacy. An autonomous right to data protection makes it easier to differentiate between the specific substantial guarantees concerned and, thus, react to the threats against these guarantees with different protection instruments.

As illustrated before, the German Constitutional Court differentiates between several guarantees surrounding the individual's privacy, such as: the right to the inviolability of the home; the right to confidentiality of telecommunications; the right to the integrity and confidentiality of information-technological systems; and last but not least, the right to informational self-determination. The reason for why the Court differentiates between these rights is that each separate right contains a specific guarantee, and this diversity gives the Court a more comprehensive scale for: first, determining the risks for the individual concerned; second, to choose the appropriate protection instrument; and third, to weigh these guarantees

regelungskontext ab."; cf. also Britz, Informational Self-Determination between Legal Doctrine and Constitutional Case Law, pp. 284 and 285.

984 See above under point C. I. 3. b) Concept of Article 8 ECHR: Purpose specification as mechanism for determining the scope of application (i.e. the individual's 'reasonable expectation'.

against the opposing constitutional positions.[985] The European Court of Human Rights achieves a similar result, albeit referring to just one fundamental right (i.e. the right to private life under Article 8 ECHR), by applying its case-by-case approach. This approach allows the Court to elaborate on several types of cases without being strictly bound to a general definition for the scope of protection. This is an important difference to the tendencies of the European Court of Justice applying, at least with respect to Articles 7 and 8 ECFR, a deductive method coming from a general definition of the scope.[986] However, the German Constitutional Court requires, providing for a conceptual link between data protection and privacy, a common protection instrument (i.e. the individual's right to determine by him or herself the disclosure and later usage of the data related to him or her). This conceptual link makes it more difficult to elaborate on alternative and more differentiated protection instruments than without such a link.[987] If the data processing concerns other fundamental rights to freedom, in effect, these rights rather supplement the scope of protection of the right to informational self-determination, which is already rather broad and vague, instead of refining its scope.[988] Similarly, the European Court of Human Rights does not refer to other fundamental rights at all.[989] Elaborating the right to data protection under the umbrella of the right to private life, or even privacy, thus makes it more difficult to apply a differentiated approach.

In conclusion, the constitutional legislator clarified, through the separation of both rights, that there are two different guarantees. This is what De Hert and Gutwirth pointed out: the protection functions of the right to privacy and the right to data protection are structurally different. Their defi-

---

985 See above under points C. I. 2. The object and concept of protection of the German right to informational self-determination, and C. I. 1. b) bb) Balance between protection and defensive function.

986 See above under point C. I. 3. c) aa) (1) General definition of the term 'personal data' under Article 7 and 8 ECFR instead of case-by-case approach.

987 See above under point C. I. 2. f) Interim conclusion: Conceptual link between 'privacy' and 'data processing'.

988 See above under point C. I. 2. c) Right to control disclosure and usage of personal data as protection instrument?.

989 See above under point C. I. 3. b) ee) Conclusion: Assessment of 'reasonable expectations' on a case-by-case basis, referring to ECtHR, Case of Gillan and Quinton vs. the United Kingdom from 12 January 2010 (application no. 4158/05), cip. 88 to 90.

nition makes it clear that the right to data protection must be, at least substantially, autonomous from the right to privacy, and not only from the other rights to freedom and equality. Functionally, with respect to the risks caused by the processing of personal data, the right to data protection stands in the center of all other fundamental rights.

(3) Function of making specified purposes explicit

This leads to the additional requirement that the specified purpose must be made explicit to the individual concerned. The European legislator established in Article 5 sect. 1 lit. b GDPR (Article 6 sect. 1 lit. b of the Data Protection Directive) the requirement of making specified purposes explicit. As quoted previously, the Article 29 Data Protection Working Party interprets this requirement as: "The purposes of collection must not only be specified in the minds of the persons responsible for data collection. They must also be made explicit. In other words, they must be clearly revealed, explained or expressed in some intelligible form. (…) The requirement that the purposes be specified 'explicitly' contributes to transparency and predictability. (…) It helps all those processing data on behalf of the controller, as well as data subjects, data protection authorities and other stakeholders, to have a common understanding of how the data can be used."[990] Thus, this requirement builds upon the requirement of specifying the purpose and safeguards predictability and transparency of the processing of data.

However, the fundamental right to data protection under Article 8 ECFR does not explicitly mention this requirement. Section 2 only states on the requirement to specify the purpose, not to make the specified purpose explicit to the individual concerned. The European Court of Justice has also not yet explicitly decided on this requirement provided for by Article 8 ECFR. In particular, the European Court of Justice does not apply, so far, the criteria developed by the European Court of Human Rights with respect to the individual's "reasonable expectations".[991] At least with respect to the right to private life under Article 7 ECFR, in the case of "*Dig-*

990 See the Article 29 Data Protection Working Group, Opinion 03/0213 on purpose limitation, p. 17.

991 See above under point C. I. 3. c) aa) (4) Protection in (semi)-public spheres irrespective of 'reasonable expectations'.

ital Rights vs. Ireland", the Court implicitly mentioned the function of such a requirement by stressing the fact "that data retained and subsequently used without the subscriber or registered user being informed is likely to generate in the minds of the persons concerned the feeling that their private lives are the subject of constant surveillance."[992] On the one hand, this could mean that the requirement is not provided for by the right to data protection but by the right to private life under Article 7 ECFR. This would raise the question of whether this function only refers to the substantial guarantees provided for by Article 7 ECFR or equally serves as a protection for the other fundamental rights to freedom and equality.

On the other hand, the requirement to make the specified purpose explicit to the individual concerned is similar, if not identical, to the idea of the consent. This becomes apparent, at least, in the decisions of the European Court of Human Rights. In these cases, as illustrated previously, the data controller can frame the individual's 'reasonable expectations' by making its purpose of data processing explicit to the individual, and the individual can then react to it accordingly.[993] Since the constitutional legislator of the European Charter of Fundamental Rights located the data protection instruments, such as the requirement of purpose specification, not under the right to private life in Article 7 ECFR (which corresponds to Article 8 ECHR) but under Article 8 ECFR,[994] it is plausible that the mechanism of "making the purpose explicit to him or her", which equals the "framing of the individual's reasonable expectations", is also located under Article 8 ECFR. If this is the case, the question then is where this mechanism is located exactly. One solution to this question could be locating this mechanism under the consent requirement provided for by Article sect. 2 ECFR. One advantage of this approach is that this protection mechanism hence is principally applicable to all fundamental rights. On the basis of the purpose made explicit to an individual, the individual is not only able to react to risks against his or her rights to privacy, but also against his or her rights to freedom and non-discrimination.

On the other hand, an argument against this thought is that the requirement to make the purpose explicit to the individual only requires the data

---

992 See ECJ C-293/12 and C-594/12 cip. 37.

993 See above under point C. I. 3. b) cc) Particular reference to the individual's 'reasonable expectations'.

994 See above under point C. I. 3. c) bb) (1) Location of protection instruments under Article 8 ECFR.

controller to provide the information, but it does not require an additional action of the individual for example giving his or her consent. Correspondingly, the General Data Protection Regulation differentiates between the requirements to make the purpose explicit in Article 5 sect. 1 lit. b (Article 6 sect. 1 lit. b of the Data Protection Directive) and the individual's consent in Article 6 sect. 1 lit. a (Article 7 lit. a of the Data Protection Directive). However, in this regard, it should be stressed that the consent provided for by Article 8 sect. 2 ECFR does not require, explicitly, certain conditions to be met for the legitimacy of the consent, such as a formalized opt-in procedure before the data processing occurs. If the European Court of Justice applies the same or, at least, a similar approach as the European Court of Human Rights, it is rather flexible in elaborating on the requirements for the consent. This is because the considerations of the European Court of Human Rights illustrate, in this regard, that the individual must primarily be able to avoid the processing, irrespective of how the consenting action looks like in the particular case.[995] Thus, the requirements established by the General Data Protection Regulation (and the Data Protection Directive) with respect to the consent do not necessarily have to match, precisely, with those provided for by Article 8 sect. 2 ECFR. If the European legislator establishes, for the consent, stricter requirements than provided for by Article 8 ECFR, this may hence result from its margin of discretion.[996]

In conclusion, considering the requirement to make the purpose explicit as corresponding with the consent required by Article 8 sect. 2 ECFR, makes it possible to refer this requirement not only to the right to privacy under Article 7 ECFR but also to the other fundamental rights, such as to freedom and equality. Building upon the requirement of purpose specification, the purpose made explicit informs the individual (and others) in which context, covered by the specific fundamental right, the processing of data occurs. The substantial guarantee provided for by the specific fundamental right determines which purpose is legally relevant and how precisely it must be specified. This corresponds, more or less, with the point of view of some legal scholars regarding the consent required by the Data Protection Directive. Pursuant to their opinion, the data controller has to

995 See above under point C. I. 3. b) dd) Consent: Are individuals given a choice to avoid the processing altogether?.

996 See above under pint C. I. 1. b) bb) (1) The 3-Step-Tests: Assessing the defensive and protection function.

inform the individual concerned about how intensively the data processing concerns his or fundamental rights.[997] Consequently, the substantial guarantee concerned also determines further requirements for the consent, for example, whether an explicit opt-in procedure is required or an implicit opt-out procedure is sufficient in order to protect the individual's specific fundamental right.

cc) Interim conclusion: Refining the concept of protection

The approach proposed in the preceding chapters does not conflict with the concepts of protection so far developed, be it by the European Court of Justice or the German Constitutional Court. In contrast, the preceding chapters illustrated that both Courts refer to the purpose, and to further fundamental rights, in order to assess the legal relevance of the data processing. However, this concept refines the so far developed concepts of protection by the Courts because it bears several advantages.

(1) Tying into the Courts' decisions and European legislation

The European Court of Justice tends to consider the right to data protection in Article 8 ECFR as a protection instrument which serves to protect, at least, the right to private life under Article 7 ECFR.[998] This becomes apparent, for instance, in the case of "*Digital Rights vs. Ireland*" where the Court stated that Article 8 ECFR is "especially important for"[999] the right to private life under Article 7 ECFR. The precise functioning of Article 8 ECFR with respect to the right to privacy indeed remains unclear. In other decisions, the Court also took other fundamental rights into account. For example, in the case of "*Schrems vs. Facebook*", the Court considered the fundamental right to effective judicial protection under Article 47 ECFR as a right to be protected by the right to data protection in Article 8 ECFR.[1000] And in the case of "*Rechnungshof vs. ORF*", the Court consid-

997 See Dammann/Simitis, ibid., cip. 22.

998 See above under point C. I. 3. c) aa) (3) Reference to further fundamental rights under Article 7 and/or 8 ECFR.

999 See ECJ C-293/12 and C-594/12 cip. 53.

1000 See ECJ C-362/14 (Schrems vs. Facebook), cip. 95.

ered, determining the intensity of the infringement, the negative effects for the individual that might result from the publication of his or her salaries for his or her chances of 'being given employment by other undertakings'.[1001] Indeed, when the European Court of Justice refers to the right to private life under Article 7 ECFR or the right to data protection under Article 8 ECFR, it is unclear which conditions and criteria the Court actually uses.[1002] Even more so, the function of the requirement to specify the purpose remains in the European Court of Justice's decisions rather vague. In the case of "*Telekom vs. Germany*", the purpose served to pool the different possible acts of the data processing to one legal coherent unity, i.e. the publication in a telephone directory.[1003] And, in the case of "*González vs. Google Spain*", the Court referred to the purpose in order to examine whether the re-publication of the data was excessive compared with the purpose of the initial publication, without precisely examining what the purpose actually was.[1004] So far, the concept of protection proposed in this doctoral thesis does not conflict with the concept developed by the European Court of Justice but only refines it.

Indeed, the concept proposed similarly ties into the approach that the German Constitutional Court developed, at least, with respect to informational measures by the State. As previously described, the Court re-determines the broad scope of protection of the right to informational self-determination by examining whether or not the measure intended by the State either constitutes a 'specific danger for the freedom of action and of being private' or if it 'qualitatively affects a person's fundamental right' or if it can 'essentially concern the individual's interests'. If this is not the case, the informational measure does not infringe the scope.[1005] Whatever the concrete scale might be, evaluating the intensity of the infringement, the Court also takes the disadvantages for the individual into account.[1006] In order to determine the intensity of the infringement, the Court takes

1001 See ECJ C-465/00, C-138/01 and C-139/01, cip. 89.

1002 See above under point C. I. 3. c) aa) (3) Reference to further fundamental rights under Article 7 and/or 8 ECFR.

1003 See above under point C. II. 2. a) ff) Interim conclusion: Do regulation instruments dictate the scale for 'purpose specification'?

1004 See above under point C. II. 1.) ECtHR and ECJ: Almost no criteria.

1005 See above under point C. I. 2. d) Infringement by 'insight into personality' and 'particualrity of state interest'.

1006 See above under point C. I. 2. e) aa) (2) The proportionality test also takes takes the use of data at a later stage into account.

both real disadvantages into account, as well as disadvantages that the individual has reasonably to fear. The Court justifies the first aspect (i.e. real disadvantages) taking into account the fact that the State's treatment of data related to unsuspicious persons 'leads to their risk of being an object of state investigations which adds to their general risk of being unreasonably suspected'.[1007] Comparably, the processing indirectly increases the risk of being stigmatized in daily or professional life. This is in particular the case if the data treatment refers to criteria, such as religion or ethnic origin, listed in Article 3 of the German Basic Law, which guarantees the freedom of equality.[1008] Regarding the second aspect (i.e. disadvantages that the individual has to fear), the Court underlines that the individual's fear of being surveyed can result, in advance, into a bias in communication and for individuals to change and/or adapt their conduct accordingly. Such chilling effects affect not only the individual, but also communication in a civic society as a whole.[1009] In conclusion, be it for determining the infringement or its intensity in relation with the examination of its proportionality, the German Constitutional Court refers, amongst others, to further basic rights of the individuals concerned. These rights can therefore provide an objective scale in order to determine the 'purpose' of the data processing.

The purpose hence plays, in the German Constitutional Court's decisions, a decisive role for the legal relevance of the data processing and, thus, also for the risks for the other basic rights. The German Court indeed elaborated on the concept of protection of the right to informational self-determination explicitly as a right which is autonomous from other basic rights. The Court justifies this approach by considering that data processing can lead to threats for the personality before "there is a specific threat for an object of protection."[1010] In terms of the regulation of risks, the concept hence establishes a precautionary protection against unspecific risks, for the personality of the individual concerned. With respect to the right to data protection under Article 8 ECFR, the European Court of Justice did

1007 See BVerfG, 3rd of March 2004, 1 BvR 2378/98 (Big Eavesdropping Operation), cip. 227; BVerfG, 4th of April 2006, 1 BvR 518/02 (Dragnet Investigation), cip. 103.

1008 See BVerfG, 4th of April 2006, 1 BvR 518/02 (Dragnet Investigation), cip. 106.

1009 See BVerfG, 14th of July 1999, 1 BvR 2226/94 (Surveillance of Telecommunications), cip. 207; BVerfG, 3rd of March 2004, 1 BvR 2378/98 (Big Eavesdropping Operation), cip. 230.

1010 See BVerfG, ibid., cip. 63: "Eine derartige Gefährdungslage kann bereits im Vorfeld konkreter Bedrohungen von Rechtsgütern entstehen."

not (and still has not) elaborated on a similar precise concept of protection as the German Court. However, European secondary laws, such as the Data Protection Directive and the General Data Protection Regulation apply the so-called risk-based approach clarifying, in its first Articles, to protect all fundamental rights of the individuals concerned.

(2) Advantages compared to existing (unclear) concepts of protection

Understanding the requirement to specify the purpose as an instrument that seeks to discover risks caused by the processing of personal data to all fundamental rights bears several advantages. First, the approach enables the regulator to precisely select the protection instruments that effectively and efficiently protect the individual against unspecific and specific risks for his or her other fundamental rights; second, the approach simultaneously enables the regulator to choose the protection instruments which are appropriate in light of the opposing fundamental rights; and finally, the approach helps answer the question which point of view shall be relevant for determining the risks: is it the point of view of the controller or the individual concerned?

(a) Effectiveness and efficiency of protection instruments

First, the approach avoids the 'broadness' and 'vagueness' characteristics stemming from the scope of protection, be it of the German right to informational self-determination or the right to Data Protection under Article 8 ECFR. If the term 'personal data' serves as the only criteria to determine the scope, the increasing digitization in society leads to the situation that this scope becomes broader and broader. In the offline world, human actions take place in very different areas of social life. These social contexts are covered by the diversity of all fundamental rights. In contrast, the more social interaction is based on the processing of personal data, the more the fundamental right to data protection overlays, or even substitutes, the other fundamental rights. Therefore, the other, eventually more specific, rights provide a legal scale in order to determine the legal relevance of the processing of 'personal data', these do not run the risk of being substituted by Article 8 ECFR or Article 2 sect. 1 in combination with

Article 1 sect. 1 GG, respectively. Instead, they "re-specify", the scope.[1011] Furthermore, as previously described, it is not 'personal data' but information that possibly leads to an infringement of an individual's fundamental right. The reason for this is that it is not data, but the interpretation of the data pursuant to a certain context, in other words, the information constitutes the basis for social interaction. A right referring to the term 'personal data', only, must therefore be considered as a regulation instrument serving to protect the substantial guarantees which are actually endangered by the processing of data.[1012]

In light of this approach, the term 'personal data' provides two favourable effects: The first effect is that the reference to data permits to interpret the right to data protection as a subjective right. While the individual concerned cannot directly determine the information that somebody else concludes from the data related to the individual, he or she can principally determine under which conditions the data might be used.[1013] The second effect is that that the term opens the scope of application at a very early stage. Each processing of personal data therefore falls under its scope with the result that the controller has to, as a first step, specify the purposes with respect to the potential risk for the individual's fundamental rights. As a second step, the substantial guarantees endangered, as well as the intensity of risk, dictate which further regulation instruments have to be applied in order to balance the opposing fundamental rights.[1014]

(b) Appropriate concept for innovation processes

The second advantage of such a concept of protection is that it fits better to the openness of innovation processes than the current concepts of protection. Critics stress that so long as the concept of the right to informational self-determination provides an individual's right to control over the

---

1011 See above under point C. I. 3. c) cc) (2) The reason for why the scope that is too broad: Increasing digitization in society.

1012 See above under point C. I. 3. c) cc) (1) The reason for why the scope that is too vague: Difference between data and information.

1013 See above under point C. I. 3. c) cc) (3) Advantages and challenges: 'Personal data' as legal link for a subjective right.

1014 Cf. above under point C. I. 3. c) cc) (4) Possible consequence: A legal scale provided for by all fundamental rights which determine the regulation instruments under Art. 8 ECFR.

collection and usage of 'his or her' data and implies, in addition, a centralized and linear environment, the requirement of purpose specification mainly refers to the moment of collection. In contrast, in light of the decentralized and non-linear environment today, the requirement of purpose specification should be considered as a regulation instrument serving to structure the non-linear processes of a data treatment.[1015] Thus, the requirement to specify the purpose must be understood as not exclusively referring to the moment of collection, pre-determining all possible future purposes. Rather, this requirement must principally refer to all moments of the data processing. This is particularly relevant with respect to the individual's consent. As previously described, legal scholars argue with respect to the purpose(s) specified in the consent that the term 'specific', in the meaning of Article 2 lit. h of the Data Protection Directive, does not exclude future acts of usage, but rather means specific circumstances including the purpose of the processing.[1016] The question therefore is which type of threat caused by the data processing can be legitimized by the consent. If the consent legitimized unspecific risks, including a later data processing endangering an individual's specific fundamental right, which was not specified by the purpose given in the original consent, the focus on the moment of collection does not restrict the controller's scope of action. In this case, the consent would be so broad that it simply legitimizes everything. In contrast, if the consent is required only for specific risks, the moment of collection is not the exclusive moment to legally evaluate the risks because specific risks also result from later data processing.[1017] The reference to all fundamental rights of the individuals concerned, thus, principally fits better to non-linear innovation processes because this concept does not exclusively focus on the moment of collection. The reason is that the fundamental rights are typically concerned with different moments of the processing of data. The subsequent analysis will demonstrate, for example, that the collection of personal data usually concerns the individual's fundamental rights to privacy, while the later use of data related to him or her more often concern his or her fundamental rights to freedom.

1015 See Albers, ibid., cip. 121 to 123.
1016 See Dammann/Simitis, ibid., cip. 22.
1017 Cf. above under point B. II. Data Protection as a risk regulation.

(c) Excursus: Objective vs. subjective risks

Finally, this approach solves the dilemma of which perspective shall be relevant for the determination of risks: On the one hand, if the data controller keeps its own perspective, and refers to the purpose in order to achieve its interests guaranteed by its fundamental rights, it does not consider the consequences for the individual concerned that the right to data protection shall actually protect.[1018] On the other hand, the individuals concerned often estimate the consequences of the data processing differently. This leads to the result that data controllers are barely able to predict the individual estimations.[1019] In contrast, the fundamental rights of the individuals concerned serve as an objective scale in order to evaluate the risks of the data processing for the substantial guarantees (aka objects of protection). Thus, this scale enables the controller to estimate the risks of its data processing with respect to the consequences for the individual concerned more reliably.

In contrast to this approach, the European Court of Human Rights primarily refers to the individual's perspective. The processing of personal data does not infringe the individual's right to private life under Article 8 ECHR if it meets his or her 'reasonable expectations'.[1020] However, the term 'reasonable' clarifies that not all expectations of the individual has to be seen as legally relevant but only the *reasonable* expectations. The meaning of this term can again be determined from an objective point of view.[1021] The individual's 'reasonable expectations', hence, do not provide unlimited protection. The European Court of Human Rights does not refer to further fundamental rights of the individual in order to assess which of

1018 See Mehde, Handbook of European Fundamental Rights, cip. 24.

1019 Cf. Masing, Challenges of data protection, p. 2308, who considers the consent as the most appropriate regulation instrument in order to meet the plurality of moral concepts.

1020 See above under point C. I. 3. b) cc) Particular reference to the individual's "reasonable expectations".

1021 Cf. Kift, Bridging the transatlantic divide, at fn. 1, referring to the Katz test established by the US Supreme Court Supreme Court, 1967: 351, which equally refers to the individual's 'reasonable expectations'; similar, Nissenbaum, Privacy as Contextual Integrity, pp. 117/118.

his or her expectations are 'reasonable' or not.[1022] However, in principle, the other fundamental rights could serve such an objective scale.

The European Court of Justice does not refer, as demonstrated previously, to the individual's 'reasonable expectations', not even when interpreting the right to private life under Article 7 ECFR, which corresponds to Article 8 ECHR. Instead, the Court provided protection irrespective of the individuals' 'reasonable expectations'. For example, in the case of "*González vs. Google Spain*", an individual could expect today that information about him or her can be retrieved online once it is published. Possibly having this in mind, the European Court of Justice did not refer to the claimant's 'reasonable expectations' but rather to the 'psychological integrity' or another substantial guarantee concerned by the search engine's listing or profiling activity, and examined the extent of such a guarantee pursuant to the terms of 'necessity' and 'relevance'.[1023] These terms can be interpreted, be they part of a compatibility assessment implicitly conducted by the Court or not, from an objective point of view.[1024]

The European legislator does not explicitly refer to the individual's 'reasonable expectations' either. Instead, it has established, within the secondary law, the more instrumental elements, i.e. the requirement of purpose specification and purpose compatibility. In contrast, focusing on predictability, the Article 29 Data Protection Working Group considers both elements as closely connected with the individual's 'reasonable expectations'.[1025] However, the considerations by the Working Group do not mean that both elements must be interpreted, exclusively, from the individual's subjective point of view. In contrast, as set out before, the other individual's fundamental rights can provide an objective scale in order to determine whether his or her 'expectations' are 'reasonable' or not.

Finally, the same considerations can principally be applied to the concept of protection developed by the German Constitutional Court with re-

---

1022 See above under point C. I. 3. b) ee) Conclusion: Assessment of 'reasonable expectations' on a case-by-case basis, referring to ECtHR, Case of Gillan and Quinton vs. the United Kingdom from 12 January 2010 (application no. 4158/05), cip. 88 to 90.

1023 See above under point C. I. 3. c) bb) (2) Protection going beyond Article 8 ECHR.

1024 See above under point C. I. 3. c) aa) (4) Protection in (semi)-public spheres irrespective of 'reasonable expectations'?.

1025 See the Article 29 Data Protection Working Group, Opinion 03/0213 on purpose limitation, pp. 11 and 13.

spect to the right to informational self-determination. If the individual's right to 'basically determine by him or herself the disclosure and later usage of data related to him or her' is considered as an instrument protecting all other basic rights, these rights can provide an objective scale in order to determine the extent of this protection instrument. Thus, the individual could control the disclosure and later usage of data related to him or her only insofar as this is necessary for the protection of his or her other fundamental rights.

b) Fundamental rights which determine purpose requirements

After having elaborated on the refinement of the concept of protection of the right to data protection under Article 8 ECFR, this chapter continues by illustrating the interplay of this concept with the substantial guarantees provided for by the other fundamental rights to privacy, freedom and non-discrimination. In doing so, the discussion refers, from time to time, to several decisions of the German Constitutional Court. Again, this is not done, of course, in the sense that the right to data protection under Article 8 ECFR should be interpreted in light of these German decisions. Instead, these decisions shall only serve as a source of inspiration for how the European fundamental rights may be interpreted.

aa) Right to privacy (aka 'being left alone')

The European Court of Justice considers the right to data protection as "especially important for"[1026] the right to private life in Article 7 ECFR. Article 7 ECFR lists several elements guaranteeing different aspects of an individual's life: The individual's private and family life, his or her home and communications. Amongst them, the term 'private life' is considered as consisting of an autonomous concept that is however closely connected to the other terms of family life, home and communications. Legal scholars interpret it as "encompassing the physical, psychological and moral aspects of the personal integrity, identity and autonomy of individu-

---

1026 See ECJ C-293/12 and C-594/12 cip. 53.

als."[1027] The most prominent guarantee provided for by Article 7 ECFR is the protection of the individual's interest to remain confidential, in other words, to be left alone. De Hert and Gutwirth call the instruments protecting this guarantee "tools of opacity".[1028] The next-following considerations will address the question of how the guarantees of privacy determine under which circumstances the protection instruments provided for by Article 8 ECFR must be applied. In doing so, the subsequent analysis will not focus on privacy protection in relation to data that reveals, *per se*, personal information about an individual, such as about his personal characteristics or attitudes. Such a protection of privacy is, here, not exposed as problematic.[1029] Instead, the following analysis will focus on the specific context in that personal data is collected because this demonstrates how different guarantees of privacy require different scopes of protection.[1030]

(1) Unfolding specific guarantees of privacy

In the case of "*Digital Rights vs. Ireland*", the European Court of Justice differentiates between the guarantees of privacy of communications and private life provided by Article 7 ECFR and protection guaranteed by Article 8 ECFR. The Court examines, first, how the retention of the data affects the guarantee of privacy of communications stating that the data "make it possible, in particular, to know the identity of the person with whom a subscriber or registered user has communicated and by what means, and to identify the time of the communication as well as the place

---

1027 See Vedsted-Hansen, EU Charter of Fundamental Rights, cip. 7.06 A with further references.

1028 See above under point C. II. 3. a) aa) (1) Different functions of rights (opacity and transparency), referring to De Hert and Gutwirth, Privacy, data protection and law enforcement. Opacity of the individual and transparency of power, pp. 71.

1029 See, for example, the list of categories of personal data that is per se protected, above under point …(Criteria established for certain cases: Context of collection, nature of data, way of usage, and results obtained)… referring to ECtHR, Case of S. and Marper vs. the United Kingdom from 4 December 2008 (application nos. 30562/04 and 30566/04), cip. 66.

1030 See the discussion above under point C. I. 3. c) cc) Referring to substantial guarantees as method of interpreting fundamental rights in order to avoid a scope of protection that is too broad and/or too vague.

from which that communication took place."[1031] The Court subsequently observes that the data retained allows "very precise conclusions to be drawn concerning the private lives of the persons whose data has been retained"[1032], and therefore also affects the guarantee of private life under Article 7 ECFR. It comes to the conclusion that the data retention therefore "directly and specifically affects private life and, consequently, the rights guaranteed by Article 7 of the Charter.[1033] Finally, the Court affirms that the data retention also affects the right to data protection under Article 8 ECFR *per se* "because it constitutes the processing of personal data within the meaning of that article and, therefore, necessarily has to satisfy the data protection requirements arising from that article".[1034] So far, the data processing in question constitutes an infringement by the State of all three mentioned guarantees. However, there are cases where it seems to be appropriate to make a clearer difference in protection, pursuant to the specific guarantee concerned. With respect to German basic rights, for instance, the Constitutional Court provides several examples for how strictly the scope of protection and, consequently, an intrusion into the scope depends on the specific guarantee.

(a) At home: Protection of 'haven of retreat'

In the decision of "*Big Eaves Dropping Operation*", for instance, the Constitutional Court elaborates on the guarantee of inviolability of the home.[1035] In this decision, it stressed that as long as it has to judge the possible infringement of a spatial private sphere of occupants of a home, only this guarantee applies.[1036] The Constitutional Court describes this guarantee as: "Containing the right to be left alone in one's home and the right to the spoken word at home, Article 13 sect. 1 GG protects the part of the private sphere that is normally guaranteed by the general personality

1031 See ECJ C-293/12 and C-594/12 cip. 26.
1032 See ECJ C-293/12 and C-594/12 cip. 27.
1033 See ECJ C-293/12 and C-594/12 cip. 29.
1034 See ECJ C-293/12 and C-594/12 cip. 29.
1035 See the facts above under point C. I. 2. c) Right to control disclosure and usage of personal data as protection instrument?.
1036 See BVerfG, ibid., cip. 131 and 132.

right."[1037] Thus, this guarantee protects the occupants of the home, only; if the observation of a home concerns people that are not the occupants, the general personality right applies. In this case, indeed, the level of protection provided for by the general right must not be higher than such of the special fundamental right.[1038] The special protection of the home protects, for example, against a physical intrusion into the home, installation of technical means within the rooms and an eavesdropping on what happens in the home. The storage, processing and transfer of the data collected to third parties also infringes or harms Article 13 sect. 1 GG.[1039] In the event that the eavesdropping occurs from outside of the protected rooms, it only infringes or harms Article 13 GG if the communication would not be – naturally – perceivable by acoustic means. The Court clarified that "even the perception of such a communication that can be heard from outside without acoustic means can infringe the guarantee of being private. However, such communication is not protected by Article 13 GG if the person concerned makes the perception of the communication from outside by him or herself possible and thus, does not actually use the spatial sphere of privacy in order to protect him or herself."[1040]

Two aspects become apparent from these considerations: First, the guarantee of inviolability of the home protects the occupant of being left alone so long as he or she really uses the spatial sphere in order to protect him or herself; and second, the information of the occupant beforehand would not exclude an infringement of his or her fundamental right, even if he or she could leave the home in order to 'be left alone'. The reason is

1037 See BVerfG, ibid., cip. 133: "Mit dem Recht, in der Wohnung ungestört zu sein, und dem Recht am eigenen in der Wohnung gesprochenen Wort schützt Art. 13 Abs. 1 GG gerade den Teil der Privatsphäre, den sonst das allgemeine Persönlichkeitsrecht gewährleistet."

1038 See BVerfG, ibid., cip. 134.

1039 See BVerfG, 3rd of March 2004, 1 BvR 2378/98, cip. 137.

1040 See BVerfG, ibid., cip. 138: "Zwar kann auch die Wahrnehmung der aus der Wohnung nach außen dringenden und ohne technische Hilfsmittel hörbaren Kommunikation deren Privatheit beeinträchtigen. Solche Lebensäußerungen nehmen aber nicht am grundrechtlichen Schutz des Art. 13 GG teil, weil der Betroffene die räumliche Privatsphäre nicht zu seinem Schutz nutzt, wenn er die Wahrnehmbarkeit der Kommunikation von außen selbst ermöglicht."

that is the classic function of this guarantee that the individual concerned has not to leave his or her home in order to 'be left alone'.[1041]

(b) Using communications: Protection against 'filtering opinions'

In contrast, in the case of "*Surveillance of Telecommunications*", the German Court elaborates on the scope of protection by referring to the specific guarantee of privacy of telecommunications.[1042] In this case, the Court stresses that Article 10 GG is, similar to the right to inviolability of the home, a special guarantee that supersedes the general right to informational self-determination, as long as the act of collection or usage of the data falls under its scope.[1043] The Court describes the aim of this guarantee as to "avoid that the exchange of opinions and information through means of communications systems stops the individuals concerned from communicating with each other because they fear that state institutions will access the content of the communication."[1044] The Court's reasoning is particularly interesting with respect to the collection of data: "the collection itself already constitutes an infringement, as long as it provides the communication to the Federal Intelligence Service and serves as a basis for the following check against the key words. The collection does not infringe Art. 10 GG, so long as the telecommunication between German connection points is only unintentionally collected because of technical reasons and is, directly after the conditioning of the signal, technically eliminated without a trace. In contrast, the collection can even then infringe Art. 10 if the data cannot be immediately related to certain persons. The hearing be-

1041 Cf. Britz, Informational Self-Determination between Legal Doctrine and Constitutional Case Law, pp. 588 to 591.

1042 See the facts above under point C. I. 2. c) Right to control disclosure and usage of personal data as protection instrument?.

1043 See BVerfG, ibid., cip. 131:

1044 See BVerfG, ibid., cip. 135: "(Mit der grundrechtlichen Verbürgung der Unverletzlichkeit des Fernmeldegeheimnisses) soll vermieden werden, daß der Meinungs- und Informationsaustausch mittels Fernmeldeanlagen deswegen unterbleibt oder nach Form und Inhalt verändert verläuft, weil die Beteiligten damit rechnen müssen, daß staatliche Stellen sich in die Kommunikation einschalten und Kenntnisse über die Kommunikationsbeziehungen oder Kommunikationsinhalte gewinnen."

fore the court confirmed (the presumption) that the data could easily be, at a later stage, related to a person."[1045]

These considerations make, similar to the previous case, apparent how the substantial guarantee defines the scope: First, the substantial guarantee protects the users against an interception by the State in order to 'avoid that the exchange of opinions and information through (these) means of communications systems stops'; and second, the collection of the data therefore leads even then to an infringement of the scope if the content is being checked against keywords, and leads to a negative result, and the data is immediately deleted. The reason is that already the checking against keywords leading to a negative result actually consists in an 'assessment of opinions'. Therefore, this guarantee protects against each collection of content.

(c) "Privacy in (semi)-public spheres": Protection against the risks of later usage of data

Finally, as illustrated above, the scope of protection of the right to informational self-determination is wider than the right to privacy of the home because it also protects personal data that is publicly available.[1046] However, on the other hand, a precise look reveals that the right is narrower than the right to privacy of telecommunications because it does *not* protect against the collection of the data if the data is checked back against keywords with a negative result and immediately deleted. In the case of "*License Plate Recognition*", the German Court justifies this restriction of the scope of protection, focusing on the specific guarantee, and differentiates

1045 See BVerfG, ibid., cip. 160: "Eingriff ist daher schon die Erfassung selbst, insofern sie die Kommunikation für den Bundesnachrichtendienst verfügbar macht und die Basis des nachfolgenden Abgleichs mit den Suchbegriffen bildet. An einem Eingriff fehlt es nur, soweit Fernmeldevorgänge zwischen deutschen Anschlüssen ungezielt und allein technikbedingt zunächst miterfaßt, aber unmittelbar nach der Signalaufbereitung technisch wieder spurenlos ausgesondert werden. Dagegen steht es der Eingriffsqualität nicht entgegen, wenn die erfaßten Daten nicht sofort bestimmten Personen zugeordnet werden können. Denn wie die mündliche Verhandlung bestätigt hat, läßt sich auch in diesen Fällen der Personenbezug ohne Schwierigkeit herstellen."

1046 See above under point C. I. 2. c) Right to control disclosure and usage of personal data as protection instrument?.

as: "the storage of the license plate that was recorded, which provides the basis for potentially further measures, (undoubtedly) infringes the basic right. This is the intended goal of the measure if the license plate matches the key words (…). From this point in time, the license plate recorded is available for the processing by state agencies and the specific danger for the freedom of action and of being private occurs, which justifies the protection of the basic right to informational self-determination. (Word in bracket added by the author.)"[1047] The reason for why the storage of personal data, after a positive match with the keywords, infringes this basic right, but not the storage of data that did not match the keywords and was therefore immediately deleted, is the following one: this second kind of collection does not infringe the scope because the substantial guarantee does not protect the individual in being left alone in a spatial private sphere. Similarly, this guarantee does also not aim to avoid the situation whereby an individual stops changing content by means of telecommunications because a third party can intercept the connection. Instead, the right to informational self-determination focuses, in these type of cases, on protecting the individual against the risk of becoming an object of state investigation which adds to the general risk of being unreasonably suspected.[1048] This guarantee does not protect against third party access to the data *per se,* but against the creation of information bases preparing further

---

1047 See BVerfG, 11th of March 2008, 1 BVR 2047/05 and 1 BvR 1254/07, cip. 68 and 69: "Zu einem Eingriff in den Schutzbereich des Rechts auf informationelle Selbstbestimmung kommt es daher in den Fällen der elektronischen Kennzeichenerfassung dann nicht, wenn der Abgleich mit dem Fahndungsbestand unverzüglich vorgenommen wird und negative ausfällt (sogenannter Nichttrefferfall) sowie zusätzlich rechtlich und technisch gesichert ist, dass die Daten anonym bleiben und sofort spurenlos und ohne die Möglichkeit, einen Personenbezug herzustellen, gelöscht werden. Demgegenüber kommt es zu einem Eingriff in das Grundrecht, wenn ein erfasstes Kennzeichen im Speicher festgehalten wird und gegebenenfalls Grundlage weiterer Maßnahmen werden kann. Darauf vor allem ist die Maßnahme gerichtet, wenn das Kraftfahrzeugkennzeichen im Fahndungsbestand aufgefunden wird (sogenannter Trefferfall). Ab diesem Zeitpunkt steht das erfasste Kennzeichen zur Auswertung durch Staatliche Stellen zur Verfügung und es beginnt die spezifische Persönlichkeitsgefährdung für Verhaltensfreiheit und Privatheit, die den Schutz des Grundrechts auf informationelle Selbstbestimmung auslöst."

1048 Cf. BVerfG, 3rd of March 2004, 1 BvR 2378/98 (*Big Eavesdropping Operation)*, cip. 230; BVerfG, 4th of April 2006, 1 BvR 518/02 (*Dragnet Investigation*), cip. 103.

negative measures. However, this does not automatically mean that the protection instruments required by this guarantee are less strict than required by the two other guarantees of privacy. In the case of "*Video Surveillance*", the Court applied a rather strict approach, at least, regarding the consent. As illustrated before, the Court states, in this case, that even if the individual knows that he or she is filmed in the public and can avoid entering the space of the recording, this cannot be considered as if the individual had given his or her consent. From this point of view, the omission of an explicit disagreement with the recording does therefore not automatically mean an implicit consent.[1049]

Apart from the last aspect regarding the consent, this concept principally corresponds with the approach applied by the European Court of Human Rights. The European Court of Human Rights does not consider each kind of collection of personal data in the public as an intrusion of the individual's private life under Article 8 ECHR. Instead, it assesses whether the collection occurs systematically and permanently and whether it goes beyond a passer-by situation. In particular, the European Court of Human Rights takes into account whether the data collected is likely to injure an individual's reputation or is otherwise intended to be used in detriment to the individual concerned.[1050] The latter aspect became particularly relevant in the case of "*Perry vs. United Kingdom*". As illustrated before, in this case, the police had prepared a custody camera in a particular way so that it could use the video footage as a proof of evidence in a Court trial against the individual concerned.[1051] Similarly, the recording of a young man walking distressed around after having committed suicide at a junction by a CCTV camera did not raise per se the Court's concerns.[1052] In-

1049 See above under point C. I. 2. c) Right to control discolsure and usage of personal data as as protection instrument?, referring to BVerfG, 23rd of February 2007, 1 BvR 2368/06 (Video Surveillance), cip. 39 and 40.

1050 See above under point C. I. 3. b) cc) (2) Public situations: 'Systematic or permanent storage' vs. 'passer-by situations', referring to ECtHR, Case of P.G. and J.H. vs. The United Kingdom from 25 September 2001 (application no. 44787/98), cip. 57.

1051 See above under point C. I. 3. b) cc) (4) 'Unexpected use' pursuant to the purpose perceptible by the individual concerned, referring to ECtHR, Case of Perry vs. the United Kingdom from 17 July 2003 (application no. 63737/00), cip. 40, 41, and 43.

1052 See above ECtHR, Case of Peck vs. the United Kingdom from 28 January 2003 (application no. 44647/98), cip. 60.

stead, the publication of the video footage by a broadcasting company harmed his right to private life because his face was not properly masked so that family members, neighbors and colleagues recognized him.[1053] In contrast, regarding the consent, the European Court of Human Rights applies a much less strict approach than the German Constitutional Court. As illustrated before, while the German Court requires an explicit consent even for a recording in the public, the European Court of Human Rights considers whether the individual has a choice of avoiding the data collection by simply not entering the space of the data collection.[1054]

Indeed, whether the European Court of Justice considers situations where the personal data is collected in (semi)-public spheres as falling under the right to the private life in Article 7 ECFR, like the European Court of Human Rights, or the new right to data protection in Article 8 ECFR is not yet sufficiently clear. In the decisions "*SABAM vs. Scarlet*" and "*SABAM vs. Netlog*", which concerned the processing of IP addresses by an Internet service provider and a social network, the European Court of Justice refers to Article 8 ECFR only. The reason might be that the Court did not see, in these contexts, IP addresses as revealing sufficient information about the private life of the individual concerned, albeit the service providers themselves could identify the individuals concerned.[1055] In the new case "*Breyer vs. Germany*", the European Court of Justice unfortunately did not refer, explicitly, to the fundamental rights to private life or data protection under Articles 7 and 8 ECFR. It only interpreted the notion "means which may likely reasonably be used in order to identify the data subject", pursuant to the Data Protection Directive.[1056] However, at least,

---

1053 See above ECtHR, Case of Peck vs. the United Kingdom from 28 January 2003 (application no. 44647/98), cip. 62 and 63.

1054 See, on the one hand, above under point C. I. 2. c) Right to control discolsure and usage of personal data as as protection instrument?, referring to BVerfG, 23rd of February 2007, 1 BvR 2368/06 (Video Surveillance), cip. 39 and 40 and, on the other hand, under point C. I. 3. b) dd) Consent: Are individuals given a choice to avoid the processing altogether?, referring to ECtHR, Case of M.S. vs. Sweden from 27 August 1997 (74/1996/693/885) and ECtHR, Case of Gillan and Quinton vs. the United Kingdom from 12 January 2010 (application no. 4158/05).

1055 See the facts of this case above under point C. I. 1. b) aa) (2) (b) The right to data protection under Article 8 ECFR and/or the right to private life under Article 7 ECFR.

1056 See ECJ C-582/14, cip. 47 and 48.

in this regard, the European Court of Justice considers data as "personal" if the controller can "reasonably" approach intermediaries or third parties, which have additional information that enables the identification of the individual. This is particularly the case if the controller collects and stores the data in order to identify the user for the purpose of prosecution of cyber attacks.[1057] This reasoning is similar to both the before-mentioned considerations made by the German Constitutional Court and the approach applied by the European Court of Human Rights because it refers, tying into the purpose of the data processing, to the possibly negative consequences for the individual concerned. In this regard, Article 8 thus serves as a protection against the risk that data are used later, once collected and stored, which is detrimental for the individual concerned.[1058]

(2) Necessity requirement, irrespective of inconvenience

The question of under which fundamental right these cases actually fall is decisive because, again, this determines, substantially, the extent of protection. With respect to the guarantee of privacy, the European Court of Justice states, in the case of "*Digital Rights vs. Ireland*" as: "To establish the existence of an interference with the fundamental right to privacy, it does not matter whether the information on the private lives concerned is sensitive or whether the persons concerned have been inconvenienced in any way (see, to that effect, Cases C-465/00, C-138/01 and C-139/01 Österreichischer Rundfunk and Others EU:C:2003:294, paragraph 75)."[1059] Thus, an intrusion *per se* conflicts with the guarantee of privacy; this guarantee does not require further disadvantages for the individual concerned. The reason for this is that each piece of data, which is collected, reveals, in particular if processed further, more aspects about the individual's private life. The German Constitutional Court considers a similar idea, indeed, with respect to the right to informational self-determination. In the case of "*License Plate Recognition*", the Court considers the collection of further data as an extension of the intrusion of this right and the

1057 See above under point C. II. 1. b) aa) (1) (c) The case of "*Breyer vs. Germany*", referring to ECJ C-582/14, cip. 31 to 49.

1058 See above under point C. I. 3. c) aa) (2) (b) Protection against collection, storage, and subsequent use.

1059 See ECJ C-293/12 and C-594/12 (Digital Rights vs. Ireland), cip. 88.

revelation of further information by means of processing of that data as a deepening of the intrusion.[1060]

Consequently, the European Court of Justice makes it clear that "so far as concerns the right to respect for private life, the protection of that fundamental right requires, according to the Court's settled case-law, in any event, that derogations and limitations in relation to the protection of personal data must apply only in so far as is strictly necessary (…)."[1061] Thus, first of all, it must be stressed that the European Court of Justice locates this requirement under the right to private life under Article 7 ECFR, and not under the right to data protection under Article 8 ECFR. This allocation makes sense in light of the fact that each datum collected constitutes a further intrusion into the individual's privacy. Hence, the requirement limits the extent of the infringement or harm for the individual's privacy by requiring that the data controller is only allowed to collect and process data that is absolutely necessary for its purpose. In conclusion, the necessity requirement does not primarily result from the principle of proportionality of law, which explains why the Court applies it for both the collection of personal data by public and private entities.[1062] Instead, the requirement results, in particular with respect to the private sector, from the substantial guarantee of privacy.

(3) 'Framing' privacy expectations

Another aspect where the guarantee of privacy concerned essentially determines the data protection instruments refers to the consent. As illustrated previously, the European Court of Human Rights refers to the individuals "reasonable expectations", in order to assess whether a state or private action intrudes into an individual's privacy and, thus, infringes or harms his or her fundamental right. For this assessment, the specification of the

1060 See above under point C. I. 2. c) Infringement by 'insight into personality' and 'particularity of state interest'?, referring to BVerfG, 11th of March 2008, 1 BVR 2047/05 and 1 BvR 1254/07 (License Plate Recognition), cip. 74.

1061 See ECJ C-293/12 and C-594/12 cip. 52; affirmed in the subsequent case of "*Schrems vs. Ireland*", ECJ C-362/14, cip. 92.

1062 See ECJ C-293/12 and C-594/12 (Digital Rights vs. Ireland), cip. 52; ECJ C-473/12 (IPI vs. Englebert), cip. 39; ECJ C-92/09 and C-93/09 (Schecke vs. Germany), cip. 77 und 8; ECJ C-73/07 (Satakunnan Markkinapörssi und Satamedia), cip. 56.

purpose and, even more so, the fact of whether or not the intruder makes the (real) purpose explicit plays a decisive role. The purpose made explicit to the individual "frames" his or her "reasonable expectations" and thereby determines the scope of protection of the right to private life under Article 8 ECHR. This assessment mechanism principally applies to all guarantees of privacy, be it in the individual's business premises, when using communications or being in the public. The mechanism results in the situation that the information of the individual about the purpose to intrude into the 'home' or to intercept his or her 'communications' principally excludes a violation of his or her right to private life under Article 8 ECHR. Indeed, the mechanism requires that the individual has a choice. A warning of an intrusion does not exclude the infringement or harm if the individual cannot avoid it. As previously described, the European Court of Human Rights appears to apply a rather liberal approach in this regard. The Court considers, for example, that an individual can avoid the search of his or her bag in relation with an airplane access control by not choosing to travel by plane.[1063]

(a) Research on the individual's decision making process (consent)

The far-reaching effects of this approach may be the reason for why the European Court of Justice did not, so far, refer to the individual's "reasonable expectations", either with respect to the right to private life under Article 7 ECFR or with the right to data protection in Article 8 ECFR.[1064] Indeed, even if this reasoning might apply to many situations, it would be highly arguable, for example, to expect that individuals can leave their private homes or omit to take a phone call. Thus, the problem of this mechanism is that it requires only that the individuals has a choice, which leads to the result that the controller could exclude the violation of their right to private life simply by warning them beforehand. In contrast, German legal scholars stress that the specific guarantees of privacy, such as of the 'home' and 'communications', safeguard that individuals maintain a chance to retreat into such 'spheres of privacy'. Only such 'spheres of pri-

---

1063 See above under point C. I. 3. b) cc) Particular reference to the individual's "reasonable expectations".

1064 See above under point C. I. 3. c) aa) (4) Protection in (semi)-public spheres irrespective of 'reasonable expectations'?.

vacy' enable the individual to freely decide which aspects of his or her behavior shall be 'public' and which aspects shall be reserved to such 'havens of retreat'.[1065] These considerations forbid a data controller to exclude an infringement of the right to private life by simply informing the individual about its intrusion.

However, the principle developed by the European Court of Human Rights became clear, and the question rather is how to determine these 'spheres of privacy' with respect to the specific substantial guarantee and, consequently, how the corresponding protection instruments must be applied in order to be effective. Referring to the individual's consent as the main protection instruments foreseen, in this regard, by the right to data protection under Article 8 ECFR,[1066] the question hence is which requirements shall apply for the consent?

This question can be unfolded in more specific questions. The preceding analysis of the Courts' decisions revealed the following "ladder of protection" regarding the individual's consent:

- Is it sufficient if the controller informs the individual about the intrusion into his or her private sphere leaving him or her the choice to leave this sphere?;
- Or should the individual have the chance to stay and just object to the intrusion?;
- Or should the controller be forbidden to intrude into the private sphere until the individual gave his or her prior consent?;
- Or should the possibility to consent to an intrusion be forbidden overall?; and
- Finally, which (further) conditions must be met in order to meet the specific guarantee of privacy concerned?

Indeed, these questions cannot be answered by legal research alone, at least, not comprehensively. Tying into the statement of the European Court of Justice that the right to data protection is "especially important for"[1067] the right to private life under Article 7 ECFR, legal research can

---

1065 See Britz, ibid., p. 588 and 589; Albers, ibid., cip. 71; see also the considerations under point B. III. 1. The individual's autonomy and the private/public dichotomy, referring to Priscilla Regan (1995), Legislating Privacy, Chapel Hill: University of North Carolina Press, pp. 226 and 227.

1066 See above under point C. II. 3. a) bb) (3) Function of making purpose explicit to the individual.

1067 See ECJ C-293/12 and C-594/12 cip. 53.

assist in elaborating on the substantial guarantees of privacy. However, the question of which protection instruments most effectively and efficiently protect such a specific guarantee must also be answered empirically. The following examples shall illustrate how the European legislator does not only refer, indeed, to the specific substantial guarantee concerned, but, of course, also to the factual circumstances that decide on whether certain protection instruments are effective and efficient. This results from the duty of protection of the State which requires that ,the measures provided for by the legislator must be sufficient for an adequate and effective protection and must be, in addition, based on an accurate investigation of facts and on reasonable estimations'.[1068]

(b) First example: The legislature's considerations on the use of 'cookies'

The first example refers to the use of cookies. Before the amendment of the ePrivacy Directive by the Civil Rights Directive, Article 5 sect. 3 authorized 'the storing of information, or the gaining of access to information already stored, in the terminal equipment of a subscriber or user' if "the subscriber or user concerned is provided with clear and comprehensive information (…) *inter alia* about the purposes of the processing, and is offered the right to refuse such processing by the data controller." In this regard, it should be stressed that the European legislator considered the pure information as an appropriate instrument avoiding an infringement of the individual's fundamental rights or, at least, balancing the opposing fundamental rights. In recital 24, the legislator stated that the devices of the individual and "any information stored on such equipment are part of the private sphere of the users requiring protection under the European Convention (…). So-called spyware, web bugs, hidden identifiers and other similar devices can enter the user's terminal without their knowledge in order to gain access to information, to store hidden information or to trace the activities of the user and may seriously intrude upon the privacy of these users. The use of such devices should be allowed only for legitimate purposes, with the knowledge of the users concerned." Thus, the legislator did not consider, in 2002, the consent as the only instrument guaranteeing

1068 See above under point C. I. b) bb) (1) The 3-Step-Tests: Assessing the defensive and protection function, referring to Calliess, ibid., cip. 6 with reference to BVerfGE 88, 203, cip. 159.

the individual's private sphere. However, a couple of years later, it considered that the pure information was not as effective as supposed. Therefore, it required, in the Civil Rights Directive from 2009, the individual's prior consent.[1069]

(c) Second example: Considerations surrounding 'unsolicited communications'

Article 13 of the ePrivacy Directive provides another illustrative example for the interplay between legal elaboration on a substantial guarantee and empirical research on how these guarantee should be met in practice. Section 1 requires the controller, who uses automated calling machines, fax or email for the purposes of direct marketing, to gather prior consent from its subscribers or users. In its recital 40, the legislator justifies this strict requirement as a protection instrument against intrusion into the individual's privacy. However, the following considerations illustrate that the intrusion per se, does not require the consent, but rather, the additional relationship between the little efforts on behalf of the controller and the significant annoyance for the individual caused by this form of marketing: "These forms of unsolicited commercial communications may on the one hand be relatively cheap to send and on the other hand may impose a burden and/or costs on the recipient. Moreover, in some cases their volume may also cause difficulties for electronic communications networks and terminal equipment." Consequently, recital 42 clarifies that the consent may not be necessary for other forms of direct marketing, which "are more costly for the sender and impose no financial costs on subscribers and users, such as person-to-person voice telephony calls". These considerations take, from an objective point of view, the efforts by the controller into account, which may either enhance or hinder the direct marketing actions and, thus, the extent of the intrusion into the individual's privacy. The legislator does not consider the prior consent of the individual concerned as necessary because of the substantial guarantee of privacy alone. Instead, the legislator takes, in a typifying manner, the practical circumstances into account, in particular, under which conditions and through which protection instruments the individual is effectively able to protect him or herself.

1069 See Article 2 sect. 5 as well as recital 66 of the Civil Rights Directive.

Correspondingly, Article 13 sect. 2 of the ePrivacy Directive explicitly abolishes the requirement of the individual's prior consent. Section 2 states: "(…) where a natural or legal person obtains from its customers their electronic contact details, in the context of the sale of a product or a service, in accordance with (…/ the Data Protection Directive), the same natural or legal person may use these electronic contact details for direct marketing of its own similar products or services provided that customers clearly and distinctly are given the opportunity to object, free of charge and in any easy manner, to such use of electronic contact details at the time of their collection and on the occasion of each message in case the customer has not initially refused such use." In this case, the reason for the fact that this regulation is more liberal is not, in the opinion of the Article 29 Data Protection Working Group, the objective expectation of the intensity of the intrusion into the individual's privacy but his or her subjective expectation (indeed, assessed from an objective point of view). In this context, the law does not require a consent to be given because the marketing actions would be 'more costly for the sender and impose no financial costs on' the individual. Rather, the individual concerned can expect that the provider of products or services that he or she has purchased will make further offers related to the initial ones.[1070] Consequently, the Working Group advocates that there may be differences in the legal ground applicable and the compatibility of further processing. These differences result from the context and the reasonable expectations. In light of this, the Working Party proposes there should be three different categories: "Direct mailings in the context of existing relationships to provide information on new (i.e. not similar) offerings or other relevant opportunities; similar direct mailings, but now on sensitive personal data, and/or automated profiles more intrusive data analytics tools; (and) the sharing of information with data brokers or other third parties in order to develop more effective segmentation in direct mailings (words in brackets added by the author)."[1071] The Working Party concludes that all cases may "be lawful, but subject to different safeguards, depending on the context of the data collection and on the relationship between the data subjects and the controllers, as well as their expectations concerning this relationship."[1072]

1070 See the Article 29 Data Protection Working Group, Opinion 03/0213 on purpose limitation, p. 34.

1071 See the Article 29 Data Protection Working Group, ibid., p. 34 and 35.

1072 See the Article 29 Data Protection Working Group, ibid., p. 34.

These examples illustrate how the factual circumstances surrounding current marketing activities determine the architecture of the decision-making process of the individual concerned in order to meet his or her substantial guarantee of privacy. In this case, the individual's objection to the direct marketing activities would not meet his or her substantial guarantee of 'being left alone' because an individual's objection would always come too late, i.e. at the moment where he or she had already received the material. However, the essential reason of having provided these two examples is to illustrate how legal and empirical research go together elaborating, on the one hand, on the substantial guarantees of privacy and, on the other hand, assessing the effectiveness of the protection instruments.

bb) Right to self-determination in public

The preceding sub-chapter already referred to the case of "*Peck vs. the United Kingdom*" in which the European Court of Human Rights affirmed a violation of the right to private life under Article 8 ECHR because of the publication of personal data (in the case, video footage showing the individual concerned). This sub-chapter examines which substantial guarantee is, in such cases of a publication of personal data, actually concerned.

(1) Clarification of substantial guarantees

Both the European Court of Human Rights, as well as the European Court of Justice usually affirm an infringement of the right to private life by the publication of personal data, be it provided for by Article 8 ECHR or by Article 7 in combination with Article 8 ECFR. However, this thesis promotes that the publication of personal data does not concern specific guarantees of privacy in the sense of a right to be left alone. Instead, the publication of personal data concerns the individual's guarantee to *influence* his or her social representation (i.e. how he or she is perceived by others) in the public. Its conceptual difference to the guarantees of privacy becomes clear with respect to photographs: While the mere taking of a photograph may infringe or harm an individual's guarantee to remain confidential in a certain 'sphere of privacy', the publication of the photograph concerns his or her ability to influence whether others notice him or her, and if so, how they *think* about him or her. The German Constitutional Court calls this guarantee a right to self-determination in the public.[1073] This right does not only refer to photographs but to any kind of medium, and is not restrained to sensitive aspects but principally refers to all aspects of the personality.[1074] This last aspect corresponds to the general considerations made by the European Court of Justice with respect to the right to private life (which does not precisely differentiate, though, between the specific guarantees).[1075] However, given that the right to private life is considered as "encompassing the physical, psychological and moral aspects of the personal integrity, identity and autonomy of individuals"[1076], it is consequent to locate such a guarantee under Article 7 ECFR and not within another fundamental right. On this basis, the subsequent analysis will discuss which protection instruments are suitable to meet this guarantee. Interestingly, all Courts, the European Court of Human Rights, the European Court of Justice, and the German Constitutional Court, essentially require the individual's consent before the publication of data related to him or her (or a law as legal basis).[1077] However, once the data is published, the concepts of protection with respect to this guarantee diverge.

(2) First publication: Strict requirements

The European Court of Human Rights principally considers the publication of personal data without the individual's consent as an infringement or harm of the right to private life under Article 8 ECHR of the individual concerned.[1078] The European Court of Justice applies a similar approach, and also provides for precise requirements regarding the necessity of the publication and the individual's consent.

1073 See Bechler, Informational Harm by Intransparent Treatment of Personal Data, pp. 134 to 136.

1074 See Bechler, ibid., pp. 134 to 136 with further references.

1075 See ECJ C-293/12 and C-594/12 (Digital Rights vs. Ireland), cip. 33.

1076 See Vedsted-Hansen, EU Charter of Fundamental Rights, cip. 7.06 A with further references.

1077 See Bechler, Informational Harm by Intransparent Treatment of Personal Data, pp. 134 to 136.

1078 See above under point C. I. 3. b) cc) (3) 'Data relating to private or public matters', 'limited use' or 'made available to the general public', referring to ECtHR, Case of Peck vs. the United Kingdom from 28 January 2003 (application no. 44647/98).

(a) Necessity of publication

Regarding the necessity requirement, the European Court of Justice already stated in the case "*Rechnungshof vs. ORF*" that the referring Court had to examine whether the disclosure of not only the salaries and pensions exceeding the certain thresholds defined by the Austrian law, but also the names of the employees concerned is actually necessary and appropriate in order to meet the aim of the authorizing law in question.[1079] While the Court referred, in this case, the final decision back to the national Court in order to answer whether the naming of the individuals was necessary for achieving the objective of the law requiring the publication, it answered in the case of "*Schecke vs. Land Hessen*" the question by its own. And while the European Court of Justice decided the first case, still on the grounds of Article 8 ECHR, at the time of the latter decision, the European Charter was already in force with the result that the Court based its decision now on the grounds of Articles 7 and 8 ECFR.[1080] In this second case, the Court examined whether or not the publication was, in light of Article 52 sect. 1 ECFR, strictly necessary for achieving the purpose of the publication. The Court first carved out the relevance of the data for the right to private life stating that "it is not disputed that the amounts which the beneficiaries concerned receive from (.../the public fund) represent part of their income, often a considerable part. Because the information becomes available to third parties, publication on a website of data naming those beneficiaries and indicating the precise amounts received by them thus constitutes an interference with their private life within the meaning of Article 7 of the Charter".[1081] The Court concluded from this and its further reasoning that the purpose of transparency would have also been met if the publication had been restricted "according to the periods for which (.../the individuals concerned) received aid, or the frequency or nature and amount of aid received."[1082] In the Court's opinion, the publication therefore was not strictly necessary and infringed the right to private life in Ar-

---

1079 See the facts above under point C. I. 3. c) aa) (3) (b) The answer depends on the type of threat posed, ECJ C-465/00, C-138/01 and C-139/01 (Rechnungshof vs. ORF), cip. 89 and 90.

1080 See the references under the point C. I. 3. c) bb) (1) Location of protection instruments under Article 8 ECFR.

1081 See ECJ C-92/09 and C-93/09 cip. 58.

1082 See ECJ C-92/09 and C-93/09 cip. 81.

ticle 7 in combination with the right to data protection under Article 8 ECFR.[1083] In conclusion, the European Court of Justice thereby applies the necessity requirement to both guarantees provided for by the right to private life under Article 7 ECFR: The specific guarantees of privacy and the guarantee of self-determination in the public, at least, with regard to the first publication of personal data.[1084]

(b) Strict requirements for consent

In the same case "*Schecke vs. Land Hessen*", the European Court of Justice also decided on the requirements surrounding the individual's consent. In particular, it examined whether the individuals concerned consented to the publication of the personal data or whether a law provided the basis for the publication. The Court assessed, precisely, whether or not the application for funding by the beneficiaries must be considered as giving their consent because "they were informed in the aid application form of the mandatory publication of the data".[1085] In this regard, the Court noted "that in the main proceedings, in their aid application forms, the applicants stated only that they were 'aware that (.../the legal provision) requiring publication of information on the beneficiaries (...)'".[1086] The Court concluded from this that the publication was not based on the applicants' consent but on the law requiring the publication.[1087] This can be seen as a strict requirement for the individual's consent. In light of the specific guarantee of self-determination in the public provided for by the right to private life, the pure information about the publication as part of a formal application process does not comply with the requirements for the consent. Instead, the Court seems to require the individuals to have given their explicit consent. This might be justified in light of the severe impact of a

1083 See ECJ C-92/09 and C-93/09 cip. 86.

1084 See, regarding the specific guarantees of privacy, above the introduction of point C. II. 3. b) aa) (2) Necessity requirement, irrespective of inconvenience, referring to ECJ C-293/12 and C-594/12 (Digital Rights vs. Ireland), cip. 52; ECJ C-473/12 (IPI vs. Englebert), cip. 39; ECJ C-92/09 and C-93/09 (Schecke vs. Germany), cip. 77 und 8; ECJ C-73/07 (Satakunnan Markkinapörssi und Satamedia), cip. 56.

1085 See ECJ C-92/09 and C-93/09 cip. 61.

1086 See ECJ C-92/09 and C-93/09 cip. 63.

1087 See ECJ C-92/09 and C-93/09 cip. 61 to 64.

publication of personal data on the right to private life of the individuals concerned.

The Court also appears to provide for similar strict requirements for the consent regarding the publication of personal data in further cases. While the Court did not explicitly discuss, in the case of "*Schecke vs. Land Hessen*", the consent with respect to Article 8 ECFR, protecting the individual's right to private life under Article 7 ECFR, it did in the case of "*Telekom vs. Germany*". As mentioned previously, this decision again referred to the publication of personal data, in the particular case, in telephone directories.[1088] However, since in this second case the data was already published based on the individuals' consent and the informational measure in question only consisted in a re-publication of the data in another directory, the Court denied that an infringement had occurred. It explicitly considered, that the consent by the individuals concerned, who must accordingly be informed, refers to the purpose of first publication and therefore covers all further processing activities for the same purpose.[1089] With respect to the information, the Court held that the data controller must inform, before the personal data is firstly published, about this purpose and the fact that the data may be transferred to third parties but will not "be used for purposes other than those for which they were collected".[1090] These are rather strict requirements, even if its precise meaning and extent remains still open.[1091]

So far, the essential point to be stressed here is that the right to data protection under Article 8 ECFR provides the necessary protection instrument, (i.e. the consent) in order to protect a specific guarantee. This specific guarantee, the guarantee of self-determination in the public determines which protection instrument the data controller must apply, and in which way. Indeed, the Court did not mention in the case of "*Telekom vs. Germany*" the right to private life provided for by Article 7 ECFR. The likely reason is that personal data has already been published before the second publication, which was the actual issue of the case. However, even

1088 See the facts of this case above under point C. I. 1. b) (2) (b) The right to data protection under Article 8 ECFR and/or the right to private life under Article 7 ECFR.

1089 See ECJ C-543/09, cip. 65.

1090 See ECJ C-543/09 cip. 66 and 67.

1091 See above under point C. I. 3. c) aa) (5) Going beyond the requirement of consent provided for under Article 8 ECHR.

if the decision did not explicitly refer to Article 7 ECFR, the requirements regarding the necessary information as a basis for the individual's consent clearly referred to the first publication, and therefore, at least implicitly, to the substantial guarantee provided for by the right to private life. The specific requirements for the individual's consent hence resulted from the specific guarantee of self-determination in the public, and not from the protection instrument *per se*.

(3) Re-publication: Weighing 'interests' against 'old and new purposes'

In the decisions of "*Rechnungshof vs. ORF*", "*Schecke vs. Land Hessen*", and "*Telekom vs. Germany*", the European Court of Justice referred to the purpose of the first publication, as a requirement provided for by Article 8 ECFR, in order to determine whether or not the publication conflicted with the specific guarantee of self-determination in the public, provided for by the right to private life under Article 7 ECFR. In particular, the purpose specified by the controller provided the legal link in order to determine the necessity of the publication. In contrast, in the case of "*González vs. Google Spain*", the Court's reasoning was less precise. The data had already been published, similar to the case of "*Telekom vs. Germany*". However, while the first publication in the case of "*Telekom vs. Germany*" was based on the individual's consent, in the case of "*González vs. Google Spain*", it was not. In this case, newspapers had published articles about Mr. González who was involved in an auction as a result of recovering social security debts. This first publication was based on an order of the Spanish Ministry of Labour and Social Affairs in order to make as many bidders as possible aware of the auction. The first publication hence depended not only on the fact that Mr. González could not pay his security debts 'but also on a number of factors beyond his control.'[1092] Thus, with respect to the considerations by the European Court of Human Rights, the European Court of Justice apparently considered, even if not explicitly, that the first publication was not based on Mr. González' consent.

The European Court of Justice examined, at first, the effects of the processing of data by Google's search engine on Mr. González' right to pri-

1092 See above under point C. I. 3. c) aa) (2) (a) Protection against first publication and profiles based on public data, referring, by means of an analogy, to ECtHR, Case of M.S. vs. Sweden from 27 August 1997 (74/1996/693/885), cip. 32.

vate life.[1093] It then answered the question of whether Mr. González can require Google to delist the articles containing information about him from its search results, given that 16 years had elapsed after the first publication of the original articles, taking the purposes of the initial publication into account. Referring to the Data Protection Directive, the Court stressed "that even initially lawful processing of accurate data may, in the course of time, become incompatible with the directive where those data are no longer necessary in the light of the purposes for which they were collected or processed."[1094] It concluded that the fundamental rights to private life and data protection under Articles 7 and 8 ECFR generally rule out "not only the economic interest of the operator of the search engine but also the interest of the general public in finding that information".[1095] In the Court's opinion, this might be only different "if it appeared, for particular reasons, such as the role played by the data subject in public life, that the interference with his fundamental rights is justified by the preponderant interest of the general public in having, on account of its inclusion in the list of results, access to the information in question."[1096] The principle of purpose specification provided for by Article 8 sect. 2 ECFR thus played an instrumental role in order to weigh Mr. González' right to private life against the opposing fundamental rights.

(a) Misconceptions in the decision of "Mr. González vs. Google Spain"

However, the Court's reasoning raises two essential questions: First, it did not precisely examine what the initial purpose was and why the later usage of that data by the search engine operator actually conflicted with this initial purpose; and second, establishing the priority rules, the Court affirmed and gave the individual a rather comprehensive right to control whether, and even more so, how others notice him or her (i.e. control his or her social representation).[1097] In particular, the Court ignored that Internet search

1093 See above under point C. I. 3. c) aa) (2) (a) Protection against first publication and profiles based on public data, referring to ECJ C-131/12 (Mr. González vs. Google Spain), cip. 80.

1094 See ECJ C-131/12, cip. 93.

1095 See ECJ C-131/12, cip. 96 and 97.

1096 See ECJ C-131/12 cip. 100.

1097 See above under points C. I. 3. c) bb) (3) Remaining uncertainty about interplay between Article 7 and 8 ECFR.

engines also create a public discourse. This fact leads to the situation that the Internet Search engines co-influence 'the role played by the data subject in public life'. Thus, while the European Court of Justice considered the public as an external factor in order to evaluate the interest of the search engine, the creation of the public is an inherent function of Internet search engines itself. This misunderstanding leads to the situation that the individuals' right to data protection enables them to comprehensively control their picture that the public has about them. Thus, "such a total control disproportionately restrains the freedom of expression and, as a consequence, the public discourse."[1098]

The reason for this misconception is that the European Court of Justice does not sufficiently indicate which substantial guarantee is actually concerned, in the particular case, by the processing of personal data.[1099] In the case of "*González vs. Google Spain*", the Court only refers to the right to private life under Article 7 ECFR, without clarifying its precise interplay with the right to data protection under Article 8 ECFR. However, as described above, one fundamental right can provide for several guarantees. The preceding chapter examined in detail the individual's guarantees of privacy. Article 7 ECFR refers, in this regard, particularly to specific 'private spheres' such as the 'home' or 'communications' of the individual concerned. In contrast, the publication of personal data does not directly concern these specific 'private spheres'. Rather, it concerns the question of to which extent an individual shall be legally allowed to influence his or her forms of social representation.[1100] In order to demonstrate the substance and limits of such a guarantee it is helpful to illustrate how the German Constitutional Court developed such a guarantee, based on the German basic personality right.[1101]

1098 See v. Grafenstein and Schulz, The Right to be Forgotten in Data Protection Law: A Search for the Concept of Protection, p. 263.

1099 See above under point C. I. 3. c) cc) Referring to substantial guarantees as method of interpreting fundamental rights in order to avoid a scope of protection that is too broad and/or too vague.

1100 See the introduction of this chapter C. II. 3. b) bb) Right to self-determination in the public.

1101 See v. Grafenstein and Schulz, ibid., p. 262.

(b) Excursus: Case law provided for by the German Constitutional Court

When the German Court weighs this guarantee against opposing basic rights, most often against the freedom of expression, it can refer to its extensively developed and differentiated case law: The Court essentially differentiates between opinions and facts, and concerning the latter, between true and untrue facts.[1102] With regard to the expression of opinions, the Court applies a priority rule in favor of the freedom of expression if the opinion expressed contributes to the public debate. In contrast, if the expression of an opinion mainly seeks to defame an individual, his or her personality right prevails. If none of these rules applies, the Court fairly weighs the colliding fundamental rights against each other. Concerning the expression of facts, the Court principally applies a priority rule for false statements favoring the personality right. Briefly: Telling the truth is principally allowed, whereas false statements are not. Indeed, the Court also makes exemptions to these rules: First, if an individual stated something untrue about another individual, but was not aware that it was wrong, and exercised the necessary care in avoiding the fault, the personality right does not principally prevail the freedom of expression, but both rights have to be fairly balanced against each other (for the press, this duty of necessary care is stricter than for individuals); this exemption hence meets the need that the public debate is often based on assumptions, and assumptions can always turn out to be wrong. Second, with respect to true facts, if they concern intimate aspects of an individual's life, for example, his or her sexual behavior, the personality right principally prevails. However, if true facts do not relate to intimate aspects, both rights have to be, here again, weighed against each other, considering, on the one hand, the intensity of the infringement for the individual concerned and, on the other hand, the public interest.[1103]

In this case, time also plays an important role. The German Constitutional Court considers several aspects in order to determine whether or not the public interest justifies the 're-publication' of a past event. For instance, concerning the social rehabilitation of criminals, it takes into account how much time has surpassed since the crime was committed and

---

1102 See overview at Grimm, The Freedom of Speech in the judicature of the German Constitutional Court (Die Meinungsfreiheit in der Rechtsprechung des Bundesverfassungsgerichts), NJW 1995, pp. 1697.

1103 See overview at Grimm, ibid., pp. 1697.

the severity of the crime; how long the convict served the sentence; as well as the way of the re-publication of the information and its impact on the individuals concerned. In this last regard, the Court considers whether or how easily the individuals concerned could be identified and, in particular, whether they run the risk of being stigmatized within society.[1104] However, this case illustrates that the German personality right does not guarantee a comprehensive control of a social image that others have about the individual concerned: "The perception of a person in public is a social construction and cannot be 'owned' by the respective person";[1105] a corresponding guarantee can thus not secure this ownership. As a consequence, the right to self-representation in public does not form a comprehensive guarantee of total disposition of the data underlying such information but rather, in relation to chances of partial self-representation.[1106]

In contrast, the reasoning by the European Court of Justice in the case of "*González vs. Google Spain*", runs the risk that individuals concerned by the processing of their data have a protection instrument at their disposal in order to comprehensively determine, instead of only influence, how they represent themselves in society. There are several reasons for this result: First, the increasing digitization in society leads to the situation that more and more opinions are expressed and dispersed through the means of data processing; second, the European Court of Justice commonly refers, determining the scope of protection of both the right to private life, as well as the right to data protection, to the term of 'personal data', only, and does not carve out the substantial guarantee which is actually concerned; third, it sets up one single priority rule in favor of the individuals concerned with one counter-exception, exclusively; this one-dimensional approach leads to the fourth situation that the Court considered, in the particular case, the 'public' as an external factor whereas it is an inherent function of Internet search engines to create this 'public', based on the search queries of others; and fifth, it did not examine, in a sufficiently precise manner, the purposes of the first publication of the articles by the newspapers and the subsequent, ongoing re-publication by the Internet search engine. This all together would have enabled the European Court of Justice to fairly balance the substantial guarantees provided for by the opposing fundamental rights.

1104 Cf. BVerfG NJW 1973, pp. 1226; 1998, pp. 2889; 2000, pp. 1859.
1105 See Bechler, ibid., pp. 174 and 175; v. Grafenstein and Schulz, ibid., p. 258.
1106 See Bechler, ibid., pp. 174 and 175; v. Grafenstein and Schulz, ibid., p. 258.

(c) Conclusion in regards to the decision of "Mr. González vs. Google Spain"

Taking these considerations into account, the circumstances of the case of "*Mr. González vs. Google*" provides the following conclusion: The re-publication of the articles containing information about Mr. González' distant past does not concern the substantial guarantee of 'privacy' but of 'self-determination in public' equally provided for by his right to private life. Legal scholars consider the term 'private life' as "encompassing the physical, psychological and moral aspects of the personal integrity, identity and autonomy of individuals."[1107] In light of his understanding, the individual's right to self-representation in public can be considered as one of the substantial guarantees provided for by the right to private life. This guarantee safeguards, in accordance with settled case-law by the European Court of Human Rights and the European Court of Justice (and the German Constitutional Court as well) that the individual is principally able to decide by him or herself whether or not personal data are firstly published. However, once personal data are legitimately published, it does not provide an individual's right to comprehensively determine how others perceive him or her in public, i.e. what they can think about him or her. As a consequence, a single priority rule in favor of the individual with the exception of "particular reasons, such as the role played by the data subject in public life"[1108] does not meet a fair balance between the opposing fundamental rights. Instead, the European Court of Justice could, comparably to the German Constitutional Court, differentiate more precisely: Facts and opinions; defaming opinions; true and untrue facts; true facts concerning intimate aspects of the individual's life etc.

Indeed, the Court took, comparably to the German case law regarding crimes committed in the distant past, the time that had elapsed since the event, as well as the intensity of the re-publication for the personality of the individual concerned and the general interest in this information, into account. However, in order to balance the substantial guarantees concerned, the Court should precisely examine the corresponding purposes. In the case of "*Mr. González vs. Google Spain*", the initial purpose was "to give maximum publicity to the auction (in that Mr. González was involved

1107 See Vedsted-Hansen, EU Charter of Fundamental Rights, cip. 7.06 A with further references.

1108 See ECJ C-131/12 cip. 100.

at the time) in order to secure as many bidders as possible". In contrast, the present purposes were different to this initial purpose: First, individual's searching for information either about Mr. González, personally, or, in general, about cases related to social security debts or compulsory auctions; second, the purpose of the publishers to keep their own articles online – a purpose which the Court obviously overlooked; and third, the purpose of the Internet search engine to provide access to any information as easily and comprehensible as possible. In light of the approach promoted in this thesis, the interests behind that purposes are not relevant for determining the purpose. These concern the guarantees provided for by the fundamental rights of the third parties as: The freedom of expression and information under Article 11 ECFR, and the freedom to conduct a business under Article 16 ECFR. Instead, the purpose of the processing is determined by the fundamental rights of the individual concerned. The examples illustrate that all these purposes commonly concerned Mr. González' guarantee of self-determination in the public. There might have been further guarantees such as provided for by his right to non-discrimination under Article 21 ECFR or his freedom to conduct a business under Article 16 ECFR. This could have been the case if there had been facts raising the concern that Mr. González ran the risk of being stigmatized or had difficulties to find employees. However, since the judgment does not refer to such facts, the determination of the purpose through these further guarantees remains hypothetical.

In conclusion, the European Court of Justice came, nevertheless, to a reasonable result, even if several elements of its reasoning are misleading. In particular, the reasoning that – beside the elements already mentioned – the re-publication infringed Mr. González' right to private life because it did not meet the requirement of being 'adequate, relevant, and not excessive in relation to the purpose for which it was initially collected' is, from a constitutional perspective, highly arguable. Indeed, the secondary law provides for this requirement but it is not necessary, per se, pursuant to his right to self-determination in the public. Article 7 lit. c of the Data Protection Directive focuses on the moment of collection of the data and runs the risk of neglecting the fundamental rights of others which have, in principle, an equally protected interest in the processing of data at a later stage. However, from a fundamental rights perspective, the final result by the European Court of Justice is reasonable because Mr. González' right to self-determination in public indeed prevailed the opposing fundamental rights. On the one hand, this was in particular the case because, in light of the criteria previously proposed, the event took place more than 16 years ago, the intensity of the harm of how he is perceived in society (i.e. his "social representation") was indeed high, and the first publication was not based on his consent but on a legal obligation. On the other hand, the interests of the other parties in this information were not so high, in particular, not the general public interest because the articles did not concern a crime, but only a compulsory auction in relation with the recovery of social security debts.

cc) Internal freedom of development

Another substantial guarantee provided for by the right to private life under Article 7 ECFR and/or the right to data protection under Article 8 ECFR concerns more internal aspects of an individual's personality. These aspects became relevant in the reasoning of the decision of "*Digital Rights vs. Ireland*". As mentioned previously, in this case, the European Court of Justice stated: "The fact that data retained and subsequently used without the subscriber or registered user being informed is likely to generate in the minds of the persons concerned the feeling that their private lives are the subject of constant surveillance."[1109]

(1) Does the German right to informational self-determination provide for such a guarantee?

These considerations apparently take up very similar thoughts provided for by the German Constitutional Court. The German Court had stressed, in its decision of "*Data Retention*" concerning the same issue as the case of "*Digital Rights vs. Ireland*", that "the individual does not know which state authority knows what, but does know that authorities can know a lot, even highly personal circumstances, about him. The legislator must meet the unspecific threat resulting from the retention of the data through efficient rules on transparency. (…) They serve, on the one hand, to diminish the threat resulting from the lack of knowledge about the real relevance of the data, to counter unsettling speculations, and to enable the individuals

---

1109 See ECJ C-293/12 and C-594/12 cip. 37.

concerned to question these measures in a public discourse. On the other hand, these requirements equally result from the principle of effective judicial relief, pursuant to Art. 10 sect. 1 GG in combination with Art. 19 sect. 4 GG. Without corresponding knowledge, the individuals concerned can neither claim against an illicit usage of data by the authorities nor for their rights to deletion, rectification or compensation."[1110] These considerations underline two aspects: First, the potential psychological effects of a secret data processing on the individual; and second that measures of transparency do not only serve to enable the individual to seek legal protection against the processing of 'his or her' data but also to avoid the 'unspecific threat of being surveyed'. In this case, the Court took this thought, as well as the corresponding measures of transparency in relation to the principle of proportionality into account. One might conclude from this that such measures do not result from an autonomous substantial guarantee, but rather constitute a criteria in the balancing exercise.

In contrast, in its first "*Decision on Population Census*", the German Constitutional Court discussed this aspect in the context of determining the substantial guarantee provided for by the right to informational self-determination. In this case, the Court stated, as described above, that this right "is especially at risk because (…) facts about personal or factual circumstances today can be enhanced by automatic data processing, technically the data (…) can be unlimitedly stored and, without any restrictions in time and space. Furthermore, the data can be, especially in the case of integrated information systems, combined with other data collections to a partly or vast profile, without the possibility for the individual to control

---

1110 See BVerfG, 2nd March 2010, 1 BvR 256/08, 1 BvR 263/08, and 1 BvR 586/08 (Data Retention), cip. 241-242: "Der Einzelne weiß nicht, was welche staatliche Behörde über ihn weiß, weiß aber, dass die Behörden vieles, auch Höchstpersönliches über ihn wissen können. Der Gesetzgeber muss die diffuse Bedrohlichkeit, die die Datenspeicherung hierdurch erhalten kann, durch wirksame Transparenzregeln auffangen. (...) Sie haben zum einen die Aufgabe, eine sich aus dem Nichtwissen um die tatsächliche Relevanz der Daten ergebende Bedrohlichkeit zu mindern, verunsichernde Spekulationen entgegenzuwirken und den Betroffenen die Möglichkeit zu schaffen, solche Maßnahmen in die öffentliche Diskussion zu stellen. Zum anderen sind solche Anforderungen auch aus dem Gebot des effektiven Rechtsschutzes gemäß Art. 10. Abs. 1 GG in Verbindung mit Art. 19 Abs. 4 GG herzuleiten. Ohne Kenntnis können die Betroffenen weder eine Unrechtmäßigkeit der behördlichen Datenverwendung noch etwaige Rechte auf Löschung, Berichtigung oder Genugtuung geltend machen."

how it should be corrected and how it is used. As a result, the possibilities of getting insights and manipulation have increased to an extent which was unknown before and which can already influence the individual because of the psychological pressure in light of the public interest. (…) The person who does not confidently know what information related to him or her is known in certain areas of his or her social environment and who cannot estimate to some degree the knowledge of potential partners of communication might be essentially restricted in his or her freedom to plan and decide in a self-determined manner. In light of the right to informational self-determination, no social or legal order would be possible if citizens would not be able to know what information others have about them."[1111]

1111 See BVerfG, 15th of December 1983, 1 BvR 209, 269, 362, 420, 440, 484/83 (Decision on Population Census), cip. 171 to 172: "Sie ist vor allem deshalb gefährdet, weil bei Entscheidungsprozessen nicht mehr wie früher auf manuell zusammengetragene Karteien und Akten zurückgegriffen werden muß, vielmehr heute mit Hilfe der automatischen Datenverarbeitung Einzelangaben über persönliche oder sachliche Verhältnisse einer bestimmten oder bestimmbaren Person personenbezogene Daten (vgl § 2 Abs. 1 BDSG) technisch gesehen unbegrenzt speicherbar und jederzeit ohne Rücksicht auf Entfernungen in Sekundenschnelle abrufbar sind. Sie können darüber hinaus - vor allem beim Aufbau integrierter Informationssysteme - mit anderen Datensammlungen zu einem teilweise oder weitgehend vollständigen Persönlichkeitsbild zusammengefügt werden, ohne daß der Betroffene dessen Richtigkeit und Verwendung zureichend kontrollieren kann. Damit haben sich in einer bisher unbekannten Weise die Möglichkeiten einer Einsichtnahme und Einflußnahme erweitert, welche auf das Verhalten des Einzelnen schon durch den psychischen Druck öffentlicher Anteilnahme einzuwirken vermögen. (Individuelle Selbstbestimmung setzt aber - auch unter den Bedingungen moderner Informationsverarbeitungstechnologien - voraus, daß dem Einzelnen Entscheidungsfreiheit über vorzunehmende oder zu unterlassende Handlungen einschließlich der Möglichkeit gegeben ist, sich auch entsprechend dieser Entscheidung tatsächlich zu verhalten.) Wer nicht mit hinreichender Sicherheit überschauen kann, welche ihn betreffende Informationen in bestimmten Bereichen seiner sozialen Umwelt bekannt sind, und wer das Wissen möglicher Kommunikationspartner nicht einigermaßen abzuschätzen vermag, kann in seiner Freiheit wesentlich gehemmt werden, aus eigener Selbstbestimmung zu planen oder zu entscheiden. Mit dem Recht auf informationelle Selbstbestimmung wären eine Gesellschaftsordnung und eine diese ermöglichende Rechtsordnung nicht vereinbar, in der Bürger nicht mehr wissen können, wer was wann und bei welcher Gelegenheit über sie weiß. (...)"

(2) Discussion on such a substantial guarantee

In legal discourse, several scholars tie into these considerations of the German Constitutional Court. Rouvroy and Poullet stress, for example, that the right to privacy serves the "capacity for both reflexive autonomy allowing to resist social pressure to conform with dominant views and for deliberative abilities allowing participation in deliberative processes".[1112] Similarly, Britz considers the un-biasedness of individual behavior as the actual substantial guarantee provided for by the right to informational self-determination.[1113] From her point of view, the right to informational self-determination does not provide a genuine and comprehensive right to decide about the revelation of personal data, but an instrument which safeguards the general and specific rights to freedom in order to protect the free development of personality. For Britz, this concept can be unfolded in two sub-categories: The external and the internal freedom of development.[1114] With respect to the second guarantee, i.e. the internal freedom of development, the German general personality right guarantees that the development of personality is able to enroll, under the conditions of its social constitution, a self-determined and "free" process. The individual's certainty being able to influence the perception of third parties regarding him or herself safeguards that he or she holds his or her self-determined development within the society as possible and worthwhile. The general personality right hence requires from the State to establish and safeguard the social pre-conditions which enables the individual to reflect and distance him or herself from own and other's expectations on his or her behavior. Indeed, there is no guarantee that the individual succeeds with his or her personal presentation in social relationships. However, the internal freedom of development is concerned in a legally relevant manner if others get a comprehensive insight into the personality of the person concerned. This might be the case if third parties get a comprehensive profile of the

1112 See Rouvroy and Poullet, The Right to Informational Self-Determination and the Value of Self-Development: Reassessing the Importance of Privacy for Democracy, p. 46.

1113 See Britz, Informational Self-Determination between Legal Doctrine and Constitutional Case Law, p. 570.

1114 See Britz, ibid., pp. 573 and 574; cf. also the "intermediate value" of the right to informational self-determination (aka privacy) stressed by Rouvroy and Poullet, The Right to Informational Self-Determination and the Value of Self-Development: Reassessing the Importance of Privacy for Democracy, pp. 85 to 61.

personality or precise and sensitive data of the individual. Thus, even if comprehensive profiles are not be generated, already the knowledge about the usage of sensitive data in certain contexts awakes stereotypes attributed to the individual concerned. In this view, the right to informational self-determination is, as Britz' underlines, not the same but functionally similar to the protection against discrimination.[1115]

Rouvroy, Poullet, and Britz commonly consider the right to privacy, aka informational self-determination, as instrumental for individual autonomy. Indeed, while Rouvroy and Poullet appear to hold an individuals' right to control over personal information, i.e. "to determine for themselves when, how, and to what extent information about them is communicated through others" as the appropriate protection instrument,[1116] Britz is reluctant to refer to such an instrument without clarifying which instrument could serve best in order to protect such a guarantee. In this regard, it is interesting to illustrate how another scholar extensively elaborates on such an alternative protection instrument. Just like the before-mentioned scholars, Bechler also ties into the considerations of the German Constitutional Court quoted before and summarizes the different aspects of protection pursued by the Court providing the individual's right to 'principally determine by him or herself to reveal his or her data' as: First, the individual's interest in privacy;[1117] second, protection against negative decisions of third parties for the individual which can result from an unlimited and uncontrolled collection and treatment of his or her data;[1118] and third, the individual lacking knowledge about what his or her social environment knows about him or her.[1119]

Picking up the last aspect of protection, Bechler promotes that this can rather be protected by means of an individual's right to transparency than by means of a right to determine the revelation of his or her data. In order to enable an individual to oversee what others know about him or her, he or she does not need to control the revelation of his or her data but only has to know what happens with the data, in other words, he or she needs a right to transparency. From Bechler's point of view, the term "informa-

1115 See Britz, ibid., pp. 571 to 573.

1116 See Rouvroy and Poullet, ibid., p. 75, and 69 quoting A. Westin, Privacy and Freedom, New York, Ateneum, 1967, p. 7..

1117 See Bechler, ibid., p. 21.

1118 See Bechler, ibid., p. 21.

1119 See Bechler, ibid., p. 20.

tional self-determination" hence should not be understood in the sense that an individual has the right to determine the information about him or herself. It rather refers to the threat for individual self-determination – as a basis for autonomous behavior – which results from information.[1120] Finally, regarding the extent of transparency, Bechler is of the opinion that such a right does not guarantee the individual to know the specific information that third parties have about him or her but only to know the data as the basis of their information. He explains this result with the fact, as mentioned above, that information is based on data that must be interpreted corresponding to the social context in order to make sense of it. Bechler concludes from this, that the individual cannot exactly know the other's subjective information but only the objective data, and therefore only the information which can be possibly concluded.[1121]

(3) Articles 7 and/or 8 ECFR: Information pursuant to insights into personality and possibilities of manipulation

With respect to the European Charter of Fundamental Rights, these considerations raise three questions: First, which fundamental right provides for such a guarantee?; second, which data or information does this right require the controller to provide or which further conditions does it have to meet?; and third, which data or information or even further requirements does the individual concerned actually need in order to exercise his or her internal freedom of development?

These questions are particularly important because the substantial guarantees of privacy, i.e. the right to be left alone, only require that the controller specifies the purpose of the collection of the data. This guarantee primarily focuses on the individual's ability to decide whether to be left alone or not, hence, whether or not to enter or remain in the space where the data is collected. This decision implies, indeed, that the individual is able to estimate the risks caused by a later use of the collected data. However, these guarantees do not primarily aim to enable the individual to know what others know about him or her in order to protect, for example, the individual against the unspecific threat of being surveyed or manipu-

1120 See Bechler, ibid., pp. 92 to 96.
1121 See Bechler, ibid., p. 97.

lated. An estimation of the risks caused by the later use of data principally requires other information than a protection of the individual's internal freedom of development. The primary question thus is in this regard which *additional* information is necessary in order to enable the individual to distance him or herself from own and other expectations.

Whether or not the European Court of Justice legally affirmed this substantial guarantee as provided for by the right to private life under Article 7 ECFR is not yet clear. In the case of "*Digital Rights vs. Ireland*", the Court discussed these aspects with respect to the intensity of the infringement of the right to private life under Article 7 ECFR. It is therefore arguable whether or not the Court considered an individual's right to transparency (i.e. to know to a certain degree what others know about him or herself) as an autonomous guarantee. At least, in light of the objective of the right to private life, "encompassing the physical, psychological and moral aspects of the personal integrity, identity and autonomy of individuals",[1122] it is plausible to locate such a guarantee under Article 7 ECFR. An alternative would be, if such a guarantee shall be recognized at all, to locate it under the right to data protection in Article 8 ECFR. The right to data protection equally serves the autonomy of an individual concerned by data processing. Furthermore, as Article 8 ECFR protects, technically the other fundamental rights of privacy, freedom and equality, the individual's internal freedom of development safeguards, substantially, his or her ability to exercise these rights.[1123] Yet another solution for this question would be to refer to the different functions of the right to private life and the right to data protection, just like De Hert and Gutwirth propose. While the right to private life serves protections instruments enabling the individual to decide on whether or not data related to him or her can be collected ("tools of opacity"), the right to data protection provides instruments enabling the individual to influence how the data can be used ("tools of transparency").[1124] Thus, the right to data protection always serves the constitutional basis for the rights to transparency. However, if the collection and processing of personal data reaches such an extent that directly affects the indi-

1122 See Vedsted-Hansen, ibid., cip. 7.06 A with further references.

1123 See above under points C. II. 3. a) aa) Intermediate function of data protection, and C. II. 3. a) bb) (2) Purpose specification discovering risks posed to all fundamental rights.

1124 See above under points C. II. 3. a) aa) (1) Different functions of rights (opacity and transparency).

vidual's "personal integrity, identity and autonomy", the individual must be able to avoid this as a whole. This might be the case if the controller combines data related to him or her to comprehensive profiles and is able to relate this to an individual's official identity (which means, is not only able to single-out a principally unknown person within an anonymous group). In this case, the controller of the data gets a particularly deep insight into the individual's unique personality. This leads to the result that a right to transparency provided for by Article 8 ECFR may not suffice to guarantee the internal freedom of development. Instead, the individual's private life under Article 7 ECFR may require that the creation of such a comprehensive profile of an officially identifiable individual must be based, in addition, on his or her consent. Here again, the right to data protection has an intermediate function for the individual autonomy, which is further determined by the other fundamental rights, i.e. the right to private life.

The requirement to specify the purpose and to make it explicit can also serve, in these cases, to meet the specific guarantee. However, here, the requirement does not serve to enable the individual to avoid the collection of personal data to take place *per se* (as is the case regarding the substantial guarantees of privacy). The requirement does not serve as legal link for the question of whether or not the first publication of the data is necessary or for examining the conditions for the re-publication of that data (as is the case regarding the substantial guarantee of self-representation in public). Here instead, the requirements to specify the purpose and to make it explicit serve, at first, as a transparency tool enabling the individual to know what the controller knows about him or her and, thus, to exercise his or her internal freedom of development. This guarantee applies, on the one hand, already to the case that the controller can single out the individual in a certain group, but not that the controller can officially identify the individual. The reason is that the risk of manipulation, for example, exists irrespective of the official identification of the individual. On the other hand, this means that this guarantee requires only rights of transparency. Only if the controller can officially identify the individual and create a vast profile about him or her, the requirement to specify the purpose and to make it explicit serves, in addition, the individual to decide on whether or not the controller is allowed to do so at all.

Focusing on the extent of transparency, be it in the form of specified purposes made explicit to the individual or alternative instruments, the question remains whether the individual has to be able to know the information, which the controller concludes from the data, or only the data basis per se. Bechler voted for the data basis, only. However, in light of the concept of the guarantee of internal freedom of development, a right to transparency might require that the individual may also know the information. From the point of view of Rouvroy and Poullet, as well as Britz, the individual must be able to reflect and distance him or herself from their own and others' expectations of them.[1125] Taking the considerations of the German Constitutional Court into account, the deeper the controller's insight into the individual's personality is, the more specific the data controller has to inform the individual about this insight. At least, the individual should be able to protect him or herself against the risk of being manipulated.[1126] This means that the individual should receive not only data but also, if necessary, the information. In any case, what kind of information the individual specifically needs and above which threshold the profiling must be considered as so extensive that it requires his or her consent cannot be answered, again, by legal research alone. Instead, these questions do not only depend on the elaboration of the substantial guarantees concerned but also on empirical research from other disciplines such as communication theory and, above all, psychology.

dd) Specific rights to freedom

Different to the 'unspecific threat 'of being surveyed or manipulated, is the situation that the individual knows that the data controller processes certain data concerning him or her for a specific purpose and stops or omits exercising a fundamental right in order to avoid disadvantages feared by him or her. Another similar type of case refers to the situation that the data controller processes the data or another individual or entity uses the information in a manner restricting the possibilities of exercising

---

1125 See above under points C. II. 3. b) cc) (2) Discussion on such a guarantee, referring to Rouvroy and Poullet, The Right to Informational Self-Determination and the Value of Self-Development: Reassessing the Importance of Privacy for Democracy, and Britz, Informational Self-Determination between Legal Doctrine and Constitutional Case Law, pp. 571 to 573.

1126 See above under point C. II. 3. b) cc) (1) Does the German right to informational self-determination provide for such a guarantee?, referring to BVerfG, 15th of December 1983, 1 BvR 209, 269, 362, 420, 440, 484/83 (Decision on Population Census), cip. 171 to 172.

or hindering the exercise of one or more of the individual's fundamental rights. Since both types of cases usually refer to specific rights of freedom, they cannot always clearly be differentiated from each other. However, while the first type is often discussed with respect to the collection of the data, the second type focuses on the later usage of the data or the information. The protection instruments provided for by Article 8 ECFR here mainly enable the individual to adapt to or protect him or herself against the informational measure and to put it up to public discussion.

(1) Focus on the collection of data: Omission by the individual of exercising their rights out of fear

Both the European Court of Justice, as well as the German Constitutional Court, consider, in their decisions, the negative effects of a certain data collection leading to an omission or cessation of the exercise of fundamental rights by the individual concerned. In legal literature, scholars tied into this reasoning transferring it to all fundamental rights to freedom.

(a) Considerations of the Courts with respect to the freedom of expression and the individuals risk of being unreasonably suspected by the State

The European Court of Justice considered in the case of "*Digital Rights vs. Ireland*" that "it is not inconceivable that the retention of the data in question might have an effect on the use, by subscribers or registered users, of the means of communication covered by that directive and, consequently, on their exercise of the freedom of expression guaranteed by Article 11 of the Charter."[1127] The German Constitutional Court similarly considered the negative effects on the exercise of fundamental rights caused by the individual's fear. In the case of "*Surveillance of Telecommunications*", the Court stressed with respect to processing of personal data by the State that "the disadvantages, which must objectively expected or feared, can already become true at the moment of knowledge. The fear of surveillance which contains the risk of recording, later processing, potential transfer, and further usage by other state agencies can already lead in

1127 See ECJ C-293/12 and C-594/12 cip. 28.

advance to a bias within communication, to a dysfunction of communication and to adaptations of personal conduct, especially here, to avoid certain content of communication or terms. (In order to determine the intensity of the infringement), not only the infringement of a multitude of individual bearers of basic rights has to be taken into account, but also the fact that the covered surveillance of the telecommunication affects the communication of the society as a whole."[1128]

Similarly, the Court argued in the case of "*Big Eavesdropping Operation*" that "the covered surveillance of the non-publicly spoken word at home does not only concern the individual but can also have effects on the communication of the society as a whole. The possibility of acoustic surveillance of the homes can result in chilling effects which also concern unsuspicious individuals because he or she can be, pursuant to the legal provisions, equally, at any time and without notice affected by the surveillance measure. As a first point, the fear of surveillance can lead to a bias in communication."[1129] In this case, the Court specified the intensity of the infringement for unsuspicious persons with respect to the risk of unreasonably suspected, as: "The recording of the communication of unsuspicious persons leads to their risk of being an object of state surveillance that adds to the general risk of being unreasonably suspected."[1130]

1128 See BVerfG, 14th of July 1999, 1 BvR 2226/94 (Surveillance of Telecommunications*)*, cip. 207: "Die Nachteile, die objektiv zu erwarten sind oder befürchtet werden müssen, können schon mit der Kenntnisnahme eintreten. Die Befürchtung einer Überwachung mit der Gefahr einer Aufzeichnung, späteren Auswertung, etwaigen Übermittlung und weiteren Verwendung durch andere Behörden kann schon im Vorfeld zu einer Befangenheit in der Kommunikation, zu Kommunikationsstörungen und zu Verhaltensanpassungen, hier insbesondere zur Vermeidung bestimmter Gesprächsinhalte oder Termini, führen. Dabei ist nicht nur die individuelle Beeinträchtigung einer Vielzahl einzelner Grundrechtsträger zu berücksichtigen. Vielmehr betrifft die heimliche Überwachung des Fernmeldeverkehrs auch die Kommunikation der Gesellschaft insgesamt."

1129 See BVerfG, 3rd of March 2004, 1 BvR 2378/98 (Big Eavesdropping Operation*)*, cip. 230: "Von der Möglichkeit zur akustischen Wohnraumüberwachung können Einschüchterungseffekte ausgehen, denen insbesondere auch der Unverdächtige ausgesetzt ist, weil auch er nach den gesetzlichen Regelungen jederzeit und ohne sein Wissen von der Ermittlungsmaßnahme betroffen werden kann. Allein die Befürchtung einer Überwachung kann aber schon zu einer Befangenheit in der Kommunikation führen."

1130 See BVerfG, ibid., cip. 227: "Wird die Kommunikation Unverdächtiger erfasst, so schafft die akustische Wohnraumüberwachung für sie das Risiko, Gegenstand

(b) Considerations on further rights of freedom

These considerations principally apply not only to the right to freedom of expression, but also to further rights of freedom. The German Constitutional Court considered already in its "*Decision on Population Census*", as quoted before: "Individual self-determination requires (...) that the individual can freely decide on his or her actions, including the freedom to genuinely act corresponding to their decisions. (...) The person who is unsure if their deviant behavior will be noted and permanently stored, used or transferred will attempt not to attract attention with such behavior. The person who is aware of being registered by the State when he or she takes part at an assembly or is part of an association will possibly give up on exercising his or her corresponding fundamental rights (...)."[1131]

Albers ties into this quote and gives several examples of how the individual's fear of negative effects might restrict or hinder him or her in exercising his or her fundamental rights. She illustrates how sociological, psychological, and economic insights might be relevant for the analysis of these effects: "The autonomous and authentic behavior of an individual grounds on his or her generalized but nevertheless context-specific expectations of the knowledge that others have about him or her. If the individual changes these expectations, he or she might also change his or her behavior (...). For example, the personal introspection writing a diary requires that nobody must fear that somebody else gets notice of his or her thoughts and uses it in other contexts. Purchasing books in libraries or participating at assemblies requires the trust of carriers of the basic rights that the Intelligence Service does not observe their behavior with the result that the information retrieved about interests of reading, participations at assemblies and political views concluded from this does not lead to later disadvantages. The transmission of information about a company to other pri-

---

staatlicher Ermittlungen zu sein, das zu dem allgemeinen Risiko hinzutritt, einem unberechtigten Verdacht ausgesetzt zu werden."

1131 See BVerfG, 15th of December 1983, 1 BvR 209, 269, 362, 420, 440, 484/83 (Decision on Population Census), cip. 170 to 172, see the original wording above under point C. I. 2. b) Autonomous substantial guarantee (cip. 341 – and, more extensively, cip. 323).

vate parties by the State can negatively affect its chances of communication and conduct on the market."[1132]

Pursuant to Albers' concept, i.e. the specific legal requirements depend on the basic right that covers: first, either the factual circumstances providing the basis of the information; or, second, the interests concerned by the retrieval and usage of the information. Albers gives the following examples: the usage of diaries principally falls under the freedom of conscience of Article 4 GG; the freedom of expression of Article 5 sect. 1 sent. 1 GG applies in the case of purchased books; the freedom of assembly of Article 8 GG covers the observation of participations at assemblies; and business documents can be protected by the freedom to conduct a business under Article 12 GG. The latter might also apply if the State or private parties publish information about a company. If the treatment of data does not refer to a certain context, but rather to a bundle of contexts or to the person concerned as such, for example in the case of 'total surveillance' or medical or genetic data, Albers stresses Article 2 sect. 1 GG can provide the necessary guarantee of protection for the personal identity.[1133]

In any event, Albers highlights that the protection of information and data guaranteed by the specific basic rights not only requires that the information and data falls under the respective scope of protection of the specific basic right and relates to the carrier of this basic right. Rather, it is also necessary to take the specific social context and the generalized, typi-

---

1132 See Albers, ibid., cip. 72: "Autonomes und authentisches individuelles Verhalten wird immer von generalisierten und zugleich kontextbezogen differenzierten Erwartungen an das Wissen begleitet, das andere über das Verhalten und die Person erzeugen. Ändern sich diese Erwartungen, findet das Verhalten überhaupt nicht mehr, anders als zuvor oder zumindest in dem Bewusstsein potenziell veränderten Wissenserwerbs anderer statt. So sind Gewissensauseinandersetzungen darauf angeiwesen, dass jemand seine Gedanken im Tagebuch ohne die Befürchtung festhalten kann, dass diese Aufzeichnungen von anderen gelesen und in anderen Kontexten ausgewertet werden. Die Ausleihe von Büchern in Bibliotheken oder die Teilnahme an Versammlungen setzen das Vertrauen der Grundrechtsträger voraus, dass ihr Verhalten nicht durch den Verfassungsschutz mit der Folge überwacht wird, dass die erlangten Informationen über Leseinteressen, Versammlungsteilnehmen, und daraus gefolgerte poltische Einstellungen später zu Nachteilen führen. Vermittelt der Staat anderen Privaten Informationen über ein Unternehmen, kann dies dessen Kommunikations- und Verhaltenschancen am Markt nachteilig verändern."

1133 See Albers, ibid., cip. 72.

cal disadvantages into account which result from the data treatment and, consequently, the retrieval and usage of the information. In addition, these disadvantages expected by the individual must be relevant from a legal perspective, which means that they must conflict with the substantial guarantee provided for by the corresponding basic rights. For example, the freedom of expression under Article 5 GG guarantees that the Intelligence Service does not collect data about book purchases in order to retrieve information about political views and to eventually use it to the detriment of the person concerned. If citizens had to fear such a usage of their data, they would probably stop purchasing books, or at least, they would do it less or in another way. In contrast, if a bookstore or library collects the data in order to control the payment or the return of the books, the collection and treatment of the data is legally irrelevant. While business documents are relevant with respect to its revelation to the company's competitors, the guaranty of freedom to conduct a business under Article 12 GG and the guarantee of property under Article 14 GG do not protect against the examination of the documents for administrative purposes if they are not transferred to private parties. As a consequence, basic rights only guarantee protection for specific social contexts: they may guarantee that the State gets no information about certain circumstances at all; they may determine the duration of the storage of personal data; they may protect against the usage of information for certain purposes; or they might protect only against the transfer of data to certain private parties.[1134] Albers elaborates her concept with respect to the processing of data and the usage of information by the State. However she highlights that the substantial guarantees can also provide state duties of protection with respect to the usage of information and data processing by third parties in the private sector. In any case, in order to determine the legal relevance of a data treatment and the usage of the information, it is necessary to differ between its corresponding contexts. The specific guarantees of basic rights provide the legal scale for this.[1135]

1134 See Albers, ibid., cip. 72.
1135 See Albers, ibid., cip. 73.

(2) Focus on the later usage of data or information: Restriction or hindrance of exercise of rights of freedom through usage of data or information

The second type of cases refers to situations where the data processing by the controller or the usage of information by other individuals or entities restricts or hinders the exercise of an individual's right of freedom. Even if it does not match exactly to this type of case, the decision of "*Rechnungshof vs. ORF*" however slightly refers to it. As described above, in this case, the European Court of Justice denied the collection and processing of the personal data by an employer of its employees, but affirmed the transfer of the data to a third party. The entity requesting the data sought to publish it. In order to determine the intensity of the infringement of the individual's right to private life under Article 8 ECHR, the Court took into account, as quoted previously, that the individuals concerned "may suffer harm as a result of the negative effects of the publicity attached to their income from employment, in particular on their prospects of being given employment by other undertakings, whether in Austria or elsewhere, which are not subject to control by the Rechnungshof."[1136]

Britz concludes from these considerations that the right to data protection under Article 8 ECHR also serves to protect the specific rights of freedom and promotes to transfer the Court's reasoning described to all other rights to freedom.[1137] In order to advocate this approach, also on the German level, she ties into the previously mentioned quote of the German Constitutional Court in the "*Decision on Population Census*" that "informational self-determination requires (…) that the individual can freely decide on his or her actions, including the freedom to genuinely act corresponding to their decisions."[1138] Britz considers that one of the components of the right to informational self-determination, the general freedom of action under Article 2 sect. 1 GG, protects against disadvantages which result from the decisions of third parties based on data and information about the individual concerned. In this respect, the right to informational self-determination provides the basic guarantee for external freedom of development. It enables the individual to influence the knowledge and perceptions of third parties in such a way that those decisions offer the indi-

1136 See ECJ C-465/00, C-138/01 and C-139/01, cip. 89.

1137 See Britz, EuGRZ 2009, p. 10.

1138 See Britz, ibid., p. 569 referring to BVerfG, ibid., cip. 170 to 172.

vidual the best options in order to conduct themselves. In this view, informational self-determination aims to avoid negative decisions of third parties for the individual maintaining or increasing his or her options to freely (inter)act. Thus, similar to Albers' concept, the freedom of action does not protect against each disadvantage, but only against such disadvantages which are legally relevant. In order to determine this legal relevance, the specific basic rights to freedom provide the necessary scale. Insofar, Britz promotes that the right to informational self-determination is an accessory right.[1139]

(3) Interim conclusion: How "privacy in public" can be further determined

The importance of this approach, which links the data protection instruments to specific rights to freedom, becomes particularly apparent with respect to the function of Article 8 ECFR. As discussed previously, scholars argue about the value of the right to data protection under Article 8 ECFR added to the European Charter of Fundamental rights. Tzanou criticizes that two main concepts currently provided for by the legal scholars De Hert and Gutwirth, as well as Rouvroy and Poullet, do not sufficiently elaborate on the value of the right to data protection autonomously from the right to private life. However, this thesis has stressed that the specific value added by the right to data protection under Article 8 ECFR is its autonomous and central function protecting against risks for the other fundamental rights. The requirement to specify the purpose of the data processing serves as the main protection instrument discovering these risks for the other fundamental rights.[1140] Having, at first elaborated on the specific guarantees of privacy, this thesis has finally discussed whether the type of cases referring to the "privacy in public" should be solved on the basis of Articles 7 and/or 8 ECFR alone or whether further fundamental rights should serve an additional scale in order to determine the protection in-

1139 See Britz, ibid., pp. 570 and 571.

1140 See above under point C. II. 3. a) aa) Intermediate function of data protection, and C. II. 3. a) bb) (2) Purpose specification discovering risks posed to all fundamental rights.

struments provided for by Article 8 ECFR.[1141] As Albers and Britz have shown, the specific fundamental rights to freedom indeed serve such an additional scale. Since this thesis promotes this concept to fit better to innovation processes, than an exclusive link to privacy (because it does not focus on the collection of personal data but takes equally later moments into account when the data is used),[1142] the following considerations illustrate why.

(a) Specific contexts of collection of personal data

So far, the collection of personal data was discussed with respect to the specific guarantees of privacy such as the privacy of the home, communications, and finally, the "privacy in public". However, Albers in particular, carved out that the collection of personal data does not only take place in the home of an individual or when he or she uses communications, which is undoubtedly protected by the right to private life under Article 7 ECFR, but also in further contexts that are covered by other fundamental rights. Transferred to European fundamental rights, the collection of personal data in the context of a library or book store, be it offline or online, is covered by the right to freedom of expressions provided for by Article 11 ECFR. The collection of personal data in the context of exercising the freedom of faith falls under Article 10 ECFR. The collection of personal data in the context of finding a spouse or founding a family relates to Article 9 ECFR. The collection of personal data concerning activities in political or civic matters is principally related to the freedom of assembly and of association under Article 12 ECFR. Article 13 ECFR covers the collection of data in the context of arts and sciences. The collection of personal data in educational contexts belongs to Article 14 ECFR. Article 15 ECFR principally applies to the collection of personal data in an employment context. It seems even plausible, in light of the many software applications currently invented for asylum seekers in Germany, to refer to the right to asylum in Article 18 ECFR in order to assess the data collection by these

1141 See above under point C. II. 3. b) aa) (1) (c) "Privacy in (semi)-public spheres": Protection against the risks of later usage of data, and C. II. 3. b) dd) (3) Interim conclusion: How "privacy in public" can be further determined.

1142 See above under point C. II. 3. a) cc) (2) (b) Appropriate concept for innovation processes.

applications.[1143] And finally, Article 16 ECFR actually provides for the more appropriate substantive requirements for the collection of personal data in an entrepreneurial context, rather than the right to private life under Article 7 ECFR, which is usually considered as providing protection of personal data in business premises.[1144]

Thus, instead of immediately referring to the rather undetermined guarantee of "privacy in public", all these before-mentioned fundamental rights come, in the first instance, into question if the collection of personal data does not take place in the home of the individual or when she or he uses communications. It is however important to stress that these rights do not cover all cases, which are discussed under the term "privacy in public". Instead, these specific rights to freedom only take over many types of cases where the collection of personal data occurs in contexts, which were usually related to "privacy in public" but actually fall under the scope of protection of such a specific right. This means that there still is a certain scope of application for that the "privacy in public" may be discussed but only insofar as no guarantee of the specific rights to freedom applies. However, coming back to the essential point: the requirement to specify the purpose thus serves to discover the risks for these specific rights. If the purpose of the data processing concerns one of these fundamental rights, its substantial guarantee determines the precision required for the specification and, eventually, further protection instruments being necessary in order to prevent the individual, i.e. the carrier of this fundamental right, against the corresponding risk.[1145]

In conclusion, so long as these specific rights apply, the question is irrelevant whether the substantive requirements applied by the European Court of Justice for the right to private life also apply to the guarantee of "privacy in public" or not. As discussed above, the European Court of Justice requires that limitations of data protection with respect the right to privacy under Article 7 ECFR must be limited to what is strictly necessary.

1143 See, for example, Bellikli, Apps wollen Flüchtlingen helfen, in Deutschland klarzukommen. Wie gut sind sie? (Apps built to help asylum seekers to get by in Germany: How good are they?), latest version retrieved on the 19th of June 2016 from http://www.bento.de/gadgets/apps-fuer-fluechtlinge-im-test-wie-hilfreich-sind-sie-120268/.

1144 See, instead of many, Vedsted-Hansen, Art. 7 – Private Life, Home, and Communications, cip. 07.11A.

1145 See above under point C. II. 3. a) bb) (2) Purpose specification discovering risks posed to all fundamental rights.

The idea behind this requirement is that each datum that is collected after the initial collection reveals, in particular if processed further, more aspects about the individual's private life.[1146] However, this thought cannot automatically be transferred to other guarantees. The fundamental rights to freedom comparably require that the collection of personal data conflicts with *their* substantial guarantees. Whether these rights require, equally, that the data collection is limited to what is strictly necessary must be answered with respect to the specific guarantee concerned. Thus, the advantage of this approach is that the diversity of specific guarantees provided for by all these fundamental rights provides for a differentiated and objective scale in order to assess which protection instruments are necessary. As Albers and Britz point out, the collection of personal data requires specific protection instruments only if the processing of data conflicts with the specific guarantees. Thus, each collection of personal data does not automatically constitute an infringement or harm of these fundamental rights. For example, the collection of personal data by a library or book store for delivery or payment purposes does not conflict with the freedom of expression and does, hence, not require further data protection instruments against specific risks for this guarantee.[1147] Similarly, the processing of personal data in an employment context for the purpose of payroll accounting does not conflict with the freedom to engage in work under Article 15 ECFR and, thus, does not require further protection.[1148]

(b) Later use of personal data in the same context

Indeed, the collection of personal data for these purposes requires protection instruments against unspecific risks resulting from the storage of that data. These unspecific risks stem from the fact that a purpose specified by the controller may not immediately reveal a specific risk for fundamental rights of freedom but can exist, even though, hidden, until a later purpose

1146 See above under point C. II. 3. b) aa) (2) Necessity requirement, irrespective of inconvenience.

1147 Cf. Albers, ibid., cip. 72.

1148 Cf. ECJ C-465/00, C-138/01 and C-139/01 (Rechnungshof vs. ORF), cip. 73 and 74.

discovers the same.[1149] Thus, even if the original purpose does not conflict, when the data is collected, with specific fundamental rights, further general conditions must be met. Only if the individual can trust that data, which was collected in a specific context, is not misused later on, the collection does not lead to an omission or cessation of the exercise of rights. This results from the above-mentioned considerations of the European Court of Justice and the German Constitutional Court. Both Courts require certain data protection rules in order to avoid chilling effects caused by the collection of personal data on the exercise of the individual's rights to freedom.[1150] Eichenhofer illustrates in detail how the concept of "trust" serves as a conceptual angle for a situation where the individual concerned cannot fully control his or her environment.[1151] In these situations, the regulator must safeguard, with respect to the issue discussed here, that the later use of personal data does not breach the trustful expectations of the individual that he or she had in the moment of collection.

This concept indeed implies that it is normatively clear which kind of later use of personal data is a misuse and, therefore, conflicts with the individuals trust and expectations. In doing so, the same principles can be applied to the later use of personal data, as was the case for the initial collection: So long as the later use of personal data does not conflict with the specific rights to privacy, freedom or equality, there is no misuse of that data. This principle logically follows from the approach referring to the substantial guarantees of fundamental rights. The processing of personal data does not, *per se*, infringe or harm a specific fundamental right of the individual concerned. Only if the later use conflicts with a substantial guarantee of the fundamental rights, is there an infringement or harm and further protection instruments must be applied. For these situations, indeed, the legislator must have established protection instruments against the specific risks that are only discovered later on. Only these protection instruments – supposing they are efficient – safeguard that the individual does not omit or cease the execution of his her fundamental rights at the

1149 Cf. above under point C. II. 3. a) bb) (2) (b) Separating unspecific from specific risks (first reason why data protection is indispensable).

1150 See ECJ C-293/12 and C-594/12 (Digital Rights vs. Ireland) cip. 28; BVerfG, 14th of July 1999, 1 BvR 2226/94 (Surveillance of Telecommunications*)*, cip. 207; BVerfG, 3rd of March 2004, 1 BvR 2378/98 (Big Eavesdropping Operation*)*, cip. 230.

1151 See at Eichenhofer, Privacy in the Internet as Protection of Trust, pp. 50 to 57.

moment of collection, only because he or she fears a potential misuse of the data later on. One of these protection instruments is, indeed, the principle of purpose limitation. As stressed before, the principle of purpose limitation principally hinders the controller to use the personal data for other purposes than originally specified. However, before analyzing in detail the function of this second component of this principle, it is necessary to clarify under which conditions the later use must be considered as pursuing another or the same purpose as originally specified.

As illustrated previously, the German Constitutional Court set up, in the decision of "*Federal Criminal Police Office Act*", three criteria for determining whether the processing of personal data by the State must be considered as pursuing another or the same purpose as specified in the moment of collection: First, the later use of personal data must be carried out by the same public agency; second, for the same task; and third, only if it pursues the protection of the same explicitly listed crimes or the same *object* of protection that was already concerned by the data collection.[1152] As stressed before, this third criterion constitutes an important liberization of the approach that the Court has formerly applied. The reason is that an object of protection, which the penalisation of an explicitly listed crime protects, is broader than the explicitly listed crime. Referring to an object of protection as the legal basis for the collection hence gives a public agency more room than referring to an explicit provision. This criteria could also be applied to the processing of personal data in the private sector. The idea behind such an analogous application is that the reference to an object of protection can help consider different acts of data processing as belonging to one context protected by a specific guarantee. The moment the specification of the purpose has discovered a specific risk caused by the collection of personal data for a fundamental right, its later use can be consid-

1152 See above under point C. II. 1. c) ee) (1) Liberalization of the strict requirement by referring to the object of protection, referring to BVerfG, BVerfG, 20th of April 2016, 1 BvR 966/09 and 1 BvR 1140/09 (Federal Bureau of Investigation Law), cip. 279: "Eine weitere Nutzung innerhalb der ursprünglichen Zwecksetzung kommt damit nur seitens derselben Behörde im Rahmen derselben Aufgabe und für den Schutz derselben Rechtsgüter in Betracht wie für die Datenerhebung maßgeblich: Ist diese nur zum Schutz bestimmter Rechtsgüter oder zur Verhütung bestimmter Straftaten erlaubt, so begrenzt dies deren unmittelbare sowie weitere Verwendung auch in derselben Behörde, (soweit keine gesetzliche Grundlage für eine zulässige Zweckänderung eine weitergehende Nutzung erlaubt)."

ered as following the same purpose, so long as it only threatens the same specific guarantee.

Indeed, this analogy is daunting because the German Court does not mean, referring to the "object of protection", the substantial guarantee provided for by fundamental rights of the individual concerned. Instead, the Court means the opposing fundamental rights that legitimize the infringement of the individual's fundamental rights. Applying the concept proposed in this thesis, the German Court hence refers to the interests of the controller covered by its own fundamental rights, not the individual's fundamental rights determining the requirement to specify the purpose.[1153] However, if the private controller could specify the purpose of collection pursuant to its interests, the purpose would not reveal the risks for the individual concerned. The controller's "task" does not help in the private sector. In the public sector, instead, as carved out previously, the Constitutional Court's approach works out because the individual concerned is able to foresee the consequences of the data processing in light of, first, the organizational law that specifies the task of the public agency and, second, the already existing laws that typify the state measures against similar threats for the object of protection.[1154] Therefore, in the private sector, it is necessary to refer to the object of protection guaranteed by the individual's fundamental rights, and not to the controller's interests protected by its opposing fundamental rights, in order to specify the purpose.

In conclusion, transferring the concept developed by the German Constitutional Court to the processing of personal data in the private sector allows, so far, the following result: So long as the later use of personal data follows purposes that refer to the same context covered by a specific guarantee as the original purpose of collection, the later use must only apply, in principle, the protection instruments required by the same specific guarantee.

1153 See above under point C. II. 1. c) ee) (1) Liberalization of the strict requirement by referring to the object of protection, referring to BVerfG, BVerfG, 20th of April 2016, 1 BvR 966/09 and 1 BvR 1140/09 (Federal Bureau of Investigation Law), cip. 279.

1154 See above under point C. II. 2. c) aa) No legal system providing for 'objectives' of data processing in the private sector.

(c) Protection instruments enabling the individual to adapt to or protect him or herself against the informational measure

The right to data protection under Article 8 ECFR hence provides, with respect to the exercise of specific rights to freedom, the individual protection against the following: First, the omission or cessation of his or her exercise of rights, usually caused by the collection of personal data because of the fear of a potential misuse of that data later on. The protection aims in this regard to hinder in general, the potential misuse of that data, and therefore gaining the trust of the individual concerned.[1155] Second, the right to data protection protects against the concrete restriction or hindrance of the exercise of rights caused by the later use of personal data as an informational basis for negative decisions. So long as the later use of personal data remains in the same context as when it is collected, in principle, the same protection instruments apply. Thus, the moment the purpose reveals a specific risk against a fundamental right to freedom, which conflicts with the substantial guarantee, the right to data protection provides the individual for the following specific protection instruments as:

First, in order to enable the individual to possibly adapt their behavior to informational measures resulting from the processing of data and the usage of the information; and second, in order to seek legal protection against these measures.[1156] These protection measures can consist in, first, information rights and duties (i.e. rights to transparency), and second, possibilities to participate in the decision-making process which leads to the hindering or restriction of exercising these rights. The requirement to make the specified purpose explicit can thus serve as a right to transparency. The more the processing of personal data risks to conflict with an individual's fundamental right to freedom, the more precisely the controller has to specify the risk and make it explicit to the individual concerned.[1157]

1155 See ECJ C-293/12 and C-594/12 (Digital Rights vs. Ireland) cip. 28 and 53 to 55, which clearly lies the focus on this trust building function of data protection law.

1156 See BVerfG, 2nd March 2010, 1 BvR 256/08, 1 BvR 263/08, and 1 BvR 586/08 (Data Retention), cip. 241; Britz, Informational Self-Determination between Legal Doctrine and Constitutional Case Law, p. 584; in contrast, the European Court of Justice devoting less attention to these concrete protection instruments, see, for example, ECJ C-293/12 and C-594/12 (Digital Rights vs. Ireland).

1157 See above under point C. II. 3. a) bb) (2) (b) Separating unspecific from specific risks (first reason why data protection is indispensable, referring to Albers,

Only if the controller makes this risk sufficiently clear, the individual concerned is able to adapt its behavior to these circumstances, seek legal protection against it, or to question the informational practice in public. This requirement thus serves as the basis for the other protection instruments.

This preparatory function of such rights to transparency is highly important because it determines what and how precisely the controller must inform the individual about the processing of their data. If the individual shall be able to correct incorrect data, he or she must only know which data is being stored by the controller; in contrast, if the individual shall be able to complete incomplete information, he or she must know the purpose, i.e. the context in which the data shall be used.[1158] Hence, it is the risk for the specific fundamental right to freedom that determines the "completeness" of a data set serving as the basis for an informational decision. Similarly, the individual must be able to adapt his or her situation to the expectations of the data controller, by changing the factual circumstances that the controller takes into account. For instance, the algorithm used by a credit scoring company uses several criteria, such as the residential address of the individual, in order to create a credit score. In this case, the individual does not have to know the general logic of the algorithm but must only know how he or she can change the factual circumstances that are decisive in order to improve his or her credit score.[1159] If this is, in the case of the individual concerned, his or her residential address, the individual has just to know this fact so that he or she can adapt and change it

Treatment of Personal Information and Data, cip. 124; cf. also Britz, Informational Self-Determination between Legal Doctrine and Constitutional Case Law, pp. 284 and 285.

1158 Cf. Article 16 GDPR.

1159 Contrary, the German Civil Supreme Court, decision from the 28th of January 2014 – VI ZR 156/13 (Schufa-Score), cip. 12 to 17 and 31 to 34, which essentially denied an individual's claim for information about the criteria underlying a credit score because of two reasons: First, the Court denied the application of Article 12 lit. a 3rd paragraph and Article 15 sect. 1 of the Data Protection Directive because the claimant did only demonstrate the processing of personal data by means of a credit scoring algorithm as a matter of the case, but not, as required by the directive, the negative decision based on the score; and second, the Court concluded, referring to § 34 of the German Federal Data Protection Law, from the genesis of this provision that the German legislator explicitly denied, in order to protect the business secret of the scoring company, an individual's right to get information about the relative importance of the criteria underlying the score.

(i.e. move, if necessary). The primary question is hence not how the algorithm works. Instead, the question is which information the individual needs to know in order to improve his or her specific situation, so that he or she can reduce a potential negative impact about him or her. Both aspects may overlap, indeed. However, principally, these are different starting points and give the chance to balance the colliding fundamental rights more appropriately (e.g. the data controller's fundamental right to property and/or freedom to conduct a business against the fundamental rights to freedom of the individual concerned).

This thought implies, indeed, that the individual can reduce the risk by changing his or her factual circumstances. In contrast, there are cases where a fact is undoubtedly correct and the only relevant one for the controller. In these cases, the individual cannot correct the incorrect data and it is useless to add further information. However, risks can arise from how an algorithm evaluates this fact therefore serving as the basis for a potentially negative decision about the individual. Buchner provides an example from the insurance industry. Here, it is common practice that insurance companies implement so-called alert services enabling them to exchange data about an insurant in cases of irregularities, for example, if they think that the insurant has committed an insurance fraud.[1160] Usually, the companies base the exchange of such data on rather broad clauses within the insurance contracts stating, for instance, that "the insurance company transfers, to the necessary extent, data related to the application documents or the execution of the contract (…) to other insurance companies (…) in order to evaluate the risk and the claims".[1161] Buchner does not consider the transfer of the data *per se* as problematic but, instead it is the choice surrounding the criteria in which the insurance company can potentially base its decision on and that in a sense is arbitrary. For example, it might be arbitrary if the insurance company considers that the age, nationality or an accident which occurred on the 'lonely plain', can already lead to it be-

1160 See Buchner, ibid., pp. 137 and 138.

1161 See Buchner, ibid., p. 139: "(...) dass der Versicherer im erforderlichen Umfang Daten, sie sich aus den Antragsunterlagen oder der Vertragsdurchführung (Beiträge, Versicherungsfälle, Risiko-/Vertragsänderungen) ergeben, ... zur Beurteilung des Risikos und der Ansprüche an andere Versicherer und/oder an den Verband (der Lebensversicherungsunternehmen(der privaten Krankenversicherung etc.) und/oder an den Gesamtverband der Deutschen Versicherungswirtschaft zur Weitergabe dieser Daten an andere Versicherer übermittelt."

ing categorized as suspicious criteria.[1162] In order to meet this risk, Buchner proposes that the treatment of data in the context of alert services should be authorized on the basis of legal provisions specifying which criteria these alert service providers are allowed to use in order to evaluate the risk or to control potential fraud. He provides examples for such legal criteria as: Proven cases of insurance fraud, an enforceable extraordinary termination of insurance contracts, or agreements on surcharges because of special risks. In any case, if alert service providers cannot prove the legitimacy of certain data for their own decision-making process, they are not allowed to use it. Buchner submits, hence, the burden of proof rests with the controller.[1163]

While Buchner stresses an important point, he does not reveal the reason underlying his concern. The reason for his concern refers to the question of whether the mathematical-statistic method used, in order to calculate the risks by the decision-maker, produces a valid result. There may be doubts on the validity of the results from both a normative and a factual perspective:

For instance, if an insurance company reveals, based on algorithmic calculations, a correlation between an accident on the 'lonely plane' and an insurance fraud, this might well be an indicator of fraud. However, from a normative perspective, it seems less valid than the criteria proposed by Buchner, such as a proven case of insurance fraud. The algorithm used must therefore indicate a degree of validity. One starting point for such a scale is, certainly, the difference between correlation and causality. While a correlation indicates a certain, often indirect, relationship between two events, causality requires that one event causes, directly, the other one.[1164] Using the before-mentioned example: while causality says that an accident on the 'lonely plane' leads to an insurance fraud, a correlation of both events can be explained by further factors, such as the lack of witnesses. The lower validity of the correlations does not mean, indeed, that they have no value. As said before, it can be an important indicator for the decision-maker. However, such differences must be clear and they can serve

1162 See Buchner, ibid., p. 140.

1163 See Buchner, ibid., pp. 143 to 147 referring, in footnote 143, to § 35 sect. 2 sent. 2 no. 2 of the German Fedeeal Data Protection Law.

1164 See, just as one example, Mayer-Schönberger and Cukier, Big Data: A Revolution That Will Transform How We Live, Work, and Think, Chapter "Correlations", pp. 87 to 125.

an important link for regulation. For example, the particular circumstances in a certain context may require, in light of the fundamental to freedom concerned, the controller to verify whether there is a causal link between the criteria taken into account and the result of the risk calculation. In contrast, in other cases, it might be sufficient that the controller only has to demonstrate that there is a correlative link between the criteria and the result. In any case, when the regulator weighs the opposing fundamental rights, in practice, the burden of proof can play a key role for such a conflict resolution.

Another factor that can be relevant for the conflict resolution process is the error rate of the algorithm used for the decision-making. This factor refers to the factual aspects raising doubts on the validity of a decisional result. Focusing on the processing of personal data in big data environments, Krasnow Waterman and Bruening illustrate, in detail, the risk of error rates arising in the process of a data analysis. They principally differentiate between the moments of collection and the aggregation of personal data, the analytical process itself, and the application of the gathered information.[1165] Regarding the collection of personal data, Krasnow Waterman and Bruening list the following factors that can particularly bear a risk: first, data is corrupted when entering the data base, i.e. deleted, unreadable or modified; second, data may be entered inaccurately, i.e. into the wrong fields (like a birth day in the field of the postal code); third, different systems based on different conventions are merged changing the meaning of data, e.g. different indications of dates in the USA and in Europe (month-day, instead of day-month). When the data is actually processed itself, Krasnow Waterman and Bruening stress, in particular, the following factors: first, in order to understand the output, it is necessary to contextualize the output with respect to the input (for instance, since data bases such as Google's search results or Twitter messages represent certain categories like gender or geography, these representations must also be taken into account for the end results); second, the selection and combination of different algorithms produce different error rates (by the way, some algorithms

1165 See Krasnow Waterman and Bruening, Big Data analytics: risks and responsibilities, IDPL 2014 (Vol. 4, no. 2), using the term "phases", while this thesis prefers the term "moments" because it less implies a linear process "from the collection to the application phase" but indicates the possibility that the process jumps, in a non-linear way, back and forth.

indicate an error, but others not even do so).[1166] In conclusion, in order to understand the validity of the results of a data analysis, the user of this information has to know the error rates from all steps in the process. For example, if an algorithm used by a credit scoring company or alert service provider consists of three steps with a failure rate of 5 % for each step, the overall failure rate is 15 %. This means that an individual's score indicating the probability of a credit failure or an insurance fraud of 35 % actually lies between 20 and 50 % (supposing the failure rate is added and not multiplied).[1167]

This example is not intended to verify that those probability calculations are useless for decision-makers. In contrast, these calculations may come to the conclusion that even a probability of 20 % is high enough and proves the individual unworthy of credit or the insurance claim. However, in light of the private autonomy of an individual negotiating contracts, which is seriously threatened by the potentially negative decision, the error rate can be one important indicator for the legitimacy of the processing of data and the use of information. In light of the conflicting fundamental rights, it depends then on the particularities of the context which possibilities the individual should have in order to contest the decision made by the controller: Which criteria are certainly legitimate and which are certainly not? Which entity assesses, if at all, the error rate (the controller or an independent third party like a data protection authority or consumer rights agency)? Will the results remain confidential or be published and, if so, to whom? Who carries the burden of proof in cases of doubt? Etc. In any case, Dietlein particularly stresses, with respect to the private sector, that fundamental rights to freedom do not provide for certain protection instruments. Instead, it is primarily the legislator who must balance the opposing fundamental rights by means of ordinary law.[1168] If the legislator cannot specify itself the protection instruments in sufficient detail, be it because of a lack knowledge, rapidity of technological and economic development or another reason, it has to delegate this task to another entity who in turn needs to lay down criteria in order to strike a suitable balance between the conflicting fundamental rights.[1169]

1166 See Krasnow Waterman and Bruening, ibid., pp. 90 to 92.
1167 Cf. Krasnow Waterman and Bruening, ibid., pp. 93.
1168 See Dietlein, The Doctrine of Duties of Protection of Basic Rights, pp. 81 to 84.
1169 See above under point A. II. 2. The regulator's perspective.

ee) Rights to equality and non-discrimination

Last but not least, this sub-chapter treats the issue of how the fundamental right to non-discrimination determines the function of the requirement to specify the purpose. In contrast to the fundamental rights to privacy and freedom, rights to equality do not cover certain spatial, medial, or social contexts but rather concern the way how decisions are made. They are therefore related to the situations discussed previously where the processing of personal data serves as a basis for potentially negative decisions. However, in contrast to protection instruments serving against risks for the exercise of fundamental rights to freedom, the fundamental right to non-discrimination often refers to criteria that the individual concerned cannot avoid at all. For instance, an individual is able to principally change his or her residential address or omit an action that is relevant for the controller and/or decision-maker. In contrast, the individual cannot change his or her personality having the elements listed in Article 21 ECFR (or it requires remarkable efforts), such as: sex, race, colour, ethnic or social origin, genetic features, language, religion or belief, political or any other opinion, membership of a national minority, property, birth, disability, age or sexual orientation. At least, the constitution does not expect to change or hide these elements. In light of this consideration, this sub-chapter examines how the right to non-discrimination can be related to the right to data protection under Article 8 ECFR, with particular respect to the private sector.

(1) In the public sector: Criteria for intensity of infringement

Regarding the State, the German Constitutional Court took, in the decision of "*Dragnet Investigation*", similar criteria listed by the basic right of equality under Article 3 GG into account in order to determine the intensity of an infringement of the right to informational self-determination. The Court stated, in this regard: "The intensity of an infringement of the right to informational self-determination depends, amongst other criteria, which information is concerned, in particular how relevant this information is for the personality of the individual concerned *per se* and in combination with further information (…). All information concerned by the dragnet investigation are related to persons and provide, combined with further information, insights into the personality. Information with further aspects protected by fundamental rights such as (sex, parentage, race, language, homeland and origin, faith or religious or political opinions) by Art. 3 sect. 3 or Art. 140 GG are especially relevant for the personality. The category of ‚special kinds of personal data' under § 3 sect. 9 BDSG (essentially referring to the criteria mentioned above) mirrors this idea".[1170] The German Constitutional Court concludes from this that "the infringement authorized by the law for the dragnet investigation is of considerable importance with respect to the content of both the data received as well as the data combined. The same applies to the further information which can be obtained through the combination and matching of the different data sets."[1171] In this regard, Britz particularly underlines the importance of protection because people quickly associate the criteria listed in the law with negative stereotypes about the individual. In her opinion, the right to informational self-determination is, as mentioned before, functionally similar to the protection against discrimination.[1172]

(2) In the private sector: 'Tool of opacity' vs. private autonomy?

However, the effects of this fundamental right on private parties, which process personal data, is less clear. Dietlein stresses that the general right

1170 See BVerfG, 4th of April 2006, 1 BvR 518/02 (Dragnet Investigation), cip. 92 to 94: "Das Gewicht eines Eingriffs in das Recht auf informationelle Selbstbestimmung hängt unter anderem davon ab, welche Inhalte von dem Eingriff erfasst werden, insbesondere welchen Grad an Persönlichkeitsrelevanz die betroffenen Informationen je für sich und in ihrer Verknüpfung mit anderen aufweisen, und auf welchem Wege diese Inhalte erlangt werden. (...) Sämtliche durch die Rasterfahndung betroffenen Informationen haben einen Personenbezug und erlauben durch ihre Verknüpfung mit anderen Informationen persönlichkeitsbezogene Einblicke. Eine besondere Persönlichkeitsrelevanz kommt vor allem Informationen zu, die sich auf anderweitig, etwa in Art. 3 Abs. 3 GG oder in Art. 140 GG in Verbindung mit Art. 136 Abs. 3 WRV verfassungsrechtlich geschützte Bereiche beziehen. Dies findet auf einfachgesetzlicher Ebene etwa in der Kategorie der "besonderen Arten personenbezogener Daten" gemäß § 3 Abs. 9 BDSG Ausdruck, (wozu nach dieser Vorschrift Angaben über die rassische und ethnische Herkunft, über politische Meinungen, religiöse oder philosophische Überzeugungen, über eine Gewerkschaftszugehörigkeit und über die Gesundheit oder das Sexualleben zu zählen sind.)".

1171 See BVerfG, ibid., cip. 95.

1172 See already above under point C. II. 3. b) dd) Focus on the later usage of data or information: Restriction or hindrance of exercise of rights of freedom through usage of data or information, referring toBritz, ibid., pp. 572 and 573.

to equality under Article 3 sect. 1 GG, which is similar to the fundamental right to equality under Article 20 ECFR, only addresses the power of the State and, thus, state authorities. In contrast, the criteria listed under sections 2 and 3 of Article 3 GG, which are similar to the right to non-discrimination under Article 21 ECFR, contain a core value that can have an indirect effect on the private sector. They require the State to establish instruments that protect individuals against harm of these "tabooed" elements of their personality.[1173]

The European Data Protection Directive mainly does so by requiring the individual's consent. As mentioned previously, De Hert and Gutwirth consider the provisions on the processing of „sensitive data" (again equivalent to the criteria listed above) as an exception from the rule that data protection serves as a tool of transparency. The processing of these types of data strictly depends, in their opinion, on the individual's consent, as a tool of opacity, because it „bears a supplementary risk of discrimination. "[1174] Tzanou additionally notes that discriminatory aspects are also addressed in Article 15 of the Data Protection Directive, which concerns automated decision-making and equally foresees the individual's consent.[1175] However, despite these affirmations, it is doubtful that the individual's consent is the appropriate instrument protecting the individual against risks caused by the processing of data, which reveals such elements of his or her personality. This is in particular the case because the revelation of such information does, in particular in big data-driven innovation processes, depend less on the collected data per se than on its combination, and may only indirectly refer to the criteria (e.g. only the zip code of a certain area is processed, where, however, an ethnic minority lives).[1176] In these cases, an individual is hardly able, at least in the moment of collection, to forbid or influence the decision-making process. Therefore, the individual's consent does not appear to be the most effective protection instrument. Instead, it seems to be more effective if the processing of this kind of data depends on objective requirements. These objective requirements might

1173 See Dietlein, ibid., pp. 84 to 86.

1174 See De Hert and Gutwirth, ibid., p. 79.

1175 See Tzanou, Data protection as a fundamental right next to privacy? 'Reconstructing' a not so new right, p. 92.

1176 See Krasnow Waterman and Bruening: Big Data analytics: risks and responsibilities, IDPL 2014 (Vol. 4, no. 2), p. 94.

prohibit the processing of this data as a whole, or establish certain conditions for the processing.

In any case, Buchner stresses that the individuals' rights of non-discrimination must be balanced with the private autonomy guaranteed, at least, by German Basic Law in favor of the private parties processing the personal data. He highlights that the German General Equal Treatment Act – which transposes several European directives into German private law[1177] – does not actually aim to protect against all kinds of discrimination, but only against discrimination that cannot be based on a justifiable reason. Buchner concludes from this that the so-called discrimination in the insurance industry which differentiates its insurance policies on the basis of genetic codes of their insurants or in the financial market adapting the interest rates to the credit scores of potential debtors, is actually justifiable so long as mathematical-statistic methods can prove the link between the characteristics in question and the calculated risk.[1178] This criteria leads back, indeed, to the discussion held previously.

(3) Interim conclusion: Additional legitimacy requirement for the data-based decision-making process

The preceding sub-chapter discussed the legitimacy of using personal data as a basis for automated decision-making in light of the specific fundamental rights to freedom concerned by the decision. The discussion came to the result that the legitimacy depends, on the one hand, on the substan-

1177 See the Council Directive 2000/43/EC of 29 June 2000 implementing the principle of equal treatment between persons irrespective of racial or ethnic origin, Council Directive 2000/78/EC of 27 November 2000 establishing a general framework for equal treatment in employment and occupation, Directive 2002/73/EC of the European Parliament and of the Council of 23 September 2002 amending Council Directive 76/207/EEC on the implementation of the principle of equal treatment for men and women as regards access to employment, vocational training and promotion, and working conditions, and Council Directive 2004/113/EC of 13 December 2004 implementing the principle of equal treatment between men and women in the access to and supply of goods and services.

1178 See Buchner, Informational self-determination in the private sector, pp. 195 and 196 with reference to contrary opinions by Baeriswyl, RDV 2000, 6 /, 10), Podlech/Pfeifer, RDV 1998, 139 (140), Wittig, RDV 2000, 59 (62), Scholz in Roßnagel, Handbuch Datenschutzrecht, Kap. 9.2 Rn. 37.

tial guarantee specifically concerned and, on the other hand, on the particularities of the decision-making process. For example, the individual's ability to change the circumstances underlying the potentially negative decision of the controller or decision-maker, or the error rate of the algorithms that they use.[1179] However, in contrast to these cases, an individual cannot avoid that his or her personality consists of characteristics that are listed under the right to non-discrimination of Article 21 ECFR. Rather, the law protects him or her against harm suffered only because he or she has such personal characteristics. This means that the assessment of whether a discrimination based on such a data processing is legitimate or not must be stricter than when taking the fundamental rights of freedom into account. It would be going too far to elaborate in detail on the criteria for this assessment.[1180] However, a starting point could be, as mentioned before, to differentiate between correlation and causality. Buchner appears to accept each link between the characteristic in question and a risk calculated by the controller on the basis of a mathematical-statistical method. In contrast, it could be doubted whether a correlation between the criteria listed under Article 21 ECFR, and a risk to the controller's interests is enough to justify a discrimination. Instead, a bottom line could be that a proof of causality between the characteristic and the risk for the decision-maker serves as an objective reason for the discriminatory practice. This approach would not exclude mathematical-statistic methods as a whole from automated decision-making processes, but only those methods that cannot prove causality. At least, these stricter pre-conditions for a mathematical-statistic proof would meet the stricter normative requirements for the legitimacy of discriminations based on criteria listed in the right to non-discrimination under Article 21 ECFR.

In conclusion, it became clear that the individual's consent serves less, at least in big data environments concerning Article 21 ECFR, as a "tool of opacity" against the collection of personal data, than as a further requirement restraining the room of action for the data controller and decision-maker. This is particularly the case, if the processing reveals that individuals run the risk of being negatively stigmatized. The requirement to

---

1179 See above under point C. II. 3. b) dd) (3) (c) Protection instruments enabling the individual to adapt to or protect him or herself against the informational measure.

1180 See, instead, Britz, Justice in the individual case versus generalization: limits of constitutional law for statistical discrimination.

specify the purpose functions, hence, here again, as a protection instrument discovering the risk of discrimination for the individual concerned. From this point of view, the requirement to make the purpose explicit to the individual, ensures, at least, that a discriminatory decision-making process does not occur in an 'illegitimate and socially irreprehensible' way because it leaves the individual outside of that process.[1181]

c) Conclusion: Purpose specification during innovation processes

In conclusion, the requirement to specify the purpose is a protection instrument serving to discover risks caused by the processing of personal data and the usage of information for the individual's autonomy, further specified by his or her fundamental rights to privacy, freedom, and non-discrimination. Covering different spatial, medial, and social contexts, the specific rights to privacy and freedom determine the data protection instruments provided for by Article 8 ECFR and, thus, the precision of the purpose being specified by the controller. An exception to this rule consists in the right to non-discrimination that does not cover a certain context, but relates to certain elements of the individual's personality concerned by a decision based on information. Thus, the fundamental right to non-discrimination can apply, in principle, to all contexts covered by the guarantees to privacy and freedom. Irrespective of this exception, it is possible, indeed, that the processing of data or use of information concerns several guarantees, simultaneously. The following chart shall illustrate the interplay of guarantees:[1182]

1181 Cf. Buchner, ibid., p. 195, referring to the legislative background text for the draft of the German General Equal Treatment Act proposed by the German Federal Government (Bundestagsdrucksache 15/4538, p. 28).

1182 This graphic chart is licensed under the Creative Commons Attribution-ShareAlike 4.0 International License; doi: https://doi.org/10.5281/zenodo.1194679.

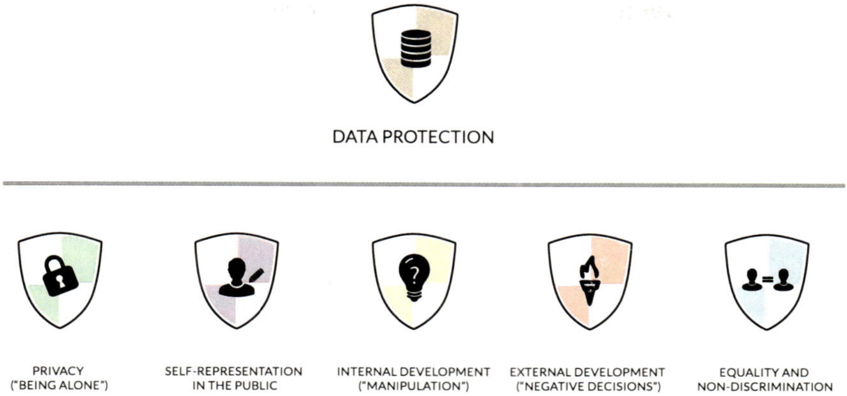

This concept of protection of the fundamental right to data protection under Article 8 ECFR is appropriate, in particular, in light of the approach regulating data-driven innovation. This approach aims not only to protect the individual against the risks caused by data-driven innovation, but also, that the risk protection instruments enhance innovation or, at least, do not unnecessarily hinder innovation.[1183] In the private sector, the colliding fundamental rights of the individual concerned and the data controller require the regulator to balance the protection function of the individual's fundamental rights against the defensive function of the controller's fundamental rights.[1184] In light of this assessment, the proposed concept of protection of the fundamental right to data protection does not only lead to a more effective protection for the individual concerned, but also allows implementing protection instruments in a way that infringe the data controller's fundamental rights less intensively.

The reason for this is that this concept of protection does not focus, exclusively, on the moment the personal data is collected, but equally takes the risks caused by the later usage of the personal data into account; and certain risks occur, as demonstrated in this chapter, often, not in the moment the data is collected, but at later stages. This is particularly the case with respect to risks against the individual's fundamental rights to freedom. But also his or her internal freedom of development or fundamental

1183 See above under point A. II. 1. Legal research about innovation.

1184 See above under point C. I. 1. B) bb) (1) The 3-Step-Test: Assessing the defensive and protection function.

right to non-discrimination may specifically be affected, only in a later stage. On the one hand, the protection instruments can thus be more effectively applied against the corresponding risks caused by the specific data processing. On the other hand, the data controller is not required to apply all protection instruments as soon as the data collection occurs, irrespective of the specific risks that the collection causes for the individual. In particular, the requirement to specify the purpose constitutes a relatively low regulatory burden on the data controller because this requirement only obliges the controller to gather the information necessary in order to assess the risk.[1185] All further protection instruments depend then on the result of this risk assessment.

In conclusion, applying the protection instruments provided for by the fundamental right to data protection to the risks against the other fundamental rights enables a more efficient regulation, in particular, of *how* the personal data is used. Indeed, this concept not only makes protection against the collection of personal data unnecessary.[1186] This is particularly the case if the collection of personal data amounts to an intrusion into an individual's specific private sphere, such as at his or her home or when she or he uses means of communication. However, taking equally the specific risks caused by the later use into account makes, in particular, the specification of the purpose the moment the data is collected a much less complex task or, in other words, a much more achievable task. In any case, taking the later use of personal data into account, leads us to the question on the function of the requirement to limit the later use of data to the purpose previously specified.

III. Requirement of purpose limitation in light of the range of protection

The preceding chapter elaborated on a concept of protection that analyzed the function of the requirements of, primarily, purpose specification and, subsequently, making the specified purpose explicit to the individual concerned. It was demonstrated how the substantial guarantees provided for

---

1185 See above under point B. II. 3. c) Interim conclusion: Fundamental rights determining the appropriateness of protection.

1186 Cf. Roßnagel, Data protection in computerized everyday life, pp. 179 and 180, who stresses the necessity to extend the focus of protection from the moment the personal data is collected to the question of how the data is processed.

by specific fundamental rights to privacy, freedom and non-discrimination can provide a legal scale in order to determine which purposes of the processing of personal data are legally relevant and how precisely, as well as under which circumstances, data controllers have to specify the said purpose. This chapter draws the attention to the function of the requirement of limiting the later usage of the data to the purposes previously specified.

1. Different models of purpose limitation and change of purpose

Similarly to the functions of purpose specification and making the specified purposes explicit, the functions of the requirement of purpose limitation also depend on the concept of protection provided for by the corresponding fundamental rights. This thesis treats, in essence, three different models regarding how the principle of purpose limitation may be implemented: The model applied by the European Court of Human Rights referring to the individual's 'reasonable expectations'; the model provided for by the European Data Protection Directive requiring that the later use of data must not be incompatible with the initial or preceding purpose; and the German model principally requiring strict purpose identity developed by the German Constitutional Court with respect to the right to informational self-determination. As set out previously, the concepts of protection provided for by the European Convention on Human Rights, the European Charter of Fundamental Rights and the German Basic Law differ to each other, and consequently, so do the functions of purpose limitation.

a) European models: 'Reasonable expectations' and purpose compatibility

On the European level, the European Charter of Fundamental Rights does not require, at least not explicitly, the limitation of the later use of data to the initial or a preceding purpose. In particular, the right to data protection under Article 8 ECFR only requires the data controller to specify the purpose of the data processing.[1187] However, in contrast, the Data Protection Directive, as well as the General Data Protection Regulation do. Article 6

1187 See also Bygrave, Data Privacy Law, p. 153 (fn. 39), who however allocates the second component of the principle of purpose limitation (i.e. to limit the later

sect. 1 lit. b of the directive and Article 5 sect. 1 lit. b of the regulation require that personal data must not be processed further in a way that is incompatible with the initial purpose. The European Court of Human Rights provides for yet another approach by requiring, in light of the right to private life under Article 8 ECHR, that the later use of data must meet the individual's 'reasonable expectations'. Hence, both approaches do not generally require the identity of purposes. The essential difference between these requirements is that the requirement of purpose identity gives, in principle, less flexibility to the controller. Purpose compatibility and the individual's 'reasonable expectations' require an assessment of whether or not the later use of the data is compatible or incompatible with the original purpose or meets or does not meet the individual's "expectations". Both tests may lead to the result, in the one case, that the later use of data must be strictly limited to the original purpose (purpose identity) or, in another case, may differ from the original purpose.[1188]

aa) Change of purpose pursuant to ECtHR and ECJ

The European Court of Human Rights implicitly had applied the test of purpose compatibility in several decisions. In contrast, the European Court of Justice has not yet referred to such a requirement.

(1) ECtHR: 'Reasonable expectations' as a main criteria

As analyzed before, the European Court of Human Rights does not set out precise criteria in order to specify the purpose and, accordingly, to carry out the compatibility assessment.[1189] The reason for this is that the European Court of Human Rights primarily refers to the individual's 'reasonable expectations'. The requirements of purpose specification, i.e. making the purpose explicit and purpose compatibility are sub-elements of the assessment of whether or not the usage of data meets the 'reasonable expec-

---

data processing to the original purpose) under the "fairness" criterion, which is explicitly mentioned under Art. 8 sect. 1 ECFR.

1188 Cf. Article 29 Data Protection Working Group, Opinion 03/0213 on purpose limitation, p. 21.

1189 See above under point B. II. 1. a) ECtHR and ECJ: Almost no criteria.

tations' of the individual concerned.[1190] In order to answer this question, the Court usually "attached importance to whether the (… / personal data) amounted to an intrusion into the applicant's privacy, whether (… / it) related to private or public matters and whether the material thus obtained was envisaged for a limited use or was likely to be made available to the general public."[1191]

In summary, the limited re-use of personal data, which was collected and stored for another limited purpose, usually does not infringe Article 8 ECHR. For example, in the case of "*Friedl vs. Austria*", the later use of a photo of an individual, once taken during an application process for a driver's license, in order to identify him or her in a criminal proceeding does not interfere with his or her reasonable expectation. The Court, in particular, took into account that the photo in question had not "been made available to the general public or would be used for any other purpose."[1192] In contrast, the unforeseen use of personal data for publication purposes, such as broadcasting, conflicts with the 'reasonable expectations' of the individual concerned.[1193] However, even the limited use of personal data, which is not a publication, can interfere with one's 'reasonable expectations'. For instance, a covered voice recording during a formal derogation in a police station, in order to identify the individual concerned interferes with his or her 'reasonable expectation'.[1194] And similarly, the use of video footage filmed with a secretly prepared custody camera in order to identify the individual concerned also conflicts with his or her 'reasonable expectations'.[1195]

In all of these cases, the usage of the data would not have infringed the individual's reasonable expectations if the controller had made its real purpose explicit to the individual, so that he or she could have adapted his or

1190 See summary above under point C. I. 3. b) ee) Conclusion: Assessment of 'reasonable expectations' on a case-by-case basis.

1191 See ECtHR, Case of Peck vs. the United Kingdom from 28 January 2003 (application no. 44647/98), cip. 61.

1192 See ECtHR, Case of Peck vs. the United Kingdom from 28 January 2003 (application no. 44647/98), cip. 61.

1193 See ECtHR, Case of Peck vs. the United Kingdom from 28 January 2003 (application no. 44647/98), cip. 60.

1194 See ECtHR, Case of P.G. and J.H. vs. The United Kingdom from 25 September 2001 (application no. 44787/98), cip. 59.

1195 See ECtHR, Case of Perry vs. the United Kingdom from 17 July 2003 (application no. 63737/00), cip. 39 and 41.

her behavior to the situation. Thus, these examples do not actually refer to the requirement of purpose compatibility but to purpose specification. However, these cases illustrate that the European Court of Human Rights considers the use of personal data for another purpose other than for why it was apparently collected, as interfering with the individual's 'reasonable expectations'. In conclusion, applying a case-by-case approach, the European Court of Human Rights does not explicitly refer to the requirement of purpose compatibility. Instead, the main criteria are the individual's 'reasonable expectations'. In assessing whether the use of data meets the 'reasonable expectations', the Court implicitly compares the later use of data with the initial purpose, applying the principles previously described.[1196]

(2) ECJ: Reference to data protection instruments instead of 'reasonable expectations'

The European Court of Justice does not strictly apply the principles developed by the European Court of Human Rights with respect to Article 8 ECHR. Instead, the Court has started to elaborate on the particularities of the concept of protection provided for by Articles 7 and 8 ECFR.[1197] It was stressed before that Article 7 ECFR corresponds to Article 8 ECHR, whereas Article 8 ECFR is only based on it.[1198] It was apparent from the analysis regarding the Court's decisions that the European Court of Justice tends to consider the right to data protection under Article 8 ECFR as a regulation instrument serving, at least, the right to private life under Article 7 ECHR. Applying this approach, the European Court of Justice does not explicitly refer to the 'reasonable expectations' considered by the European Court of Human Rights. Rather, the Court refers to the data protection instruments provided for by Article 8 ECFR and the secondary law specifying and extending these protection instruments.[1199]

1196 Cf. above under point C. I. 3. b) ee) Conclusion: Assessment of 'reasonable expectations' on a case-by-case basis.

1197 See summary above under point C. I. 3. c) bb) Interim conclusion: Article 8 ECFR as a regulation instrument?

1198 See above under point C. I. 3. a) Genesis and interplay of both rights.

1199 Cf. above under point C. I. 3. c) bb) (2) Protection going beyond Article 8 ECHR.

(a) Are the terms ‘necessity’, ‘adequacy’ and ‘relevance’ used as objective criteria for the compatibility assessment?

Interestingly, the European Court of Justice did not refer, so far, to the compatibility assessment, nor did it refer to the individual’s ‘reasonable expectations’. In particular, in the case of “*Mr. González vs. Google Spain*”, the Court did not refer, at least not explicitly, to this requirement and not even to the compatibility assessment. Instead, the Court referred to other requirements provided for by Article 6 of the Data Protection Directive. As quoted previously, the Court stated that “it follows from those requirements, laid down in Article 6(1) lit. c) to (e) (…/of the Data Protection Directive), that even initially lawful processing of accurate data may, in the course of time, become incompatible with the directive where those data are no longer necessary in the light of the purposes for which they initially were collected or processed. That is in particular where they appear to be inadequate, irrelevant or no longer relevant, or excessive in relation to those purposes and in the light of the time that has elapsed.”[1200] Thus, the Court did not explicitly refer to the compatibility requirement (it mentions the compatibility with the directive). However, the requirements of ‘necessity’, ‘adequacy’, and ‘relevance’ of the later processing might be the criteria needed for its implicit assessment. The reason for this assumption is that the compatibility assessment typically applies if the later use of data deviates from the initial purpose, (what was apparently the case in this decision). This would be an interesting result because these criteria would determine the compatibility of the later use with the initial purpose from an objective view more than from the subjective individual’s expectation. The ‘necessity’, ‘adequacy’, or ‘relevance’ of the later use of data does not depend on the individual’s perspective but only on the initial purpose specified by the controller. And the determination of what is ‘necessary’ in order achieve the purpose thus depends on an objective point of view. In any case, since the European Court of Justice did not precisely examine what the initial purpose was, the compatibility assessment remained, if it was a compatibility assessment, rather vague.[1201]

1200 See ECJ C-131/12, cip. 93.

1201 See above under point C. I. 3. c) aa) (2) Protection against first publication and profiles based on public data.

(b) Purpose identity for the consent

In contrast, in the case of "*Telekom vs. Germany*", the Court explicitly commented on the extent of the principle of purpose limitation. Indeed, this case referred not to an initial purpose provided for by law (i.e. the publication of information about Mr. González in daily newspapers), but specified within the individual's consent. The Court stated, referring exclusively to Article 8 ECFR, that the individual's consent authorizing the publication of information about him or her in a public directory also covers the transfer of that information to another undertaking which publishes the data in another directory. With respect to the extent of the principle of purpose limitation, the Court's statement on the duties of information now becomes clearer than before.[1202] The controller of the data must inform, "before the first inclusion of the data in the public directory, of the purpose of that directory and of the fact that those data will may be communicated to another telephone service provider and that it is guaranteed *that those data will not, once passed on, be used for purposes other than those for which they were collected with a view to their first publication* (underlining by the author)."[1203] Thus, irrespective of the question of whether a missing of this last (underlined) requirement leads to the invalidity of the consent, the requirement makes clear that the later use is limited to the initial purpose. The Court therefore requires, apparently, strict purpose identity with respect to the individuals consent. Indeed, what this requirement means in light of the risk-based approach promoted in this thesis will be answered later on.[1204]

1202 See above under point C. I. 3. c) aa) (5) Going beyond the requirement of consent provided for under Article 8 ECHR.

1203 See ECJ C-543/09 (Telekom vs. Germany), cip. 66 and 67.

1204 See beneath under point C. III. 2. a) bb) Refinement of current concepts of protection, and C. IV. 3. b) aa) (2) Extent of consent limiting the later use of data (instead of being illegal as a whole).

bb) Compatibility assessment required by the Data Protection Directive with respect to the opinion of the Art. 29 Data Protection Working Party

Since the European Court of Justice has not yet provided clear criteria, it is even more important to examine in detail the opinion of the Article 29 Data Protection Working Group on the compatibility assessment. Its opinion mainly refers to Article 6 sect. 1 lit. b sent. 1 of the Data Protection Directive. However, in light of the fact that Article 6 sect. 4 of the General Data Protection Regulation establishes the criteria proposed by the Working Group with respect to the purpose compatibility assessment under the directive, it is very likely that the Group's opinion is also applied in order to interpret the regulation. In any case, the Working Group provides its opinion because of the differences of how the Member States implemented the principle of purpose limitation. For example, while Belgium treats the principle under the notion of 'reasonable expectation', Germany and the Netherlands apply balancing tests. And the United Kingdom, and Greece, link the requirement to the principles of transparency, lawfulness and fairness of the data processing.[1205]

In order to give a common direction, the Working Group defines the function of purpose compatibility, referring to the specification of the purpose, as: "If a purpose is sufficiently specific and clear, individuals will know what to expect: the way data are processed will be predictable. (…) Predictability is also relevant when assessing the compatibility of further processing activities. In general, further processing cannot be considered predictable if it is not sufficiently related to the original purpose and does not meet the reasonable expectations of the data subjects at the time of collection, based on the context of the collection."[1206] Thus, in the opinion of the Working Group, the requirement of purpose compatibility ensures, together with the specification of the purpose, that the individual is able to predict the treatment of data related to him or her. In light of the reasoning by the European Court of Justice, which does not explicitly refer, so far, to the individual's 'reasonable expectations', this function appears to tie into the concept of protection provided for by the European Court of Human Rights.

1205 See Article 29 Data Protection Working Group, Opinion 03/0213 on purpose limitation, p. 10.

1206 See Article 29 Data Protection Working Group, ibid., p. 13.

(1) Preliminary analysis: Pre-conditions and consequences

With respect to the general requirement of purpose compatibility provided for by Article 6 sect. 1 lit. b sent. 1 of the Data Protection Directive, the Working Group proposes several pre-conditions for its assessment. At first, the Working Group stresses that the directive does not differentiate between the 'original purpose' and 'purposes defined subsequently'. The Working Group concludes from this that the purpose specified the moment the data is collected is the only reference which answers the question of whether or not a later processing is compatible with the initial purpose of collection. Consequently, the Working Group differs between the "collection, and all other subsequent processing operations (including for instance the very first typical processing operation following collection – the storage of data)" and concludes from this that "any processing following collection, whether for the purposes initially specified or for any additional purposes, must be considered 'further processing' and must thus meet the requirement of compatibility."[1207] The Working Party appears to consider this approach as providing for an effective protection instrument. However, at a more detailed glance, this might be arguable because it excludes purposes being specified after the collection as reference for additional tests of compatibility. In contrast, in light of the diversity of risks caused by the processing of data today, there might also be a need for protection against such data processing for purposes that are, after the collection, changed over time. Theoretically, it could be possible that a very later processing indeed is compatible with the purpose originally specified, but not with a purpose which was specified between the original purpose and before the "new" current purpose. This theoretical assumption makes it arguable to compare the later purpose only with the original purpose specified the moment when the data was collected.

In contrast, the Working Group promotes a more flexible approach in relation to two other aspects. Firstly, it stresses that the directive does not impose "a requirement of compatibility" but that the legislator instead "chose a double negation: it prohibited incompatibility." The Working Group concludes from this a more liberal approach stating: "By providing that any further processing is authorized as long as it is *not incompatible* (and if the requirements of lawfulness are simultaneously also fulfilled), it

1207 See Article 29 Data Protection Working Group, ibid., p. 21.

would appear that the legislators intended to give some flexibility with regard to further use."[1208] Unfortunately, the Working Group does not specify in more detail why this approach provided for by the double negation may give more flexibility to the data controller than the positive formulation of 'purpose compatibility'. For instance, this might be the case because the data controller did not have to guarantee, positively, the overall compatibility but only to exclude, negatively, circumstances that would make the later use incompatible. These different types of duties could furthermore result into different burdens of proof: While the positive guarantee might enable the individual concerned to prove a violation of his or her rights by only proving one aspect excluding the compatibility, the negative duties may enable the controller to exonerate itself by only proving that it had fulfilled these negative duties. Indeed, these questions must, so far, remain open.

Second, the Working Group treats the question of whether the compatibility assessment should apply a formal or substantive methodology. It describes the two different types as: "A formal assessment will compare the purposes that were initially provided for, usually in writing, by the data controller with any further uses to find out whether these uses were covered (explicitly or implicitly). A substantive assessment will go beyond formal statements to identify both the new and the original purpose, taking into account the way they are (or should be) understood, depending on the context and other factors."[1209] The Working Group considers that the formal method is more neutral and objective, however, it appears to be too rigid. In particular, the Working Group fears that the formal method "may encourage controllers to specify the purpose in increasingly more legalistic ways, with a view to ensure a margin for further data processing than to protect the individuals concerned."[1210] In contrast, the substantive method "may also enable adaptation to future developments within society while at the same time continuing to effectively safeguard the protection of personal data."[1211] Favoring the substantive method, the Working Group continues specifying the criteria serving to carry out the substantive compatibility assessment. Interestingly, the formal method described leads to nothing less than to the strict requirement of purpose identity. The later usage

1208 See Article 29 Data Protection Working Group, ibid., p. 21.
1209 See Article 29 Data Protection Working Group, ibid., p. 21.
1210 See Article 29 Data Protection Working Group, ibid., p. 22.
1211 See Article 29 Data Protection Working Group, ibid., p. 22.

of the data is incompatible with the original purpose if it is not 'covered' by this purpose. In light of the Working Group's statement that this method, i.e. the requirement of purpose identity, 'may encourage controllers to specify the purpose in increasingly legalistic ways', it is interesting to see which criteria the Working Group considers in order to avoid this result.

Finally, the Working Group clarifies that a failure to comply with the requirement of purpose compatibility leads to the unlawfulness of the later use of data. Such use therefore is not permitted. Furthermore, the Working Group stresses that the requirement of purpose compatibility provided for by Article 6 sect. 1 lit. b) of the Data Protection Directive is cumulative to the legal grounds required by its Article 7. Hence, the data controller cannot legitimize an incompatible further use of data by grounding it on a legal basis provided for by Article 7 of the Data Protection Directive.[1212] The Working Group justifies this cumulative requirement by referring to the status of the requirement of purpose compatibility as an essential principle commonly recognized in the EU, and globally. It also stresses that Article 8 ECFR comparably requires, to be considered cumulatively the specification of purposes and the legitimate basis provided for by law.[1213] Unfortunately, these considerations do not precisely explain why the concepts of protection provided for by fundamental rights, be it by the right to privacy under Article 7 ECFR, the right to data protection under Article 8 ECFR, or another fundamental right, require, cumulatively, the compatibility of purposes (not purpose specification), as well as a legal basis for the treatment of data. The considerations do not even explain why the fundamental rights require one of these requirements *per se*, particularly in the private sector.[1214] However, an answer to the question of why, or under which circumstances, both requirements may be necessary in light of the substantial guarantees endangered by data processing will be developed later on.

1212 See Article 29 Data Protection Working Group, ibid., p. 36.

1213 See Article 29 Data Protection Working Group, ibid., p. 11.

1214 Cf. already the similar question regarding the requirement of purpose specification above under point C. II. 1. b) bb) (1) Preliminary note: Clarifying conceptual (mis)understanding.

(2) Example: The expectations of a customer purchasing a vegetable box online

Before examining its criteria for the substantive compatibility assessment, the Working Group gives three introductory examples. In the basic example, "a customer contracts an online retailer to deliver an organic vegetable box each week to their home. After the initial 'collection' of the customer's address and banking information, these data are 'further processed' by the retailer each week for payment and delivery. This obviously complies with the principle of purpose limitation and requires no further analysis."[1215] The Working Group stresses that the processing obviously complies with the principle of purpose limitation because it "clearly meets the reasonable expectations of the data subjects, even if not all details were fully expressed at the start."[1216] In this example, this is indeed the case because it actually complies, even if the Working Group does not mention this explicitly, with the strict requirement of purpose identity. The later use of data simply pursues, on a formal level, the initial purpose.

In the second example, the retailer "wishes to use the customer's email address and purchase history to send them personalized offers and discount vouchers for similar products including its range of organic dairy products. He also whishes to provide the customer's data including their name, email address, phone number, and purchase history to a business contact which has opened an organic butchery business in the neighborhood."[1217] The Working Group considers in this extended example that "the retailer cannot assume that this further use is compatible and some additional analysis is necessary with the possibility of different outcomes (e.g. in case of 'internal' use or transfer of the data)."[1218] The Working Group stresses, justifying its conclusion, that "the greater the distance between the initial purpose specified at collection and the purposes of further use, the more thorough and comprehensive the analysis will have to be".[1219] So far, without giving further guidance for answering the question on how to measure the 'distance' between the purposes, the Working Group ads that "there may be also a need to include additional safeguards

1215 See Article 29 Data Protection Working Group, ibid., p. 22.
1216 See Article 29 Data Protection Working Group, ibid., p. 22.
1217 See Article 29 Data Protection Working Group, ibid., p. 23.
1218 See Article 29 Data Protection Working Group, ibid., p. 23.
1219 See Article 29 Data Protection Working Group, ibid., p. 22.

to compensate for the change of purpose (e.g. to provide additional information and explicit options for the data subject)."[1220]

In the third example, "the vegetable box customer also buys a range of other organic products on the retailer's website, some of which are discounted. The retailer, without informing the customer, has implemented an off-the-shelf price-customization software solution, which – among other things – detects whether the customer is using an Apple computer or a Windows PC. The retailer then automatically gives greater discounts to Windows users." The Working Party considers this "unrelated purpose (allowing secret 'price-discrimination'), (../as) problematic."[1221] As a consequence, it concludes from these examples the need for criteria allowing "practical assumptions ('rules of thumb')" in order to determine the "expectations of a reasonable person in the situation of the data subject".[1222]

(3) Criteria for the substantive compatibility assessment

In order to provide such 'rules of thumb', the Working Group has collected, analyzed and summarized the criteria being "already widely used in practice" amongst the EU Member States.[1223] The Group stresses that the list of criteria proposed for the substantive compatibility assessment is not exhaustive but rather "highlights the typical issues that may be considered in a balanced approach".[1224] As a consequence, the compliance with one of these criteria alone does not suffice with this approach; instead, the assessment as a whole, decides on whether or not the final result complies with the requirement of purpose compatibility.[1225]

(a) First criteria: 'Distance between purposes'

The first criteria refers to the 'distance' between the purpose of the later use of data and the original purpose at the moment of collection. The

1220 See Article 29 Data Protection Working Group, ibid., p. 22.
1221 See Article 29 Data Protection Working Group, ibid., p. 23.
1222 See Article 29 Data Protection Working Group, ibid., p. 23.
1223 See Article 29 Data Protection Working Group, ibid., p. 23.
1224 See Article 29 Data Protection Working Group, ibid., p. 27.
1225 See Article 29 Data Protection Working Group, ibid., p. 26.

Working Group again stresses, in this regard, that it would be insufficient if the assessment of the initial purpose only referred to the textually specified purpose. The reason is that data controllers, in practice, often do not actually write the purpose down, in a satisfying way, if at all. Instead, the assessment should refer to the "substance of the relationship between the (real) purposes of collection and the purposes of further processing (word in brackets added by the author)."[1226] In the Group's opinion, "this may cover situations where the further processing was already more or less implied in the initial purposes, or assumed as a logical next step in the processing according to those purposes".[1227] In fact, even if the Working Party refers to these situations in order to illustrate how the 'distance' between purposes might be determined, these situations actually refer, here again,[1228] to the requirement of purpose identity. If the further processing is 'implied in the initial purpose', it pursues a sub-purpose or even is a 'mean' of the broader initial purpose.[1229] Unfortunately, the Working Group does not give further guidance for how to measure the 'distance' between purposes. It recognizes, indeed, that there might be "situations where there is only a partial or even non-existent link with the original purposes."[1230] However, exactly for these situations, where there really is a change of purpose, the Working Group proposes, only, to "take account of the factual context and the way in which a certain purpose is commonly understood by relevant stakeholders in the various situations under analysis."[1231] This statement does thus not provide an objective legal scale in order to measure the 'distance' taken by a change of purpose.

(b) Second criteria: 'Context and reasonable expectations'

Regarding its second criteria, the Working Group refers to the factual circumstances, i.e. the context of the data collection and the individual's reasonable expectation about how the data will be used. In this regard, the

1226 See Article 29 Data Protection Working Group, ibid., p. 23.
1227 See Article 29 Data Protection Working Group, ibid., p. 24.
1228 See above under point C. III. 1. a) bb) (2) Example: The expectations of a customer purchasing a vegetable box online.
1229 Cf. above under the point C. II. 2. c) bb) Differentiating between the terms of 'purpose', 'means', and ,interests'.
1230 See Article 29 Data Protection Working Group, ibid., p. 24.
1231 See Article 29 Data Protection Working Group, ibid., p. 24.

Working Group considers the relationship between the data controller and the individual concerned as essential, as well as the transparency measures that exist in the particular case. In doing so, the Working Group refers to "what would be customary and generally expected practice in the given", for example, "(commercial or other) relationship."[1232] The examination of the relationship includes the role of the data controller, such as a lawyer or a medical doctor, the service or product offered, as well as the balance of power. In this last regard, the Working Group considers whether or not the data had to be collected on the basis of a legal provision or, in the case of a contractual relationship, how easily the individual concerned could terminate the contract and seek another contractual partner. Comparably, if the collection of data was based on the individual's consent, the Working Party takes into account "to what extent the consent was freely given, and on the precision of its terms."[1233] All these factors determine whether or not the individual concerned could expect his or her confidentiality, and if so, to what extent.

These considerations raise many questions. For example, it may be doubted that the individual's freedom to disclose the data plays a role at all for examining whether or not he or she could expect a later change of purpose. In both cases, be it where the individual voluntarily consented to the data processing for a certain purpose, or was enforced by law, the later use for another purpose might always be unexpected. In this regard, the Working Group stated that if the later use is based on a legal provision, it considers that "legal security and predictability in general might suggest that the further use is appropriate, even if the data subjects might not have been aware of all consequences involved."[1234] In particular, this statement conflicts with the Working Group's own opinion that the compatibility of purposes and the legal basis for the later use of data must be considered as cumulative requirements. If not, the compatibility assessment risks being obsolete for all cases where the later use of data can be based on one of the legal grounds listed under Article 7 of the Data Protection Directive, such as for the performance of a contract, or in order to take steps prior to entering a contract. This would allow, for example, a potential contractor of the individual to process all data necessary for estimating the risk of non-payment, irrespective of where the data originates. Even Article 7 lit. f

1232 See Article 29 Data Protection Working Group, ibid., p. 24.
1233 See Article 29 Data Protection Working Group, ibid., p. 24.
1234 See Article 29 Data Protection Working Group, ibid., p. 25.

of the Data Protection Directive, which covers the processing of data for the legitimate interests of the controller, provides, as a legal provision, a certain degree of 'legal security and predictability'. Insofar, the Working Party appears to apply a rather liberal approach.

This liberal approach also becomes apparent with respect to the individual's consent. In this respect, the Working Group appears to consider a legitimate change of purpose even if the original purpose was specified in the consent. Assumptions can therefore be made about the legal nature that the Working Group considers regarding the consent. If the consent is a bilateral agreement,[1235] the data controller cannot usually change this agreement unilaterally.[1236] In contrast, the Working Group appears to consider the consent as a unilateral waiver of fundamental rights possibly giving more room for a change of purpose than a bilateral agreement.[1237] In this case, of course, it must be discussed to what extent such a waiver of fundamental rights is possible. This will likely depend on the impact that such a waiver has on the individual's further execution of his or her fundamental right. In any case, this question will also be addressed later on.[1238]

(c) Third criteria: 'Nature of data and impact on data subjects'

The third criteria is the nature of the data and the impact of the further processing on the individual. With respect to the first aspect, the Working Group states: "In general, the more sensitive the information involved, the narrower the scope for compatible use would be."[1239] Evaluating whether or not the further processing involves sensitive data, the Working Group does not only refer to special categories of data protected under Article 8 of the Data Protection Directive, such as data revealing racial or ethnic origin or relating to health or criminal convictions, but also to other data

---

1235 Cf. above the concept provided for by the German Constitutional Court regarding the private sector under point C. I. 2. e) bb) In the private sector: The contract as an essential link for legal evaluation.

1236 See, for example, in German civil law the restrictions for a unilateral determination of contractual conditions under §§ 315 et seq. BGB.

1237 Cf. above under point C. I. 3. b) dd) Consent: Are individuals given a choice to avoid the processing altogether?.

1238 See beneath under point C. IV. 3 b) aa) Consent: "Later processing covered by specified purpose?".

1239 See Article 29 Data Protection Working Group, ibid., p. 25.

which need, in its opinion, special protection, such as data related to vulnerable persons (e.g. children, asylum seekers, the elderly, or the mentally ill) or data revealing particularly personal information (e.g. communication or location data). With respect to the second aspect, the Working Group takes both negative and positive consequences into account. Regarding the negative consequences, the Working Group lists several subcriteria as: "These may include potential future decisions or actions by third parties, and situations where the processing may lead to the exclusion or discrimination of individuals. In addition to adverse outcomes that can be specifically foreseen, emotional impacts also need to be taken into account, such as the irritation, fear and distress that may result from a data subject losing control over personal information, or realizing that it has been compromised. Relevant impact in a larger sense may also involve the way in which data are further processed: such as whether the data are processed by a different controller in another context with unknown consequences, whether the data are publicly disclosed or otherwise made accessible to a large number of persons, or whether large amounts of personal data are processed or combined with other data (e.g. in case of profiling, for commercial, law enforcement or other purposes), particularly if such operations were not foreseeable at the time of collection."[1240]

All of these considerations appear to be, at a first glance, obvious. However, the problem is how to justify them from a legal perspective. As long as these 'stand alone' without being justified pursuant to a consistent legal concept of protection, they appear to be arbitrarily selected. In this regard, the conclusion that the Working Group draws is particularly interesting. It states: "Again, in general, the more negative or *uncertain* the impact of further processing might be, the more unlikely it is to be considered as compatible use (underlining by the author)."[1241] With this statement, the Working Group clearly contradicts the conceptual idea, which requires stricter protection if the danger is more specific and intense.[1242] Instead, the protection provided for by the compatibility assessment is stricter so long as the less specific the threat is for the individual's right to

---

1240 See Article 29 Data Protection Working Group, ibid., pp. 25 and 26.

1241 See Article 29 Data Protection Working Group, ibid., p. 26.

1242 Cf. above under point C. I. 2. e) aa) In the public sector: Interplay between the three principles clarity of law, proportionality, and purpose limitation, referring, in particular, to BVerfG, 11th of March 2008, 1 BVR 2047/05 and 1 BvR 1254/07 (License Plate Recognition), cip. 95.

data protection (i.e. 'the more uncertain the impact of further processing might be'). Indeed, there might be three reasons for this conclusion.

First, it may implicitly refer to its previous consideration regarding 'the irritation, fear and distress that may result from a data subject losing control over personal information'. In this regard, the more uncertain the outcome of a later use of data is the more the individual may be distressed.[1243] Second, in doing so, the Group might indirectly refer to the function of purpose specification enhancing predictability. If the later use of data was not predictable for the individual, it is not likely to be compatible with the initial purpose.[1244] Thirdly, the Working Group might have had considerations related to the principle of clarity of law in mind. For example, as illustrated previously, the German Constitutional Court requires the State to pre-determine all purposes of the data processing. If the purpose specified the moment the data is collected is broad and does not exclude serious infringements (by the later use of the data), the law authorizing the data collection must also meet the strict requirements for these serious infringements.[1245] However, the principle of clarity of law applies to the State, only, and not to private parties. Since any action by the State must be based, irrespective of the details of the concept of the German right to informational self-determina-tion, on a law, such a law must indeed not be uncertain in order to meet the principle of clarity of law. In contrast, in the private sector, data controllers are not bound to the principle of clarity of law. Thus, if this really is the reason of the Working Group's consideration, this would impose the principle of clarity of law on private parties.[1246]

(d) Fourth criteria: 'Safeguards ensuring fairness and preventing undue impact'

The Working Group finally draws attention to the measures "that have been applied by the controller to ensure fair processing and to prevent any

1243 See Article 29 Data Protection Working Group, ibid., pp. 25 and 26.

1244 See Article 29 Data Protection Working Group, ibid., p. 13.

1245 See BVerfG, 11th of March 2008, 1 BVR 2047/05 and 1 BvR 1254/07 (License Plate Recognition), cip. 95 to 97.

1246 Cf. above under point C. II. 2. b) Further ambiguities and possible reasons behind the same.

undue impact on the data subjects."[1247] The Working Group considers these safeguards as important, in particular, because it is "an inherent characteristic of a multi-factor assessment (..) that deficiencies at certain points may in some cases be compensated by a better performance on other aspects. (…) Appropriate additional measures could thus, in principle, serve as 'compensation' for a change of purpose or for the fact that the purposes have not been specified as clearly in the beginning as they should have been. This might require technical and/or organizational measures to ensure functional separation (such as partial or full anonymization, pseudonymization, and aggregation of data), but also additional steps taken for the benefit of the data subjects, such as increased transparency, with the possibility to object or provide specific consent." With respect to the specification or change of purpose, the Working Group stresses that "a first necessary (but not always sufficient) condition towards ensuring compatibility is to re-specify the purposes. Often it is also necessary to provide additional notice to the data subjects and – depending on the circumstances and the legal basis of the further processing – it may be necessary to provide an opportunity to allow them to opt-in or opt-out. In some cases, requesting a specific separate consent for the new processing may, in particular, help compensate for the change of purpose. That is, a new legal basis under Article 7(a) can, in some situations, contribute to compensate for the incompatibility. It is important to reiterate, however, that the requirements of compatibility under Article 6(1)(b) and the requirement of an appropriate legal basis under Article 7 are cumulative. That is, a new legal basis alone cannot legitimize an otherwise incompatible further use."[1248]

These considerations are interesting in relation to two particular aspects: On the one hand, the Working Group loosens up its opinion on the requirement of purpose specification. In this regard, it actually advocates, as quoted previously, "that the purposes must be specified prior to, and in any event, not later than, the time when the collection of personal data occurs" and "must be detailed enough to determine what kind of processing is and is not included within the specified purpose, and to allow that compliance with the law can be assessed and data protection safeguards applied".[1249] It only confesses, so far, that "the degree of detail in which a

1247 See Article 29 Data Protection Working Group, ibid., p. 26.
1248 See Article 29 Data Protection Working Group, ibid., p. 26 and 27.
1249 See Article 29 Data Protection Working Group, ibid., p. 16.

purpose should be specified depends on the particular context in which the data are collected and the personal data involved."[1250] The Working Group appears now to re-balance this rather strict approach through its substantive compatibility assessment: The data controller is allowed to re-specify the original purposes that it had not sufficiently specified before through (depending on the particular case), first, notifying the individual concerned about the more specific purposes and, second, giving him or her the opportunity to opt-in or opt-out. Indeed, this re-balancing approach does not conflict with the requirement of purpose specification. The Working Party stressed that a purpose that was not sufficiently precise does not automatically lead to the unlawful processing of data. Instead, "it will be necessary to reconstruct the purposes of processing, keeping in mind the facts of the case."[1251]

On the other hand, the Working Group appears to consider situations where the individual cannot legitimize a change of purpose, not even through his or her consent. The reason for this assumption is that the Working Group cumulatively refers to the requirement of purpose compatibility and the legal grounds listed under Article 7 of the Data Protection Directive, without excluding the individual's consent under Article 7 lit. a.[1252] However, while it appears to be reasonable that any further processing of data must not only be compatible with the original purpose, but also be based on a legal provision under Article 7 sent. 1 lit. b to f of the directive, it is arguable if this cumulative requirement also applies to the individual's consent foreseen under Article 7 lit. a. The reason is that the requirement of purpose compatibility aims to ensure, in the Working Group's own opinion, that the individual is able to expect the later usage of the data and to exercise his or her rights 'in the most effective way'. Exemplifying such an 'effective way', it considers the possibility of the individual to object to the data processing.[1253] In order to achieve this aim, the individual's possibility to consent (which classically means opt-in) to a change of purpose is even more effective than his or her right to object (i.e. opt-out). Thus, there is no reason to forbid a later use of data, even if it is firstly not compatible with the original purpose, if the individual con-

1250 See Article 29 Data Protection Working Group, ibid., p. 16.
1251 See Article 29 Data Protection Working Group, ibid., p. 18.
1252 See the previous paragraphs referring to Article 29 Data Protection Working Group, ibid., p. 26 and 27.
1253 See Article 29 Data Protection Working Group, ibid., pp. 13 and 14.

sents to it. If the later use of data was not allowed, even if the individual gives his or her consent, the requirement of purpose compatibility would formulate into a formal and over-restrictive, if not paternalistic instrument substituting the individual's explicit will.

(4) Excursus: Compatibility of 'historical, statistical or scientific purposes'

Regarding the safeguards being implemented in order to comply with the requirement of purpose compatibility, the Data Protection Directive provides itself a rule regarding 'historical, statistical, and scientific purposes'. Article 6 sect. 1 lit. b sent. 2 of the directive states that further processing for those purposes "shall not be considered as incompatible provided that Member States provide appropriate safeguards". Article 5 sect. 1 lit. b sent. 2 of the General Data Protection Regulation contains the same rule. However, Article 98 of the regulation specifies this rule. On the one hand, its section 1 exemplifies appropriate safeguards, such as in order to ensure the principle of data minimisation and pseudonymisation. On the other hand, its sections 2 to 4 derogates certain rights of the individual concerned such as the right to rectification, data portability and to object the data processing. Whether or not the recommendations made by the Working Group with respect to Article 6 sect. 1 lit. b sent. 2 of the directive can equally be applied to Article 5 sect. 1 lit. b sent. 2, as well as Article 98 of the General Data Protection Regulation, is not clear. The recommendations shall however be illustrated in order to give a picture of the Working Group's thought process.

(a) Specification of the compatibility assessment (even prohibiting positive effects)

The Working Group advocates the notion to understand Article 6 sect. 1 lit. b sent. 2 of the directive, not as an exception to the general requirement of purpose compatibility, but rather as a specification of the rule. Thus, this provision does not authorize, in general, the further processing of personal data for historical, statistical or scientific purposes. Instead, the Working Group considers a substantive compatibility assessment (as well as one of the legal grounds listed under Article 7 of the Data Protection

Directive) as necessary also with respect to these purposes.[1254] The Working Group applies a comparably strict approach with respect to recital 29 of the directive. This recital states, in its second sentence, that the safeguards applied for the processing of data for historical, statistical or scientific purposes must "rule out the use of the data in support of measures or decisions regarding any particular individual". The Working Group is of the opinion that this requirement does not only refer to negative but also positive 'measures or decisions regarding any particular individual'.[1255] In any case, the Working Group stresses that it belongs to the EU Member States to specify the safeguards necessary for the compliance with the compatibility assessment and considers its scope of action as: "This specification is typically provided in legislation, which could be precise (e.g. national census or other official statistics) or more general (most other kinds of statistics or research). In the latter case, this leaves room for professional codes of conduct and/or further guidance released by the competent data protection authorities."[1256]

(b) Safeguards corresponding to the characteristics of the purposes

With a view to the particular safeguards that should be applied, the Working Group continues to specify the characteristics of 'historical', 'statistical' and 'scientific' purposes as: "'Statistical purposes' in particular, cover a wide range of processing activities, from commercial purposes (e.g. analytical tools of websites or big data applications aimed at market research) to public interests (e.g. statistical information produced from data collected by hospitals to determine the number of people injured as a result of road accidents). Data processing for 'historical purposes' may require, on the one hand, safeguards beyond anonymization such as security measures, in particular, restricted access if it concerns, for instance, court files or archives evidencing oppressive regimes. On the other hand, there may be little risk for individuals if the research refers to historic figures or familiar history. Regarding 'scientific purposes', the Working Group considers the specific needs of the controller resulting from the research question as: "Some research may require raw microdata, which are only partially

1254 See Article 29 Data Protection Working Group, ibid., p. 28.
1255 See Article 29 Data Protection Working Group, ibid., p. 28.
1256 See Article 29 Data Protection Working Group, ibid., p. 28.

anonymized or pseudonymised. In some cases, the research purpose can only be fulfilled if the pseudonymisation is reversible: for example, when research subjects need to be interviewed at a later stage in a longitudinal study. Other research, however, may require less detail, and therefore allow a higher level of aggregation and anonymization. Further publication of research results should, as a rule, be possible in such a way that only aggregated and/or otherwise fully anonymized data will be disclosed."[1257]

(c) Hierarchy of safeguards: From anonymization to functional separation

The Working Group finally lists and examines the possible safeguards that should be applied in order to meet, on the one hand, the characteristics of the research question and, on the other hand, to 'rule out the use of the data in support of measures or decisions regarding any particular individual'. The Working Group proposes a hierarchy of most important measures as: "Full anonymisation (including a high level of aggregation) is the most definite solution. It implies that there is no more processing of personal data and that the Directive is no longer applicable. Full anonymisation may, however, not be possible due to the nature of the processing (e.g. where there may be a need to re-identify the data subjects or a need to use more granular data that, as a side effect, may allow indirect identification). Furthermore, anonymisation is increasingly difficult to achieve with the advance of modern computer technology and the ubiquitous availability of information. (…) Partial anonymisation or partial re-identification may be the appropriate solution in some situations when complete anonymisation is not practically feasible. (…) Directly identifiable personal data may be processed only if anonymisation or partial anonymisation is not possible without frustrating the purpose of the processing, and further provided that other appropriate and effective safeguards are in place."[1258] The Working Party lists additional measures such as:[1259]

- Encryption.
- Coding or encryption as well as separate storage of keys themselves.

1257 See Article 29 Data Protection Working Group, ibid., p. 29.
1258 See Article 29 Data Protection Working Group, ibid., pp. 30 and 31.
1259 See Article 29 Data Protection Working Group, ibid., p. 32.

- Access control (technically, organizationally and legally safeguarded).
- Consent as exclusive legitimate basis for the processing of sensitive data.

In order to implement these additional measures, the term 'functional separation' plays an essential role. This is particularly the case if the data cannot be fully anonymized and there are several parties involved in the data processing. The Working Group stresses for "this context, some research projects may require very precise protocols (rules and procedures) to ensure a strict functional separation between participants in the research and outside stakeholders. This may include technical and organizational measures, such as securely key-coding the personal data transferred and prohibiting outside stakeholders from re-identifying data subjects (as in the case of clinical trials and pharmaceuticals research) and possible other measures."[1260] In conclusion, since the Working Group considers the special provision regarding 'historical, statistical, and scientific purposes' not as exception from the compatibility assessment, but as its specification, data controllers should take all these measures into account in order to also comply with the general compatibility assessment.

cc) Purpose identity required by the ePrivacy Directive

In contrast to the requirement of purpose compatibility provided for by the Data Protection Directive, the ePrivacy Directive requires, in principle, the identity of purposes. So long as the data controller processes the four types of data (and for certain purposes) listed in the ePrivacy Directive, it's further use of data is strictly limited to the purposes specified within the authorizing law.

(1) Strict purpose identity for the processing of 'communication data', 'traffic data' and 'location data other than traffic data'

As set out previously, Article 5 of the ePrivacy Directive permits the processing of 'communications and the related traffic data' only under the following conditions:

1260 See Article 29 Data Protection Working Group, ibid., p. 29.

1. Always if it is based on the user's consent (sect. 1 sent. 2);
2. Its storage only if it is necessary for the conveyance of a communication (sect. 1 sent. 3);
3. The recording of communications and related traffic data carried out in the course of lawful business practice for the purpose of evidence of a commercial transaction or of any other business communication if it is legally authorized (sect. 2); and
4. Finally, the storing of information, or the gaining of access to information already stored, in the terminal equipment of a subscriber or user, here again, on the basis of his or her consent, for the sole purpose of carrying out the transmission of a communication over an electronic communications network, or if it is strictly necessary for the provider of an Information Society service explicitly requested by the subscriber or user to provide the service' (sect. 3).

Article 6 of the ePrivacy Directive authorizes, in essence, the processing of 'traffic data' only if it is:

1. Made anonymous the moment where it is no longer needed for the purpose of the transmission of a communication (sect. 1);
2. For the purposes of subscriber billing and interconnection payments (sect. 2);
3. And for the purposes of marketing electronic communications services or for the provision of value added services as long as it is necessary for the marketing or service or if the subscriber or the user has given his or her prior consent (sect. 3); in the last respect, article 2 lit. g of the directive defines the term of 'value added service' as "any service which requires the processing of traffic data or location data beyond what is necessary for the transmission of a communication or the billing thereof."

Concerning the third type, location data other than traffic data, the requirements are the strictest. Article 9 of the ePrivacy Directive authorizes its processing only if it is made anonymous or with the consent of the subscribers or users.

(2) The individual's consent as an exclusive legal basis for a change of purpose

It became apparent in the preceding illustration that the processing of personal data is actually allowed always if it is based on the individual's consent. This is particularly important for a change of purpose: If the data controller wants to process the data for another purpose than specified within the law or in an individual's consent that he or she has provided, the data controller must base this change of purpose, again, on the individual's consent. The data controller can, hence, not base the data processing on another legal basis, such as a general clause for its legitimate interests, by applying the compatibility assessment.

dd) Interim conclusion: A lack in the legal scale for compatibility assessment

As analyzed above, the European Court of Human Rights does primarily refer to the individual's 'reasonable expectations' in order to assess an infringement of his or her right to private life. In doing so, the Court inherently examines, first, the purpose initially specified by the controller, second, to which extent the later use deviates from this initial purpose and though conflicts, third, with the expectations of the individual.[1261] In contrast, the European Court of Justice does not refer, so far, to the 'reasonable expectations' mechanism.[1262] Furthermore, the wording of Article 8 ECFR reveals that the right to data protection provides for the requirement of purpose specification, only. It does not mention, at least not explicitly, the individual's 'reasonable expectations' or the requirement of purpose compatibility. Hence, the European Court of Justice is principally free to discuss this requirement under the following two options: Either, under the right to private life in Article 7, which corresponds to Article 8 ECHR (eventually, also under further fundamental rights to freedom and equality that may be specifically concerned); or under the right to data protection in Article 8 ECFR, which is only based on Article 8 ECHR.

An examination of secondary law reveals three particular aspects: First, as mentioned previously, both the Data Protection Directive and the General Data Protection Regulation aim to protect not only the right to private life, but also other fundamental rights. While the directive states in its Article 1 sect. 1 that "Member States shall protect the fundamental rights and

---

1261 See above under point C. I. 3. b) ee) Conclusion: Assessment of 'reasonable expectations' on case-by-case basis.

1262 Cf. above under point C. I. 3. c) bb) (2) Protection going beyond Article 8 ECHR.

freedoms of natural persons, and in particular their right to privacy with respect to the processing of personal data", Article 1 sect. 2 of the regulation clarifies to protect "fundamental rights and freedoms of natural persons and in particular their right to the protection of personal data."[1263] Second, in doing so, the European legislator tied, possibly, into the concept of protection provided for by Article 8 ECHR, however not establishing the individual's 'reasonable expectations', but the inherent requirements of purpose specification and purpose compatibility. Interestingly, in the decision of "*González vs. Google Spain*", the European Court of Justice did not even assess, at least not explicitly, the requirement of purpose compatibility. Instead, the Court referred to other requirements such as the 'relevance', 'adequacy', and 'necessity' of the later data processing. The reference to these requirements enables, principally, the Court to assess the appropriateness of the data processing from a more objective point of view than by referring to the individual's 'reasonable expectations'.[1264] However, third, with respect to the individual's consent, which is explicitly provided for by Article 8 ECFR, the European Court of Justice requires purpose identity. Indeed, what this means, in light of the risk-based approach proposed in this thesis, will be examined later on.

The Article 29 Data Protection Working Group considers, in contrast to the European legislator, the compatibility assessment as closely connected with the individual's 'reasonable expectations' and, thus, apparently ties into the concept of protection provided for by the European Court of Human Rights with respect to Article 8 ECHR.[1265] However, as analyzed previously, the term of 'reasonable expectations' is quite vague and lacks a legal scale in order to help to determine which expectations are 'reasonable' and which are not. Unfortunately, the further criteria proposed by the Working Group in order to carry out the compatibility assessment are not more specific. The Group proposes, for example, to measure the 'distance' between the original purpose and the later usage. In fact, this criteria is

---

1263 See already above under point C. II. 1. b) dd) Data Protection Directive and General Data Protection Regulation, referring to the discussion about this terminological (and conceptual) shift from "privacy" to "data protection" at González-Fuster, The Emergence of Data Protection as a Fundamental Right of the EU.

1264 See above under point C. III. 1. a) aa) (2) ECJ: Reference to data protection instruments instead of 'reasonable expectations', referring to ECJ C-131/12, cip. 93.

1265 See Article 29 Data Protection Working Group, ibid., p. 13.

just the same as the second criteria referring to the 'reasonable expectations' but in another form: The broader the distance between the new and the initial purpose is, the less the individual has to expect that the data processing now occurs for this new purpose. Similarly, the terms 'context', 'nature of the data', and 'impact on the individual' do not provide for more reliable criteria. They equally lack a legal scale for answering questions as: which context is legally relevant for the data processing and requires which protection instruments?; and which data is sensitive, and which impact on the individual is legally relevant.[1266] Only an objective legal scale can reliably reduce the high legal uncertainty resulting from the bundle of criteria because it structures these criteria and helps to answer which protection instruments must be applied in a particular case.

There are further problematic aspects of the compatibility assessment that result from a general lack of clarity in regards to the legal scale. One aspect is that the Working Group exclusively refers, in order to assess the later use of personal data, to the initial purpose. Declaring the moment of collection of the data to the main reference for the protection instrument(s), irrespective of the specific risks existing at that time, the Group excludes protection against the before mentioned case: theoretically, it is possible that the "new" current purpose is indeed compatible with the initial purpose, but not with a purpose that was specified after the collection but before this new purpose. At least, the complexity of modern data economy makes it possible that the transfer of data from the initial context into the current context does not interfere with the individual's 'reasonable expectations', however, the transfer of that data from another intermediary context does. Another problematic aspect is that the Working Group does not justify, on the grounds of analytical legal reasoning, why the compatibility assessment and the legal basis which the data processing must be based on are cumulative and not alternative requirements. Such a cumulative requirement is particularly questionable with regard to the consent. The Working Group appears to consider that the individual's consent cannot always legitimize non-compatible purposes. This is arguable because the individual's explicit consent is actually more precise than his or her 'reasonable expectations' and, thus, the stronger form of his or her expression of autonomy. Therefore, the consent given at a later stage by an indi-

1266 See above point C. III. 1. a) bb) (3) Criteria for the substantive compatibility assessment, and already under point B. III. 5. Values as normative scale determining "contexts" and "purposes".

vidual should usually substitute the 'reasonable expectations' that he or she already had when the data was first collected.[1267]

In conclusion, without an objective legal scale, it is impossible to answer the question of how to interpret the requirement in Article 6 sect. 1 lit. b of the Data Protection Directive that personal data must not be 'further processed in a way incompatible with those purposes" originally specified. The same problem will arise with the homologue requirement under Article 5 sect. 1 lit. b of the General Data Protection Regulation. The General Data Protection Regulation only repeats, in its Article 6 sect. 4, the same bundle of criteria as already proposed by the Working Group with respect to the directive. In this regard, a particular question is: under which circumstances is it necessary to require data controllers to strictly limit the later data processing to the initially specified purpose and when is it appropriate to allow them to process the data, later on, so long as this is not incompatible with the initial purpose?

b) German model: Purpose identity and proportionate change of purpose

Prior to elaborating on a possible solution for the questions posed precedingly, it is useful to examine the principle of purpose limitation provided for by German law. As already mentioned by the Article 29 Data Protection Working Group, the German legislator did not directly transpose the requirement of purpose compatibility into German ordinary law but instead, applied a balancing test. The next chapter will examine in detail how the German legislator carried out these balancing tests within the ordinary law applicable in the private sector. In order to find a potential reason for why the German legislator has established balancing tests instead of establishing, explicitly, the requirement of purpose compatibility, the second chapter will examine the principle of purpose limitation with respect to the concept of protection of the German right to informational self-determina-tion. Perhaps, just as with respect to the requirement to specify the purpose, the German legislator referred to conceptual elements of this German right rather than to the European concept of protection, which was not yet comparably developed. Finally, alternative concepts

1267 See above under point C. III. 1. a) bb) (1) Preliminary analysis: Pre-conditions and consequences.

provided for in legal literature will be considered in order to give insights into the diversity of functions that the principle of purpose limitation can basically have. This may provide a source of inspiration for elaborating on the function of the principle of purpose limitation with respect to the European Charter of Fundamental Rights.

aa) Change of purpose in the private sector pursuant to ordinary law

As mentioned previously, the German Constitutional Court has developed the principle of purpose limitation with respect to the State. In contrast to the European approach, the German Court principally requires, elaborating on the concept of the right to informational self-determination, the identity of purposes and makes, in a second step, exemptions from this strict requirement allowing a change of purpose so long as this change is not disproportionate. Examining ordinary data protection laws, the German legislator appears to have transposed these requirements, not only in the public sector, but also in the private sector. While the Telecommunication Law and Telemedia Law require the identity of purposes (corresponding to the ePrivacy Directive), the Federal Data Protection Law provides, by means of the balancing tests, for a more liberal approach exempting several purposes of data processing from the strict requirement of purpose identity. This approach leads to a rather complex legal system of requirements, exceptions and counter-exceptions.

(1) Strict purpose identity required by Telemedia Law and Telecommunication Law

The ePrivacy Directive does not regulate, as mentioned previously, Information Society services. In contrast, the Telemedia Law does, by extending the requirements provided for by the ePrivacy Directive also to so-called telemedia services (which is similar to Information Society services). Article 12 sect. 2 of the Telemedia Law establishes the general requirement that a "service provider is only allowed to use personal data collected for the purpose of providing telemedia services for other purposes if it is authorized by the Telemedia Law or another legal provision explicitly referring to the Telemedia Law or if it is based on the user's consent." Outside the Telemedia Law, there are no such provisions. Inside the

Telemedia Law, there is Article 14 sect. 2, regarding data related to a contract, and, concerning usage data, Article 15 sect. 5 sent. 4.[1268] These provisions mainly authorize a change of purpose for the purposes of criminal prosecution, defense of danger, and the execution of immaterial property rights. In contrast, the German Telecommunication Law does not foresee a general requirement of purpose identity. However, the requirement of purpose identity results from the provisions that authorize the processing of telecommunication data for specific purposes as illustrated previously.[1269]

(2) The more nuanced approach established by the Federal Data Protection Law

The Federal Data Protection Law also does not explicitly provide for a general requirement of purpose identity. The German legal scholar v. Zezschwitz underlines that this requirement results, rather, from the systematic overview of the different provisions with respect to the constitutional requirements provided for by the right to informational self-determination and the protection of the individual's privacy.[1270] Explicitly, the German Federal Data Protection Law only establishes the requirement of purpose specification, for the data controller's own purposes in Article 28 sect. 1 sent. 2 and for third parties purposes under Article 29 sect. 1 sent. 2.[1271] Article 28 sect. 2 and sect. 5 sent. 2, as well as Article 29 sect. 4 furthermore regulate under which conditions the data controller is allowed to use the data for other purposes than initially specified. Legal scholars criticize the broadness of the balancing tests established in these provisions authorizing a change of purpose. Bergmann et alt. consider, for example, the provision as an "practically, unlimited exemption from the re-

1268 See Schreibauer, Federal Data Protection Law and further Provision, § 12 TMG, cip. 6 to 9.

1269 See above under pojnt C. II. 1. c) aa) Purposes of processing authorized by the Telecommunication Law.

1270 See v. Zezschwitz, Concept of normative Purpose Limitation, cip. 6.

1271 See already above under point C. II. 1. c) cc) (1) Three basic legitimate grounds.

quirement of purpose limitation".[1272] Simitis concludes from the regulation that the principle of purpose limitation is "actually abolished".[1273]

The reason for this criticism is that these provisions essentially require the same legal conditions for a change of purpose as was already necessary when the data was collected.[1274] Pursuant to these provisions, the later use of data for another purpose than initially specified, is allowed under the following two alternative conditions:

1. The purpose change is "necessary to safeguard justified interests of the controller of the filing system and there is no reason to assume that the data subject has an overriding legitimate interest in his data being excluded from processing" or
2. "the data are generally accessible (…), unless the data subject's legitimate interest in his data being excluded from processing or use clearly outweighs the justified interest of the controller".

Thus, only the purpose foreseen under Article 28 sect. 1 sent. 1 no. 1 ("when needed to create, carry out or terminate a legal obligation or quasi-legal obligation with the data subject") does not justify a change of purpose. However, Article 28 sect. 2 foresees in its no. 2 and 3 further exemptions from the requirement of purpose identity. For example, a change of purpose is equally allowed if it is "necessary to protect the legitimate interests of a third party and there is no reason to believe that the data subject has a legitimate interest in excluding transfer or use" (no. 2 lit. a). In light of the broadness of these provisions, some legal scholars promote the notion to restrictively interpret these balancing tests, given the compatibility assessment required by the Data Protection Directive. For example, Bergmann et alt. promote that a new purpose different to the initial one principally conflicts, as a general rule, with the confidentiality interests of the individual concerned.[1275] In any event, in order to interpret the German law, which transposes the European directive, it is necessary to elabo-

---

1272 See Bergmann/Möhrle/Herb, BDSG, § 28 Rn. 493: "Allerdings sieht Satz 2 die Möglichkeit von Zweckänderungen vor, was aufgrund der praktisch grenzenlosen Durchbrechung des Zweckbindungsprinzips nicht nur (...)."

1273 See Simitis, Federal Data Protection Law, § 28 cip. 284.

1274 See article 28 sect. 2 and sect. 5 sent. 2 as well as article 29 sect. 4, all of them referring to article 28 sect. 1 sent. 1 no. 2 and 3.

1275 See Bergmann/Möhrle/Herb, BDSG, § 28 Rn. 497; see also Simitis, ibid., cip. 290.

rate on reliable criteria that help interpret the European compatibility assessment.

For certain types of purposes, the German Federal Data Protection Law requires a stricter limitation of purposes. For example, for marketing and address trading purposes, Article 28 sect. 3 sent. 7 limits the later use of data to the initial purpose, that means, it requires purpose identity. For purposes of market research in favor of third parties, Article 30a sect. 2 provides for a three-layered limitation:

1. Personal data which do not originate from publically available sources may only be used for the specific research project for which it was collected;
2. In contrast, the later use of data from publically available sources is not limited to the specific research project, instead, this data may be used for any kind of 'market research';
3. Finally, data collected for 'market research' may only be used for other purposes if the data is made anonymous.

For research purposes in general, Article 28 sect. 2 no. 3 authorizes, on the one hand, a change of purpose "if scientific interest in conduct of the research project substantially outweighs the interest of the data subject in excluding the change of purpose and if the research purpose cannot be attained by other means or can be attained thus only with disproportionate effort." On the other hand, Article 40 sect. 1 forbids, once the data was used for such a research purpose, its use for another purpose. Indeed, the extent of this requirement is debated amongst legal scholars. In particular, it is discussed whether this requirement refers to 'research purposes' as such, allowing the re-use of that data also for other research projects, or whether it goes one step beyond limiting the re-use of the data to the specific research project for that it was initially used.[1276] Proposing a compromise, some legal scholars only require a substantial link between the initial and the subsequent research project. These scholars seek to broaden the scope of research action while avoiding, simultaneously, that data initially used for medical research may be used, for instance, for military research.[1277] However, even if this approach moderates between both contrasting positions, it lacks not only reliable criteria in order to determine

1276 See Greve (Auernhammer), § 40 cip. 11.

1277 See Greve (Auernhammer), § 40 cip. 11 as well as Lindner, Data protection in the Federal State and the Länder, § 40, cip. 23.

the substantial link required, but also a convincing reason for why such a substantial link is necessary from a legal point of view.

Finally, Article 31 requires a strict purpose limitation for "personal data stored exclusively for the purposes of data protection control or data security or to ensure the proper operation of a data processing system". This requirement is particularly relevant with respect to employees working in the IT environment. For example, protocol data exclusively stored in relation with access control systems must not be used for other purposes such as for monitoring the employees. Since this requirement is considered as a statutory prohibition within the meaning of article 134 of the German Civil Law, private parties, such as the employer and the employee cannot demolish this prohibitive requirement by means of bilateral agreements. However, some legal scholars argue that it is possible to bilaterally agree that this kind of data is *not exclusively* stored for data security purposes but also for further purposes. In this case, the strict requirement of purpose identity provided for by article 31 of the Federal Data Protection Law shall not apply.[1278]

In conclusion, the Federal Data Protection Law does not require a strict purpose limitation. The reason is that the law authorizes the change of purpose almost under the same conditions the data that was already collected. Only for certain types of purposes, such as for research purposes, does the law establish exemptions from this rule limiting the later use of the data to the initial purpose. Therefore, there are two questions: first, why did the legislator establish such a double-layered system?; and second, do the balancing tests, as a part of this double-layered system, differ to the European compatibility assessment?

bb) Comparison with the principles developed by the German Constitutional Court for the public sector

In order to answer this question, it is necessary to examine the function of the principle of purpose limitation within the concept of protection of the right to informational self-determination. So far, there is only one decision by the German Constitutional Court that provides for an extensive reasoning on the effects of this right in the private sector. This decision mainly

1278 See Eßer, Federal Data Protection Law and further Provisions, § 31 cip. 7 and 8.

referred to the specification of the purpose and not to the second component, i.e. the limitation of the later use to the original purpose.[1279] Therefore, this chapter focuses on the principle of purpose limitation with respect to the public sector in order to find criteria that might help understand the function of the principle of purpose limitation also in the private sector.

(1) Strict requirement of purpose identity limiting the intensity of the infringement

In Germany, as already stated, the principle of purpose limitation principally requires the identity of purposes. This strict requirement of purpose identity results from the particularities of the concept of protection of the German right to informational self-determination. As stated previously, the German Constitutional Court considers that this right "supplements and broadens the constitutional protection of freedom of action and of being private by expanding it already to the level of danger for the personality" before there is a specific threat for an object of protection.[1280] In order to implement this guarantee, the Constitutional Court sets up an individual's 'right to basically determine by him or herself about the disclosure and the usage of his or her personal data' as the main protection instrument.[1281] As a consequence, the German Constitutional Court principally considers each act of collection and processing by the State – such as the storage, filtering, and transferal – of personal data as an infringement of

1279 See illustrated above under point C. I. 1. b) aa) (3) German Basic Rights.

1280 See BVerfG, 11th of March 2008, 1 BVR 2047/05 and 1 BvR 1254/07 (License Plate Recognition), cip. 64: "Dieses Recht flankiert und erweitert den grundrechtlichen Schutz von Verhaltensfreiheit und Privatheit; es lässt ihn schon auf der Stufe der Persönlichkeitsgefährdung beginnen. Eine derartige Gefährdungslage kann bereits im Vorfeld konkreter Bedrohungen von Rechtsgütern entstehen."

1281 See BVerfG, 15th of December 1983, 1 BvR 209, 269, 362, 420, 440, 484/83 (Decision on Population Census), cip. 173; cf. equally BVerfG, 14th of July 1999, 1 BvR 2226/94 (Surveillance of Telecommunications), cip. 136 and BVerfG, 3rd of March 2004, 1 BvR 2378/98 (Big Eavesdropping Operation), cip. 132 and BVerfG, 4th of April 2006, 1 BvR 518/02 (Dragnet Investigation), cip. 64 and BVerfG, 13th June 2007, 1 BvR 1550/03 (Retrieval of Bank Account Master Data), cip. 63; BVerfG, 1 BvR 2027/02 (Release of Confidentiality), cip. 31.

the scope of protection.[1282] Given that such a right shall not be an absolute right but rather be considered with regard to its function in society as a whole, the Court seeks to restrain the broadness of its scope in two ways. First, by precisely determining which acts actually infringe the scope of protection and, thus, by prudently restricting the scope of protection. And second, by using a balancing exercise, taking the intensity of the infringement into account. For both ways, the specification of the purpose provides an essential legal link. However, since the criteria for determining the infringement itself are not yet clearly developed by the Court,[1283] the specification of the purpose plays a more important role in order to determine the intensity of the infringement.[1284] In this regard, the requirement of purpose limitation builds upon the requirement of purpose specification and limits the intensity of the infringement.[1285]

In the cases of "*License Plate Recognition*", "*Retrieval of Bank Account Master Data*", and "*Surveillance of Telecommunications*", the German Constitutional Court clarifies how the requirement of purpose identity limits the intensity of the infringement referring to the interplay of the principle of clarity of law and the principle of proportionality. In the first mentioned case, the Court stressed that "the individual has only to accept infringements of his or her right if they are based on a constitutionally legal provision. The legal requirements depend on the type and intensity of the infringement of the basic right. They (the requirements) refer, on the one hand, to the required clarity of law and, on the other hand, to the principle of proportionality (words in brackets added by the author)."[1286] Both prin-

1282 See Härting, Purpose limitation and change of purpose in data protection law, p. 3284; and above under point C. I. 2. c) Right to control disclosure and usage of personal data as a protection instrument.

1283 See above under point C. I. 2. d) Infringement by 'insight into personality' and 'particularity of state interest'.

1284 See above under point C. I. 2. e) aa) In the public sector: Interplay of the three principles clarity of law, proportionality, and purpose limitation.

1285 See Britz, Informational Self-Determination between Legal Doctrine and Constitutional Case Law, p. 584.

1286 See BVerfG, 11th of March 2008, 1 BVR 2047/05 and 1 BvR 1254/07 (License Plate Recognition), cip. 75: "Der Einzelne muss jedoch nur solche Beschränkungen seines Rechts hinnehmen, die auf einer verfassungsmäßigen gesetzlichen Grundlage beruhen. Die Anforderungen an die Ermächtigungsgrundlage richten sich nach der Art und Intensität des Grundrechtseingriffs (..). Sie betreffen zum einen die gebotene Normenbestimmtheit und Normenklarheit (..) und zum anderen den Grundsatz der Verhältnismäßigkeit (..)."

ciples therefore interact with each other. If the legal provision is unclear because it does not exclude purposes that intensively infringe the right to informational self-determination, the examination of whether or not the provision meets the requirement of proportionality must also take these purposes into account.[1287] In the second mentioned case, the Court made clear the interplay of the principle of clarity of law and the principle of purpose limitation. It stated: "If a legal provision authorizes an infringement of the right to informational self-determination, the principle of clarity of law has a specific function to provide a sufficiently precise determination of the purpose of usage for the information concerned. It hence supplements the constitutionally required purpose limitation with respect to the information retrieved."[1288] In the third mentioned case, the Court finally specified the function of the requirement of purpose limitation as: "Since the protection (…) does not end in the moment a state agency has become aware of the event of communication, the requirements provided for by this fundamental right also apply to the transfer of that data and information which has been retrieved (…). This is even more important in light of the fact that the transfer does not only regularly lead to an extension of the public agencies or persons which are informed about the communication but also to a change of usage context which means additional and potentially higher disadvantages than in the original context."[1289]

1287 See BVerfG, ibid., cip. 163.

1288 See BVerfG, 4th of April 2006, 1 BvR 518/02 (Retrieval of Bank Account Master Data), cip. 73: "Ermächtigt eine gesetzliche Regelung zu einem Eingriff in das Recht auf informationelle Selbstbestimmung, so hat das Gebot der Bestimmtheit und Klarheit die spezifische Funktion, eine hinreichend präzise Umgrenzung des Verwendungszwecks der betroffenen Informationen sicherzustellen. Auf diese Weise wird das verfassungsrechtliche Gebot der Zweckbindung der erhobenen Information verstärkt."

1289 See BVerfG, ibid., cip. 139: "Da die Kommunikation ihren von Art. 10 GG vermittelten Geheimnisschutz nicht dadurch verliert, daß bereits eine staatliche Stelle von dem Fernmeldevorgang Kenntnis erlangt hat, beziehen sich die Anforderungen des Grundrechts auch auf die Weitergabe der Daten und Informationen, die unter Aufhebung des Fernmeldegeheimnisses erlangt worden sind. Das gilt um so mehr, als es sich bei der Weitergabe regelmäßig nicht nur um eine Ausweitung der Stellen oder Personen, die über die Kommunikation informiert werden, sondern um die Überführung der Daten in einen anderen Verwendungszusammenhang handelt, der für die Betroffenen mit zusätzlichen, unter Umständen schwereren Folgen verbunden ist als im ursprünglichen Verwendungszusammenhang."

In conclusion, the principle of purpose limitation primarily results from the individual's right to principally 'determine by him or herself about the disclosure and later usage of the data'. This mechanism would be undermined if the controller of the data processing was not limited to the purpose initially specified.[1290] With respect to the State, the principle of clarity of law supplements this principle requiring a sufficiently precise determination of the purpose of the later use. Thus, the strict requirement of purpose identity limits, in terms of proportionality of law, the intensity of the infringement.

(2) Proportionate change of purpose

However, in the same decision of "*Surveillance of Telecommunications*", the Court also clarified that "the principle of purpose limitation does not generally exclude a change of purpose. Indeed, such a change of purpose must also be based on a legal provision that is formally and substantively proportionate with the basic law. This requirement means that a change of purpose is justified by prevailing public interests. The new purpose of usage must refer to the tasks and capability of the public agency to which the data are transferred and be sufficiently clear. Furthermore, the purpose of usage for which the data are collected and the changed purpose of usage must not be incompatible with each other."[1291] The change of purpose would hence be disproportionate if it would circumvent a legal prohibition of collecting data.[1292] In the case of "*Data Retention*", the Court exemplified this requirement as: "A transfer of the telecommunication data re-

---

1290 Cf. Forgó et al., Purpose Specification and Informational Separation of Powers, pp. 11 and 12.

1291 See BVerfG, ibid., cip. 140: "Zwar schließt der Grundsatz der Zweckbindung Zweckänderungen nicht rundweg aus. Sie bedürfen jedoch ihrerseits einer gesetzlichen Grundlage, die formell und materiell mit dem Grundgesetz vereinbar ist. Dazu gehört, daß die Zweckänderungen durch Allgemeinbelange gerechtfertigt sind, die die grundrechtlich geschützten Interessen überwiegen. Der neue Verwendungszweck muß sich auf die Aufgaben und Befugnisse der Behörde beziehen, der die Daten übermittelt werden, und hinreichend normenklar geregelt sein. Ferner dürfen der Verwendungszweck, zu dem die Erhebung erfolgt ist, und der veränderte Verwendungszweck nicht miteinander unvereinbar sein (...)."

1292 See, for example, BVerfG, 10th of March 2008, 1 BvR 2388/03 (Behördliche Datensammlung – Data collection by public authorities), cip. 91 to 93.

ceived to other (state) agencies can be only authorized by law if it serves the execution of tasks for that a direct access to the data (by the other agency) would also be directly allowed."[1293] However, in the preceding case of "*Surveillance of Telecommunications*", the Court had already clarified that this constitutional proportionality test must also take the means into account that the state agencies may apply in order fulfill the respective purposes and, as a consequence, which data precisely is transferred. In this case, the Intelligence Service was authorized to collect large sets of data for the less intensively infringing purpose of strategic control. In contrast, the other state agency was authorized to collect limited data for the more intensively infringing purpose of prevention, investigation, and prosecution of crimes. Thus, the Court considered the second purpose as more intensively infringing the right to informational self-determination than the purpose of strategic control. The question therefore was whether or not, and if so, to what extent the Intelligence service was allowed to transfer its data to the other agency or, in other words, under which conditions this was a disproportionate change of purpose.[1294]

The German Constitutional Court affirmed that this transfer of limited data was not incompatible or, in the Court's current words, was compatible with the original purpose as: "The purposes (of prevention and prosecution of crimes changed later on) are compatible with the original purposes which justified the collection of the data (…). The surveillance of telecommunication that the Intelligence Service is allowed to carry out even in the absence of a specific suspicion indeed is legitimate only for (the purpose) of strategic control. Its essence consists in the fact that it does not lead to measures taken against certain persons but refers to international situations of danger about that the federal government shall be informed. Only this limited purpose justifies the broadness and severity of the infringement of basic rights. If they pursued from the beginning to prevent and prosecute crimes, the provisions (authorizing the data collection) would not be justified on the grounds of Article 10 GG. (…) However, Ar-

1293 See BVerfG, 2nd March 2010, 1 BvR 256/08, 1 BvR 263/08, and 1 BvR 586/08 (Data Retention), cip. 236: "Eine Weitergabe der übermittelten Telekommunikationsverkehrsdaten an andere Stellen darf gesetzlich dementsprechend nur vorgesehen werden, soweit sie zur Wahrnehmung von Aufgaben erfolgt, deretwegen ein Zugriff auf diese Daten auch unmittelbar zulässig wäre (...)."

1294 See BVerfG, 14th of July 1999, 1 BvR 2226/94 (Surveillance of Telecommunications) cip. 233 to 235.

ticle 10 GG does not exclude any transfer of data to public agencies that are not allowed to survey telecommunications even in the absence of specific suspicions (…). Since the Intelligence Service collects, applying its legitimate means, a multitude of telecommunications that are irrelevant for the receiving agencies, though, it must be guaranteed that these (receiving agencies) do not get access to the complete data set. In contrast, the transfer of information being, as a result of due diligence, relevant for the prevention, investigation or prosecution of crimes to public agencies listed under (…/the offended law) does not conflict with the original purpose even if this is different to the new purpose."[1295] In light of these considerations, the Court came to the conclusion that the law authorizing the change of purpose, i.e. the data transfer, was proportionate because it limited the

---

1295 See BVerfG, ibid., cip. 233 to 235: "Die Zwecke sind ferner mit dem ursprünglichen Zweck, der die Erhebung der Daten unter Beschränkung des Fernmeldegeheimnisses gerechtfertigt hat (...), vereinbar. Zwar ist die verdachtslose Fernmeldeüberwachung, die der Bundesnachrichtendienst vornehmen darf, nur zur strategischen Kontrolle zulässig. Ihr Charakteristikum besteht darin, daß sie nicht auf Maßnahmen gegenüber bestimmten Personen abzielt, sondern internationale Gefahrenlagen betrifft, über die die Bundesregierung unterrichtet werden soll. Nur dieser begrenzte Verwendungszweck rechtfertigt die Breite und die Tiefe der Grundrechtseingriffe. Zielten sie von vornherein auf Zwecke der Verhinderung oder Verfolgung von Straftaten, ließe sich die Befugnis dazu nicht mit Art. 10 GG vereinbaren (...). Grundrechtsgebotene Beschränkungen des Einsatzes bestimmter Erhebungsmethoden dürfen nicht dadurch umgangen werden, daß Daten, die mit einer solchen Methode rechtmäßigerweise zu bestimmten Verwendungszwecken erhoben worden sind, in gleicher Weise auch für Zwecke zugänglich gemacht werden, die einen derartigen Methodeneinsatz nicht rechtfertigen würden. Art. 10 GG schließt aber nicht jegliche Übermittlung an Behörden aus, denen eine verdachtslose Fernmeldeüberwachung nicht zusteht oder nicht zugestanden werden dürfte. Da der Bundesnachrichtendienst aufgrund der ihm gestatteten Methode notwendig eine Vielzahl von Fernmeldevorgängen erfaßt, die von vornherein für die Empfangsbehörden irrelevant sind, muß allerdings sichergestellt sein, daß diesen nicht der Zugang zu dem vollen Datenbestand eröffnet wird. Dagegen widerspricht es dem Primärzweck nicht, daß diejenigen Erkenntnisse, die - obwohl unter anderen Gesichtspunkten erhoben - für die Verhinderung, Aufklärung oder Verfolgung von Straftaten relevant sind, nach sorgfältiger Prüfung an die in § 3 Abs. 5 G 10 genannten Behörden weitergegeben werden. Mit den Vorgaben der angegriffenen Übermittlungsregelung - Übermittlungsschwelle sowohl nach § 3 Abs. 5 Satz 1 als auch nach § 3 Abs. 3 Satz 1 G 10, besondere Prüfung durch einen Bediensteten mit Befähigung zum Richteramt in § 3 Abs. 5 Satz 2 G 10 - sind die insoweit zu stellenden Anforderungen erfüllt."

transfer to cases where: First, concrete circumstances exist giving rise to the suspicion that an individual plans to commit, is committing or has committed a certain crime listed in the law; and second, these requirements must be proven, before the data transfer, by a person being qualified to hold judicial office.[1296]

In the last recent case of "*Federal Criminal Police Office Act*", the Constitutional Court also refined this part of the concept of protection surrounding the principle of purpose limitation. As illustrated previously, the Court had clarified the criteria to be considered in order to answer the question of whether a later use of data pursues the same purpose as in the moment of collection of the data or whether it must be considered as a change of purpose. If the data is used by the same public agency, for the same task, and serves the same object of protection as already specified in the legal provision authorizing the collection of that data, the later use does not constitute a change of purpose.[1297] However, if the later use constitutes, pursuant to these criteria, a change of purpose, there is a new infringement of the same basic right that the data collection had infringed. So far, the Court clarifies this as: "A change of purpose must thus comply with the basic right that was decisive for the collection of the data. (…) The legal provision authorizing a change of purpose has to meet the principle of proportionality. Doing the balancing exercise, the importance of this law must correspond to the severity of the infringement of the data collection. Information that has been gathered by a particular severe infringement can be used, correspondingly, only for a particular important purpose."[1298] In conclusion, if the later use of data serves, for example, an-

1296 See BVerfG, ibid., cip. 235.

1297 See above under point C. II. 1. c) ee) (1) (d) Liberalization of the strict requirement by referring to the object of protection, referring to BVerfG, 20th of April 2016, 1 BvR 966/09 and 1 BvR 1140/09 (Federal Bureau of Investigation Law), cip. 277 to 282.

1298 See BVerfG, ibid., cip. 285 and 286: "Zweckänderungen sind folglich jeweils an den Grundrechten zu messen, die für die Datenerhebung maßgeblich waren. (Das gilt für jede Art der Verwendung von Daten zu einem anderen Zweck als dem Erhebungszweck, unabhängig davon, ob es sich um die Verwendung als Beweismittel oder als Ermittlungsansatz handelt (…).) Die Ermächtigung zu einer Zweckänderung ist dabei am Verhältnismäßigkeitsgrundsatz zu messen. Hierbei orientiert sich das Gewicht, das einer solchen Regelung im Rahmen der Abwägung zukommt, am Gewicht des Eingriffs der Datenerhebung. Informationen, die durch besonders eingriffsintensive Maßnahmen erlangt wurden, können auch nur zu besonders gewichtigen Zwecken benutzt werden (…)."

other object of protection than the collection and therefore constitutes a change of purpose, the importance of this new object of protection must correspond to the severity of the infringement that the direct collection of this data would have caused.[1299]

With respect to the reason for the change of purpose, the Court applies the same justification as illustrated previously:[1300] The later use of the data for another purpose does not require the same reason as for its collection, such as a specific danger. Instead, the principle of proportionality requires only that "the data provide, be it per se or in combination with further information of the public agency, for a specific investigative reason."[1301] This might be the case for the investigation of crimes or the prevention of dangers for an object of protection that correspond, in their importance, to those for that the data was collected.[1302] Indeed, here again, if the data collection led to an infringement of the basic rights to the inviolability of the home or the confidentiality and integrity of information technological systems, its later use for another purpose requires again a specific danger or even urgent danger.[1303]

The Court's considerations show that the German Constitutional Court also differentiates between the assessments of whether a change of purpose is 'compatible' or 'incompatible' with the original purpose. While the Court at first required, in general, that "the purpose of usage for which the data are collected and the changed purpose of usage must not be incompatible with each other"[1304], it finally affirmed the compatibility as: "The purposes (of pretention and prosecution of crimes changed later on) are compatible with the original purposes which justified the collection of

1299 See BVerfG, ibid., cip. 288.

1300 See above under point C. II. 1. c) ee) (1) (d) Liberalization of the strict requirement by referring to the object of protection.

1301 See BverfG, ibid., cip. 289: "Verfassungsrechtlich geboten, aber regelmäßig auch ausreichend, ist insoweit, dass sich aus den Daten - sei es aus ihnen selbst, sei es in Verbindung mit weiteren Kenntnissen der Behörde - ein konkreter Ermittlungsansatz ergibt."

1302 See BVerfG, ibid., cip. 288.

1303 See BVerfG, ibid., cip. 291.

1304 See BVerfG, 14th of July 1999, 1 BvR 2226/94 (Surveillance of Telecommunications), cip. 140: "Ferner dürfen der Verwendungszweck, zu dem die Erhebung erfolgt ist, und der veränderte Verwendungszweck nicht miteinander unvereinbar sein (...)."

the data (…).”[1305] Though, the Court apparently uses the first term in the meaning of a general requirement and the second term referring to the result of its assessment in a specific case. This might be another difference between both terms adding to the aspects mentioned previously.[1306]

(3) Identification marks as a control-enhancing mechanism

In order to guarantee the requirement of purpose limitation and the legitimacy of the proportionality test for an eventual change of purpose, the German Constitutional Court requires the following: “the purpose limitation can only be guaranteed if the data can be, after its collection, identified as a result of the infringements of the privacy of telecommunications. The constitution hence obliges (the public agencies) to set identification marks.”[1307] In this regard, the Court argued “without such an obligation, the data and information collected (…) could be stored in a way and/or mixed with other data and information with the result that their origin (…/and consequently the original purpose of their collection) could not be identified anymore. In doing so, the purpose limitation (…) would be undermined.”[1308] As a consequence, this obligation does not apply if its aim is already met. This was, for example, the case in the decision of “*Email Confiscation*” (Beschlagnahme von Email).

1305 See BVerfG, ibid., cip. 223: “Die Zwecke sind ferner mit dem ursprünglichen Zweck, der die Erhebung der Daten unter Beschränkung des Fernmeldegeheimnisses gerechtfertigt hat (…), vereinbar.”

1306 See above under point C. III. 1. a) bb) (1) Preliminary analysis: Pre-conditions and consequences, referring to a similar differentiation made by the Article 29 Data Protection Working Group, ibid., p. 21.

1307 See BVerfG, 2nd March 2010, 1 BvR 256/08, 1 BvR 263/08, and 1 BvR 586/08 (Data Retention), cip. 141: “Die Zweckbindung läßt sich nur gewährleisten, wenn auch nach der Erfassung erkennbar bleibt, daß es sich um Daten handelt, die aus Eingriffen in das Fernmeldegeheimnis stammen. Eine entsprechende Kennzeichnung ist daher von Verfassungs wegen geboten.”

1308 See BVerfG, ibid., cip. 257: “Ohne eine derartige Pflicht könnten die aus G 10-Meldungen stammenden Daten und Informationen nach der in § 3 Abs. 7 G 10 geregelten Prüfung ihrer Relevanz in einer Weise abgespeichert werden oder sich mit anderen Daten und Informationen vermischen, daß ihre Herkunft aus einer strategischen Fernmeldekontrolle nicht mehr erkennbar ist. Die in § 3 Abs. 3 G 10 vorgesehene Verwendungsbeschränkung wäre damit unterlaufen.”

> In this case, the public prosecution investigated an individual suspected of having committed the crimes of fraud and breach of trust. In the course of the investigations, a judicial court admitted a warrant for confiscating data carriers, in particular, in order to analyze emails that were stored on the servers of an email service provider and belonged to the claimant who was not the suspected person of the investigation. The claimant filed a constitutional complaint against the confiscation alleging an infringement of his basic rights to confidentiality of telecommunications, Art. 10 GG, and to informational self-determination. He argued, in particular, that the confiscation was disproportionate because he was not the suspected person.[1309]

The German Constitutional Court denied the claim. The Court argued that the confiscation indeed infringed the claimant's basic right to confidentiality of telecommunications under Art. 10 GG. However, the infringement was based on the provisions of the Code of Penal Procedure and, thus, on a parliamentary law. Furthermore, the confiscation met the procedural requirements necessary for a proportionate infringement of the right to confidentiality of telecommunications under Art. 10 GG.[1310] In particular, the Court stated that the obligation to set identification marks is not necessary for the confiscation of emails stored on the server of the provider. The reason is that the requirement of purpose limitation is already met on the basis of the penal law procedure. In the course of this procedure, it is also possible to trace the processed data back to its origin of collection.[1311] Therefore, it was not necessary to set explicit identification marks in order to meet the principle of proportionality.

cc) Alternative concepts provided for in German legal literature

As stated previously, the German Constitutional Court developed these requirements of purpose identity, proportionate change of purpose, and the supplementing requirements of setting identification marks with respect to the State. The German legislator has reacted to these requirements by precisely and, consequently, extensively regulating the processing of personal data by the State within the ordinary law. However, the result is a "flood

---

1309 See BVerfG, 16th of June 2009, 2 BvR 902/06 (Email Confiscation), cip. 19 to 29.

1310 See BVerfG, ibid., cip. 40 and 41.

1311 See BVerfG, ibid., cip. 102.

of regulation"[1312] which nevertheless does not comply, in the opinion of many critics, with needs of the State to appropriately act in an Information Society.[1313] As a consequence, several legal scholars propose alternative concepts for how to implement the principle of purpose limitation. Indeed, all these proposals refer to a treatment of data by the State. However, an examination of these concepts might also help in order to understand the function of the principle of purpose limitation in the private sector and find possible regulation instruments, which assist in balancing the opposing interests of data controllers and the individuals concerned.

(1) Purpose identity and informational separation of powers

The legal scholars Forgó, Krügel and Rapp principally acknowledge the requirement of purpose identity as a consequence of the right to informational self-determination providing individuals the right to basically determine by themselves the collection and, even more important, later usage of 'their' data. This is, in their opinion, the intention of the German Constitutional Court if it requires the State to strictly limit the later usage of personal data to the purpose initially specified. However, Forgó et al. admit that there are actually no reliable criteria that provide certainty in order to specify the purpose, not even on the public sector. They propose to specify the purpose not from the perspective of the state, which usually refers to categories of administrative organization, but from the perspective of the individual concerned.[1314] Using an eGovernment example, the authors illustrate how this approach avoids a conceptual shift away from the strict requirement of purpose identity by giving, however, more room for state agencies providing their electronic services in favor of the citizen.[1315]

1312 See, instead of many, Hoffmann-Riem, New Concept of Data Protection, pp. 513 to 517, who mainly uses the term "Verrechtlichung".

1313 See, for example, Albers, Treatment of Personal Information and Data, cip. 68; Forgó and Krügel, Subjective purpose limitation: Data protection – Brake or motor of E-Government?, pp. 732 to 735; Eifert, Purpose Compatibility instead of Purpose Limitation, pp. 140 and 141.

1314 See Forgó et al., Purpose Specification and Informational Separation of Powers, pp. 11 and 12.

1315 See Forgó et al., ibid., pp. 37 and 38.

(a) Purpose specification by the individual instead of the controller

Forgó et alt. particularly criticize that the current approach focusing on the specification of the purpose from the perspective of the State, which determines the purpose by means of the authorizing law, does not allow to process data for purposes other than for that which it was collected, even if the citizen concerned actually wants the processing to take place. They argue, referring to the example of § 14 sect. 2 of the German Federal Data Protection Law (BDSG), that even if this provision authorizes certain changes of a given purpose by the State, it does not give the public agencies the necessary scope of action in order to sufficiently exploit the potential of electronic government services. § 14 sect. 2 BDSG allows, for instance, in its no. 2 the change of purpose if it is based on the individual's consent and in its no. 3 if " it is evident that this is in the interest of the data subject and there is no reason to assume that he or she would withhold consent if he or she knew of such other purpose". Forgó et al. consider, on the one hand, that the individual's consent required by the first provision does not sufficiently meet the practical needs because it requires, pursuant to § 4a BDSG, several formal requirements such as in written form.[1316] They stress that this is even then the case if the law foresees the form of electronic signatures instead of writing. They doubt the electronic signature provides for a suitable solution, in light of the high costs for its technical implementation, the slow progress of implementation in Germany and the negative experiences in other States.[1317] On the other hand, they argue that even if the evidence test under § 14 sect. 2 no. 3 BDSG does not require the individual's consent referring to the interest of the individual concerned, it is still stricter than the compatibility test required on the European level.[1318]

Instead of interpreting the German provisions in light of the European directive and thus applying the compatibility assessment, Forgó et alt. advocate to tie into the approach of the German right to informational self-determination, but to take the perspective of the individual into account, not of the controller. The specification of the purpose from the perspective of the individual instead of the controller corresponds, in their opinion, more effectively to the aim providing the individual a right to determine

1316 See Forgó et al., ibid., p. 38.
1317 See Forgó et al., ibid., p. 45.
1318 See Forgó et al., ibid., pp. 31 and 32.

by him or herself the usage of 'his or her' data. In doing so, they underline that such a "subjective" purpose is not equal to the individual's explicit or implicit consent agreeing to a purpose, which is specified by the controller, but it is his or her own "individual specification" of the purpose. The individual has thus not to estimate the risks by reading the consent provided for by the controller, but can determine on his or her own the extent of the data processing. They conclude from this that their approach, which builds on the individual's "subjective" purpose, implements the idea of informational self-determination in practice better than the classic understanding of the individual's consent.[1319]

(b) Principle of purpose limitation and informational separation of powers

Forgó et alt. justify their approach by referring to the actual function of the principle of purpose limitation. They stress that the German Constitutional Court developed the strict requirement of purpose limitation with respect to the State in order to guarantee the "informational separation of powers". They define the term as "the systematic differentiation of the public administration and its information processes in order to seal themselves off against each other".[1320] The informational separation of powers serves to limit the power of the State by hindering its public agencies to boundlessly aggregate information about its citizens. According to this principle, public agencies are only allowed to process information if it is necessary to fulfill their tasks. The specific legal competences of public agencies hence are not only formal rules of law, but also an inherent part of the informational separation of powers.[1321] The basic right to informational self-determination and the informational separation of powers are, in light of these considerations, closely connected to each other: The principle of clarity of law obliging the legislator to 'precisely and specifically determine in certain areas the purpose of the data processing' supplements the principle of purpose limitation and thereby procedurally guarantees that citizens are able to know which public agencies process the data and to which extent. The principle of informational separation of powers guarantees this aim on

1319 See Forgó et al., ibid., pp. 37 to 39.
1320 See Forgó et al., ibid., p. 16 with further references, pp. 115 et seq.
1321 See Forgó et al., ibid., pp. 16 and 17 with further references.

an organizational level, traditionally, by referring to the legal competencies for the specific public agencies' tasks.[1322]

Forgó et alt. refer to the German Constitutional Court which already stated in its first "*Decision on Population Census*" as: "An obligation for the provision of personal data requires that the legislator precisely and specifically determines in certain areas the purpose of usage and should ensure that the information is suitable and necessary for achieving this purpose. (…). All (public) agencies collecting personal data in order to perform their tasks are restrained to the minimum which is necessary for achieving their given goals. The usage of the data is restricted to the purpose provided for by the provision."[1323] They conclude from these considerations that the legislator is not necessarily obliged to refer to the legal competences of public agencies which were traditionally applied in order to 'precisely and specifically determine the purpose in certain areas' in order to 'perform their tasks'. Rather, the legislator can also choose other organizational and procedural measures if these measures equally meet the constitutional requirements. In the opinion of Forgó et alt., this is in particular the case if the technical development provides for measures which, first, enable the individuals to specify themselves the purpose of the data processing, as most effective form of self-determination, and, second, safeguard the principle of informational separation of powers.[1324]

1322 See Forgó et al., ibid., pp. 19 and 20 as well as 53.

1323 See BVerfG, 15th of December 1983, 1 BvR 209, 269, 362, 420, 440, 484/83 (Decision on Population Census), cip. 179 and 180: "Ein Zwang zur Angabe personenbezogener Daten setzt voraus, daß der Gesetzgeber den Verwendungszweck bereichsspezifisch und präzise bestimmt und daß die Angaben für diesen Zweck geeignet und erforderlich sind. (Damit wäre die Sammlung nicht anonymisierter Daten auf Vorrat zu unbestimmten oder noch nicht bestimmbaren Zwecken nicht zu vereinbaren.) Auch werden sich alle Stellen, die zur Erfüllung ihrer Aufgaben personenbezogene Daten sammeln, auf das zum Erreichen des angegebenen Zieles erforderliche Minimum beschränken müssen. Die Verwendung der Daten ist auf den gesetzlich bestimmten Zweck begrenzt. (...)"

1324 See Forgó et al., ibid., pp. 54 to 58.

(c) Example of re-registration: Collection and transfer of data on the citizen's request

Forgó et al. illustrate the challenges caused by the current legal situation and a possible solution on the example of re-registrations that citizens want to carry out before a public authority of their choice when they change their place of domicile. The challenges for such a "one-stop-solution" are, first, the diversity of public agencies each of them competent for another specific registration task and, second, the decentralized organization of information about the individual's corresponding circumstances.[1325] Pursuant to the current legal framework, the public agency, which does not have the legal competencies in order to carry out this task, is not allowed to process the data, i.e. collect and transfer it to the competent authority.[1326] One solution could be to forego the separation of specific administrative competences and to centralize the information management system. Forgó et alt. indeed consider this radical solution as a severe infringement of the principle of purpose limitation guaranteed by the basic right to informational self-determination. As a consequence, they propose an alternative solution. In their opinion, all public agencies should be authorized by law to collect and transfer data to the competent authority, under two conditions: First, the public authority may collect and transfer the data, only on the citizen's request; and second, technical-organizational measures safeguard the informational separation of powers. In order to meet the first requirement, they promote that the public agency contacted first by the citizen must provide the necessary information about the different tasks that can be initiated by the citizen and then carried out by which competent authority. In order to fulfill the second requirement, the agency contacted by the citizen has, first, to delete the data immediately after its transfer to the competent authority. Second, it must be technically and organizationally safeguarded that nobody else than the competent authority or the official in charge, respectively, gets access to the data and that these authorities process the data only in order to carry out their task which was initiated by the citizen. Finally, the different acts of the data processing must be documented in order to serve the informational basis for later control.[1327]

1325 See Forgó et al., ibid., pp. 40 to 42.
1326 See Forgó et al., ibid., p. 43.
1327 See Forgó et al., ibid., pp. 53 to 58.

(2) Compatibility of purposes

The legal scholar Eifert also criticizes, with respect to the State, the concept of protection of the right to informational self-determination, which leads to the situation that each act of data processing and every change of purpose must be based on the individual's consent or an authorizing law. This results, in his opinion, in a flood of regulation and, subsequently, to a situation which is contrary to what was actually intended by the legislator. The result is not more protection but a lack of protection and transparency leading to a detriment for the individual concerned.[1328]

(a) Criticism of the "subjective" purpose approach

However, Eifert disagrees with the approach proposed by Forgó et al. He stresses that the specification of the purpose from the individual's perspective broadens the scope of action of the State, going beyond the legal provisions which already authorize, as mentioned previously, the data processing if "it is evident that this is in the interest of the data subject and there is no reason to assume that he or she would withhold consent if he or she knew of such other purpose" (§ 14 sect. 2 no. 3 BDSG). This approach risks, in addition, being abused in the moment the State only supposes the "subjective purpose" of the individual, while the authority actually acts in its own interests. From a juridical-technical perspective, Eifert admits that it might be possible to differentiate between the individual's consent and his or her "subjective" purpose. As a consequence, it is principally possible to set up different legal requirements without undermining the one or the other instrument. However, he stresses that both instruments actually are expressions of the same substantial guarantee, i.e. the individual's autonomous self-deter-mination. Eifert therefore doubts that it makes sense to set up different legal requirements for the same individual autonomous decision. In particular, he criticizes that the requirements for the "subjective" purpose are less strict than for the consent and not reverse. This result conflicts, in his opinion, with the overall scheme of the concept of protection: While the "subjective" purpose determines, as a first step, the scope of protection and consequently its infringement, the individual's

---

1328 See Eifert, Purpose Compatibility instead of Purpose Limitation, pp. 140 to 142.

consent justifies the infringement, as a subsequent step. If the "subjective" purpose provides the basis for the consent, its legal requirements should be stricter and not less strict than for the subsequent instrument.[1329]

(b) Compatibility instead of identity of purposes

Eifert therefore proposes an alternative approach. Instead of referring to the individual's "subjective" purpose, he wants to keep on specifying the purpose from the perspective of the controller and, simultaneously, to loosen up the strict requirement of purpose identity. He stresses that the German Constitutional Court itself does not generally require the strict identity of purposes but rather "that the purpose of the collection and the changed purpose of usage must be 'proportionate to each other'."[1330] However, Eifert criticizes the strict approach of the Court requiring the State to base each change of purpose on a (eventually newly enacted) legal provision.[1331] His theoretical starting point for refining the German concept of protection is the shift of focus from the 'individual's right to basically determine by him or herself the usage of data' toward a guarantee of autonomous decisions and freedoms of action. Such a guarantee does not require the State to base the treatment of each single datum on a law, because it does not refer to the datum *per se* but rather to the context of usage and its situational risk for the individual's right of self-representation. Comparable to Albers, Eifert thus promotes that the specific basic rights to freedom primarily serve as the legal scale for legal regulation protecting against these risks. He concludes from this shift within the concept of protection that the purpose compatibility would be the more appropriate requirement than the strict identity of purposes. The requirement of purpose compatibility provides, in his opinion, a fair balance between the interests of the individual concerned to foresee the later data usage and the State need to flexibly react to atypical situations and future trends.[1332]

1329 See Eifert, ibid., pp. 142 and 143.
1330 See Eifert, ibid., p. 144.
1331 See Eifert, ibid., p. 144.
1332 See Eifert, ibid., pp. 144 to 146.

(c) Supplementing protection instruments

Eifert considers several supplementing instruments as necessary in order to re-balance the broader room of action of the State. In particular, he stresses measures of transparency, data quality, and common definitions for certain types of compatible purposes as complementary instruments. With respect to transparency measures, Eifert underlines the importance of information duties that the controller has to meet and must hence not depend on the individual's initiative. Thus, they are different from the individual's right to obtain access or retrieve certain information that the individual has to actively exercise. The reason is that if an original purpose can be legitimately changed, the public authority using the data for this new purpose does not have to collect the data directly from the individual. Instead, it usually retrieves the data from another authority that had directly collected the data. Though, the individual concerned cannot foresee that another authority uses the data for a new purpose and is not able to exercise his or her right to information. Therefore, the authority itself, using the data for a new purpose, must inform the individual concerned.[1333] Eifert admits that the question of how the public authorities have to inform the individual in practice is challenging. Since it is not the law which informs the individuals concerned in a general and abstract way about the data treatment, the public agencies themselves have principally to inform each individual about each treatment of the data for another purpose than the original. The question of how to avoid that the potential flood of information does not overwhelm the individual will be the matter of the future case.[1334]

With respect to the second requirement to implement measures for the data quality in order to re-balance the broader scope of action of the State, Eifert stresses, at first, the important function of the requirement of purpose identity. This strict requirement safeguarded that the usage of data was always limited to its original context. Thus, the fact that public authorities had principally to collect new data from the individual concerned if they pursued another purpose guaranteed that the data was always correct with respect to the new usage context.[1335] In light of this, the German Constitutional Court made sure, by requiring for each change of purpose

1333 See Eifert, ibid., p. 147.
1334 See Eifert, ibid., pp. 147 and 148.
1335 See Eifert, ibid., p. 148.

an authorizing law being subject to another proportionality test, that the legislator proves the quality of data with respect to this new context. However, Eifert considers that such a measure for guaranteeing data quality must not necessarily be taken by the legislator. It is also possible to set up such control (and correction) mechanisms within the public agencies themselves. In this regard, Eifert considers to enrich the data with further meta- information about the original context in order to avoid a misinterpretation of its meaning by another authority. In addition, the information duties become relevant again because they enable the individual concerned to correct the data by themselves. Eifert comes to the conclusion that the more sensitive the data is, and the more important its role is for the controller, the stricter the mechanisms must be in order to guarantee the data quality.[1336]

After having examined several of these instruments, Eifert comes to the core question resulting from his approach: How can one define the purposes being compatible to each other? He considers it is difficult to find criteria which help to define those purposes in practice, since the definition of those purposes depends on the specific context of the usage of data and the correspondingly endangered basic rights. Eifert concludes from this that it is only possible to develop certain methods and proposes to map, as a first step, the actual needs for data, as well as the data flux. This is possible, at least, with respect to the State, because the State Organizational Laws already determines for which the tasks a public agency is allowed and/or must act, and, thus, collect and further processes personal data.. On this basis, it would be possible to find some principles limiting the compatibility of certain purposes.[1337]

(3) Purpose identity and change of purpose as 'a threshold for duty of control'

Finally, Albers, in turn criticizes the approach of purpose compatibility. In her opinion, rules concerning the change of purpose primarily serve as 'thresholds for duties of control'.[1338]

1336 See Eifert, ibid., pp. 148 to 150.
1337 See Eifert, ibid., p. 151.
1338 In German: "Aufmerksamkeitsregeln".

(a) Criticism of purpose compatibility

In Albers' opinion, in order to maintain the quality of data when it is re-used in another context, the strict requirement of purpose identity, combined with legal rules authorizing the change of purpose works better than the looser approach of purpose compatibility. The reason is that the stricter approach enforces the controller of the data to examine more precisely what the original purpose is, and whether or not the new purpose differs to this original one.[1339]

(b) Specification, identity and change of purpose as equivalent regulation instruments

However, Albers stresses that the stricter approach of purpose identity, combined with legal rules authorizing the change of purpose must not be understood as 'rule and exception'. In her opinion, the requirement of purpose identity is neither the rule, nor is the change of purpose the exception. The requirements of purpose specification, purpose identity, and change of purpose rather are different components of a regulation instrument serving to combine the different acts of a data treatment to a legally relevant unity, in other words, gives meaning to actions.[1340] At first, the specification of purposes helps the controller to determine the relevant context of knowledge and action based on the processing of data. Secondly, the specified purpose determines, from a legal perspective, which of the different acts of data processing constitute a legal unity and which must be differentiated from each other. The requirement of purpose identity supplements this structural function of purpose specification, on a temporary level. This means that the data controller not only has to (legally) structure its treatment the moment the data is collected, but also later on is obliged to always refer to the precedent purpose(s). Albers stresses that the legislator can focus, combining these two functions, on different aspects and provides two examples: While § 14 sect. 1 BDSG limits the later usage of data to the purpose of its collection, § 7 sect. 2 sent. 2 of the Law of Toll Collection on Federal Highways (BFStrMG) limits the data processing to explicitly listed purposes. In Albers' opinion, the require-

1339 See Albers, Treatment of Personal Information and Data, cip. 123.
1340 See Albers, ibid., cip. 123.

ment of purpose identity can thus be implemented in different ways: on the one hand (this is the classic understanding of purpose identity), the legislator can require that data is used only for the purpose originally specified. On the other hand, it is also possible to forbid that certain purposes are combined. Finally, the authorization of a change of purpose constitutes a further component for the regulation of the data treatment. This instrument necessarily re-balances the limitations of the two precedent instruments enabling the State to adequately react to the circumstances changing over time.[1341] Therefore, an authorization of a purpose change is not the exception to the strict requirement of purpose identity. Instead, the specific needs for protection of the individuals concerned determine under which conditions 'his' or 'her' data might be transferred from one context into another one, generating further information.[1342]

(c) The opposing fundamental rights providing for the objective legal scale

With this last aspect, Albers refers to the legal scale determining the need of protection. Since the changed purpose must equally be specified, Albers considers the requirement of purpose specification as the starting point for this determination. Comparably to Eifert, she does not apply the approach of specifying the "subjective" from the perspective of the individual concerned. Instead, the specific basic rights provide for the necessary scale. These define, with regard to further regulation instruments, such as measures of transparency and participation, how precisely the purpose must be specified, which purposes must be identical, can be changed or must not be combined.[1343] In doing so, Albers also takes, however, the State's tasks and capacities into account. In her opinion, it depends also on the fact whether the State acts, for instance, in the area of administrative execution, risk prevention or planning. The precision of purpose specification, strict purpose limitation and the possibilities to change the purpose also depend on these contexts of regulation.[1344]

1341 See Albers, ibid., cip. 123.
1342 See Albers, ibid., cip. 129.
1343 See Albers, ibid., cip. 126.
1344 See Albers, ibid., cip. 124.

dd) Interim conclusion: Right to control data causing a 'flood of regulation'

The preceding analysis of the principle of purpose limitation developed by the German Constitutional Court with respect to the State provides a likely reason for why the German legislator did not directly transfer the requirement of purpose compatibility into German ordinary law and instead adopted the balancing test approach. The balancing tests result, basically, from the concept of protection of the right to informational self-determination requiring, on the one hand, the identity of purposes and, on the other hand, allowing the change of purpose so long as it is proportionate. Indeed, the principle of proportionality only binds the State and not private individuals. Therefore, establishing the same principle for the processing of personal data in the private sector, the legislator recognizes a wider scope of action for the processing of personal data by private individuals than the State.[1345] In doing so, the legislator re-balances the strict requirement of purpose identity by a multitude of wide exemptions for the change of purposes. The result is a double-layered system allowing, as a first step, the processing of data for the initial purpose and limiting the later use to this initial purpose, and then, as a second step, allowing the change of purpose for the same purpose originally authorized. Comparable to the public sector, this 'flood of regulation' makes the law very difficult to understand. Instead of such a system, it would principally be possible not to differentiate between original and subsequent purposes but simply allow all processing operations for the same specific purposes as listed in the law.

Indeed, the alternative concepts provided for in legal literature give further reasons for why the German legislator has chosen, possibly, the current system. First, Forgó et al. illustrate the strong connection between the strict requirement of purpose identity and the constitutional scope of action of the State. They recognize that the strict requirement of purpose identity results from the concept of protection of the German right to informational self-determination providing the individual a right 'to basically determine by him or herself the collection and later usage of his or her data'. This mechanism would be undermined, in their opinion, if the data controller was not limited to the purpose initially specified. Furthermore,

1345 Cf. above under point C. I. 1. b) bb) (1) The 3-Step-Test: Assessing the defensive and protection function.

Forgó et al. stress the important function of this requirement by safeguarding the 'informational separation of powers' of the State. The requirement of purpose identity hence guarantees that citizens are able to know which public agencies process the data and to which extent. The Constitutional Court implements this guarantee requiring that the legislator, first, has to "precisely and specifically determine(..) in certain areas the purpose of use (.../and, second, the public) agencies which collect personal data in order to perform their tasks are restrained to the minimum which is necessary for achieving their given goals (.../and therefore the use of data) is restricted to the purpose provided for by the provision".[1346] In the opinion of Forgó et al., the principle of informational separation of powers traditionally guarantees this aim on an organizational level by referring to the legal competencies for the specific tasks of the public agencies.[1347] In light of this function of the principle of purpose limitation, they propose, in order to broaden the scope of action for the State, to specify the purpose not from the perspective of the controller but, subjectively, from the individual's perspective. Such a 'subjective' purpose does not have to be expressed in the individual's consent. Instead, the individual can also express his or her purpose without the formal requirements. A further condition is that technical-organiza-tional measures safeguard that no other agency or individual gets access to the data and, thus, the requirements for the 'informational separation of powers' are met.[1348] In conclusion, this function makes it clear that even if the concept of protection provides the individual a right to 'determine by him or herself the collection and later use of data', the individual does not have to exercise this right exclusively by the

1346 See BVerfG, BVerfG, 15th of December 1983, 1 BvR 209, 269, 362, 420, 440, 484/83 (Decision on Population Census), cip. 179 and 180: "Ein Zwang zur Angabe personenbezogener Daten setzt voraus, daß der Gesetzgeber den Verwendungszweck bereichsspezifisch und präzise bestimmt und daß die Angaben für diesen Zweck geeignet und erforderlich sind. Damit wäre die Sammlung nicht anonymisierter Daten auf Vorrat zu unbestimmten oder noch nicht bestimmbaren Zwecken nicht zu vereinbaren. Auch werden sich alle Stellen, die zur Erfüllung ihrer Aufgaben personenbezogene Daten sammeln, auf das zum Erreichen des angegebenen Zieles erforderliche Minimum beschränken müssen. Die Verwendung der Daten ist auf den gesetzlich bestimmten Zweck begrenzt. (...)"

1347 See Forgó et alt., Purpose Specification and Informational Separation of Powers, pp. 19 and 20 as well as 53.

1348 See above under point C. III. 1. b) cc) (1) (b) Principle of purpose limitation and informational separation of powers.

consent but can do it also in other forms, provided for that potential further requirements of the concept of protection are safeguarded.

In contrast, Eifert proposes a shift within the concept of protection. Instead of providing the individual a right to control 'his or her' data, the mechanisms safeguarding the concept of protection, i.e. the individual's autonomy, should rather enable the individual to control his or her risks caused by the processing of data. Comparable to Albers, Eifert promotes that the specific basic rights to freedom primarily provide the legal scale in order to evaluate these risks. He concludes from this shift within the concept of protection that the requirement of purpose compatibility is more appropriate than the stricter requirement of purpose identity. In his opinion, the requirement of purpose compatibility provides a balance between the interests of the individual concerned to foresee the later use of data and the state's need to flexibly react to atypical situations and future trends. Indeed, this conceptual shift requires that further mechanisms such as of transparency, as well as data quality are met, and common definitions for the compatibility of purposes exist. Eifert stresses, for example, the importance of information duties for the case that a public agency does not collect personal data directly from the individual concerned but retrieves it from another agency. This idea reveals an important point and should equally apply if the same public agency that has collected the personal data uses that data for another purpose than originally specified. The reason is that even if the data was directly collected from the individual, he or she cannot foresee that the authority uses the data for another purpose. Also in this case, the agency itself should thus inform the individual.

Promoting the requirement of purpose compatibility, Eifert criticizes the approach of a "subjective" purpose because the difference made between several forms of expressing informational self-determination would not make sense in his opinion.[1349] However, Eifert overlooks that such different forms of expression are possible, indeed. An individual is not restricted in controlling his or her risks by giving his or her consent as formally required by Article 4a of the German Data Protection Law. Instead, he or she can also do it otherwise, irrespective of such formal requirements. The question simply is which mechanism enables best the individual to control his or risks with respect to the specific situation.

1349 See above under point C. III. 1. b) cc) (2) (b) Criticism of the "subjective" purpose approach.

Finally, Albers equally promotes to focus not on data, but on the risks that are determined by the specific fundamental rights of freedom. In her opinion, the principle of purpose limitation functions, together with the change of purpose, as 'thresholds for duties of control'. Since the strict requirement of purpose identity enforces the data controller to more precisely examine the initial (or preceding) purpose(s), she prefers the stricter requirement to the "looser" approach of purpose compatibility. In addition, this approach may be considered, from a regulator's point of view, as easier to implement by means of ordinary law than the approach of purpose compatibility. The reason is that the looser approach of purpose compatibility must be re-balanced by several additional measures in order to guarantee the quality of data processed with respect to the different usage contexts.[1350] In any case, as a consequence of her risk-based approach, Albers stresses that the requirement of purpose identity neither is the rule, nor is a change of purpose an exception to this rule. Instead, building upon the specification of the purpose, both mechanisms interact with each other serving to legally combine or separate the multitude of acts of a data treatment to relevant (and meaningful) unities.[1351]

In conclusion, this function might provide another reason for why the German legislator provided for such a complicated regulation of data processing in the private sector. As mentioned above, the German legislator has established a double-layered system: as a first step, it allows the processing of data for initial purposes by limiting the later use to these initial purposes; as a second step, it essentially allows the change of purpose under the same legal condition as previously allowed. Instead of such a system, it would be possible not to differentiate between original and subsequent purposes, but to simply allow all processing operations for the same purposes listed in the law. However, the legislator has probably chosen the more complicated system because it enforces the controller to examine, more strictly, whether the new purpose of its later processing operations still complies with the law. In any case, and irrespective of the question whether this system actually achieves this aim – which could be doubted in light of that controllers do not understand the regulation – Albers' conclusion is not correct that the requirement of purpose compatibility would not achieve the same result. In fact, the substantive compatibility assess-

1350 See above under point C. III. 1. b) cc) (2) (c) Supplementing protection instruments.

1351 See Albers, Treatment of Personal Information and Data, cip. 123.

ment requires, amongst other aspects, to measure the 'distance' between the original purpose and the later data processing.[1352] Thus, irrespective of the scale for measuring the distance, the criteria equally requires from the data controller to precisely examine what the original purpose was and whether the later use of data is compatible or not with this initial purpose.

2. Solution approach: Controlling risks that add to those specified previously

The alternative concepts of protection provided for in German literature refer altogether to the processing of personal data by the State. However, these alternative concepts clarified the diversity of potential functions that the principle of purpose limitation can have. This decomposition of potential functions help, in turn, clarify which of these functions essentially applies to the public sector, only, and which functions should equally apply in the private sector. This helps finally answer the question of which of these functions should be further elaborated on regarding the concept of protection provided for by the European Charta of Fundamental Rights.

a) Conceptual shift: From the exclusion of unspecific risks to the control of specific risks

There are three particular questions on how to elaborate on the concept of protection with respect to the principle of purpose limitation: First, which functions have both approaches, in light of the previously proposed risk-based approach, i.e. the strict requirement of purpose identity and the "looser" requirement of purpose compatibility; second, how far this finding might be transposed to the concepts of protection developed by the European Court of Human Rights, the EU legislator (with particular respect to the General Data Protection Regulation), as well as the German Constitutional Court; and third, which of these concepts fit best, in light of its potentially refined function, to innovation processes in non-linear and decentralized environments. Referring to the moment as being decisive when evaluating risks, this question considers whether the principle of

1352 See above under point C. III. 1. a) bb) (3) (a) First criteria: 'Distance between purposes'.

purpose limitation should serve to exclude all unspecific risks as soon as the data is collected, or rather control specific risks, taking into account the potential later processing of that data.

aa) Different types of changes of purpose in light of different types of risks

With respect to the first question, this thesis promotes focusing on the risks caused by the processing of personal data, rather than on a control of that data *per se*. Even if personal data can serve as an appropriate legal link for protection instruments, it is the risks caused by data processing that constitute the actual target of the concept of protection guaranteeing the individual's autonomy.[1353]

(1) Purpose compatibility as an "umbrella assessment"

Eifert advocates that the requirement of purpose compatibility fits better to such a concept of protection rather than the stricter requirement of purpose identity.[1354] At least, in the private sector, the identity of purposes does indeed not fulfill the function of safeguarding the 'informational separation of powers' by the State. In this regard, there is no general need for the requirement of purpose identity.[1355] Furthermore, in contrast to Albers' considerations, the strict requirement of purpose identity does not require the controller to precisely examine the conditions for a change of purpose more than the test of purpose compatibility. In contrast, both methods require the same 'duties of control' because the substantive compatibility assessment proposed by the Working Group equally requires the controller to compare the later use of personal data with the original purpose.[1356]

1353 See above under point C. I. 3. c) cc) (3) Advantages and challenges: 'Personal data' as legal link for a subjective right, and C. II. 3. a) Regulative aim: Data protection for the individual's autonomy.

1354 See above under point C. III. 1. b) cc) (2) (b) Compatibility instead of identity of purposes.

1355 See above under point C. III. 1. b) dd) Interim conclusion: Right to control data causing a 'flood of regulation'.

1356 See above under point C. III. 1. b) dd) Interim conclusion: Right to control data causing a 'flood of regulation'.

However, for the regulator, it might be easier to establish the strict requirement of purpose identity than of purpose compatibility. On the one hand, one reason for this assumption is that a regulation by means of the "looser" requirement of purpose compatibility appears to be more complex because it must be re-balanced by additional requirements, such as of transparency and data quality. It must also be clarified with respect to the question of which purposes are compatible and which are not.[1357] On the other hand, this assumption turns out to be correct only if there is no objective scale that would help determine these additional requirements. If there is an objective scale, it is principally possible to typify these requirements and even compatible and incompatible purposes, respectively. Typifying these requirements on the basis of an objective scale, hence helps the regulator to fulfill its task so that this task is, at least, not too complex.

This leads to the previously proposed concept of data protection serving all fundamental rights to privacy, freedom and non-discrimination. Pursuant to this concept, the individual's fundamental rights do not only provide an objective scale for the specification of the original purpose, but also for the other protection instruments.[1358] As a consequence, the individual's fundamental rights do equally provide an objective scale for all subsequent purposes and, thus, in order to determine the additional requirements for the compatibility assessment. On the basis of this objective scale, it is possible to determine in which situations the individual concerned needs further protection measures, such as measures of transparency and data quality. It is also possible, in principle, to typify which purposes are compatible with each other and which are incompatible. In this regard, there indeed is, just as Albers advocates, no general rule and exception relationship between purposes that must either be identical or that can be considered as compatible or incompatible. Instead, these questions depend on the risk for the respective substantial guarantee concerned by the data processing.[1359]

1357 See above under point C. III. 1. b) dd) Interim conclusion: Right to control data causing a 'flood of regulation'.

1358 See above under point C. II. 3. a) cc) (2) (b) Appropriateness for innovation processes.

1359 Cf. above under point C. III. 1. b) cc) (3) (b) Specification, identity and change of purpose as equivalent protection instruments, and C. III. 1. b) cc) (3) (b) The opposing fundamental rights providing for the objective legal scale.

(2) Custer's and Ursic's taxonomy: "Data recycling, repurposing, and recontextualization"

Before coming to the requirements provided for by specific substantial guarantees for the compatibility assessment, it is necessary to further clarify the terminology in order to differentiate between different ways to use the personal data later on. Previously, this thesis elaborated on a risk-based approach determined by the individual's specific fundamental rights that determine the context in that the data processing occurs. The requirement to specify the purpose safeguards that risks arising in these contexts against the individual's fundamental right are discovered in a timely manner so that the individual and/or the controller can still avoid that the potential risk turns into harm.[1360] This part of this thesis clarifies, focusing on the compatibility assessment, in more detail the terminology regarding the later use of the personal data and further different types of risk.

The legal scholars Custer and Ursic propose, in particular, the following taxonomy for the "re-use" of personal data: First, the most simple form is, in their opinion, "using the same data in the same way more than once."[1361] They call this type of re-use "data recycling" and provide the example of personal data collected for billing purposes, which is re-used on a monthly, quarterly or annual basis. In contrast, they refer to the term "re-purposing" if the collected data is used for another purpose, for example, if the previously-mentioned insurance company uses the same data in order to analyze the individual risk of its patients of falling ill and, thus, personalize the prices for its insurance policies. For these cases of "re-purposing", Custer and Ursic consider, typically, that an additional consent of the individual concerned or another legitimate basis provided for by law is necessary.[1362] Finally, if the personal data is re-used in another context, for example, if the insurance company sells the data to another company or uses the data for advertising purposes, this may raise, in the authors' opinion, "issues of contextual integrity, since data may have a different meaning or may be interpreted differently in another context."[1363]

1360 See above under point C. II. 3. b) dd) (3) (b) Later use of personal data in the same context.

1361 See Custer and Ursic, Big data and data reuse: a taxonomy of data reuse for balancing big data benefits and personal data protection, p. 5.

1362 See Custer and Ursic, ibid., p. 5.

1363 See Custer and Ursic, ibid., p. 6.

Both authors stress that the Data Protection Directive does not differentiate between the "repurposing" of data and its "recontextualization" but, instead, principally requires the same legal conditions, such as the individual's consent. In contrast, Custer and Ursic highlight the different risks arising from the repurposing of personal data and its recontextualization. In the case of "recontextualization", the likelihood increases that errors will occur when interpreting the meaning of the data; and the individual is, additionally, less able to exercise his or her data protection rights because the transfer of data into another context decreases transparency.[1364] Both authors come to the conclusion that the differentiation between different types of data re-use helps interpret privacy principles, such as the principle of purpose limitation because this may be, "in a way, not specific enough".[1365] In particular, they propose that the difference of risks requires the controller to ask for the individual's consent in cases of recontextualization of personal data much more explicitly than for cases of repurposing. And, for most cases of data recycling, in turn, the individual's consent could even be assumed.[1366]

With respect to the "recycling" of personal data, it is compelling to see that the legal requirements proposed by Custer and Ursic differ, from a comparative point of view, to that established by the German Constitutional Court with respect to the processing of personal data by the State. This difference is interesting only from a *comparative* point of view, of course, because Custer and Ursic refer to another constitutional regime than the German Constitutional Court. It is, however, interesting because it demonstrates another potential difference between legal requirements for the data processing by private parties and the State. The German Court applies a rather strict approach with respect to the State, even if it has slightly liberalized it in the last case of "*Federal Criminal Police Office Act*". In this case, the Court required, with respect to the re-use of personal data by the same public agency and for the same purpose, only an "investigative reason". Only if the collection of the data has lead to a particularly severe infringement of the individual's basic rights, such as of his or her right to the inviolability of the home, the re-use of data requires the same reason for the "recycling" as for its collection (e.g. a specific or even an urgent dan-

1364 See Custer and Ursic, ibid., p. 6.
1365 See Custer and Ursic, ibid., pp. 10 and 11.
1366 See Custer and Ursic, ibid., p. 11.

ger).[1367] In contrast, the approach by Custer and Ursic is more liberal because it never requires a special reason for the re-use of data. This is justified because Custer and Ursic refer to the re-use of personal data by private parties and not the State. Consequently, the principle of clarity of law, from which the requirements for the reason of the data processing result, does not apply.[1368]

Finally, it should be stressed that Custer and Ursic correctly highlight an important point regarding the difference of risks caused by the repurposing and recontextualization of personal data, and its consequences for the protection instruments necessary in order to protect the individual against the corresponding risk. Methodologically, these considerations are similar to that of the Article 29 Data Protection Working Group, which equally refers to the context of the data processing, the "distance" between an original purpose and another purpose, and the fact how far the individual concerned could foresee the re-use of the data.[1369] The justification of the stricter requirements for cases of re-contextualiza-tion also corresponds to the reasoning by Eifert who stressed the issue of transparence and data quality as well.[1370] So far, the value added by Custer and Ursic therefore is mainly terminological. However, it is the terminological difference that helps to also clarify the difference regarding the phenomenological, as well as the normative level. This is the essential value added by Custer and Ursic to this work. Indeed, they do not explain how a context can be defined, or how to measure the distance between purposes, or determine the expectations of the individual concerned. However, this will be done here.

1367 See above under point C. II. 1. c) ee) (1) (d) Liberalization of the strict requirement by referring to the object of protection, referring to BVerfG, 20th of April 2016, 1 BvR 966/09 and 1 BvR 1140/09 (Federal Criminal Police Office Act), cip. 283 and 289.

1368 Cf. above under point C. II. 1. c) ee) (1) (a) Function of purpose specification (basic conditions), referring to BVerfG, 20th of April 2016, 1 BvR 966/09 and 1 BvR 1140/09 (Federal Bureau of Investigation Law), cip. 285; see already BVerfG, 13th June 2007, 1 BvR 1550/03 (Retrieval of Banking Account Matser Data), cip. 71, 73 and 74.

1369 Cf. Custer and Ursic, ibid., p. 6, and above under point C. III. 1. a) bb) (3) Criteria for the substantive compatibility assessment, referring to Article 29 Data Protection Working Group, Opinion 03/0213 on purpose limitation.

1370 See above under point C. III. 1. b) cc) (2) (c) Supplementing protection instruments, referring to Eifert, Purpose Compatibility instead of Purpose Limitation, pp. 147 to 151.

(3) Clarification of an objective scale: "Same risk, higher risk, and another risk"

As proposed before, the function of the requirement to specify the purpose is to reveal a potential risk for a substantial guarantee (aka. specific object of protection) of the individual's fundamental rights. The substantial guarantee of a fundamental right to privacy or freedom determines, in particular, the context of the data processing. Thus, the diversity of all fundamental rights together provide the framework for the purpose being specified by the controller. The higher the risk is for a substantial guarantee, the more precise the purpose must be specified.[1371]

The controller is indeed free to specify the purpose more precisely than required. However, pursuant to the substantive methodology promoted by the Article 29 Data Protection Working Group for the compatibility assessment, one must not formally stick to the concrete formulation stipulated by the data controller. Instead, the purpose must be interpreted in light of the circumstances of the particular the case.[1372] This is the moment where the terminology proposed by Custer and Ursic can help: so long as the later use does not cause a new risk than revealed before, the later use pursues, from a substantive point of view, the same purpose and can therefore be considered as "data recycling". Instead, the moment the re-use of the data causes a new risk, there is a substantive change of purpose: If the re-use causes a higher risk for the same substantial guarantee than revealed before, this kind of re-use can be called "re-purposing". If the re-use causes a risk for another (new) object of protection, this can be called a "recontextualization".

In the case of data recycling, or respectively, if there is a formal change of purpose, only, the required protection instruments remain the same. The reason is that the formally re-stipulated purpose does not reveal another risk than already specified before. In contrast, if the re-specification of the purpose reveals a higher risk for the same object of protection or a risk for another substantial guarantee, this requires additional or other protection

---

1371 See above under point C. II. 3. a) bb) Purpose specification as a risk regulation instrument.

1372 See above under point C. III. 1. a) Preliminary analysis: Preconditions and consequences, referring to the Article 29 Data Protection Working Group, Opinion 03/0213 on purpose limitation, pp. 21 and 22, who prefers the substantive methodology to a formal methodology.

instruments. These instruments depend, here again, on the substantial guarantee concerned. Therefore, a risk for another substantial guarantee indeed requires, in principle, different protection instruments or more protection than just a higher risk for the same substantial guarantee. For instance, the individual's consent for a re-purposing, i.e. if the data processing remains in the same context, does not have to be as explicit as if the data causes a risk for another (new) substantial guarantee. In contrast, the revelation of a risk for another substantial guarantee, or respectively, a re-contextualization requires stricter protection instruments.[1373] This might be a particularly strict 'duty of control', specific measures safeguarding the data quality, and or transparency.[1374]

Applying this risk-based approach, the principle of purpose limitation serves to control risks caused by the later use of personal data that were not revealed before. So far, both requirements of purpose identity and purpose compatibility are suitable in order to fulfill this function. However, the next considerations show that both approaches focus, conceptually, on different moments of the data processing.

bb) Refinement of current concepts of protection

This approach could principally be incorporated in all current concepts of protection surrounding the principle of purpose limitation, be it under the right to data protection in Article 8 ECFR, the right to private life in Article 8 ECHR or the German right to informational self-determination.

(1) Article 8 ECFR and European secondary law

On the level of the European Charter of Fundamental Rights, the constitutional legislator has clarified, establishing the autonomous Article 8 ECFR, that the right to data protection is independent from the right to private life under Article 7 ECFR. The central function of the right to data

1373 Cf. above under point C. III. 1. a) bb) (3) (d) Fourth criteria: 'Safeguards ensuring fairness and preventing undue impact', referring to the Article 29 Data Protection Working Group, Opinion 03/0213 on purpose limitation, pp. 25 and 26.

1374 Cf. above under point C. III. 1. b) dd) Interim conclusion: Right to control data causing a 'flood of regulation'.

protection can thus serve equal protection for all other fundamental rights against the risks of data processing.[1375] Indeed, Article 8 ECFR itself does not establish the overall principle of purpose limitation but the requirement of purpose specification only. The European Court of Justice was reluctant, so far, to explicitly interpret the principle of purpose limitation. In essence, the Court only clarified that the individual's consent requires purpose identity.[1376]

(a) "Purpose identity" forbidding additional risks (than specified before)

So far, this thesis has not clarified what this requirement means in light of the proposed risk-based approach. However, applying this approach, purpose identity means that the later use of data must not cause an additional risk to the purpose specified before. Purpose identity does not only forbid a new risk for another substantial guarantee, but also a higher risk for the same substantial guarantee. Therefore, "purpose identity" does not only require that the data processing has to remain in the same context, rather, purpose identity additionally requires that there is no risk at all that adds to the risk as specified previously. So far, the compatibility assessment enables, thus, the data controller to determine substantive "purpose identity": the data controller can indeed formally stipulate the purpose, differently, but substantively, the purpose of the later use can be considered as identical to the preceding purpose, so long as the new purpose does not reveal an additional risk to the individual fundamental rights as previously specified.

(b) Further protection instruments that can avoid purpose incompatibility

However, the so-called compatibility assessment provided for by European data protection laws goes beyond an assessment of purpose identity. As illustrated previously, the ePrivacy Directive only allows the process-

---

1375 Cf. above under point C. II. 3. a) bb) (2) (c) Central function with respect to all fundamental rights (second reason why data protection is indispensable of data protection II).

1376 See above under point C. III. 1. a) aa) (2) ECJ: Reference to data protection instruments instead of ,reasonable expectations.

ing of personal data either for the purposes explicitly listed in the law or on the basis of the individual's consent. In both cases, the data controller is not allowed to process the data for another purpose if this causes a new risk. In contrast, the Data Protection Directive, as well as the General Data Protection Regulation allows the data controller to process the personal data so long as it is not incompatible with the initial purpose. Thus, even if the data controller processes personal data for another purpose, which is, from a substantive point of view, not identical to the preceding purpose, the data controller can base its processing on another legal provision so long as it is not incompatible with the initial purpose. In this regard, the general clause for the data controller's 'legitimate interests' is particularly relevant. Indeed, whether the later processing is definitely incompatible with the preceding purpose depends on balancing the colliding fundamental rights.[1377]

The processing of personal data for another purpose other than for why it was originally collected is not incompatible so long as the interest pursued with the change of purpose outweighs the risks caused by it. In order to assess these risks, all fundamental rights of the individual concerned must be taken into account. This means, in particular, to consider not only the (potentially) new risk caused by the change of purpose against another substantial guarantee, but also to the fundamental right that was (potentially) already concerned the moment the data was collected.[1378] For example, if the data was collected by intruding into the individual's privacy of communications, this harm potentially becomes more intensive with a substantive purpose change.[1379] Thus, whether the controller's interest pursued with the change of purpose positively passes the balancing exercise does not only depend on the potentially new risk for another substantial guarantee of the individual concerned, but also on the increased risk or harm for the substantial guarantee that was already formerly concerned. Indeed, the outcome of this assessment can be influenced, in particular, by implement-

1377 Cf. above under point C. I. 1. b) aa) (3) (c) Balancing the colliding constitutional positions.

1378 Cf. above under point C. III. 1. b) bb) (2) Proportionate change of purpose, referring to BVerfG, 20th of April 2016, 1 BvR 966/09 and 1 BvR 1140/09 (Federal Bureau of Investigation Law), cip. 288.

1379 Cf. above at the introduction of point C. II. 3. b) aa) (2) Necessity requirement, irrespective of inconvenience, referring, by means of an example, to BVerfG, 11th of March 2008, 1 BVR 2047/05 and 1 BvR 1254/07 (License Plate Recognition), cip. 74.

ing further protection instruments reducing the risks for the individual concerned.

(c) Systemizing the criteria for the compatibility assessment

Correspondingly, in order to carry out the compatibility assessment, the General Data Protection Regulation establishes under its Art. 6 sect. 4, just as the Article 29 Data Protection Working Group has earlier proposed regarding the Data Protection Directive, several criteria such as the 'safeguards ensuring fairness and preventing undue impact'. Beside these safeguards implemented by the controller, the regulation lists the following criteria: the 'distance' between the purposes, the 'context' of the data processing, as well as the 'reasonable expectations' of the individual concerned, the 'nature of the data' and the 'impact on the data subjects'. Indeed, as illustrated before, this bundle of criteria is neither coherent nor does it provide for legal certainty.[1380]

However, on the basis of the approach advocated in this thesis, it is possible to systemise the criteria. As already stressed in the introduction, the data controller's 'purpose' and the 'context', in which the data processing takes place, are actually two different links for legal regulation of the same phenomenon. The purpose links the current context of the data processing with a future context, in which the data shall be used.[1381] If the re-specified purpose of the controller reveals a higher risk than specified previously, the purpose is, from a normative standpoint, substantively different. If the re-specified purpose reveals a risk for another substantial guarantee of an individual's fundamental right, the personal data is even going to be used in another context than before.[1382] The fundamental rights of the individual concerned define which context is legally relevant and how

1380 See above under point C. III. 1. a) bb) (3) Criteria for the substantive compatibility assessment, and compare also the critique of the criteria proposed by the Forum Privatheit, White Paper – Data Protection Impact Assessment, above under point C. II. 3. a) bb) (1) (c) Criticism: Incoherence of risk criteria.

1381 See above under point B. III. 4. Clarifying the relationship between "context" and "purpose".

1382 See above under point C. III. 2. a) aa) (3) Clarification of an objective scale: "Same risk, higher risk, and another risk".

specifically the purpose must be specified.[1383] Thus, the approach referring to all fundamental rights to privacy, freedom and equality provides an objective scale not only for the definition of the context, but also for measuring the ‚distance' between the purposes.

Similarly, the fundamental rights also determine which expectations of the individual concerned are 'reasonable' and which are not. The individual does not have to reasonably expect that the later use of personal data leads to a higher risk or another risk than previously specified by the data controller.[1384] Comparably, the fundamental rights define the 'nature of the data'. If personal data reveals *per se,* intimate information about an individual such as his or her DNA, the specific protection for this kind of data results from the substantial guarantee of private life under Article 7 ECFR, that also covers the privacy of intimate information.[1385] If the processing of certain types of data leads to the risks of discrimination of an individual in social life, it is the fundamental right to non-discri-mination under Article 21 ECFR that defines this category. And if certain data concern, as such, specific fundamental rights to freedom, such as information about an individual's religion, it is Article 10 ECFR that determines this as a special data category.

The fundamental rights also provide an objective scale in order to assess which impact of the data processing on the individual concerned is legally relevant. For example, if the collection of personal data intrudes into an individual's privacy, such as at his or her home, such an intrusion harms his or her right to privacy of the home under Article 7 ECFR and, indeed, in this regard, "it does not matter whether the information on the private lives concerned is sensitive or whether the people concerned have been inconvenienced in any way".[1386] The reason is that the rights to privacy (more or less) guarantee that the individual is being left alone, irrespective of any further harm.[1387] Correspondingly, protection of a specific

1383 See above under point C. II. 3. a) bb) (2) Purpose specification discovering risks posed to all fundamental rights.

1384 Cf. above under point C. II. a) cc) (2) (c) Excursus: Objective vs. subjective risks.

1385 See above the introduction of point C. II 3. b) aa) Right to privacy (aka 'being left alone'), referring, as an example, to ECtHR, Case of S. and Marper vs. the United Kingdom from 4 December 2008 (application nos. 30562/04 and 30566/04), cip. 66.

1386 See ECJ C-293/12 and C-594/12 cip. 33.

1387 Cf. above under point C. II. 3. b) aa) Right to privacy (aka 'being left alone').

right to freedom against a certain use of information gathered by data processing requires that the processing conflicts with its substantial guarantee that means, the individual suffers harm in terms of that he or she is restrained in exercising this fundamental right.[1388]

Finally, as a consequence, the substantial guarantees also determine the protection instruments that shall prevent harm from occurring against the individual. If the respecification of the purpose reveals a new risk against a fundamental right, the controller has to implement protection measures that avoid, or at least reduce, that risk.[1389] In conclusion, Article 8 ECFR does not explicitly establish the principle of purpose limitation, but only the requirement of purpose specification. However, the fundamental right to privacy, freedom and non-discrimination determine which data protection instruments are necessary in order to protect the individual against new risks that were not revealed before.

In conclusion, in many cases, the criteria proposed by the Article 29 Data Protection Working Group, and now established under Article 6 sect. 4 of the General Data Protection Regulation, may refer to the same phenomenon, for example, the "purpose" that specifies the "context" of the data processing. However, when carrying out the compatibility assessment, each criteria can shed light on another decisive aspect. For example, the context does not yet say anything about the fact of whether or not the data processing leads to a higher risk for the substantial guarantee (covering the context) than specified before. This can be more precisely determined by referring to the "purpose". Comparably, the "nature of data" may especially help clarify when the transfer of certain data from one context into another one is particularly "sensitive" for the individual concerned. The term "impact" focuses on the question of whether, and if so, how intensively the later use of data conflicts with the substantial guarantee concerned. All criteria together hence constitute an extremely helpful set of "analytical instruments" in order to carve out the particularities of data processing in a specific case. This is the value of the criteria; however, without an objective legal scale, they would float freely in an argumentative space.

1388 See above under point C. II. 3. b) dd) Specific rights to freedom.

1389 Cf. above under point C. II. 3. a) cc) (2) (a) Effectiveness of protection instruments.

(2) Right to private life under Article 8 ECHR and the right to informational self-determination

This risk-based approach could also be incorporated, principally, in the other current concepts of data protection surrounding the principle of purpose limitation. The European Court of Human Rights does not refer, to other fundamental rights, in particular, not in order to specify the purpose.[1390] However, the Court's case-by-case approach referring to categories such as 'intrusion into privacy' or 'publication' illustrates that the European Court of Human Rights indeed elaborates on differentiated categories of protection.[1391] In principle, the Court could furthermore refer to other fundamental rights in order to elaborate on additional categories for the assessment of the individual's 'reasonable expectations'.[1392] This approach would make it possible to refer to the right to private life under Article 8 ECHR in order to provide for precautionary protection instruments in favor of the other fundamental rights long before there is a discovery of a specific risk to them.[1393] In light of this approach, the later use of personal data would conflict with the individual's 'reasonable expectations' if it causes a new risk for his or her fundamental rights that he or she had not to expect. This concept is very similar to the concept proposed with respect to Article 8 ECFR.

Also the concept of the German right to informational self-determination can be refined, correspondingly. At a first glance, this concept indeed excludes the approach of purpose compatibility. The approach of purpose identity results, as a general requirement, in the private sector not from the 'informational separation of state powers' but from the individual's 'right

1390 See above under point C. I. 3. b) ee) Conclusion: Assessment of 'reasonable expectations' on a case-by-case basis, referring to ECtHR, Case of Gillan and Quinton vs. the United Kingdom from 12 January 2010 (application no. 4158/05), cip. 88 to 90.

1391 Cf. above under point C. I. 3. c) aa) (1) General definition of the term "personal data" under Articles 7 and 8 ECFR.

1392 See above under point C. II. a) cc) (2) (c) Excursus: Objective vs. subjective risks.

1393 Cf. above under point C. II. 3. a) bb) (2) (b) Separating specific from unspecific risks.

to control the disclosure and use of the data related to him or her'.[1394] Forgó et al. consider that this determination right would be undermined if the later usage was not strictly limited to the originally specified purpose. However, at a second glance, one main challenge of this stricter concept is to find criteria in order to reliably specify the purpose. If the requirement of purpose identity does not refer to data *per se,* but to the risks originally specified, its effects on the scope of action of the controller are less strict. The reason is that there is no substantive change of purpose. This means, the purpose is substantively identical so long as the data processing does not reveal an additional risk to the individual's fundamental rights.[1395] Indeed, if the respecification of the purpose reveals an additional risk, the controller is principally not allowed to process the data for this (substantively) changed purpose. In this case, the German legislator has to establish legal provisions in order to proportionately balance the colliding fundamental rights. In doing so, it could apply, again, the approach promoted in this thesis referring to all basic rights of the individual concerned.[1396]

cc) Applying a 'non-linear perspective'

Even if the risk-based approach promoted in this thesis can basically be incorporated in the current concepts of protection applied by the European Court of Human Rights and the German Constitutional Court, there remains a slight disadvantage compared to the approach of purpose compatibility proposed in this thesis with respect to the European Charter of Fundamental Rights. Both current concepts focus on the moment of collection as the main starting point for the legal evaluation of risks and, thus, principally conflict with the non-linearity of innovation processes.[1397] In contrast, the requirement of purpose compatibility does not focus, in principle,

1394 See above under points C. III. 1. b) bb) (1) Strict requirement of purpose identity limiting the intensity of the infringement, and C. III. 1. b) dd) Interim conclusion: Right to control data causing a 'flood of regulation'.

1395 Cf. above under point C. III. 2. a) aa) (3) Clarification of an objective scale: "Same risk, higher risk, and another risk".

1396 Cf. above under point C. II. 3. a) cc) (1) Tying into the Courts' decisions and European legislation.

1397 See above under point C. I. 2. d) Purpose specification as the essential link for legal evaluation; cf. the cases illustrated under point C. I. 3. b) cc) Particular reference to the individual's "reasonable expectations"; as well as on the level of

on the moment of collection, but instead on the subsequent moments and therefore is, theoretically, more open toward innovation. Indeed, this difference might only be significant on a theoretical level, without further impact in practice. However, it was already stressed that there might be at least one case where this slight theoretical difference plays a role in practice.

As stressed previously, the Article 29 Data Protection Working Group promotes the idea that we have to examine the compatibility of all later uses of personal data with respect to the first collection. In doing so, it overlooks the possibility that the current purpose may be compatible with the original purpose, but not with another purpose specified in between. The Working Group apparently focuses on the moment of collection because it ties into the individual's 'reasonable expectations': The logical starting point for the individual's expectations about what could happen with data related to him or her always is the moment of collection.[1398] Similarly, an understanding of the German concept of protection guaranteeing an individual's right to 'basically determine by him or herself the disclosure and later usage of the data' equally focuses on the moment of collection'. In particular, the legal scholar Albers criticizes this approach promoting a shift of focus in data protection law away from a linear to a non-linear conception of data processing activities.[1399]

Thus, the conceptual difference between, on the one hand, the 'reasonable expectations' mechanism and the informational self-determination right and, on the other hand, the compatibility assessment is the moment that is considered as decisive for the legal evaluation of the risks. In order to guarantee the individual's autonomy, both his or her 'reasonable expectations', as well as his or her informational self-determination right protect the individual's confidence in how the data will be used. Both concepts of protection exclude all of the risks that were not discovered at the initial moment of collection. The individual's 'reasonable expectations', as well as self-determination right require the controller to specify, the moment of

---

ordinary law under point C. II. 2. b) cc) Arguable focus on data collection for legal evaluation in the private sector.

1398 See above under point C. III. 1. a) bb) (1) Preliminary analysis: Pre-conditions and consequences.

1399 See above under point C. I. 2. f) Conceptual link between ,'privacy' and ,'data protection', referring to Albers, Treatment of Personal Information and Data, cip. 121 to 123.

collection, the intended use and, consequently, the related risk. The purpose limits the later use of data to this risk: If the purpose reveals the risk for a specific substantial guarantee, the controller must not process the data in a way leading to a higher or another risk; and if the purpose specified in the moment of collection reveals no specific risk at all, the later usage of the data must also not lead to a specific risk. Both requirements hence exclude all risks that were not specified in the moment of collection. Only the mechanisms used to reach this goal are different: In the one case, the concept protects the individual because he or she could not expect the later risk or infringement, and in the other case, because he or she could not determine it. In contrast, the requirement of purpose compatibility does not necessarily tie into the moment of collection, excluding all unspecific risks. Instead, the requirement of purpose compatibility focuses, first, on the moment of the later use, subsequently compares, second, the related risks with the risks precedingly specified and, finally, turns onto the question of how a newly discovered risk can be excluded (or reduced) through specific protection instruments.

In conclusion, all three requirements can be understood as controlling the risks caused by the data processing. However, while the individual's 'reasonable expectations' and the right to 'determine the disclosure and later usage of the data' primarily serve to exclude, in the moment of collection, all undiscovered risks, the requirement of purpose compatibility allows one to focus, first, on the control of specific risks caused by the later use of data. Thus, while the first two concepts protect the individual by excluding all risks, that were not specified, the requirement of purpose compatibility provides protection by controlling specific risks that may occur later on.

b) Substantial guarantees: Providing criteria for a compatibility assessment

Such a non-linear approach applied for the compatibility assessment requires precisely to examine which kind of data processing causes which risk. In order to answer this question, the fundamental rights to privacy, freedom and non-discrimination provide an objective scale in order to determine which purposes are, from an objective point of view, compatible or incompatible. Thus, the substantial guarantees provided for by all fundamental rights determine the criteria for the compatibility assessment. In order to protect the individual's autonomy, the result might be, in the one case, strict purpose identity, in another case, the exclusion of certain data for a certain use and in yet another case no restriction at all. The next subchapters will examine which substantial guarantee provides, in principle, for which requirement.

aa) Right of 'being left alone': 'Reasonable expectations' determined by risks

As illustrated previously, the substantial guarantees of privacy (i.e. rights of being left alone) provided for by Article 7 ECFR protects the individual against arbitrary intrusions into his or her private spheres. Article 7 ECFR certainly applies in situations in the individual's private home or when he or she uses means of communications. Whether the European Court of Justice refers to situations in the public equally to Article 7 ECFR or the right to data protection under Article 8 ECFR is not yet sufficiently clear. In any case, applying the concept of protection proposed in this thesis, many cases of "privacy in public" can rather fall under the specific rights to freedom than the right to private life.[1400] However, if these cases do not fall under specific rights to freedom, the answer to the previous question can be significant, for example, with respect to the requirements for the consent and the requirement that "derogations and limitations (of the right to private life) in relation to the protection of personal data must apply only in so far as is strictly necessary (…)."[1401] The reason for this is that both aspects are, in turn, decisive regarding the purpose compatibility requirement. The European Court of Justice requires for the individual's consent strict purpose identity.[1402] This means that if the controller refers, in order to legitimize an intrusion into the privacy of the individual, to his or her consent, it is not allowed to substantively change the purpose. In light of the concept of protection proposed in this thesis, the later use of data must

1400 See above under point C. II. 3. b) dd) (3) Interim conclusion: How "privacy in public" can be further determined.

1401 See above under point C. II. 3. b) aa) (2) Necessity requirement, irrespective of inconvenience, referring to ECJ C-293/12 and C-594/12 (Digital Rights vs. Ireland), cip. 52; affirmed in the subsequent case of "*Schrems vs. Ireland*", ECJ C-362/14, cip. 92.

1402 See above under point C. III. 1. a) aa) (2) (b) Purpose identity for the consent, referring to ECJ C-543/09 (Telekom vs. Germany), cip. 66 and 67.

not lead to a higher risk for the same object of protection or a risk for another one.[1403] The second before-mentioned requirement that 'derogations and limitations (of the right to private life) in relation to the protection of personal data must apply only in so far as is strictly necessary (…)' determines further whether a change of purpose leads to a higher risk for the same object of protection. If the change of purpose reveals further information about the individual's private life, the change of purpose 'extends' the privacy intrusion and, thus, immediately realizes a higher risk for the individual concerned than specified before.[1404] In this sense, this requirement equals the requirement of purpose identity.

Indeed, the controller can broaden its scope of action already, the moment that the data is collected through specifying, originally, the intrusion into the privacy in broad terms. As stressed before, the specific object of protection (aka substantial guarantee) of privacy constitutes the framework for the specification of the purpose.[1405] For example, it would be sufficient if the controller specified the purpose by stating that the collection of certain types of data (also to be specified) amounts to an intrusion into the individual's home. This is a rather broad purpose, indeed. However, this is justified, in light of the individual's autonomy, because there is another substantial guarantee concerned that safeguards that the individual is able to know which information the controller specifically retrieves about him or her: the guarantee of the individual's internal freedom of development.[1406] The advantage resulting from these two overlapping substantial guarantees is threefold: First, the individual's consent does not have to be drafted in an over-complex way because it simply refers to the essential risk; second, the controller's later scope of action is not overly restricted; and third, the individual concerned constantly stays up-to-date regarding the current knowledge that the controller retains about him or her. In contrast, if the controller specifies, when the data is first collected, a narrow purpose, its scope of action is more restricted. In this case, the change of purpose is substantive if it reveals more information about the

---

1403 See above under point C. III. 2. a) aa) (3) Clarification of an objective scale: "Same risk, higher risk, and another risk".

1404 See already above under point C. II. 3. b) aa) (2) Necessity requirement, irrespective of inconvenience.

1405 See above under point C. III. 2. a) aa) (3) Clarification of an objective scale: "Same risk, higher risk, and another risk".

1406 See above under point C. II. 3. b) cc) Internal freedom of development.

individual's private life. The controller must then reduce the risk caused by the change of purpose by additional protection measures. For example, the controller might choose an anonymization technique which excludes that the processing reveals further information about the individual's private life.[1407]

Finally, there is another type of case where the controller wants to use the data in a way that does not only 'extend' the intrusion into the individual's privacy but also causes a risk for further fundamental rights. If the controller has based the data processing on the individual's consent, the purpose specified in the consent must reveal the risk for the object of protection of these further fundamental rights. The reason is, again, that the European Court of Justice requires purpose identity regarding the consent. However, if the controller has based the processing not on the individual's consent but, for example, on an authorizing law, the question is whether or not this substantive change of purpose is incompatible with the original purpose (which had only specified a risk for the guarantee of privacy). The answer depends on the specific guarantee of privacy concerned by the data collection. Supposing the European Court of Justice applied an approach comparable to that by the German Constitutional Court, it may differentiate this position as: first of all, the controller's interest pursued with the new purpose must be so important that it had equally legitimized the collection of the data; second, since the individual's privacy of the home is especially important (serving as a 'haven of retreat'), the compatibility assessment is particularly strict if the collection of the data has amounted into an intrusion of the individual's home;[1408] and third, if the collection of the data interfered with the guarantee of privacy of communications, the purpose compatibility also depends on the question of whether the new risk caused by the change of purpose risks to lead to a bias in the communication between individuals.[1409] Thus, in any case, the substantial guaran-

---

1407 See, in more detail how the specific substantial guarantees also determine the anonymization technique that is necessary in order to exclude the scope(s) of protection, beneath under point C. IV. 1. Scope of application and responsibility (Article 8 sect. 1 ECFR).

1408 Cf. above under point C. III. 1. b) bb) (2) Proportionate change of purpose, referring to BVerfG, 20th of April 2016, 1 BvR 966/09 and 1 BvR 1140/09 (Federal Bureau of Investigation Law), cip. 291.

1409 Cf. above under point C. II. 3. b) aa) (1) (b) Using communications: Protection against 'filtering opinions', referring, by means of an example, to BVerfG, 14th of July 1999, 1 BvR 2226/94 (Surveillance of Telecommunications), cip. 160.

tee of privacy specifically concerned determines the (eventually additional) requirements for the compatibility assessment and, consequently, which protection measures are necessary in order to minimize or even avoid the related risk.

In conclusion, there are two main types of cases where the data controller potentially harms the individual's right to privacy under Article 7 ECFR: First, if the data collection intrudes into the individual's privacy and he or she is not able to decide on whether or not the controller may collect the data. Second, the individual could decide on the collection of the data for a certain purpose, but the controller uses the data later for another purpose leading to another or more intensive risk and the individual is, again, not able to decide on that new risk. In any case, such an infringement of the individual's substantial guarantee of privacy under Article 7 ECFR can be justified on the basis of the controller's opposing fundamental rights. These conflicts of the opposing fundamental rights must be regulated by an authorizing law.

bb) Self-representation in the public: A balancing exercise instead of purpose determination

Regarding the substantial guarantee of self-representation in the public, there essentially are two different types of cases: The first type of cases refers to the first publication of personal data; the second type refers to the re-publication of personal data that was already legally published. The European Court of Justice requires that the first publication of personal data must be based on the individual's consent or another legitimate basis provided for by law.[1410] Here again, if the first publication of the personal data was based on the consent, the later use of that data is principally limited to the purpose originally specified.[1411]

In contrast, if the first publication was not based on the individual's consent, the decision of "*Mr. González vs. Google Spain*" illustrates that a later use of data by a private party is not, *per se,* limited to the purpose for

---

1410 See above under point C. II. 3. b) bb) (2) First publication: Strict requirements, referring to ECJ C-92/09 and C-93/09 (Schecke vs. Germany), cip. 61 to 64; and ECJ C-465/00, C-138/01 and C-139/01 (Rechnungshof vs. ORF), cip. 89 and 90.

1411 See above under point C. III. 1. a) aa) (2) (b) Purpose identity for the consent.

that it was firstly published. The European Court of Justice did not examine in detail the initial and the later purpose. However, the facts of this case made clear that the initial publication occurred, upon an order by the Ministry of Labor and Social Affairs, by newspapers in order to attract attention of as many bidders for the auction as possible. In contrast, later on, the newspapers, the Internet search engine, and the users of the search engine pursued, since the auction had already taken place, purposes different to the initial one. Interestingly, the Court did not refer to the compatibility assessment, but to the requirement that the later use must be 'adequate, relevant, and not excessive in relation to the purpose for which it was initially collected'. The Court affirmed that the individual's right to private life under Article 7 ECFR, and his or her right to data protection under Article 8 ECFR, generally rule out the opposing economic interests of the search engine, as well as the information interests of its users, except where there is a preponderant interest of the public in that information, for example, because of the social role that the individual plays in public life.[1412] The decision is highly arguable if this general rule is considered as prevailing or determining the result of the purpose compatibility assessment.[1413] The reason for this doubt is that such a general priority rule is, in the final analysis, similar to the general requirement of purpose identity, which then allows, only exceptionally, a change of purpose, as already criticized.[1414] In the case of re-publication of personal data, this rule-and-exception relationship provides the individual with a rather comprehensive right to determine his or her social representation in the public. This conflicts with the substantial guarantee of self-representation in the public, which is actually concerned and only guarantees, once the data is published legally, the individual certain chances of influencing his or her representation in society. Whether these chances are unconstitutionally limited or not depends on a fair balance taking both the circumstances of the first publication and of the re-publication into account.[1415] In order to

1412 See ECJ C-131/12 cip. 97.

1413 See the discussion whether or not the requirements are part of the general compatibility assessment above under point C. III. 1. a) aa) (2) (a) 'Necessity-adequacy-relevance' as objective criteria for the compatibility assessment?.

1414 Cf. above under point C. III. 1. b) cc) (3) (b) Specification, identity and change of purpose as equivalent regulation instruments.

1415 See above under point C. II. 3. b) bb) (3) Re-publication: Weighing 'interests' against 'ald' and new purposes.

achieve this objective, the compatibility assessment provides for a more flexible balancing framework than a general priority rule.

In conclusion, there are, again, two main types of cases where the data controller potentially harms the individual's right to self-representation in the public: First, if it publishes information about the individual and this is not based on the individual's consent. And second, if the information was already published, and the data controller re-publishes it in a way that conflicts with the risk that was specified in the individual's consent, i.e. unduly restrains the individual's ability to influence his or her social representation in public. In any case, in this regard, it is particularly important to stress that the first publication, as well as the re-publication of the information can always be justified, even without consent, in light of the controller's opposing fundamental rights. These rights are often, in these type of cases, the fundamental freedom to expression and information. These conflicts of the opposing fundamental rights must then, again, be balanced by an authorizing law.

cc) Internal freedom of development: Specific instead of preliminary information

The internal freedom of behavior protects the individual against the unspecific threat knowing that others know something about him or her but not knowing what they know exactly.[1416] The European Court of Justice similarly stressed that such a situation is "likely to generate in the minds of the persons concerned the feeling that their private lives are the subject of constant surveillance."[1417] And the German Constitutional Court required, referring to the increased insights into the personality and possibilities of manipulation, that the individual has to "confidently know what information related to him or her is known in certain areas of his or her social environment" and to "estimate to some degree the knowledge of potential partners of communication".[1418]

1416 See above under point C. II. 3. b) cc) Internal freedom of development, referring, by way of an example, to BVerfG, 2nd March 2010, 1 BvR 256/08, 1 BvR 263/08, and 1 BvR 586/08 (Data Retention), cip. 241.

1417 ECJ C-293/12 and C-594/12 cip. 37.

1418 BVerfG, 15th of December 1983, 1 BvR 209, 269, 362, 420, 440, 484/83, cip. 170 to 172.

The requirement of purpose identity can indeed provide protection for such a guarantee, in particular, if it is required formally. If the data controller is strictly bound to the purpose it has initially stipulated, the individual can know, to a certain degree, what others know about him or her. The strict requirement of purpose identity, hence, can principally provide the individual the certainty, at least to some degree, about what information certain individuals know about him or her. However, this certainty can equally be provided for by other instruments of transparency, for example, rights and duties of information. These measures might be even more efficient since they principally refer to all moments of the data processing covering the current information, and not only to the moment of collection, where the purpose describes a future situation. Only if the information gathered becomes so vast that a right to transparency does not meet the individual's internal freedom of behavior, this may affect his or her fundamental right to private life under Article 7 ECFR in a way that requires the controller to retrieve his or her consent.[1419] Indeed, the Article 29 Data Protection Working Group also sees the requirement of purpose compatibility as a tool of transparency.[1420] However, the controller does not have to safeguard transparency by only applying strict purpose identity. Instead, the controller can also apply alternative protection instruments that safeguard transparency, which gives the controller more room when using personal data for other purposes than specified previously. Thus, alternative instruments of transparency can equally reduce the complexity of the compatibility assessment.

In any case, all transparency measures must ensure that the individual concerned is able to reflect and distance him or her from own and others' expectations. That means that the transparency measures have to reveal the extent and deepness of insights by others into the personality enabling the individual to protect him or herself against the risk of manipulation. How this aim is to be achieved is a question that cannot only be answered on a legal basis but must also be examined empirically.[1421] In conclusion,

---

1419 See above under point C. II. 3. b) cc) (3) Articles 7 and/or 8 ECFR: Information pursuant to insights into personality and possibilities of manipulation.

1420 See above at the introduction under point C. III. 1. a) bb) Compatibility assessment required by the Data Protection Directive, referring to the Article 29 Data Protection Working Group, Opinion 03/0213 on purpose limitation, p. 13.

1421 See above under point C. II. 3. b) cc) (3) Articles 7 and/or 8 ECFR: Information pursuant to insights into personality and possibilities of manipulation.

if the data controller does not sufficiently provide the information necessary for the individual to distance him or herself from his or her own and other's expectations, the data controller harms the individual's right to internal freedom of behavior. However, again, such harm might be justified by the data controller's colliding fundamental rights. This can be the case if the controller does not want to reveal information that is simultaneously protected by its own right to property (e.g. for the logic of a patented algorithm) or to conduct a business (e.g. for business secrets). These conflicts of the opposing fundamental rights must again be balanced by authorizing legal provisions.

dd) External freedoms of behavior: Purpose identity as one potential element amongst several protection instruments

Different to the 'unspecific threat' 'of being surveyed' is the situation that the individual knows that the data controller processes certain data related to him or her for a specific purpose and therefore stops, or omits exercising a fundamental right in order to avoid the disadvantages reasonably feared by him or her. Another similar type of case refers to situations where the data controller processes the data or another individual or entity uses the information in a manner restricting the possibilities of exercising an individual's fundamental right. Since both types of cases refer to specific rights of freedom, they cannot always be clearly differentiated from each other. However, while the first type is often discussed with respect to the collection of the data, the second type focuses on the later usage of the data or the information.[1422] As stressed before, the protection instruments provided for by the right to data protection under article 8 ECFR mainly enable the individual to: First, adapt his or her behavior to the informational measure; and second, seek protection against these measures.[1423]

In order to meet these aims, the requirement of purpose identity can play an important role. The moment personal data is collected, the requirement of purpose identity safeguards that the individual can trust that the data controller does not use the data later on for another purpose that in-

1422 See above the introduction of point C. II. 3. b) dd).

1423 See above under point C. II. 3. b) dd) (3) (c) Protection instruments enabling the individual to adapt to or protect him or herself against the informational measure.

creases the risk that the individual has accepted or even causes a so far unknown risk for another fundamental right to freedom. However, in these cases, the compatibility assessment particularly helps to assess which further protection instruments the data controller can implement in order to reduce or even avoid the additional risk. The rights to freedom thus serve the necessary scale in order to determine the further protection instruments. These instruments can be rights or duties of information, rights to correct wrong or misleading data and to delete it, or prohibitions to combine certain purposes or types of data by transferring it from one context into another one. The strict requirement of purpose identity hence is only one protection instrument amongst several others that come into question in order to meet the specific guarantees. In light of this, it should be stressed that purpose identity as an exclusive and general requirement could not only disproportionately restrict the scope of action of data controllers, but also restrict the individual's possibilities of protection.

In conclusion, the data controller harms an individual's specific fundamental right to freedom if it processes the data in a way that conflicts with its object of protection (aka substantial guarantee). However, if the individual does not consent to such harm, this might nevertheless be justified on the basis of the controller's colliding fundamental rights. These conflicts of the opposing fundamental rights must again be regulated by an authorizing law. In any case, with respect to potential harm and, in particular, the balancing exercise, further protection instruments such as of information, participation, and judicial review play a particularly important role.

ee) Equality and non-discrimination: Specifying incompatible purposes in the course of social life

In contrast the fundamental right to non-discrimination appears to require, at least more often than the fundamental rights to freedom, that certain purposes must not be combined. As discussed previously, several legal scholars consider the individual's consent as a 'tool of opacity' as the appropriate protection instrument in order to protect the individual against risks of being discriminated in social life. In contrast to this approach, this thesis promotes the notion that the fundamental right to non-discrimination should primarily be considered as requiring protection instruments that regulate the way how informational (possibly discriminatory) decisions are made. Second, if 'tools of opacity' are necessary in order to protect the individual against the risk of discrimination, these tools should not depend on the individual's consent, but rather on objective requirements provided for by law. The reason for this is that many discriminatory effects happen indirectly and are, therefore, hardly foreseeable by the controller and, even more so, by the individual.[1424] This is even more the case if discriminatory effects happen only in the course of time. In daily life, the criteria listed under Article 21 ECFR have not always the same relevance for discriminatory purposes. Often, the importance of a criteria in relation with a discriminatory practice depends on certain events that suddenly show up in human history. For instance, the criteria of being Islamic provides the basis for discriminatory practices mainly since terrorists have started to commit terroristic attacks in the name of their god. A data controller, as well as an individual, can hardly predict these events and, thus, retrieve the consent for this type of data for this purpose, in advance.

In any case, if the requirement of purpose identity is interpreted pursuant to the risk-based approach as proposed in this thesis, it can provide an appropriate (objective) 'tool of opacity'. If such an event occurs after the data is collected and therefore turns the formerly "normal" personal data now into sensitive data, this new risk requires the controller not to process the data in a discriminatory way. In order to increase legal certainty, the regulator, or a regulated self-regulation entity could also set up, respectively, legal provisions or private standards that list such specific purposes being incompatible.[1425] For instance, such a list might prohibit the transfer of information about the probability that a woman is pregnant from whatever context (e.g. an online purchasing context) into an employment context.[1426] The background reason for this is that it is possible to calculate, today, based on a woman's purchase behavior the probability that she is pregnant, and even in which month the pregnancy occurred. This is possible because women typically start buying specific products

1424 See above under point C. II. 3. b) ee) (2) In the private sector: 'Tool of opacity' vs. private autonomy?, referring to Krasnow Waterman and Bruening: Big Data analytics: risks and responsibilities, IDPL 2014 (Vol. 4, no. 2), p. 94.

1425 See the different strategies of state regulation and regulated self-regulation above under point A. II. 2. The regulator's perspective.

1426 See Kühling, Data protection in a future world of ubiquitous data processing, p. 165, with further examples referring to information about an HIV infection or a recovered alcoholic disease; Grafenstein v., The Principle of Purpose Limitation between Openness toward Innovation and the Rule of Law, p. 792.

when they become pregnant or are pregnant in a certain month.[1427] However, in an employment context, particularly, when applying for a job, employers are not allowed to ask whether the applicant for the job is pregnant or not.[1428] Therefore, in order to avoid that the employer circumvents this prohibition by retrieving the corresponding data, for example, from a drug store, data protection laws could clarify that the use of such data for employment purposes is incompatible with the original purpose. As mentioned previously, in Germany, the General Equality Act (AGG) transposes several European directives into German ordinary law and provides for similar provisions. These can therefore provide a basis for a data protection regulation that clarifies, correspondingly, the incompatibility of purposes.[1429]

In conclusion, the data controller harms the individual's right to non-discrimina-tion if it processes the data in a way that causes a specific risk for the individual concerned being discriminated in social life. However, again, this can be justified on the basis of the data controller's own fundamental rights. In this regard, it is necessary to scrutinize whether the discrimination is based, from a normative perspective, on a justifiable reason or not.[1430]

c) Conclusion: Purpose limitation in decentralized data networks

The preceding analysis has demonstrated that the strict requirement of purpose identity can indeed provide protection for all of the substantial guarantees mentioned in the analysis. This is even then the case if this requirement is not interpreted in a formal way, i.e. providing an individual's right to control the usage of 'his or her' data, but more substantively, within the meaning of an individual's control of risks caused by the data processing. So far, the compatibility assessment enables one to assess purpose identity, i.e. whether the later data processing causes a new risk to the in-

1427 See, for example, at Duhigg, The Power of Habit, pp. 228 to 244.

1428 See BAG (Federal Labour Court), decision from the 15th of October 1992 (2 AZR 227/92), and BAG, decision from the 6th of February 2003 (2 AZR 621/01).

1429 Cf. Buchner, Informational Self-Determination, p. 116, who indeed stresses that these conflicts may often be better solved by means of the Social State principle, and not by data protection law.

1430 See above under point C. 2. b) ee) Rights to equality and non-discrimination.

dividual's fundamental rights than specified before. However, the approach provided for, at least, by the Data Protection Directive and the General Data Protection Regulation goes beyond such a narrow assessment of purpose identity. This approach principally allows the data controller to process the data also for substantively different purposes so long as this is not incompatible with the original purpose. In order to assess potential purpose incompatibility, the individual's fundamental rights to privacy, freedom and non-discrimination play a decisive role. Compared to the requirement of purpose specification, this is even more the case because the fundamental right to data protection under Article 8 ECFR itself does not require the data controller to limit the later data processing to the original purpose. On the level of fundamental rights, this requirement thus results from the substantial guarantees provided by the other fundamental rights.[1431]

It is also clearer that there are, beside the strict requirement of purpose identity, alternative protection instruments, which can equally protect the substantial guarantees. Even more so, some guarantees such as the individual's internal freedom of development can be protected even more so, for example, by a right to transparency than by strict purpose identity. The reason is that such a right to transparency enables the individual not only to get information about the intended processing once, the moment the data is collected, but is constantly up-dated about the knowledge that the data controller retrieves, on the basis of its ongoing data processing.[1432] The concept of protection proposed for the right to data protection under Article 8 ECFR hence leads, here again, to the situation that the regulation extends protection from the moment of collection to the way *how* the data is used later on.[1433] In many situations, these alternative protection instruments might thus be more appropriate than the strict requirement of purpose identity: on the one hand, they may infringe the data controller's fun-

---

1431 Cf. Bygrave, Data Privacy Law, p. 153 (fn. 39), who also considers that the second component of the principle of purpose limitation (i.e. to limit the later data processing to the original purpose) is provided on the level of fundamental rights, but as part of the fairness" criterion that is explicitly mentioned under Art. 8 sect. 1 ECFR.

1432 Cf. Roßnagel, Data protection in computerized everyday life, p. 180.

1433 See, already with respect to the requirement of purpose specification, above under point C. II. 3. c) Conclusion: Purpose specification during innovation processes, referring to points A. II. 1. Legal research about innovation, and C. I. 1. b) bb) (1) The 3-Step-Test: Assessing the defensive and protection function.

damental rights less, and on the other hand, they may provide for more effective and efficient protection to the individual's fundamental rights. Indeed, this understanding does not make currently established laws, such as the ePrivacy Directive, disproportionate only because the directive requires strict purpose identity. The legislator has a large margin of discretion when establishing protection instruments in the private sector. However, the European legislator may take these considerations into account when establishing a new law or, in particular, amending the ePrivacy Directive.[1434]

In conclusion, the function of the principle of purpose limitation is not, in light of the risk-based approach proposed in this thesis, to exclude all possible risks the moment the data is collected, but rather to control specific risks caused by the later usage of the data. Insofar, the purpose compatibility requires the data controller to assess whether or not a change of purpose causes a new risk for the individual's fundamental rights to privacy, freedom or non-discrimination. If the compatibility assessment discovers such a new risk, it depends on the colliding fundamental rights and, in particular, on the substantial guarantees concerned, which determine the protection instruments that the data controller should implement in order to avoid that the new purpose is considered as incompatible with the preceding purpose(s).

Finally, this approach is also particularly suitable for innovation processes occurring in private de-centralized environments. The reason is that the transfer of data from one data controller to another one is not principally forbidden. Instead, the legitimacy of the data transfer primarily depends, again, on the question of whether the transfer creates a new risk for the individual's fundamental rights and, if this is the case, on the protection instruments applied. If the transfer does not create a new risk for the individual's fundamental rights, the transfer is not problematic. In contrast, in the public sector, the transfer of personal data from one agency to another agency is, in general, much more problematic. This difference results from the principle of the informational separation of powers. In the private sector, this principle does not apply. In Germany, for example, the tasks of the public agency specified within the law provides, beside the

1434 See the "Summary report on the public consultation on the Evaluation and Review of the ePrivacy Directive" retrieved on the 11th of September 2016 from https://ec.europa.eu/digital-single-market/en/news/summary-report-public-consultation-evaluation-and-review-eprivacy-directive.

object of protection for that the processing serves, an essential link for limiting the later usage of the data.[1435] The State is not allowed, in light of its constitution, to aggregate information about its citizens in an unlimited way. In contrast, private data controllers are not bound to the principle of informational separation of powers, but are limited only if the data processing causes a threat against fundamental rights of the individual concerned. Thus, the transfer of personal data from one private party to another one does not constitute harm *per se* for the individual concerned, but only if this causes a new risk to his or her fundamental rights. The data controllers, hence, must make sure, when transferring, storing and further processing personal data, that this does not cause an additional risk to that as previously specified.[1436]

IV. Data protection instruments in non-linear environments

The preceding chapters analyzed the function of the requirements of purpose specification and purpose limitation with respect to the concept of protection of the right to data protection under Article 8 ECFR. This chapter examines how both requirements may, or should be implemented, in the private sector, by specific regulation instruments. In doing so, the first sub-chapter clarifies the scope of protection of the right to data protection, as well as its specific protection instruments with respect to the other fundamental rights to privacy, freedom, and non-discrimination. It will also be clarified who is principally responsible for implementing these protection instruments. The subsequent sub-chapter addresses the question of the effects of these protection instruments on the private sector, which regulatory approach comes into question and, in particular, the interplay of the individual's consent and legal provisions in order to balance the colliding fundamental rights. Finally, the last sub-chapter examines in detail, with

---

1435 See above under points C. II. 3. c) ee) (1) (d) Liberalization of the strict requirement by referring to the object of protection, referring to BVerfG, 20th of April 2016, 1 BvR 966/09 and 1 BvR 1140/09 (Federal Bureau of Investigation Law), cip. 281.

1436 Cf. Roßnagel, Data protection in computerized everyday life, pp. 188 to 191, who stresses the "informational architecture" as a significant factor for determining the risks caused by the data processing in modern collaborative societies; see also above under point …(Hierarchy of safeguards: From anonymization to 'functional separation')….

respect to the individual's decision-making process, overall, the interplay of several protection instruments.

1. Scope of application and responsibility (Article 8 sect. 1 ECFR)

The right to data protection under Article 8 ECFR provides the individual with the necessary instruments in order to protect against the risks caused by data processing against his or her other fundamental rights of privacy, freedom and non-discrimination. Thus, the definition of the term 'personal data' sets, on the one hand, the threshold of protection for the individual concerned. On the other hand, the term also determines the requirements conflicting, in principle, with societal needs for information. Therefore, the definition of the term must strike a balance between these two opposing constitutional positions.[1437] This chapter builds on the considerations made in previous chapters regarding the fact that the term "personal data" is extremely vague and broad.[1438] As a first step, this chapter will examine the practical problems resulting from the current definition. As a second step, the chapter elaborates on a potential solution for the conflict described. As illustrated previously, the purpose is usually considered as one important factor determining the scope of protection. However, the approach promoted in this thesis will demonstrate that the purpose is not only "one important factor" but a decisive mechanism in order to fairly balance between the opposing fundamental rights.

1437 See the Article 29 Data Protection Working Group, Opinion 4/2007 on the concept of personal data, p. 5.

1438 See above under point C. I. 3. c) cc) (1) The reason for why the scope is too vague: Difference between data and information, referring to Pombriant, Data, Information and Knowledge – Transformation of data is key, pp. 97 and 98, who adds, furthermore, the third dimension of subjective "knowledge"; Albers, Treatment of personal information and data, cip. 8 to 15; Britz, Informational Self-Determination between Legal Doctrine and Constitutional Case Law, pp. 567 and 568.

a) Problems in practice: A balance between too much and too little protection

As stressed previously, the European Court of Justice does not yet clearly differentiate between the substantial guarantees of the right to private life under Article 7 ECFR and the right to data protection under Article 8 ECFR and, thus, between the different scopes of protection.[1439] In the case of "*Schecke vs. Land Hessen*", referring to the term of 'personal data', the Court defines the scope of protection as: "The right to respect for private life with regard to the processing of personal data, recognized by Article 7 and Article 8 of the Charter, concerns any information relating to an identified or identifiable individual".[1440] Secondary data protection laws refer, in order to assess whether an individual is identifiable or not, to 'all the means reasonably likely to be used'. And, the European Court of Justice clarified, also in this regard, several aspects, in particular, in relation to the processing of IP addresses.[1441] However, examining, in more detail, the criteria discussed in legal literature still makes it very clear the fact that the scope of protection, referring to the term 'personal data', only, either provides too much or too little protection against the risks caused by the processing of that data.[1442] This becomes abundantly clear if one examines the different types of data that may be related to an individual and, correspondingly, the conditions under that 'personal data' can be considered as 'anonymized'.

aa) How data may be related to an individual

The Article 29 Date Protection Working Group assesses three elements in order to answer the question of whether data *relate* to an identified or

1439 See above under point C. I. 3. c) bb) (3) Remaining uncertainty about interplay between Article 7 and 8 ECFR.

1440 See ECJ C-92/09 and C-93/09 cip. 52.

1441 See recital 26 of the Data Protection Directive and recital 26 of the General Data Protection Regulation, as well as ECJ C-582/14, illustrated in more detail above under point C. II. 1. b) aa) (1) Scope of protection: 'Personal data'.

1442 Cf. Pahlen-Brandt, Pahlen-Brandt, Contribution to the discussion aon "personal data", p. 36, who only refers to the arbitrariness on part of the controller; however, the same thought applies to the data protection authority monitoring the data processing.

identifiable individual: The data is considered as *relating* to an individual, first, if the data itself contains the information about an individual ("content" element) or, second, if the data controller wants to relate, at a later stage, the data to an individual ("purpose" element) or, third, the use of the data is likely to affect rights or interests of an individual ("result" element).[1443] In order to assess whether or not the data relates to an *identified or identifiable* individual, the Working Group examines how far the individual can be distinguished from other individuals: The individual is identified if he or she can clearly be distinguished from all other individuals; in contrast, if the individual cannot be clearly distinguished from all other individuals, but only by further identifiers, be it directly or indirectly, he or she is only identifiable. The Working Group stresses that such an assessment depends on the context. For example, while a unique name clearly distinguishes a person from all other individuals, a common name does not. In this case, further identifying factors such as an address or birthday are necessary in order to clearly distinguish the individual from others.[1444] The General Data Protection Regulation has taken up this approach clarifying, in recital 26 sent. 3, that the "singling out" of an individual in a certain group is one of the means that can 'reasonably likely to be used'.

The informatics scholar Buchmann exemplifies how actually rare it is, in light of the criteria described, that data do not relate to an identifiable individual or, correspondingly, that a data controller can exclude the application of data protection laws. He gives the example that a young man is asked to participate in a survey about rock concerts. The young man had joined five Heavy Metal concerts in the last year and one concert of Britney Spears. The young man considers the last concert as a delicate detail of his private life that he does not want to reveal to his friends. Consequently, the young man asks the conductor of the survey, who wants to publish the results, to delete his name. The conductor of the survey agrees. However, the problem with this type of anonymization, is that the friends of the young man could recognize the pattern of his rock concerts that he visited and, consequently, discover the additional (so far, hidden) information about the Britney Spears concert. Therefore, the young man asks to hide this pattern but the conductor of the survey denies his request. The reason is that if the survey looses this essential information, the real pat-

1443 See the Article 29 Data Protection Working Group, Opinion 4/2007 on the concept of personal data, pp. 10 and 11.

1444 See the Article 29 Data Protection Working Group, ibid., pp. 10 and 11.

terns will actually be hidden (i.e. changed). So, the young man decides not to participate in the survey… and is surprised: His Heavy Metal friends read the survey and ask him whether or not he visited a concert by Britney Spears. How could they get this clue? The reason is that the survey revealed that many people who visited the same five Heavy Metal concerts also visited the Britney Spears concert.[1445]

This example not only illustrates the difficulties that a controller faces when trying to avoid that data relates to an individual. Rather, it reveals that each datum can always be related to a person, irrespective of from where it originally stems. This becomes particularly apparent, first, with respect to facts that primarily relate to objects, processes or events, and not to an individual. For example, the location or economic value of a house, or the functioning of a car do primarily not relate to an individual. However, the moment a financial bank uses the information about a house in order to calculate the mortgage rate for an individual, or an insurance company uses information about a car in order to assess an individual's insurance claim, will this data become personal data.[1446] A second example of how data or information might be related to an individual refers to subjective opinions.[1447] This consideration is particularly relevant with respect to profiling based on context-predicting algorithms. Such an algorithm produces, based on the precedent behavior of the individual concerned, as well as the correlating behavior of third parties, probabilities about the future behavior of the individual.[1448] Prominent examples are, in the banking sector, the evaluation of the reliability of potential debtors, in the insurance industry, estimations on the health risk of insurants, and, in the employment sector, assessments of the reliability of employers.[1449] Legal scholars discuss whether or not such a "subjective opinion" ("subjective opinion" because the result of this algorithm is not a fact but an estimation about an individual's behavior) must be considered as personal data related to an individual. On the one hand, this might not be the case be-

1445 Cf. Buchmann, How can privacy be measured?, p. 510 (with a slightly different example).

1446 Cf. the Article 29 Data Protection Working Group, Opinion 4/2007 on the concept of personal data, pp. 9 and 10.

1447 See for example, the Article 29 Data Protection Working Group, Opinion 4/2007 on the concept of personal data, p. 6; Skistims et al., DuD 2012, pp. 31.

1448 See Skistims et al., Data Protection Compliance of Context-Predicting Algorithms, DuD 2012, pp. 32.

1449 See Article 29 Data Protection Working Group, ibid., p. 6.

cause this information is not necessarily true or verified. On the other hand, these legal scholars argue that data protection laws provide for access, correction and deletion rights even regarding incorrect data. If these laws protect against incorrect data, they also protect against subjective opinions, as a consequence.[1450] They justify this approach by considering that an opinion (aka estimation) that an individual behaves, in the future, in one or another way affects his or her right of self-determination just like the use of incorrect data.[1451]

In conclusion, if all these types of data can be related to an individual, then the scope of protection of ordinary data protection laws is unlimited, more precisely, the scope of application actually requires the "processing of data", only, and not the "processing of personal data". The same considerations apply, in principle, to the scope of protection of the right to data protection under Article 8 ECFR.

bb) Anonymization of personal data

Correspondingly, the definition leading to an almost unlimited scope of protection also becomes apparent in the discussion on the anonymization of "personal data". Interestingly, the Data Protection Directive does not explicitly differentiate between 'personal data' and 'anonymized data'. A definition of 'anonymized data' would assist data controllers in avoiding the application of data protection laws. However, some legal scholars justify the absence of such a definition in the directive, on the grounds that no legal provision explicitly refers to it. Furthermore, its definition was already disputed during the legislation process. Originally, the term was defined within the meaning that personal data becomes anonymized only if the identification of the data was disproportionality costly. Some scholars had criticized that this definition would change over time because the more technological development progresses, the easier it is for a re-identification to be possible.[1452] The upcoming General Data Protection Regulation apparently ties into these considerations when it clarifies, on the one hand, in recital 26, that the regulation shall "not apply to anonymous in-

1450 See the Article 29 Data Protection Working Group, Opinion 4/2007 on the concept of personal data, p. 6; see also Skistims et al., DuD 2012, pp. 12.

1451 See Skistims et al., ibid., pp. 32 (33) with further references.

1452 See Ehmann/Helfrich, ibid., Art. 2, cip. 22 et seqq.

formation, namely information which does not relate to an identified or identifiable natural person or to personal data rendered anonymous in such a manner that the data subject is not or no longer identifiable“ (sent. 5) but refers, on the other hand, in relation to the assessment of ’whether means are reasonably likely to be used to identify the individual’ to "the time of the processing and technological developments" (sent. 4). Some critics conclude from this that it is actually impossible to avoid, by anonymizing personal data, the application of the regulation, because technology today can always trace anonymized data back to an individual.[1453] Thus, from this point of view, it indeed appears not to make much sense to differentiate between ‚personal data’ and ’anonymized data’.

The considerations by the Data Protection Group regarding certain anonymization techniques appears to affirm this “pessimistic” point of view. Their opinion assesses the effectiveness of anonymization techniques pursuant to the following three questions: first, “is it still possible to single out an individual”; second, “is it still possible to link records relating to an individual”; and third, can information be inferred concerning an individual?”[1454] The critics El Emam and Álvarez stress that these three questions actually imply a “zero risk” approach. Even if the Working Group pretends to only require “proper” anonymization techniques, the wording used in its opinion appears not to accept a remaining risk of identification. Since zero risk is practically not achievable, and not required legally, both critics promote to clarify the level of risk that is acceptable when personal data is anonymized.[1455] They exemplify this – in their opinion – overprotective approach with respect to each one of the criteria proposed:

With respect to the first criteria of whether it is still possible to single out an individual, both authors criticize the approach by the Working Group to take *any third party* into account.[1456] They recognize that the Working Group also takes, indeed, the context into account. However,

---

1453 See Härting, Data Protection Regulation: The new data protection law in operational practice, cip. 291.

1454 See the Article 29 Data Protection Working Group, Opinion 05/2014 on Anonymisation Techniques, p. 3.

1455 See El Emam and Álvarez, A critical appraisal of the Article 29 Working Party Opinion 05/2014 on data anonymization techniques, pp. 74 and 75; cf. also the different risk regulation approaches discussed above under point B. II. Data protection as a risk regulation.

1456 See the Article 29 Data Protection Working Group, ibid., p. 9.

they stress that the context refers, in this regard, to the concrete data processing but does not specify which other third parties have to be taken into account and which parties do not. Consequently, not only do "intruders" coming from the specific context of the data processing need to be taken into account, but all possible "intruders". Both critics therefore promote, in contrast, to clarify that only the context of the concrete data processing is relevant. This would make it possible to precisely define, during the risk assessment, the scenarios of re-identification attacks: "deliberate (motivated intruder), inadvertent, and accidental."[1457] Regarding the second criteria, i.e. of whether personal data can be linked to each other, El Emam and Álvarez criticize that the Working Group obviously considers, in general, such a link of personal data as a negative characteristic of data processing. In contrast, the ability to link data is a necessary prerequisite for many processing purposes, in particular, for longitudinal studies. Both authors therefore promote not to destroy the "longitudinal patterns", hindering the link of data, but to use alternative anonymization techniques, for instance, pseudonymization of the data.[1458]

Regarding the third criterion, i.e. the "inference" criterion, El Emam and Álvarez quote a statement of the Working Group, that the Group has made with respect to the use of anonymized data for profiling purposes, as: "even though data protection laws may no longer apply to this type of data, the use made of datasets anonymised and released for use by third parties may give rise to a loss of privacy. Special caution is required in handling anonymised information especially whenever such information is used (often in combination with other data) for taking decisions that produce effects (albeit indirectly) on individuals."[1459] The Working Group subsequently proposes two anonymization techniques in order to prevent conclusions to be drawn from anonymised data. These techniques pursue the notion to eliminate the accuracy of statistical data.[1460] El Emam and Álvarez highlight that these anonymization techniques hinder, in advance,

---

1457 See El Emam and Álvarez, ibid., pp. 83 and 84.

1458 See El Emam and Álvarez, ibid., pp. 85 and 86 referring to K El Emam and L Arbuckle, Anonymizing Health Data: Case Studies and Methods to Get You Started (O'Reilly, Sebastopol 2013); Khaled El Emam, Guide to the De-Identification of Personal Health Information (CRC Press (Auerbach), Boca Raton 2013).

1459 See the Article 29 Data Protection Working Group, ibid., p. 11.

1460 See the Article 29 Data Protection Working Group, ibid., pp. 18 and 19.

each kind of possible use of data for statistical purposes, which do not even have a negative impact on individuals.[1461] Both critics therefore instead propose to establish certain governance mechanisms that hinder, at a later stage, that such methods are used in a way impairing the fundamental rights of individuals. Since it is the later use of originally anonymized data that relates that data to individuals again, such a governance model would very probably have to apply the purpose compatibility assessment.[1462]

In conclusion, the criticism points to one common conceptual starting point for the approach pursued by the Data Protection Working Group: The Group is of the opinion that one should take the specific context of data processing into account but actually, it does not. Its overall approach is to avoid, as early as possible, that data can generally be related to an individual, directly or indirectly. It leads to an extremely broad scope of protection of data protection laws and makes it extremely difficult for the controller to avoid the applicability of the laws. However, the next chapter will show that there is a good reason for this approach, and another possible solution, besides restricting the scope of application, in general, for the problem of over-regulation resulting from such a broad scope.

cc) Again: The problem of a "yes-or-no-protection" solution

The reason for this approach is that the scope of protection decides on whether there is protection at all or not for the individual concerned. As analyzed previously, data protection laws belong, conceptually, to the regulation of risks.[1463] If the risk of potential harm shall be avoided, in advance, or at least reduced, protection against risks must extend to moments where it is effective and efficient. Indeed, because of the broad extent of risk regulation instruments, this kind of regulation runs, in turn, the risk to create a heavy regulatory burden, in particular, in the private sector. With respect to the public sector, this problem was previously discussed with respect to the German Constitutional Court's attempts to restrict the broad

1461 Cf. the example given by Buchmann above under point C. IV. 1. a) aa) How data may be related to an individual.

1462 See El Emam and Álvarez, ibid., pp. 78 and 79.

1463 See above under point B. II. Data protection as a risk regulation.

scope of protection of the right to informational self-deter-mination by narrowly defining an infringement of its scope.[1464]

As illustrated, the German Constitutional Court refers, in order to determine an infringement of the scope, to the 'state interest, with respect to the overarching context and with respect to the purpose', and to the fact of whether this constitutes a 'specific danger for the freedom of action and of being private'; or if it 'qualitatively affects a person's fundamental right'; or if this can 'essentially concern the individual's interests'.[1465] Indeed, if the German Court does not consider a certain act of data processing as an infringement of the scope, there is no protection against the processing. Such a restriction of the scope bears the risk of denying protection *per se* instead of applying different protection instruments. This might be the reason for why the German Court appears, so far, to be ambiguous or reluctant to narrowly define an infringement of the scope.[1466]

b) Alternative solution: Scope(s) pursuant to the type of risk

However, the approach proposed in this thesis also provides a resolution for this conflict, i.e. safeguarding preventative and precautionary protection, on the one hand, and avoiding an over restrictive regulation, on the other hand. This thesis advocates that data controllers should refer to all fundamental rights of the individual concerned in order to determine which purpose of its data processing is legally relevant and how precisely it must be specified, i.e. which risk the data processing creates and under which circumstances it is allowed. This concept of protection provided for by the right to data protection under Article 8 ECFR also assists in answering the question how the scope should be defined. Hence, the purpose of the processing also determines which data relate to an individual and which do not. The next chapter will illustrate that one reason for the Data Protection Working Group's too general criteria lies in the lack of differentiation between the different levels of protection. In order to demon-

---

1464 See above under point C. I. 2. d) Infringement by 'insight into personality' and 'particularity of state interest'.

1465 See above under point C. I. 2. d) Infringement by 'insight into personality' and 'particularity of state interest'.

1466 See above under point C. I. 3. c) cc) (3) Advantages and challenges: 'Personal data' as legal link for a subjective right.

strate this, the following considerations will first illustrate an approach proposed by Britz with respect to the German right to informational self-determination. On this basis, it will be shown how the function of the principle of purpose limitation, as pointed out previously, can help to clarify the scope of application with respect to Article 8 ECFR.

aa) Theoretical starting point: Different levels of protection

With respect to the German right to informational self-determination, Britz elaborates on different levels of protection, referring to the external freedom of development protected by this right. Pursuant to her understanding of the concept of protection of the right to informational self-determination, the treatment of data and usage of information is legally relevant if it leads to negative decisions by third parties or hinders the un-biased behavior of the individual concerned.[1467] Thus, the right to informational self-determination protects against informational behavior that leads to specific disadvantages for the individual concerned.[1468]

In this regard, Britz stresses the fact that the German Constitutional Court usually determines the causality between the informational measure and the disadvantages for the individual by the specific purpose for why data is collected or processed.[1469] However, this does not mean that the collection of personal data must immediately lead to specific disadvantages for the individual in order to fall under the scope of the right to informational self-determination. In contrast, the scope already applies if the processing might provide the basis for possible negative decisions at a later stage.[1470] Britz refers, in this regard, to the Court's consideration that 'the right to informational self-determination supplements and broadens a protection of freedom of action and of being private by extending its scope

---

1467 See above under point C. II. 3. b) cc) (2) Discussion on such a guarantee, referring to Britz, Informational Self-Determination between Legal Doctrine and Constitutional Case Law, pp. 573 and 574.

1468 See Britz, ibid., p. 575.

1469 Cf. above under point B. III. 4. Clarifying the relationship between "context" and "purpose", with reference to BVerfG, 15th of December 1983, 1 BvR 209, 269, 362, 420, 440, 484/83 ("Volkszählungsurteil"), cip. 158 and 159.

1470 See, for example, BVerfG, 4th of April 2006, 1 BvR 518/02 ("Rasterfahndung"), cip. 64 and 65, as well as BVerfG, 13th June 2007, 1 BvR 1550/03 ("Kontostammdatenabfrage"), cip. 64 and 65.

already at the level of danger before a concrete threat of specific objects of protection exists'.[1471] In Britz' opinion, this statement makes it abundantly obvious that specific disadvantages are, in principle, irrelevant for affirming or denying protection against the risks of data processing.[1472]

(1) Pro and cons for precautionary protection against abstract dangers

Britz recognizes that such a pre-protection against abstract disadvantages is indeed likely to improve protection against negative decisions of third parties, as well as the individual's fear of such negative decisions, which can lead to a bias in his or her behavior. In order to avoid negative decisions, the requirement of specific disadvantages for protection might sometimes be, indeed, too late. Since each decision is actually made on the basis of data and information, the non-regulated processing of data always increases the probability or likely outcome to conclude negative decisions. Furthermore, a precautionary protection against abstract dangers can also promote, in Britz' opinion, the individual's un-biased behavior because it avoids that individuals fear that the data related to them can be misused.[1473] However, Britz points out that such an abstract concept of protection leads to the situation in which each act of collection and treatment of data and each usage of information becomes legally relevant and had to be, as a consequence, regulated by the State.[1474]

She therefore advocates the notion of requiring precautionary protection against abstract dangers only in cases of special danger. In her point of view, even the German Constitutional Court seeks to re-balance the wide scope of protection. This can either be done by narrowing the definition of infringements, or at a later stage of the assessment, when the Court balances the colliding fundamental rights.[1475] Summarizing the correspond-

1471 Cf. above under point C. I. 2. b) Autonomous substantial guarantee, referring to BVerfG, 13th June 2007, 1 BvR 1550/03 ("Kontostammdatenabfrage"), cip. 64.

1472 See Britz, ibid., p. 576 with reference also to BVerfG, 4th of April 2006 ("Rasterfahndung"), 1 BvR 518/02 and BVerfG, 13th June 2007, 1 BvR 1550/03 ("Kontostammdatenabfrage").

1473 See Britz, ibid., pp. 576 and 577; cf. above under point C. II. 3. b) dd) (3) (b) Later use of personal data in the same context.

1474 See Britz, ibid., p. 577.

1475 Cf. above under points C. I. 2. d) Infringement by 'insight into personality' and 'particularity of state interest' and C. I. 2. e) aa) In the public sector: Interplay

ing reasoning in German legal literature, Britz justifies her protection-limiting approach with the following arguments:[1476] Fundamental rights principally do not protect against all dangers; a comprehensive precautionary protection would lead to a comprehensive regulation; uncertainty about other's information is no 'pathological condition' but the normal state within a society; total certainty about other's information is not attainable.[1477] Another aspect is provided for by the German Constitutional Court itself which stated that it is primarily the individual concerned who must undertake measures protecting him or herself. The individual's interest must furthermore be balanced with the colliding interests of third parties involved.[1478] Britz finally underlines that even if protection by fundamental rights pursuant to the specific usage context of the information is weaker than comprehensive precautionary protection, it is not ineffective.[1479]

(2) Abstract precautionary protection only in cases of special danger

Britz summarizes several topics discussed in legal literature with respect to special dangers and concludes from these topics several types of cases that justify, exceptionally, or even require a precautionary protection against abstract dangers:[1480]

(a) In contrast to the considerations of the German Constitutional Court, there might be a special danger even if the (state) interest for the data concerned is not yet so particular that it qualitatively concerns an in-

between the three principles clarity of law, proportionality, and purpose limitation..

1476 See Britz, ibid., p. 578.

1477 See Britz, ibid., p. 578 with references esp. to Hoffmann-Riem, New Concept of Data Protection, pp. 514 et sequ. as well as 528; Eifert, Purpose Congruence instead of Purpose Limitation, pp. 140 et. sequ.

1478 Cf. above under points C. I. 1. b) aa) (3) (b) Priority of contractual agreements and the imbalance of powers, C. I. 1. b) aa) (3) (c) Balancing the colliding constitutional positions, C. I. 1. b) bb) (1) The 3-Step-Test: Assessing the defensive and protection function.

1479 See Britz, ibid., p. 579.

1480 See Britz, ibid., pp. 579 to 581.

dividual's fundamental right;[1481] this can be the case if the later context of the data use and the disadvantage resulting from the intensity of the infringement can be, from an abstract but realistic point of view, foreseen.

(b) Certain data and information cause a special risk for the individual concerned even if the concrete purpose of their usage is not yet known, such as information about prior criminal convictions, severe deceases, participation at assemblies or political views.

(c) In addition, the secrecy of the collection of data and information lead to special dangers because the individual concerned is not able to adapt his or her behavior pursuant to the expectations of the controller and cannot correct incorrect data or influence the information or claim against it.

(d) In view of the error rate, the usage of statistical processes and their combination with other personal data in order to retrieve further information are especially dangerous, too.

(e) With respect to the reasoning of the German Constitutional Court, the collection and storage of particularly large databases is similarly considered as especially dangerous because they provide for the controller, from the individual's point of view, uncontrollable possibilities of combination and usage of data, for example, in the case of profiling; the special danger can result from both the quantity of the persons concerned and the data and information about one single individual because it runs the risk of producing errors, which can lead to wrong and disadvantageous decisions; the sheer amount of personal data and information also enables the controllers of that data to intensively control the individuals concerned.

(f) Finally, infringements of special spheres of confidentiality bear special dangers because the individuals concerned consider these as possibilities to maintain their privacy. They trust in them in order to protect themselves against the revelation of 'their' information.[1482]

1481 Cf. above under point C. I. 2. d) Infringement by 'insight into personality' and 'particularity of state interest', with reference to BVerfG, 4th of April 2006, 1 BvR 518/02 (Dragnet Investigation), cip. 69.

1482 Comparably to Albers' approach, Britz considers these spheres as mainly protected by specific basic rights such as the right to privacy of correspondences of Art. 10 GG and the guarantee of inviolability of the home of Art. 13 GG; cf. above under point C. II. 3. b) aa) (1) Unfolding specific guarantees of privacy.

Britz concludes that the German right to informational self-determination does not only protect against specific disadvantages but also against special abstract dangers. In her opinion, the German Constitutional Court equally tends to take, more and more, not the right to informational self-determination as such into account, but also refers to the other, more specific, basic rights.[1483] Britz concludes from this that it is not each data treatment or usage of information that is legally relevant, but only if it specifically infringes or consists in a special risk for a certain right to freedom.[1484]

(3) Advantages of a nuanced approach

Indeed, Britz' terminology described is not comprehensively clear. In particular, it remains unclear whether the German right to informational self-determination should protect the basic rights to freedom against infringements and special abstract dangers, only, or also against specific risks. A protection against specific risks makes sense because its preventative protection instruments are located between precautionary protection and protection against infringements that may often be too late.[1485] However, so far, the essential point that Britz makes clear is that the level of protection (i.e. protection against infringements, specific risks, or special abstract dangers) defines the scope of application of the protection instrument.

This differentiation leads to the solution indicated previously. As advocated in this thesis, the protection instruments provided for by the right to data protection under Article 8 ECFR depend on the other rights to privacy, freedom and non-discrimination. One of these protection instruments is the requirement to specify the purpose. It enforces the data controller to assess the risks caused by its data processing. For this assessment to take place, the substantial guarantees provided for by all fundamental rights provide the objective scale. So long as it remains unclear which substan-

1483 See, indeed, the summary above under point C. I. 2. d) Infringement by 'insight into personality' and ‚particularity of state interest', and C. I. 2. e) aa) (2) The proportionality test also takes takes the use of data at a later stage into account.

1484 See Britz, ibid., p. 581.

1485 See the different types of protection instruments pursuant to the different types of threat above under point B. II. 3. German legal perspectives: Different protection instruments for different types of threat.

tial guarantee the data processing concerns, the processing leads only to an unspecific risk. In contrast, if the purpose concerns a substantial guarantee, the risk is specified. The requirement of purpose specification hence turns, given the current data processing intended by the data controller, unspecific risks into specific risks.[1486] In conclusion, the protection of the individual's autonomy guaranteed by the right to data protection provides: first, protection instruments against unspecific risks; and second, instruments protecting against specific risks. The different levels of risk and, if there is a specific risk, the fundamental right to privacy, freedom, or non-discrimination specifically concerned thus provide the criteria determining the scope of protection.

This concept solves, to an essential extent, the question under which circumstances data must be considered as relating to an individual. In this regard, the purpose of the controller hence provides, indeed, an essential link in order to determine the scope of protection.[1487] Thereby, the concept avoids the pitfall that the scope of protection exclusively depends on the subjective purpose of the controller. Some legal scholars suspect insofar that the controller could circumvent the application of data protection laws by simply specifying the purpose of the data processing in a way that would pretend not to relate to an individual.[1488] The concept proposed here hinders such a circumvention because the specification of the purpose does not exclusively depend on the controller's subjective will. Instead, the requirement to specify the purpose obliges the controller to assess whether or not its processing operation intended causes a risk for an individual's specific fundamental right or not. If the controller hides a specific risk and does thus not apply the necessary protection instruments, the processing is illegal. Thus, the objective legal scale determined by the individual's fundamental rights avoids that the controller circumvents the legal requirements.

1486 See above under point C. III. 2. a) cc) Applying a 'non-linear perspective'.

1487 See Karg, The personal datum as a legal link for regulation – An anachronism of data protection?, p. 265; cf. also above under point C. I. 2. d) Infringement by 'insight into personality' and 'particularity of state interest'.

1488 See Karg, The personal datum as a legal link for regulation – An anachronism of data protection?, p. 257, referring to Forgó/Krügel, MMR 2010, pp. 17 ff. (21); Bergt, The question on "identifiable persons" as main problem of data protection, pp. 368/369.

Another advantage of this concept is that it fits to the non-linearity of innovation processes. It protects more efficiently the individual concerned and, simultaneously, does not unnecessarily restrict the scope of action of the data controller. In this regard, Pohle criticizes, for example, that current concepts of data protection focus, with respect to the definition of the scope of protection and the term of "personal data", too much on the moment the data is collected, and instead they should focus on the later use of data concerning an individual. Pursuant to Pohle's historical analysis, one reason for this misconception comes from the understanding of public organizations which act as strictly rational entities. Dating back to the early discussions on data protection, most legal scholars implied, in Pohle's opinion, Weber's concept of economic rationality. This led many scholars to the conclusion, that a regulation of personal information could focus on the moment of collection because the whole process could simply be determined by the purpose specified when the data is collected. From this perspective, hence, there was no need to define the scope of application of data protection instruments with respect to the later use of data.[1489] Today, the gap of protection resulting from this focus on the moment of collection, when determining the scope of protection, is well known. It is the reason for why the Article 29 Data Protection Working Group interprets the term "personal data" so extensively taking the possibility into account

1489 See Pohle, Personal Data Not Found: Person-related decisions as an over-due refinement of data protection, p. 16, referring, amongst other authors, to Wilhelm Steinmüller at al. "Grundfragen des Datenschutzes", Gutachten im Auftrag des Bundesministeriums des Innern, BT-Drs. VI/3826, Anlage 1. 1971, S. 49; Ernst Benda, "Privatsphäre und Persönlichkeitsprofil", in: Menschenwürde und freiheitliche Rechtsordnung, Festschrift für Willi Geiger zum 65. Geburtstag (ed. Gerhard Leibholz et al.), Tübingen: J. C. B. Mohr (Paul Siebeck), 1974, pp. 23 to 44 (27); Adalbert Podlech, "Aufgaben und Problematik des Datenschutzes", in: Datenverarbeitung im Recht 5 (1976), pp. 23 to 39 (p. 25); James B. Rule et al., The Politics of Privacy, New York Elsevier, 1980, pp. 25 et sequ.; M. G. Stone and Malcolm Warner, Politics, Privacy, and Computers, in: The Political uarterly 40.3 (1969), pp. 256 to 267 (258); summarized in Pohle, "Die immer noch aktuellen Grundfragen des Datenschutzes", p. 49; cf. also above under point C. I. 2. f) Interim conclusion: Conceptual link between 'privacy' and 'data processing' referring to Albers, Informational Self-Determination, cip. 121 to 123, and Hoffmann-Riem, Protection of the Confidentiality and Integrity of Information Technological Systems, p. 1009 and 1010, as well as 1014.

that anonymized data might be related, only in the future, to an individual.[1490] However, the ambiguous broadening of the scope, which results from the unclear concept of protection, runs the risk of over-regulation.[1491] Both negative effects, i.e. for the individuals concerned and the data controllers, can be avoided if the diversity of all fundamental rights are taken into account in order to determine the scope of application of data protection laws, and its protection instruments. The reason for this is, as mentioned previously, that the fundamental rights typically apply at different moments of the data processing.[1492]

bb) Differentiating between the general scope of protection and the application of specific protection instruments

This chapter will demonstrate the approach defining the scope of protection of data protection instruments by referring to the different types of threat, and if there is a specific risk, the context of the data processing determined by the fundamental right concerned. In order to find a balance between the protection of individuals concerned and the societal need for information,[1493] this thesis hence promotes a different approach: On the first level, the general scope of protection applies, requiring the data controller to specify the purpose in order to assess the risk, and providing for further precautionary instruments against unspecific risks. On the second level, the substantial guarantees provided for by the other fundamental rights to privacy, freedom and non-discrimination determine the scope of application for the specific preventative protection instruments.

1490 See above under point C. IV. 1. 1. a) aa) How data may be related to an individual, and C. IV. 1. 1. a) bb) Anonymization of personal data, referring to the Article 29 Data Protection Working Group, Opinion 4/2007 on the concept of personal data, pp. 10 and 11, as well as ibid., Opinion 05/2014 on Anonymisation Techniques, p. 3.

1491 See above under point C. IV. 1. b) aa) (1) Pro and cons for precautionary protection against abstract dangers, referring to Britz, ibid., p. 577.

1492 See above under point C. II. 3. a) cc) (2) (b) Appropriate concept for innovation processes.

1493 See the Article 29 Data Protection Working Group, Opinion 4/2007 on the concept of personal data, pp. 4 and 5.

(1) General scope of protection enabling specification of purpose (aka risk)

Since the specification of the purpose is the necessary pre-condition for the risk assessment, the concept of protection must not circumvent the assessment by defining a restrictive scope.[1494] Therefore, a broad definition of the scope is necessary, for example, covering data even if only a third party can identify the individual or anonymous data is later related to an individual. However, such a broad scope of protection does not impose, so far, a disproportionate regulatory burden on data controllers. The reason is that the main requirement is, in the first instance, the specification of the purpose only. This requirement does not overly restrict the scope of action of data controllers because further protection instruments are necessary only if there are additional risks. The broad scope of protection does thus not lead, per se, to the application of all protection instruments for all kinds of data processing. Indeed, if there are further risks, the additional protection instruments required restrain the controllers' scope of action more than the requirement to specify the purpose. However, this more extensive and/or intensive restriction is justified in light of these risks against the individual's fundamental rights additionally (and specifically) concerned by the data processing.[1495]

Such an approach consisting of a broad general scope of protection providing the basis for the risk assessment and a subsequent risk-based specification of the protection instruments, guarantees a fair balance between the individual's need for protection and the needs within society for a free flux of information. The Article 29 Data Protection Working Group similarly promotes this approach with respect to the scope of the Data Protection Directive. As stressed previously, Article 1 of the directive aims to not only protect the individual's right to privacy, but to all fundamental rights and freedoms with respect to the processing of personal data. The Working Group highlights the function of this aim as: "This is a very important element to take into account in the interpretation and application of the rules of (... / the directive). It may play a substantive role in determin-

1494 See above under point C. II. 3. a) bb) (2) (b) Separating unspecific from specific risks; cf. Härting and Schneider, Data Protection in Europe: An Alternative Draft for a General Data Protection Regulation, p. 3.

1495 See above under point C. I. 1. b) bb) Balance between defensive and protection function.

ing how to apply the provisions of the Directive to a number of situations where the rights of individuals are not at risk, and it may caution against any interpretation of the same rules that would leave individuals deprived of protection of their rights."[1496] The diversity of all fundamental rights thus helps, in the opinion of the Working Group, to assess the risks caused by the processing of personal data, as well as the corresponding protection instruments. This approach solves a large part of the question of how to interpret, in general, the scope of protection because the scope of application of protection instruments against specific risks can be determined precisely by the substantial guarantee specifically concerned. Only regarding unspecific risks, it remains difficult for the controller to avoid the scope, overall. However, this difficulty is justified, as stressed before, because the requirements against unspecific risks impose a lighter regulatory burden on the data controllers.

(2) Application of protection instruments determined by specific risks

Interpreting the term 'personal data' pursuant to the fundamental right of privacy, freedom, or non-discrimination specifically concerned solves both problems mentioned previously: first, the specific fundamental rights provide for the criteria that are necessary for determining under which conditions an individual is 'identified or identifiable'; and second, this context-specific definition of the scope avoids that protection is excluded in cases where it is actually needed. As mentioned previously, with respect to the first problem, the Article 29 Data Protection Working Group states: "In general terms, a natural person can be considered as 'identified' when, within a group of persons, he or she is 'distinguished' from all other members of the group."[1497] The problem of this general definition is that it requires two further criteria in order to identify a person: First, there must be one common criteria that defines who belongs to the group and who does not; second, there must be one other criteria uniquely distinguishing the individual from the other group members in order to be 'singled out'. Both criteria lead to the result that the definition of the term 'personal data' highly depends on the specific context.[1498] And both criteria are, simulta-

1496 See the Article 29 Data Protection Working Group, ibid., p. 4.
1497 See the Article 29 Data Protection Working Group, ibid., p. 12.
1498 See the Article 29 Data Protection Working Group, ibid., p. 13.

neously, the reason for the second problem, i.e. that the current definition of the term 'personal data' excludes the application of protection instruments even if substantial guarantees require them. The subsequent considerations will demonstrate both problems, as well as its possible solution.

(a) Rights to privacy

As illustrated previously, the substantial guarantees of privacy of the home, communications, and "in the public" can be distinguished from each other.[1499] The differences also influence the scope. For example, the guarantee of inviolability of the home may provide the following two criteria: First, this guarantee protects the individual of being left alone only so long as he or she really uses the private sphere in order to protect him or herself; and second, the guarantee only protects the occupants, not third parties, such as guests which can use their own homes in order to be left alone. The conclusion with respect to the scope of protection is that this guarantee does not obviously require that the intruder knows who the occupant is.[1500] This aspect is particularly relevant with respect to the initial question regarding the criteria which identify an individual in order to determine the scope of protection. The moment an intrusion of the home occurs, typical identifiers, such as the name of the occupant, is irrelevant for denying or affirming protection. What is only relevant is that the individual concerned by the data processing is the occupant of the home and that he or she wants to be alone. An anonymization of data collected through an intrusion into an individual's home can thus exclude the scope of application of corresponding protection instruments only if it safeguards that no inferences about the individual can be concluded from that data.[1501] This idea may less strictly be applied to the later use of data. The reason for this is that all information about the individual retrieved from that data indeed constitutes and extends harm for his or her right to privacy of the home.

1499 See above under point C. II. 3. b) aa) (1) Unfolding specific guarantees of privacy.

1500 See above under point C. II. 3. b) aa) (1) (a) At home: Protection of 'haven of retreat', referring, by way of an example, to BVerfG, 3rd of March 2004, 1 BvR 2378/98 (Big Eavesdropping Operation), cip. 131 to 138.

1501 Cf. the anonymization techniques discussed by the Article 29 Data Protection Working Group, Opinion 05/2014 on Anonymisation Techniques, pp. 18 and 19.

However if this information cannot be related, for example, to a 'single household' anymore, this might not conflict, at least not so intensively, with this substantial guarantee.[1502]

In contrast, the substantial guarantee to privacy of communication may provide different criteria: In this regard, the fact that the individual concerned can be 'identified or identifiable' and, though, be 'distinguished from other members of the same group' may be more relevant. First, the common criteria defining who belongs to this group and who does not, refers to 'users of means of communication'. The substantial guarantee of privacy of communications protects these users against an interception by third parties in order to 'avoid that the exchange of opinions and information through (these) means of communications systems stops or is being changed'; therefore, if a third party filters the content pursuant to certain keywords, this leads to a negative result and the data is immediately deleted, this can nevertheless infringe the substantial guarantee of the fundamental right because the data processing consists in an 'assessment of content' exchanged between the communicating partners. Only if an anonymization technique safeguards that the content filtered cannot be traced back to an individual, this excludes the scope of application because no third party can use the information retrieved from the content against this individual.[1503] Instead, if the data can be related, later on, to an individual, further protection instruments are needed. In particular, the data controller must make sure that the later use of data does not lead to the situation that the individual concerned stops communicating because he or she fears certain disadvantages at a later stage.[1504]

(b) Right of self-representation in the public

Only the substantial guarantee of self-representation in the public requires, *per se*, that the data published relate to an identified or identifiable indi-

---

1502 See above under point C. III. 2. b) aa) Right of 'being left alone': 'Reasonable expectations'.

1503 See above under point C. III. 2. b) aa) Right of 'being left alone': 'Reasonable expectations', referring, by way of an example, to BVerfG, 14th of July 1999, 1 BvR 2226/94 (Surveillance of Telecommunications), cip. 131, 135, and 160.

1504 Cf. above under point C. III. 2. b) aa) Right of 'being left alone': 'Reasonable expectations'.

vidual. In these cases, the public, or simply certain persons, must be able to recognize the individual concerned in order to affirm the application of protection instruments.[1505] Hence, it depends on various social contexts whether or not an individual's family, neighbors or colleagues are able to relate published data to him or her. The examples as illustrated previously demonstrate how difficult it is for the data controller to exclude the scope of application. First, even if the data do not contain an identifier directly revealing the identity of the individual, such as a unique name, third parties are often able to recognize, based on further information, a pre-known pattern and discover the individual's identity. Second, even if the data does not relate per se to an individual, third parties can always relate it to the individual on the basis of their own opinion.[1506] Correspondingly, the anonymization technique used in order to exclude the scope of application of protection instruments depend on these specific social contexts in which the individual interacts. However, in this regard, it is important to underline that the regulator cannot exclude all risk.[1507] Controllers also cannot exclude all risks caused by the processing of personal data.[1508] This corresponds to the substantial guarantee of self-representation in the public that does not guarantee the individual to comprehensively control his or her picture in society but only to influence it to a certain extent.[1509] If the individual has no guarantee to comprehensively control his or her picture in society, he or she cannot fully control the risk that others might relate certain data to him or her.

(c) Internal freedom of behavior

The importance of defining the scope of application of protection instruments pursuant to the specific substantial guarantee concerned, can equal-

---

1505 See, for example, ECtHR, Case of Peck vs. the United Kingdom from 28 January 2003 (application no. 44647/98), cip. 62 and 63.

1506 See above under point C. IV. 1. a) aa) How data may be related to an individual, referring to Buchmann, How can privacy be measured?, p. 510.

1507 See above under point B. II. 3. German legal perspectives: Different protection instruments for different types of threat.

1508 See above the criticism by El Emam and Álvarez, A critical appraisal of the Article 29 Working Party Opinion 05/2014 on data anonymization techniques, pp. 74 and 75, under point C. IV. 1. a) bb) Anonymization of personal data.

1509 See above under point C. II. 3. b) bb) Right of self-determination in public.

ly be demonstrated with regard to the internal freedom of behavior. As illustrated previously, such a guarantee enables the individual to know what others know about him or her. This guarantee aims to empower the individual to distance him or her from their own and others' expectations and, particularly, protect him or herself against the risk of being manipulated. The discussion held previously left open the idea of whether or not this guarantee requires that the individual knows the data or the information that others have about him or her.[1510] In other terms, it can be asked which kind of data should be considered as 'personal data' defining the scope of application of the corresponding protection instruments.

The example of personalized online advertising demonstrates how strongly the answer depends on the specific risk determined by the substantial guarantee. For personalized online advertising, the controller processes data related to an internet user in order to create a profile about an individual's behavior and position advertising on the individual's screen pursuant to this profile. Such data can be, as listed before: Identifiers, for example, the IP address referring to the user; information about the beginning, the end, and the extent of the use such as the time, data volume or downloads; or information about the specific use of the services, such as the specific websites visited.[1511] In order to answer the question of which kind of knowledge the controller (i.e. online advertiser) has about the individual concerned, it is necessary to understand how these profiles are created. In this regard, Article 4 sect. 12 lit. b of the draft of the Data Protection Regulation from the 30th of June 2014, provides a useful explanation defining a profile as: "a set of data characterizing a category of individuals that is intended to be applied to a natural person". In light of this definition, the categories characterizing certain attitudes applied to an internet user is the knowledge that the controller has about this user, not the data as such. Applying the definition of 'personal data' proposed by the Article 29 Data Protection Working Group, the criteria distinguishing this user from all other users captured by the advertiser thus is a placeholder, only. In contrast, the real name of the internet user is, so far, irrelevant for the controller. The reason is that the controller only needs a placeholder, in order to place the 'right' advertisement to the 'right' user, whoever he or she is in the 'real world'. Consequently, the real name does, in this context, not

1510 See above under point C. II. 3. b) cc) Internal freedom of behavior.

1511 Cf. above under point C. II. 1. c) bb), referring to Schreibauer, Federal Data Protection Law and further Provisions, § 11 TMG, cip. 6 to 10.

play a role for the substantial guarantee of internal freedom of development because the risk of manipulation exists irrespective of whether or not the controller knows the name or address of the individual.[1512]

Interestingly, in these cases, German law and the German Data Protection Working Group consider the name of the individual concerned, i.e. his or her real identity, as the main reference in order to deny or affirm protection. As illustrated previously, Article 12 of the German Telemedia Law authorizes the processing of such 'usage data' if it is based on the user's consent or a legal provision. Article 15 sect. 3 allows, as legal provision, the processing of such data for the purpose of advertising if the data is pseudonymized and the user does not object to the processing. Pursuant to Article 3 no. 6a of the Federal Data Protection Law, the term 'pseudonymization' means "the replacement of the name and other identifiers through a place holder in order to exclude the identification of the individual concerned or, at least, to make it significantly more difficult."[1513] It is important to stress, in this regard, that the German Working Group does not consider IP addresses as a 'place holder' but as an 'identifier'.[1514] Therefore, the data controller must not combine the 'pseudonymized' data with the IP address or another identifier such as the name of the user retrieved, for example, from the internet shop. The protection provided for by Article 15 sect. 3 of the Telemedia Law hence seeks, mainly, to avoid that the data collected cannot be related to a 'real' individual with a 'real' name and address. This approach provides for a different protection than the substantial guarantee of internal freedom of behavior. The substantial reason for why the user's 'real' name should be, for these type of cases, relevant and why the pseudonymization of that data should exclude further protection instruments such as a more detailed right to transparency indeed remains unclear.

1512 See also Härting, Profiling: a proposal for an intelligent regulation.

1513 Article 3 no. 6a of the Federal Data Protection Law states as: "Pseudonymisieren ist das Ersetzen des Namens und anderer Identifikationsmerkmale durch ein Kennzeichen zu dem Zweck, die Bestimmung des Betroffenen auszuschließen oder wesentlich zu erschweren."

1514 Eßer, Federal Data Protection Law and further Provisions, cip. 30, with further references.

(d) Rights to freedom and non-discrimination

The fundamental rights to freedom and non-discrimination equally provide for the criteria necessary in order to decide whether an individual can be singled out or not, though, whether the data processed by the controller is 'personal' or not. For example, Article 10 ECFR guarantees everyone the right to freedom of thought, conscience and religion including to practice it, be it in public or in private. Article 15 ECFR guarantees everyone the right to engage in work and to pursue a freely chosen or accepted occupation. Article 21 protects against any discrimination based on any ground such as sex, race, colour, ethnic or social origin, genetic features, language, religion or belief, political or any other opinion, membership of a national minority, property, birth, disability, age or sexual orientation. In order to protect an individual against specific risks to these rights, the individual must act in a social role which is covered by this fundamental right, and the data processing has to conflict with the substantial guarantee provided for by the right.[1515] The individual's identity is determined, in all these cases, by the substantial guarantee. This might be the case because the individual acts in the social role of a believer or a potential employee, which is covered by Article 15 or 21 ECFR respectively. In contrast, further criteria providing additional aspects of an individual's identity, such as his or her official name or address are not relevant, at least not primarily, for protection against the risks for these guarantees. Therefore, if the controller wants to avoid the scope of application, it must use an anonymization technique that safeguards that the individual concerned cannot be singled out with respect to the other carriers of the substantial guarantee concerned. If the individual can be singled out, the data is not anonymized and the controller must assess further whether, and if so, in which way the processing of the personal data conflicts with the substantial guarantee. Corresponding to the conflict, the controller must implement further protection instruments.

1515 Cf. above under point C. II. 3. b) dd) Specific rights to freedom, and C. II. 3. b) ee) Rights to equality and non-discrimination.

(3) Again: General scope of protection requiring data security (against unspecific risks)

Beside these specific risks there remain, however, unspecific risks that require precautionary instruments in addition to the requirement to specify the purpose, i.e. the risk. As illustrated previously, if the specification of the purpose does not reveal, at a certain moment, a specific risk for the fundamental rights to privacy, freedom and non-discrimination, there is still the unspecific risk that the data is used, later on, in a way causing a specific risk against an individual's fundamental right. This is the reason why Britz considers that a precautionary protection against abstract dangers is always likely to improve protection. Nevertheless, because of a potential over-regulation, Britz promotes to establish precautionary instruments against abstract dangers only for cases of special danger.[1516]

Indeed, many of the cases listed by Britz refer, in light of the concept of protection proposed in this thesis, to specific risks. For example, intrusions into an individual's special spheres of confidentiality (see lit. f) leads less to an abstract risk than to an infringement of the rights to privacy of the home or communications. This is in particular the case, if the intrusion occurs in secret (see lit. c) because the individual concerned is not able to decide whether or not he or she wants to avoid the intrusion into his or her private sphere.[1517] Another example refers to the use of statistical methods (see lit. d), which primarily lead, particularly if used for profiling purposes, to a specific risk against an individual's internal freedom of development and, potentially, his or her right to non-discrimina-tion.[1518] The example of processing information about an individual's criminal convictions, severe deceases, the participation at assemblies or political views (see lit. b), leads, in the first instance, to specific risks against his or her privacy, freedom of assembly and association, freedom of expression, as well as, if published, right to self-determination in the public.[1519] In all

---

1516 See above under point C. IV. 1. b) aa) (2) Abstract precautionary protection only in cases of special danger, referring to Britz, Informational Self-Determination between Legal Doctrine and Constitutional Case Law, pp. 576 and 577.

1517 See above under point C. II. 3. a) bb) (3) Function of making specified purposes explicit.

1518 See above under points C. II. 3. b) cc) Internal freedom of development, and C. II. 3. b) ee) Rights to equality and non-discrimination.

1519 See, as a whole, above under point C. II. 3. b) Fundamental rights which determine purpose requirements.

these cases, the processing of data does not lead, applying the approach proposed here, to an unspecific but rather to a specific risk. However, Britz also provides an example, which leads to a point being useful for this thesis. In her opinion, precautionary protection is also necessary if the disadvantages can be, from an abstract and realistic point of view, foreseen, even if the interest of the controller in the data is not yet so particular that it qualitatively concerns an individual's fundamental right (see lit. a).

This last example describes the situation where the controller does not yet pursue the data processing which leads to a specific risk against a substantial guarantee. However, it is always possible, particularly in a non-linear environment, that the controller, be it the collector of the data or another entity, pursues such a processing operation later on. Therefore, the data controller must always implement precautionary protection instruments that are necessary in order to avoid that later protection instruments against specific risks are undermined. These precautionary measures, beside the requirement to specify the purpose, are recognized by all Courts, as analyzed before. The European Court of Human Rights requires, pursuant to the right to private life under Article 8 ECHR, that data controllers implement safeguards against abuse by any further usage of the data.[1520] The European Court of Justice discusses such an 'effective protection of the data retained against the risk of abuse and against any unlawful access and use of that data' with respect to the right to data protection provided for by Article 8 ECFR.[1521] And the German Constitutional Court stated, in the case of "*Data Retention*", that the German Basic Law does not prohibit per se the retention of personal data if the ordinary law, which authorizes the data retention, provides sufficiently clear rules, in particular, in relation to data security. In the particular case, the Court considered that the retention required an especially high standard of data security because the data attracted, in light of its multifunctional informative value, the attention of many different stakeholders. In particular, if the stakeholders are private entities, the Court took into account that these entities have little incentive to maintain a high level of data security in light of the corresponding costs. In order to maintain a particularly high standard of data security, the Court proposed, amongst other factors, the sys-

1520 See, for example, ECtHR, Case of Z. vs. Finland from 25 February 1997 (application no. 22009/93), cip 95; ECtHR, Case of M.S. vs. Sweden from 27 August 1997 (74/1996/693/885), cip. 41.

1521 See ECJ C-293/12 and C-594/12 (Digital Rights vs. Ireland), cip. 66.

temic separation of the data, its encryption, a secure access control, and an irreversible documentation.[1522]

These decisions primarily referred to the processing of personal data by the State. However, the function of the requirements discussed in the decisions principally applies also to the private sector. The encryption of personal data and/or secure access control safeguards that unauthorized entities do not obtain access to the data. The documentation of, in particular, the processing purpose ensures that each controller coming next in the life cycle of personal data is able, once having retrieved the documentation, to assess the unspecific risk of the processing currently intended with respect to the preceding processing.[1523] The separation of the data storage reduces the risk that an unauthorized entity gets, once having obtained access to one data silo, access to all data at once.[1524] In any case, the specific security requirements depend, again, on the corresponding risk.[1525] Even if this risk is unspecific and, therefore, as proposed in this thesis, the current purpose cannot further specify the risk, it can nevertheless be "contextualized" by the specific provenance of the data. The data's provenance and, thus, its general importance (i.e. sensitivity) for the individual concerned can be determined by the purposes *precedingly* specified (and documented). The preceding purposes determine in which context, covered by one or more of the individual's specific fundamental rights to privacy, freedom, or non-discrimination, the data was collected and/or processed and, though, the nature of the data and its relation to the individual. This infor-

1522 See BVerfG, 2nd March 2010, 1 BvR 256/08, 1 BvR 263/08, and 1 BvR 586/08 (Data Retention), cip. 222 and 224.

1523 Cf. above under point C. III. 1. b) bb) (3) Identification marks as a control-enhancing mechanism.

1524 The functional separation of data might also be necessary in order to guarantee the pseudonymization of data, and/or in light of certain specific substantial guarantees: for example, in the public sector, the functional separation of personal data will often be necessary in order to guarantee strict purpose identity resulting from the informational separation of powers, cf. above under point C. III. b) cc) (1) (b) Principle of purpose limitation and informational separation of powers; and in the private sector, functional separation of personal data may be necessary in order to avoid the retrieval of further information about an individual's private life and, thus, an increased risk for his or her right to private life, cf. above under point C. III. 2. b) aa) Right of 'being left alone': 'Reasonable expectations', referring to C. II. b) aa) (2) Necessity requirement, irrespective of inconvenience.

1525 Cf. Schneider, Data security – a forgotten area of regulation?, pp. 10 to 12.

mation combined with typical risk scenarios enables the controller to implement security measures that are both necessary and sufficient. Finally, in this regard, another aspect that was already mentioned by Britz becomes relevant. The more personal data the controller stores about one or more individuals (see lit. e), the higher is the unspecific risk and the higher the security level must be.[1526] Such a contextualization of unspecific risks makes it possible to adapt the security measures to the particularities of a specific case and to fairly balance the rights and interests of an individual concerned with that of entities who process data related to him or her.

By way of example: if an entity, such as a cloud computing service provider, receives data without being able to relate that data to an individual, pursuant to the definition proposed previously, for instance, because the data is completely encrypted, additional security measures might be less or even not required; in contrast, the more that data might be related to an individual, pursuant to the (unspecific) risk scenarios, as described previously, it must implement security measures, accordingly.[1527]

c) Excursus: Responsibility (“controller” and “processor”)

The previous example demonstrates, indeed, the tight connection between the scope of protection and the responsibility for implementing the corresponding protection instruments. However, differentiating between different types of risks also helps to answer the question of who is legally responsible for the processing of personal data and, correspondingly, implementing the necessary protection instruments. In this regard, data protection laws usually differentiate between the roles of the ‘controller’ and ‘processor’.[1528] As mentioned above, the Data Protection Directive and

1526 Cf. Roßnagel, Data protection in computerized everyday life, pp. 185 to 188, who promotes a risk-based precautionary protection with respect to the probability that data may be re-identified; cf. also, with respect to the risk of "identity theft“, Härting, Profiling: a proposal for an intelligent regulation, pp. 534/535; and regarding the number of individuals concerned, Forum Privatheit, White Paper – Data Protection Impact Assessment, p. 27.

1527 Cf. Hon, Millard, and Walden, Who is responsible for ‘personal data’ in cloud computing?, in particular, pp. 15/16, who discuss this question in relation to the question on data protection responsibility.

1528 See above under point C. II. 1. b) aa) (2) Liability for ‚data processing’: ’Controller’ and ’processor’.

the General Data Protection Regulation define a 'controller' as "the natural or legal person, public authority, agency or any other body which alone or jointly with others determines the purposes and means of the processing of personal data".[1529] In contrast, the processor is "a natural or legal person, public authority, agency or other body which processes personal data on behalf of the controller".[1530] The processor is therefore bound to the purpose specified by the controller and is allowed to specify the means only; if the processor determines itself the purpose or an essential part of means, it becomes itself controller carrying full legal responsibility.[1531] Referring to this concept, the law essentially assigns legal responsibility to the entity that is, pursuant to the factual circumstances of the particular case, in control of the data processing. However, despite this conceptual clarity, in many cases, it is unclear which entity carries which specific duty of protection.[1532] This ambiguity becomes particularly apparent when one attempts, as demonstrated previously, to differentiate between 'purposes' and 'means'. Its precise meaning is important because the Data Protection Working Group refers to both terms in order to clarify who carries the responsibility.[1533] However, without an objective legal scale, it is impossible to reliably differentiate between both terms because a 'purpose' can always be considered as the 'means' for another, broader 'purpose'.[1534]

Therefore, in order to clarify who carries which kind of legal responsibility for the processing of personal data, some legal scholars promote to refine the concept of 'controller' and 'processor'. Jandt and Roßnagel propose, for example, to differentiate more precisely between different forms

1529 See Article 2 lit. d of the Data Protection Directive as well as Article 4 sect. 7 sent. 1 of the Data Protection Regulation.

1530 See Article 2 lit. e of the Data Protection Directive as well as Article 4 sect. 8 of the Data Protection Regulation.

1531 See above under point C. II. 1. b) aa) (2) Liability for ‚data processing': 'Controller' and 'processor', referring to Article 29 sect. 2 and 10 of the General Data Protection Regulation.

1532 See Jandt and Roßnagel, Data protection in social networks – Collective responsibility for data processing, pp. 160 and 165.

1533 See above under point C. II. 1. b) aa) (2) Liability for 'data processing': 'Controller' and 'processor', referring to Article 29 Data Protection Working Group, "Opinion 1/2010 on the concepts of 'controller' and 'processor'", p. 14.

1534 See above under point C. II. 2. c) bb) Differentiating between the terms of 'purpose', 'means', and 'interests'.

of joint responsibility when several controllers are involved in the processing of personal data. In doing so, they introduce the terms of 'cumulative' and 'collective' responsibility: The term 'cumulative' responsibility means that all controllers are responsible, each one of them, for the same processing of the same data. In contrast, 'collective' responsibility means, in cases of collaborative data processing, that each controller is responsible for certain types of data for specific phases of the processing.[1535] Blume even proposes to change the roles of 'controller' and 'processor', overall. In his opinion, the 'processor' should carry more responsibility, than it does in light of the current concept, because it is the entity that is closest to the data processing and, therefore, best able to guarantee "that the data subject is ensured sufficient rights and security against data misuse".[1536] In any case, the approach proposed here helps, by differentiating between different types of risks, to further clarify and justify the refinement of the concept of responsibility.

(1) Cumulative responsibility for precautionary protection

In light of this approach, each entity processing personal data is, per se, responsible for implementing the precautionary protection instruments against unspecific risks. There are two reasons for such a cumulative responsibility: First, each entity must specify the purpose of the processing in order to assess whether its data processing reveals a specific risk for the individual concerned. This duty also applies, in particular, to the processor because the processor can only verify, on the basis of its own purpose, whether it pursues the same purpose as specified by the controller or not. If the processor's own purpose reveals that its data processing causes a new risk, be it a higher risk for the same substantial guarantee, or for another substantial guarantee not previously thought of, the processor becomes responsible for this new specific risk and, hence, itself a controller.[1537] Consequently, the substantial guarantee also determines, which means the controller itself must specify so that the processor, who correct-

1535 See Jandt and Roßnagel, ibid., pp. 161.
1536 See Blume, An alternative model for data protection law: changing the roles of controller and processor, p. 296.
1537 Cf. above under point C. III. 2. a) aa) (3) Clarification of an objective scale: "Same risk, higher risk, and another risk".

ly carries out the data processing pursuant to the given purposes and means, causes no new risk to the individual concerned. Second, since the controller can only be responsible for the risks that it has specified itself, the processor must implement, parallel to the controller, the necessary precautionary security protection instruments against unspecific risks. The reason for this is that each entity who gets into contact with the data (what may mean, who gets a copy of the data), must itself ensure that no unauthorized third party gets access to that data stored and/or misuses it in one or the other way.[1538] Both the controller and the processor are thus responsible, cumulatively, for unspecific risks resulting from the data processing.[1539]

(2) Cooperative responsibility for preventative protection

In contrast, if several entities process the same data but for different purposes, each entity is, in principle, responsible only for the specific risk that it creates. In this regard, the substantial guarantee concerned determines which controller must implement the necessary protection instrument in order to avoid or, at least, reduce the risk, accordingly.[1540] Taking the example of a social network: if a user of the social network collects data from another individual and publishes that data, the user is responsible for applying the protection instruments required by the individual's right to self-determination in public and must, for instance, retrieve the individual's consent. In contrast, if the social network uses the same data in order to create a profile about the individual and deliver him or her personalized advertising, the social network is responsible for implementing protection instruments that safeguard the individual's internal freedom of development. This could be information about the profile shown to the individual next to the advertising.[1541] In contrast to some critics' opinions, the pro-

1538 Cf. Blume, ibid., p. 296.

1539 Cf. Jandt and Roßnagel, Data protection in social networks – Collective responsibility for data processing, p. 161, who use the term of ‚cumulative responsibility' if several entities are equally responsible for the same processing of the same personal data.

1540 Cf. above under point B. II. 3. c) Interim conclusion: Fundamental rights determining appropriateness of protection, referring to Jaeckel, Duties of Protection in German and European Law, pp. 85 to 88 as well as 165 and 166.

1541 Cf. Jandt and Roßnagel, ibid., p. 161.

cessing of that same data can hence clearly be distinguished.[1542] It is not necessary that both controllers (i.e. the social network and the user) are cumulatively responsible for both specific risks. Instead, each controller is responsible for the specific risk that it creates.

However, certain cases may require the controllers to coordinate their corresponding protection instruments in order to ensure that preventative protection for the individual against specific risks is, from a holistic point of view, effective and efficient. This may often mean that protection must not be too late. The following example of alert services in the insurance industry, which is provided for by Buchner, demonstrates the necessity of such a cooperative protection. Buchner criticizes the flaw of protection in the insurance industry that results from the anonymization of data. This problem originates from how the insurance industry organizes the process of data exchange. The alert service provider itself does not receive any personal data but only anonymized codes. The moment when an insurance company registers an irregularity evaluating an insurance claim, it only checks the code related to the insurant with the alert service and, in the case of a match, directly connects itself with the other insurance company(ies) which had registered the code at the alert service before because of a similar "irregularity" of the insurant. As a consequence, the alert service itself is not, pursuant to the current interpretation of data protection law, the data controller. Buchner criticizes, in contrast to other legal scholars, that this process does not improve, but rather worsens the situation for the individual concerned because he or she cannot control the flux of information by accessing it at one centralized entity, but has to collect the different pieces from all potential entities that come into question.[1543] Therefore, Buchner argues that the question of which entity infringes the 'privacy' of the individual concerned by relating data to his or her identity, is actually not decisive for determining which entity must be the data controller. Instead, it is decisive which entity is in the center of the data process and therefore able to effectively let individuals participate in that process with respect to its consequences. Consequently, he promotes that the law needs to be clarified: so that the alert service providers, such as in the insurance

1542 See Weichert, Information-technological collaboration and data protection responsibility, p. 607.

1543 See Buchner, Informational self-determination in the private sector, pp. 141 to 143.

industry, shall be the legally relevant controller.[1544] The reason for this claim lies, here again, in the specific risk that determines which entity is responsible for implementing the appropriate protection instruments. Applying the approach promoted in this thesis, it is the alert service provider who causes the specific risk for the individual concerned: the moment the alert service provider informs an insurance company about an "irregularity" related to an individual, irrespective of whether the service provider can relate itself the data to the individual or not, this information creates a certain picture in the „collective mind" of the insurance company and any protection against this picture may come too late.[1545] In this moment, the insurance company becomes aware that something might be wrong with the individual's insurance claim; and the individual had no possibility, before, to verify whether or not the data justifies the mind set of the company or to influence it. Therefore, the entities within the insurance industry involved in the processing of the personal data must organize the alert system in a way so that the individual concerned is effectively able to correct the data or the misconceptions before 'irregularities' are exchanged. This could be done, for instance, if the alert service stored not only the codes, but also further information, and the individual was able to react to this information before it is transferred to third parties such as the insurance companies.

2. Legitimacy of processing of personal data (Article 8 sect. 2 ECFR)

The preceding chapter clarified the interplay between, on the one hand, a broad scope of protection of the right to data protection under Article 8 ECFR providing for the requirement of purpose specification and further precautionary instruments against unspecific risks and, on the other hand, the scopes of application of preventative protection instruments determined by specific risks for the fundamental rights to privacy, freedom and non-discrimination. For this concept, the risk-oriented function of the prin-

---

1544 See Buchner, ibid., p. 143.

1545 Cf. the considerations by Miller, Personal Privacy in the Computer Age: The Challenge of a New Technology in an Information-Oriented Society, p. 1221, and Grimm, Data protection before its refinement, p. 586, illustrated above under point B. II. 1. Risk terminology oscillating between "prevention" and "precaution".

ciple of purpose limitation plays a decisive role. This chapter examines different regulatory approaches coming into question that determine the legitimacy of data processing on the private sector: Does the fundamental right to data protection require the State to forbid all kinds of collection and processing of personal data and to make only certain exceptions?[1546] Or, do the opposing rights of third parties, which collect and process personal data, require that their actions are principally free and only certain kinds of it fall under specific regulations?[1547] And, finally, which role does the individual's consent actually play compared with other legal provisions regulating the processing of personal data?

a) Same measures but differently applied in the public and private sector

Article 8 sect. 2 ECFR appears to answer, at a first glance, these questions in favor of a general prohibition rule for the data processing. This Article requires that personal data must be processed fairly for specified purposes and on the basis of the consent of the person concerned, or some other legitimate basis laid down by law. However, the European Charta of Fundamental Rights principally does not directly bind private parties but only the State. In the private sector, it is principally the State that is being required to establish protection instruments that fairly balance the opposing fundamental rights of private parties.[1548] In particular, it is still unclear whether the European Court of Justice follows this principle or considers, exceptionally, a direct effect of the right to data protection under Article 8 ECFR on the private sector.[1549]

1546 See, for example, De Hert and Gutwirth, Data Protection in the Case Law of Strasbourg and Luxemburg: Constitutionalisation in Action, p. 70; as well as Karg, The renaissance of the prohibition principle in data protection, pp. 78 and 79.

1547 See, for example, Masing, Challenges of data protection, p. 2307.

1548 See above under point C. I. 1. b) aa) Third-party effect, protection and defensive function.

1549 See above the introduction under point C. I. 1. b) aa) (2) (b) The right to data protection under Article 8 ECFR and/or the right to private life under Article 7 ECFR, referring to Britz, Europeanisation of Data Protection Provided for by Fundamental Rights?, p. 8; v. Danwitz, The Fundamental Rights to Private Life and to data Protection, p. 585; ECJ C-101/01 (Lindqvist); ECJ C-275/06 (PROMUSICAE); Kokott and Sobotta, The distinction between privacy and data protection in the jurisprudence of the CJEU and the ECtHR, p. 225, stressing only

As illustrated previously, legal scholars discuss, even if it was clear that Article 8 sect. 2 ECFR has an indirect effect on the private sector, whether there should be, irrespective of the effects of fundamental rights, an equal or equivalent level of data protection in the private and the public sector. Pursuant to the first opinion, the level of protection and regulation instruments are the same for both the public and private sector. In relation to the second opinion, different regulation instruments are applied in order to achieve a higher, lower, or the same level of protection in the private sector.[1550] Buchner finally disapproves both alternatives because the indirect effect of fundamental rights not only leaves a large margin for appreciation to the legislator in finding the right instruments for the balance of the opposing rights on the private sector. This balancing exercise also means that fundamental rights are not an absolute rights, but always relates to opposing constitutional positions. The result is that fundamental rights always lack an objective scale that would actually be the pre-condition for answering the question of whether there should be a higher, lower or equivalent level of protection.[1551]

aa) Different risks in the public and private sector

While Buchner's considerations highlight an important aspect, these opinions do actually not conflict with each other. The reason for this is that they refer, in light of the concept proposed in this thesis, to two different aspects of the regulation: On the one hand, the processing of personal data indeed creates a new *and* common threat on both the public and private sector, i.e. the informational accumulation of power on behalf of the controller.[1552] In order to re-balance this accumulation of power, procedural requirements such as of purpose specification, purpose limitation, and the individual's consent or another basis laid down by law are indeed suitable measures protecting against both the risks caused by data processing in the

---

an indirect effect on the private sector; in contrast, De Hert and Gutwirth, Data Protection in the Case Law of Strasbourg and Luxemburg: Constitutionalisation in Action, pp. 69 and 70, which appear to consider a direct effect on the private sector.

1550 See Buchner, ibid., pp. 44 and 45 with further references, 57 and 58.

1551 See Buchner, ibid., pp. 57 and 58.

1552 Cf. Trute, JZ 1998, p. 826.

public and the private sector. On the other hand, a more detailed view reveals that the specific circumstances of such a potential abuse of aggregated power are principally different in the public and private sector.[1553] And, as a consequence, the substantial requirements determining *how* the procedural protection instruments must be implemented in order to appropriately protect against this diversity of risks, are also different. Thus, while the protection instruments are principally the same on the public and private sector, they are applied differently. And since the substantial concept of protection is also different on both sectors, it is impossible to measure whether those (differently applied) protection instruments lead, in the end, to a higher, equal, or lower level of protection.

Thus, in order to correctly apply the protection instruments provided for by the fundamental right to data protection, it is necessary to assess the risk in light of the substantial guarantees concerned. In this regard, Buchner provides illustrative examples for how different the risks may be, on the one hand, in the private sector, and on the other hand, on the public sector: First, only the State has the power to directly enforce its decisions by formal legal instruments. Second, while the State builds upon a monopoly with respect to public services, commercial companies compete in the private sector. This makes the State more powerful toward individuals concerned than private companies, given that private companies have no monopoly on the products and/or services demanded by the individuals concerned (if a private company holds a monopoly, there are other laws, such as anti-trust regulation, which aim to re-balance these power inequalities[1554]). Third, Buchner refers to the fact that the way the State treats data is not a value-free process. In Buchner's opinion, the state has an idealistic and norm-oriented picture of its citizens, expressed through legal order. In contrast, in the private sector, there is a multitude of private companies that determine the value of personal data differently. In principle, even if all the private companies pursue financial goals, the value of a per-

---

1553 See above under point C. I. 1. b) cc) Equal or equivalent level of protection compared to state data processing, referring, on the one hand, to De Hert and Gutwirth, Privacy, data protection and law enforcement. Opacity of the individual and transparency of power, pp. 77 and 78, and on the other hand, to Buchner, Informational self-determination in the private sector, pp. 72 to 74.

1554 In this regard, it is indeed possible to take the power inequalities into account that result from the aggregation of personal data, how it was recently addressed by the ammended anti-trust law in Germany.

sonal characteristic, such as compulsive gambling, is rather different for a gambling service provider than for a private bank granting loans. Buchner concludes that the consequences for an individual being evaluated by the State as a good or bad citizen are worse than as a good or bad customer by ‘the market’. He stresses the high intensity of State infringements in light of the – not only potential – totality of State surveillance as well as its proven lack of legitimacy.[1555]

Irrespective of whether or not these examples are, under all circumstances, correct, they demonstrate that power inequalities are different on the public and the private sector. This does again not mean that there are less or fewer power inequalities on the private sector than on the public sector, but only, that they are different. Therefore, even if the procedural protection instruments are the same, they have to be differently applied in the private and public sector. As a consequence, with respect to the interplay between the public and the private sector, the attention must indeed be drawn to the problem of State access to data stored by private parties. The more data that is collected by private entities, the more the State wants to gain access to it. However, this does not require, primarily, restricting the collection of data in the private sector. In the opposite, such a justification for a restriction of data processing in the private sector would likely render these requirements disproportionate.[1556] The reason for this is that there is an alternative solution that is more effective and infringes less the private data controllers’ fundamental rights: imposing stricter rules on the State in relation to the way it accesses such data.[1557]

1555 See Buchner, ibid., pp. 64 to 72; see also Grimm, Data protection before its refinement, p. 587.

1556 Cf. above under point C. I. 1. b) bb) (1) The 3-Step-Test: Assessing the defensive and protection function.

1557 See Mantelero and Vaciago, The "Dark Side" of Big Data: Private and Public Interaction in Social Surveillance, pp. 161 to 169; Buchner, ibid., pp. 72 to 74; see, in particular, Peters, Effective protection of fundamental rights and efficient criminal prosecution in relation to acess to electronic data stored by private third parties.

bb) Example: Requirements to specify the purpose and limit the processing at a later stage

This result, i.e. that the same protection instruments must be differently applied, was already demonstrated in the preceding analysis: For example, the requirement to specify the purpose does not only apply to the processing of personal data by the State, but also to the processing by private parties. The reason is that the purpose specified by the controller provides the legal link for any evaluation of risks caused by data processing, irrespective of whether this happens in the public or the private sector.[1558] However, with respect to the question of how the controller must specify the purpose, different criteria are applied to the processing of personal data by the State and private parties. The difference results from diverse situations in which the State and private parties act. For example, while the tasks of public agencies, which are specified further in Organizational State Law, limit the extent of state data processing, beside the object of protection for that the data processing serves, private data controllers do not have such a reference system at their disposal in order to specify the purpose.[1559] In this regard, the requirement applied by the German Constitutional Court that "the legislator has to determine especially the purpose of usage of the data in a precise manner and specifically *in relation to certain areas*" (underlining added by the author) becomes clearer.[1560] This term refers, with respect to data processing by public agencies, to the tasks and competences of the public agencies. In contrast, in the private sector, it is more helpful for data controllers to specify 'certain areas of social life' in light of the individual's fundamental rights concerned by the processing of per-

1558 See summary above under point C. II. 3. a) cc) (1) Tying into Courts' decisions and European legislation.

1559 See above under point C. II. 2. c) aa) No legal system providing for 'objectives' of data processing in the private sector, and C. II. 1. c) ee) (1) (d) Liberalization of the strict requirement by referring to the object of protection, referring, amongst others, to BVerfG, 20th of April 2016, 1 BvR 966/09 and 1 BvR 1140/09 (Federal Bureau of Investigation Law), cip. 281.

1560 See BVerfG, 4th of April 2006, 1 BvR 518/02, cip. 145: "Bei Eingriffen in das Grundrecht auf informationelle Selbstbestimmung - wie auch in die Spezialgrundrechte der Art. 10 und 13 GG - hat der Gesetzgeber insbesondere den Verwendungszweck der Daten bereichsspezifisch und präzise zu bestimmen (...)."

sonal data.[1561] Another example refers to the discussion on purpose identity and compatibility. In the public sector, the strict requirement of purpose identity primarily serves to guarantee the 'informational separation of powers'.[1562] Thus, the requirement of purpose identity, building on the requirement to specify the purpose, hinders the State to boundlessly aggregate information about its citizens.[1563] In light of this function, the strict requirement of purpose identity does not have to be equally applied in the private and public sector. Instead, in principle, a more flexible approach, such as referring to a purpose compatibility assessment serves better to balance the opposing fundamental rights of private parties.[1564]

cc) Legal-technical constraints surrounding the prohibition rule

In light of these differences, it is essential to also examine pursuant to which approach (such as a prohibition rule) further protection instruments surrounding the principle of purpose limitation should be implemented in the private sector. For example, De Hert and Gutwirth are of the opinion that "there is a prohibition rule, which is generally subject to exceptions. This second set of tools is particularly useful for regulating relationships between private actors. As a starting point for such relationships, it should be accepted that these actors have equal claims to liberty and are in principle capable of protecting their own liberty interests. Individual consent and ad hoc balancing are suitable instruments to reconcile the liberty interests at stake. Only after careful consideration and with solid arguments, for instance with regard to unequal power relationships, should governments interfere and impose 'hard norms' or 'choices' resulting from categorical balancing."[1565] This consideration is similar to that of the German

---

1561 See above under point C. II. 3. a) Regulative aim: Data protection for the individual's autonomy.

1562 See above under point C. III. 1. b) dd) Interim conclusion: Right to control data causing a 'flood of regulation'.

1563 See, in particular, above under point C. III. 1. b) cc) (1) (b) Principle of purpose limitation and informational separation of powers.

1564 See above under point C. III. 2. c) Conclusion: Purpose limitation in decentralized data networks.

1565 See De Hert and Gutwirth, Data Protection in the Case Law of Strasbourg and Luxemburg: Constitutionalisation in Action, p. 70.

Constitutional Court, which equally considers the individual's consent as the primary protection instrument in the private sector.[1566]

However, in the public sector, the 'prohibition rule' principally results from the requirement provided for by constitutional law that each state act infringing the scope of protection of an individual's fundamental right must be approved by parliamentary law (so-called defensive function of fundamental rights). This also is the reason for why Buchner requires that the State should not be allowed to base its data processing on the individual's consent because this undermines its limitations provided by parliamentary law. In contrast, in the private sector, the individual's consent might indeed be the more suitable protection instrument for his or her autonomy.[1567] In contrast, in the private sector, the legislator must safeguard that there is a regulation which balances the conflicting fundamental rights (so-called protection function).[1568] Therefore, the prohibition rule must equally be examined in light of the approach of regulating innovation in the private sector and, in particular, the colliding fundamental rights.

b) Possible approaches of regulation in the private sector

Buchner consequently stresses that there is actually no constitutional requirement for either approach, in the private sector. In particular, he points out that the first approach (i.e. an equal level of protection, which leads, also in the private sector, to the requirement that each kind of processing of personal data must be based on a legitimate basis laid down by law), may not even necessarily lead to a restrictive regulation. General exceptions provided for by law, such as for the 'legitimate interests' of a data controller, and the possibility to receive the individual's consent can lead to the situation where this requirement does not play an effective role in data protection regulation. However, from his point of view, each of the

---

1566 See above under point C. I. 1. b) aa) (3) (b) Priority of contractual agreements and the imbalance of powers, referring to BVerfG, 1 BvR 2027/02 (Release of Confidentiality), cip. 34 to 36.

1567 See above under point C. I. 1. b) cc) Equal or equivalent level of protection compared to state data processing?, referring to Buchner, Informational self-determination in the private sector, pp. 62 and 63.

1568 See above under point C. I. 1. b) bb) Balance between defensive and protection function; in particular, Dietlein, The Doctrine of Duties of Protection of Basic Rights, p. 111 to 117.

two options provide two contrasting 'approaches of regulation'. If the regulation generally prohibits each kind of data processing and only permits certain exceptions, the law is interpreted differently than if it principally allows data processing and only prohibits certain types of it.[1569] For example, a legal exception to a general rule is usually interpreted narrowly.[1570] This means that it is difficult for the data controller to interpret an exceptional authorization of data processing extensively. In contrast, it is more difficult for the individual concerned by data processing to interpret a provision, which exceptionally prohibits a certain processing operation, in an extensive way in order to protect him or her against the processing. Another example concerns the burden of proof. One or the other regulatory approach may lead to the result that either the individual must demonstrate that the controller did not apply the law, or the controller must demonstrate that it did apply the law.[1571]

aa) Classic instruments: Specific legal provisions, broad legal provisions, and/or consent

Whatever the approach will be, Buchner considers three ways of how to implement one or the other approach in the private sector: First, the legislator can establish, balancing itself the opposing rights, detailed and sector-specific regulations (be it by means of authorizing or prohibiting provisions); second, it can provide general provisions which must then be interpreted (i.e. by the private parties concerned, data protection authorities or judicial courts); third, it can provide a regulatory infrastructure enabling an individual to efficiently decide by him or herself under which conditions he or she discloses personal data to another and, hence, how to balance his or her fundamental rights with the controller's opposing rights.[1572] Buchner discusses the advantages and disadvantages of the first two options: Detailed provisions are good, in his opinion, for regulating

1569 See Buchner, ibid., pp. 80 and 81.

1570 See, regarding the European level, the in-depth analysis by Herberger, "Exceptions have to be interpretetd narrowly" – The considerations by the European Court of Justice.

1571 Cf. above under point C. III. 1. a) bb) (1) Preliminary analysis: Pre-conditions and consequences.

1572 See Buchner, ibid., p. 96.

the routine treatment of data, because there is no need to undertake a balancing exercise, as the treatment of data is always the same. However, this kind of detailed regulation cannot cover unknown kinds of data treatment, as the need to carry out a balancing exercise is required with respect to the circumstances of the particular issue at hand. In contrast, general provisions can principally cover unknown kinds of data treatment because their wording is sufficiently *general*. However, because of this, general provisions do not provide legal certainty. In light of these disadvantages, Buchner favors the last option: The individual's consent enables private parties to balance their opponent rights and interests themselves with respect to a particular issue at hand.[1573] Building upon these considerations, two aspects shall be clarified, in the following two sections, with respect to the regulation of data-driven innovation.

bb) Conceptual shift: From a legal basis to 'legitimacy assessment'

First, the individual's consent does not always guarantee that the individual concerned is really able to appropriately balance the opponent fundamental rights, on his or her own. Balboni et al. stress, in particular, that the individual's consent may often substitute a real balancing of conflicting fundamental rights that would lead to appropriate protection. This is particularly the case if the individual cannot effectively manage the data processing because it takes place too often and rapidly.[1574] Balboni et al. are even of the opinion that the legal system of data protection laws itself hinders a real balancing exercise by the individual concerned and the data controller because the system considers the individual's consent as a legal basis for data processing and is, therefore, "logically separate from the actual level of protection provided to the data subject." The authors draw from this separation their conclusion "that processing can take place lawfully (with a valid legal basis) but without what the authors would consider 'appropriate' protections. Thus, in the case of data subject consent as a legitimate ground for processing personal data, the data subject's self-determined decision to agree to processing his own data may prevail over a

1573 See Buchner, ibid., pp. 97 to 102.

1574 See Balboni et al., Legitimate interest of the data controller New data protection paradigm: legitimacy grounded on appropriate protection, p. 255.

possible lack of protection for his personal data."[1575] In this regard, it should be stressed that the authors use the term "appropriate", apparently, not within the meaning of being "constitutionally legal", in light of the opposing fundamental rights. Instead, the authors rather use this term, apparently, in the meaning of political legitimacy.

In any case, this thought similarly applies to the legitimate grounds listed under Article 7 lit. b to e of the Data Protection Directive, as well as Article 6 sect. 1 lit. b to e of the General Data Protection Regulation. These legitimate grounds allow the purpose specified (within the corresponding provision) to prevail, generally, over the individual's fundamental rights.[1576] Only the general clause under Article 7 lit. f of the directive and Article 6 sect. 1 lit. f of the regulation allows, in principle, for a different balancing test. However, appropriate protection for the individual depends, here, in practice, mainly on the data controller's subjective view.[1577] In light of this potential lack of "appropriate" protection, Balboni et al. praise the conceptual shift within the concept of protection established by the General Data Protection Regulation. This shift combines, in their opinion, "legitimate processing modalities" (mainly the principles established under Article 5 of the regulation, such as the principle of purpose limitation) with the controller's and processor's obligation to conduct a so-called "legitimacy assessment" for the data processing. They consider such an assessment as required under Chapter IV of the regulation, in particular, by the risk-based "responsibility" approach under Article 24.[1578] This approach shifts, pursuant the view of Balboni et al., the "legal assumption regarding the personal data processing regime (...) from the principle that ‚processing is prohibited unless...', to ‚processing is permitted provided that...'."[1579] Balboni et al. correspondingly propose that this "assessment must take into consideration the ultimate level of data protection that could effectively be guaranteed, and ask whether the level of protection provided to personal data under the proposed scenario, can still be deemed 'appropriate'."[1580]

1575 See Balboni et al., ibid., p. 246.
1576 See Balboni et al., ibid., p. 254.
1577 See Balboni et al., ibid., pp. 253 and 254.
1578 See already above under point B. II. 1. Risk terminology oscillating between "prevention" and "precaution".
1579 See Balboni et al., ibid., pp. 258.
1580 See Balboni et al., ibid., pp. 246.

This conceptual shift indeed fits better to innovation processes than the exclusive focus on the individual's consent or a legal provision as the necessary basis for the legitimacy of data processing. The reason is that the classic understanding of a 'legitimate basis laid down by law' often focuses on the moment of collection.[1581] However, many risks caused by the later processing of data cannot be comprehensively foreseen when the data is first collected.[1582] Instead, the principle of "accountability" requires the controller (as well as processor) to safeguard the effective and efficient application of data protection principles during the whole data process.[1583] In conclusion, the consent alone does not necessarily lead to appropriate protection of the individual. Instead, it must be seen together with further protection instruments in order to achieve the result that Buchner promotes: a fair balancing of the conflicting fundamental rights.

cc) Side note: State regulated self-regulation increasing legal certainty

The second aspect to be clarified with respect to Buchner's criticism of broad legal terms is the following: Buchner criticizes broad legal terms because they increase legal uncertainty. However, legal uncertainty can be reduced, again, by mechanisms of regulated self-regulation.[1584] In fact, taking the considerations by Balboni et al. regarding the consent into account, the consent requirement also goes hand in hand with legal uncertainty. This is particularly the case, if the validity of the consent or the data processing based on it, respectively, depends on an overall "legitimacy assessment". The preceding analysis demonstrated that there are various questions surrounding, in particular, the principle of purpose limitation that must be answered on a case-by-case assessment and leads, consequently, to legal uncertainty. For instance, it is unclear under which conditions the controller has to notify the individual about an intrusion into his

---

1581 See above under point C. II. 2. b) cc) Arguable focus on data collection for legal evaluation in the private sector.

1582 See above under point B. II. Data protection as a risk regulation.

1583 See already the Article 29 Data Protection Working Group, Opinion 3/2010 on the principle of accountability.

1584 See above under point A. II. 2. The regulator's perspective, referring to Eifert, Regulation Strategies, cip. 52 to 71.

or her privacy excluding an infringement.[1585] The same question arises with respect to the processing of data leading to a specific risk for fundamental rights of freedom and equality. These questions refer, amongst other aspects, to the degree of precision of the purpose, as well as additional requirements that the controller has to meet.[1586] Further questions refer to the compatibility assessment.[1587]

However, the function of reducing legal uncertainty does not necessarily require, in regard of these preceding aspects, a comprehensive regulation of all kinds of processing of personal data. Instead, the legislator can also establish an "open" regulation providing, as a first step, examples that typify certain purposes of data processing that are either legal or illegal. As a second step, the legislator can establish one or several general rules covering cases where the data controller processes the data for a purpose that is not explicitly regulated by the law (be it because it is not explicitly prohibited or allowed). These general rules should then provide more general criteria in order to assist other entities to determine whether data processing is prohibited or allowed and/or under which conditions.[1588] In conclusion, if the legislator does not precisely define the criteria itself in relation to what is considered to be legal or illegal data processing, it should, at least, provide for more general criteria and combine these substantive criteria with procedural mechanisms to enable others to then specify these general criteria.[1589] With respect to the General Data Protection Regulation, the European legislator did so by providing mechanisms for the establishment of codes of conducts and certificates.[1590] In light of these considerations, legal uncertainty is not a valid argument against implementing certain regulation instruments. In contrast, as illustrated previously, broad legal terms, just as principles, as well as the indi-

1585 See the discussion on 'opt-in' and 'opt-out' procedures above under point C. II. 3. b) aa) (3) 'Framing' privacy expectations.

1586 See above under point C. II. 3. b) dd) (3) (c) Protection instruments enabling the individual to adapt to or protect him or herself against the informational measure.

1587 See above under point C. III. 1. b) cc) (2) Compatibility of purposes.

1588 See the contrary approach of a closed regulation under Article 7 of the Data Protection Directive and, in principle, also under Article 6 of the General Data Protection Regulation.

1589 See above under point A. II. 2. The regulators perspective, referring to Eifert, Regulation Strategies, cip. 52 to 71.

1590 See Articles 40 to 43 of the regulation.

vidual's consent can all be suitable instruments for regulating innovation. As a first step, such instruments are open toward innovation if they leave enough room for data controllers to find the appropriate solution of protection. As a second step, if combined with mechanisms of regulated self-regulation, data controllers are able to increase legal certainty.[1591]

dd) Interplay of consent and legal provisions

Thus, the legislator is principally free in regulating data-driven innovation by either establishing a general prohibition rule with certain exceptions, or, in reverse, by principally allowing the processing of personal data except in situations where certain kinds of data processing are explicitly prohibited. In order to implement the one or the other regulatory approach, the legislator can establish either very specific provisions or rather broad legal terms, or set up the requirement to gather the individual's consent. Upon this basis, the interplay of the individual's consent and legal provisions shall now be examined in more detail.

In this regard, it must firstly be stressed that the consent itself imperatively requires, as a protection instrument, a legal provision that prohibits certain kinds of data processing if the consent shall be an exclusive legal basis legitimizing these kinds of processing. The reason for this is, from a legal-technical point of view, that the controller is only obliged to gather the consent if it is not allowed to process the data otherwise. In this case, where the consent shall be an exclusive legal basis for data processing, the legislator must thus prohibit such kinds of data processing if it seeks to make the processing dependent on the individual's consent. Without such a legal obligation, the individual concerned would have no exclusive control over the corresponding risks, by either giving or not giving his or her consent.[1592] In contrast, if the regulator comes to the result that certain kinds of data processing do not exclusively require the individual's consent or leaves it open to debate, the consent is not a concurring alternative (in the meaning of an 'exclusive' legal basis) but a complementary regu-

1591 See above under point A. II. 2. The regulators perspective, referring to Eifert, Regulation Strategies, cip. 52 to 71.

1592 Cf. Karg, ibid., p. 78, who requires, indeed, that all kinds of data processing must be subordinated the individual's consent, irrespective of the corresponding risk.

lation instrument. This is the case, for example, with respect to the legal basis listed under Article 7 of the Data Protection Directive, as well as Article 6 sect. 1 of the General Data Protection Regulation. The Data Protection Working Group principally considers all legal basis listed under Article 7 of the directive, thus, including the consent and the general clause for the controller's 'legitimate interests', as equally applicable.[1593]

Such a complementary interplay of legal provisions, like the general clause, and the individual's consent is important if the legislator does not clarify itself which kind of processing of personal data shall certainly be allowed or not, and under which specific conditions. The reason for this is that there are situations where the individual's consent does not function as a legitimate basis for data processing.[1594] This can be the case if the individual does not give his or her consent,[1595] or the consent is not valid because it was not given voluntarily,[1596] but the data controller has a legitimate interest in the data processing. A similar situation occurs if the individual withdraws his or her consent or objects to the processing of data,

1593 See Article 29 Data Protection Working Group, Opinion 06/2014 on the notion of legitimate interests of the data controller under Article 7 of Directive 95/46/EC, pp. 13/14.

1594 See, regarding the overriding interests, at Brownsword, Consent in Data Protection Law: Privacy, Fair Processing and Confidentiality, pp. 85 to 87; that the complementary interplay actually is necessary so long as the legislator does not exclude these "fallacy" cases is mostly overlooked in the debate, see, for example, the summary at Radlanski, The concept of consent in the reality of data protection law, pp. 201 to 209.

1595 See the example of negative information about an insurant exchanged in the insurance industry at Buchner, ibid., pp. 143 to 147.

1596 See the discussion on the criteria for the voluntariness of the consent, for example, at Kamp and Rost, Criticism of the individual's consent – An interjection on a ficticious legal basis in asyymetric power relations, pp. 82 and 83, who promote rather strict requirements, similar to Article 7 sect. 4 GDPR; in contrast, see the more liberal approach applied, with respect to the private sector, the German Constitutional Court above under point C. I. 1. b) aa) (3) German Basic Rights, referring to BVerfG, 1 BvR 2027/02 (Release of Confidentiality), cip. 34 to 40, and regarding the public sector the approach of the European Court of Human Rights above under point C. I. 3. b) dd) Consent: Are individuals given a choice to avoid the processing altogether?, referring to ECtHR, Case of Gillan and Quinton vs. the United Kingdom from 12 January 2010 (application no. 4158/05), cip. 65 and 87, as well as ECtHR, Case of M.S. vs. Sweden from 27 August 1997 (74/1996/693/885), cip. 32.

but the controller has a legitimate interest in the processing.[1597] If the legislator does not explicitly exclude these cases from a general "consent requirement", it must provide further legal provisions that balance the colliding fundamental rights.

c) Interim conclusion: Balancing the colliding fundamental rights

In conclusion, this sub-chapter focused on the legal necessity of the individual's consent or another basis laid down by law for the processing of personal data. In the private sector, the legislator principally has a large margin of discretion for choosing its regulatory approach: It can decide for a comprehensive regulation exclusively allowing certain kinds of data processing or, in contrast, can forbid certain purposes. It can also establish self-regulation instruments such as the individual's consent or, more general, by authorizing private entities specifying the conditions under which certain types of data processing are legal or not. Such co-regulation mechanisms are, as a first step, principally open to innovation and, as a second step, enable data controllers to increase legal certainty. In this regard, the individual's consent fits principally into the idea of innovation processes: the individual is able, pursuant to the circumstances of the particular case, to assess by him or herself the risk caused by the data processing and, thus, whether to consent to it and under which conditions.[1598]

However, first of all, the preceding discussion made clear that so long as the legal provision, which requires the consent, does not explicitly exclude cases where the consent does not properly work legitimizing the data processing, the data controller must be able to refer to complementary legal provisions in order to achieve a fair balance of the individual's protection against its own colliding fundamental rights. Situations where the consent does not properly work in balancing the colliding fundamental rights occur if the data controller has a legitimate interest in the data pro-

1597 See Buchner, Informational self-determination in the private sector, pp. 233 to 243 with reference to Simitis, BDSG, § 4a Rn. 90, Ohly, Einwilligung, S. 176; cf. Bergmann/Möhrle/Herb, Datenschutzrecht, § 4a BDSG Rn. 24; Gola, DuD 2001, 278 (279), Gola/Schomerus, BDSG § 4a Rn. 18; Schaffland/Wiltfang, BDSG, § 4a Rn. 26; Simitis in ders. BDSG § 4a, Rn. 94 ff; Tinnefeld/Ehrmann/Gerling, Datenschutzrecht, S. 324.

1598 See Masing, Challenges of data protection, p. 2308.

cessing but the individual concerned, first, does not give his or her consent, or second, the consent is not valid because it was not given voluntarily, or third, the individual withdraws his or her consent or objects the data processing. If the legislator does not (or cannot) determine these cases in advance, the individual's consent must not be the only protection instrument that balances the colliding fundamental rights, but there must be another complementary means providing the conditions under that the data processing can finally be considered as legitimate.

The European Data Protection Directive and the General Data Protection Regulation currently provide for a comprehensive regulation prohibiting, in general, the processing of personal data and making, at second instance, certain exceptions from this rule. In doing so, the legislator did not determine the cases where the individual's consent should be an exclusive legitimate basis for data processing (and was probably not able to do so, in light of its knowledge deficiencies in highly dynamic innovative environments). Thus, the individual's consent and the legal provisions authorizing the processing of personal data, in particular, the general clause for the controller's 'legitimate interests', complement each other. In any case, legal scholars stress the conceptual shift, within the General Data Protection Regulation, away from the „legal assumption (...) that ‚processing is prohibited unless...', to ‚processing is permitted provided that...'."[1599] This shift becomes particularly apparent, amongst others, in the accountability principle under Article 24 of the regulation, and leads to the situation that the legitimacy assessment for the data processing does not mainly focus, anymore, on the moment of collection but takes the data process as a whole into account.[1600] What this specifically means for the assessment will be illustrated in the following chapter.

3. The individual's "decision-making process" (in light of the GDPR)

In order to illustrate the 'legitimacy assessment', as introduced before, this chapter takes the "individual's decision-making process" as a whole into account. At first, two different procedures implementing the consent are examined, the so-called opt-in and opt-out procedures. However, instead

1599 See Balboni et al., ibid., pp. 258.

1600 See already the Article 29 Data Protection Working Group, Opinion 3/2010 on the principle of accountability.

of deciding for one or the other procedure, both functions will be assessed in light of the overall decision-making process of the individual who seeks to manage the risks caused by the processing of data concerning him or her. In doing so, the principle of purpose limitation, as interpreted in this thesis, again is particularly useful. The reason for this is that the principle of purpose limitation originates from the consent. In early discussions about the concept of the consent, legal scholars considered it as a condition in itself that the consent must refer to a particular context and, though, to a specific purpose. Otherwise it was unclear to what the individual concerned was consenting to.[1601] Only later, did legal scholars apply this "artifact" of the consent to all kinds of processing of personal data, irrespective of whether this is based on the individual's consent or not.[1602] Thus, after having clarified, in general, the function of the principle of purpose limitation, in view of non-linear environments, this function may now help, vice versa, implement the consent in a way suitable for these environments. In any case, this risk-oriented function of the principle of purpose limitation helps not only clarify how the individual's consent should be implemented, but also with respect to additional protection instruments. This chapter concludes these considerations by coming back to the question posed in the introduction and the second part "B. II. 2. Regulation of innovative entrepreneurship" of which regulatory strategy serves best in order to specify the individual's decision-making process overall.

1601 See Pohle, Purpose limitation revisited, p. 141, referring to Oscar M. Ruebhausen und Orville G. Brim Jr. (1965). "Privacy and Behavioral Research", Columbia Law Review 65.7, pp. 1184 to 1211.

1602 See Pohle, ibid., p. 142, referring to Wilhelm Steinmüller et al. (1971), Grundfragen des Datenschutzes: Gutachten im Auftrag des Bundesministeriums des Innern – Fundamental questions of data protection: report on behalf the German Ministry of the Interior, BT-Drs. VI/3826, Anlage 1, and Datenschutzkommission des Deutschen Juristentages (1974), Grundsätze für eine Regelung des Datenschutzes: Bericht der Datenschutzkommission des Deutschen Juristentages – Principles for a regulation of data protection: report of the Data Protection Commission of the German Jurists Conference, München, C. H. Beck Verlag, p. 27.

a) Static perspective: Opt-in or opt-out procedure for consent?

In legal literature, it is highly debated in which manner the individual has to consent in order to legitimize the data processing: Must the individual give his or her consent prior to the processing or is it sufficient if he or she does not object?

aa) Classic discussion regarding current data protection laws

The Data Protection Directive defines in its Article 2 lit. h the term 'consent' as "any freely given specific and informed indication of his wishes by which the data subject signifies his agreement to personal data relating to him being processed". Article 4 sect. 11 of the General Data Protection Regulation essentially adopts this definition and clarifies, indeed, that the individual's indication of his or her wishes must not only be specific and informed but also *unambiguous* and that the individual might give it *by statement or by a clear affirmative action*. The requirement that the individual's consent must be unambiguous plays an essential role in comparison to the consent required for the processing of special categories of personal data. Article 8 sect. 2 lit. a of the Data Protection Directive, as well as Article 9 sect. 2 lit. a of the General Data Protection Regulation require an 'explicit' consent. From the perspective of the Data Protection Working Group, the term 'explicit' means that the individual must take some positive action, be it orally or in writing. Hence, the presence of a pre-ticked box is not sufficient.[1603] In contrast, for data other than sensitive data, Article 7 lit. a of the directive, as well as the General Data Protection Regulation, only require an 'unambiguous' consent. Legal scholars conclude from this comparison that the consent needed for the processing of personal data that is not sensitive can therefore also be given in an implicit form, as long as it is unambiguous.[1604]

The Working Group also considers, regarding the unambiguity requirement laid down in the directive: "This requirement enables data controllers to use different types of mechanisms to seek consent, ranging from statements to indicate agreement (express consent), to mechanisms that re-

---

1603 See the Article 29 Data Protection Working Group, Opinion 15/2011 on the definition of consent, p. 35.

1604 See the opponent opinion by Ehmann/Helfrich, ibid., Art. 7, cip.12 et seqq.

ly on actions that aim at indicating agreement."[1605] However, it adds that a "consent based on an individual's inaction or silence would normally not constitute valid consent, especially in an on-line context. (…) For example, this is the case with the use of pre-ticked boxes or Internet browser settings that are set by default to collect data."[1606] The consent must furthermore be given prior to the collection of the data; however, it can be also given during the data processing when there is a new purpose.[1607] Indeed, these considerations do not explain why the decision of a website user to proceed, after having been informed about the data processing, in using the website shall not be considered an 'action indicating his or her agreement' but as 'inaction or silence'. Furthermore, the considerations do not answer the question of whether the consent must be given prior to each kind of processing of personal data or whether it is possible to differentiate pursuant to the specific risk that the processing causes against a fundamental right to privacy, freedom, or non-discrimination of the individual concerned. In particular, does the last consideration regarding the change of purpose mean that the individual gives, for the first time, his or her consent only if there is a change of purpose?

Correspondingly to these questions, there is an ongoing discussion in legal literature of how to categorize the so-called opt-out consent, which is often used in practice. In contrast to the so-called opt-in consent, an opt-out consent does not require, for example, on a website, that the individual actively ticks a box in order to indicate his or her consent to the data processing. Instead, it is sufficient that the individual continues to use the website and does not, in addition, tick a box in order to actively disagree with the processing. The essential difference between both forms of consent, thus, is the degree of action of the individual or, in other words, how explicitly he or she has to consent to the data processing.[1608] In light of this, scholars discuss whether an opt-out consent can be seen as an implicit consent such as required under Article 7 lit. a of the Data Protection Directive and under Article 6 sect. 1 lit. a of the General Data Protection Regulation or whether it must be considered as an objection to the data process-

1605 See the Article 29 Data Protection Working Group, ibid., p. 35.
1606 See the Article 29 Data Protection Working Group, ibid., p. 35.
1607 See the Article 29 Data Protection Working Group, ibid., p. 34.
1608 Cf. Radlanski, The concept of consent in the reality of data protection law, pp. 18 to 20.

ing.[1609] Both laws foresee, beside the right of the individual to withdraw his or her consent, a right to object to the data processing if the processing is not based on the consent but on a legal provision such as the general clause for the data controller's 'legitimate interests'.[1610] In the UK, an opt-out procedure is seen as an implicit but valid consent and provides, therefore, a legal basis for the data processing. In contrast, in Germany, an opt-out procedure is not considered as an individual's consent but only as the implementation of his or her right to object the data processing if the processing is based, for instance, on the general clause for the data controller's 'legitimate interests'.[1611]

bb) Further approaches considered by the legislator and Constitutional Courts

The preceding analysis has already shown that the European legislator, as well as the different Courts (i.e. European Court of Human Rights, European Court of Justice, and German Constitutional Court) apply different approaches when deciding on this issue.[1612] For example, on the European level, the ePrivacy Directive only required, in its version from 2002, the data controller to inform the individual about the use of cookies (supposing, apparently, that the website user could decide, on this basis, to stop using the website). In contrast, in its amended version from 2009, it went

1609 See Kosta, Construing the Meaning of "Opt-Out" – An Analysis of the European, U.K. and German Data Protection Legislation, pp. 16 and 17.

1610 See Article 14 of the Data Protection Directive, and Article 21 of the General Data Protection Regulation.

1611 See Kosta, Construing the Meaning of "Opt-Out" – An Analysis of the European, U.K. and German Data Protection Legislation, pp. 16 and 17, with further references to Rosemary Jay, Data Protection Law and Practice (3rd edn Sweet & Maxwell London 2007), para. 3-65, regarding the UK situation, and, regarding the German view point, Stefan Hanloser, "'opt-in' im Datenschutzrecht und Wettbewerbsrecht – Konvergenzüberlegungen zum Einwilligungsbegriff bei der E-Mail Werbung", Computer und Recht (CR) (2008), pp. 714-715.

1612 See, however, Kosta, ibid., p. 29, referring to Roger Brownsword, "The cult of consent: fixation and fallacy" (2004), 15 King's Law Journal, p. 233, who comes to the conclusion as: "In reality, only the 'opt-in' consent is a real consent under the meaning of the Data Protection Directive, while any 'opt-out' clause should not be confused or in any way linked to the right of consent, but should be treated as a means for the exercise of the right to object."

one step beyond requiring the individual's consent because it was seen as the more effective protection instrument.[1613] Similarly, the ePrivacy Directive requires the use of automated calling machines, fax, or email for the purpose of direct marketing the individual's prior consent. In contrast, other forms of direct marketing that are not as cheap and easy to send, and do not impose financial costs on the individual concerned, do not necessarily require consent.[1614] And indeed, the European Court of Human Rights appears to apply a rather liberal approach when considering, regarding the right to private life under Article 8 ECHR, that an individual would be able to avoid a search of his or her bag at the airport by not choosing to travel by plane.[1615]

In contrast, the German Constitutional Court applies a rather strict approach when it states, for example, that an individual cannot be considered as consenting to being filmed by a public video camera if it knowingly and voluntarily enters the space recorded and does not explicitly disagree with the filming. In the German Court's point of view, if an individual does not explicitly object to a certain processing of data, this does not automatically mean that the individual consents to it.[1616] However, with respect to the processing of personal data by private parties, the German Constitutional Court also considers, more flexibly, different ways of how an individual could decide on the processing. For example, with respect to the release of confidentiality, the Court stated that the individual must not necessarily give his or her consent toward his or her insurance company when the insurance contract is concluded. Instead, the insurance company could also implement alternative or supplementary mechanisms such as: specific re-

---

1613 See above under point C. II. 3. b) aa) (3) (b) Examples: the legislature's considerations on the use of 'cookies' referring to Article 5 sect. 3 of the ePrivacy Directive as well as recital 24, and to Article 2 sect. 5 as well as recital 66 of the Civil Rights Directive.

1614 See above under point C. II. 3. b) aa) (3) (c) Example: Considerations surrounding 'unsolicited communications', referring to Article 13 sect. 1 of the ePrivacy Directive as well as recitals 40 and 42.

1615 See above under point C. I. 3. b) dd) Consent: Are individuals given a choice to avoid the processing altogether?, referring to ECtHR, Case of Gillan and Quinton vs. the United Kingdom from 12 January 2010 (application no. 4158/05), cip. 65.

1616 See above under point C. I. 2. c) Right to control disclosure and usage of personal data, referring to BVerfG, 23rd of February 2007, 1 BvR 2368/06 (Video Surveillance), cip. 39 and 40.

leases of confidentiality upon particular requests, which must refer to the specific institutions involved; or by a mechanism informing the individual so timely that he or she is still able to object the retrieval of personal data by the insurance company from the other institution; or by a mechanism where the other institution does not provide the information about the individual directly to the insurance company but, before, to the individual who can then decide to add information and forward it to the insurance company or not.[1617]

cc) Requirements illustrated so far, with respect to different guarantees

A similar discussion amongst German legal scholars referred, in particular, to the principle of purpose limitation, as was analyzed before. These scholars discussed whether there might be different forms of how an individual can provide their consent to the processing of personal data.[1618] In any case, instead, of answering specifically how the individual has to consent, the aim of this analysis was to only clarify that the regulator can indeed require different ways of how the individual should decide on whether the data is processed or not, and under which conditions.[1619] The analysis conducted in this thesis went therefore on to illustrate this fact with respect to the substantial guarantees provided for by the different fundamental rights to privacy, freedom, and non-discrimination.[1620] However, so far, this was done from a rather static point of view, i.e. the analysis had referred to only one substantial guarantee specifically concerned. The analysis has thus not yet addressed the question of how the individual should

1617 See above under point C. I. 2. d) bb) In the private sector: the contract as an essential link for legal evaluation, referring to BVerfG, 1 BvR 2027/02 (Release of Confidentiality), cip. 59 and 60.

1618 See above under point C. III. 1. b) dd) Interim conclusion: Right to control data causing a ‘flood of regulation’, referring, on the one hand, to Forgó et al., Purpose Specification and Informational Separation of Powers, pp. 53 to 58, and, on the other hand, to Eifert, Purpose Compatibility instead of Purpose Limitation, pp. 142 and 143.

1619 See the opponent opinion above under point C. III. 1. b) cc) (2) (a) Criticism of the "subjective“ purpose approach, referring to Eifert, Purpose Compatibility instead of Purpose Limitation, pp. 142 to 143.

1620 See above under point C. II. 3. b) aa) (3) (a) Research on the individual’s decision making process (consent), and C. II. 3. b) bb) (2) (b) Strict requirements for consent.

be involved if the processing of data is used for purposes that lead to a new risk for his or her fundamental rights, at least not extensively.[1621] This implies a dynamic point of view.

b) Dynamic perspective: Interplay of several protection instruments

The dynamic point of view on the individual's involvement in the data processing is taken in this part of this thesis. In doing so, the object of his or her consent will firstly be analyzed: Does the consent of the individual refer to personal data as such or risks caused by the data processing? An answer to this question will significantly influence the extent of the consent, i.e. the controller's room of action when using the data later on. In this regard, the risk-based approach elaborated with respect to the principle of purpose limitation plays, again, an important role. It helps clarify under which conditions the use of personal data for another purpose than previously specified requires another legitimate basis and, if based on the individual's consent, which procedure (i.e. opt-in or opt-out). In addition, it helps to further clarify the interplay of the individual's consent with legal provisions that equally authorize the processing (in particular, the general clause for the ‚legitimate interests' of the controller), his or her right to object the data processing, as well as further measures of transparency and participation.

aa) Consent: "Later processing covered by specified purpose?"

As shown previously, amongst legal scholars it is common ground that the controller must inform which data it collects or processes, in which manner, and for what purposes, before the individual consents to it.[1622] How-

---

1621 See only above under point C. III. 2. a) aa) (2) Custer's and Ursic's taxonomy: "Data recycling, repurposing, and recontextualization", referring to Custer and Ursic, Big data and data reuse: a taxonomy of data reuse for balancing big data benefits and personal data protection, p. 11.

1622 See above under point C. II. 1. b) cc) Purposes of processing specified when consent is given, referring to Article 29 Data Protection Working Group, Opinion 15/2011 on the definition of consent, and Dammann/Simitis, ibid., cip. 22; as well as under point C. II. 1. c) dd) (3) Discussion on degree of precision of specified purpose, with further references.

ever, two aspects shall now be clarified: The first aspect concerns the object of the consent, i.e. whether the individuals consents to the processing of data *per se* or, instead, to the risks caused by the data processing and specified by the processing purpose. In this regard, the considerations of legal scholars shall be stressed, who criticize the 'fallacy of the necessity of the consent'. This fallacy leads to the situation where data controllers have to gather the individual's consent for almost everything, which in turn leads to the situation that individuals are overwhelmed by the sheer number of consents they are asked to provide.[1623] Brownsword particularly advocates that what determines whether data processing is "morally permissible is not the presence or absence of consent but the application of background duties (or rights)."[1624] Tying into this approach, this thesis demonstrates that the specific fundamental rights to privacy, freedom, and non-disrimination of the individual concerned help determine whether an individual's consent is necessary. These rights hence determine the context of the data processing and the risk caused by it, which in turn helps assess which kind of action the individual has to take, in other words, how explicitly the individual has to provide his or her consent.[1625] The second aspect treats the extent of the consent provided. As stressed before, several legal scholars consider the consent provided to be unlawful as a whole if

1623 See Brownsword, Consent in Data Protection Law: Privacy, Fair Processing and Confidentiality; furthermore, Balboni et al., Legitimate interest of the data controller New data protection paradigm: legitimacy grounded on appropriate protection, p. 255; Buchner, Informational self-determination in the private sector, 176 to 183.

1624 See Brownsword, ibid., p. 91.

1625 See, regarding the importance of the context in order to determine the requirements for the consent, Kosta, Construing the Meaning of "Opt-Out" – An Analysis of the European, U.K. and German Data Protection Legislation, p. 18, referring to Joel Reidenberg and Paul Schwartz, "Data protection law and online services: regulatory responses" (Brussels 1998), p. 80, available online at http://ec.europa.eu/justice/policies/privacy/docs/studies/regul_en.pdf (last accessed on 29 March 2015); cf. also Article 29 Data Protection Working Group, Opinion 15/2011 on the definition of consent, pp. 21 to 25; regarding rights that determine the context, above under point B. III. 5. Values as normative scale determining "contexts" and "purposes", and C. II. 3. a) Solution approach: Purpose specification as a risk-dsicovery process; and regarding the kind of activity taken by the individual in order to consent, above under C. IV. 3. a) aa) Classic discussion regarding current data protection laws.

the specified purpose is not sufficiently precise.[1626] In contrast to this approach, this thesis has cast doubt on whether such imprecise purpose makes the consent unlawful as a whole. Instead, it is necessary to assess whether or not the purpose made explicit in the consent covers the risk caused by the later use of data.[1627] The purpose specified in the consent hence does not determine whether the consent is illegal as a whole or not, but whether or not the later data processing can be based on the consent.

(1) Risks as object of consent (not data)

In order to assess both aspects, it is necessary to clarify the function of the individual's consent. Several legal scholars stress its function as an expression of the individual's autonomy.[1628] The German legal scholar Ohly refers to two ethical reasons for the necessity of autonomous decisions. From a deontological perspective, this necessity results from human dignity. The individual's ability to decide about his or her own affairs constitutes the individual's human dignity and has therefore to be respected by the society. From a utilitarian perspective, the individual's ability to decide their own affairs increases, based on the assumption that everybody prefers autonomy to heteronomy, the common welfare.[1629]

However, in light of Constitutional Law, the individual's ability to discard their rights is often discussed as a 'waiver' of fundamental rights and

---

1626 See above C. II. 2. b) cc) Arguable legal consequences considered for consent, with further references; as well as Buchner, ibid., p. 242 who is of the opinion that the consent is illicit "if the data controller did not duly inform about all necessary circumstances which are decisive for the data processing" ("Nur wenn die verantwortliche Stelle ihrer Pflicht zu einer umfassenden Aufklärung über alle entscheidungsrelevanten Umstände der Datenverarbeitung nicht nachgekommen sein sollte, ist ihr das Risiko zuzurechnen, dass die Datenverarbeitung aufgrund unwirksamer Einwilligung von Anfang an unzulässig ist.").

1627 See above C. II. 3. b) dd) Arguable legal consequences surrounding the validity of the consent.

1628 See the Article 29 Data Protection Working Group, Opinion 15/2011 on the definition of consent, pp. 8/9; Brownsword, Consent in Data Protection Law: Privacy, Fair Processing and Confidentiality, p. 87, who stresses the consent as a consequence of an ethical will theory of rights; Ohly, Consent in Private Law, pp. 69 and 70.

1629 See Ohly, ibid., pp. 69 and 70.

correspondingly scrutinized in legal discourse.[1630] However, Ohly stresses the misleading connotation of this term and clarifies that an individual who provides his or her consent does not necessarily waive the fundamental right concerned as a whole, but rather, legitimizes a specific action, be it by the State or private companies, that infringes or harms that fundamental right. The effects of the consent are therefore less far reaching than what many critics worry about.[1631] With respect to German Basic Law, legal scholars furthermore discuss whether the right to discard their affairs guaranteed by basic rights results from the substantial guarantee specifically concerned, from the general freedom of action, or from the general personality right.[1632] With a particular view to the consent, Ohly favors the first approach. In his opinion, the object of protection (aka substantial guarantee) and the right to self-determination closely relate to each other: a right to self-determination isolated from a specific object of protection looses its contours. In contrast, the more specific the object of protection is (to which the individual's right of self-determination refers), the more effective becomes the function of his or her consent.[1633] In relation to this thesis, the question of under which basic right the individual's right to self-determination is located does not have to be answered. The individual's consent is, regarding the processing of data related to him or her, explicitly provided for by Article 8 sect. 2 ECFR. However, the essential aspect for this thesis is that the individual has to know what the infringement or risk actually is if his or her consent shall legitimize the risk, or even the infringement.[1634] These considerations therefore help answer the question surrounding the object and extent of the individual's consent in data protection law.

This thesis carved out that the right to data protection protects, on the one hand, against unspecific risks, and, on the other hand protects the individual against specific risks to his or her fundamental rights to privacy, freedom, and non-discrimination. In order to make the right to data protec-

---

1630 See also above C. I. 3. b) Concept of Article 8 ECHR: Purpose specification as a mechanism for determining the scope of application (i.e. the individual's 'reasonable expectation'), and C. III. 1. a) bb) (3) (b) Second criterion: 'Context and reasonable expectations' at the end.

1631 See, for example, at Lynskey, The Foundations of EU Data Protection Law, pp. 188-190, with further references.

1632 See Ohly, Consent in Private Law, pp. 94 and 95.

1633 See Ohly, Consent in Private Law, pp. 191.

1634 See Ohly, Consent in Private Law, pp. 230 and 231.

tion more effective, this thesis promotes the notion that one must determine its protection instruments with respect to the specific risks for the substantial guarantees provided for by all these fundamental rights.[1635] This approach fits to Ohly's considerations who stresses, similarly, that the right to self-determination looses its contours without reference to specific objects of protection. Following Ohly's considerations, the individual's self-determination, aka consent, provided for by the right to data protection gets more effective, the more specific the object of protection is to which the consent refers. This means with respect to the question posed above: If the consent shall legitimize an infringement of or risk against a specific guarantee, the individual's consent must refer to this infringement or risk; if the individual does not understand the infringement or risk, he or she cannot consent to it. Indeed, the consent must not necessarily refer to infringements of or risks to specific substantial guarantees. If the controller does not reveal an infringement or risk, the consent does simply not legitimize such an infringement or risk that may result from the processing of that data afterwards.[1636] Clarifiying what an individual actually consents to (i.e. risks caused by the data processing against the specific fundamental rights, not the data processing *per se*) is often overlooked in the debate about the extent of the individual's consent, and overall, about the extent of individual control.[1637]

(2) Extent of consent limiting the later use of data (instead of being illegal as a whole)

This leads to the question on the extent of the individual's consent: if a later use of data leads to a risk or harm not covered by the consent, this does not make the consent unlawful as a whole. Instead, the consent simply does not legitimize this risk or harm. This result also complies with general principles of civil law: Before coming to the question of whether or not the individual's consent is null and void the consent must be interpreted,

1635 See above C. I. 1. c) cc) Referring to substantial guarantees as method of interpreting fundamental rights in order to avoid a scope of protection that is too broad and/or too vague.

1636 See also above C. III. 2. a) cc) Applying a 'non-linear perspective'.

1637 See, instead of many others, Lynskey, The Foundations of EU Data Protection Law, pp. 177-153.

pursuant to the will of the individual concerned or, in the case of a contractual agreement, of both contracting parties.[1638] Hence, whether or not the consent covers the later use of data depends on the following three aspects: First, the intensity of the risk or harm caused by the later use of data; second, on the precision of the purpose specified in the consent, which indicates the risk; and third, what is a sub-part of the first criteria, on the protection instruments implemented in order to limit the risk caused by the later use of data. These three aspects play together when assessing whether the processing of data at a later stage is covered by the individual's consent or not: The higher the intensity of a risk or harm is, the more specific must the purpose be specified in the consent, in order to legitimize the processing of data. If the risk or infringement caused by the processing of data at a later stage is too high compared with the (too low) degree of specification of the purpose, the data controller can only implement protection instruments that reduce the intensity of the risk or harm to the lower level that is covered by the purpose specified in the consent. If the data controller is not able to reduce the intensity of the risk or harm to this lower level covered by the consent, it cannot base the data processing on the consent.

In order to determine the intensity of the risk or harm, it is possible to apply the following criteria: First of all, the quality (or nature) of the substantial guarantee concerned; correspondingly, the circumstances of the data collection (e.g. intruding into a home, intercepting communications, in the public, or another social context covered by a substantial guarantee); the degree of conflict with the individual's substantial guarantee (e.g. scanning emails for technical improvements, for marketing, or even law enforcement); the way the controller received the data (e.g. directly from the individual or from a third party); as well as the type of data (e.g. sensitive data or publically available data).[1639] In any case, in order to legitimize the risk or the infringement caused by the later processing of data,

1638 With respect to German civil law, see Ohly, Consent in Private Law, pp. 366 and 340.

1639 Cf. the criteria applied by the German Constitutional Court as illustrated above under point 2. d) aa) (2) The proportionality test also takes takes the use of data at a later stage into account.

the purpose specified in the consent must be more precise, the more intensive the risk or infringement is.[1640]

This concept corresponds to the information required by Ohly with respect to the risk caused in the context of medical treatments. Ohly lists several criteria as being relevant for the information prior to obtaining the individual's consent: The information must refer, on the one hand, to the factual circumstances (i.e. type of data, occasion and circumstances of collection and/or further processing) as well as the type, extent, process, and sure consequences of the infringement. On the other hand, the information must also refer to the risks and possible side effects of the treatment. The extent of the information depends, in turn, on several factors, such as: The more intensive a certain risk is, the more extensive the information must be; the information must be early enough in order to leave the individual concerned sufficient time for consideration; in contrast, the information is superfluous if the individual concerned already has the information; and finally, the individual can also forgo the information given.[1641]

In this regard, the question posed previously in relation to the formal requirements for the individual's consent can finally be answered. With respect to the publication of personal data in telephone directories, the European Court of Justice requires that the data controller, which has first collected and published the personal data, must inform the individual, "before the first inclusion of the data in the public directory, of the purpose of that directory and of the fact that those data will may be communicated to another telephone service provider and that it is guaranteed *that those data will not, once passed on, be used for purposes other than those for which they were collected with a view to their first publication* (underlining by the author)."[1642] So far, this thesis has interpreted these considerations that the Court requires strict purpose identity for the individual's consent. However, another question remained open: of whether this formal requirement additionally means that the consent is unlawful as a whole if the data controller does not explicitly warrant that the data is not used for another

1640 See above under point C. II. 3. a) bb) (2) (b) Separating unspecific from specific risks (first reason why data protection is indispensable), referring to Albers, Treatment of Personal Information and Data, cip. 124.

1641 See Ohly, Consent in Private Law, pp. 376 and 377.

1642 See above under point C. I. 3. c) aa) (5) Going beyond the requirement of consent provided for under Article 8 ECHR, referring to ECJ C-543/09 (Telekom vs. Germany), cip. 66 and 67.

purpose.[1643] In light of the previous analysis, the answer to this question is that this statement of the Court does not have to be interpreted as a formal requirement applying, in general, to the individual's consent. Rather, this requirement apparently results from the particularities of the specific case. As highlighted before, in this case, the data controller transferring the personal data to another private party was required to do so in light of Article 25 section 2 Universal Service Directive 2002/22/EC. Thus, the European Court of Justice appears to consider this formal requirement in light of the fact that the legislator requires the transfer of that data. The legislator is bound, in light of the defensive function of the individual's fundamental rights, to a strict proportionality assessment.[1644] It must, hence, determine the purpose specified within the authorizing law in a way excluding more intensive infringements that would be disproportionate.[1645] However, if the processing of personal data does not result from a legal obligation, there is no reason to consider such a strict requirement. If the data controller does not exclude, in such a "voluntary" case, the fact that the data might be used for other purposes, this does hence not lead, formally, to the illegitimacy of the consent.

(3) Change of purpose: Opt-out procedures for higher and opt-in procedures for other risk

However, coming back to the consent as an instrument protecting the individual against specific risks, the question is whether this protection can be differentiated further pursuant to different types of specific risks. As stressed previously, if the risk or harm caused by the later data processing does not match with the individual's consent, the data controller cannot base its processing on the consent. The reason is that the data controller pursues, from a substantial point of view, another purpose than specified in the consent. If the requirement to specify the purpose does not refer to the processing of personal data *per se* but the risks caused by the process-

---

1643 See above under point C. III. 1. a) aa) (2) (b) Purpose identity for consent.

1644 See above under point C. I. 1. b) bb) (1) The 3-Step-Test: Assessing the defensive and protection function.

1645 Cf. above under point C. III. 1. b) bb) Strict requirement of purpose identity limiting the intensity of the infringement, referring to BVerfG, 11th of March 2008, 1 BVR 2047/05 and 1 BvR 1254/07 (License Plate Recognition), cip. 163.

ing, this approach corresponds to the requirement of purpose identity applied by the European Court of Justice regarding the individual's consent.[1646]

However, the previous analysis regarding a change of purpose has shown that different types of risk can determine which protection instrument is necessary and appropriate: a substantive change of purpose can either lead to a higher risk for the same substantial guarantee, or to another risk, i.e. a risk against another substantial guarantee not previously specified in the consent.[1647] Though, in order to fairly balance the colliding fundamental rights in light of the different types of risks, it is necessary to react with a differentiated set of protection instruments.[1648] In order to legitimize a higher risk for the same substantial guarantee as specified in the consent, it is hence plausible to require a separate "consent" given by the individual only in the form of an opt-out procedure. In contrast, if the change of purpose leads to a new risk for another substantial guarantee that was not yet specified in the consent, it is appropriate to require, more strictly, an opt-in procedure.[1649] The reason for the less strict approach regarding higher risks is that the individual concerned has already given his or her consent to this kind of risk, though, is already aware that there is a risk to this substantial guarantee, and the risk has now only increased. Indeed, the effectiveness of this less strict opt-out procedure requires that the individual gets informed about the higher risk in a timely manner so that he or she can still avoid that the risk turns into harm. However, in contrast, if the change of purpose reveals another risk for another substantial guarantee, the individual concerned is not yet prepared that there is a risk to this substantial guarantee at all. Therefore, the requirements for the individual's decision-making process must not be less strict than if this other

1646 See above under point C. III. 1. a) aa) (2) (b) Purpose identity for individual's consent, referring to ECJ C-543/09 (Telekom vs. Germany), cip. 66 and 67.

1647 See above under point C. III. 2. a) aa) (3) Clarification of an objective scale: "Same risk, higher risk, and another risk".

1648 See above under point B. II. 3. c) Interim conclusion: Fundamental rights determining the appropriateness of protection.

1649 Cf. already above under point C. III. 1. a) bb) (3) (d) Fourth criteria: 'Safeguards ensuring fairness and preventing undue impact', referring to Article 29 Data Protection Working Group, ibid., p. 26 and 27.

risk had already arisen in the moment the individual has firstly given his or her consent.[1650]

bb) Clarifying recital 50 GDPR: "Separate legal basis if purpose not compatible"

This result also corresponds, basically, with the more general consideration provided for in recital 50 sent. 1 and 2 of the General Data Protection Regulation. This recital states: "The processing of personal data for purposes other than those for which the personal data were initially collected should be allowed only where the processing is compatible with the purposes for which the personal data were initially collected. In such a case, no legal basis separate from that which allowed the collection of the personal data is required." Applying the risk-based approach proposed in this thesis, the phrase "where the processing is compatible with the (preceding) purposes (...) no separate legal basis (...) is required" means that "data processing, which does not lead to an additional risk, does not require a separate legal basis". This interpretation thus means that later data processing is, at least, compatible with an original purpose if it does not lead to an additional risk than specified before. In contrast, if the data processing causes an additional risk, a separate legal basis might be necessary. For example, if the legal basis was the individual's consent, a higher risk requires an opt-out procedure, and another risk requires an opt-in procedure, as a separate basis. Indeed, in none of these cases, is it necessary to continue the purpose compatibility assessment because the individual has already assessed the circumstances of the particular case. [1651] It is the function of the consent in which the individual legitimizes the additional risk caused by the change of purpose.[1652] It does not make sense to continue the purpose compatibility assessment after the individual has already compared on his or her own the purposes and risks specified in the origi-

---

1650 Cf. above under point C. III. 2. a) aa) (2) Custer's und Ursic's taxonomy: "Data recycling, repurposing, and re-contextualization", referring to Custer and Ursic, Big data and data reuse: a taxonomy of data reuse for balancing big data benefits and personal data protection, p. 11.

1651 Cf. Masing, Challenges of data protection, p. 2308.

1652 See above under point C. IV. 3. b) aa) (1) Risks as object of consent (not data).

nal consent with the risks caused by the new purpose of the data processing.[1653]

(1) Arg. ex contrario: Is an incompatible purpose legal on a separate legal basis?

However, these considerations, so far, apply to the "consent", be it in the form of an opt-in procedure or opt-out procedure, and not, in general, to any legal basis for the data processing. Instead, the compatibility assessment does not become unnecessary only because there is a separate basis for the substantive change of purpose. In particular, recital 50 sent. 1 and 2 of the regulation do not exclude the necessity of an ongoing compatibility assessment if the change of purpose can be based on a separate legal basis. This might appear so, at a fist glance, if one draws an argumentum ex contrario from this recital: so long as the data processing is *compatible* with the preceding purpose, no separate legal basis is required; thus, ex contrario, a separate legal basis can authorize the data processing even if the later data processing is *incompatible* with the preceding purpose. However, this argumentum ex contrario is erroneous. The reason for this error is that the conclusion is imprecise regarding two aspects: The first aspect refers to the difference between the ongoing assessment process and its preliminary results. Recital 50 refers to a result of the assessment. If a change of purpose can be based on the same legal basis because it is compatible, this does not mean that the data processing that is not compatible with the preceding purpose can always be legitimized by a separate legal basis. Instead, the ongoing assessment might come to the result that the later processing is compatible, given that further requirements laid down in another legal basis are met. However, the ongoing assessment may also come to the result that the later data processing is under no circumstances compatible with the preceding purpose, i.e. incompatible at all. This leads to the second aspect of why the argumentum ex contrario is imprecise, and that concerns the terminological difference between "purposes that are not compatible" and "incompatible purposes".

1653 See instead the Article 29 Data Protection Working Group, ibid., p. 26 and 27, criticized above under point C. III. 1. a) bb) (3) (d) Fourth criteria: 'Safeguards ensuring fairness and preventing undue impact'.

(2) Differentiating between "not compatible" and "incompatible" purposes

The difference between both terms was already stressed before. The Article 29 Data Protection Working Group apparently views in both notions a difference underlining that the Data Protection Directive does not impose, when implementing the purpose limitation principle, "a requirement of compatibility" but that the legislator instead "chose a double negation: it prohibited incompatibility." The Working Group draws from this a more flexible approach stating: "By providing that any further processing is authorized as long as it is *not incompatible* (and if the requirements of lawfulness are simultaneously also fulfilled), it would appear that the legislators intended to give some flexibility with regard to further use."[1654] Similarly, the German Constitutional Court makes a difference between both terms, even if it remained, so far, unclear how both notions precisely correlate to each other. In the case of "*Surveillance of Telecommunications*", the German Court first requires, in general, that purposes must not be incompatible with each other. In contrast, after its assessment, the Court finally came to the conclusion that the current purposes were, in the specific case, compatible with each other.[1655] In this part of this doctoral thesis, the difference now becomes clearer: While the first notion "not incompatible" applies as a general requirement, the second notion "compatible" (or "not compatible") refers to a specific case and leaves it open whether or not this case would be decided differently under other or further circumstances or conditions.

(3) Assessment of safeguards that ensure that purposes do not (definitely) become incompatible

In conclusion, if recital 50 states that no separate legal basis is necessary so long as the processing of personal data is compatible with the original

1654 See above under point C. III. 1. a) bb) (1) Preliminary analysis: Pre-conditions and consequences, referring to Article 29 Data Protection Working Group, Opinion 03/0213 on purpose limitation, p. 21.

1655 See above under point C. III. 1. b) bb) (2) Proportionate change of purpose, referring to BVerfG, 14th of July 1999, 1 BvR 2226/94 (Surveillance of Telecommunications), cip. 140 and 223.

purpose, it does not simultaneously say that an incompatible purpose could always be authorized by a separate legal provision. Instead, it is then necessary to assess whether and, if so, under which further circumstances and/or requirements the processing of that data for another purpose can be authorized. The recital itself does not say under which circumstances or which (other or further) legal requirements provided for by the separate legal basis the new purpose might be compatible with the preceding purpose. It only repeats, in its last sentence, the requirements that the Article 29 Data Protection Working Group has already proposed and that are now officially established in Article 6 sect. 4 of the General Data Protection Regulation. As stressed previously, this particularly depends, amongst other aspects, on the existence of appropriate protection instruments.[1656] In the end, the requirement that the later data processing must not be incompatible thus is, in light of the preceding considerations, the ultimate end of the ongoing compatibility assessment. This ultimate end may only be a theoretical one because it is hardly possible to say in practice, assessing the particularities of each case, that a certain data processing is under no circumstances compatible with an original purpose.

cc) Legal basis and opt-out: Change of purpose

The consent therefore can be a useful instrument for both the individual concerned by data processing and the controller in order to find themselves a sound balance of their colliding fundamental rights. The controller can ask the individual for his or her consent legitimizing the risk caused by its data processing. However, if the individual does not provide his or her consent, the consent is not valid because it was not given voluntarily, or the individual withdraws the consent, the data controller must be able, if it has a legitimate interest in the processing, to legitimize it otherwise. For example, it can refer to the general clause, by entering into the following balancing exercise.

1656 See above under point C. III. 1. a) bb) (3) Criteria for the substantive compatibility assessment, referring to Article 29 Data Protection Working Group, ibid., pp. 27 ff.

(1) Opt-out: A risk-reducing protection instrument

The general clause is applicable only if the interests of the controller covered by its own fundamental rights are not overridden by the risk caused by its data processing against the individual's fundamental rights. In contrast, if the controller pursues interests, which are overridden by the risk that its data processing causes against the individual's fundamental rights, the controller can implement protection instruments reducing this risk to a lower level, when the data processing passes the balancing test.[1657] In this regard, the individual's right to object to the data processing can also be seen as such a risk reducing instrument because it enables the individual to manage the risk on his or her own.[1658] Indeed, an individual's right to object the data processing (i.e. an opt-out procedure) may be less efficient than an opt-in procedure, however, it is not inefficient.[1659] This is particularly the case because the data controller must inform the individual in a timely manner so that the individual is able to avoid that the risk turns into harm.[1660] Consequently, if the data controller also excludes the individual's possibility to opt-out from the risk caused by the processing, the balancing exercise gets stricter. It's own fundamental rights must override, taking further safeguards into account, the increased risk of the individual, which arises from the fact that the individual is not even able to manage the risk by his or her objection.

Current data protection laws regulate this issue, correspondingly: For example, the general clauses under Article 7 lit. f of the Data Protection Directive and Article 6 sect. 1 lit. f of the General Data Protection Regulation allow the processing of personal data so long as the legitimate interests of the controller are not overridden by the risk against the individual's fundamental rights. In contrast, if the data controller wants to exclude the

---

1657 See above under point C. IV. 2. c) Interim conclusion: Balancing the colliding fundamental rights, referring to Article 29 Data Protection Working Group, Opinion 06/2014 on the notion of legitimate interests of the data controller under Article 7 of Directive 95/46/EC, pp. 42 to 44; as well as Article 29 Data Protection Working Group, Opinion 3/2010 on the principle of accountability.

1658 See Buchner, ibid., p. 234.

1659 See above under point C. IV. 3. a) aa) Classic discussion regarding current data protection laws, referring to Kosta, Construing the Meaning of "Opt-Out" – An Analysis of the European, U.K. and German Data Protection Legislation.

1660 Cf. above under point B II. 3. c) Interim conclusion: Fundamental rights determining the appropriateness of protection; and Buchner, ibid., pp. 246 and 247.

individual's right to object the data processing, it must have, pursuant to Article 21 of the regulation, "compelling legitimate grounds for the processing which override", vice versa, the individual's fundamental rights. This stricter requirement "re-balances" the fact that the exclusion of the right to object suspends, in addition to the irrelevance of the individual's consent, another opportunity of the individual to manage the risks by him or her own. Keeping this in mind, it will now be illustrated, in four separate examples, how an opt-out procedure helps carry out the balancing exercise.

(2) Examples: New risks not covered by consent (in light of the specified purpose)

In the first two cases, the processing of personal data was already based on the individual's "consent" because it has caused a specific risk for an individual's fundamental right. In the first case, later on, the controller substantively changes the purpose, which leads to a higher risk for the same substantial guarantee. In this case, the data controller must inform the individual (about the risk and his or her right to withdraw the consent) in a timely way so that he or she is still able to avoid that the risk turns into harm. If the individual receives the information and does not withdraw his or her consent, this can be considered as another legitimate basis for the higher risk. In contrast, if the individual withdraws their consent, the individual explicitly indicates that he or she does not agree with the higher risk and the data controller looses the legitimate basis for the data processing. The controller can pursue the new purpose only if it has an interest covered by its own fundamental right that is so "compelling" that it overrides the *higher* risk to the individual's substantial guarantee.

In the second case, the data processing has also already been based on the individual's consent. However, in this case, the data controller changes the purpose in a way, which leads to a risk for another substantial guarantee and thus requires an opt-in procedure. If the individual does not provide his or her consent, the data controller can only base the data processing for this new purpose on the general clause if the new risk, which is caused by this change of purpose, against the other substantial guarantee and does not override the controller's own fundamental right. In this balancing exercise, it is not sufficient to simply balance the controller's interest against the risk of the individual, which is now specified by the current purpose. Instead, it is necessary to take into account the particular risk that arises specifically because the data is transferred from one context into another. In light of the fact that the preceding purpose has already specified a risk for another (the first) substantial guarantee, one has to scrutinize whether the risk for the new substantial guarantee additionally conflicts with the guarantee previously concerned. Thus, the overall risk can be higher than if only the new substantial guarantee had been taken into account. However, in favour of the data controller, one has to also take into account that the individual still has a right to object the processing. This right reduces (even if less efficiently than an opt-in procedure) the risk for the individual because it enables him or her to manage the increased risk by him or herself. Whatever the end risk will be, again, the data controller has to inform the individual in such a timely manner that he or she is still able to avoid that this risk turns into harm. The controller can only exclude the individual's right to object if it has a legitimate interest covered by its own fundamental rights that is so compelling that it overrides the overall risk against the individual's substantial guarantees. In light of the potential accumulation of risks caused by the substantial change of purpose, this might not very often be the case.

(3) Examples: New risks not covered by a former applicable provision

The preceding considerations can similarly be applied to the third and fourth cases. In these two cases, the preceding purpose was based on a legal provision. In the third case, the data controller has already based the preceding data processing on a legal basis. If the data controller changes the purpose in a way, which leads to a higher risk for the same substantial guarantee, it must inform the individual (about the risk and his or her right to object) in such a timely way that he or she can still avoid that the higher risk turns into a harm. If the individual does not object, this can be considered as a separate legal basis legitimizing the higher risk for the same substantial guarantee as already concerned. The data controller can exclude the individual's right to object if it has a legitimate interest that is so compelling that it overrides the risk to the individual's fundamental rights. Finally, in the fourth case, the change of purpose leads to a new risk against another substantial guarantee. The data controller can again base this new data processing, for example, on the general clause so long as this other risk does not override the controller's fundamental rights. The general clause can hence provide a legal basis for both the original purpose and the new purpose. However, the data controller must carry out, each time, the balancing exercise and, in addition, for the substantive change of purpose, strictly carry out the compatibility assessment. If the data controller wants to exclude, furthermore, the individual's right of objection, again, its own interest must override the overall risk to all individual's fundamental rights.

dd) Information duties and further participation rights

So far, there are two moments where the data controller has a particular interest to reduce the risks caused by its processing: First, if the controller wants to base the processing on an already existing consent of the individual concerned, but the purpose, i.e. the risk, is not specified, in the consent, in a sufficiently precise way. In this case, the data controller cannot base the data processing on the individual's consent if the risk is higher than specified in the consent. Therefore, the controller may seek to reduce the risk to a lower level, where it is just covered by the purpose specified. The second moment becomes relevant if the data controller does not obtain the individual's consent, however, has a legitimate interest in the processing, but the interest is overridden by the risk caused by its processing against the individual's fundamental rights. In this case, the controller might seek to reduce the risk to a lower level, where it is covered, for example, by the general clause as provided for by the Data Protection Directive and the General Data Protection Regulation. In both cases, opt-out procedures play an important role because they provide a separate legal basis and reduce the risk overall. The reason for this function is that an opt-out procedure enables the individual concerned to control specific risks on his or her own, in particular, if indicated by the controller as soon as they occur. Of course, opt-out procedures are not the only protection instrument enabling individuals to manage on their own the risks. Further protection instruments can be an individual's right to information, having data deleted, rectified, and/or completed, as well as the corresponding duties of the controller. In this regard, the data controller's duty to provide information to the individual concerned and the individual's right to rectify data related to him or her, as provided for by the General Data Protection Regulation, shall now be described.

(1) Controller's duties of information

The General Data Protection Regulation foresees, particularly in its Articles 12 to 14, that the information duties of the data controller apply to all kinds of data processing, in principle, irrespective of the specific risks to the individual's fundamental rights to privacy, freedom or equality. Generally, the moment the controller obtains personal data, be it collected directly from the individual or indirectly from another source, the controller must essentially inform the individual about the following aspects (section 1 of Articles 13 and 14 GDPR):

- the identity and contact details of the controller;
- the purposes and the legal basis of the processing;
- the recipients or categories of recipients of the personal data (if any);
- the categories of data concerned (if the personal data have not been directly obtained from the individual);
- the interests of the controller if the processing is based on the general clause (if the data have been directly obtained from the individual)

In relation to these aspects, the controller has to inform the individual only once, irrespective of whether it processes the data for another purpose or not. In contrast, the controller must essentially inform the individual, not only at the moment it obtains the personal data, but each time when it processes the data for another purpose than originally specified, about the new purpose, and the following aspects ("necessary for a fair and transparent processing", pursuant to section 2 combined with section 3 and 4 of Articles 13 and 14 GDPR, respectively):

- The period of time for that the data will be stored;
- About the source from where the data originated (if the data have not been directly obtained from the individual);
- The existence of the rights to object to the processing, request access to and rectification of personal data or deletion of that data as well as to lodge a complaint;
- If the processing is based on the individual's consent, the right of withdrawal;
- The interests of the controller if the data is based on the general clause (if the data have not been directly obtained from the individual);
- The existence of automated decision-making, including profiling, and (at least) if this refers to special categories of personal data or the automated decision is *solely* based on automated processing *and* produces

legal or similarly significant effects on the individual, information about:
- the significance of these effects, as well as
- meaningful information about the logic involved.

These duties of information principally apply, irrespective of the specific risks. However, the following considerations will demonstrate how this information can or should be customized, respectively, and how these duties can or should be interpreted in order to structure best the decision-making process of the individual who manages the risks caused by the data processing.

(a) Data collection: Customizing information in relation to daily decision-making processes

Overall, these duties can make a lot of sense. For example, if the data controller informs the individual concerned, at the moment of collection, about the processing purpose, the individual can indeed verify whether this intrudes into his or her private spheres, such as at home or in communications. Equally, if the controller seeks to publish the data, the information is the necessary pre-condition that the individual can give his or her consent. In comparison, if the purpose of data collection reveals a risk for an individual's fundamental right to freedom, this also enables the individual to protect him or herself against the risk, be this by means of his or her consent or by other protection instruments. In the public, in particular, if the purpose of collection does not reveal a specific risk to the individuals fundamental rights to privacy, freedom or non-discrimination, the information guarantees that the individual does not suffer from the unspecific threat that the data might be misused later on (this indeed requires the controller to implement further precautionary protection instruments against the unspecific risks). However, the extent of these information duties bear the risk that the individual gets bombed with too much information. With respect to the collection of personal data, it is hence decisive how to provide the information in a way that enables the individual to efficiently manage all these risks in the course of his or her daily decision-making processes. In this regard, it will be the challenge for future research what? finding out how these duties may be customized, using the mechanisms for the individual's decision-making process.

(b) Change of purpose: Interpreting information duties regarding specific risks

In particular, with respect to the change of purposes, the duties run the risk of an overload of information for the individual concerned. If the data controller informed the individual about each formal purpose change, irrespective of whether or not this causes a specific risk for the individual, the individual runs the risk of not being aware of information that might once be relevant.[1661] With respect to the change of purpose, this "management risk" of the individual can be solved by interpreting the information duties in light of the risk-based approach proposed here. The controller should inform the individual not about each formal change of purpose, but only if there is a substantive change of purpose, i.e. if this causes a new risk against the individual's fundamental rights. It depends then on the specific risk which further protection instruments the controller has to implement.[1662]

(c) Profiling and automated decision-making

Finally, it will be challenging to interpret the information duties and customize the information, in particular, with respect to the storage and accumulation of personal data by the data controller. The General Data Protection Regulation requires the controller to inform the individual about: first, the existence of automated decision-making, including profiling; and second, (at least) if this refers to special categories of personal data, or the automated decision is *solely* based on automated processing *and* produces legal or similarly significant effects on the individual, information about the significance of these effects, as well as meaningful information about the logic involved. With respect to the profiling component, this requirement meets the substantial guarantee of the internal freedom of behavior rather well: The individual's internal freedom of behavior guarantees that he or she can know, to a certain extent, what others know about him or

---

1661 See already above under point C. III. 1. b) cc) (2) (c) Supplementing protection instruments, referring to Eifert, ibid., pp. 147 and 148.

1662 Cf. above under point C. III. 1. b) cc) (2) (c) Alternative concepts: Purpose compatibility: Supplementing protection instruments, referring to Eifert, Purpose Compatibility instead of Purpose Limitation, p. 147 and 148.

her. However, this guarantee is not restricted, in the first instance, to cases where the information is based on sensitive data or used for decisions that produce significant effects on the individual. However, such a guarantee aims to enable the individual to distance themselves from their own and other expectations of them. Thus, it might be reasonable that the legislator typified this guarantee by considering that mainly decisions based on this kind of data or producing significant effects on the individual create such expectations that are relevant for him or her. Nevertheless, there remain several questions on the precise meaning of the following terms: in particular, the "significance" of effects on the individual; the "logic involved" in the automated decision-making; and an automated decision that is "solely" based on data processing.

The first and second terms indeed are difficult to interpret. Pursuant to the considerations made previously, one could say, at least, that the effects are significant if the individual has so little information about what others know about him or her that he or she is restricted in distancing him or herself from own and other's expectations. This is particularly the case, if others are able to manipulate the individual because of the knowledge asymmetry they achieved on the basis of the information they gathered about the individual. Thus, the individual has to know, at least, the criteria under which the data controller categorizes the individual's behavior in the profiling system. However, it will be the challenge of future research to find out which information is necessary and appropriate in order to find a strike balance between the colliding fundamental rights. This question on how to appropriately balance the conflicting fundamental rights cannot be answered by legal research alone. Instead, it will be necessary to also find out, empirically, together with other research disciplines, which information the individual actually needs in order to distance him or herself from their own and others' expectations.

From this angle, it may also possible to examine in more detail what the third term means, that the automated decision must (not) be "solely" based on the data processing. This term apparently aims to avoid that the individual becomes a mere object of information. If there is a human entity who verifies the decision, the individual is not a mere object of automated data processing, but the decision is made by humans even if it is based on data processing. However, the question is how the data controller has to structure the process of its automated decision-making with the result that the decision is not considered as "solely" based on data processing. For example, it could be considered as an illegal circumvention of the law if the data controller could simply exclude the clause by taking an employee who looks over the process, only superficially, in order to verify the decision. In any case, in this regard, it is important to stress that the legal provision does not generally exclude the information duty. Instead, the provision provides a bottom line: *at least*, if the decision-making is solely based on data processing, the data controller has to provide for the information as previously described. This makes it possible to interpret the provision as requiring the information – even if the decision-making process is not solely based on data processing – if the information is necessary to safeguard the individual's internal freedom of behavior.

Last but not least, it is worth stressing, that the individual's right "not to be subject to a decision based solely on automated processing, including profiling", pursuant to Article 22 of the Data Protection Regulation, is narrower than the corresponding information duty of the controller. The individual has this right *only* if this type of data processing "produces legal effects concerning him or her or similarly significantly affects him or her". Thus, there is no bottom line (by referring to the term "at least") that allows to interpret this provision as requiring, for example, the individual's consent also in further cases where there is a risk for the individual's internal freedom of behavior. One might also doubt whether or not the individual's consent is the appropriate protection instrument, in particular, if the processing involves special categories of personal data leading to a risk for his or her right to non-discrimination. Instead, one could also think about particularly strict requirements regarding the justifiable reason for the discrimination.[1663] However, these strict requirements may already result, if interpreted in light of the risk-based approach proposed here, from the principles set up under Article 5 sect. 1 lit. c and d of the regulation that require that the data processing must be adequate, relevant, and accurate. Furthermore, Article 22 sect. 3 of the regulation foresees additional protection instruments, in particular, with respect to the individual's consent, requiring the data controller to implement "suitable measures to safeguard the data subject's rights and freedoms and legitimate interests, at least the right to obtain human intervention on the part of the controller, to express his or her point of view and to contest the decision."

1663 See above under point C. II. 3. b) ee) (c) Interim conclusion: Additional legitimacy requirement for the data-based decision-making process.

(2) Individual's right to rectification

In more general terms, Article 16 of the General Data Protection Regulation provides for similar protection instruments. Establishing the so-called right to rectification, this Article states: "The data subject shall have the right to obtain from the controller without undue delay the rectification of inaccurate personal data concerning him or her. Taking into account the purposes of the processing, the data subject shall have the right to have incomplete personal data completed, including by means of providing a supplementary statement." Taking the individual's fundamental rights into account, this right to rectification is particularly important in order to safeguard his or her right to self-representation in the public, as well as specific rights to freedom and non-discrimination. If the data controller is allowed to publish personal data, irrespective of the individual's consent, the individual can at least require that this data is accurate. In addition, the right to have incomplete data completed plays a decisive role in order to safeguard the individual's right to influence his or her social representation, i.e. how others perceive and think about him or her. Interestingly, Article 16 of the regulation explicitly refers to the purpose of the data processing. An answer to the question of which information the individual must be able to add in order to influence his or her social representation indeed depends on the respective purpose of the publication, or the social context to that the purpose refers. In particular, if this social context is covered by a specific fundamental right to freedom, its substantial guarantee concerned helps determine which additional information the individual must be able to add in order to reduce the specific risk and, correspondingly, to maintain, with respect to this context, the best options of conduct. Finally, the provision even recognizes that published data might just be related later on to an individual, for example, in the form of an opinion. In this case, it does indeed not make sense for the individual to correct wrong data but to add a "supplementary statement".

c) Conclusion: Specifying the decision-making process (Art. 24 and 25 GDPR)

In order to answer the question of how self-protection instruments, such as the consent, and authorizing legal provisions play together in order to appropriately balance the colliding fundamental rights, this chapter examined several protection instruments. All these instruments together must be taken into account in order to assess whether or not an individual is able to effectively and efficiently manage the risks caused by the processing of data related to him or her. Decomposing the overall aim of data protection to protect the individual's autonomy into different types of risks makes it possible to customize the protection instruments with respect to the whole 'decision-making process' of the individual.

By differentiating between the different types of risks, this clarifies that the risks do not have to be regulated all at once the moment when the data is collected. Instead, it is possible to require and to implement protection instruments in the course of the personal data's life cycle, separated in time. The individual's consent certainly is one of the most prominent protection instruments because it enables the individuals to manage the risks on their own as an expression of their own autonomy. However, it depends on the specific risk against the individual's fundamental rights whether or not his or her consent is necessary, and if so, how he or she should provide it. Ohly particularly stresses that the specific guarantee concerned can answer the question of how to implement the individual's consent in practice. The classic understanding of the consent to be given prior to the processing (opt-in procedure) and an individual's right to object the processing (opt-out procedure) are, indeed, two expressions of the same idea (i.e. autonomy or self-determination). However, it depends on the particular circumstances of the specific case, the specific guarantee concerned by the processing, as well as on the controller's opposing fundamental rights which procedure is necessary and appropriate.[1664] For example, the individual's guarantee of privacy of the home requires, in principle, rather strict requirements for the consent if the collection of data amounts into an intrusion into his or her home.[1665] In contrast, other guarantees of privacy or fundamental rights to freedom may require less strict conditions for the validity of the individual's decision.[1666] In particular, regarding later data processing, it was shown that a change of purpose leading to a higher risk

1664 See Ohly, Consent in Private Law, pp. 195 and 196.

1665 See above under point C. II. 3. b) aa) (1) (a) At home: Protection of 'haven of retreat'.

1666 See above under point C. II. 3. b) aa) (3) 'Framing' privacy expectations.

for the same substantial guarantee as already concerned before might require an opt-out procedure, only.[1667]

Determining a procedure for the individual's decision-making process, that appropriately balances the opposing fundamental rights, becomes complex, in particular, if the data processing is additionally (or even solely) based on legal provisions. In this regard, the preceding chapter posed the question of which criteria must be applied when interpreting the self-protection instruments, such as the individual's consent, and legal provisions authorizing the data processing. Indeed, the less the individual concerned is able to protect him or herself against the risks caused by data processing, the stricter the authorizing legal provisions must be interpreted.[1668] However, overall, the question cannot be answered, in general, but must be assessed with respect to the particularities of the specific case. For example, further protection instruments, such as an individual's right to rectify data related to him or her can re-balance the shift of decision-making power back from the controller to the individual.[1669] In any case, one has not only to take the individual's consent, but all protection instruments together into account in order to assess the overall legitimacy of the data processing.[1670]

In this regard, the principle of responsibility established under Article 24, as well as the principle of data protection-by-design under Article 25 of the General Data Protection Regulation will play a decisive role. This is particularly the case because the protection instruments specifically provided for by the regulation are, actually, only a selection of a broader set of instruments. For example, the information rights and duties do not comprehensively address the risks resulting from 'profiling'. It was shown, in this regard, that information about the failure rate or, in other words, the validity of the results based on such an algorithm can also reduce the risk that individuals are "scored" inappropriately.[1671] The regulation indeed re-

1667 See above under point C. IV. 3. b) cc) Legal basis and opt-out: Change of purpose.

1668 See above under point C. I. 1. b) bb) (1) The 3-Step-Test: Assessing the defensive and protection function.

1669 See above under point C. IV. 3. b) dd) (2) Individual's right to rectification.

1670 See above under point C. IV. 2. b) bb) Concpetual shift: From a legal basis to a 'legitimacy assessment'.

1671 See above under point C. II. 3. b) dd) (3) (c) Protection instruments enabling the individual to adapt to or protect him or herself against the informational measure.

quires the data controller to inform the individual, under certain circumstances, about the logic of the algorithm. However, information such as described before should actually provided, in the first place, to the third party that makes the informational decision concerning the individual. The regulation foresees, in contrast, that this information is primarily provided to the individual. It can thus be doubted whether the individual is able to inform, on its own behalf, the third party timely enough, thus, before this party gets the score and makes its decision. Such problems thus must be solved, in light of Article 24 and Article 25 of the regulation, by applying technical and organisation measures that appropriately address such risks. In light of this, the question of how to customize this process indeed is the bottom line for future research.[1672]

1672 See Sandfuchs, ibid., p. 248.

D. Empirical approach in order to assist answering open legal questions

The preceding analysis highlighted, from time to time, which aspects cannot be answered by legal research alone.[1673] In summary, these aspects concern, in particular, the following questions: Under which conditions does the processing of personal data lead to a risk against an abstract constitutional position, such as democracy or solidarity?; in which cases is the individual typically not able to autonomously decide at all?; or how should data controllers specify the individual's decision-making process in order to enable them to effectively and efficiently manage the risks caused by the processing?; and finally, how must the corresponding mechanisms of regulated self-regulation be designed enabling data controllers to turn the specification of these requirements into a competitive advantage?

In order to answer these questions, it is necessary to collaborate with researchers from other research disciplines, using their theoretical concepts and methodological research designs. While researchers from social sciences may assist in assessing the risks caused by data processing and the appropriate protection instruments, researchers from economics may assist in examining the effects of the protection instruments on innovation processes.[1674] This chapter first illustrates different risk assessment methodologies, and focuses, subsequently, on the multiple-case study approach that appears to be best suited to bridge the research regarding the risks caused by innovation with research on the effects of risk protection instruments on innovation processes. Finally, the chapter concludes with a draft on how this methodology could be applied to the examples given in the

1673 See, in particular, above under point C. I. 1. c) Interim conclusion: Interdisciplinary research on the precise object and concept of protection,C. II. 3. b) aa) (3) (a) Research on the individual's decision making process (consent), C. II. 3. b) cc) (3) Articles 7 and/or 8 ECFR: Information pursuant to insights into personality and possibilities of manipulation, C. IV. 3. c) Conclusion: Specifying the decision-making process (Art. 24 and 25 GDPR).

1674 Cf. above under point A. II. 2. The regulator's perspective, B. I. Innovation and Entrepreneurship, B. II. Data protection as a risk regulation.

introduction of this thesis. In this regard, the idea of standardizing "purposes" of data processing will be discussed, in particular.

I. Clarifying different risk assessment methodologies

In order to illustrate different risk assessment methodologies, it is useful to differentiate between the object of the assessment and the methods applied for the assessment. This differentiation helps obtain a clearer picture about how different methods may be chosen or combined in order to assess the risks for a certain object of the risk assessment.

1. Different objects of risk assessments

Clarifying the object of a risk assessment assists, in particular, to differentiate between several assessments foreseen in data protection laws. For example, the General Data Protection Regulation foresees in its Article 35 the so-called data protection impact assessment. This assessment also refers to the risks caused by the processing of personal data, just as the requirement to specify the purpose and to limit the later data processing to this purpose, under Article 5 sect. 1 lit. b of the regulation. Thus, what is the difference between these two risk assessment methodologies?

a) Risk-based approach of purpose specification and limitation (Art. 5 sect. 1 lit. b GDPR)

As proposed in this doctoral thesis, the principle of purpose limitation consists of two components: The first component is the requirement to specify the purpose of the data processing. The function of this requirement is to discover specific risks caused by the data processing against the individual's fundamental rights to privacy, freedom and non-discrimination. The second component requires the data controller not to process personal data in way that is incompatible with the initial purpose. The function of this requirement is to control the risks caused by the later data processing compared to the risk originally specified. Thus, again, what is, in light of this approach, the difference between this kind of risk assessment and the data protection impact assessment, pursuant to Article 35 of the General Data Protection Regulation?

b) Data Protection Impact Assessment (Art. 35 GDPR)

The first difference is that the data protection impact assessment constitutes a formalized procedure for the risk assessment. Article 35 sect. 1 of the General Data Protection Regulation states: “Where a type of processing in particular using new technologies, and taking into account the nature, scope, context and purposes of the processing, is likely to result in a high risk to the rights and freedoms of natural persons, the controller shall, prior to the processing, carry out an assessment of the impact of the envisaged processing operations on the protection of personal data. A single assessment may address a set of similar processing operations that present similar high risks.” Section 3 provides three examples where a data protection impact assessment is required, in particular: First, with respect to an especially extensive form of profiling; second, in regard to processing of sensitive personal data; and third, with respect to a systematic monitoring of publicly accessible on a large scale. If this pre-assessment leads to the result that the data processing intended causes a high risk for the individual’s fundamental rights, the controller is required to conduct a formalized impact assessment as specified in section 7 of Article 35. In this regard, pursuant to section 9, the controller shall also “seek the view of data subjects concerned or their representatives on the intended data processing”. The regulation does not specify how these views shall be sought. However, if this formalized assessment affirms that there indeed is a high risk against the individuals’ fundamental rights, the data controller must consult (again pursuant to a formalized procedure) the data protection authority, whose function is to safeguard that the high risk caused by the intended data processing is mitigated, pursuant to Article 36 of the regulation. Finally, section 11 of Article 35 of the regulation requires the controller to repeat the assessment, at least, if it changes the original purpose of the processing.

In light of these formalized requirements, the German White Paper on the Data Protection Impact Assessment correctly stresses the importance of clarifying what this assessment substantively refers to.[1675] This question shall first be answered with respect to the principle of purpose limitation as established under Article 5 sect. 1 lit. b of the regulation. The German White Paper also provides guidance in this regard. It stresses that the data protection impact assessment refers, in essence, to the risk that personal data is processed in way that goes *beyond* the purpose specified by the controller. It considers that this might be the case because the data is processed by unauthorized third parties but also if the data is used, internally, in the data controller's organization in an illegitimate way. In light of this, the White Paper proposes to concentrate, elaborating on a methodology for the data protection impact assessment, on assessing the underlying motives that may exist on behalf of other departments in the data controller's organization and, in particular, the access to processing procedures and the personal data itself by public security agencies, competing private companies or research institutes.[1676] The White Paper therefore recommends to take, in particular, the following aspects into account in order to assess the risk that data protection rules might not be applied: First, the motivation of the organisation to change the purpose in an illegitimate way; second, the operative possibilities and opportunities within the organisation to illegitimately change the purpose; third, processing of personal data in third countries with a potentially lower level of protection (e.g. control mechanisms and judicial remedy); and fourth, the level of IT protection measures with particular respect to resolution mechanisms for conflicts between IT security (on behalf of business processes) and operative implementation of the individual's data protection rights.[1677]

In conclusion, the data protection impact assessment established under Articles 35 to 36 of the General Data Protection Regulation requires a formalized procedure for the assessment of risks that go beyond the purpose compatibility assessment. While Article 5 sect. 1 lit. b of the regulation requires the data controller to specify the purpose of the data processing with respect to the risks against the individual's fundamental rights, and to constantly control the later risks caused by the later data processing, this "first order" risk assessment however does not tackle the broader risk that the data controller may not appropriately apply these requirements. Against this broader ("second order") risk, the Data Protection Impact As-

1675 See Forum Privatheit, White Paper – Data Protection Impact Assessment, p. 29.
1676 See Forum Privatheit, ibid., p. 23.
1677 Cf. Forum Privatheit, ibid., p. 35.

sessment provides for a three layered regime of protection: First, a formalized procedure for the risk assessment; second, the data controller's duty to consult the data protection authority if the formalized assessment discovers a high risk; and third, by special fines applicable, pursuant to Article 83 sect. 4 lit. a of the regulation, if the data controller does not comply with the first two requirements.

c) Further methodologies (technology assessment and surveillance impact assessment)

Indeed, both risk assessments refer "only" to the fundamental rights of individuals concerned by the data processing. However, as stressed before, there can equally be risks caused by the processing of personal data against further aspects that may, from a social point of view, be relevant, such as abstract constitutional positions. Those abstract constitutional positions might be concerned by the data processing, in particular, with respect to the principle of democracy and the social state principle.[1678] The German White Paper differentiates, in this regard, the data protection impact assessment as required by Article 35 of the regulation from scientific assessments, such as technology assessments. These assessment methodologies particularly seek to reveal risks that are not yet known before and also refer to further aspects such as justice, as well as costs or public security.[1679] Similarly, Wright, Friedewald and Gellert give an overview about the so-called Surveillance Impact Assessment, which was developed in the SAPIENT project and consists in an advanced risk assessment methodology. This methodology seeks to address "not only issues of privacy and data protection, but also ethical, social, economic, and political issues."[1680]

1678 See above under point C. I. 1. b) bb) (2) A first review: decomposing the object and concept of protection, as well as B. III. 1. The individual's autonomy and the private/public dichotomy.

1679 See Forum Privatheit, ibid., p. 30, referring to Finn, R. L.; Wright, D.; Friedewald, M. (2013): Seven types of privacy. In: Gutwirth, S.; Leenes, R. et al. (ed.): European Data Protection: Coming of Age. Dordrecht: Springer, pp. 3 to 32, as well as Wright, D.; Kroener, I.; Friedewald, M. et al. (2014). A guide to surveillance impact assessment — How to identify and prioritise for treatment risks arising from surveillance systems. Deliverable 4.4. SAPIENT Project.

1680 See Wright, Friedewald and Gellert, Developing and testing a surveillance impact assessment methodology, p. 40.

However, in this regard, it shall be stressed, again, that it essentially depends on how the object and concept of data protection is defined, whether issues concerning the society as a whole, such as of individuality or solidarity, are covered by data protection or not.[1681] Correspondingly, Wright, Friedewald and Gellert recognize themselves that "both privacy and data protection are not only fundamental rights but are also highly complex concepts around which public opinion is diverse, fluid and often tied to other issues".[1682] It is, thus, the main challenge of interdisciplinary research to find out what is the object and concept of data protection. In any case, it can be helpful to involve the stakeholders concerned by data processing in order to clarify, at least, the concept of protection.[1683]

In conclusion, both risk assessments, i.e. the assessment inherent in the principle of purpose limitation and the data protection impact assessment under Article 35 of the regulation, refer to the individuals' fundamental rights and freedoms. However, the General Data Protection Regulation states, in its Article 1 sect. 2, to protect the individuals' fundamental rights and freedoms, beside their right to data protection. In this regard, thus, it is up to legal research in order to determine whether: the principle of purpose limitation and the data protection impact assessment only directly covers the individual's fundamental rights to privacy, freedom and non-discrimination; or whether it, indirectly, by taking a broader interpretation of the fundamental right to data protection, covers further aspects such as democracy and solidarity. Indeed, this thesis focuses on data protection instruments protecting the individual against risks against his or her specific fundamental rights. Which abstract constitutional positions precisely are protected by the fundamental right to data protection and which mechanisms come into question in order to protect these positions might be examined, in more detail, in other works.

1681 See above under point C. I. 1. b) bb) (2) A first review: decomposing the object and concept of protection, as well as B. III. 1. The individual's autonomy and the private/public dichotomy.

1682 See above under point C. I. 1. b) bb) (2) A first review: decomposing the object and concept of protection, as well as B. III. 1. The individual's autonomy and the private/public dichotomy.

1683 See Wright, Friedewald and Gellert, ibid., pp. 47 and 48.

2. Different assessment methods

This leads to the different methods coming into question in order to carry out a risk assessment. In Germany, the legal scholar Roßnagel examines such means, by focusing on technology assessments as a legal research discipline. His considerations refer to totally unknown risks against regulatory aims, and it can hence be argued whether or not this approach also applies to the risk assessment as proposed for the principle of purpose limitation, as well as the data protection impact assessment required under the General Data Protection Regulation. However, Roßnagel's considerations help, in any case, to get a clearer picture about the methods that can be applied, in principle, to any risk assessment. In particular, this approach is interesting because it examines how and by which means technological development can be influenced in such a way that it does not hinder but rather enables regulatory aims. Thus, comparable to the approach of the "regulation of innovation", as applied in this thesis, technology assessments as a research discipline shall also provide scientific evidence for regulatory decisions.[1684]

Indeed, Roßnagel stresses, similar to Voßkuhle's opinion illustrated in the introduction of this thesis, that the empirical results do not necessarily bind the lawyers assessing whether the technology complies with the law or not. There are two reasons for this cautious attitude: First, the public or the individuals concerned may under-estimate the risks and, therefore, praise the technology even if they are risky. And second, it is possible that the technology assessment does not provide for consistent results. This inconsistency must not be used as an argument against protection. Instead, here again, it then depends on the law to decide on whether it provides protection against such uncertain risks or not.[1685] However, coming to the means being appropriate for a technology assessment, Roßnagel gives an overview by describing, in particular, the following methods: Case studies, theories from social sciences, and expert and stakeholder participation.

1684 See Roßnagel, Technology assessment as a legal research discipline, p. 98.

1685 See Roßnagel, ibid., pp. 267 to 269; cf. already above under point C. II. 3. c) Interim conclusion: Fundamental rights determining the appropriateness of protection.

a) Examining abstract constitutional positions from a social science perspective

Roßnagel stresses that case studies may be particularly useful in order to describe the effects on the particular individual who uses a technology – but not on society as a whole. The reason for this failure is that they cannot describe, *per se*, the cumulative and synergetic effects of the usage of technology by several individuals. Indeed, Roßnagel does not neglect the value of case studies *per se*. Instead, he makes clear that without further theories from the social sciences it is impossible to draw conclusions from these specific cases to society as a whole. For such conclusions, it is necessary to interpret the results of the case studies in light of more general theories developed in research disciplines such as of communication psychology or communication sociology, and developmental psychology, which focus on the interdependencies between technology, individuals, and the society.[1686] These social research disciplines may ground their theories, in turn, on empirical research providing the data basis either as a bottom line for their hypothesis or for verifying their hypothesis.[1687] In any case, the moment causal relationships or (at least) correlations between socio-technological conditions and certain consequences are discovered, legal research can transpose these findings to its own research in order to assess whether these consequences and, thus, the conditions conflict with the regulatory aims, and how to react to it.[1688] These considerations are highly relevant with respect to abstract constitutional positions, such as democracy and solidarity that might be covered by data protection as a fundamental right.[1689] In order to find out whether data processing really threatens those values or not and, if so, how to reduce or even avoid such a threat, it is thus necessary to tightly work together with these social science research disciplines.

1686 See Roßnagel, ibid., pp. 176 and 177.

1687 Cf. Baxter and Jack, Qualitative Case Study Methodology: Study Design and Implementation for Novice Researchers, pp. 544 and 545; Eisenhardt and Graebner, Theory Building From Cases: Opportunities and Challenges, p. 25.

1688 Cf. Roßnagel, ibid., p. 181.

1689 See above under point C. I. 1. b) bb) (2) A first review: decomposing the object and concept of protection.

b) Pre-structuring interests through multiple-stakeholder and expert participation

Another method consists in the participation of stakeholders concerned by the use of a technology and expert groups. For gathering this kind of practice knowledge, Roßnagel lists four reasons: First, certain consequences of the use of certain technologies can only be foreseen on the basis of the practice knowledge from all stakeholders concerned; in this regard, it is often a question of political powers of whether all interests of the stakeholders concerned are covered in the solution finding process. Second, an answer to the question of whether or not the use of a technology results into a risk also depends on the subjective perception of the stakeholders concerned. Third, the use of a technology affects, usually, these stakeholders, differently. If not all interests of the stakeholders concerned are represented, it is hardly possible to fairly balance conflicting interests. Finally, the participation of all stakeholders concerned increases their willingness to accept the result of the technology assessment. In order to avoid these procedural risks or, vice versa, guarantee the success of the technology assessment, Roßnagel refers to the following iterative process: After a first examination of the current state of the art reported in literature, it is helpful to discuss this analysis with experts from the various interest groups concerned. On this basis, the technology assessment has to be refined, and this result must be discussed again. This process can be repeated until most conflicts or misconceptions are eliminated. In order to achieve this aim, it is recommended to also inform the public about the ongoing assessment and to take its feedback into account.[1690] In conclusion, multi stakeholder workshops may be a suitable means in order to pre-structure not only the divergent interests, but also the risks resulting from these interests and the protection instrument that balance best this conflict of interest.

c) Specifying 'decision-making process' by user-centered development of data protection-by-design

With particular respect to the possibilities to regulate technologies, Roßnagel highlights that information and communication technologies are

1690 See Roßnagel, ibid., pp. 182 to 185.

particularly suitable for a regulation by design. A regulation by design means that legal requirements can be implemented into the technology itself. Thus, with a particular view to information and communication technologies, there is no 'yes' or 'no' of being compliant with the law but, instead, there are several possibilities to adjust the technology in a way that meets the regulatory aim. In order to avoid paternalizing end users of these technologies, Roßnagel stresses that their interest should particularly be respected. Furthermore, information and communication technologies are particularly suitable for an iterative process of implementing legal requirements into their technological design. The reason is that these technologies are already being developed, mainly, by applying these iterative methods.[1691] Thus, the development of these technologies allows, in particular, an interactive and iterative process with risk assessment methodologies. Roßnagel highlights, indeed, an important aspect: as further these development processes get, the more difficult it becomes to implement legal requirements into the technological design.[1692]

Correspondingly, Margraf and Pfeiffer, two engineering scholars for IT security, advocate involving end-users of these technologies as early as possible into the technological development process. Giving the example of IT security, both authors stress the bad usability of those measures as one of the essential problems for achieving the regulatory aim.[1693] In order to illustrate the challenges related to usable security measures, they give the following specific example of encryption technologies: In an empirical study, end users of email services were asked to implement an email encryption technology. In order to function properly, this technology requires an end-user to generate a public and a private key. The users must send the public key to their communication partners enabling them to encrypt their emails designated for the user, and to verify the authenticity of the encrypted emails that the users send to them. In turn, the private key enables users to decrypt the emails that they receive from their communication partners, and to generate the code that is necessary for the verification of the email's authenticity. Amongst 12 end-users of this study, three users have sent their private key and seven users have used the public key in or-

1691 Cf. above under point A. I. 4. a) Coming from a practical observation: Startups and non-linear innovation processes.

1692 See Roßnagel, ibid., pp. 182 to 185.

1693 See Margraf and Pfeiffer, User-centric development for the Internet of Things, p. 246.

der to encrypt their emails: nobody was able to fulfill all of the required tasks. The encryption technology missed its aim totally.[1694]

Margraf and Pfeiffer conclude from this study that the main challenge for the success of security measures is to implement these measures in a way that does not overcharge the user of the technology. Referring to Saltzer and Schroeder, the authors stress one essential principle for the usability of privacy- and security-by-design: The so-called psychological acceptability principle. This principle contains two elements. The first element requires a user-interface that is easy to use. The second element requires that the internal mechanisms of the technology must be designed in a way that it corresponds with the expectations of the user.[1695] Margraf and Pfeiffer stress that this second element becomes more important the less technologies provide for a user-interface (such as currently happening in the Internet of Things). In conclusion, in order to safeguard that the internal mechanisms of a technology, which aims to implement privacy- and security-by design requirements, corresponds with the expectations of the user, the individual must be involved, as early as possible, in the technological development process.[1696] This technical approach corresponds to the considerations made previously with respect to the individual's decision-making process: If the individual concerned by the processing of personal data shall be able to effectively and efficiently manage the corresponding risks, this process must be designed in a way that the individual intuitively understands it.[1697]

Margraf and Pfeiffer propose to differentiate between the following three "trust-layers" in order to more specifically assess under which conditions the user accepts the privacy- and security-by-design measures, in

---

1694 See Margraf and Pfeiffer, User-centric development for the Internet of Things, pp. 246 and 247, referring to A. Whitten, J.D. Tygar: Why Johnny can't encrypt: A usability evaulation of PGP5.0. In 8th USENIX Security Symposium: Usenix, 169 to 184, 1999.

1695 See Margraf and Pfeiffer, ibid., p. 247, referring to J.H. Saltzer and M.D. Schroeder: The Protection of Information in Computer Systems. Proc. IEEE 63 (Sept. 1975), 1278 to 1308. Issue 9.

1696 See Margraf and Pfeiffer, User-centric development for the Internet of Things, p. 246.

1697 See above under point C. IV. 3. c) Conclusion: Specifying the decision-making process (Art. 24 and 25 GDPR).

other words, its usability:[1698] On the layer of "situational trust", the acceptance (that means, in this regard, usability) depends on the specific design of privacy- and security measures. However, the design is not the only aspect that should be taken into account. On the layer of "learned trust", the user has "learned" how certain mechanisms work or, on this basis, whether or not he or she can trust these pre-known mechanisms. This layer is particularly relevant with respect to the brand and reputation of data controllers. The user trusts in the data protection conformity of a certain data processing, pursuant to the cognitive association he or she has with the data controller's brand or reputation. In this regard, data protection certificates and seals are also particularly relevant because the user learns whether he or she can trust the data processing or not, if this occurs under a certain certificate or seal. Finally, the user's acceptance of data protection-by-design measures depends on "dispositional trust" that the user has, based on his or her personality. For example, if the user originates from a conservative milieu, it is likely that he or she trusts more in a seal given by a public authority than a private company. In contrast, if the user belongs to a modern-skeptical milieu, he or she trusts, likely, less in a seal given by public authorities than in the fact that the protection mechanisms are publically accessible so that scientific institutions can verify it.[1699]

3. Interim conclusion: Unfolding complexity

The preceding illustration of different methods for a risk assessment makes it clear that such an assessment can be rather complex. Basically, this complexity corresponds with the complexity of the technology and of the risks caused by the data processing, respectively. However, the preceding considerations have also shown that it is possible to adjust the assessment methods to the corresponding object of assessment. If the object of assessment is to research the risks caused by the processing of personal

1698 See Margraf and Pfeiffer, ibid., p. 247, referring to M. Friedewald, O. Raabe, P. Georgieff et al.: Ubiquitäres Computing: Das "Internet der Dinge" – Grundlagen, Anwendungen, Folgen, Berlin: Edition Sigma (Studien des Büros für Technikfolgen-Abschätzung beim Deutschen Bundestag, 31), 2010.

1699 See Margraf and Pfeiffer, ibid., p. 248, referring to Deutsches Institut für Vertrauen und Sicherheit im Internet (DIVSI): Milieu-Studie zu Vertrauen und Sicherheit im Internet, 2013.

data against abstract constitutional positions, such as democracy or solidarity, indeed, it will not only be necessary to conduct case studies. Instead, it will probably be necessary to work closely together with social science research disciplines, which may also conduct representative surveys at large, in order to understand a possible relation between the data material gathered from these case studies and/or surveys and the variety of theoretical concepts describing the functioning of democratic civil societies. Comparably, if the object of assessment is to capture and weigh potentially conflicting interests related to the data processing, the involvement of stakeholders concerned may be an appropriate means. Of course, each method has its difficulties. Roßnagel doubts, for example, that the theoretical concepts developed, so far, in social science research disciplines are already sufficiently advanced in order to explain, in a satisfying way the interrelationship between societal values, individuals, and technology, as a whole. However, in contrast, specific components of these theories may well suit a specific research approach.[1700] In turn, multi-stakeholder processes face the challenge, amongst others, of being rather complex and time consuming, which principally conflicts with lean and iterative development cycles for the technology in question.[1701]

In any case, in light of the variety of empirical (and interdisciplinary) research methodologies and methods, it is a primary task of legal researchers, who focus on the regulation of data-driven innovation, to find the research methodology and methods that are appropriate for answering their research questions.[1702] In light of the research questions posed in this thesis, the only method that was, so far, not yet examined in detail, appears to be particularly suitable: case studies. The main reason for this is not that case studies can simultaneously provide the basis for the two other means previously described (they may provide either a source of data for proving scientific evidence of theoretical concepts for the society at large, or as an illustration for potential points of interest conflicts between the stakeholders involved). Rather, in contrast to these other methods, case studies appear to be particularly suitable because of the following two reasons: First, they might particularly help understand *why* and *how* certain phenomena relate to each other; and second, they could be, in terms of co-

1700 See Roßnagel, ibid., pp. 182 to 185.
1701 Cf. Forum Privatheit, ibid., pp. 30 and 35.
1702 Cf. Hoffmann-Riem, Innovation Responsibility, p. 39; Roßnagel, ibid., pp. 287 and 288.

ordinated efforts, a less complex means. This could make case studies particularly suitable for de-folding very complex objects of assessments, such as in relation to non-linear innovation processes.[1703]

As illustrated before, the research approach of regulating innovation is, in light of its conceptual structure, a rather complex one. It does not only treat the question of protection against risks caused by data-driven innovation, but also, on the question of how such a regulation must be shaped in order to be open to or even enhance innovation. This approach hence adds another level to the question of how to protect individuals against the risks. The preceding analysis has carved out where the interplay between instruments regulating the processing of personal data becomes particularly clear: with respect to the question of how the individual's decision making process should be specified. On the one hand, thus, it is an open legal question of how this process must be designed, specifically, in order to provide the individual concerned by the data processing effective and efficient protection against the related risks.[1704] On the other hand, this room of flexibility provides data controllers the opportunity to find themselves the best solution and, therefore this kind of regulation is principally open toward innovation (at least, more open than classic if-then rules).[1705] Indeed, as illustrated in the preceding chapter "B. I. 2. Regulation of innovative entrepreneurship" of this thesis, this broader room of action decreases legal certainty, and this can in turn hinder entrepreneurial innovation processes. Thus, a promising solution could be to combine this principally broader room of action, which the principle of purpose limitation leaves, with further mechanisms increasing legal certainty in turn. Such a combination of regulation instruments may not only open to, but even, enhancing entrepreneurial innovation.[1706] For understanding this complex interplay, case studies can hence be a suitable means if the assumption turns

1703 Cf. Baxter and Jack, Qualitative Case Study Methodology: Study Design and Implementation for Novice Researchers, pp. 544 and 545; Eisenhardt and Graebner, Theory Building From Cases: Opportunities and Challenges, pp. 26 and 27.

1704 See above under point C. IV. 3. c) Conclusion: Specifying the decision-making process by means of regulated self-regulation.

1705 See above under point A. II. 2. The regulator's perspective, referring to Eifert, Regulation Strategies, cip. 59 and 60.

1706 See above under point B. I. 2. b) Principles between openness toward innovation and legal uncertainty.

out to be correct that they can explain, in particular, the *why* and *how* of phenomena.

II. Multiple-case-studies: Combining research on risks with research on innovation processes

A case study approach indeed faces certain challenges. Roßnagel stresses, for example, that the interdependencies of technology with its environment are often too complex so that it is hardly possible to describe it in a comprehensive and detailed manner, simultaneously. In his opinion case studies can therefore provide a basis for hypothetical risk scenarios. However, with particular respect to information and communication technologies, which are used in daily life, it is highly difficult to conduct those risk scenarios. He gives three reasons for this challenge: first, these technologies are usually used in very different contexts which makes it difficult to typify the risk-scenarios; second, the individual concerned, whose conduct is hardly predictable, constitutes an additional factor, influencing the technology assessment; and third, the interests of the stakeholders involved in the use of these technologies are, often, highly diverse.[1707] Nevertheless, Roßnagel stresses, in conclusion, that is not impossible to draw general conclusions from case studies. However, this may only be possible as the problem and the solution found are structurally generalizable and representative.[1708] This leads to the question of how case studies should be designed and conducted in order to provide such generalizable and representative results.

1. Reason for the case study approach

The economists Eisenhardt and Graebner particularly address this question – by refining it: How can theory, which is built on case studies, be generalized if the cases are not representative of all existing cases within this issue? They answer this question, hence, by refining the purpose of this empirical research method: The purpose of using a case study design "is to

---

1707 See Roßnagel, ibid., pp. 176 and 177.
1708 See Roßnagel, ibid., p. 188.

develop theory, not to test it".[1709] In light of this, case studies indeed "typically answer research questions that address 'how' and 'why'" of complex relationships amongst phenomena. In contrast, case studies are less suited "to address the questions 'how often,' and 'how many,' and questions about the relative empirical importance of constructs."[1710]

The philosophical approach that underlies a case study design may help explain this in a more illustrative way. In a nutshell, case studies are based on a constructivist paradigm, which understands reality as a "social construction". Thus, a case study can particularly suit this paradigm because it enables researchers to closely work together with the participants, whose actions shall be studied: Researchers can observe the participants in certain contexts in order to understand their view on reality and, though, the meaning of their actions.[1711] These considerations affirm the assumption made before that case studies can be a suitable means in order to understand, in particular, the complex functioning of the principle of purpose limitation as an instrument regulating innovation: On the one hand, case studies can assist, asking end-users of a data-driven technology, in answering the question of how data controllers should implement this principle by designing the individuals' decision-making process in a way that enables them to effectively and efficiently protect themselves against the data protection risks. On the other hand, case studies can help one to understand, by asking entrepreneurs who implement, as the controllers of the data processing, these requirements into their technologies, how they can use this room of action. In particular, under which conditions this room of action may not only be considered as giving more room for innovation but as even enhancing innovation?

1709 See Eisenhardt and Graebner, Theory Building From Cases: Opportunities and Challenges, p. 27.

1710 See Eisenhardt and Graebner, ibid., pp. 26 and 27.

1711 See Baxter and Jack, Qualitative Case Study Methodology: Study Design and Implementation for Novice Researchers, p. 545, with further references; cf. also Mayer-Schönberger, The Law as Stimulus: The Role of Law in Fostering Innovative Entrepreneurship, pp. 181 ff.

2. Generalizing the non-representative cases

These considerations confirm that case studies can be a suitable means for legal research on innovation. The question of how findings from such case studies can be generalized, remains still open. There are several techniques in order to make case study research more generalizable. Eisenhardt and Graebner recommend, in particular, to combine several cases to a single case study. In their opinion, "theory-building from multiple cases typically yields more robust, generalizable, and testable theory than single-case research."[1712] The reason is that only the relationships replicated across all or most cases has to be considered as relevant for generalization.[1713] With respect to the data gathered, through a multiple-case study design, the use of different data sources additionally increases the quality of the results because it reduces the bias of the information. For example, interviews with stakeholders concerned are a highly appreciated data source because they constitute an efficient way to receive "rich, empirical data".[1714] However, in order to avoid that the results of the analysis of interviews are limited to the subjective view of the interviewees, it is recommended to interview not only several individuals from different organizational levels and departments, in the same entity, but also from other relevant stakeholders outside the entity.[1715] Applying these recommendations to the research questions of this thesis, it is plausible to not only refer to the individuals concerned by data processing and people in the data controller's organization, but also to external observers. In particular, investors may provide, beside the individuals', an additional interesting data source because their powers often constitute a significant factor influencing how data controllers deal with data protection requirements. For example, if investors consider personal data processed by the data controller as an essential asset of their investment, they might require data controllers to comply with data protection law, just as they consider immaterial property rights as an essential economic value regarding their investment.[1716]

1712 See Eisenhardt and Graebner, ibid., p. 27.
1713 See Eisenhardt and Graebner, ibid., p. 30.
1714 See Eisenhardt and Graebner, ibid., p. 28; see also Baxter and Jack, ibid., p. 554.
1715 See Eisenhardt and Graebner, ibid., p. 28.
1716 See above under point B. I. 2. c) Interim conclusion with respect to the principle of purpose limitation.

3. Designing the case studies

Baxter and Jack finally provide guidance as to how case studies should be designed: In order to make sure that the cases selected can answer the research questions, as well as to determine the extent of generalization, it is necessary to determine a so-called unit of analysis, i.e. the "case". In doing so, Baxter and Jack recommend, for example, to clarify whether an individual (or entity) shall be analyzed, or whether a program, or process shall be analyzed.[1717] This question helps determine the unit of analysis for the empirical approach proposed in this thesis. The primary research question of this thesis concerns a "program", i.e. the functioning of the principle of purpose limitation established by the law. So far, this thesis has examined the following two questions, legally:

1. *What is the meaning and function of the principle of purpose limitation on the private sector, in light of the object and concept of protection of data protection law?*
2. *In order to find a balance between the societal need for data-driven innovation and protection against its risks, what regulation instruments should transpose the principle of purpose of limitation in the private sector?*

However, while the legal analysis could comprehensively answer the first of these research questions, the preceding analysis has demonstrated that the second research question cannot be answered by legal research alone. The remaining open questions essentially are, as summed up previously, how a data controller must specify the individual's decision-making process in order to effectively and efficiently protect the individual against related risks, and whether, or if so, under which conditions the specification of this process enhances its innovative activities. In order to answer these questions, it is now necessary to choose two sub-units of analysis: first, the process of the individual managing his or her risks in a certain context, and second, the innovation process of the data controller designing the individual's decision-making process. For the multiple-case study approach, these two phenomena are thus the two appropriate units of analysis.

After having determined the units of analysis, Baxter and Jack recommend to precisely define which aspects shall not be taken into account.

1717 See Baxter and Jack, ibid., p. 554.
See Eisenhardt and Graebner, ibid., pp. 545 and 546.

This helps avoid that the case finally becomes too broad. In order to avoid this problem, it is useful to provide for "boundaries", such as: by time and place; activity and context; and by definition.[1718] Boundaries are, apparently, helpful for the research questions of this thesis because these questions require, empirically, two units of analysis (even if they may partly overlap). Therefore, boundaries help "curb" the already broad approach resulting from such a doubled (or bridging) unit of analysis. Taking the examples given in the introduction of this doctoral thesis, it is possible to determine the cases pursuant to the following aspects: the time-frame in which the users use the products of the startups, as well as in which the startups process the data and conduct its innovative activities (e.g. developing and improving the product and/or business model); the place where the product is used (i.e. marketed) and where the startup is situated and operates; the specific activities of the users in their decision-making processes, and the startup's ongoing development process specifying the decision-making process of the individual (regarding the implementation of the principle of purpose limitation) and its efforts to turn this into a competitive advantage; the context in which the individual acts (which means, in particular, his or her substantial guarantees concerned by the processing), as well as the essential contextual parameters for the startup (e.g. the applicable law, customer segment, market, personal network); and, of course, the definitions of these terms (in particular, of the "principle of purpose limitation" as proposed in this thesis, of the term "business model", etc.).

Finally, the ultimate challenge of conducting a multiple-case study is to convincingly link the "rich" empirical data to distinct propositions that contribute to the research question. Eisenhardt and Graebner stress, in this regard: "If the researcher relates the narrative of each case, then the theory is lost and the text balloons. So the challenge in multiple-case research is to stay within spatial constraints while also conveying both the emergent theory that is the research objective and the rich empirical evidence that supports the theory."[1719] How the empirical findings may be linked to such distinct propositions shall be exemplified in the following chapter, by taking the examples of the startups mentioned in the introduction of this thesis.

1718 See Baxter and Jack, ibid., p. 554.
1719 See Eisenhardt and Graebner, ibid., p. 29.

III. Researching the effects of data protection instruments in regards to innovation processes

After having demonstrated that – and how – case studies can provide a suitable means in order to explain the complex interplay of regulation instruments and innovation, the approach shall now be illustrated taking the startups mentioned in the introduction as examples. As previously stressed, the legal analysis conducted in this thesis could comprehensively answer the first research question on the function of the principle of purpose limitation. In contrast, legal analysis alone cannot comprehensively answer the second research question of how the regulation instruments should be implemented on the private sector, in order to balance best the opposing fundamental rights. At least, it became clear that the instruments implemented for the decision-making process of the individual concerned constitute an essential object for such an interdisciplinary research approach: in first instance, it became clear that there are several remaining open questions regarding the effectiveness and efficiency of the protection instruments and that one has to put the end-user of these protection instruments into the center of the research process in order to find appropriate solutions.[1720] In second instance, one can now examine how this room of action can be used in order to turn this openness toward innovation into a situation that even enhances innovation.

1. Enabling innovation: Contexts, purposes, and specifying standards

The preceding chapter "B. I. 2. Regulation of innovative entrepreneurship" has carved out that this room of action is principally open toward innovation, but decreases legal certainty, which in turn principally hinders entrepreneurial innovation. The essential question therefore is how to combine the principle of purpose limitation that is basically open toward innovation with mechanisms that enhance legal certainty and, thus, innovation.[1721]

1720 See above under point D. I. 2. c) Specifying 'decision-making process' by user-centered development of privacy-by-design.

1721 See above under point B. I. 2. c) Interim conclusion with respect to the principle of purpose limitation.

a) Enabling data controllers to increase legal certainty

The entrepreneurial theories described before shed further light on this question.[1722] In the entrepreneurial environment, the law serves a condition for business opportunities.[1723] Correspondingly to the logics of causation and discovery, the regulatory "command-and-control" strategy provides the entrepreneur precise criteria of how to apply the law: Entrepreneurs must "discover" these criteria and build their products pursuant to them in a "causal-linear" process. However, in highly dynamic and non-linear environments, this regulation strategy risks turning into red tape with the result that legal certainty does not enhance but hamper innovation processes. In contrast, the legislator can also build on the creation and effectuation aspects of entrepreneurial behavior by establishing principles or broad legal terms and, correspondingly, through certain mechanisms that enable entrepreneurs to specify themselves how to apply the over-arching aim, and, thus, increase, by their own, legal certainty.[1724] Entrepreneurs have then to use the mechanisms that are "effectively" at their disposal and "create" their own criteria in order to make sure that the way they seek to reach the over-arching aim meets the legislator's expectations. Data controllers are hence able to increase themselves legal certainty, which increases their innovative capacities.

b) Enhancing competition on the "data protection" market

This leads, in addition, to a situation where the legislator helps itself create a market of innovation: By setting the over-arching aims, such as by the principle of purpose limitation, and leaving entrepreneurs sufficient room for its specific application, the regulator uses the creativity of private markets producing a variety of possible solutions.[1725] From a New Institutional Economics perspective, Wegner illustrates under which conditions a

1722 See above under point B. I. 1. Process of innovative entrepreneurship.
1723 Cf. above under points B. I. 1. a) Key Elements for the entrepreneurial process, and B. I. 1. d) Entrepreneurial Contexts: The Law as one influencing factor in innovation processes amongst others.
1724 See above under point A. II. 2. The regulator's perspective.
1725 See Wegner, Dynamic Markets and their Persistent Openness to Innovation, pp. 74 and 75.

regulator is able to enable such an innovative capacity.[1726] He argues that in light of the evolutionary nature of innovations, an economy's innovative capacity depends on the velocity of private entities to react to three constantly ongoing changes: First, to perceive current changes of scarce resources; second, to predict future changes; and third, on the basis of this information, to constantly re-allocate its resources. From this point of view, it is, a priori, impossible to centralize the knowledge necessary in order to determine future changes and, thus, the later profits of today's investments. The market as a whole thus cannot avoid that single investments fail; in contrast, the failure of investments is an essential pre-condition for the private entities' ability to learn.[1727] Wegner concludes from this that the legislator has only limited abilities to actively enable specific innovations: since it cannot centralize the necessary knowledge for such an active innovation politics, it can only guarantee the existence of competition in the market, and thus, that the market participants are able to make autonomous entrepreneurial decisions. Instead, if the legislator provides the company with a certain way of how they have to meet the regulatory aim, it minimizes their capacity to react to changes in their environment and, thus, their capacity of innovation.[1728] The regulatory strategy of "command-and-control" is therefore not able to maintain a market that constantly produces new ways of how the principle of purpose limitation is applied. This is another reason for why the legislator should be reluctant to define itself, too narrowly, the individual's decision-making process, beside the reason that such requirements can paternalize the individual concerned.[1729]

From this point of view, and given that no third parties' fundamental rights are threatened,[1730] it is the consumers' choice about the quality of products or services, i.e. the data protection level applied, which decides

1726 See Wegner, ibid., p. 73.

1727 See Wegner, ibid., pp. 74 and 75.

1728 See Wegner, ibid., pp. 76 to 80.

1729 Cf. the criticism of state-given decision-making processes ('choice architectures') at Neumann, Libertarian Paternalism – Theory and empiricism with respect to decision-making architectures designed by the State, pp. 41 to 55 and 97 to 100, as well as Sandfuchs, Privacy against one's will?, pp. 223 to 226, both referring to Thaler and Sunstein, Nudge – Improving Decisions About Health, Wealth, and Happiness.

1730 See above under point C. I. 1. b) bb) (2) A first review: decomposing the object and concept of protection.

on the success of innovations. This leads to a certain product and service variability of different qualities: If there is no common quality standard provided for by law, consumers who actually prefer a lower quality (for example, for a cheaper price) do not have to buy products or services of higher quality (and therefore for the likely higher price).[1731] Hence, the private entities create themselves, be it with the participation of the regulator (co-regulation) or without it (self-regulation), certain quality standards. These standards can then signal, for instance, in the form of certificates, the corresponding quality to the consumer.[1732] Indeed, the transaction costs that consumers have when they want to prove the quality in question can be prohibitively high. For instance, this might be the case if there is no common scale that helps compare the differences in quality. This case becomes particularly relevant with respect to the risks caused by the processing of personal data that most consumers are unable to foresee.[1733] Another case refers to the situation where the market for a certain product is so fragmented, that even if there was a common scale that principally makes a comparison of products possible, the consumer loses the overview.[1734]

However, addressing the first-mentioned problem, this thesis has elaborated on an objective legal scale that enables one to determine the specific risks caused by data processing and, as a consequence, to compare different levels of protection that data controllers may have implemented against such a risk. With respect to the second problem, consumer and/or data protection bodies may provide for a solution: If the market of different standards, such as in the form of certificates, is so fragmented that the consumers run the risk of loosing the overview, these bodies could evaluate the standards, compare and rank them, again, on the basis of the objective legal scale. This ranking signals the consumers, in an overview, which standards provide for which level of protection.

1731 See Wegner, ibid., pp. 84 and 85.

1732 See Wegner, ibid., pp. 85 and 86; Roßnagel, Data protection in computerized everyday life, p. 195.

1733 See above point A. I. 5 Interim conclusion: Uncertainty about the concept of protection and its legal effects.

1734 See Wegner, ibid., pp. 80 to 82.

c) Remaining questions in relation to the effects of legal standards

In conclusion, the legislator may thus not only provide for regulation instruments being open to innovation, such as principles or broad legal terms, but also enhance innovation through the establishment of mechanisms, such as standardization procedures as part of certificates. These mechanisms are able to enhance innovation on two levels: On the first level, standardization mechanisms enable entrepreneurs to create themselves legal certainty, which enhances their innovative capacities. On the second level, the legislator creates a market of innovation by creating and maintaining competition of different forms and levels of protection surrounding the principle of purpose limitation.

Indeed, there remain several questions about the effects of such standards.[1735] With respect to the legal effects, Eifert examines not only principles but also broad legal terms, where private standards play a role. This comparison provides greater assistance in order to obtain a better understanding about the possible variety of legal effects. Regarding broad legal terms, Eifert stresses, it usually belongs to legal courts to specify these terms. They fully control all interpretative executions of such terms by public agencies. However, in order to specify the terms, the Courts often refer to rules or standards set up by private entities, without acknowledging a direct legal effect of these rules or standards. Instead, they often serve as criteria for assessing the burden of proof or, at least, a reference for the judicial reflection.[1736] Such standards may play a role with respect to purposes specified within the law itself, such as marketing purposes in the ePrivacy Directive.[1737] In contrast, with respect to principles, private standards often serve to officially specify the principles. In these cases,

1735 See the definition of athe term "standard" by the International Organization for Standardization (ISO) and the International Electrotechnical Commission of Standardization (IEC) as a "document, established by consensus and approved by a recognized body, that provides, for common and repeated use, rules, guidelines or characteristics for activities or their results, aimed at the achievement of the optimum degree of order in a given context", retrieved on the 20th January 2017 from http://www.iso.org/sites/ConsumersStandards/1_standards.html.

1736 See Eifert, Regulation Strategies, cip. 61 to 63.

1737 See already under point C. I. 1. a) The interplay between European Convention for Human Rights, European Charter of Fundamental Rights and German Basic Rights, and see further examples above under point C. II. 2. a) cc) Further examples for different scales applied in order to specify the purpose.

there is often a functional separation of the entities dealing with private standards: one entity sets up private standards; the second entity seeks to apply the standards (e.g. entrepreneurs); and the third entity controls whether or not the second entity correctly applies this standard. Thus, the "control issue" is not carried by a public agency, but instead by private entities. Public agencies then control everything as a whole, whilst primarily focusing on the controlling entities.[1738] For example, the General Data Protection Regulation provides for several provisions regulating such standardization processes under its Article 40 to 42.

However, beside these general observations, there are many questions open to be answered by research. One question concerns the legitimacy of these private standards with respect to their legal effects. Since the legislator, who acts on the basis of democratic legitimacy, establishes broad objectives and, thus, is not able to guarantee, substantively, that private standards meet its objectives in detail anymore, it must guarantee the fulfillment of its objectives through procedural requirements. The General Data Protection Regulation addresses this problem, partly, by requiring the participation of the competent data protection authority in the standardization process, such as for codes of conducts and certificates under its Articles 40 to 42. In contrast, with respect to broad legal terms, such as purposes specified within the law itself, there are no such requirements. In any case, the question remains valid as to how standards can additionally be legitimized. One way for doing so, is by establishing so-called multi-stakeholder processes.[1739] As mentioned before, in these processes, the individuals concerned by the private standard are able to influence its establishing procedure. Of course, there are further remaining questions, such as how the multi-stake-holder process must be organized so that all interests of the individuals concerned by the standard are represented.[1740]

Another debated question is whether such standards may provide for the same level of protection as data protection law or must go beyond that

1738 See Eifert, ibid., cip. 91 ff.

1739 See above under point D. I. 2. b) Pre-structuring interests through multiple-stakeholder and expert participation.

1740 See Eifert, ibid., cip. 68, and Belli, A Heterostakeholder Cooperation for Sustainable Internet Policymaking.

legal level of protection.[1741] For example, Hornung and Hartl are of the opinion that standards can only fulfill their function as a market incentive if they provide for a higher level of protection than established by data protection law. They argue that the incentive consists in the marketing advantage that only exists, in their opinion, if the standard signaled to the consumers provides for a higher level of protection than what they could expect provided for by law. From this point of view, the "level of protection" provided for by law is a minimum level of protection.[1742] Irrespective of whether this general assumption is correct or not and without going into too much detail, the category of a fixed "level of protection" does not appear to fit the characteristics of a principle. As described before, a principle provides an objective, which, as its main characteristic, leaves room for the entities to find different ways of applying the principle. This allows, in essence, three different types of varieties: First, varieties of protection instruments applied with respect to different dangers, risks or threats for the individual concerned; second, given a certain danger, risk or threat, varieties of instruments ensuring the same level of protection (e.g. a private data broker acting on behalf of the individual concerned instead of a data protection authority); and third, given a certain danger, risk or threat, varieties of protection instruments leading to different levels of protection (e.g. opt-out instead of opt-in mechanisms). In light of this nature of legal principles, it does actually not make sense referring to a "minimum level of protection".

Finally, from an empirical perspective, there is not much research, if at all, on the practical effects of data protection standards on innovation processes. Blind examines, the effects of technical standards on innovation.[1743] Differentiating between several characteristics of standards (i.e. compatibility, minimum quality, variety reduction and information), he proposes the following overview on possible effects on innovation:

1741 See Hornung and Hartl, Data Protection through Market Incentives – in Europe, too?, ZD May 2014, who differentiate between audits referring to procedures ("dynamic character") and certificates referring to certain products or services ("static character").

1742 See Hornung and Hartl, ibid., pp. 220 and 221.

1743 See Blind, The Impact of Standardization and Standards on Innovation.

	Positive Effects on Innovation	Negative Effects on Innovation
Compatibility/Interoperability	Network externalities Avoiding lock-in in old technologies Increasing variety of system products Efficiency in supply chains	Monopoly power Lock-in in old technologies in case of strong network externalities
Minimum Quality/Safety	Avoiding adverse selection Creating trust Reducing transaction costs	Raising rival's costs
Variety Reduction	Economies of scale Critical mass in emerging technologies and industries	Reducing choice Market concentration Premature selection of technologies
Information	Providing codified knowledge	

Table: Types of Standards and their Effects on Innovation[1744]

How far these findings might be transferred to legal standards such as of data protection law is, indeed, another question. It appears to be plausible, at least, that legal standards, which typify the conditions under which a certain use of personal data meets the principle of purpose limitation, has similar impacts on innovation. For example, in the context of Smart Cities, a standard for the processing of personal data for the purpose of "creating social heat maps" might also have a positive impact on the network externalities of applications for traffic management. A plausible reason for this assumption could be that such a standard increased the legal certainty for startups (such as illustrated in the introduction, the social heat map application for traffic management) retrieving, transferring and exchanging corresponding data.

In any case, the interplay between legal certainty as an entrepreneurial incentive, compliance with the law (or its specific application) as a competitive advantage, and the functioning of co-regulation instruments on the private market is a rather complex issue. Therefore, the following examples, which were already mentioned in the introduction, shall help illustrate how the empirical case study approach, as proposed in this thesis, may answer some of these questions.

1744 Following Blind, ibid., p. 10, who refers to Swann, G. M. P. (2000), The Economics of Standardization: Final Report for Standards and Technical Regulations Directorate Department of Trade and Industry, Manchester Business School.

2. Demonstration on the basis of the examples provided for in the introduction

Applying the structure of this thesis, the following demonstration will first illustrate, for each single startup (i.e. "case"), how the specific application of the principle of purpose limitation can legally be analyzed. Subsequently, it will be demonstrated which remaining open questions could be answered by the empirical approach proposed above. With a particular view to the legal analysis, it shall be stressed that this analysis does not assess the compliance of the data processing with current data protection laws, except where it is explicitly stressed. Furthermore, the analysis does not go into much technical detail either. In particular, questions of data protection instruments against unspecific risks are not tackled in much detail. The focus of this analysis rather lies on exemplifying how the requirements to specify the purposes and to limit the later processing to the initial purposes may be met, in light of *specific* risks against the individual's fundamental rights.

a) Example of "personalized advertising"

In the first example, a startup sought, in the beginning, to analyze the usage behavior of the users of its mobile app in order to personalize image advertising. The users should be able to choose different background pictures for their mobile phones (so-called wall paper). If the users showed preferences for certain themes, the image advertising should match these themes, i.e. the corresponding user profiles. The startup wanted to sell these personalized image advertising spaces to companies from the advertising industry.[1745]

aa) Preliminary legal analysis

In light of the function of the principle of purpose limitation proposed in this thesis, the data processing can be analyzed pursuant to the specific risk that the purpose specified discovers.

1745 See above under point A. I. 4. b) aa) The unpredictable outcome of entrepreneurial processes.

(1) Initial product and business model: Internal freedom of development

The purpose described above discovers a risk for the users' guarantee of internal freedom of development. In particular, the processing of that data does not refer to the users' communications because the users' preferences are analyzed on the data collected irrespective of a communication process.[1746] The data only relates to their choice of background pictures on the phone. The data analysis does not refer, so far, to data related to criteria listed under Article 21 ECFR, nor does it reveal such information. Finally, the startup does not publish the collected data nor the profiles; in particular, it does not make the data available to their business partners from the advertising industry.

The appropriate instrument protecting the users against the risk for their internal freedom of development consists in providing for the information that the startup has about them. The information about their profiles, i.e. preferences shown for certain themes and, consequently, categories for the personalized image advertising, enables the users to know what the startup knows about them and, in particular, to protect themselves against the risk of being manipulated by the advertising.[1747] The startup could hence specify the purpose and make it explicit to the users as:

> "We collect and process data about your preferences that you show when using our app in order to, first, create a profile about your preferences and, second, personalize image advertising based on this profile. (We do not provide this data to our advertising partner from which we receive the image advertising.)[1748] In order to understand the profile that we create for your personalized advertising, you can always see here/below the current state of which categories we have created on which types of data collected in your case."

1746 Cf. BverfG, decision from the 22nd of August 2006, 2 BvR 1345/03 (IMSI Catcher), cip. 55 to 62.

1747 See above under point C. II. 3. b) cc) (3) Articles 7 and/or 8 ECFR: Information pursuant to insights into personality and possibilities of manipulation.

1748 From a substantial point of view, this sentence in brackets is not absolutely necessary because private data controllers do not have to exclude, explicitly and in advance, like state data controllers, further possible purposes, see above under point C. IV. 3. b) aa) (2) Extent of consent limiting the later use of data (instead of being illegal as a whole). However, private data controllers can, of course add this sentence in order to create more trust on behalf of the individual concerned. See also Article 13 sect. 1 lit. e and Article 14 sect. 1 lit. e GDPR.

This information should, as usual, be made available before the download of the app and be accessible when the app is installed on the phone. The blue highlighted term “here” or “below” leads the user, as promised, to the visualized information that is always kept up-to-date. On the basis of this information, the user is always able to understand why he or she receives these kind of advertising images and not others. This information is necessary but also sufficient in order to meet the users’ guarantee of internal freedom of development and, in particular, in order to protect them against the risk of being manipulated by the advertising. Since these profiles reveal only a small aspect of the user’s personality, and single out the individual only amongst the other users of the app, the processing does not directly affect the user’s private life. Thus, there is no further need for a formalized process for the individual’s prior and explicit consent. However, if the profiles become, in the course of time, so comprehensive and/or reveals particular aspects of the users’ private life that this causes a higher risk for their substantial guarantee, the startup must send an explicit message to the users informing them about this higher risk and their possibility to opt-out, at least, from this higher risk. Indeed, when there is a higher risk for this substantial guarantee cannot be answered by legal research alone but should be determined together with other research disciplines.[1749]

(2) Change of product and business model: No substantive change of purpose

As illustrated in the introduction, the startup has changed, in the course of its development process, the functioning of its app, as well as its business model. The wall paper function of the app should now serve as an entry point for the user following the links to different media, such as music, newspaper articles, and still, image advertising. The startup sought to get a percentage from their media partners when its users purchase, having followed the link, a media product. This purpose did not reveal a new risk for another specific guarantee. In particular, the data processing did not concern the users’ privacy of communications because the technological link

1749 See abve under point C. II. 3. b) cc) (3) Articles 7 and/or 8 ECFR: Information pursuant to insights into personality and possibilities of manipulation.

between the devices and the servers of the media partner still did not reveal a specific risk for the communication of their users.[1750] Another question is whether this new purpose constitutes a higher risk for the same substantial guarantee as already concerned before or not: the users' internal freedom of behavior. On the one hand, the new purpose covered, in addition to the personalized delivery of images, links to partners from the media industry. Insofar, one can say that the advertising is more intrusive because it makes it easier for the user to purchase a product advertised in the images. On the other hand, the user is able to recognize by him or herself the link to the offers made by the media partners. Either, he or she clicks on the link or not. Therefore, one could doubt whether this creates an additional risk of being manipulated or not. However, in terms of transparency and accountability, the startup should, at least, adapt the already existing protection instruments. This means, the startup should inform its users about this (only formal) new "purpose" and add this information to the already existent text described above. The copulation of this information makes it easier, if the data is used, later on, for further purposes, to trace the recent purpose back to all preceding purposes.

So long as the development process for the product and the business model does not reveal a risk for another guarantee than that of the internal freedom of development, the startup can proceed as described before.

bb) Open legal questions ('propositions')

Indeed, there remain several specific questions that cannot be answered by legal analysis alone. These specific questions can be used, turned around, as propositions for the case study. There are two overall questions of this study: First, how should the startup specify the purpose and, thus, the conditions for the data processing in order to enable the individual to effectively and efficiently manage the risks against his or her internal freedom of behavior? And second, under which conditions can the startup turn this, by means of standardization, into a competitive advantage?

1750 Cf. BVerfG, decision from the 22nd of August 2006, 2 BvR 1345/03 (IMSI Catcher), cip. 59 and 60.

(1) Standardization of "personalized marketing" purpose

The first question can be answered by assessing, together with the startup and its users, the following proposition: In order to enable the users to effectively and efficiently manage the risk caused by data processing for the purpose of "personalized marketing" against their internal freedom of behavior, the following aspects must be determined.

- At first, it must be clear which entity gets access to the information about the user. As described before, this is the startup itself. However, if further entities shall obtain access to the information, such as advertising or media partners, it must be clarified which entity is best suited for informing the user about which entity of them has which knowledge about the user.
- Correspondingly, it must be clarified about what the individual is informed of. If the user is able to know what others know about him or her, he or she has to know, at least, the profiling criteria under which personal data is categorized and which make him or her "unique", in relation to the other users in the profiling system. Furthermore, the user also needs information about where the data originates from and what type it is. The reason for this, is that it also determines the information about the individual. Finally, the user should know which entity specifically has that information.
- Furthermore, it must be clarified which protection instruments against unspecific risks the startup implements, as well as potential partners of the startup who receive the data or the information about the user. If the startup and, possibly, its partners, do not implement protection instruments against unspecific risks, the user cannot trust that the data and/or information is not misused, later on, because a third party gets access to that information without providing for the necessary protection instruments. Thus, the startup (or another entity that is better suited to inform the user) must inform the user also about these precautionary protection instruments. In this regard, also the information that no further entities than explicitly specified are able to access that information can enhance the user's trust that the information is not going to be misused.
- Finally, it must be assessed, how this information should be presented to the individual so that he or she is able, in terms of cognitive capacities available in the daily online life, to understand that information.

(2) Competitive advantage

Simultaneously and/or subsequently, the second question can be answered by assessing the following proposition: In order to enable the startup turning the standardization of this purpose into a competitive advantage, the advantages received for the implementation of the principle of purpose limitation and/or disadvantages avoided must outweigh, from the perspective of the startup, the efforts spent for it.

- With respect to the efforts, it is first necessary to decide whether the startup initiates itself a standardization process or whether it applies an existing standard. While the application of an existing standard enables the startup to signal a certain level of protection to its users, the initiation of the standardization process provides for an additional opportunity: The startup can influence this standard in favour of the specific risk and its specific needs, and potentially profit from a first mover effect. However, it is also more costly, if the startup standardizes itself the purpose.
- In any case, with respect to the advantages received and disadvantages avoided, it is possible to take, beside positive effects such as decreased transaction costs in light of higher legal certainty, the following network partners of the startup into account: Users, business partners, and investors.
  - Does the application of the standard help the startup to decrease the complexity of its entrepreneurial process, and if so to which extent? In particular, how decisive is legal certainty that they apply the law and are certainly not fined by a data protection authority?
  - With respect to users, it will be interesting to assess in which form the users of the app may favour the specific standard: Do they pay a higher price?; or do they use, more extensively, the app and therefore reveal more information about them?; do users prefer the startup's app to another product on the market that has no standardized level, or even a lower level of protection?
  - With respect to business partners, it will be interesting to see, for example, whether there are positive network externalities: Do business partners start exchanging personal data for the same standardized purpose for "personalized marketing"? Does this create a positive effect on the startup's data quality or increase the variety of products based on that data processing? Does it increase the startup's income, overall?

- Finally, do investors of the startup positively evaluate the economic value of the startup because it can certify the compliance of the data processing with data protection law?

Only if the startup comes to the conclusion that its advantages received or disadvantages avoided (e.g. fines because of data protection breach or legal uncertainty) outweighs the efforts spent for the standardization of that purpose or the application of an already existent corresponding standard, the startup is able to turn the legal requirements surrounding the principle of purpose limitation into a competitive advantage.

b) Example of "anonymized data for statistic/research purposes"

In the second example, a startup retrieved personal data from the social network Facebook via an API in order to create a social heat map. This heat map should predict how many people will be at a certain place and at a certain time. The startup sought to sell, pursuant to the first business idea, the social heat map to taxi drivers enabling them to plan their driving routes more efficiently. The data retrieved via the API related to geo-locations that Facebook users, who were organizing an event or attending such an event, have made public. This data was not anonymized when the startup gathered it, but the startup anonymized the data, immediately after having retrieved it, by deleting its references to the social profiles of the Facebook users.

aa) Preliminary legal analysis

In light of the function of the principle of purpose limitation proposed in this thesis, the data processing can be analyzed pursuant to the specific risk that the purpose specified discovers.

(1) Processing of public personal data: Self-determination in public

Since this data had been published before the startup retrieved it, the purpose of the data processing revealed a risk for the users' guarantee of self-determination in public. In light of this guarantee, it is important to note that the users published the data themselves. Facebook provides, at least with respect to the function of organizing or attending an event, information for ensuring that the users are aware of the publication. Therefore, the first requirement provided for by this guarantee is met in that the first publication must be based on the users' consent (or, which is not relevant here, another legitimate basis provided for by law). Indeed, the startup's processing purpose did not concern the first publication of the personal data but its re-publication. In this regard, it is decisive that the startup had anonymized the data before it sold the social heat map to taxi drivers. So far, the purpose did not reveal a risk for the users whose data had been analyzed so that the startup did not have to implement further protection mechanisms. If the startup had not anonymized the data, it should have compared, taking the above-mentioned criteria into account, the original purpose of the first publication with the new purpose of the re-publication.[1751] However, since the startup anonymized the data, this mechanism did not play a role.

Nevertheless, the users' guarantee of self-determination in public also takes the possibility into account that personal data can be attributed, later on, by third parties, such as friends, family members, or colleagues. This leads to the moment where the taxi driver, once he or she has purchased the data, can attribute the data to the passengers.

(2) The taxi driver: Attributing anonymized data to passengers

The question of which form of anonymization excludes an application of data protection instruments provided for by Article 8 ECFR is particularly relevant with respect to the guarantee of self-determination in public. The reason is that the publication of data results in the situation that everybody else is principally able to relate the data back to the individual concerned. However, it depends on the anonymization technique which kind of additional information enables other individuals to de-anonymize or re-identify the data. As described above, the possibility to re-identify anonymized data can also be described in terms of risk. From a substantial perspective, the guarantee of self-determination in public hence determines which

1751 See above under point C. II. 3. b) bb) (3) Re-publication: Weighing 'interests' against 'old and new purposes'.

anonymization technique is necessary in order to avoid or, at least, reduce the risk for this guarantee.[1752]

In the case of the startup, there was a very low risk, at least a low risk being legally relevant for the individual's guarantee of self-determination in public. The reason is that the processing of the anonymized data leading to a possible re-attribution of that data to an individual concerned does not provide for an additional risk for his or her guarantee. A taxi driver picking up a passenger at an event because he or she was recommended to do so by the social heat map does not know more than if he or she had read the information published on Facebook by him or herself. The taxi driver simply gets notified that the individual concerned, i.e. the passenger, really was at the event. Indeed, the taxi driver would not be able to 'monitor' the published Facebook events by him or herself, in particular, not without such an algorithm. Thus, the data processing indeed enables the taxi driver to relate the data to a passenger, once he or she is at the location. However, this does not conflict with the passengers' right to self-determination in public. This might be the case if the processing leads to a serious interference of the individual's private life, for example, by connecting "a vast number of aspects" of his or her private life, which could not have been so easily connected otherwise, and by rendering this information ubiquitous.[1753] Another case can be that the processing reveals a single information (hence, no vast profile) but this information is particularly relevant for the personality of the individual concerned.[1754] However, the data processing by the startup, and the relation of that data to the passengers by taxi drivers did not constitute such a serious interference with the passengers' private lives. The purpose of the startup was to create a statistical social heat map, thus, the opposite of a personal profile (this was the reason for why the personal data could be anonymized). And the relation of that anonymized data "back" to the individual does not reveal a particularly relevant aspect of his or her private life. This is even then the case if the taxi driver picked up the passenger at a "delicate" location because the driver shows up at this location only because there is a statistic probability

1752 See above under point C. IV. 1. b) bb) (2) (b) Right of self-representation in the public.

1753 Cf. ECJ C-131/12 (Mr. González vs. Google Spain), cip. 80.

1754 Cf. Britz, Informational Self-Determination between Legal Doctrine and Constitutional Case Law, p. 572; BVerfG, 4th of April 2006, 1 BvR 518/02 (Dragnet Investigation), cip. 92 to 94.

that there will be enough people so that it is worth to adjust the driving route toward this location. This additional knowledge provided for by the social heat map is not particularly relevant for the passenger's personality.

In conclusion, so long as the purpose of the startup did not reveal another risk for the fundamental rights of the users of the social network, the startup did not have to apply any further protection instruments. In particular, it was not necessary to make the purpose explicit because there was no need for the users to adapt themselves to the informational measure or to contest it.[1755]

bb) Open legal questions ('propositions')

Here again, there remain, at least, a few specific questions that cannot be answered by legal analysis alone. The two overall questions of this case study are: First, how should the startup specify the purpose and, thus, the conditions for the data processing in order to reassure the individuals concerned, as well as the business customers of their application that the use of this application complies with data protection law? And second, under which conditions can the startup turn this, by means of standardization, into a competitive advantage?

(1) Standardization of "statistical" or "scientific" purposes

The first question could be answered by assessing, together with the startup, the following proposition: In order to increase legal certainty with respect to the data processing for "statistic" purposes, the following aspects must be determined.

- First of all, it must be clear to which extent it is possible, at all, to standardize the purpose of data processing for "statistics" or "scientific research". In particular, if the "anonymized" data is intended to be published, the risk that data is re-identified depends, first, in the context where the personal data originates; second, the technique used in order to anonymize the data; and third, the context in which the anonymized

1755 See above under point C. II. 3. b) dd) (3) (c) Protection instruments enabling the individual to adapt to or protect him or herself against the informational measure.

data is used. Therefore, a standard regarding "statistical" or "scientific" purposes has to be determined, at least, pursuant to these three categories. In the case of the startup, it appears hence to be plausible to limit the standard to personal data collected from social networks, and the publication of that data – anomyized, with a certain anonymization technique that must be specified – for the use in a Smart City, or more narrow, Smart City Traffic Management environment. In other cases, it might be necessary to specify the use of that data in more detail. For example, if the data shall be used for statistics in a military context, it is possible that this use conflicts, even if the data is collected in the (online) public and in an anonymized form, with the freedom of thought, conscience and religion under Article 10 ECFR of an individual. This can be the case if an individual is a deeply convinced pacifist, does not want that data originally related tom him or her is used in a military context, and did not know, when the personal data was collected, or could not avoid, that this data will once be used, in an anonymized form, for the statistics purposes in a military context.[1756] However, since this is not particularity the case, here, it does not have to be discussed which protection instruments might be necessary in order to protect Article 10 ECFR of an individual. So far, a limitation of the standard for "statistic" purposes to the criteria as proposed before seems to be sufficient.

- Indeed, the main challenge for this standard is to determine which anonymization technique reduces the risk of re-identification to a level where it is acceptable in light of the individuals' right to self-determination in public. One possible method is to assess, in the case study, by interviewing users of social networks, which risk scenario they are able to accept. These risk scenarios, and the results gathered from the inter-

1756 The reference to the individual's right to freedom of thought, consience, and religion can thus solve the question of which 'research project' is still covered by the 'research' purpose as discussed above under point C. III. 1. b) aa) (2) The more nuanced approach established by the Federal Data Protection Law, referring to Greve (Auernhammer), § 40 cip. 11 as well as Lindner, Data protection in the Federal State and the Länder, § 40 Rn. 23; in contrast, the Article 29 Data Protection Working Group apparently wants to exclude any impact on the individual, as described above under point C. III. 1. a) bb) (4) (a) Specification of the compatibility assessment (even ecluding positive effects), referring to Article 29 Data Protection Working Group, Opinion 03/0213 on purpose limitation, p. 28.

views, should additionally be re-assessed, with data protection authorities as well as experts from the field of anonymization, because of their higher expertise. The case study might lead to the result that further precautionary protection instruments are necessary in order to lower the risk further. For example, the startup might be obliged to give third parties access to that anonymized data only under the condition that they do not process the data in order to re-identify it.

– Finally, it must be determined whether, and if so, in which way the public must be informed about the data processing taking place under this specific standard. As illustrated previously, the data processing by the startup is not required to inform the individuals concerned, specifically. However, it may be necessary to inform the public in general, in order to re-assure users of social networks, once they get notified about the data processing, that pre-cautionary measures against the risk of a re-identification of the data are met. Only this information avoids that users suffer from the unspecific threat that the data might be misused, in the future. One solution could be that the social networks inform its users about the usage of that data under this specific standard. Another or additional way could be that the customers using that anonymized data inform, in a general manner, the public about it.

(2) Competitive advantage

Similar to the preceding case study, the second question can be answered by assessing the following proposition: In order to enable the startup turning the standardization of this purpose into a competitive advantage, the advantages received for the implementation of the principle of purpose limitation and/or disadvantages avoided must outweigh, from the startup's perspective, the efforts spent for it. In this regard, it is principally possible to apply the same propositions as already proposed in relation to the preceding case study. However, two particularities shall be highlighted. First, it might be particularly interesting to assess whether, and if so, to which extent the proposed standard will enhance a positive feedback from the business customers of the startup. This may be particularly interesting because passengers might find it "creepy" if they find out that their taxi driver plans his or her driving route on the basis of personal data (that they might have) published on Facebook, without further safeguards. Second, it will be interesting to assess in more detail whether the standard is "sufficiently broad" enabling the startup to develop further business cases under the same standard (e.g. further categories of local public transport services, but also shops and restaurants). Such a flexibility is important because it would mean, otherwise, that the startup had again to standardize the purpose or to apply again an already existing standard. This would essentially increase the efforts spent.

In any case, if the startup comes to the conclusion that its advantages received or disadvantages avoided outweighs the efforts spent for the standardization of that purpose or the application of an already existing standard, it is able to turn the requirements surrounding the principle of purpose limitation into a competitive advantage, i.e. the principle has an innovation-enhancing effect.

c) Example of "scoring in the employment context"

Similar to the previous example, another startup gathered personal data that was already publically available. However, in this case, the individuals concerned have published the personal data not in a social but in professional networks. Furthermore, in contrast to the startup previously described, this startup did not anonymize the data. Rather, the startup processed that data, such as about steps of the users' carrier and their former places of residence, in order to create profiles about them. Based on mathematical-statistic methods, the profile of a user contained information about the estimated degree of professional experience in a certain area, the probability that he or she would change the current employer and/or his or her place of residence for another job. The startup sought to sell access to these profiles to human resource departments in order to assist companies to find new appropriate employees. Thus, this data was not anonymized and a negative impact was foreseeable because the information could appear so unattractive to an employer that it would not invite the individual concerned, albeit the individual might be interested in the job.

aa) Preliminary legal analysis

In light of the function of the principle of purpose limitation proposed in this thesis, the data processing can be analyzed pursuant to the specific risk that the purpose specified discovers.

(1) Re-publication of personal data: fair balance instead of a priority rule

This case is similar to the situation in the case of "*González vs. Google Spain*". As illustrated before, in this case, the European Court of Justice stated that a re-publication of personal data harms the individual's right to private life, if the re-publication is excessive in relation to the purpose of the first publication. In particular, the European Court set up, a priority rule in favor of the individual concerned affirming an individual's right to be delisted from search engine results, except if he or she plays an important role in public. Transferring this principle to the profiles created by the startup, the creation of the profiles and its usage by the startup's customers may be seen as excessive because of the negative foreseeable impact. The users of the social networks hence had, at least, a right to be de-listed from the startup's database because most of them do not play an important role in public.

In contrast, this doctoral thesis has criticized this approach as being oversimplified and referred, providing an example of a more differentiated approach, to criteria developed by the German Constitutional Court with respect to the German right to self-determination in public. The German Court at first differentiates, in this regard, as illustrated previously, between opinions and facts. In relation to the expression of opinions, the Court applies a priority rule favoring the freedom of expression if they contribute to the public debate. If the expression of an opinion primarily aims to defame an individual, his or her personality right prevails. If none of both rules apply, the German Court fairly weighs the conflicting fundamental rights.[1757] Applying this balancing exercise to the example of the startup, the discussion could develop as follows: First, it can be argued whether the result of the algorithm should be considered as a fact or an opinion.[1758] In order to answer this question, in general, the German Constitutional Court asks whether the statement can be subject to an obligation of proof: Opinions cannot be proven, but facts (also "internal" facts such as sentiments) can. In light of this criteria, it is clear that the personal data

1757 See above under point C. II. 3. b) bb) (3) (b) Excursus: Case law provided for by the German Constitutional Court, referring to Grimm, The Freedom of Speech in the judicature of the German Constitutional Court (Die Meinungsfreiheit in der Rechtsprechung des Bundesverfassungsgerichts), NJW 1995, pp. 1697.

1758 Cf. above under point C. IV. 1. a) aa) How data may be related to an individual.

used, such as the steps of carrier, places of residence and the number of former employees, are facts. However, the score based on these facts indicating, for example, the degree of expertise in a professional area is more arguable. On the one hand, the score is based on a certain mathematical-statistic method and can thus be understood and reproduced, objectively. However, this only proves whether the result is correct pursuant to the method. In contrast, the choice of the method used and, equally, the choice of the data analyzed in order to achieve a certain "forecast value" are valuing choices.[1759] This speaks in favor of considering these scores as opinions. Supposing this last consideration is correct, the subsequent question is whether the risk for the guarantee of self-determination arises from the valuing score or from the underlying facts. Since an employer looks, at first, at the score and, only, as a second step, at the underlying facts, it can be argued that the risk results from the expression of the opinion, i.e. the score, rather than from the underlying facts. The reason for this consideration is that the reduction of efforts that an employer has to spend analyzing the underlying data is, actually, the main value of the algorithm.

Therefore, it must be assessed whether a priority rule applies to this "opinion" or the opposing fundamental rights must fairly be weighed against each other. One question is, in this regard, whether this score primarily aims to defame the individual concerned. With respect to the startup, its score is based on a mathematical-statistic method that has not the function to "defame" the individuals concerned. Therefore, the priority rule in favor of the individual does not apply. Hence, the other question is whether the opinion contributes to the public debate. If this is not the case, the priority rule in favor of the freedom of expression does not apply, either, and the conflicting fundamental rights have to be fairly balanced against each other. In this regard, further fundamental rights should also be taken into account. At this moment, it becomes apparent that the individual's freedom to find an occupation provides essential criteria for the balancing exercise. The reason is that even if the scores are principally available for everybody who pays the service of the startup, the information is particularly relevant for a certain social context, only: The employment- or work-related context covered by Article 15 ECFR. Thus, rather than the question of whether the scores contribute to the public debate *per se* or

1759 See Krasnow Waterman and Bruening: Big Data analytics: risks and responsibilities, IDPL 2014 (Vol. 4, no. 2), p. 92.

not, here, the specific freedom to find an occupation specifically determine the data protection instruments enabling the individual to influence his or her social representation in this work-related context. This leads us to the question of which instruments are necessary in order to find a fair balance between the opposing fundamental rights.

(2) Freedom to find an occupation: Participation instruments

Previously it was discussed in general, which instruments are appropriate for protecting individuals against the risks for their fundamental rights to freedom. In summary, if the controller or decision-maker reveals a risk, they must enable the individual concerned to adapt him or herself to the informational measure, contest and/or question it in public. These instruments shall now be illustrated with respect to the freedom to find an occupation under Article 15 ECFR: If a decision-maker in the human resource department informed the individual about the risk regarding his or her freedom to find an employment, it would be too late. The reason is that the employer has already received the information about the individual, and the individual could only react, afterwards. Therefore, the startup has to notify, before transferring the information to third parties, the individual about the transfer in order to enable the individual to avoid that the risk turns into harm. The startup could provide this notice, for example, via text messages within the professional networks. The startup could specify the purpose as:

> "Hi …, we would like to present you our new service for your profile. In order to help you find out which new carrier chances are out there, we process personal data that you have published under your profile about your current and former steps of carrier, places of work and employers. Based on this data we create a score about your professional experience, the likeliness of your interest for a new job offer, worldwide. If you would like to see your score, just click this link to our website where you can register with your LinkedIn and/or Xing account. If you would like to improve or adapt your score to your current situation, you can always correct the data you publish under your professional profile(s), and add new skills. So far, we do not take further score categories or categories of data into account. If you are interested in extending your profile and chances of your carrier, just contact us and we will do our best to extend your profile to further categories!"

Indeed, this text raises two essential questions. The first question refers to the extent of information that the individual needs to know about the functioning of the score. In essence, the participation rights described with this information correspond to the right to correct wrong data and complete incomplete data. Furthermore, the user is also able to delete correct data, which he or she considers as having a negative impact on his or her score. The user is also able to see his or her score, so that he or she can evaluate which types of potential employers most probably prefer which skills or willingness to move and, thus, which data to add, change or delete. However, in order to effectively influence the score, the individual must be able to understand, at least, to a certain extent, the functioning of the score. Thus, it is decisive to assess which information the individual specifically needs. Indeed, this information right must be balanced against the opposing fundamental rights of the startup. The logic of the score might be protected by a patent, or as a business secret. In this balancing exercise, alternative protection instruments can also be taken into account. One alternative instrument could be, if the startup does not want to reveal the specific information about the functioning of the score that is needed by the individual, to provide information about the statistical reliability of the score. If the potential employer can see the degree of probability that the individual concerned really has the skills indicated in the score, this reduces the risk for the individual of not getting the employment offer even if he or she was an appropriate candidate.

Indeed, this alternative does not improve the position of the individual in his or her decision-making process with respect to these risks. This leads to the second question in relation to the text as shown above. Some readers may already have noted that this solution does not foresee a possibility for the user to forbid the creation of the score and the making available of this score to third parties. Hence, this solution does not implement an individual's right to be de-listed from the startup's database. Instead, the individual can only decide on whether he or she deletes data from his or her profile in the professional network, providing the basis for the scores, or not. This is a limited possibility for the individual to opt out-from the data processing. This opt-out procedure is limited because the individual can only opt-out from the startup's data processing if he or she deletes, in his or her profile within the professional network, all the data being relevant for the score. The following considerations shall exemplify how this question might be discussed, i.e. whether this opt-out procedure is sufficient in order to meet the individual's freedom to find an occupation or not.

First, the individual must have, as proposed previously, a right to opt-out from the data processing if this leads to a higher risk for the same substantial guarantee as already concerned before. In contrast, if the data processing leads to a risk against another substantial guarantee that was not specified before, the requirements are stricter, thus, an opt-in procedure may be necessary.[1760] With respect to the startup, its data processing leads to a higher risk for the same substantial guarantee "only". The purpose of the data collection and of its first publication within the professional network already referred to the professional context covered by Article 15 ECFR. Indeed, the original purpose did not make it explicit that there was a specific risk for this fundamental right. The users probably did not foresee, precisely, the risk of a third party creating scores with a potentially disadvantageous result, and which can be compared with scores of other users. However, the users knew, when publishing the personal data, that third parties will compare their profiles with others and, of course, will use this information as a basis for all kind of work-related decisions. Thus, even if this risk adds to the former situation because the score makes the comparison with a potentially negative result much easier than before, it is still the same guarantee of Article 15 ECFR that is at risk. Hence, an opt-out procedure might be sufficient.

However, this does not yet answer the question of whether it sufficiently meets the right to opt-out if the individual can delete, in the professional network, the data being relevant for the score. An answer to this question depends on the weighing of the individual's fundamental right to find an occupation under Article 15 against the startup's and employers' fundamental right to conduct a business under Article 16 ECFR. On the one hand, one might require that the individual is also able to object the creation of the score by the startup and its transfer to third parties, and is thus not obliged to "delete" his or her profile in the professional network. On the other hand, one might come to the conclusion that it is sufficient if the individuals concerned are able to: decide on whether to publish the data or not in the professional network; to delete some of this information or add further information; to see their score created by the startup; and evaluate the impact of this score for their future possibilities to exercise their fundamental right under Article 15 ECFR. Both options are plausible, and the

---

1760 See above under point C. IV. 3. b) aa) (3) Change of purpose: Opt-out procedures for higher and opt-in procedures for other risk.

balancing of the colliding fundamental rights may come to the result that both options are, from a fundamental right's perspective, possible.[1761] Indeed, the General Data Protection Regulation establishes an individual's right to object the data processing, pursuant to Article 21. If the startup bases its data processing on the general clause for its legitimate interests or the interests of the potential employers, the individual's right to object can be excluded only if it can demonstrate "compelling legitimate grounds for the processing which override the interests, rights and freedoms of the data subject".

bb) Open legal questions ('propositions')

In light of the preliminary legal analysis, this case study should be designed, in particular, by focusing, on the one hand, on this decision-making process for the individual, and, on the other hand, on the impact on the startup's business model if this process is going to be changed.

(1) Standardization of "profiling potential employees"

The reason for this particular focus on the balance between the conflicting fundamental rights is that not only the risks for the individuals are particularly high, but also the impact of the startup's business model is significant if it was required to get the individuals more involved. So far, the value proposition of the application offered by the startup mainly refers to business customers. The possibility of the individuals concerned to delete personal data in their profiles within the professional network and to add further information is rather a side effect of this value proposition. In contrast, if the individuals have a right to opt-out from the data processing or the startup is even required to ask for the individuals' consent (in the meaning of opt-in), this turns the value proposition actually around. In this moment, the individual is able to keep its profile in the professional network as it is and, though, to freely decide on whether he or she wants the

1761 Cf. the variety of options exemplified by the German Constitutional Court, above under point C. I. 2. d) bb) In the private sector: The contract as an essential link for legal evaluation, referring to BVerfG, 23rd of October 2006, 1 BvR 2027/02 (Release of Confidentiality), cip. 59 and 60.

"service" or not. This leads to the result that the startup could be obliged, factually, to change its value proposition in a way which enables individuals to actively design their score, in order to keep these users in its "system".

Indeed, in particular, if individuals only have a right to opt-out, and are not asked for their consent, it may equally be possible that few individuals exercise their right to opt-out. This could lead to the situation that the few individuals, who opt-out, suffer harm from not being invited to job interviews only because the employer gets no score about them. This would hence be a situation where an opt-in procedure is required in order to 'nudge' individuals not to participate in the application, or even to forbid the individuals to consent. As stressed before, this can be justified if it is necessary to protect fundamental rights of third parties (i.e. the individuals who are not invited to job interviews only because there is no score about them). However, this is, so far, only a hypothesis, which can barely be assessed in case studies, today. And correspondingly, at least, a prohibition of the individuals' consent would not only harm, intensively, the individuals' but also the startup and employers' fundamental rights.

(2) Signaling legal certainty (to the "workers' council")

Therefore, it will be interesting to assess, in a case study, whether, and if so, which further incentives there may be for the startup to apply alternative protection instruments (e.g. information about the score's reliability). This might be the case if the startup's sales force fails, for example, when facing the workers' council of their customers, at least, in Germany. If the workers' council of the customer comes to the conclusion that the use of the application of the startup by the human resources department must be approved by the council, this might be a decisive incentive for the startup to re-assure the council that everything is compliant with the law. One important signal could be, in this regard, to standardize the purpose of that data processing, getting the data protection authority involved. And the data protection authority might approve the standard only if further protection instruments are set in place.

In conclusion, here again, there remain a few specific questions that cannot be answered by legal analysis alone. The two overall questions of this case study can be: First, how should the startup specify the purpose and, thus, the conditions for the data processing in order to re-assure its business customers that the use of this application complies with data protection law? And second, under which conditions can the startup turn this, by means of standardization, into a competitive advantage? Only if the startup comes to the conclusion that its advantages received or disadvantages avoided outweighs the efforts spent for the standardization of that purpose or the application of an already existent corresponding standard, it is able to turn the legal requirements surrounding the principle of purpose limitation into a competitive advantage. Only in this case, the principle of purpose limitation has an innovation-enhancing effect.

5. Summary: Standardizing "purposes" of data processing

After having illustrated how these three cases could be studied, the question is which common patterns could arise in order to ascertain the general results?

At a first view, it appears to be difficult, indeed, to draw common patterns from these three cases. The reason for this first impression is that each case presented actually concerns another substantial guarantee: In the first case, the data processing leads to a risk against the internal freedom of behavior; in the second case, the anonymization technique used essentially determines the risk to the right to self-determination in public; and in the third case, the processing primarily causes a risk against the individuals' freedom to find an occupation. This diversity makes it difficult to draw generalizations, for instance, for the design of the individual's decision-making process. The situation would be different if all cases referred, instead, to the same substantial guarantee concerned by the data processing. For example, if in all cases the processing of personal data concerned a risk for the individual's internal freedom of behavior, but in different settings, it would be possible to generalize what information individuals need, in general, in order to distance themselves from own and other expectations.

However, second, there are certain commonalities. These commonalities refer altogether to the question of how purposes can be standardized, at all. Indeed, that the standardization of "purposes" stands in the center of this discussion is no coincidence. Previously, it was already stressed that standards appear to be an appropriate instrument increasing legal certainty for both the individuals concerned and the data controllers. The reason is that they signal, on the one hand, a certain level of protection to the individual concerned and, on the other hand, reduce transaction costs of data controllers for complying with the law.[1762]

In any case, the preceding analysis made it clear that those standards do not refer to a certain product, procedure, or company.[1763] Instead, the standards discussed above refer to the purpose of the data processing. Referring to a purpose, instead of to a company, for instance, is possible, in particular, because the purpose is determined by the risk-based approach proposed in this thesis. In light of this approach, the primary question is not which company processes personal data or in which product or procedure the data is processed, but which substantial guarantee is at risk. This approach thus makes it possible, for example, to freely exchange personal data between different companies or products so long as the necessary protection instruments against this specific risk are met, thus, so long as this exchange does not cause a higher risk for the same substantial guarantee, or even a risk for another substantial guarantee.[1764] In conclusion, if personal data is processed under a standardized purpose, as proposed here, this means that both the individuals concerned and data controllers, which are part of this "purpose"-oriented system, are reassured that all data processing occurs under the same conditions.

The case studies also give the impression that it will be easier to standardize initial purposes than subsequent purposes, in particular, if the later data processing does not lead to a risk for another substantial guarantee that was not specified before. In all three cases illustrated before, the later data processing leads, "only," if at all, to a higher risk for the same substantial guarantee. The assessment of the risk against just one substantial guarantee is less complex than if several substantial guarantees have to be taken into account. This is in particular the case if a new risk for another

1762 See above under point D. III. 1. Enabling innovation: Contexts, purposes, and specifying standards"; in this regard, it shall be stressed, again, that the term "standard" does not necessarily mean an official standard provided for by an official standardization organisation such as the International Organization for Standardization (ISO); instead, a private standard can also be given the concrete form of a code of conduct or certificate or seal.

1763 See Hornung and Hartl, Data Protection through Market Incentives – in Europe, too?, ZD May 2014, who differentiate between audits referring to procedures ("dynamic character") and certificates referring to certain products or services ("static character").

1764 See above under point C. III. 2. c) Conclusion: Purpose limitation in decentralized networks.

substantial guarantee simultaneously increases the risk for a substantial guarantee that was already concerned before.[1765] However, it is not impossible to standardize, in addition, under which conditions personal data can be processed for another purpose causing a risk for another substantial guarantee that was not concerned before. These questions may become particularly relevant if private parties want access to certain personal data, for instance, in order to use it in the new context of "dispute resolution under civil law".

In any case, another common pattern will concern the question on the scope of risk that the standard covers: the standardization of purposes requires determining which processing purpose is covered and, thus, which risk. This definition influences two essential aspects of a standard: One the one hand, it determines the extent of trust that individuals and data controllers are allowed to have in the specific standard. If a certain standard guarantees that certain risks will not occur, individuals and data controllers can trust in this assurance. In contrast, if a certain standard does not tackle certain risks, individuals and controllers cannot trust that this risk will not occur because the standard does simply not cover this other risk. On the other hand, the definition of the standard determines the extent of efforts that must be spent in order to standardize the purpose and the corresponding conditions for the data processing. The broader the scope of risks is that a standard shall cover, the more complex the standardization process gets, and the more complex it is for companies to apply the standard, finally. Therefore, it will be necessary to assess the right balance between the broadness of risks covered and the complexity of the standardization process or the application of this standard. This balance will be decisive, at least, with respect to Articles 40 and 42 of the General Data Protection Regulation. As mentioned before, these provisions establish certain regulated self-regulation mechanisms enabling private associations of categories of data controllers and/or processors to draw up their own code of conduct or to provide for data protection certificates. Both provisions state that the "specific needs of micro, small and medium-sized enterprises shall be taken into account", when establishing such codes of conducts or certification procedures.[1766] One solution to reduce the com-

1765 Cf. above under point C. IV. 3. b) cc) (2) Examples: New risks not covered by consent (in light of the specified purpose), and C. IV. 3. b) cc) (3) Examples: New risks not covered by a former applicable provision.

1766 See Art. 40 sect. 1 and Art. 42 sect. 1 sent. 2 GDPR.

plexity of these procedures, avoiding that these smaller enterprises are overwhelmed, is to limit the scope of risks that the underlying standards cover.

Finally, there remains one last, but however very important, aspect to be clarified. It was shown that legal requirements, such as specified in standards, can enhance innovation, at least, so long as they do not turn "red tape". It was also illustrated that principles, like the principle of purpose limitation, are not "red tape" because they leave, in general, a certain room of action to the data controller, which is able to implement the principle pursuant to the particularities of a specific case. However, it may occur, indeed, that a change of purpose specifically endangers an individual's substantial guarantee so intensively that the principle of purpose limitation forbids the processing of data for this new purpose, overall. The data controller that has no overriding interest may perceive this restriction as a regulation turning "red tape" but this perception does not outweigh the individual's fundamental rights, of course. As stated in the introduction, the regulation of innovation does not require that each regulatory effect is open toward innovation or even enhances innovation. In contrast, the regulation of innovation makes primarily sure that the law does not *unnecessarily* hinder innovation, and in the second place, that it even enhances innovation.[1767]

1767 See above under point A. II. 1. Legal research about innovation, referring to Hoffmann-Riem, ibid., 260 and 261; cf. also Brownsword and Yeung, Regulating Technologies: Tools, Targets, and Thematics, p. 21.

E. Final conclusion: The principle of purpose limitation can not only be open towards but also enhancing innovation

This doctoral thesis has examined the principle of purpose limitation provided for by data protection law from the perspective of a "regulation of innovation". This approach examines both the risks caused by innovation and whether risk protection instruments are appropriate with respect to its effects on innovation processes. In light of this approach, this thesis has posed the question on, first, the function of the principle of purpose limitation in light of Article 8 ECFR, and second, which regulation instruments serve best, when implementing the principle of purpose limitation in the private sector, in order to balance the colliding fundamental rights of the data controller and the individual concerned. Pursuant to the previous analysis, the principle of purpose limitation is a regulation instrument that seeks, as a first step, to protect the individual's autonomy against the risks caused by the processing of data related to him or her with respect to his or her other fundamental rights. As a second step, it leaves sufficient room for data controllers to find the best solution for protection with respect to the particularities of the specific case. This scope of action enables, combined with co-regulation instruments, data controllers to turn the principle of purpose limitation into an innovation-enhancing mechanism.

The first component of the principle of purpose limitation requires the controller to specify the purpose of the data processing. This requirement is a precautionary protection instrument obliging the data controller to discover specific risks caused by its processing against the individual's (other) fundamental rights to privacy, freedom and non-discrimination. Whether the data controller must apply further protection instruments and, if so, which instruments precisely, and how, depend on the risk discovered by the specification of the purpose. How precisely the controller has to specify the purpose thus depends on the risk against the individual's other fundamental rights. For example, if the risk discovered by the purpose against a specific fundamental right to privacy or freedom requires the individual's consent, the purpose specified within the consent must precisely indicate the risk for this fundamental right. The data controller can reduce the risk against this right by implementing further protection instruments, such as further rights of information or participation of the individual in the data processing. This may be necessary in order to find a legitimate balance between the risks against the individual's fundamental rights specifically concerned and the controller's fundamental rights and, thus, in order to legitimize the data processing, overall.

The second component of the principle of purpose limitation, i.e. the requirement to limit the data processing to the preceding purpose, aims to limit the risk caused by the later data processing to the risks previously discovered. Whether a risk caused by the later processing of personal data is compatible with the risk previously discovered or incompatible, depends, on the individual's fundamental rights to privacy, freedom and/or non-discrimination specifically concerned, on further protection instruments implemented by the data controller, and on the controller's opposing fundamental rights. For example, if the purpose pursued with the later processing discovers a higher risk for the same substantial guarantee (aka object of protection) of an individual's fundamental right to privacy, freedom and/or non-discrimination as previously concerned, the data controller may implement further protection instruments enabling the individual to manage the higher risk (e.g. informing the individual about this higher risk and giving him or her the possibility to opt-out from this risk). In contrast, if the new purpose discovers a risk for another substantial guarantee that was not concerned before, the requirements for such a change of purpose may be stricter. Particularly in this case, not only the new risk to this other substantial guarantee must be taken into account, but also whether the change of purpose additionally increases the risk for the guarantee initially concerned. The accumulation of risks might lead to the result that the change of purpose still is, in light of further protection instruments installed and the data controller's opposing fundamental rights, compatible with the preceding purpose, or is, definitely, incompatible.

This approach is a more refined approach than the current concepts of protection and therefore bears several advantages: First of all, referring the data protection instruments to risks against all the individual's fundamental rights avoids the situation that the scope of protection of the fundamental right to data protection becomes, in light of the increase of digitization in society, more and more, broad and vague. Since social interaction occurs, increasingly, on the basis of the processing of personal data, this approach makes it possible to differentiate, similar to the analogue world, protection pursuant to the different social contexts covered by the diversity of all fundamental rights. The approach thus provides an objective legal scale in order to reliably assess the risks caused by data processing. In doing so, it helps to determine the scope of protection and also provides answers to further questions, such as which entity processing personal data must implement which kind of protection instruments. Such an objective legal scale is the first pre-condition for providing legal certainty.

The second advantage of this approach is that it provides a solution for the question of at which moment during the processing of data the regulation should apply: Is it necessary to regulate all potential risks the moment personal data is collected? Or is it sufficient to regulate the later use of that data? This question was already discussed in the 1970'ies and still is debated passionately.[1768] For example, Hoofnagle recently criticized, in a blog post titled "*The Potemkinism of Privacy Pragmatism*", the use-regulation approach because these "regulations offer no real protection, because businesses themselves get to choose what uses are appropriate" and, "understood in context, are part of what appears to be a general strategy to eliminate legal responsibility for data companies."[1769] These considerations are insofar correct as there is no objective legal scale determining when, in the life-cycle of a personal datum, a specific risk for certain fundamental rights occur and how these risks can be controlled before it irreversibly turns into a harm for the individual. In contrast, the previous analysis demonstrated that the fundamental rights of the individual concerned are typically concerned in different stages of the data processing: while the classic rights to privacy, such as at home or of communications, are typically concerned the moment that personal data is collected, a risk against the fundamental rights to freedom rather arises through the later use of data. This differentiated approach thus enables a regulation that is not only more effective, in favor of the individual concerned, but also more open toward data-driven innovation. The reason for this is that data controllers are hardly able to predict, when the data is first collected, all possible future purposes of data processing because the outcome of innovation processes is hardly predictable. However, in light of the approach proposed in this thesis, the principle of purpose limitation does not require data controllers to predict all possible purposes, in advance, because the

---

1768 See above under point B. II. Risk terminology oscillating between 'prevention' and 'precaution', referring, amongst others, to Miller, Personal Privacy in the Computer Age: The Challenge of a New Technology in an Information-Oriented Society, p. 1221.

1769 See Hoofnagle, The Potemkinism of Privacy Pragmatism: Civil liberties are too important to be left to the technologists.

principle does not exclusively refer, with respect to the evaluation of the risks, to the moment of collection, but to all later moments, equally.

This leads to the third advantage because the proposed approach is not only open toward innovation but is also able to enhance innovation. On the basis of an objective legal scale, data controllers are able to specify the principle of purpose limitation with respect to the particularities of its specific data processing. Indeed, this does not disburden them from the so far required case-by-case assessment. However, by means of regulated self-regulation mechanisms data controllers can set up private standards for specific cases that are, however, generalizable. How this can be done in a reliable, scientific way was demonstrated in the last chapter of this thesis. In particular, applying a multiple case-study approach makes it possible to standardize certain purposes of data processing in a way that guarantees that the individual's decision-making process is so designed that individuals can effectively and efficiently manage the risks caused by the data processing (i.e. determined by the corresponding purposes). Such standards, be it in the form of a certificate, a code of conduct or binding corporate rules, specify the conditions of the data processing and can thus signal to the individual concerned, as well as business customers of the data controller, the level of data protection. Data controllers can hence create themselves legal certainty and use this as a competitive advantage on the market.

Finally, such standards simultaneously provide the basis for two additional advantages. First, they provide the basis for further privacy-enhancing technologies. If machines shall, one day, manage the risks on behalf of the individual concerned, the purpose of the data processing and, thus, all further requirements must be formalized, at least, to a certain extent, in order to enable machines to communicate the requirements to each other. In particular, formalizing purposes makes it possible that a third party (potentially, a machine), which receives personal data from another party (or machine), can obtain all purposes previously specified in an automated way. Indeed, this does not automatically safeguard that the principle of purpose limitation is actually met. However, the documentation of the preceding purpose is the necessary pre-condition for the purpose compatibility assessment; and in a world of ubiquitous computing, it is hardly imaginable how all the corresponding purposes are documented and exchanged, otherwise.[1770] To which extent this requires manufacturers to implement the technological parameter into the soft- and hardware that they produce, is another question.[1771] In any case, standardizing purposes will be, in light of the decisive role that the requirement of purpose specification plays in data protection laws, an essential pre-condition for the success of data protection-by-design.

Last but not least, pursuant to Article 46 sect. 2 of the General Data Protection Regulation, such standards can safeguard the transfer of personal data to third countries. In particular, with respect to the USA (but also, soon, to the UK), such standards may particularly help increase legal certainty for the exchange of personal data. Mainly focusing on Nissenbaum's context-based approach, this thesis has shown that the general discussions about the object and concept of the privacy and/or data protection approaches are, actually, not so distinct as it seems. The outcomes of both approaches often are, in practice, rather similar.[1772] In light of the similarities, standards may therefore help, indeed, further bridge the transatlantic divide, be it under a data protection or privacy regime.[1773]

1770 See Roßnagel, Data protection in computerized everyday life, pp. 162/163 and 165.

1771 See Roßnagel, Data protection in computerized everyday life, p. 192; Schulz and Dankert, ‚Governance by Things' as a challenge to regulation by law.

1772 See Maxwell, Principles-based regulation of personal data: the case of ‚fair processing', p. 213.

1773 Cf. Kift, Bridging the transatlantic divide.

Bibliography

All quoted German texts are translated by the author.
All URLs were last accessed on 23rd January 2017.

Acquisti, Alessandro / *Grossklags,* Jens: What Can Behavioral Economics Teach Us about Privacy?, in: Sabrina De Capitani di Vimercati / Stefanos Gritzalis / Costas Lambrinoudakis / Alessandro Acquisti (eds.), Digital Privacy – Theory, Technologies, and Practices, New York i.a.: Auerbach, 2008, pp. 363–377, quoted as: *Acquisti and Grossklags, What Can Behavioral Economics Teach Us about Privacy?, p.*

Albers, Marion: Informationelle Selbstbestimmung, Baden-Baden: Nomos, 2005, quoted as: *Albers, Informational Self-Determination, p.*

Id.: § 22 – Umgang mit personenbezogenen Informationen und Daten, in: Wolfgang Hoffmann-Riem / Eberhard Schmidt-Aßmann / Andreas Voßkuhle (eds.), Grundlagen des Verwaltungsrechts, Band 2 – „Informationsordnung, Verwaltungsverfahren, Handlungsformen", 2nd edition, München: C.H. Beck, 2012, quoted as: *Albers, Treatment of Personal Information and Data, cip.*

Alvarez, Sharon / *Barney,* Jay B.: Discovery and Creation: Alternative Theories of Entrepreneurial Action, in: Strategic Entrepreneurship Journal 1 (1-2) (2007), pp. 11–26, quoted as: *Alvarez and Barney, Discovery and Creation: Alternative Theories of Entrepreneurial Action, p.*

Appel, Ivo: Aufgaben und Verfahren der Innovationsfolgenabschätzung, in: Innovation und Recht III – Innovationsverantwortung, Berlin: Duncker & Humblot, 2009, pp. 147–181, quoted as: *Appel, Tasks and Procedures of the Innovation Impact Assessment, p.*

Article 29 Data Protection Working Party (set up under Article 29 of Directive 95/46/EC): Statement on the role of a risk-based approach in data protection legal frameworks, 30 May 2014, 14/EN, WP 218, URL: http://ec.europa.eu/justice/data-protection/article-29/documentation/opinion-recommendation/files/2014/wp218_en.pdf, quoted as: *Article 29 Data Protection Group, Statement on the role of a risk-based approach in data protection legal frameworks, p.*

Id.: Opinion 03/0213 on purpose limitation, 2 April 2013, 00569/13/EN, WP 203, URL: http://ec.europa.eu/justice/data-protection/article-29/documentation/opinion-recommendation/files/2013/wp203_en.pdf, quoted as: *Article 29 Data Protection Working Group, Opinion 03/0213 on purpose limitation, p.*

Id.: Opinion 4/2007 on the concept of personal data, 20 June 2007, 01248/07/EN, WP 136, URL: http://ec.europa.eu/justice/policies/privacy/docs/wpdocs/2007/wp136_en.pdf, quoted as: *Article 29 Data Protection Working Group, Opinion 4/2007 on the concept of personal data, p.*

Id.: Opinion 05/2014 on Anonymisation Techniques, 10 April 2014, 0829/14/EN WP216, URL: http://ec.europa.eu/justice/data-protection/article-29/documentation/opinion-recommendation/files/2014/wp216_en.pdf, quoted as: *Article 29 Data Protection Working Group, Opinion 05/2014 on Anonymisation Techniques, p.*

Id.: Opinion 15/2011 on the definition of consent, 13 July 2011, 01197/11/EN, WP187, URL: http://ec.europa.eu/justice/data-protection/article-29/documentation/opinion-recommendation/files/2011/wp187_en.pdf, quoted as: *Article 29 Data Protection Working Group, Opinion 15/2011 on the definition of consent, p.*

Id.: Opinion 06/2014 on the notion of legitimate interests of the data controller under Article 7 of Directive 95/46/EC, 9 April 2014, 844/14/EN, WP 217, URL: http://ec.europa.eu/justice/data-protection/article-29/documentation/opinion-recommendation/files/2014/wp217_en.pdf, quoted as: *Article 29 Data Protection Working Group, Opinion 06/2014 on the notion of legitimate interests of the data controller under Article 7 of Directive 95/46/EC, p.*

Id.: Opinion 3/2010 on the principle of accountability, 13 July 2010, 00062/10/EN, WP 173, URL: http://ec.europa.eu/justice/data-protection/article-29/documentation/opinion-recommendation/files/2010/wp173_en.pdf, quoted as: *Article 29 Data Protection Working Group, Opinion 3/2010 on the principle of accountability, p.*

Balboni, Paolo / *Cooper,* Daniel / *Imperiali,* Rosario / *Macenaite,* Milda: Legitimate interest of the data controller New data protection paradigm: legitimacy grounded on appropriate protection, in: International Data Privacy Law 3 (4) (2013), pp. 244–261, quoted as: *Balboni et al., Legitimate interest of the data controller New data protection paradigm: legitimacy grounded on appropriate protection, p.*

Baldwin, Robert / *Cave,* Martin / *Lodge,* Martin: Understanding Regulation – Theory, Strategy and Practice, 2nd edition, Oxford: Oxford University Press, 2013, quoted as: *Baldwin and Cave, Understanding Regulation – Theory, Strategy and Practice, p.*

Baxter, Pamela / *Jack,* Susan: Qualitative Case Study Methodology: Study Design and Implementation for Novice Researchers, in: The Qualitative Report 13 (4) (2008), pp. 544–559, quoted as: *Baxter and Jack, Qualitative Case Study Methodology: Study Design and Implementation for Novice Researchers, p.*

Bäcker, Matthias: Grundrechtlicher Informationsschutz gegen Private, in: Der Staat 51 (1) (2012), pp. 91–116, quoted as: *Bäcker, Constitutional Protection of Information regarding Private Parties, p.*

Bechler, Lars: Informationseingriffe durch intransparenten Umgang mit personenbezogenen Daten, Halle an der Saale: Universitätsverlag Halle-Wittenberg, 2010, quoted as: *Bechler, Informational Harm by Intransparent Treatment of Personal Data, p.*

Belli, Luca: A heterostakeholder cooperation for sustainable internet policymaking, in: Internet Policy Review 4 (2) (2015), pp. 1–21, quoted as: *Belli, A Heterostakeholder Cooperation for Sustainable Internet Policymaking.*

Bergmann, Dr. Lutz / *Möhrle,* Roland / *Herb,* Prof. Dr. Armin: Datenschutzrecht, Loseblattsammlung, 53th edition, Berlin: Boorberg , 2017, quoted as: *Bergmann/Möhrle/Herb, BDSG*

Bergt, Matthias: Die Bestimmbarkeit als Grundproblem des Datenschutzrechts – Überblick über den Theorienstreit und Lösungsvorschlag, in: Zeitschrift für Datenschutz 5 (8) (2015), pp. 365–371, quoted as: *Bergt, The question on „identifiable persons" as main problem of data protection, p.*

Bernsdorff, Norbert: Art. 8, in: Jürgen Meyer (ed.), Charta der Grundrechte der Europäischen Union, 3rd edition, Baden-Baden: Nomos, 2011, quoted as: *Bernsdorff, European Charter of Fundamental Rights, Art. 8 cip.*

Bethge, Herbert: Grundrechtskollisionen, in: Detlef Merten / Hans-Jürgen Papier (eds.), Handbuch der Grundrechte in Deutschland und Europa – Band III „Allgemeine Lehren II", Heidelberg: C.F. Müller Verlag, 2009, § 72, quoted as: *Bethge, § 72 – Collision of Basic Rights, cip.*

Blank, Steve: Why the Lean Start-Up Changes Everything, Harvard Business Review 2013, URL: https://hbr.org/2013/05/why-the-lean-start-up-changes-everything , quoted as: *Blank, Why the Lean Start-up Changes Everything, p.*

Id.: Four Steps to the Epiphany – Successful Strategies for Products that Win, 2nd edition, 2006, URL: http://web.stanford.edu/group/e145/cgi-bin/winter/drupal/upload/handouts/Four_Steps.pdf, quoted as: Blank, *Four Steps to Epiphany, p.*

Blind, Knut: The Impact of Standardization and Standards on Innovation, in: Manchester Institute of Innovation Research (ed.), Compendium of Evidence on the Effectiveness of Innovation Policy Intervention, 2013, URL: http://www.innovation-poli cy.org.uk/compendium/section/Default.aspx?topicid=30, quoted as: *Blind, The Impact of Standardization and Standards on Innovation, p.*

Blume, Peter: An alternative model for data protection law: changing the roles of controller and processor, in: International Data Privacy Law 5 (4) (2015), pp. 292–297, quoted as: *Blume, An alternative model for data protection law: changing the roles of controller and processor, p.*

Boos, Carina / Kroschwald, Steffen /Wicker, Magda: Datenschutz bei Cloud Computing zwischen TKG, TMG und BDSG – Datenkategorien bei der Nutzung von Cloud-Diensten, in: Zeitschrift für Datenschutz 3 (5) (2013), 205–209, quoted as: *Boos et al., Data protection and cloud computing pursuant to the Telecommunication Law, Telemedia Law, and Federal Data Protection Law, p.*

Boyd, Danah / *Crawford,* Kate: Critical Questions for Big Data, in: Information, Communication and Society 15 (5) (2012), pp. 662–679, quoted as: *Boyd and Crawford, Critical Questions For Big Data, p.*

Braithwaite, John / *Coglianese,* Cary / *Levi-Faur,* David: Can regulation and governance make a difference?, in: Regulation and Governance 1 (1) (2007), pp. 1–7, quoted as: *Braithwaite et al., Can regulation and governance make a difference?, p.*

Britz, Gabriele: Informationelle Selbstbestimmung zwischen rechtswissenschaftlicher Grundsatzkritik und Beharren des Bundesverfassungsgerichts, in: Edmund Brandt / Martin Eifert / Bernd Holznagel i.a. (eds.), Offene Rechtswissenschaft, Tübingen: Mohr Siebeck, 2010, quoted as: *Britz, Informational Self-Determination between Legal Doctrine and Constitutional Case Law, p.*

Id.: Europäisierung des grundrechtlichen Datenschutzes?, in: Europäische Grundrechte-Zeitschrift 36 (1-4) (2009), pp. 1–11, quoted as: *Britz, Europeanisation of Data Protection Provided for by Fundamental Rights?, p.*

Id.: Das Grundrecht auf Datenschutz in Art. 8 der Grundrechtecharta, in: Der Hessische Datenschutzbeauftragte (ed.), Dokumentation der Fachtagung „Datenschutz in Deutschland nach dem Vertrag von Lissabon“ am 9. Dezember 2008, URL: https://www.datenschutz.hessen.de/download.php?download_ID=188, quoted as: *Britz, The Fundamental Right to Data Protection in Article 8 ECFR, p.*

Id.: Einzelfallgerechtigkeit versus Generalisierung: Verfassungsrechtliche Grenzen statistischer Diskriminierung, Tübingen: Mohr Siebeck, 2008, quoted as: *Britz, Justice in the individual case versus generalization: limits of constitutional law for statistical discrimination, p.*

Brownsword, Roger: Regulating Technologies: Tools, Targets, and Thematics, in: Roger Brownsword / Karen Yeung (eds.), Regulating technologies: legal futures, regulatory frames and technological fixes, Oxford: Hart, 2008, pp. 3-22, quoted as: *Brownsword and Yeung, Regulating Technologies: Tools, Targets, and Thematics, p.*

Id.: Consent in Data Protection Law: Privacy, Fair Processing and Confidentiality, in: Serge Gutwirth / Yves Poullet / Paul de Hert / Cecile de Terwangne / Sjaak Nouwt (eds.), Reinventing Data Protection?, New York i.a.: Springer, 2009, pp. 83–110, quoted as: *Brownsword, Consent in Data Protection Law: Privacy, Fair Processing and Confidentiality, p.*

Buchmann, Erik: Wie kann man Privatheit messen? Privatheitsmaße aus der Wissenschaft, in: Datenschutz und Datensicherheit 39 (8) (2015), pp. 510–514, quoted as: *Buchmann, How can privacy be measured?, p.*

Buchner, Benedikt: Informationelle Selbstbestimmung im Privatrecht, Tübingen: Mohr Siebeck, 2006, quoted as: *Buchner, Informational self-determination in the private sector, p.*

Burgkardt, Felix: Grundrechtlicher Datenschutz zwischen Grundgesetz und Europarecht, Hamburg: Dr. Kovac, 2013, quoted as: *Burgkardt, Data Protection between German Basic Law und Union Law, p.*

Bygrave, Lee A.: Data Privacy Law – An International Perspective, Oxford: Oxford University Press, 2014, quoted as: *Bygrave, Data Privacy Law, p.*

Callies, Christian: Schutzpflichten, in: Detlef Merten / Hans-Jürgen Papier (eds.), Handbuch der Grundrechte in Deutschland und Europa – Band II „Grundrechte in Deutschland – Allgemeine Lehren I“, Heidelberg: C. F. Müller, 2006, § 44, quoted as: *Callies, Duties of Protection, cip.*

Cate, Fred H. / *Cullon,* Peter / *Mayer-Schönberger,* Viktor: Data Protection Principles for the 21st Century – Revising the 1980 OECD Guidelines, Oxford Internet Institute 2014, URL: https://www.oii.ox.ac.uk/archive/downloads/publications/Data_Protection_Principles_for_the_21st_Century.pdf, quoted as: Cate/Cullon/Viktor Mayer-Schönberger, Data Protection Principles for the 21st Century, p.

Center for Information Policy Leadership: The Role of Risk Management in Data Protection – Paper 2 of the Project on Privacy Risk Framework and Risk-based Approach to Privacy, 2014, URL: https://www.informationpolicycentre.com/files/Uploads/Documents/Centre/The_Role_of_Risk_Management_in_Data_Protection_FINAL_Paper.PDF, quoted as: *Center for Information Policy Leadership, The Role of Risk Management in Data Protection – Paper 2 of the Project on Privacy Risk Framework and Risk-based Approach to Privacy, p.*

Christl, Wolfie: Kommerzielle Digitale Überwachung im Alltag, Studie im Auftrag der Bundesarbeitskammer Wien, 2014, URL: http://crackedlabs.org/dl/Studie_Digitale_Ueberwachung.pdf, quoted as: *Christl, Commercial Digital Surveillance in Daily Life.*

Costa, Luiz: Privacy and the precautionary principle, in: Computer Law & Security Review 28 (2012), pp. 14–24, quoted as: *Costa, Privacy and the precautionary principle, p.*

Custer, Bart / *Ursic,* Helena: Big data and data reuse: a taxonomy of data reuse for balancing big data benefits and personal data protection, in: International Data Privacy Law 6 (1) (2016), pp. 1–12, quoted as: *Custer and Ursic, Big data and data reuse: a taxonomy of data reuse for balancing big data benefits and personal data protection, p.*

Dammann, Ulrich / *Simitis,* Spiros: EG-Datenschutzrichtlinie, Baden-Baden: Nomos, 1997, quoted as: *Dammann/Spirits, EU Data Protection Directive, ,Chapter', cip.*

Danwitz, Thomas von: Die Grundrechte auf Achtung der Privatsphäre und auf Schutz personenbezogener Daten – Die jüngere Rechtsprechung des Gerichtshofes der Europäischen Union, in: Datenschutz und Datensicherheit 39 (9) 2015, pp. 581–585, quoted as: *v. Danwitz, The Fundamental Rights to Private Life and to data Protection, p.*

De Hert, Paul / *Gutwirth,* Serge: Data Protection in the Case Law of Strasbourg and Luxemburg: Constitutionalisation in Action, in: Serge Gutwirth / Yves Poullet / Paul de Hert / Cecile de Terwangne / Sjaak Nouwt (eds.), Reinventing Data Protection?, New York i.a.: Springer, 2009, pp. 3–44, quoted as: *De Hert and Gutwirth, Data Protection in the Case Law of Strasbourg and Luxemburg: Constitutionalisation in Action, p.*

Id.: Privacy, data protection and law enforcement. Opacity of the individual and transparency of power, in: Erik Claes / Antony Duff / Serge Gutwirth (eds.), Privacy and the criminal law, Antwerp/Oxford: Intersentia, 2006, pp. 61–104, quoted as: *De Hert and Gutwirth, Privacy, data protection and law enforcement. Opacity of the individual and transparency of power, p.*

Dietlein, Johannes: Die Lehre von den grundrechtlichen Schutzpflichten, Berlin: Duncker & Humblot, 2005, quoted as: *Dietlein, The Doctrine of Duties of Protection of Basic Rights, p.*

Dijk, Niels van / *Gellert,* Raphaël / *Rommetveit,* Kjetil: A risk to a right? Beyond data protection risk assessments, in: Computer Law & Security Review 32 (2) (2016), pp. 286–306, quoted as: *van Dijk, Gellert and Rommetveit, A risk to a right? Beyond data protection risk assessments, p.*

Dopfer, Martina / *von Grafenstein*, Maximilian / *Richter,* Nancy / *Schildhauer,* Thomas / *Tech,* Robin / *Trifonov,* Stefan / *Wrobel,* Martin: Working Paper „Fördernde Und Hindernde Faktoren Für Internet-Enabled Startups. (Supporting and Hindering Factors for Internet-Enabled Startups.), 2015, URL: https://papers.ssrn.com/sol3/papers.cfm?abstract_id=2759911,

quoted as: *Dopfer et al., Supporting and hindering factors for internet-enabled startups, p.*

Drucker, Peter F.: The Discipline of Innovation, in: Harvard Business Review, Reprint 98604 (1998), first published in 1985, URL: https://hbr.org/2002/08/the-discipline-of-innovation, quoted as: *Drucker, The Discipline of Innovation, p.*

Duhigg, Charles: Die Macht der Gewohnheit – Warum wir tun was wir tun (English original title: The Power of Habit), Berlin: Berlin Verlag, 2012, quoted as: *Duhigg, The Power of Habit, p.*

Eckhoff, Rolf: Der Grundrechtseingriff, Köln i.a.: Carl Heymanns, 1992, quoted as: *Eckhoff, The Infringement of Fundamental Rights, p.*

EDRi / access / Privacy International / Fundacja Panoptykon: Data Protection Broken Badly, 2015, URL: https://edri.org/files/DP_BrokenBadly.pdf, quoted as: *EDRi / access / Privacy International / Fundacja Panoptykon: Data Protection Broken Badly.*

El Emam, Khaled / *Álvarez,* Cecilia: A critical appraisal of the Article 29 Working Party Opinion 05/2014 on data anonymization techniques, in: International Data Privacy Law 5 (1) (2015), pp. 73–87, quoted as: *El Emam and Álvarez, A critical appraisal of the Article 29 Working Party Opinion 05/2014 on data anonymization techniques, p.*

Ehmann, Eugen / *Helfrich,* Markus: EG Datenschutzrichtlinie, Köln: Otto Schmidt, 1999, quoted as: *Ehmann/Helfrich, EU Data Protection Directive, „Chapter", cip.*

Eichenhofer, Johannes: Privatheit im Internet als Vertrauensschutz, in: Der Staat 55 (1) (2016), pp. 41–67, quoted as: *Eichenhofer, Privacy in the Internet as Protection of Trust, p.*

Eifert, Martin: Zweckvereinbarkeit statt Zweckbindung als Baustein eines modernisierten Datenschutzrechts, in: Walter Gropp / Martin Lipp / Heinhard Steiger (eds.), Rechtswissenschaft im Wandel – Festschrift des Fachbereichs Rechtswissenschaft zum 400jährigen Gründungsjubiläum der Justus-Liebig-Universität Gießen, Tübingen: Mohr Siebeck, 2007, pp. 139–152, quoted as: *Eifert, Purpose Compatibility instead of Purpose Limitation, p.*

Id.: Regulierungsstrategien, in: Wolfgang Hoffmann-Riem / Eberhard Schmidt-Aßmann / Andreas Voßkuhle (eds.), Grundlagen des Verwaltungsrechts – Band I „Methoden – Maßstäbe – Aufgaben – Organisation", 2nd edition, München: C.H. Beck, 2012, § 19, quoted as: *Eifert, Regulation Strategies, p.*

Id.: Innovationsfördernde Regulierung, in: Martin Eifert / Wolfgang Hoffmann-Riem (eds.), Innovation und Recht II – Innovationsfördernde Regulierung, Berlin: Duncker & Humblot, 2009, pp. 11–19, *quoted as: Eifert, Innovation-enhancing Regulation, p.*

Eisenhardt, Kathleen M. / *Graebner,* Melissa E.: Theory Building From Cases: Opportunities and Challenges, in: Academy of Management Journal 50 (1) (2007), pp. 25–32, quoted as: *Eisenhardt and Graebner, Theory Building From Cases: Opportunities and Challenges, p.*

Eßer, Martin: § 31, in: Martin Eßer / Philip Kramer / Kai von Lewinski (eds.), Auernhammer – Bundesdatenschutzgesetz, 4th edition, Köln: Carl Heymanns, 2014, quoted as: *Eßer, Federal Data Protection Law and further Provisions, cip.*

European Union Agency for Fundamental Rights / European Court of Human Rights / Council of Europe: Handbook on European data protection law, Luxembourg: Publications Office of the European Union, 2014, quoted as: *Handbook on European data protection law, p.*

Eurobarometer: Entrepreneurship in the EU and beyond, Flash EB Series #283, 2010, URL: http://ec.europa.eu/public_opinion/flash/fl_283_en.pdf, quoted as: Eurobarometer: Entrepreneurship in the EU and beyond.

Expert Group on Fundamental Rights: Affirming Fundamental Rights in the European Union, Time to Act, Luxembourg: Office for Official Publications of the European Communities, 1999, URL: http://bookshop.europa.eu/en/affirming-fundamental-rights-in-the-european-union-pbCE2199181/downloads/CE-21-99-181-EN-C/CE2199181ENC_001.pdf;pgid=y8dIS7GUWMdSR0EAlMEUUsWb00008BR_Mmdd;sid=q4ng-7rouAbg__TN3ld-XNjN5ur-ib07rVo=?FileName=CE2199181ENC_001.pdf&SKU=CE2199181ENC_PDF&CatalogueNumber=CE-21-99-181-EN-C, quoted as: *Expert Group on Fundamental Rights, p.*

Fagerberg, Jan: Innovation: A Guide to the Literature, in: Jan Fagerberg / David C. Mowery (eds.), The Oxford Handbook of Innovation, Oxford: Oxford University Press, 2004, pp. 1–26, quoted as: *Fagerberg, Innovation: A Guide to the Literature, p.*

Federal Communications Commission: Internet Protocol Version 6: IPv 6 for Consumers, 25 October 2016, URL: https://www.fcc.gov/consumers/guides/internet-protocol-version-6-ipv 6-consumers, quoted as: *Federal Communications Commission: Internet Protocol Version 6: IPv 6 for Consumers.*

Folz, Hans-Peter, Artikels 3, 15, 16, and 21 EU-GR Charta, in: Christoph Vedder / Heintschel von Heinegg, Wolff (eds.), Europäisches Unionsrecht – EUV / AEUV / Grundrechte-Charta, Baden-Baden: Nomos Verlag, 2012, quoted as: *Folz, Articles 3, 15, 16, and 21 ECFR – Freedom to Conduct a Business, cip.*

Forgó, Nikolaus / *Krügel,* Tina / *Rapp,* Stefan: Zwecksetzung und informationelle Gewaltenteilung, Baden-Baden: Nomos Verlag, 2006, quoted as: *Forgó et al., Purpose Specification and Informational Separation of Powers, p.*

Forgó, Nikolaus / *Krügel,* Tina: Die Subjektivierung der Zweckbindung: Datenschutz – Bremsblock oder Motor des E-Government, in: Datenschutz und Datensicherheit 29 (12) (2005), pp. 732–735, quoted as: *Forgó and Krügel, Subjective purpose limitation: Data protection – Brake or motor of E-Government?, p.*

Forum Privatheit: White Paper, Datenschutz-Folgenabschätzung: Ein Werkzeug für einen besseren Datenschutz, 2016, URL: https://www.forum-privatheit.de/forum-privatheit-de/texte/veroeffentlichungen-des-forums/themenpapiere-white-paper/Forum_Privatheit_White_Paper_Datenschutz-Folgenabschaetzung_2016.pdf, quoted as: *Forum Privatheit, White Paper – Data Protection Impact Assessment, p.*

Franzius, Claudio: Modalitäten und Wirkungsfaktoren der Steuerung durch Recht, in: Wolfgang Hoffmann-Riem / Eberhard Schmidt-Aßmann / Andreas Voßkuhle (eds.), Grundlagen des Verwaltungsrechts – Band I „Methoden – Maßstäbe – Aufgaben – Organisation", 2nd edition, München: C.H. Beck, 2012, § 4, quoted as: *Franzius, Modes and Impact Factors for the Control through Law, cip.*

Fueglistaller, Urs / *Müller*, Christoph / *Müller*, Susan / *Volery*, Thierry / assisted by *Röschke*, Arik: Basics, in: Fueglistaller, Urs / Müller, Christoph / Müller, Susan / Volery, Thierry (eds.), Entrepreneurship – Modelle, Umsetzung, Perspektiven, 4th edition, Wiesbaden: Springer Gabler , 2016, Grundlagen, quoted as: *Fueglistaller et al., Entrepreneurship – Basics, p.*

Fueglistaller, Urs / *Müller*, Christoph / *Müller*, Susan / *Volery*, Thierry / assisted by *Fust*, Alexander: Basics, in: Fueglistaller, Urs / Müller, Christoph / Müller, Susan / Volery, Thierry (eds.), Entrepreneurship – Modelle, Umsetzung, Perspektiven, 4th edition, Wiesbaden: Springer Gabler , 2016, Innovation und Entrepreneurship, quoted as: *Fueglistaller et al., Entrepreneurship – Innovation and Entrepreneurship, p.*

Müller, Christoph / *Fueglistaller*, Urs / *Müller*, Susan / *Volery*, Thierry, in: Fueglistaller, Urs / Müller, Christoph / Müller, Susan / Volery, Thierry (eds.), Strategie und Geschäftsmodell, in: Entrepreneurship – Modelle, Umsetzung, Perspektiven, 4th edition, Wiesbaden: Springer Gabler , 2016, Grundlagen, quoted as: *Müller et al., Entrepreneurship – Strategy and business model, p.*

Gartner, William B.: What are we talking about when we talk about entrepreneurship?, in: Journal of Business Venturing 5 (1) (1990), pp. 15–28, quoted as: *Gartner, What are we talking about when we talk about entrepreneurship?, p.*

Id.: A Conceptual Framework for Describing the Phenomenon of New Venture Creation, in: The Academy of Management Review 10 (4) (1985), pp. 696–706, quoted as: *Gartner, A Conceptual Framework for Describing the Phenomenon of New Venture Creation, p.*

Gasser, Urs: Cloud Innovation and the Law: Issues, Approaches, and Interplay, Berkman Center Research Publication No. 2014-7, URL: https://papers.ssrn.com/sol3/papers.cfm?abstract_id=2410271, quoted as: *Gasser, Cloud Innovation and the Law: Issues, Approaches, and Interplay, p.*

Gellert, Raphaël: Data protection: a risk regulation? Between the risk regulation of everything and the precautionary alternative, in: International Data Privacy Law 5 (1) (2015), pp. 3–19, quoted as: *Gellert, Data protection: a risk regulation? Between the risk regulation of everything and the precautionary alternative, p.*

Gola, Peter / *Schomerus,* Rudolf: Bundesdatenschutzgesetz, Kommentar, 12th edition, München: C.H.Beck, 2015, quoted as: Gola/Schomerus, Federal Data Protection Law, § 28 BDSG cip.

González-Fuster, Gloria: The Emergence of Data Protection as a Fundamental Right of the EU, Cham i.a.: Springer, 2014, quoted as: *González-Fuster, The Emergence of Data Protection as a Fundamental Right of the EU, p.*

Globig, Klaus: Der Auskunftsanspruch des Betroffenen als Grundrecht, in: Hans-Wolfgang Arndt (ed.) Völkerrecht und deutsches Recht – Festschrift für Walter Rudolf zum 70. Geburtstag, München: C.H. Beck, 2001, pp. 441–465, quoted as: *Globig, Basic Right to Information, p.*

Grafenstein, Maximilian von / *Schulz,* Wolfgang: The right to be forgotten in data protection law: a search for the concept of protection, in: International Journal for Public Law and Policy 5 (3) (2015), pp. 249–269, quoted as: *v. Grafenstein and Schulz, The right to be forgotten in data protection law: a search for the concept of protection, p.*

Id.: Das Zweckbindungsprinzip zwischen Innovationsoffenheit und Rechtssicherheit – Zur mangelnden Differenzierung der Rechtsgüterbetroffenheit in der Datenschutzgrund-VO, in: Datenschutz und Datensicherheit 39 (12) (2015), pp. 789–795, quoted as: v. Grafenstein, The Principle of Purpose Limitation between Openness toward Innovation and the Rule of Law, p.

Greve, Dr. Holger : § 40, in: Martin Eßer / Philip Kramer / Kai von Lewinski (eds.), Auernhammer – Bundesdatenschutzgesetz, 4th edition, Köln: Carl Heymanns, 2014, quoted as: *Greve (Auernhammer), cip.*

Grimm, Dieter: Der Datenschutz vor einer Neuorientierung, in: JuristenZeitung 68 (12) (2013), pp. 585–592, quoted as: *Grimm, Data protection before its refinement, p.*

Gusy, Christoph: Informationelle Selbstbestimmung und Datenschutz: Fortführung oder Neuanfang?, in: Kritische Vierteljahresschrift für Gesetzgebung und Rechtswissenschaft 83 (1) (2000), pp. 52–64, quoted as: *Gusy, Informational Self-Determination and Data Protection: Continuing or New Beginning?, p.*

Härting, Niko: Zweckbindung und Zweckänderung im Datenschutzrecht, in: Neue Juristische Wochenschrift 68 (45) (2015), pp. 3284–3288, quoted as: *Härting, Purpose limitation and change of purpose in data protection law, p.*

Id.: Datenschutz-Grundverordnung: Das neue Datenschutzrecht in der betrieblichen Praxis, Köln: Otto Schmidt, 2016, quoted as: *Härting, General Data Protection Regulation: The new data protection law in business practice, cip.*

Id.: Profiling: Vorschläge für eine intelligente Regulierung – Was aus der Zweistufigkeit des Profiling für die Regelung des nicht öffentlichen Datenschutzbereichs folgt, in: Computer und Recht 30 (8) (2014), pp. 528–536, quoted as: *Härting, Profiling: a proposal for an intelligent regulation, p.*

Härting, Niko / *Schneider,* Jochen: Data Protection in Europe: An Alternative Draft for a General Data Protection Regulation – Alternatives to the European Commission's Proposal of 25 January 2012, Computer Law Review International 14 (2013) Supplement 1, pp. 1-38, quoted as: *Härting and Schneider, Data Protection in Europe: An Alternative Draft for a General Data Protection Regulation, p.*

Hallinan, Dara / *Friedewald,* Michael: Public Perception of the Data Environment and Information Transactions – A selected-survey analysis of the European public's views on the data environment and data transactions, in: Communications & Strategies 88 (4) (2012), pp. 61–78, quoted as: *Hallinan and Friedewald, Public Perception of the Data Environment and Information Transactions – A selected-survey analysis of the European public's views on the data environment and data transactions, p.*

Vested-Hansen, Jens: Article 7 – Respect for Private and Family Life, in: Steve Peers / Tamara Hervey / Jeff Kenner / Angela Ward (eds.), The EU Charter of Fundamental Rights, A Commentary, Oxford i.a.: Hart 2014, pp. 196-225, quoted as: *Vested-Hansen, EU Charter of Fundamental Rights, cip.*

Hartog, Chantal / *van Stel,* André / *Storey,* David J.: Institutions and Entrepreneurship: The Role of the Rule of Law, 2010, URL: http://ondernemerschap.panteia.nl/main/publication/bestelnummer/h201003, quoted as: *Hartog et al., Institutions and Entrepreneurship: The Role of the Rule of Law, p.*

Herberger, Marie: "Ausnahmen sind eng auszulegen" – Die Ansichten beim Gerichtshof der Europäischen Union, Berlin: Duncker & Humblot, 2017, quoted as: *Herberger, "Exceptions have to be interpretetd narrowly" – The considerations by the European Court of Justice, p.*

Heun, Sven-Erik: §§ 88, 95, 96 TKG, in: Martin Eßer / Philip Kramer / Kai von Lewinski (eds.), Auernhammer – Bundesdatenschutzgesetz, 4th edition, Köln: Carl Heymanns, 2014, quoted as: *Heun, Federal Data Protection Law and further Provisions, ‚Chapter', cip.*

Hoffmann-Riem, Wolfgang: Informationelle Selbstbestimmung in der Informationsgesellschaft – Auf dem Wege zu einem neuen Konzept des Datenschutzrechts, in: Archiv des öffentlichen Rechts 123 (4) (1998), pp. 513–540, quoted as: *Hofmann-Riem, New Concept of Data Protection, p.*

Id.: Rechtswissenschaftliche Innovationsforschung als Reaktion auf gesellschaftlichen Innovationsbedarf, in: Martin Eifert / Wolfgang Hoffmann-Riem (eds.), Innovation und rechtliche Regulierung, Baden-Baden: Nomos, 2002, pp. 26–47, quoted as: *Hoffmann-Riem, Jurisprudential Research on Innovation as Reaction to a Societal Need for Innovation, p.*

Id.: Innovationsoffenheit und Innovationsverantwortung durch Recht – Aufgaben rechtswissenschaftlicher Innovationsforschung, in: Archiv des öffentlichen Rechts 131 (2) (2006), pp. 255–277, quoted as: *Hoffmann-Riem, Openness toward Innovation and Responsibility for Innovation by means of Law, p.*

Id.: Der grundrechtliche Schutz der Vertraulichkeit und Integrität eigengenutzter informationstechnischer Systeme, JuristenZeitung 63 (21) (2008), pp. 1009–1022, quoted as: *Hoffmann-Riem, Protection of the Confidentiality and Integrity of Information Technological Systems, p.*

Hoffmann-Riem, Wolfgang / *Fritzsche*, Saskia: Innovationsverantwortung – Zur Einleitung, in: Martin Eifert / Wolfgang Hoffmann-Riem (eds.), Innovation und Recht III – Innovationsverantwortung, Berlin: Duncker & Humblot, 2009, pp. 11–41, quoted as: *Hoffmann-Riem, Innovation Responsibility, p.*

Hofmann, Bernhard: Zweckbindung als Kernpunkt eines prozeduralen Datenschutzansatzes, Baden-Baden: Nomos, 1991, quoted as: *Hofmann, Purpose Limitation as Anchor Point for a Procedural Approach in Data Protection, p.*

Hofmann, Jeanette / *Katzenbach,* Christian / *Gollatz,* Kirsten: Between coordination and regulation: Finding the governance in Internet governance, in: New Media & Society 2016, pp. 1–18, quoted as: *Hofmann, Katzenbach and Gollatz, Between coordination and regulation: Finding the governance in Internet governance, p.*

Hon, W Kuan / *Millard,* Christopher / *Walden,* Ian: Who is responsible for 'personal data' in cloud computing? The cloud of unknowing, Part 2, in: International Data Privacy Law 2 (1) (2012), pp. 3–18, quoted as: *Hon, Millard, and Walden, Who is responsible for 'personal data' in cloud computing?, p.*

Hood, Christopher / *Rothstein,* Henry / *Baldwin,* Robert: The Government of Risk – Understanding Risk Regulation Regimes, Oxford: Oxford University Press, 2001, quoted as: *Hood, Rothstein, and Baldwin, The Government of Risk – Understanding Risk Regulation Regimes, p.*

Hoofnagle, Chris Jay, The Potemkinism of Privacy Pragmatism: Civil liberties are too important to be left to the technologists, 2014, URL: http://www.slate.com/articles/technology/future_tense/2014/09/data_use_regulation_the_libertarian_push_behind_a_new_take_on_privacy.html, quoted as: *Hoofnagle, The Potemkinism of Privacy Pragmatism: Civil liberties are too important to be left to the technologists.*

Hornung, Gerrit / *Hartl,* Korbinian: Datenschutz durch Marktanreize – auch in Europa? Stand der Diskussion zu Datenschutzzertifizierung und Datenschutzaudit, in: Zeitschrift für Datenschutz 4 (5) (2014), pp. 219–225, quoted as: *Hornung and Hartl, Data Protection through Market Incentives – in Europe, too?, ZD May 2014, p.*

Jaeckel, Liv: Gefahrenabwehrrecht und Risikodogmatik – Moderne Technologien im Spiegel des Verwaltungsrechts, Tübingen: Mohr Siebeck, 2010, quoted as: *Jaeckel, Prevention of Danger through Law and Legal Conceptualization of Risk, p.*

Id.: Risiko-Signaturen im Recht – Zur Unterscheidbarkeit von Gefahr und Risiko, JuristenZeitung 66 (3) (2011), pp. 116–124, quoted as: *Jaeckel, Differentiating between Danger and Risk, p.*

Id.: Schutzpflichten im deutschen und europäischen Recht – Eine Untersuchung der deutschen Grundrechte, der Menschenrechte und Grundfreiheiten der EMRK sowie der Grundrechte und Grundfreiheiten der Europäischen Gemeinschaft, Baden-Baden: Nomos, 2001, quoted as: *Jaeckel, Duties of Protection in German and European Law, p.*

Jandt, Silke / *Roßnagel,* Alexander: Datenschutz in Social Networks – Kollektive Verantwortlichkeit für die Datenverarbeitung, Zeitschrift für Datenschutz 1 (4) (2011), pp. 160–166, quoted as: *Jandt and Roßnagel, Data protection in social networks – Collective responsibility for data processing, p.*

Jarass, Hans D.: Vor Art. 1, Art. 1 GG, in: Jarass, Hans D. / Pieroth, Bodo (eds.), Grundgesetz für die Bundesrepublik Deutschland – Kommentar, München: C.H. Beck, 2012, quoted as: *Jarass in: Jarass/Pieroth, GG, Art.*

Jarchow, Thomas / *Estermann,* Beat: Big Data: Chancen, Risiken und Handlungsbedarf des Bundes – Ergebnisse einer Studie im Auftrag des Bundesamts für Kommunikation, 26 Oktober 2015, URL: https://www.uvek.admin.ch/dam/uvek/de/dokumente/anlaesse/2015-ab-juli/BFH%20Big%20Data%20Studie.pdf.download.pdf/BFH_Big-Data-Studie.pdf, quoted as: *Jarchow and Estermann, Big Data: Chances, Risks and Need for Action of the Swiss Confederation, p.*

Kamp, Meike / *Rost,* Martin: Kritik an der Einwilligung – Ein Zwischenruf zu einer fiktiven Rechtsgrundlage in asymmetrischen Machtverhältnissen, in: Datenschutz und Datensicherheit 37 (2) (2013), pp. 80–84, quoted as: *Kamp and Rost, Criticism of the individual's consent – An interjection on a ficticious legal basis in asyymetric power relations, p.*

Karg, Moritz: Die Rechtsfigur des personenbezogenen Datums – Ein Anachronismus des Datenschutzes?, in: Zeitschrift für Datenschutz 2 (6) (2012), pp. 255–260, quoted as: *Karg, The personal datum as a legal link for regulation – An anachronism of data protection?, p.*

Id.: Die Renaissance des Verbotsprinzips im Datenschutz, in: Datenschutz und Datensicherheit 37 (2) (2013), pp. 75–79, quoted as: *Karg, The renaissance of the prohibition principle in data protection, p.*

Kift, Paula: Bridging the transatlantic divide in privacy, in: Internet Policy Review 2 (3) (2013), pp. 1–7, quoted as: *Kift, Bridging the transatlantic divide, at fn.*

Kirby, Michael: The history, achievement and future of the 1980 OECD guidelines on privacy, in: International Data Privacy Law 1 (1) (2011), pp. 6–14, quoted as: *Kirby, The history, achievement and future of the 1980 OECD guidelines on privacy, p.*

Kloepfer, Michael: Recht ermöglicht Technik – Zu einer wenig beachteten Funktion des Umwelt- und Technikrechts, in: Natur und Recht 1997, pp. 417–418, quoted as: *Kloepfer, Law enables Technology – About an understimated function of environmental and technology law, p.*

Kokott, Juliane / *Sobotta,* Christoph: The distinction between privacy and data protection in the jurisprudence of the CJEU and the ECtHR, in: International Data Privacy Law 3 (4) (2013), pp. 222–228, quoted as: *Kokott and Sobotta, The distinction between privacy and data protection in the jurisprudence of the CJEU and the ECtHR, p.*

Kollmann, Tobias / *Stöckmann,* Christoph / *Linstaedt,* Jana / *Kensbock,* Julia: European Startup Monitor 2015, URL: http://europeanstartupmonitor.com/fileadmin/presse/download/esm_2015.pdf, quoted as: Kollmann et al., European Startup Monitor 2015, p.

Kosta, Eleni: Construing the Meaning of „Opt-Out" – An Analysis of the European, U.K. and German Data Protection Legislation, in: European Data Protection Law Review 1 (1) (2015), pp. 16–31, quoted as: *Kosta, Construing the Meaning of „Opt-Out" – An Analysis of the European, U.K. and German Data Protection Legislation, p.*

Kramer, Philip: §§ 4a, 28 BDSG, in: Martin Eßer / Philip Kramer / Kai von Lewinski (eds.), Auernhammer – Bundesdatenschutzgesetz, 4th edition, Köln: Carl Heymanns, 2014, quoted as: *Kramer, Federal Data Protection Law and further Provisions, ,Chapter', cip.*

Kranenborg, Herke: Article 8 – Protection of Personal Data, in: Steve Peers / Tamara Hervey / Jeff Kenner / Angela Ward (eds.), The EU Charter of Fundamental Rights, A Commentary, Oxford i.a.: Hart 2014, quoted as: *Kranenborg, Article 8 – Protection of Personal Data, cip.*

Kühling, Jürgen: Datenschutz in einer künftigen Welt allgegenwärtiger Datenverarbeitung – Aufgabe des Rechts?, in: Die Verwaltung 40 (2) (2007), pp. 153–172, quoted as: *Kühling, Data protection in a future world of ubiquitous data processing, p.*

Kuner, Christopher / *Cate,* Fred H. / *Millard,* Christopher / *Svantesson,* Dan Jerker B. / *Lynskey,* Orla: Editorial – Risk management in data protection, in: International Data Privacy Law 5 (2) (2015), pp. 95–98, quoted as: *Kuner et al., Risk management in data protection, p.*

Id.: Editorial – The data protection credibility crisis, in: International Data Privacy Law 5 (3) (2015), pp. 161–162, quoted as: *Kuner et al., The Data Protection Credibility Crisis, IDPL 2015 Vol. 5 no. 3, p.*

Kutscha, Martin: Datenschutz durch Zweckbindung – Ein Auslaufmodell?, in: Zeitschrift für Rechtspolitik 32 (4) (1999), pp. 156–160, quoted as: *Kutscha, ZRP, vol. 4, 1999, pp. 156–160, Data Protection through Purpose Limitation – An Obsolescent Model?, p.*

Ladeur, Karl-Heinz: Das Umweltrecht der Wissensgesellschaft: Von der Gefahrenabwehr zum Risikomanagement, Berlin: Duncker & Humblot, 2005, pp. 209–233, quoted as: *Ladeur, The Environmental Law of the Knowledge Society: From the protection against dangers to the management of risks, p.*

Lenaerts, Koen / *Gutiérrez-Fons,* José Antonio: The Charter in the EU Constitutional Edifice, in: Steve Peers / Tamara Hervey / Jeff Kenner / Angela Ward (eds.), The EU Charter of Fundamental Rights, A Commentary, Oxford i.a.: Hart 2014, pp. 1600–1637, quoted as: *Lenaerts and Gutiérrez-Fons, The Charter in the EU Constitutional Edifice, p.*

Levie, Jonathan / *Autio,* Erkko: Regulatory Burden, Rule of Law, and Entry of Strategic Entrepreneurs: An International Panel Study, in: Journal of Management Studies 48 (6) (2011), pp. 1392–1419, quoted as: *Levie and Autio, Regulatory Burden, Rule of Law, and Entry of Strategic Entrepreneurs: An International Panel Study, p.*

Lewinski, Kai von: § 1 BDSG, Vorb. § 88 TKG, in: Martin Eßer / Philip Kramer / Kai von Lewinski (eds.), Auernhammer – Bundesdatenschutzgesetz, 4th edition, Köln: Carl Heymanns, 2014, quoted as: *v. Lewinski, Federal Data Protection Law and further Provisions, ,Chapter', cip.*

Id.: Die Matrix des Datenschutzes, Tübingen: Mohr Siebeck, 2014, quoted as: *v. Lewinski, The Matrix of Data Protection, p.*

Lindner, Josef Franz: Datenschutzrecht in Bund und Ländern, Kommentar, München: C.H. Beck, 2013, quoted as: *Lindner, Data protection in the Federal State and the Länder, cip.*

Lipshaw, Jeffrey M.: Why the Law of Entrepreneurship Barely Matters, in: Western New England Law Review 31 (3/7) 2009, pp. 701-715, quoted as: *Lipshaw, Why the Law of Entrepreneurship Barely Matters.*

Luhmann, Niklas: Zweckbegriff und Systemrationalität, Tübingen: Mohr Siebeck, 1968, quoted as: *Luhmann, The Concept of Purpose and System Rationality, p.*

Lynskey, Orla: The Foundations of EU Data Protection Law, Oxford: Oxford University Press, 2015, quoted as: *Lynskey, The Foundations of EU Data Protection Law, p.*

Mantelero, Alessandro / *Vaciago,* Giuseppe: The „Dark Side" of Big Data: Private and Public Interaction in Social Surveillance – How data collections by private entities affect governmental social control and how the EU reform an data protection responds, in: Computer Law Review International 14 (6) (2013), pp. 161–169, quoted as: *Mantelero and Vaciago, The „Dark Side" of Big Data: Private and Public Interaction in Social Surveillance, p.*

Margraf, Marian / *Pfeiffer,* Stefan: Benutzerzentrierte Entwicklung für das Internet der Dinge, in: Datenschutz und Datensicherheit 39 (4) (2015), pp. 246–249, quoted as: *Margraf and Pfeiffer, User-centric development for the Internet of Things, p.*

Matscher, Franz: Methods of Interpretation of the Convention, in: Ronald St. J. Macdonald / Franz Matscher / Herbert Petzold (eds.), The European System for the protection of human rights, Dordrecht i.a.: Kluwer Academic, 1993, pp. 63–81, quoted as: *Matscher, Methods of Interpretation of the Convention, p.*

Masing, Johannes: Herausforderungen des Datenschutzes, Neue Juristische Wochenschrift 65 (32) (2012), pp. 2305–2311, quoted as: *Masing, Challenges of data protection, p.*

Mayer-Schönberger, Viktor: The Law as Stimulus: The Role of Law in Fostering Innovative Entrepreneurship, in: Journal of Law and Policy for the Information Society 6 (2) (2010) pp. 153–188, quoted as: *Mayer-Schönberger, The Law a s Stimulus: The Role of Law in Fostering Innovative Entrepreneurship, p.*

Mayer-Schönberger, Viktor / *Cukier,* Kenneth: Big Data: A Revolution That Will Transform How We Live, Work, and Think, New York: Houghton Mifflin Harcourt, 2013, quoted as: *Mayer-Schönberger and Cukier, Big Data: A Revolution That Will Transform How We Live, Work, and Think, p.*

Maxwell, Winston J.: Principles-based regulation of personal data: the case of ‚fair processing', in: International Data Privacy Law 5 (3) (2015), pp. 205–216, quoted as: *Maxwell, Principles-based regulation of personal data: the case of ‚fair processing', p.*

Mehde, Veith: Datenschutz, in: Sebastian F. Heselhaus / Carsten Nowak (eds.), Handbuch der Europäischen Grundrechte, München: C.H. Beck, 2006, § 21, quoted as: *Mehde, Handbook of European Fundamental Rights, cip.*

Miller, Arthur R.: Personal Privacy in the Computer Age: The Challenge of a New Technology in an Information-Oriented Society, in: Michigan Law Review 67 (6) (1969), pp. 1089–1246, quoted as: *Miller, Personal Privacy in the Computer Age: The Challenge of a New Technology in an Information-Oriented Society, p.*

Moroz, Peter W. / *Hindle,* Kevin: Entreneurship as a Process: Toward Harmonizing Multiple Perspectives, in: Entrepreneurship Theory and Practice 36 (4) (2012), pp. 781–818, quoted as: *Moroz and Hindle, Entreneurship as a Process: Toward Harmonizing Multiple Perspectives, p.*

Murray, Andrew D.: Conceptualising the Post-Regulatory (Cyber)state, in: Roger Brownsword / Karen Yeung (eds.), Regulating Technologies – Legal Futures, Regulatory Frames and Technological Fixes, Oxford i.a.: Hart Publishing, 2008, pp. 287–316, quoted as: *Murray, Conceptualising the Post-Regulatory (Cyber)state, p.*

Id.: The Regulation of Cyberspace – Control in the Online Environment, Abingdon i.a.: Routledge–Cavendish, 2007, quoted as: *Murray, The Regulation of Cyberspace – Control in the Online Environment, p.*

Neumann, Robert: Libertärer Paternalismus – Theorie und Empirie staatlicher Entscheidungsarchitektur, Tübingen: Mohr Siebeck, 2013, quoted as: *Neumann, Libertarian Paternalism – Theory and empiricism with respect to decision-making architectures designed by the State, p.*

Neveling, Stefanie / *Bumke,* Susanne / *Dietrich,* Jan-Hendrik: Ansätze wirtschaftswissenschaftlicher und soziologischer Innovationsforschung, in: Martin Eifert / Wolfgang Hoffmann-Riem (eds.), Innovation und rechtliche Regulierung. Schlüsselbegriffe und Anwendungsbeispiele rechtswissenschaftlicher Innovationsforschung, Baden-Baden: Nomos, 2002, pp. 364–413 quoted as: *Neveling et alt., Economic and Sociological Approaches of Innovation Research, p.*

Niedobitek, Matthias: Entwicklung und allgemeine Grundsätze, in: Detlef Merten / Jürgen Papier (eds.), Handbuch der Grundrechte in Deutschland und Europa – Band VI/1 „Europäische Grundrechte I", Heidelberg i.a.: C.F. Müller, 2010, § 159, quoted as: *Niedobitek, Development and General Principles, cip.*

Nissenbaum, Helen: Privacy in Context – Technology, Policy, and the Integrity of Social Life, Stanford: Stanford University Press, 2010, quoted as: *Nissenbaum, Privacy in Context, p.*

Id.: Respect for Context as a Benchmark, in: Beate Roessler / Dorothea Mokrosinska (eds.), Social Dimensions of Privacy – Interdisciplinary Perspectives, Cambridge: Cambridge University Press, 2015, pp. 278–302, quoted as: *Nissenbaum, Respect for Context as a Benchmark, p.*

Id.: Privacy as Contextual Integrity, in: Washington Law Review 97 (1) (2004), pp. 101–139, quoted as: *Nissenbaum, Privacy as Contextual Integrity, p.*

OECD: Data-Driven Innovation for Growth and Well-Being. What Implications for Governments and Businesses?, Directorate for Science, Technology and Innovation Policy Note, October 2015, URL: http://www.oecd.org/sti/ieconomy/PolicyNote-DDI.pdf, quoted as: *OECD: Data-Driven Innovation for Growth and Well-Being.*

Id.: OECD Science, Technology and Industry Outlook 2014, URL: http://www.oecd.org/sti/oecd-science-technology-and-industry-outlook-19991428.htm, quoted as: *OECD: Science, Technology and Industry Outlook 2014, p.*

Id.: The OECD Privacy Framework, 2013, URL: http://www.oecd.org/sti/ieconomy/oecd_privacy_framework.pdf, quoted as: *The OECD Privacy Framework, p.*

Pahlen-Brandt, Ingrid: Datenschutz braucht scharfe Instrumente – Beitrag zur Diskussion um „personenbezogene Daten", in: Datenschutz und Datensicherheit 32 (1) (2008), pp. 34–40, quoted as: *Pahlen-Brandt, Contribution to the discussion aon „personal data", p.*

Papier, Hans-Jürgen: Drittwirkung der Grundrechte, in: Detlef Merten / Hans-Jürgen Papier (eds.), Handbuch der Grundrechte in Deutschland und Europa – Band II „Allgemeine Lehren I", Heidelberg: C.F. Müller, 2006, § 55, quoted as: *Papier, Third-Party Effect of German Basic Rights, cip.*

Peters, Emma: Wirksamer Grundrechtsschutz und effektive Strafverfolgung beim Zugriff auf elektronische Daten in Speichern privater Dritter (im Kontext der Grundrechte des Datenbetroffenen) (working title, manuscript, forthcoming 2017), quoted as: *Peters, Effective protection of fundamental rights and efficient criminal prosecution in relation to acess to electronic data stored by private third parties, p.*

Plath, Dr. Kai-Uwe, Kommentar zum BDSG und zur DSGVO sowie den Datenschutzbestimmungen von TMG und TKG, 2nd edition, Köln: Verlag Dr. Otto Schidt KG, 2016, quoted as *Plath, §* cip.

Pohle, Jörg: Zweckbindung revisited, in: Datenschutz Nachrichten 38 (3) (2015), pp. 141–145, quoted as: *Pohle, Purpose limitation revisited, p.*

Id.: Personal Data Not Found: Personenbezogene Entscheidungen als überfällige Neuausrichtung im Datenschutz, in: Datenschutz Nachrichten 39 (1) (2016), pp. 14–19, quoted as: *Pohle, Personal Data Not Found: Person-related decisions as an over-due refinement of data protection, p.*

Pombriant, Denis: Data, Information and Knowledge – Transformation of data is key, in: Computer Law Review International 14 (4) (2013), pp. 97–102, quoted as: *Pombriant, Data, Information and Knowledge – Transformation of data is key, p.*

Raab, Charles D. / *De Hert,* Charles: Tools for Technology Regulation: Seeking Analytical Approaches Beyond Lessig and Hood, in: Roger Brownsword / Karen Yeung (eds.) Regulating Technologies – Legal Futures, Regulatory Frames and Technological Fixes, Oxford i.a.: Hart Publishing, 2008, pp. 263–285, quoted as: *Raab and De Hert, Tools for Technology Regulation, p.*

Radlanski, Philip: Das Konzept der Einwilligung in der datenschutzrechtlichen Realität, Tübingen: Mohr Siebeck, 2016, quoted as: *Radlanski, The concept of consent in the reality of data protection law, p.*

Rauhofer, Judith: Of men and mice: Should the EU data protection authorities' reaction to Google's new privacy policy raise concern for the future of the purpose limitation principle?, in: European Data Protection Law Review 1 (1) (2015), pp. 5–15, quoted as: *Rauhofer, Of men and mice: Should the EU data protection authorities' reaction to Google's new privacy policy raise concern for the future of the purpose limitation principle?, p.*

Ries, Eric: The Lean Startup: How Today's Entrepreneurs Use Continuous Innovation to Create Radically Successful Businesses, New York: Random House, 2011, quoted as: *Ries, The Lean Startup, p.*

Rouvroy, Antoinette / *Poullet,* Yves: The Right to Informational Self-Determination and the Value of Self-Development: Reassessing the Importance of Privacy for Democracy, in: Serge Gutwirth / Yves Poullet / Paul de Hert / Cecile de Terwangne / Sjaak Nouwt (eds.), Reinventing Data Protection?, New York i.a.: Springer, 2009, pp. 45–76, quoted as: *Rouvroy and Poullet, The Right to Informational Self-Determination and the Value of Self-Development: Reassessing the Importance of Privacy for Democracy, p.*

Roßnagel, Alexander: Das Gebot der Datenvermeidung und -sparsamkeit als Ansatz wirksamen technikbasierten Persönlichkeitsschutzes?, in: Martin Eifert / Wolfgang Hofmann-Riem (eds.), Innovation, Recht und öffentliche Kommunikation – Innovation und Recht IV, Berlin: Duncker & Humblot, 2011, pp. 41–66, quoted as: *Roßnagel, The Requirement of Data Minimization, p.*

Id.: Datenschutz in einem informatisierten Alltag – Gutachten im Auftrag der Friedrich-Ebert-Stiftung, 2007, URL: http://library.fes.de/pdf-files/stabsabteilung/04548.pdf, quoted as: *Roßnagel, Data protection in computerized everyday life, p.*

Id.: Rechtswissenschaftliche Technikfolgenforschung – Umrisse einer Forschungsdisziplin, Baden-Baden: Nomos, 1993, quoted as: *Roßnagel, Technology assessment as a legal research discipline, p.*

Roßnagel, Alexander / *Pfitzmann,* Andreas / *Garstka,* Hansjürgen: Modernisierung des Datenschutzrechts – Gutachten im Auftrag des Bundesinnenministeriums des Innern, Bundesinnenministerium des Innern, 2001, URL: https://www.bfdi.bund.de/SharedDocs/VortraegeUndArbeitspapiere/2001GutachtenModernisierungDSRecht.pdf?__blob=publicationFile, quoted as: *Roßnagel, Garstka and Pfitzmann, Modernization of data protection law – report on behalf of the Federal Ministry of the Interior (2001), p.*

Rost, Martin: Standardisierte Datenschutzmodellierung, in: Datenschutz und Datensicherheit 35 (6) (2012), pp. 433–438, quoted as: *Rost, Standardized Modeling of Data Protection, p.*

Rost, Martin / *Bock,* Kirstin: Privacy by Design und die Neuen Schutzziele: Grundsätze, Ziele und Anforderungen, in: Datenschutz und Datensicherheit 35 (1) (2011), pp. 30–35, quoted as: *Rost and Bock, Privacy by Design and the New Protection Goals: Principles, objectives, and requirements, p.*

Rost, Martin / *Pfitzmann,* Andreas: Datenschutz-Schutzziele—revisited, in: Datenschutz und Datensicherheit 33 (6) (2009), pp. 353–358, quoted as: *Rost and Pfitzmann, Data Protection Goals – revisited, p.*

Rudolf, Walter: Recht auf informationelle Selbstbestimmung, in: Detlef Merten / Hans-Jürgen Papier (eds.), Handbuch der Grundrechte in Deutschland und Europa – Band IV „Einzelgrundrechte I", Heidelberg: C.F. Müller, 2011, § 90, quoted as: *Rudolf, Right to Informational Self-Determination, cip.*

Ruiz-Miguel, Carlos: El derecho a la protección de los datos personales en la Carta de Derechos Fundamentales de Unión Europea: Análisis crítico, in: Revista de Derecho Comunitario Europeo 7 (14) (2003), pp. 7–43, quoted: *Ruiz-Miguel, El derecho a la protección de los datos personales en la Carta de Derechos Fundamentales de Unión Europea: Análisis crítico, p.*

Rupp, Martin: Die grundrechtliche Schutzpflicht des Staates für das Recht auf informationelle Selbstbestimmung im Pressesektor, Saarbrücken: Alma Mater, 2013, quoted as: *Rupp, The State Duty of Protection for the Right to Informational Self-Determination in the Press Sector, p.*

Sandfuchs, Barbara: Privatheit wider Willen?, Tübingen: Mohr Siebeck, 2015, quoted as: *Sandfuchs, Privacy against one's will?, p.*

Sarasvathy, Saras D.: Causation and Effectuation: Toward a Theoretical Shift from Economic Inevitability to Entrepreneurial Contingency, in: Academy of Management Review 26 (2) (2001), pp. 243–263, quoted as: *Sarasvathy, Causation and Effectuation, p.*

Schneider, Jens-Peter: Stand und Perspektiven des europäischen Datenverkehrs- und Datenschutzrechts, in: Die Verwaltung 44 (4) (2011), pp. 499–524, quoted as: *Schneider, Status of and Perspectives for the European Data Traffic and Data Protection Law, p.*

Schneider, Jochen: Die Datensicherheit – eine vergessene Regelungsmaterie? Ein Plädoyer für Aufwertung, stärkere Integration und Modernisierung des § 9 BDSG, in: Zeitschrift für Datenschutz 1 (1) (2011), pp. 6–12, quoted as: *Schneider, Data security – a forgotten area of regulation?, p.*

Schreibauer, Marcus: Vorb. § 11, §§ 11, 12 TMG, in: Martin Eßer / Philip Kramer / Kai von Lewinski (eds.), Auernhammer – Bundesdatenschutzgesetz, 4th edition, Köln: Carl Heymanns, 2014, quoted as: *Schreibauer, Federal Data Protection Law and further Provisions, cip.*

Schulz, Wolfgang / *Dankert,* Kevin: Governance by Things' as a challenge to regulation by law, in: Internet Policy Review 5 (2) (2016), pp. 1–19, quoted as: *Schulz and Dankert, ‚Governance by Things' as a challenge to regulation by law.*

Schumpeter, Joseph: Capitalism, Socialism & Democracy, 5th edition, London i.a.: Routledge, 2003, quoted as: *Schumpeter, Capitalism, Socialism & Democracy, p.*

Schweizer, Rainer J.: Allgemeine Grundsätze, in: Detlef Merten / Hans-Jürgen Papier (eds.), Handbuch der Grundrechte in Deutschland und Europa – Band VI/I „Europäische Grundrechte I", Heidelberg i.a.: C. F. Müller, 2010, § 138, quoted as: *Schweizer in: Handbook of Basic Rights – Europe I, §;*

Id.: Die Rechtsprechung des Europäischen Gerichtshofs für Menschenrechte zum Persönlichkeits- und Datenschutz, in: Datenschutz und Datensicherheit 33 (8) (2009), pp. 462–468, quoted as: *Schweizer, European Convention and Data Protection, p.*

Simitis, Spiros: Die informationelle Selbstbestimmung – Grundbedingungen einer verfassungsrechtlichen Kommunikationsordnung, in: Neue Juristische Wochenschrift 37 (8) (1984), pp. 398–405, quoted as: *Simitis, NJW 1984, p.*

Id.: Bundesdatenschutzgesetz, Baden-Baden: Nomos, 2014, quoted as: *Simitis, Federal Data Protection Law, cip.*

Singer, Slavica / *Amorós,* José Ernesto / *Moska Arreola,* Daniel: Global Entrepreneurship Monitor – 2014 Global Report, URL: http://www.gemconsortium.org/report, quoted as: Singer et al., Global Entrepreneurship Monitor – 2014 Global Report.

Skistims, Hendrik / *Voigtmann,* Christian / *David,* Klaus / *Roßnagel,* Alexander: Datenschutzgerechte Gestaltung von kontextvorhersagenden Algorithmen, in: Datenschutz und Datensicherheit 36 (1) (2012), pp. 31–36, quoted as: Skistims et al., *Data Protection Compliance of Context-Predicting Algorithms, p.*

Solove, Daniel J.: Understanding Privacy, Cambridge, Massachusetts: Harvard University Press, 2008, quoted as: *Solove, Understanding Privacy, p.*

Stentzel, Rainer: Das Grundrecht auf ...? Auf der Suche nach dem Schutzgut des Datenschutzes in der Europäischen Union, in: Privacy in Germany 3 (5) (2015), pp. 185–190, Union quoted as: *Stentzel, The Fundamental Right to ...? The Search of the Object of Protection of Data Protection in the European Union, PinG 05.15, p.*

Streinz, Rudolf / *Michl,* Walther: Art. 4 EUV, Art. 6 AEUV, Art. 51 GRCh, in: Streinz (ed.), EUV/AEUV Kommentar, 2nd edition, München: C.H. Beck, 2012, quoted as: *Streinz/Michl, in: Streinz, EUV/AEUV, cip.*

Thaler, Richard H. / *Sunstein,* Cass R.: Nudge – Improving Decisions About Health, Wealth, and Happiness, New Haven i.a.: Yale University Press, 2008, quoted as: *Thaler and Sunstein, Nudge – Improving Decisions About Health, Wealth, and Happiness, p.*

Thierer, Adam: Privacy Law's Precautionary Principle Problem, in: Maine Law Review 66 (2) (2014), pp. 467–486, quoted as: *Thierer, Privacy Law's Precautionary Principle Problem, p.*

Trute, Hans-Heinrich: Der Schutz personenbezogener Informationen in der Informationsgesellschaft, in: JuristenZeitung 53 (17) (1998), pp. 822–831, quoted as: *Trute, JZ 1998, p.*

Tzanou, Maria: Data protection as a fundamental right next to privacy? 'Reconstructing' a not so new right, in: International Data Privacy Law 3 (2) (2013), pp. 88–99, quoted as: *Tzanou, Data protection as a fundamental right next to privacy? 'Reconstructing' a not so new right, p.*

Veil, Winfried: DS-GVO: Risikobasierter Ansatz statt rigides Verbotsprinzip – Eine erste Bestandsaufnahme, in: Zeitschrift für Datenschutz 5 (8) (2015), pp. 347–353, quoted as: GDPR: Risk-based approach instead of rigid principle of prohibition, p.

Vodafone Institute for Society and Communications: Big Data – A European Survey on the Opportunities and Risks of Data Analytics, 2016, URL: http://www.vodafone-institut.de/wp-content/uploads/2016/01/VodafoneInstitute-Survey-BigData-en.pdf, quoted as: *Vodafone Institute for Society and Communications: Big Data – A European Survey on the Opportunities and Risks of Data Analytics, p.*

Voßkuhle, Andreas: Neue Verwaltungsrechtswissenschaft, in: Wolfgang Hoffmann-Riem / Eberhard Schmidt-Aßmann / Andreas Voßkuhle (eds.), Grundlagen des Verwaltungsrechts – Band I „Methoden – Maßstäbe – Aufgaben – Organisation", 2nd edition, München: C.H. Beck, 2012, pp. 1–63, quoted as: *Voßkuhle, New Regulatory Approach of Administrative Law, p.*

Wegner, Gerhard: Nachhaltige Innovationsoffenheit dynamischer Märkte, in: Martin Eifert / Wolfgang Hoffmann-Riem (eds.), Innovationsfördernde Regulierung – Innovation und Recht II, Berlin: Duncker & Humblot, 2009, pp. 71–91, quoted as: *Wegner, Dynamic Markets and their Persistent Openness to Innovation, p.*

Weichert, Thilo: Informationstechnische Arbeitsteilung und datenschutzrechtliche Verantwortung – Plädoyer für eine Mitverantwortlichkeit bei der Verarbeitung von Nutzungsdaten, in: Zeitschrift für Datenschutz 4 (12) (2014), pp. 605–610, quoted as: *Weichert, Information-technological collaboration and data protection responsibility, p.*

Welter, Friederike: Contextualizing Entrepreneurship – Conceptual Challenges and Ways Forward, in: Entrepreneurship Theory and Practice 35 (1) (2011), pp. 165–184, quoted as: *Welter, Contextualizing Entrepreneurship, p.*

Wente, Jürgen: Informationelles Selbstbestimmungsrecht und absolute Drittwirkung der Grundrechte, in: Neue Juristische Wochenschrift 37 (25) (1984), pp. 1446–1447, quoted as: *Wente, NJW 1984, p.*

Westin, Alan F.: Privacy & Freedom, New York: Atheneum, 1967, quoted as: *Westin, Privacy and Freedom, p.*

Wolff, Heinrich Amadeus: § 28 BDSG, in: Heinrich Amadeus Wolff / Stefan Brink (eds.), Datenschutzrecht in Bund und Ländern – Kommentar, München: C.H. Beck, 2013, quoted as: *Wolff, § 28 BDSG, cip.*

World Economic Forum: Insight Report: Enhancing Europe's Competitiveness – Fostering Innovation-Driven Entrepreneurship in Europe, January 2014, URL: http://www3.weforum.org/docs/WEF_EuropeCompetitiveness_InnovationDrivenEntrepreneurship_Report_2014.pdf, quoted as: *World Economic Forum: Insight Report: Enhancing Europe's Competitiveness – Fostering Innovation-Driven Entrepreneurship in Europe.*

Wright, David / *Friedewald,* Michael / *Gellert,* Raphaël: Developing and testing a surveillance impact assessment methodology, in: International Data Privacy Law 5 (1) (2015), pp. 40–53, quoted as: *Wright, Freidewald and Gellert, Developing and testing a surveillance impact assessment methodology, p.*

Zezschwitz, Friedrich von: Konzept der normativen Zweckbegrenzung, in: Alexander Roßnagel (ed.), Handbuch Datenschutzrecht: Die neuen Grundlagen für Wirtschaft und Verwaltung, München: C.H. Beck, 2003, pp. 219–268, quoted as: *v. Zezschwitz, Concept of Normative Purpose Limitation, cip.*